Wm Stanley

THE BROOKINGS INSTITUTION

The Brookings Institution—Devoted to Public Service through Research and Training in the Social Sciences—was incorporated on December 8, 1927. Broadly stated, the Institution has two primary purposes: the first is to aid constructively in the development of sound national policies; and the second is to offer training of a super-graduate character to students of the social sciences. The Institution will maintain a series of co-operating institutes, equipped to carry out comprehensive and inter-related research projects.

The responsibility for the final determination of the Institution's policies and its program of work and for the administration of its endowment is vested in a self-perpetuating board of trustees. It is the function of the trustees to make possible the conduct of scientific research under the most favorable conditions, and to safeguard the independence of the research staff in the pursuit of their studies and in the publication of the results of such studies. It is not a part of their function to determine, control, or influence the conduct of particular investigations or the conclusions reached; but only to approve the principal fields of investigation to which the available funds are to be allocated, and to satisfy themselves with reference to the intellectual competence and scientific integrity of the staff. Major responsibility for "formulating general policies and co-ordinating the activities of the various divisions of the Institution" is vested in the president. The by-laws provide also that "there shall be an advisory council selected by the president from among the scientific staff of the Institution and representing the different divisions of the Institution."

THE INSTITUTE OF ECONOMICS

OF

THE BROOKINGS INSTITUTION

PUBLICATION No. 85

UNION POLICIES AND INDUSTRIAL MANAGEMENT

SUMNER H. SLICHTER

WASHINGTON, D.C.

THE BROOKINGS INSTITUTION

1941

Printed in the United States of America

George Banta Publishing Company

Menasha, Wisconsin

DIRECTOR'S PREFACE

This volume grows out of a study begun some years ago when Professor Slichter, on leave of absence from Cornell University, was a temporary member of the staff of the Institute of Economics. The original project was focused on the policies and attitudes of trade unions with reference to production. But since any such policy expresses itself through a variety of practices and shop rules embodying those practices, it became clear that production policy could not be appraised except on a basis of a fuller analysis of a wide range of relationships between trade unionists and employers. In its present form, the volume presents a comprehensive discussion of both the content and the process of collective bargaining except as to wage rates.

During recent years, experience has widened and interest deepened in the whole problem of devising more adequate machinery for the peaceful adjudication of labor differences. To the consideration of this problem, Professor Slichter brings both profound knowledge and deep wisdom gained from many years of close association in the ranks of workers as well as employers. We trust the volume will prove helpful to all who are concerned in understanding and utilizing effectively the methods already evolved in the field of industrial jurisprudence and, in due time, contributing to their improvement.

EDWIN G. NOURSE
Director

Institute of Economics
December 1940

v

ACKNOWLEDGMENT

The preparation of this study has extended over a considerable period of time and has involved much field work in a wide variety of industries. Many persons in these industries have contributed generously of their time in discussing problems and policies confronting employers and unions. Records of many enterprises and organizations have been made available. It is impossible to enumerate all of those who have co-operated. Among those who have been particularly generous are:

James Maloney, President, and Harry Jenkins, Secretary, Glass Bottle Blowers' Association of the United States and Canada; W. P. Clarke, former President, American Flint Glass Workers' Union.

John P. Frey, President, Metal Trades Department, American Federation of Labor.

Don H. Taylor, Executive Director of the New York Employing Printers' Association, Inc.; Woodruff Randolph, Secretary, and W. R. Trotter, former Director of Research, International Typographical Union; E. J. Volz, President of the International Photo-Engravers' Union.

E. J. Brown, former Business Agent of the Milwaukee local, International Brotherhood of Electrical Workers (and now President of the international union); C. G. Norman, Chairman, Board of Governors, Building Trades Employers' Association of the City of New York; M. H. Hedges, Director of Research, International Brotherhood of Electrical Workers.

Emil Rieve, former President, and William Smith, Secretary, American Federation of Hosiery Workers; Frazier MacIver, Vice-President, Phoenix Hosiery Company.

John Carmody, former Production Manager of The H. Black Company; Meyer Perlstein, former Manager, and Abraham W. Katovsky, present Manager of the Joint Board of the Cleveland Ladies' Garment Workers' Union; Julius Hochman, Manager of the Joint Board of the Dress and Waistmakers' Union, New York.

O. S. Beyer, Jr., former Technical Adviser to the Railway Employes' Department, American Federation of Labor; John Roberts,

Chief of Motive Power, Canadian National Railways; Colonel G. H. Emerson, Chief of Motive Power and Equipment, Baltimore and Ohio Railroad Company; A. J. Hills, Chief of Personnel, Canadian National Railways; B. M. Jewell, President of the Railway Employes' Department; R. J. Tallon, President, Division 4, Railway Employes' Department; William J. McGee, former President, H. L. Alberty, former Secretary, and H. J. Doyle, present President, Baltimore and Ohio System Federation; J. Corbett, President, Canadian National System Federation; R. C. Gaeth, President, Chicago and North Western System Federation.

Willard Hotchkiss, former Executive Director of the National Industrial Federation of Clothing Manufacturers; Morris Greenberg, Vice President, Hart, Schaffner, and Marx; B. Nitka, Production Manager, B. Kuppenheimer and Company, Inc.

John P. O'Connell, former Business Agent of the textile workers' local at the Naumkeag Steam Cotton Company.

Clinton S. Golden and Harold J. Ruttenberg of the Steel Workers' Organizing Committee.

The list might be greatly extended. A few of those who have been particularly generous in helping are no longer living. Among them are George W. Perkins, President of the Cigar Makers International Union; Fred C. Butler, Manager, Cleveland Garment Manufacturers' Association; F. A. Silcox, Executive Director, New York Employing Printers' Association, Inc.; and Michael Keough, President of the International Molders' Union.

The tables in Chapters II, III, and IV are mainly the work of my assistants, Mr. James Healy and Miss Nina Mulcare. My wife has prepared the index and I am indebted to her for many invaluable suggestions throughout the preparation of the manuscript.

Sumner H. Slichter

Harvard University
    December 1940

CONTENTS

CHAPTER I

EMERGENCE OF A SYSTEM OF INDUSTRIAL JURISPRUDENCE

Collective bargaining, as carried on by labor unions with employers, has two principal aspects. In the first place, it is a method of price-making—making the price of labor. In the second place, it is a method of introducing civil rights into industry, that is, of requiring that management be conducted by rule rather than by arbitrary decision. In this latter aspect, collective bargaining becomes a method of building up a system of "industrial jurisprudence." Through the institution of the state, men devise schemes of positive law, construct administrative procedures for carrying them out, and complement both statute law and administrative rule with a system of judicial review. Similarly, laboring men, through unions, formulate policies to which they give expression in the form of shop rules and practices which are embodied in agreements with employers or are accorded less formal recognition and assent by management; shop committees, grievance procedures, and other means are evolved for applying these rules and policies; and rights and duties are claimed and recognized. When labor and management deal with labor relations analytically and systematically after such a fashion, it is proper to refer to the system as "industrial jurisprudence." It is solely with this second aspect of collective bargaining that we are concerned in the present volume. The price- or wage-making aspect of collective bargaining is essentially a separate subject, although we shall have occasion in later chapters to comment on certain points of contact between the two phases of collective bargaining.

THE MODERN WORKER'S DEMAND FOR PROTECTIVE RULES

Wage earners have many specific purposes in seeking to build up a system of industrial jurisprudence. They wish to protect their organizations against being weakened by employers who might discriminate against union members; to strengthen their organizations by making union membership an aid to employment; to allocate limited opportunities to work; to make more work for themselves; to protect themselves against the cost and impact of technological change. Underlying these specific purposes, however, and far more important, is the desire of the workers for protection against the arbitrary and uncontrolled discretion of management. It is the desire of the modern worker for such protection which gives the real significance to the system of industrial jurisprudence which collective bargaining has built up. The workers of today in American industry are increasingly men who have had some high school training. Between 1890 and 1940 the annual number of high school graduates increased thirty-fold. A large proportion of the new entrants into industry have completed a high school course and nearly all of them have had at least one or two years of high school work. Workers of this kind expect management to be conducted in accordance with rules. Furthermore, they expect to help make the rules and to have an opportunity to appeal to a proper person when, in their judgment, the rule has not been observed. In short, the days are coming to an end when the boss's word, no matter how unreasonable, is law. Modern business management must expect to operate within the framework of a system of industrial jurisprudence.

The system of industrial rights and duties which collective bargaining endeavors to establish deals with such matters as entrance to the trade, hiring, training, promotion, reduction of staff, technological change, and methods of compensation. The specific policies pursued by different unions and the rules which they seek to enforce differ greatly. Some unions are deeply interested in controlling entrance to the trade. Others may not concern themselves with this matter. Most unions are interested in controlling hiring, but a few are not and there are differences in the control exercised by different unions over hiring. A few unions seek to compel employers to engage help from a union office or from a union-controlled hiring hall; others simply demand that employers give preference to union members; still others are content if the employer hires men who agree to join the union on being hired or after serving a probationary period. Some unions make no effort to control the reduction of staff by employers; others insist upon seniority rules (of which there are several types); others demand that the work be divided; and still others prefer a combination of seniority and equal division of work. There are several ways in which these two principles may be combined. Some unions endeavor to enforce make-work rules; others have a definite policy against such rules.

The introduction of technological change into industry produces various policies. Some unions oppose technological changes; others seek to compete with new methods and new processes by making concessions on old methods; still others seek to control the introduction of new machinery and methods. Not infrequently a combination of these several policies is simultaneously pursued. Some unions are opposed to piecework or bonus systems; others prefer them. Still others are opposed to payment by time in some industries or some branches of industry and prefer piecework, or other methods of payment by results, in other branches of industry. Where payment is by the piece, unions seek to build up rules for protecting the pieceworkers against the negligence and inefficiency of management, and against impediments and interruptions to production which are beyond the control of the workers.

To some extent these variations in union policies and union rules are simply the result of differences in experience or differences in the intelligence and foresight of union leadership. There is discernible a trend for unions to base their policies upon an exploration of the facts and on a more careful and realistic consideration of the long-run effects of their policies. This trend is part of the natural maturing of unions. Hence some differences in policy among unions are attributable to differences in their stage of development. Most differences in union rules and policies, however, are the result, not of differences in leadership or maturity of the union, but of differences in conditions between industries. It is not an accident that some unions (such as those in the building trades) insist far more than others upon controlling hiring by employers. Likewise, it is not an accident that some unions (such as the printing pressmen or the building trades unions) make little or no effort to control layoffs by employers. It is not an accident that the unions in the needle trades seek to enforce equal division of work during periods of business shrinkage and do not in general demand seniority rules. It is not an accident that over a period of time there has been a tendency for many unions to limit the seniority principle by the equal-division-of-work principle and the equal-division-of-work principle by the seniority principle. It is not an accident that the glass bottle blowers' union pursued a policy of competition toward some machines, such as the Owens automatic, and a policy of control toward other machines, such as the feed and flow device. It is not an accident that some unions prefer piecework when others oppose it. These variations in policy are the result of variations in conditions. It is desirable to establish generalizations concerning the relationships between union policies and the conditions which produce them.

EFFECTS OF UNION WORKING RULES AND THE PROBLEMS RAISED BY THEM

Naturally the system of industrial jurisprudence developed by collective bargaining has a multitude of effects and creates many problems for both unions and employers. Does the control exercised over entrance to the trade and over hiring increase or diminish the supply of trained mechanics? How does it affect the quality of the training? How do union restrictions on hiring affect the ability of employers to select the best qualified men? How does the control of hiring and of layoffs affect the mobility of labor and the ease with which the working force adjusts itself to market shifts or to changes in the location of industries? Do union policies toward technological change cause the rate at which new inventions are applied to come closer to the optimum rate or farther from it? Do union policies toward technological change mitigate or aggravate the displacement of labor by these changes?

The most frequent complaint of employers concerning union shop rules and policies is that they limit the efficiency of labor and reduce the output of industry. Some sacrifice of production is undoubtedly desirable in order that men may have protection from arbitrary management. The security that can be obtained only in that way is undoubtedly worth a great deal. Furthermore, it must be remembered that industry produces men as well as goods and that the kind of men which a democratic community needs may not be produced in shops which are small oriental despotisms. Nevertheless, it is obviously desirable to reduce the conflict between civil rights and production in industry to a minimum. How serious is this conflict and what can be done to minimize it?

Union rules may restrict production in several ways. In the first place, they may interfere with the freedom of management to pick the best men available and to stimulate efficiency by rewarding superior performance and penalizing poor performance. In the second place, they may restrict the ability of management to introduce more productive methods and machinery. In the third place, they may deliberately make work by imposing restrictions on output or by requiring excessive crews. In the fourth place, they may restrict production because they may have become obsolete.

The fact that a rule may limit the output of a given plant does not necessarily mean that it limits the output of industry as a whole. Seniority rules are a good example. Many plants could probably get more output if they were free to drop some of their older men. Nevertheless, these men, if dropped, would probably be less productive anywhere else than they are in the plants where they have served for many years. Likewise, the fact that trade unions may restrict the rate at which new machinery and processes are introduced does not necessarily mean that the product of industry is being limited, as employers, left to themselves, may make changes at a rate faster than the optimum. It is important to consider the economic consequences of trade union rules from the standpoint of the community as a whole as well as from the standpoint of the individual employer.

Changes in technology and markets, the rise of new forms of competition and new methods of doing business are constantly making some shop rules and policies out of date. Obsolete rules may produce unintended consequences of great importance—sometimes consequences exactly the opposite of those originally intended. And yet it is not always easy to modify obsolete rules, partly because they come to be regarded as ends and partly because they create vested interests within the union and sometimes among groups of employers. Keeping shop rules and policies adjusted to industrial changes is one of the most important problems of collective bargaining.

RELATION OF UNION SHOP RULES AND POLICIES TO COMPETITION BETWEEN UNION PLANTS AND OTHER PLANTS

Labor unions are confronted with the problem of protecting their members not only against arbitrary management but also against loss of employment as a result of competition of non-union plants and of new products from other industries. Often they have also the problem of helping their members in high-cost union plants hold their jobs in the face of the competition of low-cost union plants. These problems arise partly because wage scales in union plants are higher than in non-union, partly because the system of industrial jurisprudence created by collective bargaining limits in some respects the efficiency of union plants, partly because of the invention of new products and methods and the changes in taste that are constantly occurring, and partly because of the great differences in plant and managerial efficiency among union concerns. In some instances these problems arise because the very plants which the unions are most successful in organizing are least able to resist because their competitive position is weak—due to poor management, obsolete plant and equipment, insufficient capital, or other reasons.

If unions ignore the effect of competition upon the employment of their members, the gains conferred on employees by a working rule may be partially or entirely offset by the loss of employment for which the rule is responsible. Some unions have been slow to become aware of the problem of protecting their members against competition. Some of them have overlooked the fact that in a constantly changing environment the rule which represented a great victory for the union yesterday may be a threat to the security of its members today. Many unions have been misled by the fact that the immediate elasticity of the demand for labor is much less than the elasticity over a period of several years. Hence they have overestimated the cost differentials which one plant can stand in competition with other plants whether in the same industry or in other industries. There are several reasons, however, for concluding that

the plant demand for labor is quite elastic, at least when periods
of several years are involved, and the history of collective bargaining in this country is full of instances of unions, such as the
old window glass workers' union, the upholstery weavers' union,
or the cigar workers' union, which destroyed themselves or made
themselves weak by imposing excessive costs on employers.[1] For
many other unions the problem of competition, particularly the
competition of non-union plants, has been a serious one.

Recognition of the problem of competition from non-union
plants, from low-cost union plants, and from other industries has
been gradually spreading among trade unions and has affected their
policies in building up a system of industrial jurisprudence. It has
caused a few unions to impose make-work rules and restrictions on
employers in an attempt to create new jobs as fast as competition
and market shifts destroy old ones; it has caused some unions to
limit the restrictions imposed upon managerial discretion; it has
caused some unions to abandon rules that had become obsolete and
burdensome; it has caused a few unions to adopt the deliberate
policy of keeping trade agreements as short and simple as possible
and of relying upon the administrative method of settling cases in
the light of individual facts as they arise.

During the last twenty years a few unions have attempted to
deal with the problem of competition from other industries, from
low-cost union plants, and from non-union plants by developing
systematic co-operation with management for the purpose of increasing production and reducing costs. Important instances of such co-
operation appeared during the twenties in the needle trades, on a

---

[1] One reason for high long-term elasticity of the demand for labor is competition
between the old and the new—the most pervasive form of competition in our
economy and the one most completely neglected in economic treatises. A second
is the ever-growing pervasiveness of inter-product competition. As the number
of products invented by industry increases and the number of substitutes for each
article becomes larger, the elasticity of demand for each article tends to rise. A third
reason is the rise of large buyers who purchase to their own specifications from the
lowest bidder (often doing the development work on the product themselves). In
competition for the business of such buyers small differences in costs are of decisive
importance. A fourth reason for high long-term elasticity of the demand for
labor is the rapid spread of organized industrial research with its tendency
to increase the elasticity of substitution both between products and between
factors of production. As the technical schools turn out an increasing number
of better trained men, the elasticity of substitution will continue to increase.

few railroads, and in the textile industry. More recently there has been a considerable spread of the policy to the steel industry, the seamless hosiery industry, and elsewhere. The policy is still new and experimental and there is uncertainty concerning the contribution which unions are willing and able to make to the reduction of costs and to the increase of output, and even concerning the willingness of managements to accept the help of the unions. Nevertheless the policy of union-management co-operation may acquire great importance during the next several decades.

PLAN OF THE BOOK

This book is divided into two principal parts. The first part (Chapters II to XI) deals with the content of the system of industrial jurisprudence which collective bargaining has built up, with the conditions that have produced different rules and policies, and with the principal effects and problems created by specific rules and policies. The second part of the book (Chapters XII to XIX) examines the relation of the system of industrial jurisprudence to the ability of union plants to hold their own in competition with non-union plants, with low-cost union plants, and with the products of other industries, and analyzes the efforts of unions to deal with the effect of competition upon the employment of their members in so far as these efforts take the form of shop rules and policies rather than wage concessions. Since by far the most serious competitive menace faced by trade unions and union employers is from non-union plants, special attention will be given to this problem. As the most promising effort of unions to deal with the effect of competition upon the employment of their members has been systematic co-operation with management for the purpose of increasing production and reducing costs, this policy will be examined in some detail. Four principal experiments in union-management co-operation will be studied for the purpose of setting forth the methods employed, the problems encountered, and the results achieved, and an effort will be made to appraise the outlook for this policy.

CHAPTER II

CONTROL OF ENTRANCE TO THE TRADE

Attempts to control entrance to the trade are confined in the main to craft unions—that is, to organizations composed of members of a particular trade. Industrial unions, as a rule, make no such efforts, because the vast majority of their members are specialists of various sorts who must acquire their training on the job. An exception to this generalization is the United Mine Workers of America which, although an industrial union, has endeavored to control admission to the occupation of mining by miners' certificate laws. Such laws increase the bargaining power of the union by limiting the ability of employers to defeat strikes by hiring strikebreakers.

The efforts of unions to regulate the entrance to trades take three principal forms: (1) the regulation of apprenticeship; (2) the regulation of the use of helpers and the work of helpers; (3) the support of license laws which forbid the practice of the trade by persons not holding a license or a certificate of competency.

EXTENT OF REGULATION OF APPRENTICESHIP

Early in the century 70 out of 120 unions then affiliated with the American Federation of Labor attempted to regulate apprenticeship.[1] In 1936, such regulation was attempted by only 66 out of 156 national unions in the United States.[2] These figures must not be interpreted as reflecting indifference of trade unions to apprenticeship where it exists: they simply mean that in most occupations training is acquired in other ways. Virtually every union in occupations for which apprenticeship is usual makes some effort to regulate it, but very few of these unions make the serving of an apprenticeship a prerequisite to membership. Of Motley's group of 70 unions regulating apprenticeship, only 19 required apprentice training for membership;[3] among the 56 in the 1929 group,

[1] J. M. Motley, *Apprenticeship in American Trade Unions*, p. 53.
[2] For the names of these 66 unions, see the appendix.
[3] *Apprenticeship in American Trade Unions*, p. 60.

9

only 8 made it a prerequisite to membership and several of the 8 did not adhere rigidly to the policy.[4]

The reason most apprenticeship-regulating unions do not require applicants for admission to have completed an apprenticeship is that they control only a small part of the entire trade. Consequently, their ability to increase their bargaining power depends largely upon their success in absorbing non-union workers. Under these circumstances, it would be suicidal to enforce highly restrictive admission requirements. A few strong locals may be in a position to do so, especially in the building trades where there is little inter-market competition, but even these restrictions often encounter opposition from the national unions. Consequently, most unions which regulate apprenticeship simply stipulate that candidates for membership must have served an apprenticeship *or the equivalent*—thereby opening the doors to the men who have "picked up" the trade in small towns or by shifting from employer to employer. The few national unions requiring completion of an apprenticeship for admission to the union are all organizations which control a very large proportion of the entire trade.

METHODS OF LIMITING THE NUMBER OF APPRENTICES

Some limit on the number of apprentices is necessary in order to protect the union's standard rate. Otherwise employers could undercut the standard rate by employing a high proportion of apprentices. Unions attempt to restrict the number of apprentices by three principal methods: (1) by direct restrictions on the number; (2) by requiring a minimum term of apprenticeship; (3) by controlling the wages of apprentices.

Limitations on the number of apprentices are usually imposed by agreements between employers and the union. The limitation ordinarily takes the form of a ratio of apprentices to journeymen regularly employed—such as not more than 1 apprentice to 5 or 6

---

[4] These organizations were: Journeymen Barbers' International Union of America; Amalgamated Lithographers of America; International Association of Marble, Stone, and Slate Polishers, Rubbers, and Sawyers, Tile and Marble Setters' Helpers, and Terrazzo Workers' Helpers; International Association of Operative Plasterers and Cement Finishers of the United States and Canada; International Photo-Engravers' Union of North America; International Plate Printers, Die Stampers, and Engravers' Union of North America; International Union of Stove Mounters of North America; American Wire Weavers' Protective Association.

journeymen. In addition, however, some agreements set a maximum number of apprentices that may be employed in the plant regardless of the number of journeymen. For example, the agreement may specify that the employer shall hire not more than 1 apprentice to every 5 journeymen regularly employed but that in no case shall the number of apprentices in the shop exceed 5. In some cases (especially where the shop is large) a maximum limit

RESTRICTIONS IN 611 TRADE AGREEMENTS ON NUMBER OF APPRENTICES

I. BY RATIO ONLY

Ratio of Apprentices to Journeymen	All Trades	Building Trades	Printing Trades	Other Trades in Manufacturing	Miscellaneous Trades
1 to 4 or less..........	176	72	71	26	7
1 to 5.................	128	19	68	38	3
1 to 6.................	18	3	12	3	—
1 to 7, 8, or 9.........	40	17	16	6	1
1 to 10, 11, 12, 13, or 14.	34	13	13	8	—
1 to 15 or more........	13	3	1	8	1
Total..............	409	126	182	89	12

II. BY RATIO AND ABSOLUTE LIMIT

Maximum Number of Apprentices Permitted in a Department or a Shop	All Trades	Building Trades	Printing Trades	Other Trades in Manufacturing	Miscellaneous Trades
1....................	57	16	32	7	2
2....................	44	22	18	4	—
3....................	51	20	26	5	—
4....................	19	6	13	—	—
5 to 9...............	26	3	22	1	—
10 or more...........	5	1	4	—	—
Total..............	202	68	115	17	2

may be placed upon the number of apprentices who may be employed in any given department.

As indicated by the accompanying table, in 409 of 611 trade agreements in various industries, or slightly more than two-thirds, the number of apprentices was limited merely by a ratio, but in 202 it was limited by both a ratio and an absolute maximum for the shop or department.

A limit on the number of apprentices means little unless the term of apprenticeship is also specified. Consequently, simultaneously with a restriction on numbers, unions also seek to regulate the term of apprenticeship. It might be expected that unions would be interested in making the term of apprenticeship as long as possible in order to discourage boys from entering the trade. This, however, is not true. If the term is made too long, the employer makes a handsome profit by paying apprentice wages to boys who, in the latter years of their apprenticeship, possess almost the skill of journeymen. This encourages employers to train as many boys as the ratio permits and also subjects the union to strong pressure

RESTRICTIONS IN 611 TRADE AGREEMENTS ON LENGTH OF APPRENTICESHIP

Number of Years of Apprenticeship	All Trades	Building Trades	Printing Trades	Other Trades in Manufacturing	Miscellaneous Trades
Less than ½.............	3	—	—	2	1
½ to 1.................	7	2	1	4	—
1 to 2.................	18	7	2	5	4
2 to 3.................	59	20	12	25	2
3 to 4.................	87	57	7	20	3
4 to 5.................	175	85	43	43	4
5 to 6.................	256	20	229	7	—
6 or over.............	6	3	3	—	—
Total..............	611	194	297	106	14

from employers to liberalize the ratio. Most important of all, it creates the temptation for boys who have learned the trade but who cannot obtain journeymen's wages in a union shop to leave and seek employment in non-union shops. Consequently, trade unions do not find it advantageous to insist on too long a term of apprenticeship.

The terms specified in the sample of 611 agreements are indicated in the accompanying table. It will be seen that more than two-thirds of these agreements specify terms of from 4 to 6 years.

A few unions have sought to limit the number of apprentices by pushing their wages so high that employers do not find it economical to train many boys. Both the glass bottle blowers' union and the flint glass workers have pursued this policy.[5]

[5] The introduction of semi-automatic machines and later the Owens automatic and finally the "feed and flow" devices into the glass bottle industry, their effect

In addition to these general methods of limitation there are various minor ways in which unions occasionally restrict the number of apprentices. Some unions, especially those in the building trades, do not permit an employer to indenture apprentices until he has been in business a year.[6] An indirect restriction occasionally found in the building trades is the requirement that the employer must give apprentices steady work the year round or pay them for the time lost.[7] Naturally it is exceedingly difficult for a contractor to

---

upon the union, and the union's policy toward these machines are discussed below in Chaps. VII, VIII, and IX. When machines for making bottles began seriously to displace the bottle blowers, the union naturally became exceedingly anxious to discourage the training of apprentices. In 1909, and again in 1912, the union induced the manufacturers to agree that no new apprentices would be started during the next year. Each of these agreements was obtained, however, only because the union in that year consented to a substantial reduction in wages. Beginning in 1913, the union made an important change in its apprentice policy. The bottle blowers had been paid by the piece, and the piece rates for apprentices were only half the rates paid to journeymen for doing the same work. After a year's experience, however, an apprentice could produce nearly as much as a journeyman. (G. E. Barnett, *Chapters on Machinery and Labor*, p. 97. See also U. S. Congress, *Report of the Industrial Commission on the Relations and Conditions of Capital and Labor Employed in Manufactures and General Testimony*, 1901, Vol. VII, "Testimony," p. 110.) Obviously, it was profitable for employers to hire as many apprentices as the union rules permitted. In order to check the influx of boys into the dying trade, the union secured an agreement that apprentices would be paid 75 per cent of the journeymen's piece price and that the term of apprenticeship would be reduced from 50 working months to 40. This removed most of the profit from training apprentices, and the apprenticeship ratio became of little importance. (Barnett, *Chapters on Machinery and Labor*, p. 99.)

Some branches of the flint glass workers' union have regulated the number of apprentices through the control of piece rates. The lamp workers' branch, for example, imposed only one restriction on the training of apprentices, namely, that apprentices receive the same piece rates as journeymen. (U. S. Department of Commerce and Labor, *Regulation and Restriction of Output*, Eleventh Special Report of the Commissioner of Labor, 1904, p. 652.) Under the circumstances no employer wished to train apprentices. The flint glass workers' union has restricted the number of apprentices in the press ware department of the industry by an agreement that apprentices shall be paid 90 per cent of the regular piece price and that the term of apprenticeship shall be only twelve months. (U. S. Bureau of Labor Statistics, *Trade Agreements, 1927*, Bulletin No. 468, p. 87.) When apprentices are paid by the piece and at piece rates below the standard rates, the union has a strong interest in making the term of apprenticeship short.

[6] See, for example, the agreement of the bricklayers' and plasterers' Local No. 3 (U. S. Bureau of Labor Statistics, *Trade Agreements, 1926*, Bulletin No. 448, p. 33) and the agreement of Local No. 31 of the United Brotherhood of Carpenters and Joiners (the same, p. 36).

[7] Such a provision is found in the agreements of the bricklayers' and plasterers' Local No. 21 of Chicago, effective Apr. 7, 1925; of the electrical workers' Local No. 141 of Wheeling, W.Va., effective May 1, 1925; and of the operative plas-

give steady employment to many apprentices. Quite commonly unions do not permit apprentices on night shifts and do not permit journeymen engaged on the night shifts to be counted in determining the number of apprentices that the employer may have. In most industries such a restriction is of little importance, but in the printing industry, where the use of night shifts is frequent, it makes a substantial difference in the ratio of apprentices to journeymen. The agreement of the potters' union with the United States Potters' Association requires that any manufacturer who is unable to secure a journeyman must apply at the union office before starting an apprentice.[8] Between 1919 and 1927 the agreements of the Philadelphia photo-engravers' union provided that an apprentice might not be indentured in a branch of the trade if a journeyman in that branch were unemployed in Philadelphia.[9]

These minor restrictions on apprenticeship are often offset in some measure by other provisions in the union apprenticeship rules. For example, a union which permits a ratio of 1 apprentice to every 5 or 6 journeymen may permit every employer, however small his force, to have at least 1 apprentice. The provisions of agreements defining the ratio of apprentices to journeymen commonly read: 1 apprentice to every x journeymen *"or major fraction thereof."*

REASONABLENESS OF UNION APPRENTICESHIP LIMITS—THE GENERAL PROBLEM

Is not any restriction on the number of apprentices undesirable from the standpoint of the community? If a restriction does not limit the number of apprentices, it is useless; if it does, it prevents some employers from hiring as much labor as they otherwise would employ. In the latter event does the restriction not bring about an uneconomical distribution of labor?

It may be admitted without hesitation that limits on the number of apprentices, if carried too far or applied at the wrong time, may

terers' and cement finishers' Local No. 31 of Pittsburgh, effective Apr. 1, 1925. (U. S. Bureau of Labor Statistics, *Trade Agreements, 1925*, Bulletin No. 419, pp. 24, 32, and 49.) In Cleveland the provision has been included in the agreements in the bricklaying, carpentry, painting, plumbing, and electrical trades.

[8] The national union maintains an employment bureau where out-of-work members file their names.

[9] Charles Leese, *Collective Bargaining among Photo-Engravers in Philadelphia*, p. 143. Since 1927 this restriction has been dropped.

prevent the most economical distribution of labor among occupations. It does not follow, however, that all limits on the number of apprentices are undesirable. In the absence of limits employers are able to give preference to apprentices over journeymen. Up to a certain point this might tend to correct maladjustments in the distribution of labor introduced by union wage scales. Carried too far, however, the preference of apprentices over journeymen shortens the trade life of the journeymen. For example, in times of depression, employers, in the absence of apprenticeship regulation, are likely to keep apprentices at work and to lay off journeymen.[10] Likewise if employers are free to hire apprentices without limit, the older craftsmen have difficulty in getting back into the trade when business revives. In this way the trade skill of many of the older men is lost to the community and they are compelled to make their living at occupations for which they are not particularly suited. This is obviously not economical.

It is often said that union apprenticeship rules prevent industries from training as many apprentices as they need. The number of apprentices which an industry needs depends upon the proportion of boys who complete their apprenticeship and become journeymen, the rate at which the number of journeymen's jobs is rising or falling, the rate at which journeymen are retiring or leaving the industry, and the extent to which the supply of journeymen is being augmented by immigration and may be expected to be augmented in years to come. Various trades differ substantially in these respects, but accurate data concerning the needs of various trades are virtually non-existent. At one time several studies of apprenticeship needs in the printing trades were made for the New York Employing Printers' Association, and occasional rough estimates have been made by committees of employers. By and large, however, there is no reliable information concerning the number of

---

[10] A conspicuous instance of this seems to have occurred in Chicago during the depression of 1893-94. Many building tradesmen had been attracted to Chicago by the construction of the World's Fair buildings. As a result of complaints that employers were keeping apprentices at work and laying off journeymen, a survey of the city was made by a joint committee representing the bricklayers and the contractors. They found 642 journeymen and 710 apprentices at work. (Andrew Lanquist, "Observation on the Apprentice Problem," *The American Contractor*, Feb. 11, 1922, Vol. XLIII, p. 22.)

apprentices whom it would be necessary to start each year in various trades in order to maintain a given number of journeymen or to increase them by a given amount. The apprenticeship ratios in trade union agreements are not ordinarily based upon statistical investigations of the trade and are not modified with changes in business conditions. Consequently, one should not expect these ratios to be accurately adjusted to the needs of the trades.

Although the reasonableness of union apprenticeship regulations must be tested in the light of particular conditions in particular trades, it is possible to make rough tests of their reasonableness. One must take account, of course, of *both* the ratio of apprentices to journeymen and the term of apprenticeship. For example, a ratio of 1 to 5 and a term of 4 years would permit a shop with 100 journeymen to make a maximum of 5 journeymen a year, whereas if the term were 2 years, the shop could make a maximum of 10 journeymen a year.

The number of new journeymen admitted to a trade in a given time (say, a year) for each given number (say, 100) of journeymen employed in the trade may be called the journeyman accession rate. Among our sample of 611 agreements, the most usual ratio of apprentices to journeymen was 1 to 4 or less in all trades except miscellaneous manufacturing trades, where it was 1 to 5.[11] The most usual term of apprenticeship was 4 to 5 years except in the printing trades, where it was 5 to 6 years. The great majority of those agreements specifying between 4 and 5 years specified 4 years and of those specifying 5 to 6 years specified 5 years.[12] These terms may be taken as the most usual length. The most usual ratios when combined with the most usual apprenticeship terms prevailing in the several trades would permit the following accession rate per 100 journeymen employed:

Building trades 6.25
Printing trades................................ 5.00
Other trades in manufacturing 5.00
Miscellaneous trades 6.25

These figures, of course, apply only in those cases where both the apprentice ratio and the apprentice term stipulated in the agree-

[11] See above, p. 11.
[12] The same.

ment are the most usual ratio and the most usual term, but they may be regarded as fairly typical because some agreements permit more journeymen to be trained and others less. It should be emphasized too that these figures are maxima because they assume that *every* apprentice completes his term and becomes a journeyman and that every employer trains as many apprentices as the rules permit.

As a general rule, an employer does not wish to have so many apprentices that he is compelled to lay off one or two of them every time he drops a few journeymen. Consequently, the number of apprentices actually permitted by the ratio is the number that can be kept when operations are at a moderately low level. This is likely to be at least 20 per cent less than would be permitted by the application of the ratio to the average force of journeymen.

An appreciable minority of apprentices never complete their training. The employer may, of course, promptly replace each apprentice who drops out, but the effect is to raise the average period required to train a journeyman and to reduce the number of journeymen made each year. Representative data are lacking on the proportion of apprentices who fail to complete their training, but the maximum estimates above of the number of new journeymen who could be trained under the usual union rules should be reduced at least 20 per cent in order to allow for the fact that some apprentices do not finish their training.

A further deduction from the theoretical maximum accession rate should be made to allow for the failure of many employers to start apprentices in years of poor business.[13] It is difficult to determine how large this deduction should be, because accurate data are again lacking. A deduction of one-third, however, would be conservative.

If the theoretical maximum figures are reduced by one-fifth for the unwillingness of employers to take more apprentices than can be kept steadily at work and if the resulting figure is reduced by one-fifth for the failure of all apprentices to complete the course and

[13] In such years the unions themselves object to apprentices' being started. During the recent severe depression many unions made agreements with employers that new apprentices would not be started. Hence union rules are restrictive unless they permit enough apprentices to be started in good years to make up for the failure to start them in bad years.

if the last figure is reduced one-third for the failure of employers to start the permitted number of apprentices in bad years, the "practical" maximum accession rates per 100 journeymen permitted by the apprentice ratio becomes only 43 per cent of the theoretical maximum. In the case of the most usual ratios and terms in the several trades quoted on page 16, it would be as follows:

Building trades 2.69
Printing trades 2.15
Other trades in manufacturing 2.15
Miscellaneous trades 2.69

How many new journeymen are needed each year to replace the old journeymen who die, retire, or are promoted to supervisory positions? Trade life varies, of course, in different occupations. Among 100 men between the ages of 22 and 65 who are distributed with respect to age as are the gainfully employed in mechanical and manufacturing pursuits, there is approximately one death per year. In addition, a number retire, go into business for themselves, or are promoted, but reliable figures concerning withdrawals and promotions are not available. The number of withdrawals must vary considerably among industries. It is probable that they are at least twice as numerous as the deaths, and in some occupations where trade life is short they must considerably exceed the deaths. If we assume that withdrawals and promotions are twice as numerous as deaths, then the attrition rate among journeymen is about 3 per cent a year. If the assumptions on which these rough estimates are based are approximately correct, then the conclusion follows that typical union agreements fall slightly short of permitting sufficient replacements to maintain a stationary working force. But the fact should be stressed that reliable data are lacking on the proportion of apprentices who complete their training and become journeymen; on the proportion of journeymen who leave various trades each year; and on the allowances that should be made for the failure of employers to take on apprentices in years of poor business or to have more apprentices than can be kept steadily employed.

Although in industry after industry unions and employers are setting apprentice ratios and terms with only the vaguest notions as to how many apprentices the trade requires, some of them realize the need for careful statistical information. In his report to the 1926 convention of the International Photo-Engravers' Union, Mr. E. J. Volz, at that time vice-president of the union, said:

There have also been periods . . . when the supply over-balanced the demand. . . . The question of the proper number of apprentices to meet the ordinary demand without over-manning the industry can be best determined when considered over a period of years and should be approached in an effort to meet the legitimate needs of the industry during periods of business activity without undue overtime or stress and with a minimum of unemployment with its resultant hardships during periods of depression.[14]

In his report to the thirtieth convention of the International Printing Pressmen's and Assistants' Union, President Berry said:

. . . the theory of one apprentice to ten journeymen is unsound and impractical; and likewise the theory that no office shall have more than four apprentices irrespective of the number of journeymen employed is inadequate. These things should be settled by fact and not by theory, and an apprenticeship is a matter that involves the future of the organization and the well-being of the industry, and it is impracticable and unsound upon the part of our organization in convention to attempt to arbitrarily determine what shall be or what shall not be, since the apprenticeship is so vital to three parties, to wit, to the apprentice, to the industry, and to the union.[15]

The convention decided to base the regulation of the number of apprentices upon the needs of the industry, arrived at by a calculation of the normal growth and demand of the industry, the death and retirement rate of journeymen pressmen, and other factors.[16]

At the time of the establishment of the pressmen's school in New York City under the auspices of the pressmen's union and the

[14] International Photo-Engravers' Union of North America, *Reports of Officers and Convention Proceedings*, 1926, pp. 47-48. Mr. Volz in 1940 was president of the union.
[15] International Printing Pressmen's and Assistants' Union, *Reports of Officers to Thirtieth Biennial Convention*, 1924, p. 96.
[16] In accordance with this policy, a flexible apprentice rule was written into the constitution of the union. The rule reads as follows: "Apprenticeship shall be calculated by the physical demand based upon the requirements of the business through expansion, by death, by retirement, or incapacitation, and all apprenticeship regulations shall be approved by the Board of Directors."

New York Employing Printers' Association, an attempt was made to estimate the number of apprentices needed in the cylinder pressrooms of the job and commercial printing industry. The results were:

Cause	Apprentices Needed Each Year per 100 Journeymen
Death	.80
Total disability	.20
Journeymen leaving industry	.50
Apprentices leaving industry	.50
Growth of industry	.79
Total	2.79

Both sides agreed that the total was only approximately accurate, and for practical purposes 3 per cent was accepted as the figure to be used. With 2,500 journeymen, 75 new journeymen were needed each year. As the apprenticeship period was four years, this meant something more than 300 apprentices in training—or a ratio of about 1 apprentice to 8 journeymen.[17]

REASONABLENESS OF UNION APPRENTICESHIP LIMITS— THE RATIO OF APPRENTICES TO JOURNEYMEN

A rough test of the reasonableness of union apprenticeship limits is provided by comparing the apprentice-journeyman ratios in union agreements with the ratio of the number of gainfully employed malts in the apprentice age group to the number in the journeyman age group. For purposes of this comparison persons of less than 23 years of age may be regarded as in the apprentice age group and persons of 23 or over as in the journeyman age group. The part of the gainfully employed population which concerns us is that engaged in manufacturing and mechanical pursuits. The comparison is of limited significance because it does not take into account the effect of the actual duration of apprenticeship. Assuming, however, that apprenticeship lasts in all cases until the twenty-third birthday,

[17] An attempt to adjust the number of entrants to the decline in an industry was made under the Mining Act of 1926 in Great Britain. Power was given the minister to make regulations, but after consultation with representatives of the industry he accepted instead a formal undertaking by the principal employers in the industry to carry out the intention of the section of the act by restricting new entrants to: (1) persons under 18; (2) disabled ex-service men in search of disability pensions; (3) mining students; (4) persons employed in the industry before Apr. 30, 1926. (T. S. Chegwidden and S. Myrddin-Evans, *The Employment Exchange Service of Great Britain*, p. 170.)

do union apprentice-journeyman ratios permit all gainfully employed males to serve an apprenticeship of this length?

In 1930 there were engaged in manufacturing and mechanical pursuits (exclusive of owners, supervisors, or common laborers) 1,085,480 males in the apprentice age group (less than 23 years of age) and 7,608,155 in the journeyman age group—a ratio of 1 to 7.[18] This estimate undoubtedly exaggerates the number of persons in the apprenticeship age group because many workers complete their apprenticeship before the beginning of their twenty-third year.[19]

In 409 of the 611 apprenticeship agreements examined, the only direct limit upon the number of apprentices was a maximum ratio of apprentices to journeymen. Yet in 322 of these 409 cases, or 79 per cent, the maximum ratio was 1 to 6 or less than 6. In 176, or 43 per cent, the ratio was 1 to 4 or less. Thus in a vast majority of cases the union apprentice ratio was substantially

---

[18] It was assumed that three-fifths of the gainfully employed classified by the census of occupations as 20-24 years inclusive were 20, 21, or 22 years of age. This probably overestimates the number by a slight amount because some persons do not enter industry until they are 21 or more. Certain classes of workers among which there is no apprenticeship were excluded. These include manufacturers and officials, managers and superintendents, foremen and overseers, and laborers. In a few instances, the census classifies apprentices and journeymen as separate occupations. In these cases all persons reported by the census as apprentices, *regardless of age*, were counted as apprentices and added to those in the apprentice age groups.

[19] It may be argued that the error caused by counting as apprentices some journeymen who are less than 23 years of age is counteracted by the fact that some workers 23 years of age or over who were reported as journeymen probably are apprentices. But the latter number is likely to be negligible. Among the workers actually reported as apprentices, the proportion who were 23 years of age or over (on the assumption of equal distribution by years within the age group 20 to 24 years) was as follows: blacksmiths, 14.07 per cent; boilermakers, 30.3 per cent; carpenters, 14.7 per cent; electricians, 13.0 per cent; machinists, 12.5 per cent; plumbers, 23.4; tinsmiths and coppersmiths, 12.0; apprentices to other building and hand trades, 12.0; jewelers, 9.2; printers and bookbinders, 13.6 per cent; other apprentices in manufacturing, 13.1 per cent. (Derived from U. S. Department of Commerce, *Fifteenth Census of the United States: 1930, Population*, Vol. V, General Report on Occupations, pp. 118-19.) The census makes the following comment on the apprentice figures: "A child returned as pursuing a trade, the mental or physical requirements for the pursuit of which usually are not possessed by a person of his age, was classified as an *apprentice* and not as a *journeyman* in the designated trade. The figures for apprentices, therefore, include many who were not specifically returned as apprentices. It is probable, also, that some of these returned as *journeymen* and classified as *apprentices* were, in fact, neither journeymen nor apprentices, but *helpers* or *operatives*." (*Fifteenth Census of the United States: 1930, Population*, Vol. V, p. 343.)

Occupation	Ratio of Estimated Number of Gainfully Employed Males 10–22 Years of Age, Plus Apprentices of Any Age, to Gainfully Employed Males Age 23 and Over	Number of Union Agreements with Specified Maximum Ratio of Apprentices to Journeymen					
		1 to 4 or Less	1 to 5	1 to 6	1 to 7 up to 1 to 9 Inclusive	1 to 10 up to 1 to 14 Inclusive	1 to 15 or More
Bakers	1 to 4.68	5	1	2	—	—	1
Barbers	1 to 10.18	—	—	—	—	—	—
Blacksmiths, forge men, and hammermen	1 to 19.77	—	1	1	—	—	—
Boilermakers	1 to 15.32	—	5	6	—	—	—
Brick and stone masons and tile layers	1 to 11.52	1	1	—	—	—	—
Buffers and polishers	1 to 7.32	—	1	—	3	1	—
Cabinet makers	1 to 12.18	—	—	—	—	—	—
Carpenters	1 to 17.78	2	1	—	4	1	—
Compositors, linotypers, and typesetters	1 to 3.42	10	21	7	9	6	1
Coopers	1 to 12.20	—	—	—	—	1	1
Electricians	1 to 6.05	16	1	—	—	—	—
Electrotypers, stereotypers, and lithographers	1 to 6.55	23	1	—	2	1	—
Engravers	1 to 6.45	—	35	1	3	—	—
Glass blowers	1 to 10.57	—	—	—	—	—	—
Jewelers, watchmakers, gold and silversmiths	1 to 8.30	—	—	—	—	—	—
Loom fixers	1 to 21.09	—	—	—	—	—	—
Machinists	1 to 7.99	1	16	—	—	5	—
Molders	1 to 14.72	—	5	—	—	—	—
Painters, glaziers, and varnishers (building)	1 to 10.71	—	—	—	—	—	—
Paper hangers	1 to 11.24	—	—	—	—	—	—
Pattern and model makers	1 to 9.86	—	—	—	1	—	—
Plasterers	1 to 10.55	3	—	—	—	—	—
Plumbers, gas, and steam fitters	1 to 7.73	7	1	1	—	—	—
Pressmen and plate printers	1 to 6.23	19	1	4	2	3	—
Roofers and slaters	1 to 7.99	2	—	—	—	—	—
Stonecutters	1 to 11.15	11	1	2	2	5	—
Tinsmiths and coppersmiths	1 to 7.12	16	3	—	—	—	—
Toolmakers and die setters	1 to 10.67	—	—	—	—	—	—
Upholsterers	1 to 4.47	4	4	—	—	—	—

[a] *Fifteenth Census of the United States: 1930, Population,* Vol. V, pp. 118–27.

greater than the ratio between the gainfully employed persons in the apprentice age groups to those in the journeyman age groups. This means that the permissible ratio was high enough to allow all workers below 23 to be apprentices. But allowance must be made for the fact that the actual apprentice ratio over a period of years is likely to be less than half the theoretical maximum.

A general comparison of apprentice ratios and the age distribution of workers is somewhat unsatisfactory because it fails to take account of the differences in the age distribution of the workers in various trades. The table on page 22 presents a comparison of the apprenticeship ratios in 295 union agreements with the distribution of workers between the apprentice and journeyman age group in certain trades for which census data are available.[20] In the case of one trade, compositors, linotypers, and typesetters, a reliable comparison is impossible.[21] This leaves 241 agreements which can be compared with the census ratios. Of these, 215 provide a ratio of apprentices to journeymen lower than the ratio of males in the apprentice age group to those in the journeyman age group.

The estimates of the ratios of workers in the apprentice age groups to workers in the journeyman age groups, presented in the table on page 22, may be summarized as follows:

Unweighted average ratio for all 29 trades	1 to 8.59
Trades in which ratio is 1 to less than 4	1
Trades in which ratio is 1 to less than 7	7

[20] In estimating the number in the apprentice age group the assumption is continued that three-fifths of the persons in the 20-24 age group are below 23 years of age. Where apprentices are classified separately, *all of them*, regardless of age, are counted in the apprentice age group.

[21] The number of apprentices in this trade is greatly overstated because the census groups together printers' and bookbinders' apprentices. Journeymen bookbinders, however, are not included with the compositors and are not classed as a separate occupation. Apparently they were included among semi-skilled workers in printing establishments. The ratio for compositors, linotypers, and typesetters, therefore, is the ratio of all printers' and bookbinders' apprentices plus all compositors, linotypers, and typesetters under 23 years of age to compositors, linotypers, and typesetters who are 23 years of age or over. It is probable that the number of workers properly in the apprentice age groups should be less than 35,000 instead of 41,615. This would make the ratio 1 to 4.05. If all of the agreements of the Typographical Union in the table are compared with this ratio, 10 out of 54 are found to have a lower ratio.

Another overstatement probably occurs in the case of the machinists' apprentices. The census reports that "many of the machinists' apprentices probably are machine tenders."

Trades in which ratio is 1 to more than 7 22
Trades in which ratio is 1 to less than 10 14
Trades in which ratio is 1 to less than 12 22
Trades in which ratio is 1 to less than 15 25

It will be noted that in 22 out of the 29 trades, the number of persons in the apprentice age groups is less than one-seventh of the number in the journeyman age groups. Yet it will be recalled that in 322, or 79 per cent, of the 409 apprentice agreements where the ratio was the only direct limit on the number of apprentices, the ratio was 1 to 6 or less.

REASONABLENESS OF UNION APPRENTICESHIP LIMITS—
THE TERMS OF APPRENTICESHIP

One frequently encounters the assertion that unions restrict entrance to the trade by requiring unreasonably long terms of apprenticeship. Whether a long term of apprenticeship reduces or increases the number of apprentices depends upon whether the limiting factor is the willingness of boys to serve an apprenticeship or the employers' willingness to take apprentices. If the former, a long term reduces the number of apprentices; if the latter, it tends to increase the number, because the longer the term, the less as a general rule is the employer's cost of training boys. Only in the latter years of his apprenticeship does a boy produce enough to pay the cost of his wages and training.[22] Evidence to be presented in the next section points to the conclusion that the number of apprentices is usually controlled by the unwillingness of employers to train boys. Under such conditions a long term is not a limiting factor.

What is a reasonable term of apprenticeship depends partly upon the care with which apprentices are selected, the opportunities which they are given for learning the trade, the thoroughness and completeness with which they are expected to master the trade, and the amount of productive work they are expected to do as apprentices in order to pay for their training.

There has been a slow tendency to reduce the length of apprenticeship. In medieval England, the customary length was

---

[22] A leading representative of the New York Employing Printers states that in the job printing industry a six-year apprenticeship is not seriously restrictive because it gives the employer a year's work at 75 per cent of journeyman's wages. If a boy is going to make a journeyman printer, he will have acquired journeyman skill at the end of five years or not at all.

seven years. This was also the length prescribed in the Statute of Artificers passed in 1562. In colonial America the seven-year period was common even in the early eighteenth century. A study of 198 indentures in New York dated between 1718 and 1727 showed that only 9 were for less than seven years, 120 were for seven years, and 69 for more than seven years.[23] But the term has been gradually becoming less, and today few unions require an apprenticeship of more than five years. Indeed in our sample of 611 agreements, only six, or less than 1 per cent, prescribed a term of six years or more, and the most usual length was five to six years. In the state of Wisconsin, where the indenture and training of apprentices has been regulated by the state since 1911, the rules set up by joint employer-labor committees provide in most trades for a four-year term. The recently established Federal Committee on Apprentice Training has established joint committees of employers and labor representatives in several industries to draw up apprenticeship standards. These committees show a disposition to set the term of apprenticeship at five years. Undoubtedly, more intensive training of apprentices would permit the training time to be reduced considerably (possibly to three years) in most cases, but such an arrangement would be prohibitively expensive to the employer because he would receive much less productive work from the boys. The higher the wages of apprentices, the longer, of course, is the term that is necessary to make it worth while for employers to train them.

Since it is impossible to appraise the term of apprenticeship prescribed by each union agreement in the light of what the boys are expected to learn and the facilities for teaching them, the best way to test their reasonableness is to compare them with the length of apprenticeship courses in non-union enterprises. Such a comparison is presented in the table on page 26.[24]

In general there is little difference in the terms of apprenticeship required by the unions and by non-union employers. In both the building trades group and the metal trades group, the most usual period of apprenticeship in non-union plants as well as union

---

[23] P. H. Douglas, *American Apprenticeship and Industrial Education*, p. 40.

[24] The information concerning the length of apprenticeship courses in non-union plants was obtained by correspondence with the managements.

Occupation	Length of Term under Union Agreements						Length of Term in Non-Union Shops					
	Total	Less than 3 Years	3 to 4 Years	4 to 5 Years	5 to 6 Years	6 Years or Over	Total	Less than 3 Years	3 to 4 Years	4 to 5 Years	5 to 6 Years	6 Years or Over
Building trades												
Bricklayers........	15	—	10	5	—	—	1	1	—	—	—	—
Carpenters........	16	—	2	14	—	—	4	1	2	1	—	—
Electricians.......	24	—	6	17	1	—	8	2	1	5	—	—
Painters..........	29	1	16	10	1	1	1	—	—	1	—	—
Sheet metal workers.	22	—	—	19	3	—	7	—	1	6	—	—
Total............	106	1	34	65	5	1	21	4	4	13	—	—
Metal trades												
Blacksmiths.......	2	—	1	1	—	—	5	—	1	4	—	—
Boilermakers......	11	—	—	11	—	—	4	—	1	3	—	—
Machinists (including tool makers)..	22	—	—	22	—	—	28	—	4	24	—	—
Molders..........	4	—	—	4	—	—	3	—	2	1	—	—
Patternmakers.....	1	—	—	—	1	—	8	—	—	8	—	—
Total............	40	—	1	38	1	—	48	—	8	40	—	—

plants is four to five years. Among the non-union plants, there is no instance in which the term is as much as five years; among the trade union apprenticeship agreements, only 1 out of 40 in the metal trades and 6 out of 106 in the building trades provide a term of five years or longer. In the building trades 35 out of 106 union agreements, or 31 per cent, and 8 out of 21 non-union shops, or 38 per cent, provide a term of less than four years; in the metal trades 1 out of the 40 union agreements and 8 out of 48 non-union apprenticeship courses provide a term of less than four years. On the whole, the short terms of apprenticeship are slightly more frequent in the non-union shops and the long terms slightly more numerous among the union agreements. But the general conclusion must be that the difference between the two is slight.

In considering the reasonableness of apprenticeship terms required by trade unions, one should note that the term may actually be six months or a year less than the period specified in the union agreement. The reason is that the union may require the employer to pay almost journeyman's wages to apprentices during the last six months or year of their apprenticeship. This, of course, makes boys more willing to serve an apprenticeship, but it makes employers less willing to train apprentices. The agreements of the railroad shopcrafts provide that apprentices at the beginning of their last year shall be paid about 82 per cent and during the last six months about 90 per cent of the journeyman's rate of pay. This means that apprentices during their last year receive substantially more than journeymen in many non-union plants. In the photo-engraving industry, where a five-year term is the rule, some of the agreements provide that fifth-year apprentices shall receive about a dollar an hour. The agreement in effect in Philadelphia from January 1, 1929 to December 31, 1934, for example, provided that fifth-year apprentices should receive $45 for a week that varied from 40 to 45 hours. Although this was substantially below the journeyman's minimum of $60, it was considerably above the rates received by skilled journeymen in many other trades. In fact, as late as 1923 the minimum rate for journeyman photo-engravers in Philadelphia was only $45 a week.

REASONABLENESS OF THE ABSOLUTE LIMITS ON
THE NUMBER OF APPRENTICES

In 202 out of 611 agreements examined, an absolute limit was placed upon the number of apprentices that might be employed in a shop or a department. In order to judge the reasonableness of these limits it would be necessary to know the number of journeymen employed in each of the union shops, but unfortunately this information is not available. In 101 of the 202 agreements covered in the table on page 11 the limit was two or less per shop or department, and in 152 three or less. When the maximum is set so low, there is a strong presumption that it is unreasonably restrictive. Nevertheless, proof is lacking, and in defense of these low limits it may be urged that many of them apply in industries where there is a large proportion of small shops. For example, 16 of the 57 agreements which permitted only one apprentice to a shop were in the building trades and 32 were in the printing trades—industries in which small concerns abound. In one case, the limit of one apprentice to a shop applied in a declining industry: it was enforced by the horseshoers' union. The reasonableness of an absolute limit on the number of apprentices depends also upon the duration of the term of apprenticeship. An agreement of the fur workers' union, for example, which imposed a maximum limit of five apprentices to the shop, required a term of only six months.[25] Clearly such a short term destroys much of the restrictiveness in the limit of five.

DO EMPLOYERS TRAIN AS MANY APPRENTICES AS
UNION RULES PERMIT?

This study would obviously be incomplete without a comparison between the number of apprentices actually hired by employers and the number permitted by trade union rules. Inquiries in a considerable number of industries show that employers, with rare exceptions, hire far fewer apprentices than the rules permit. The reader should be warned, however, against construing this as conclusive evidence that the rules as a whole do not restrict the number of apprentices. The effective limitation may be indirect and may be found in the wage scales which make the compensation of ap-

[25] Agreement of Locals 1, 5, 10, and 15 in New York City, effective February 1927 to February 1929, U. S. Bureau of Labor Statistics, *Trade Agreements, 1927*, Bulletin No. 468, pp. 72-74.

prentices high relative to that of journeymen and in other provisions such as the requirement in some building trade agreements that the employer give steady work to the apprentices.

The evidence is overwhelming that few employers hire as many apprentices as union rules allow. In the building industry even during the boom of the twenties, the failure of employers to hire as many apprentices as union rules permitted was almost universal.[26] The late Mr. Burt Fenner, former chairman of the Apprenticeship Commission of the New York Building Congress, described the situation in the construction industry of New York City as follows:

At the present time the greatest obstacle to progress, strange as it may seem, is the indifference of employers. . . . They applaud the work of the Commission and contribute to its financial support, but when they are appealed to to take on one or two apprentices and make themselves responsible for their training, they find some reason for refusing, or postponing action.[27]

Mr. J. E. Merrick of Louisville, speaking at a convention of the National Association of Sheet Metal Contractors, said:

The union has begged us time and again to get together and agree upon training apprentices. Not a shop in my city has ever given the proposition due consideration. The boy must have an incentive to learn the trade. The average employer today is responsible for the shortage of mechanics in our line.[28]

In Washington, D.C., in the midst of the boom there were less than 35 per cent of the permissible number of apprentices in training in the painting trade, only 50 per cent among the lathers, and only 65 per cent among the electricians.[29]

In Detroit, the union ratio of 1 apprentice bricklayer to 5 journeymen, with a maximum of 5 apprentices to any one contractor, permitted in 1927 over 500 apprentices, but less than 200

[26] The complaint that employers fail to hire as many apprentices as permitted by union rules is not new. The Massachusetts census for 1885 indicated that none of the building trades had even half as many apprentices as the union rules usually permitted and in most of the trades there were only one-fourth as many. W. E. Weyl and A. M. Sakolski, *Conditions of Entrance to the Principal Trades*, U. S. Bureau of Labor Statistics, Bulletin No. 67, p. 762 n.

[27] Oregon Association of Building and Construction, *A Prospectus for 1924*, p. 5.

[28] *The American Pressman*, September 1923, Vol. XXXIII, No. 10, p. 32.

[29] Mary Conyngton, "Apprenticeship in the Building Trades in Washington, D.C.," *Monthly Labor Review*, January 1925, Vol. XX, p. 4.

were in training.[30] The largest open-shop contractor employed no apprentices whatever. In the plastering trade in Detroit, the Bureau of Labor Statistics found that more than half of the contractors were not training apprentices and in the painting trade found no indentured apprentices in any of the large union shops.[31] In 1925, the Apprenticeship Commission of the New York Building Congress pointed out that in the painting and decorating trade, where the union had a membership of over 10,000, there were only 193 apprentices, and in carpentry and joinery, with a union membership of about 31,000, there were but 1,500 enrolled apprentices.[32] The commission reported at the end of 1924 that in the majority of seven trades in which apprentice schools had been started, the number of apprentices had increased from 100 to 300 per cent since 1922.[33] There had been no changes in the union rules.

A survey of apprenticeship in the commercial printing industry by the United Typothetae of America in 1920 revealed that 36 per cent of the plants had no apprentices. The ratio of apprentices to journeymen was 1 to 8.3 in the composing room, 1 to 14.6 in the press room, 1 to 9.4 in the bindery, and 1 to 10.3 in all departments.[34] At the 1925 convention of the American Photo-Engravers' Association (the employers' organization and not to be confused with the union) Commissioner Flader said:

Employers as a class are responsible for the failure to employ all the apprentices allowed in agreements, and their general indifference to apprentices and the manner of their training, helps to bring about the shortage of skilled labor of which we hear so much complaint.[35]

The association adopted a resolution "most vigorously urging all employing photo-engravers to employ their full quota of apprentices and to give strict attention to the proper training of more and better workmen."[36] In 1924, the agreement between the New York cylinder pressmen in the book and job industry allowed 1

---

[30] U. S. Bureau of Labor Statistics, *Apprenticeship in Building Construction,* Bulletin No. 459, p. 56.

[31] The same, pp. 57, 59.

[32] New York Building Congress, *Building Congress News,* Apr. 1, 1925, p. 3.

[33] The same, Dec. 10, 1924, p. 1.

[34] *Typothetae Bulletin,* November 1921, Vol. XV, p. 65.

[35] *Photo-Engravers' Bulletin,* Vol. XV, p. 48.

[36] The same, p. 245.

apprentice to every 4 journeymen or major fraction thereof, except that on certain conditions shops having only one or two journeymen might employ an apprentice. There were approximately 2,500 members in the union. This permitted about 500 to 600 apprentices. The actual number, however, was 108. The agreement in the New York photo-engraving industry allowed 1 apprentice to every 5 journeymen in job shops. Although there were 1,279 journeymen on the day shifts in these shops, there were only 195 apprentices. In the composing rooms of the job printing industry in New York, in the spring of 1922, there were 174 apprentices, or 24 short of the quota permitted by the union rule, and in the press rooms 37 apprentices, or 61 less than the quota. The president of the printing pressmen's union, speaking at the New York Club of Printing-house Craftsmen on January 21, 1926, criticized the failure of employers to hire sufficient apprentices in the press rooms. He pointed out that there should be at least 240 pressmen apprentices in the union shops in the job and commercial printing industry in New York and that at the time there were 158.[37]

Occasionally one finds unions going out of their way to encourage employers to hire the full quota of apprentices permitted by union rules. Between January 1923 and April 1926, the number of apprentices registered with the bricklayers' union increased from 5,409 to 13,360, largely as a result of a joint drive by the Mason Contractors' Association of the United States and Canada and the bricklayers' union. The help of the local unions was obtained by pointing out to them that commercial trade schools would spring up and that boys would learn the trade outside the jurisdiction of the union unless the locals encouraged apprentice training.[38]

It would be unfair and misleading, however, to blame the shortage of apprentices simply upon the employers. Behind the reluctance of employers to train apprentices are economic conditions. The apprentice is an expense at least for the first two years and the employer who trains apprentices is by no means certain whether the boys he trains will remain in his service or enter the employ of his competitors. Sometimes the union rules themselves limit the

[37] *Printing*, Jan. 30, 1926, Vol. XXXV, p. 29.
[38] See the *American Contractor*, Dec. 13, 1924, p. 32, and July 31, 1926, p. 23.

ability of the employer to hold apprentices—as when the seniority rules grant no seniority to the apprentice on becoming a journeyman after four or five years of training.[39] In a few trades, such as some branches of building construction, employers may prefer a shortage of workers to a surplus because an oversupply of journeymen leads men to become contractors and thus to create a "surplus" of contractors.

In Great Britain some of the strong employers' associations compel each employer to train his share of apprentices. The employers' associations in the United States have not been strong enough to do this. Germany has gone so far as to impose a tax on employers who do not take apprentices.[40] There have been occasional agreements between unions and employers' associations in the United States requiring that each employer keep a certain number of apprentices. Such provision was included in the agreement made July 17, 1924 between the Publishers' Association of New York and the International Printing Pressmen and Assistants' Union. The Publishers' Association is composed of New York City newspaper publishers. The agreement provided that each "office may have one apprentice for each six journeymen or fraction thereof and *shall* have at least one apprentice for every ten journeymen or major fraction thereof."[41] Another way of handling the apprentice problem is through co-operative plans which spread the cost over all competitors in the market. Such a plan exists in the Cleveland building industry.

NUMBER OF APPRENTICES IN UNION AND IN NON-UNION SHOPS

The most satisfactory way of testing the restrictiveness of union apprenticeship rules is to compare the number of apprentices in union shops with the number in non-union shops. Unfortunately data for such a comparison are meager.

There is some evidence that in the commercial branch of the

[39] The question of how much seniority to give apprentices on completing their apprenticeship has been a source of considerable controversy. As indicated above, many agreements do not permit apprentices to accumulate any seniority as journeymen. A fairer arrangement is to permit two years of apprenticeship to count as one year of seniority as a journeyman. Thus an apprentice on completing a four-year apprenticeship would have two years' seniority as a journeyman.

[40] *The Economist*, July 31, 1937, Vol. CXXVIII, p. 229.

[41] Italics added. *Monthly Labor Review*, December 1924, Vol. XIX, p. 1301.

photo-engraving industry apprentices are more numerous in non-union shops. This industry presents a peculiar situation. The union has such complete control of the photo-engravers (over 90 per cent are members) that non-union employers are compelled to provide their labor supply by training a large number of apprentices. At any rate, in 1920, Mr. Matthew Woll (then president of the International Photo-Engravers' Union) estimated that in the non-union shops there was nearly one apprentice to one journeyman—about 500 of each.[42] The union usually permits only one apprentice to five journeymen. In the newspaper branch of the industry, on the other hand, the non-union shops do not appear to train apprentices. In his report to the 1924 convention, President Woll stated that in union newspaper shops the union contracts permitted 65 apprentices and 51 were employed, but that 54 open-shop newspapers employed no apprentices.[43]

In every other industry for which data are obtainable apprentices appear to be far more numerous relative to journeymen in union plants than in non-union. The survey of apprenticeship in the printing industry, made by the United Typothetae in 1920, disclosed that 42 per cent of the non-union plants and 31 per cent of the union plants had no apprentices. Among the non-union plants there was one apprentice to eleven journeymen; among all shops, union and non-union, one apprentice to ten journeymen.[44] The Bureau of Labor Statistics, after investigating apprenticeship in the building trades in 19 cities, reported:

It is much harder to find an apprentice in an open than in a closed shop. Only three open-shop contractors were encountered in the course of the investigation who had more apprentices than they would have been granted under union agreement.[45]

For the railroads, figures are available in the annual reports filed by the roads with the Interstate Commerce Commission. The table on page 34 shows the number of journeymen per apprentice during 1929 in the maintenance-of-way equipment forces of 18 roads which

---

[42] International Photo-Engravers' Union of North America, *Officers' Reports and Convention Proceedings*, 1925, p. 17.

[43] The same, *Reports of Officers and Convention Proceedings*, 1924, p. 14.

[44] *Typothetae Bulletin*, November 1921, Vol. XV, pp. 65-66.

[45] U. S. Bureau of Labor Statistics, *Apprenticeship in Building Construction*, p. 9.

operated under union agreements in that year and 25 non-union roads.[46] The figures are based upon averages of the number of men employed on the fifteenth of each month during the year.

EXTENT OF APPRENTICE TRAINING IN THE MAINTENANCE-OF-EQUIPMENT FORCES OF
RAILROADS IN 1929

Union Roads	Number of Journeymen per Apprentice	Non-Union Roads	Number of Journeymen per Apprentice
Chesapeake and Ohio.......	6.9	Southern Pacific..........	5.1
Western Pacific............	7.4	Missouri Pacific...........	6.4
Chicago and Alton.........	7.6	Northern Pacific..........	7.9
Southern Railway.........	8.6	Louisville and Nashville.....	8.7
Chicago and Great Western..	9.0	Union Pacific.............	8.8
Cleveland, Cincinnati, Chicago, and St. Louis.......	10.1	Atchison, Topeka, and Santa Fe....................	9.8
Seaboard Air Line..........	10.6	Great Northern...........	10.5
Baltimore and Ohio.........	13.2	Chicago, Rock Island, & Pacific....................	10.6
New York, Chicago, and St. Louis..................	13.2	Denver and Rio Grande.....	10.8
Chicago and North Western..	13.9	Illinois Central............	12.0
Chicago, Indianapolis, and Louisville...............	14.3	Lehigh Valley.............	13.4
Erie.....................	14.6	Pere Marquette............	14.0
Buffalo, Rochester, and Pittsburgh..................	17.7	Norfolk and Western.......	14.4
New York Central.........	17.8	Chicago, Burlington, & Quincy.................	14.9
Chicago, Milwaukee, St. Paul, and Pacific.............	17.9	Delaware, Lackawanna, & Western...............	15.5
Grand Trunk Western......	19.4	Wabash..................	15.6
Hocking Valley............	22.9	Virginian.................	16.7
Michigan Central..........	25.9	New York, New Haven, & Hartford................	17.4
		Atlantic Coast Line........	18.2
		Boston and Maine..........	32.7
		Delaware and Hudson......	47.5
		Chicago and Eastern Illinois.	71.9
		Wheeling and Lake Erie.....	76.1
		Pennsylvania.............	76.2
		New York, Ontario, and Western................	89.4

Among the ten roads having the fewest journeymen per apprentice, five are union roads and five non-union, but among the ten having the largest number of journeymen per apprentice seven are non-union roads and only three union. The median ratio of apprentices to journeymen lies between 1 to 13.2 and 1 to 13.9 for union roads and is 1 to 14.4 for non-union. Thus the union roads on the whole trained more apprentices than the non-union.

[46] Practically all of the roads listed as non-union in 1929 have since signed agreements with the shopcrafts unions.

EXTREME RESTRICTIONS ON APPRENTICESHIP

Although our survey shows that union rules limiting the number of apprentices are not on the whole unreasonable, no one knows how far unions might be willing to go in restricting the number of apprentices *if they had the power*. Taking human nature as it is, however, one would expect unions which have a strong monopolistic position drastically to limit the entrance to the trade. The experience of the now defunct National Window Glass Workers and of some building trades locals confirms this generalization. Several years ago, the Bureau of Labor Statistics reported that

the building trades unions in St. Louis have a very definite policy of "keeping the trade in the family" and enforce it to such an extent that a contractor declared that "a boy has as good a chance to get into West Point as into the building trades unless his father or his uncle is a building craftsman."[47]

At the twenty-ninth convention of the International Photo-Engravers' Union the executive committee was authorized to encourage a reduction in the number of apprentices to be employed.[48]

Most notable of all is the experience of the National Window Glass Workers, which at one time acquired such complete control over the labor supply that it was able to regulate the output of the entire industry. The strict union control of apprenticeship produced a shortage of skilled men when business revived in 1899 and 1900. This shortage in turn had profound repercussions upon the life of the union, for it led the American Window Glass Company to attempt to gain a preferred position in the labor market by giving the union (then known as Local Assembly No. 300) a block of stock to be paid for out of dividends, and to give the union representation on the board of directors. The union was to provide the company with sufficient skilled men to operate its plants at capacity. The preference shown to the American Window Glass Company split the union and led the members in the independent plants to form the Window Glass Workers' Association of America with which Local Assembly No. 300 waged war for several years.[49] The Win-

[47] U. S. Bureau of Labor Statistics, *Apprenticeship in Building Construction*, p. 9.

[48] *American Photo-Engraver*, October 1928, Vol. XX, p. 1047.

[49] This account is based upon "The Passing of the National Window Glass Workers," *Monthly Labor Review*, October 1929, Vol. XXIX, p. 775.

dow Glass Cutters' League, which has virtually a monopoly of labor in the field, does not (in 1940) permit apprentices to be started without the approval of the president of the League.

EFFECTS OF THE DEPRESSION ON UNION REGULATION OF APPRENTICESHIP AND THE TRAINING OF APPRENTICES

The recent depression has caused the ratios of apprentices to journeymen to be modified to reduce the number of apprentices permitted. Most of the 409 agreements included in the table on page 11 were negotiated prior to 1929. Among these agreements 176, or 43.0 per cent, specified a ratio of 1 to 4 or less, and 47, or 11.5 per cent, of 1 to 10 or more. Among 149 agreements negotiated between 1935 and 1940, 48, or 32.2 per cent, specified a ratio of 1 to 4 or less, and 61, or 41.0 per cent, of 1 to 10 or more. The depression, however, does not seem to have caused an increase in the term of apprenticeship. Among 611 agreements (referred to on p. 11) largely negotiated prior to 1929, only 28, or 4.6 per cent, prescribed an apprenticeship of less than two years and 437, or 71.5 per cent, required four years or more. Among 169 agreements negotiated between 1935 and 1940, 29, or 17.1 per cent, prescribed an apprenticeship of less than two years and 97, or 57.4 per cent, of four years or more.

The long and severe depression discouraged the training of apprentices. Both unions and unemployed were opposed to starting apprentices while journeymen of long service were out of work.[50] For example, when the depression began there were 3,600 legally indentured apprentices in the state of Wisconsin. By 1934 there were only 1,000.

The long period during which few apprentices have been trained will considerably increase the number that will need to be trained between 1940 and 1950. This number will be further increased in many trades by the national defense program. It is not unlikely that the apprentice ratios which have been adequate in ordinary times will be insufficient to permit the needs of the country to be promptly met, and that a temporary modification of the ratios will

---

[50] Examination of 650 agreements negotiated between 1935 and 1940, however, revealed only 12 cases in which the training of apprentices was specifically prohibited during the life of the agreement.

be necessary. But this modification will need to be accompanied by special inducements for employers to increase the number of apprentices.

EFFORTS OF UNIONS TO REGULATE THE TRAINING OF APPRENTICES

In addition to attempting to regulate the number of apprentices, many unions undertake to regulate the quality of training that apprentices receive and to protect the opportunity of the boys to learn the trade. In fact, interest among unions in the character of the training received by apprentices is decidedly on the increase. The rules for this purpose take a great variety of forms. For example, some trade agreements prescribe that apprentices may work only with a mechanic. Rule No. 42 of the agreement negotiated in 1919 between the United States Railroad Administration and the shopcrafts provided that two apprentices should not work together as partners and that apprentices should not be assigned to work on night shifts. The national agreement between the molders' union and the stove founders (clause 4) provides: "Each apprentice in the last year of his apprenticeship should be given a floor between two journeymen molders, and they with the foreman should pay special attention to his mechanical education in all classes of work." Some locals of the photo-engravers' union permit very few apprentices to be trained in newspaper offices on the ground that the work in them is too specialized to give the boys a good opportunity to learn the trade.

Two important obstacles in the training of apprentices have been (1) the tendency for boys to leave the shop a year or two before the expiration of their training period and to seek work as journeymen, and (2) the failure of employers to keep the boys steadily employed. Many trade agreements provide that apprentices who leave their position without the consent of their employer forfeit their right to finish their apprenticeship in any other shop within the jurisdiction of the union.[51] It has been pointed out above that the practice of apprentices' leaving before the end of their terms and obtaining employment elsewhere as journeymen discourages em-

---

[51] The constitution of the International Typographical Union provides that no apprentice shall leave one office and enter that of another employer without the written consent of the first employer and the president of the union.

ployers from training apprentices. To the extent that unions compel boys to complete their course of training, they encourage employers to train more apprentices.

The problem of assuring apprentices reasonably steady employment is important in the building trades because the volume of work done by each contractor fluctuates greatly. Attention has been called to the fact that a few unions require that employers keep apprentices steadily at work or, failing to do so, pay them their regular wages.[52] In the Cleveland building trades an effort has been made by the contractors' association to relieve the burden on the individual contractor by finding work with other contractors for the boys whom the employer does not need.[53] The agreement of the Typographical Union with the New York Employing Printers declares that apprentices must be regularly employed, if employed at all, and must not be laid off on regular working days. Some unions insist that unemployed apprentices be given preference when vacancies are filled.[54]

The most important contribution of unions to the training of apprentices consists in their efforts to see that employers give the boys an all-round training. There is need for the unions to do this because, after an apprentice has acquired proficiency at a certain part of the work, it is advantageous for the foreman to keep him busy on those operations rather than give him an opportunity to learn new ones. One might expect that top management in its own interest would see that apprentices are given a good all-round training, but experience over many years in many industries shows that most managements cannot be relied upon to do this.[55]

Failure to give apprentices opportunity to learn all branches of

[52] See p. 13.

[53] The employment directors for apprentices in the building trades had the responsibility of keeping track of new jobs that were coming along and of interviewing contractors about employing boys who were without work.

[54] The agreement between the electrical workers' union of Syracuse and the local contractors, made June 18, 1924, provided that the employer notify the union as soon as he laid off an apprentice and that unemployed registered apprentices would be assigned to employers in preference to new applicants. U. S. Bureau of Labor Statistics, *Trade Agreements, 1923-1924*, Bulletin No. 393, p. 28.

[55] Interest in employee training of all kinds has been growing, but the neglect of it is still one of the principal shortcomings of American personnel administration.

the trade means that the journeymen suffer from the competition of cheap child labor, because the wages of apprentices are based upon the assumption that the boys will be rotated and given a chance to learn rather than narrowly specialized. Furthermore, the boy who fails to obtain good training in the trade is likely, after he becomes a journeyman, to have difficulty in obtaining steady work at the union scale. The poorly trained journeyman is always a menace to the union because his difficulties in obtaining work are likely to lead him to break away from the organization and to work below the union scale. The poor mechanic who has trouble in getting work is likely also to be difficult for the union to control in times of strike. On the other hand, it strengthens the union in dealing with employers if every member is well trained and if the union controls the best mechanics in the market. Most craft unions realize this.

Sometimes the effort of the union to promote better training of apprentices simply takes the form of a rule in the agreement that each apprentice shall be given an all-round training. In this extremely rudimentary form, the union's effort is likely to be ineffective. The next step is for the agreement between the union and the employer to prescribe that the apprentice shall not spend more than a given period of time on any one machine or class of work.[56] A still further step is for the agreement to prescribe the time which apprentices shall spend on different branches of the trade. For example, the agreement between the Boston photo-engravers and the newspapers, effective May 11, 1935, specifies the type of work the apprentice shall perform each year.[57] One of the most definite and

[56] Such provisions are found in a number of the shopcraft agreements. Some of them provide that the boys shall spend not more than three months on any machine or special class of work, others not more than four, others not more than six.

[57] The agreement provides that during the first year the apprentice shall perform general apprentice work in the engraving department at the discretion of the foreman. During the second year he must work at least two hours a day at the branch he elects to follow. During the third year he must work at least three hours a day at this branch; during the fourth year at least four hours a day; and during the fifth year at least six hours a day, as the foreman directs. If it is deemed advisable, after an investigation by a committee composed of the president and the business manager of the union and two to be selected by the publishers, the boy must be granted an extension of six months' time after the completion of his five years' apprenticeship in the shop where he has been employed.

detailed regulations of the apprenticeship course is found in the agreement between the New York Typographical Union and the Printers' League Section of the New York Employing Printers, which stipulates what the boy shall do in each year of his apprenticeship.[58]

Rules regulating the training of apprentices may have little practical effect unless some one is responsible for seeing that the rules are observed. Some trade agreements provide a joint apprenticeship commission made up of representatives of the union and of the employers which is given full supervision of the training and discipline of apprentices. In case of a dispute between an apprentice and his employer, appeal may be taken by either to the joint committee, and its decision is final. Where a supervising commission exists, quarterly reports on the progress of each apprentice should be submitted to it.

An important development in the training of apprentices during the last twenty years has been the institution of apprentice schools. There are many things about most trades which boys cannot readily learn on the job. Although the boys are usually expected to work under the direction of a journeyman, some journeymen are not good teachers. Some may not be particularly interested in helping the boys, particularly when this involves some interference with the journeyman's own work. Some journeymen are reluctant to reveal all that they know. Some parts of the trade are not adapted to being taught in the shop. Shop mathematics, laying out of work, reading of blueprints are examples. For instance, the best way to teach boys

---

[58] The agreement provides that no shop shall be entitled to employ an apprentice unless it has the equipment necessary for proper instruction in the several branches of the trade. The agreement also stipulates that in the first year all apprentices shall be required to do general work in the composing room. Not less than three nor more than six months of the first year shall be spent as copy-holder and as assistant to proofreader. During the second year the apprentice shall spend at least three-fourths of his time at composition and distribution. He shall be given opportunity to set reprint and job work. In the third year he shall spend at least three-fourths of his time on the floor at hand composition and distribution and be given opportunity to set ads and job work from manuscript and to assist on make-up and composition. In the fourth year he shall be employed at least seven hours each day in hand composition, distribution, make-up, and stone work. In the fifth year he shall spend the first six months at these, and the second half of the year he shall be instructed in the operation of any type-setting or type-casting machine. One purpose of the agreement is to prevent the boys from learning to operate linotype machines until they have mastered other branches of the trade.

to read blueprints is to have them make drawings themselves. Furthermore, shop training is likely to be deficient in that the boys learn how to *do* things, but often they are not told *why* certain things are done or certain methods followed. Finally, shop training alone may fail to develop in the boys a capacity to learn for themselves—a quality of great importance, especially in rapidly changing trades.[59]

A few enterprises have established apprentice schools without the help of trade unions. In some cases, however, especially in the building trades and the printing industry, apprentice classes are conducted under the joint auspices of unions and employers. Unions are almost invariably glad to co-operate in the establishment of apprentice classes. Not only do they wish journeymen to be well trained, but they wish them to be trained under union auspices. They believe that the better and the more attractive the training in the union shops, the less likely are the boys to learn the trade in commercial trade schools, which are often recruiting agencies for non-union employers.[60] Good training also attracts a better class of boys into the trade, and the unions like this. Finally, the unions feel that formal training adds to the dignity and prestige of the trade.

One of the earliest instances of co-operative apprentice classes was in the Chicago bricklaying trade. The scarcity of journeymen led, in 1900, to a study of the apprentice problem by the joint arbitration committee of the local contractors and the bricklayers' union. Joint rules governing the training of apprentices were put into effect. Among other things they provided that the contractor should keep the apprentice at work for nine consecutive months and see to it that during the remaining three months—January, February, and March—the apprentice attended school. For the first two years he was to attend a public school and present a certificate of attend-

---

[59] Mr. Woll, former president of the photo-engravers' union, has stressed this point.

[60] Mr. Woll reported to the 1927 convention: "Control over apprentice training is of vital importance to our union. The way to strengthen and elevate the control is to make our union apprenticeship conform to the highest standards and practices. No union can afford not to make this subject one of its most important and constant interests. . . . It is urged that each union create a standing committee on apprentice training and make educational work of first order importance in their plans for the coming year." International Photo-Engravers' Union of North America, *Officers' Reports and Convention Proceedings*, 1927, p. 27.

ance from the principal to the joint arbitration board. During the last two years he was to attend a technical school acceptable to the joint arbitration board. A certificate of attendance was necessary to enable him to start work in the spring.[61] In 1903 the same plan was adopted by the union and the contractors in the carpentry trade.

During recent years scores of co-operative classes for the training of apprentices have been established. Before the great depression there were such classes in Cleveland for bricklayers, carpenters, painters, plumbers, sheet metal workers, and iron workers; in Chicago for sheet metal workers and electricians; in New York for the sheet metal workers, carpenters, painters, electrical workers, upholstery workers, plasterers, plumbers, bricklayers, and granite cutters. The sheet metal workers also had classes in Pittsburgh and Washington; the electrical workers in Atlantic City, Trenton, and Indianapolis; the carpenters in Pittsburgh and Trenton; the photoengravers in New York and Philadelphia. The national agreement between the Bricklayers' and Masons' International Union and the Tile and Mantel Contractors' Association of America, for the five years ending March 31, 1928, provided that the apprenticeship term, whenever possible, should include technical school instruction for at least one month in each of the first two years.[62] The Building Trades Department of the American Federation of Labor at its convention in 1927 decided to increase the attention paid to vocational training.[63]

Some classes for apprentice training were discontinued during the great depression, but the movement to supplement training on the job with classroom instruction is a growing one. The International Association of Machinists at its convention in 1936 approved a resolution urging the adoption of schools for apprentices by all employers.[64]

[61] Lanquist, *American Contractor*, Feb. 11, 1922, p. 22.

[62] U. S. Bureau of Labor Statistics, *Trade Agreements, 1923 and 1924*, Bulletin No. 393, p. 22.

[63] *American Federationist*, November 1927, Vol. XXXIV, p. 1297.

[64] International Association of Machinists, *Proceedings of the Nineteenth Convention*, 1936, ninth day, p. 42. The resolution also urged that apprentices receive the usual pay for time spent in school, that examinations of apprentices be made every six months, that the first failure of apprentices be sufficient to retard promotion and the second to warrant dismissal.

Many unions have co-operated wholeheartedly with the work of the Federal Committee on Apprentice Training, which is concerned with improving the training of apprentices and raising apprenticeship standards. The general policy of this committee provides that apprentices shall have at least 144 hours a year devoted to classroom study and experience. The Federal Committee functions through local, state, and national committees. Through conferences with local joint apprenticeship committees (of which there were about 1,200 in the United States in 1940), the national committee endeavors to secure the local acceptance of standards for the particular trade. The next step is to expand local standards into state standards and then to define the national standards. Sometimes, however, national standards are set up first through the co-operation of a joint committee representing the national trade association and the national trade union covering the trade. National standards have been adopted in the plumbing industry in an agreement between the Master Plumbers' Association and the United Association of Journeymen Plumbers and Steamfitters. In several other industries, national trade apprenticeship standards were in process of development in 1938. The International Typographical Union and the state federations of labor in Ohio, Indiana, Michigan, and other states have endorsed the work of the Committee on Apprentice Training. At its 1937 convention, the American Federation of Labor strongly endorsed the committee.[65] The influence of the committee seems to be in the direction of replacing four-year apprenticeship with five-year. This is of doubtful wisdom.

Several unions have set up their own apprentice classes or courses. For some years the International Typographical Union offered

[65] The Federal Committee is particularly interested in encouraging the growth of indentured apprenticeship regulated by a state law, such as the statute adopted in Wisconsin in 1911. The Wisconsin law is based upon the fact that apprentice training is education and upon the principle that it is the duty of the state to see that proper educational standards are preserved and that the apprentices receive proper training in the trade. The Wisconsin law makes the approval of the state a condition of every indenture. To assure all-round training, every indenture provides that the apprentice shall be rotated from one kind of work to another and fixes both the minimum and maximum periods of time which he may spend at any process. In 1931, Oregon passed a law similar to the Wisconsin one, but it has been a dead letter. An excellent discussion of the apprenticeship problem, with particular reference to the Wisconsin law, will be found in E. E. Witte, "Unemployment and Recovery," The Yale Review, March 1937, Vol. XXVI, pp. 475-90.

lessons in printing to its apprentices—and also to the journeyman members. Originally the course was optional. Some of the locals favored making it obligatory for apprentices. In 1925, the union finally made the course, or its equivalent, compulsory for each apprentice under 26 years of age. The course is conducted by a Bureau of Education at the national headquarters of the union. In 1927, there were more than 9,000 apprentices enrolled with the bureau.[66] The pressmen's union also requires its apprentices to take a five-year correspondence course offered by the International Trade School, which is maintained by the union at its general headquarters.

The co-operation of unions in the conducting of apprentice classes takes several forms. In a minority of cases, the unions make financial contributions. Thus an agreement between the Trenton carpenters' union and the master carpenters which required the apprentices to take a two-year night course in the School of Industrial Arts provided that half of the tuition should be borne by the local union and half by the employers.[67] Apprentices in the Chicago electrical construction trade, who attended class for eight hours a day, were paid for this attendance once every two weeks by the contractor and the union jointly. The schools for compositors and pressmen in the New York job printing industry are supported by the union, the employers' association, the city, and the federal government. Several years ago the Typographical Union was contributing $10,000 a year to the compositors' school and the New York Employing Printers a like amount; the pressmen's union was contributing $5,000 a year to the pressmen's school, and the employers' association $3,500.[68]

More important than the financial contributions from the unions is their help in enforcing regular attendance, in maintaining high

---

[66] *Typographical Journal*, January 1927, Vol. LXX, p. 13. The union requires an apprenticeship of five years. The course of lessons is for two years. The union rule requires that an apprentice be enrolled in the course by the local unions by the third year of his apprenticeship.

[67] U. S. Bureau of Labor Statistics, *Trade Agreements, 1923 and 1924*, Bulletin No. 393, p. 26. Some unions have found that night classes are not very satisfactory. The boys are too tired to do good work and attendance in the evening is difficult to maintain.

[68] Personal interview with executive director of the employers' association.

The employers' association was partly reimbursed by payments from employers who had apprentices in the school. Each employer paid $25 a year for each apprentice. The pressmen's union also collected an annual fee of $25 from each apprentice.

standards of work, handling cases of discipline, and improving the attitude of the boys toward their school work and their apprenticeship training in general. There is some disposition for the boys to regard the class work as unimportant and as less practical than work in the shop. Unless they are held strictly to account, they will not attend classes regularly. Hence one finds rules regulating attendance at classes and conduct in classes. In the Chicago bricklaying and carpentry trades, it was customary to add a day without pay to the boy's apprenticeship for every day that he was tardy or disorderly in school and to add two days for every day of unexcused absence from school.[69] The electrical workers in Atlantic City required an attendance record of 90 per cent when the boys came up to be examined for their journeyman's card. The New York sheet metal workers required an attendance of 90 per cent. The boys were advanced in pay every six months, but an apprentice who did not meet the required standard of attendance, or failed to do his class work satisfactorily, did not receive his advance. The Pittsburgh sheet metal workers required that the time lost from school be made up before the apprentice received his journeyman's card.[70] The Cleveland bricklayers and carpenters required an apprentice who had two unexcused school absences to appear before the joint committee and imposed one day's attendance at school without pay for the third offense and suspension for the fourth. For misconduct in school he was required to appear before the committee after a second offense, and after a fourth offense he was suspended for two weeks and required to attend school on his own time and to report daily to the secretary of the local.

THE HELPER PROBLEM

In some trades it is usual for the mechanics to work with helpers. If not restricted in their work, the helpers in the course of several years may learn how to do the journeyman's work. Thus working as a helper may be one way of entering a trade. But it is obvious that the helper may be a menace to the journeyman. Suppose, for example, that there are 1,000 journeymen assisted by

---

[69] Lanquist, *American Contractor*, Feb. 11, 1922, p. 23.
[70] U. S. Bureau of Labor Statistics, *Trade Agreements, 1923 and 1924*, Bulletin No. 393, p. 44.

1,000 helpers. If, in the course of several years, the helpers become capable of replacing the journeymen, there are 2,000 men capable of filling 1,000 places. Every helper under these circumstances is a potential strikebreaker, because a strike would give him a good opportunity to become a journeyman.

Unions adopt various policies toward helpers. Some organizations attempt to prevent the use of helpers; others seek to restrict their work so that they will not have an opportunity to learn the journeyman's job; still other organizations accept the helper as a man who is learning the trade and undertake to regulate the number of helpers and their work.

The hosiery workers have fought the helper in certain branches of the trade on the ground that he became a competitor for the knitter's job. At one time it was the custom in some plants for a knitter and helper to operate two knitting machines. The union opposed the extension of this system. Recent increases in the length and speed of machines made this method of operation impractical, and the issue is now dead.

The building trades and some of the railroad shopcrafts undertake to prevent helpers from becoming competitors of journeymen by regulating the work of the helper in such a way that he does not have an opportunity to learn the trade. This may be done in several ways. Most of the railroad shopcrafts, for example, carefully define the work which must be done by journeymen. Another method of preventing helpers from learning the trade is to forbid them to work alone. Furthermore, when working with a journeyman the helper may be prohibited from using the tools of the journeyman's trade. Such a rule is particularly difficult to enforce where the journeyman is paid by the piece, because the journeyman may make more money by allowing the helper to work without restriction. In fact, the skilled pieceworker is tempted to employ helpers himself and to become a sort of sub-contractor. Some unions, therefore, prohibit the use of helpers when journeymen are paid by the piece. This was done for many years by the molders.[71]

71 In the early days of the foundry industry, the employment of helpers by molders was known as the "Berkshire system." At the conference with the Manufacturers' Protective and Development Association in December 1927, the molders' union abandoned in some degree its historic position with reference to the em-

There are some cases in which the helper by the very nature of his work learns a journeyman's trade and yet where the journeyman needs a helper on many operations. In these cases the union has little alternative except to regulate the helper as an apprentice. The blacksmiths' union is an example. In order to limit the number of helpers who learn the trade, distinction may be made between the ordinary helper and the helper apprentice. The number of apprentice helpers may be limited and the time they are required to serve before becoming journeymen regulated.

EFFORTS OF TRADE UNIONS TO REGULATE ENTRANCE TO TRADES BY LAW

A number of unions attempt to control entrance to the trade by state laws or city ordinances which require anyone who practices the trade to have a license. The principal unions interested in licensing laws are the plumbers, the stationary engineers and firemen, the electricians, the barbers, and the motion picture operators. In 1923, there were laws licensing plumbers in 21 states, stationary engineers in 7 states, electricians in 4 states.[72] In 1924, sixteen states required

---

ployment of helpers by pieceworkers. Clause 23 of the conference agreement was changed to permit a helper to work with a piecework molder on certain types of floor work, such as warm air, steam or boiler work, and the ashpits, domes, and firepots of the circulating heater "with the further understanding that the helper shall not be permitted to do any part of the molder's work, or to use any part of the molder's tools excepting the shovel and riddle." The reason for the change, as given by the president, was the "unorganized condition of the furnace molders." Most furnace work was being done in non-union shops and the permission to use helpers was given "in order that union employers might be placed in a position whereby they could manufacture and sell more furnaces than they were selling." International Molders' Union, *International Molders' Journal*, November 1928, Vol. LXIV, Supplement, p. 2.

[72] I am indebted to the Legislative Reference Library of the state of Wisconsin for the following citations to state laws in effect in 1929 governing licenses to plumbers, engineers, and electricians: Arkansas, Stat. 1921, secs. 7624-9; California, Gen. Laws 1915, Art. 2838-39; Gen. Laws Suppl. 1917-21, Art. 2712a; Colorado, Stat. 1912, p. 2343 and Laws 1917, pp. 405-12; Florida, Stat. 1920, secs. 2252-55; Illinois, Stat. 1921, c. 109a, par. 1-9; Kansas, Stat. 1915, secs. 985-91; Louisiana, Stat. 1920, p. 1362; Maine, Stat. 1916, p. 450; Maryland, Code 1914, pp. 1146-48, vol. 1; Massachusetts, Gen. Laws 1921, p. 1454, vol. 11; Michigan, Comp. Laws 1915, secs. 6857-72; Missouri, Stat. 1919, secs. 8825-32; Montana, Code 1921, secs. 5183-93; New Hampshire, Stat. 1913, pp. 376-78, sec. 265; Oklahoma, Rev. Laws Suppl. 1918, secs. 6985a-1; Oregon, Rev. Laws 1920, secs. 3856-61; Pennsylvania, Stat. 1920, secs. 3522-28, 2845-52, 4415-17; South Carolina, Laws 1914 (spec. session), p. 14 and Laws 1914, p. 659; Tennessee, Code 1917, p. 953 and Code Suppl. 1920, sec. 2361a-1-26; Texas, Civil Code

licenses of barbers; in 1937, forty states.[73] In addition, many cities have passed ordinances requiring licenses of plumbers, electricians, engineers, and taxi drivers. Restrictions on entrance into these trades have a basis in reasons of safety or public health. During recent years, however, the painters' unions in some localities have attempted to secure license laws in the painting trade.

The laws regulating the issuance of licenses usually require that persons pursuing the trade shall be more than a certain age, have a minimum amount of schooling (such as eighth-grade education) and be able to read and write the English language, and, in some cases, have served an apprenticeship term of not less than a specified length. In addition, the laws usually specify that persons pursuing the trade shall be competent, and an examining board is created to examine all applicants for licenses. No careful study has been made of the administration of these laws, of their value to the public, or of the abuses that may occur in their administration.

Even among the unions which endeavor to obtain license legislation, there is some opposition to such legislation. For example, at the convention of the United Association of Journeymen Plumbers and Steamfitters in September 1928, Local No. 440 offered a resolution recommending to all city and state law-making bodies that all laws pertaining to the licensing of journeyman steamfitters and journeyman plumbers be rescinded. The committee on the state of the association, to which the resolution was referred, recommended non-concurrence, and the resolution was rejected.[74] There has been some opposition to license laws within the barbers' union, but it is growing weaker. The president of the union in his report to the fifteenth convention referred to this opposition and to the embarrassment which it caused the union in seeking to obtain legislation.[75] Several delegates at this convention spoke against licensing laws. The convention, however, endorsed a model law.

1929, sec. 991-997a and Penal Code 1920, sec. 131; Wisconsin, Stat. 1921, sec. 1409-a-5-10.

[73] Journeymen Barbers' International Union of America, *Report of the Proceedings of the Fifteenth Convention*, 1924, p. 48, and correspondence with the union.

[74] *Plumbers, Gas and Steam Fitters' Journal*, November 1928, Vol. XXXIII, p. 150.

[75] Journeymen Barbers' International Union of America, *Fifteenth Convention, Proceedings*, 1924, p. 30. The president said: "It is, indeed, a crying shame that any union journeyman barber would be against a measure that is bound to elevate and throw safeguards around the profession, and the time has come when the Inter-

Some of the opposition to licensing laws among union members arises on account of the license fee; some on the ground that the examinations are too difficult and require candidates to answer questions which many practical, competent, and experienced mechanics at the trade are not able to answer; some on the ground that the licensing laws work a hardship upon the traveling members and retard their freedom of movement. A union member going into a state or a city where a license is required may be compelled to wait several weeks or even several months before he obtains a license. Many of the barbers' license laws provide for reciprocal agreements with other states which permit the issuance of temporary working permits to barbers who come under the license laws of their own states. These persons, however, must take an examination for licenses in the state to which they migrate.

Licensing laws tend to raise wages by making it easier for unions to win strikes. The reason is obvious: since employees must be licensed, employers find difficulty in obtaining strikebreakers. This, indeed, is one reason why some unions are so keenly interested in licensing laws. It explains the importance which the United Mine Workers attach to the miners' licensing act of Illinois and the Pennsylvania act requiring a license for miners in the anthracite industry and the great interest of taxi drivers in licensing laws. Illuminating is an extract from a talk to the taxi drivers of New York by Harold F. Galbraith, leader of the Philadelphia Taxi Drivers' Union:

The future is very rosy for this union. . . . After a strong union is formed and it should ever become necessary to call a strike there can be no outside Scabs brought in, for all cab men must have a hacking license. In order to get this license the applicant must be a resident of the city for one year and thirty days must elapse before an application is granted.[76]

The use of licensing laws at times of strikes was well described by delegate Loring G. Hersay from the Providence, Rhode Island, local of the barbers' union at the fifteenth convention. Mr. Hersay said:

I have settled more strikes for my organization by being a member of the board of state barber examiners than a dozen local unions could have

---

national Union must take a firm grip on the situation and refuse support and assistance to any state working to have a Barbers' License Law enacted until the membership throughout such state stands as a unit behind the measure."

[76] *The Hosiery Worker*, Feb. 2, 1934, Vol. XII, p. 3.

done in my town, and I am secretary of my local. We have settled hotel strikes where they got scab men in there without licenses from out of town. I have gone to the police station and sworn out warrants and taken them out of the barber shops, and two hours afterward had the boss sign up. Now, those are some of the things you can accomplish by that law. I could talk here two or three hours on that, but this has been covered and I want to keep that before you. It keeps the bums out, and it keeps wages up, and the good barber gets a chance to earn a lot of good money.[77]

Do licensing laws increase or decrease the number of men in the trade? The answer is not certain. By raising the price of labor, they tend to reduce the number of jobs and this, of course, tends to reduce the number of men attached to the trade. But since workers seem disposed to judge the attractiveness of occupations more by the hourly rates of pay than by the annual earnings, high hourly rates are likely to attract more men into the trade than the employment opportunities warrant. Consequently, it is possible that license laws actually increase rather than decrease the number of men in a trade. At any rate, it seems certain that licensing laws tend to increase the number of men relative to the number of jobs. Hence they are more likely to produce a labor surplus than a labor shortage in the trade.

SOME CONCLUSIONS

From this survey of the efforts of unions to control entrance to the trade, the following principal conclusions stand out:

1. In almost no instances are union apprentice ratios based upon statistical analysis of the retirement and death rates among journeymen, the growth of the trade, or the proportion of beginning apprentices who complete their courses. Except for the census every ten years, virtually no data are available on the number of skilled men in the country. No satisfactory information is provided even by the census on the number of apprentices. Data on the attrition rate in the several trades and the length of trade life are almost non-existent. Although the number of apprentices who could theoretically be trained under the most usual ratios and terms is sufficient to meet the needs of moderately expanding trades, the num-

[77] Journeymen Barbers' International Union, *Fifteenth Convention, Proceedings,* 1924, p. 356.

ber that actually can be trained is less than half the theoretical maximum and in most cases is not sufficient to maintain the existing number of journeymen. The apprentice ratios fall far short of meeting the needs of rapidly expanding trades, of occupations in which the trade life is short, or of a sudden expansion of national defense.

2. The duration of the apprentice training required by union agreements is virtually the same as that existing in apprentice courses in non-union plants. This does not mean that the period could not be considerably shortened without sacrificing the adequacy of the training. Shortening the course, however, without reducing the quality of the training would raise the net cost of training, both because additional supervision would be necessary and because the employer would be deprived of the opportunity to recover, during the late period of the apprentice's training, part of the losses incurred during the early years of training.

3. Scattered instances of extreme restriction of entrance to the trade by unions can be found. They are not, however, numerous. Undoubtedly they would be more numerous if the unions were in a more monopolistic position. Since most unions do not completely control entrance to the trade, they must not make it too difficult for boys to learn the trade in union shops.

4. Apprentices are more numerous in union shops than in non-union shops. Hence, one must conclude that the net effect of all union rules and conditions is not to discourage the training of apprentices. On the contrary the unions seem to increase the number of apprentices trained. They do this largely because as organized groups they are able to put pressure on employers to take boys. The unions do not wish an employer to take an unlimited number of boys, but the members and their relatives and friends have sons for whom the union members seek an opportunity to learn the trade. As a rule, the union members wish to place more boys as apprentices than the employers are willing to take.

5. Although unions seem to increase the number of apprentices trained, they have made little progress in solving the problem of providing good opportunities for boys to learn skilled trades. Even in union shops, the number of apprentices is far too few to provide replacements for the journeymen. No one knows what proportion

of the journeymen in American industry have ever served a regular apprenticeship, but it is small. Most skilled men have literally "picked up" the trade. The growing obstacles to movement from plant to plant make "picking up" a trade more difficult and thus increase the need for systematic training.

6. Unions are easily interested in improving the training of apprentices, and in many cases they have helped substantially to improve it, both by requiring the employer to give more all-round training and by their own participation in the administration of apprentice courses. Effective union participation in the training of apprentices still exists in only a small minority of plants and there is room for great extension of this participation. Indeed it is a safe generalization that unions have placed too much emphasis upon the wages of apprentices and not enough on their training. Far more serious to a boy than receiving a low wage for several years is having his time taken up for four years without being taught the trade.

7. Timing the training of skilled workers is still far from solution. In depressions, when there is unemployment among journeymen, neither unions nor employers wish to start apprentices. Nevertheless, this is the time when apprentices need to be started if they are to become journeymen during periods of expanding employment. As a general rule, the expansion of the training of apprentices comes fairly late in the business cycle and boys do not become available as journeymen until employment has dropped.

8. There is great variation with respect to union policy toward helpers. Some unions are mainly concerned with preventing helpers from learning the trade. Others assume that journeymen will be replaced mainly from the ranks of helpers.

9. The administration and the effect of license laws covering the entrance to trades is still an unexplored area. There is no reason to expect that these laws under ordinary circumstances will produce a shortage of labor relative to demand for it. On the contrary, they are more likely to produce a surplus relative to demand. They are likely, however, to facilitate the raising of wages by unions in the trade. Their value as a protection to the buyers of labor is little known, but undoubtedly varies greatly.

CHAPTER III

CONTROL OF HIRING

The strategic importance of control over the opportunity to work is obvious. When wage earners are unorganized, the employer, because of the very fact that he is the employer, decides who shall be hired or laid off. Unless a union is able in some measure to limit the employer's control over either hiring or layoffs, it is not likely to survive against a hostile employer because he, by discriminating in favor of non-unionists, will make membership in the organization unattractive to the men. It is not necessary, however, that the union be able to limit the employer's discretion at *all* points. For example, a union which, for any reason, has little control over the employer's freedom to hire may protect itself by restricting his freedom to lay off. The railroad unions are one example. Likewise, a union which cannot control layoffs may protect itself by requiring that preference in hiring be given to union members—as do the unions in the building trades. As a general principle, it may be stated that a union which is unable to restrict the employer's control over the opportunity to work at *one* point will be all the more interested in limiting his control over this opportunity at other points. This chapter will discuss the efforts of unions to limit the employer's control of hiring. The following two chapters will discuss the efforts of unions to restrict the employer's freedom to make layoffs.

The contest over the control of hiring has been far more acute in the United States than in Great Britain and some other European countries. This difference seems to be explained by the great solidarity of the working class in Great Britain in contrast to the individualism of the American worker. The solidarity of British workers affects union policy in several ways. In the first place, it makes the men willing to down tools against workers who refuse to join their organizations. This enables British unions to treat the issue of union membership as a question concerning the employees only and not involving the employer. They regard a refusal to work with non-members simply as a quarrel among themselves and not ordinarily as a strike against the employer.[1] In the second place, it helps unions to hold their members so that it is less necessary to demand the closed shop in order to prevent indifferent members from ceasing to pay dues. Finally, the solidarity of the British workers makes it unnecessary for the unions to demand control of hiring in order to present a united front to the employer in case of a strike. Non-members of unions in Great Britain have ordinarily been as willing as members to respond to a strike call against a common employer, and to remain out as long as the strike was in process. Whether victorious or defeated, the men, both union and non-union, go back to work together: they do not dribble back in small groups as often happens in the case of lost strikes in the United States. The American unions have been compelled to stress the control of hiring because the effective functioning of trade unionism presupposes a more homogeneous and less individualistic working class than the United States has possessed.[2]

FORMS AND EXTENT OF RESTRICTIONS ON HIRING

The most common restriction on the employer's freedom to hire is the provision found in many trade agreements requiring that the employer hire only union members or men willing to join. This arrangement is known as the closed shop. As will be pointed out presently, there are several forms of the closed shop. A few agreements go beyond the mere closed shop and require the employer to engage his help through the union office or through hiring halls controlled by the union. Closely akin to the closed shop (and in prac-

---

[1] Although the agreements of British unions ordinarily preclude strikes against employers over matters covered by the agreement, at least until methods of adjustment provided in the agreement have been exhausted, they do not bar the members from refusing to work with non-members. This situation, of course, tends to restrain the employer from discriminating against members because, if he did, he would find himself involved with the union.

[2] In Sweden an interesting compromise was worked out in 1906 between the employers' federation, the National Federation of Employers' Associations, and the Federation of Trade Unions. The growing strength of the unions led the employers to adopt the policy of recognizing the unions. In return, the unions agreed to recognize the right of the employer to engage and dismiss workers without regard to whether they were union members or not. In other words, the open shop was traded for union recognition. The employers' federation insists upon the inclusion of this clause in all agreements negotiated by its constituent federations.

tice usually indistinguishable) is the preferential shop, under which the employer agrees to give preference in hiring (and sometimes in making layoffs) to union members. In some cases the agreement between the union and the employer may require that preference in filling vacancies shall be given to furloughed men and that these men, if qualified, shall be rehired in the order of their "seniority" or length of service with the company. This rule may or may not be part of a closed-shop agreement. It is found in most of the agreements between the railroads and their employees and in many of the agreements made with new unions during the last five or six years. Most of these agreements do not contain closed-shop clauses.[3] Some unions place restrictions on the employer's freedom to use certain tests and methods, such as physical examinations, in selecting employees. Finally, a few unions have sought to require employers to hire a certain number of older men.[4]

With respect to actual restrictions on hiring, the difference between a closed and an open shop may or may not be sharp.[5] Some employers who enter into open-shop agreements with trade unions may be quite meticulous in refusing to give the slightest encouragement to membership in the union. Other employers, while maintaining the open-shop principle, may go far in encouraging union membership. There are various ways by which the employer may do this. For example, he may have a verbal understanding with union officials to notify them of vacancies and to hire union mem-

---

[3] In fact, the requirements that furloughed men shall be given preference in filling vacancies and that they shall be rehired in the order of their seniority, together with certain other clauses in the railroad agreements, are to be regarded as substitutes for the closed shop.

[4] In 1936, the painters' union in New York City negotiated an agreement which provided that if 10 to 20 journeymen were employed by a contractor, at least one must be 55 years of age or over, and if 20 or more were employed, at least two must be 55 years of age or over. A few years ago the electrical workers' local in New York arranged to have older members of the union given preference on certain types of work. A recent agreement of the electrical workers in Cincinnati provides that every sixth man in a shop or on a job shall be not less than 50 years old.

[5] The expression "open shop" is used in several ways. Often it simply means that the employer refuses to recognize the union, but does not refuse to hire union men. Where, however, the employer enters into an open-shop agreement with the union, he is recognizing the organization. This type of open shop is obviously very different from the open shop maintained by employers who refuse to recognize unions.

bers provided suitable men are available. Some employers go a step farther and, while refusing to sign a closed or a preferential shop agreement, embody provisions in the trade agreement designed to help the union gain and hold members.[6]

More effective support to union membership may be given by requiring that all workers who join the union keep up their membership. This is done in several agreements between the International Paper Company and the two unions in the paper industry, made in October 1937, which provide: "Any permanent employee who is now in good standing in the local unions or who after this date becomes or is reinstated as a member shall be expected to maintain such membership in the union during the life of this agreement." Stronger and more complete is the standard provision used by some unions in the Congress of Industrial Organization in recent agreements.[7]

Among 169 open-shop agreements in a group of 400 agreements negotiated between 1933 and 1939, 11 provided that the employer would give consideration to union members in hiring employees or would recommend that new employees join the union, and 9 provided that present and future members of the union must keep up their membership.

PROVISIONS OF CLOSED-SHOP AGREEMENTS

The union restrictions on hiring which are most frequently brought into question are the closed shop and the preferential

[6] An agreement between a paper processing company and the printing pressmen's union contains the following provision: "The employer will advise and encourage its employees in all reasonable ways to become members of the union and to maintain good standing therein."

The agreement between the Pacific Coast Association of Pulp and Paper Manufacturers and the paper makers' and the pulp and sulphite workers' union provides that the employer "will co-operate with the local union in every proper and lawful way to assist in obtaining and retaining members."

[7] "The Company believes that its interests and the interests of its employees would be better served if all of the employees were members of the Union.

"The Company, as a matter of policy, will endeavor to persuade its employees at the said plants to become members of the Union.

"If, at any time, the Union shall furnish to the Company a list of employees who are not members of the Union, the Company agrees to advise such employees of the Company's policy and to urge them to join the Union.

"The Company believes that those of its employees who are members of the Union should pay their dues, and if the Union furnishes the Company with a list of Union members who are delinquent, the Company will endeavor to persuade such employees to pay their dues."

shop. The tables on pages 58-61 show, by industries or trades, the general "shop forms" imposed by two groups of agreements. The table on pages 58-59 covers 250 agreements negotiated by locals of over 50 national unions between 1923 and 1929; the table on pages 60-61, 400 agreements negotiated by the locals of over 50 national unions and by some federal locals between 1933 and 1939. In the first group of 250 agreements there were 78 open shop agreements, 168 closed shop, and 4 preferential shop. In the second group of 400 agreements there were 169 open shop, 215 closed shop, and 16 preferential shop.[8]

The terms of the closed-shop agreements vary, and one cannot judge the effects of these agreements without examining their provisions. Closed-shop agreements which provide simply that the employer must hire union members only are not the rule. The great majority of closed-shop agreements provide that the employer must hire union men if available. This was true of 133 out of 168 closed-shop agreements in the group negotiated between 1923 and 1929, and of 137 out of 215 negotiated between 1933 and 1938. Other closed-shop agreements provide that the employer may hire anyone, but that new employees must join the union within a given period. The CIO unions, which have particularly sponsored this form, have designated it the "union shop." Still other agreements provide that union men will be preferred and non-union men must join. The closed-shop forms in the two groups of agreements covered by the tables may be summarized as follows:

	Agreements of 1923-29	Agreements of 1933-39
Union members must be hired if available	133	137
Union members will be preferred and non-members on being hired must join	3	19
The employer may hire anyone, but non-members must join the union within a given period	12	36
Only new employees must become union members	–	15
Indefinite	20	8
Total	168	215

[8] Nine of the agreements classified as open shop require present or future employees who become members of the union to retain their membership. If one conceives of an open shop as one in which each worker is free to belong to the union or not as he pleases, these shops cannot be regarded as completely open because once a man joins the union he loses his freedom. He retains it only so long as he elects not to join.

SHOP FORMS IN 250 AGREEMENTS NEGOTIATED BETWEEN 1923 AND 1929

Industry or Trade	Grand Total	Open Shop					Closed Shop					
		Total	No Discrimination	Employer Will Consider Union Men or Recommend Joining	Present and Future Members Must Remain Members	Preferential Shop	Total	Only New Employees Must Become Union Members	Anyone May Be Hired, but Those Hired Must Join Union within Given Period	Union Men Will Be Preferred; Non-union Must Join	Union Men Must Be Hired if Available	Indefinite
BUILDING CONSTRUCTION	65	5	4	1	—	—	60	—	2	—	52	6
Bricklayers and masons	6	—	—	—	—	—	6	—	—	—	6	—
Carpenters and joiners	8	—	—	—	—	—	8	—	1	—	7	—
Electrical workers	16	5	4	1	—	—	11	—	—	—	8	3
Elevator constructors	2	—	—	—	—	—	2	—	—	—	2	—
Glaziers	1	—	—	—	—	—	1	—	—	—	1	—
Heat and frost insulator workers	2	—	—	—	—	—	2	—	—	—	2	—
Hod carriers	4	—	—	—	—	—	4	—	—	—	3	1
Hoisting engineers	6	—	—	—	—	—	6	—	1	—	5	—
Painters	6	—	—	—	—	—	6	—	—	—	4	2
Plasterers	3	—	—	—	—	—	3	—	—	—	3	—
Plumbers and steamfitters	2	—	—	—	—	—	2	—	—	—	2	—
Roofers	3	—	—	—	—	—	3	—	—	—	3	—
Sheet metal workers	4	—	—	—	—	—	4	—	—	—	4	—
Uniform Building Trades Agreement	2	—	—	—	—	—	2	—	—	—	2	—
METAL AND STONE TRADES AND MACHINERY	15	3	3	—	—	—	12	—	1	—	9	2
Boilermakers	3	—	—	—	—	—	3	—	1	—	2	—
Granite cutters	9	2	2	—	—	—	7	—	—	—	5	2
Molders	1	—	—	—	—	—	1	—	—	—	1	—
Steel workers	1	1	1	—	—	—	—	—	—	—	—	—
Stone cutters	1	—	—	—	—	—	1	—	—	—	1	—
MINING, QUARRYING, AND OIL	7	6	6	—	—	1	—	—	—	—	—	—
Mine workers	7	6	6	—	—	1	—	—	—	—	—	—
NEEDLE TRADES	18	2	2	—	1	1	14	—	2	—	9	3
Amalgamated Clothing Workers	2	1	1	—	—	—	1	—	—	—	1	—
Furriers	2	—	—	—	—	—	2	—	—	—	1	1
Glove workers	1	—	—	—	—	—	1	—	—	—	1	—
Ladies' garment workers	8	—	—	—	1	1	6	—	—	—	4	2
Tailors	2	—	—	—	—	—	2	—	2	—	—	—
Textile workers	3	1	1	—	—	—	2	—	—	—	2	—

Note: The Closed Shop columns "Only New Employees Must Become Union Members," "Anyone May Be Hired, but Those Hired Must Join Union within Given Period," "Union Men Will Be Preferred; Non-union Must Join," and "Union Men Must Be Hired if Available" fall under the heading "Those Now Employed Must Join and in Hiring New Employees."

The original table columns carry no printed headings. The data columns are reproduced left-to-right as they appear beside the occupation labels.

PAPER, PRINTING, AND BOOKBINDING	42					1	41			1	40	
Bookbinders	5						5				5	
Compositors	8						8				8	
Papermakers	2						2				2	
Photo-engravers	19					1	18			1	17	
Printing pressmen	4						4				4	
Stereotypers and electrotypers	4						4				4	
TRANSPORTATION AND COMMUNICATION	65	61	61				4		1	1	1	1
Masters, mates, and pilots	1	1	1									
Railroad workers												
(a) Engineers, firemen, conductors	17	17	17									
(b) Maintenance of way	7	7	7									
(c) Railway clerks	5	5	5									
(d) Shopcrafts	20	20	20									
(e) Switchmen	5	5	5									
Teamsters and chauffeurs	3						3		1		1	1
Telegraphers	5	4	4				1			1		
Transport workers	2	2	2									
OTHER UNIONS IN MANUFACTURING	21	1	1				20			1	16	3
Bakery and confectionery workers	4						4				3	1
Brewery, cereal, etc., workers	4						4				4	
Glass bottle blowers	2						2			1		1
Glass workers	3						3				3	
Leather workers	1						1				1	
Operative potters	2						2				1	1
Rubber workers	1	1	1									
Upholsterers and mattress workers	4						4				4	
MISCELLANEOUS	17						17		6		6	5
Barbers	5						5				1	4
Building service employees	1						1				1	
Cooks and waitresses	2						2				2	
Hotel and restaurant employees	2						2				2	
Retail clerks	7						7		6			1
GRAND TOTAL	250	78	76	1	1	4	168		12	3	133	20

59

SHOP FORMS IN 400 AGREEMENTS NEGOTIATED BETWEEN 1933 AND 1939

Industry or Trade	Grand Total	Open Shop — Total	Open Shop — No Discrimination	Open Shop — Employer Will Consider Union Men or Recommend Joining	Present and Future Members Must Remain Members	Preferential Shop	Closed Shop — Total	Closed Shop — Only New Employees Must Be Union Members	Those Now Employed Must Join, and in Hiring New Employees — Anyone May Be Hired, but Those Hired Must Join Union within Given Period	Those Now Employed Must Join — Union Men Will Be Preferred; Non-union Must Join	Those Now Employed Must Join — Union Men Must Be Hired if Available	Indefinite
METAL AND STONE TRADES AND MACHINERY	56	39	37	2	—	1	16	—	7	2	6	1
Aluminum workers	1	1	1	—	—	—	—	—	—	—	—	—
Blacksmiths	1	1	1	—	—	—	—	—	—	—	—	—
Brass workers	1	1	1	—	—	—	—	—	—	—	—	—
Die casters	1	1	1	—	—	—	—	—	—	—	—	—
Farm equipment workers	1	1	1	—	—	—	—	—	—	—	—	—
Granite workers	2	1	1	—	—	—	1	—	1	—	—	—
Jewelry workers	2	2	1	1	—	—	—	—	—	—	—	—
Machinists	17	9	8	1	—	—	8	—	2	1	5	—
Metal polishers	4	—	—	—	—	—	4	—	3	—	—	1
Molders	4	1	1	—	—	1	2	—	1	1	—	—
Silver workers	1	1	1	—	—	—	—	—	—	—	—	—
Steel workers	21	20	20	—	—	—	1	—	—	—	1	—
MINING, QUARRYING, AND OIL	14	12	9	3	—	2	—	—	—	—	—	—
Mine workers	3	3	3	—	—	—	—	—	—	—	—	—
Oil field and gas well workers	9	7	4	3	—	2	—	—	—	—	—	—
Quarry workers	2	2	2	—	—	—	—	—	—	—	—	—
NEEDLE TRADES	33	11	9	—	2	1	21	—	—	1	19	1
Clothing workers	5	—	—	—	—	—	5	—	—	—	5	—
Hat and cap workers	2	—	—	—	—	1	1	—	—	—	1	—
Hosiery workers	4	3	3	—	—	—	1	—	—	—	1	—
Ladies' garment workers	9	—	—	—	—	—	9	—	—	—	9	—
Ladies' handbag workers	3	—	—	—	—	—	3	—	—	—	2	1
Tailors	2	1	—	—	1	—	1	—	—	1	—	—
Textile workers	8	7	6	—	1	—	1	—	—	—	1	—
PAPER, PRINTING, AND BOOKBINDING	65	7	2	1	4	—	58	5	5	6	42	—
Bookbinders	2	2	2	—	—	—	—	—	—	—	—	—
Compositors	9	—	—	—	—	—	9	—	—	—	9	—
Machine printers	1	—	—	—	—	—	1	—	—	—	1	—
Paper and papermill workers	20	5	—	1	4	—	15	2	5	6	2	—
Photo- and copper-engravers	12	—	—	—	—	—	12	1	—	—	11	—
Printing pressmen	17	—	—	—	—	—	17	1	—	—	16	—
Stereotypers and electrotypers	4	—	—	—	—	—	4	1	—	—	3	—

Table columns are breakdown categories whose headers do not appear on this page. Values read left-to-right across the page.

TRANSPORTATION AND COMMUNICATION.	1	14	3	8	2	28	6			14	14	48
Longshoremen and seamen		6	1		1	8	1					9
Marine cooks	1	1				1						1
Marine engineers and firemen	1	4	1	3		5	3			1	1	9
Masters, mates, and pilots						1						1
Railroad workers			1	3						8	8	8
Teamsters		2		1	1	6	1			1	1	8
Telegraphists						2	1			2	2	5
Transport workers		1		4		5	1			2	2	7
OTHER UNIONS IN MANUFACTURING.	3	31	5	9	8	56	6	1	3	57	61	123
Automobile workers		3	2	1		6				19	19	19
Bakery and confectionery workers		8				8				1	1	7
Brewery and cereal workers		1				1	1			1	1	10
Carpet and linoleum workers	1	1										3
Chemical workers						1				1	2	1
Cork workers		1		1		2	1		2	1	1	8
Electrical and radio workers	1	4	1	1	4	10				6	6	10
Glass bottle blowers		4				4						12
Glass workers				2	4	4	4			4	4	4
Leather workers												1
Lumber workers							1			1	1	1
Pottery workers		1				3	1	1				7
Rubber workers		4	2	2		4			1	3	4	4
Shoe workers						1				2	2	2
Sugar refinery workers		1				1						1
Upholstery workers										1		1
Remington Rand workers										1	1	1
Workers' Protective Union		3										1
Miscellaneous federal labor unions	3	3	2	4		12		1	1	17	18	30
MISCELLANEOUS.	2	25	2	7		36		2	2	21	25	61
Actors, radio artists, and theatrical employees		3				3				2	2	5
Barbers		1				1						1
Bottlers	1									1	1	1
Building service employees		4		1		5				1	1	6
Cemetery workers						1						1
Cleaners and pressers		1				1						1
Cooks and waitresses	1			2						1	1	3
Department store workers						5				3	3	6
Distillery workers		2	1	2		5				1	1	1
Drug workers										1	1	2
Gas station operators		1				1			1	1	1	3
Grain and mill workers		3		2		6				2	2	8
Grocery and warehouse workers	2	3				3				1	2	5
Hospital workers		1				3				2	2	1
Hotel and restaurant workers						1		1				2
Janitors and cleaners		2							1	1	1	7
Laundry workers		2	1	2		2						4
Newspaper workers	2	2				5				2	2	2
Office and professional workers		2	1			2		1	1	1	2	4
Packinghouse workers								1			2	2
RAND TOTAL	8	137	19	36	15	215	16	9	11	149	169	400

61

When the agreement stipulates that an employer may hire a non-unionist in case unionists are not available, it may be important to define the meaning of "available." Most agreements do not do so. For example, 111 out of the 133 agreements of the twenties which require the employer to hire union men if available, and 101 out of the 137 agreements of the thirties, specify no definite waiting period. The agreement of the stereotypers' and electrotypers' Local No. 65 in Seattle, effective 1928 to 1930, gave the union one hour to supply a man. On the other hand, the agreement of Local No. 35 of the same union in Cleveland required the employer to wait ten days before hiring a non-unionist. The waiting periods provided in the agreements included in the two tables are as follows:

	Agreements of 1923-29	Agreements of 1933-39
4 hours	1	2
24 hours	5	6
36 hours	–	1
48 hours	11	15
1 week	3	2
Reasonable time	2	10
No time mentioned	111	101
Total	133	137

When a union requires that all employees be members, but permits the employer to hire non-members, it may stipulate a definite time within which new employees must join or apply for membership. This was done in 29 out of the 148 closed-shop agreements covered in the first table and in 107 out of the 207 agreements in the second table in which the terms were definite.[9] The time limits stipulated were:

	Agreements of 1923-29	Agreements of 1933-39
Before 24 hours	2	5
1 day to 1 week	3	11
Before 2 weeks	5	12
Before 3 weeks	1	20

[9] The provisions of 20 of the agreements in the first group and of 8 in the second group were indefinite on this point. Hence they were excluded from this comparison.

Before 1 month	15	49
Before 3 months	2	6
Before 6 months	1	3
At next regular union meeting	–	1
Total	29	107

In some cases the union apparently did not expect to admit non-members, because the agreement simply stipulated that non-union men would work only until union members became available. This was done in 25 out of the 148 agreements in the first group and in 8 out of the 207 in the second group.

EFFECT OF THE CLOSED OR PREFERENTIAL SHOP UPON THE SIZE OF THE LABOR SUPPLY

Admission policies of unions. The closed or preferential shop may affect the size of the labor supply available to union employers. So long as employers are free to hire non-unionists, the union has a strong incentive to attempt to persuade non-union members to join. But when an agreement requires employers to hire only union members or at least to give preference to them, the union has a temptation to practice a restrictive membership policy. The union is, of course, always eager to organize additional *shops* because that means bringing more jobs as well as more men under union control. Quite different, however, is likely to be the attitude of the union toward admitting an individual who does not come in as a result of recognition of the union by the employer for whom he works. Admitting him means that the union is dividing the employment opportunities in the union shops among just so many more men. Particularly if the volume of employment in the industry fluctuates violently, the locals are strongly tempted to limit their membership to a number for whom there is fairly steady work in union shops. If this leads union employers in busy years or busy seasons to bid wages above the union scale, the temptation of the local to restrict its membership is even greater.

One method of limiting membership is to charge a high admission fee. For example, the Perth Amboy local of the electrical workers was reported in May 1926 to have an initiation fee of $200 for inside wiremen.[10] The initiation fee of the Cleveland electrical

[10] *Journal of Electrical Workers and Operators*, May 1926, Vol. XXV, p. 237.

workers in 1920 was also $200; that of the stationary engineers, $100;[11] that of the glaziers in Cincinnati $400. In 1930, the New York local of the lathers' union attempted to collect a fee of $280.[12] Some of the locals of the motion picture operators charged an initiation fee of $500 to $600. High initiation fees, however, are probably more effective in enriching the union treasury than in keeping down membership because (1) the fees may usually be paid on the installment plan, and (2) as long as union membership is of substantial assistance to a man in getting employment, plenty of men are willing to pay even a high fee.[13]

Another method of restricting membership is for the union to refuse on one pretext or another to admit applicants. Since some national unions make the local union the judge of competence of applicants, the local can exclude men simply by refusing to accept them as competent. Men who come from other towns with the hope of remaining and following the trade may be compelled to move on because the local refuses to examine them promptly. A rule sometimes adopted by local unions is: "No applications for new members will be accepted while members of this union are out of work." Such a rule may easily be administered to compel employers to hire incompetent men before the union will admit new members.

The tendency of local unions to pursue restrictive membership policies is usually discouraged by the national officers. Since the bargaining power of the union depends upon its control of the labor supply, a union which excludes workers is undermining its own bargaining power. The national officers are usually well aware of

---

[11] Cleveland Chamber of Commerce, *The Causes of High Building Costs in Cleveland* (October 1920), p. 26.

[12] This was in violation of the national constitution of the union, which limits the initiation fees that locals may charge to $100. As a result the New York local became involved in a controversy with the national. *The Lather*, February 1931, Vol. XXXI, pp. 4, 5.

[13] A high fee may prove unexpectedly unsatisfactory to the union members. Recently one of the teamsters' locals in New England put in an initiation fee of $250 against the advice of its officers. Soon the rank and file began to ask whether their friends and relatives could not be accepted for less. This was, of course, impossible and led to the repeal of the high fee. In September 1940 a strike occurred among the carpenters engaged in the construction of cantonments at Camp Edwards, Mass., because the New Bedford carpenters' local, which had assumed jurisdiction at the project, attempted to collect an initiation fee of $75 from each carpenter. The men objected to such a large amount because the project was scheduled to be completed in 75 days.

this.[14] Some nationals prohibit their locals from charging an initiation fee of more than a given amount. The Amalgamated Clothing Workers put the limit at $10, the bricklayers at $50, and the lathers at $100.[15] But limitations on initiation fees may be circumvented by the simple device of rejecting applications for admission. The real influence of the national union must be exercised by advice—by pointing out to the local leaders the dangers of a restrictive policy. Examples of such attempts abound in trade union publications. Thus we find the Journal of the International Brotherhood of Electrical Workers saying:

> . . . several of our locals—large and small—search for every kind of excuse to keep men out of their ranks—men who are working at our trade regularly and are qualified in every way. Such locals act on the unsound theory that the more men brought into their ranks, the less work there will be for those already in the local . . . . our members will . . . never get anything like their full share out of the electrical industry until their locals let down their bars and discard some of their bewhiskered, narrow and selfish policies, and bring into their fold every qualified and worthwhile man in their communities.[16]

---

[14] How a restrictive membership policy may be a boomerang to the local is illustrated by the experience of the Brooklyn plumbers in the spring of 1927. When the men struck, the employers promptly organized a union of their own known as the Amalgamated Association of Plumbers and Gas Fitters. Most of the 300 strikebreakers employed on the first day of the strike were Brooklyn boys who had learned their trade in Brooklyn but who had never been able to join the plumbers' union. "We have been outcasts from the start," the spokesman for the men said, "and now when we may get a chance to get half-way decent work and pay, the union that repelled us before, calls upon us for assistance. Is there sound logic in their request? Have these proud unionmen who condemned us to work for non-union firms for low wages a right to expect help from us? Don't you think that it is our turn now and that we should be sent to an insane asylum if we threw away this splendid chance?" *American Labor Weekly*, June 5, 1927, p. 2.

This group later succeeded in obtaining a state charter and started work on 15 large jobs in Brooklyn. On none of the jobs on which they worked did the men in the other trades strike, although it is a cardinal rule in the building trades that union men will not work with non-unionists. *Journal of Electrical Workers and Operators*, July 1927, Vol. XXVI, p. 371.

[15] The opposite policy is pursued by the plumbers' union, which sets no maximum, but provides that no local that has been organized for more than six months may charge an initiation fee of less than $20, subject to the power of the general executive board to grant a dispensation for a period not to exceed three months.

[16] *Journal of Electrical Workers and Operators*, May 1925, Vol. XXIV, pp. 401-02.

In extreme cases where a local persists in pursuing restrictive policies against the advice or instructions of international officers, the latter may take over the operation of the local.[17]

Some locals of the musicians' union have demanded that the examinations for admission be made stricter. In his report to the convention of the union in 1928, the international president, Mr. J. N. Weber, opposed this suggestion:

Many of our older members are still of the opinion that if the examinations were stricter and the unions were composed of only such members who are able to pass them, that then their employment opportunities would be multiplied. Nothing is further from the truth. The condition in any calling, if its followers desire to be successfully organized is that all those who are active in the calling must become members of the organization.

President Weber pointed out that

artistic services are not necessary in the great part of our musicians' employment. . . . if a musician renders a service which satisfies the public, it is folly for us to set a standard on his eligibility in order to qualify as an applicant for membership in our organization.[18]

Many nationals permit an applicant who is rejected by a local union to appeal to the national. On the whole, this right is of little importance because few rejected applicants take the trouble to appeal. The disposition of the appeals, however, sheds light on the contrasting attitudes of the nationals and the locals. At the convention of the International Typographical Union in 1911, the executive council referred to the many appeals to the general executive council from rejected applicants for membership in subordinate unions:

An analysis of these cases shows that in a majority of them the unions are to blame. The executive council has been compelled to reverse the union and order the admission of the applicant on the ground that the unions do not give any reason for, or attempt to explain why the applicant was rejected. . . . The executive council is doing all in its power to build up a perfect organization of printers, and subordinate unions should not reject applicants without good and sufficient reasons.[19]

---

[17] This has been done in several instances in the International Union of Operating Engineers. See *Journal of Operating Engineers*, July 1929.

[18] *International Musician*, June 1928, Vol. XXV, p. 21; the same, May 1928, Vol. XXV, p. 1.

[19] *Typographical Journal*, Supplement, October 1911, Vol. XXXIX, p. 128.

Between January 1921 and February 1929, the general executive council passed on 76 appeals of applicants who had been rejected for membership by local unions but upheld the rejection in only 22 cases. In six of the 22, leniency was recommended and in two the rejection of the local was upheld only because the applicant had already left the jurisdiction of the local. In only 14 out of 76 cases was the rejection clearly and unqualifiedly supported. In 31 instances the rejection of the local was reversed and in 23 the local was ordered to re-ballot, and the general executive council recommended that it admit the applicant.[20]

Admission policies of unions are affected not only by the closed shop but also by the tendency of union wage scales, which are usually well above non-union rates, to attract more men into the union than can find employment in union shops.[21] This explains the paradox of a large number of local unions practicing restrictive membership policies without depriving employers of an adequate supply of labor.[22]

[20] The latter cases arose, for the most part, out of the 44-hour strike of 1922. The applicants were men who had worked in "struck" shops. In each of these cases the national upheld the rejection of the local but recommended reconsideration, expressing the opinion that "favorable action on his readmission will serve the best interests of our organization." In the years immediately preceding 1921 the decisions of the general executive board were very different. In the four years ending with 1920, the locals were upheld in ten cases and reversed in six. All six reversals occurred in 1920. During the three years 1917, 1918, and 1919, there were no reversals of local decisions on applications for admission. The reason probably was that the shortage of labor during the war period led many inadequately trained men to apply for admission. The union officers were afraid that incompetent men would gain admission to the organization in order to obtain jobs and would give the union a bad name. After the shortage of labor ceased in 1920, there was less danger of unqualified men's gaining admittance.

[21] In 1940 almost all of the teamsters' locals in southern New England had from 25 to 100 applicants and the Boston local had several hundred.

[22] As might be expected, unions are likely to pursue restrictive membership policies when a decline of demand or technological changes create a great surplus of workers in the trade. Between 1907 and 1914 the lace industry experienced a long period of depression. As a result the Amalgamated Lace Operatives' Society raised its initiation fee for curtain men to $100 and for Levers men to $200. The organization had been accepting members of foreign unions who had had three years' experience. This requirement was raised to five years. (Gladys L. Palmer, *Labor Relations in the Lace and Lace-Curtain Industries in the United States*, U. S. Bureau of Labor Statistics, Bulletin No. 399, p. 28.) The spread of automatic press-feeding machinery producing unemployment among the press assistants led press assistants' Local No. 23 of New York to cease admitting new members. "American Trade Unions and the Problem of Unemployment," *Monthly Labor Review*, March 1928, Vol. XXVI, p. 485.

The permit-card system. When there are violent fluctuations in the demand for labor, a union may desire to limit the number of its members in order to assure steady work for them. At the same time, the very fluctuations in the demand for labor will make it difficult for the union to meet the employers' needs and still restrict its membership. Some unions seek to solve this problem by permitting the employment of temporary workers who are not required to become members of the union. Among the 400 agreements in the table on pages 60-61, 61 provided for temporary workers. The length of time which temporary workers might be employed varied from one week in 4 cases to over six months in 4 cases.[23]

Similar to the system of the temporary worker is the permit system. This consists of issuing "permit cards" to non-members who are thereby allowed to work with union members. The non-members pay the union several dollars a week for their permit cards. The number of cards issued may be adjusted to the demand for labor.[24] The permit-card system tends to be confined to industries where fluctuations in the demand for labor are violent. In those industries it concentrates the available employment at slack times among union members—unless an excessive number of permit cards is issued—and concentrates the burden of unemployment upon non-members. It presupposes the existence of the closed shop and it also presupposes that the union possesses little or no control over the layoff of men by employers.

For example, a union which is able to compel employers to ration work in periods of slack employment is not likely to adopt the permit system except to a very limited extent to take care of extreme peaks in demand. Furthermore, the national unions, for reasons which will be explained presently, are opposed to the permit system. Consequently, the system is likely to develop only where the locals are in large measure independent of national control.

[23] In 4 cases the limit was one week; in 1 case the limit was two weeks; in 8 cases, up to one month; in 11 cases, up to three months; in 26 cases, up to six months; in 4 cases, over six months; and in 7 cases, no limit was set.

[24] In some cases, however, far more permit cards are issued than the demand for labor warrants. This may happen, as explained below, because the income from permit cards is a source of graft to union officials.

As a matter of fact, the permit system is pretty much confined to the building trades—an industry in which the three conditions mentioned above are present. The permit system was in effect for a number of years in the New York local of the electrical workers' union. At times the organization had more applicants for admission than it had members. Although it refused to admit these men, it allowed them to work with union men provided they carried a "privilege card," which was issued on the payment of $2.50 a week for journeymen, and $1.00 a week for helpers.[25] The permit system has also been widely used by the plumbers. At the 1924 convention the general executive board reported:

There has grown up a system among some of our local unions which has almost become a fixed institution, known as "the permit helper" which helper very seldom, if ever, becomes a member, or is given the opportunity to become a member of the United Association. These locals charge these helpers a certain amount each week for the privilege of working, which money is placed in the local treasury and used for local expense of administration.[26]

Although the permit system is attractive to the members of local unions, it weakens the union because it involves surrender by the local of a large measure of its control over the labor supply. Indeed the permit system may be described as a method by which the local union sacrifices control of the labor market for the temporary advantage of gaining steadier work for its members. Naturally no love is lost between the men who are inside the union and the men who hold permit cards, who are refused membership but are compelled to pay for the privilege of working on union jobs. Every permit-card holder is a potential strikebreaker, and many of the permit-card holders would welcome the opportunity presented by a strike to replace the union men. As time goes on, the situation becomes worse. The very existence of the permit system encourages the union to pursue a restrictive membership policy. In a few years, therefore, the union comes to be composed mainly of the older workmen who have passed the period of their

[25] State of New York, *Intermediate Report of Joint Legislative Committee on Housing Legislation*, Legislative Document No. 60, 1922, pp. 49-50.
[26] *Plumbers, Gas and Steam Fitters' Journal*, November 1924, Vol. XXXIX, p. 75.

greatest efficiency, and the youngest, strongest, and fastest work-men are found largely among the permit holders. Naturally this makes the employers more and more reluctant to continue con-tractual relations with the union and causes them to become eager for an opportunity to sever relations and replace union men with permit holders.

Since permit-card holders are not members of the union and the officials are not, therefore, responsible to them, permit cards easily become a source of graft to union officials. If they do, the system may work out in the opposite way from that intended. The union officials become interested in issuing as many of the permit cards as possible, with the result that permit-card holders may be working while good union members are idle. Of course, in this case the rank and file may attempt to vote out the officers. If the latter are making large incomes from the permit cards, however, they oppose this and the union becomes a racket.

The national unions invariably oppose the permit system. They realize that, at best, it undermines the bargaining power of the local by maintaining a number of non-union men who are hostile to the union and that, at worst, it converts the union into a racket. The national officers of the electrical workers succeeded, after a hard struggle, in abolishing the permit system in New York. The constitution of the International Union of Operating Engineers forbids the union permit system. The international has occasionally assumed special supervision over a local which has practiced the permit system in violation of the constitution.[27]

The general executive board of the plumbers' union strongly condemned the permit-helper system in its report to the 1924 convention. The board said that from time to time it had received communications from permit helpers who were anxious to join the association but who were not given the opportunity. The board stated:

The permit helper system is a very dangerous and vicious one, and dia-metrically opposed to the principles and ethics of our Association and the Organized Labor Movement, as well as being a serious menace to the advancement and progress of our own Organization.[28]

---

[27] See *Journal of the International Union of Operating Engineers*, July 1929, Vol. LVI, pp. 52-54, for mention of the cases.

[28] *Plumbers, Gas and Steam Fitters' Journal*, November 1924, Vol. XXXIX, p. 75.

The vast majority of the helpers, according to the board, never became members but remained handymen and when the opportunity presented itself naturally drifted into non-union shops, especially the large equipment concerns, where they took the place of first-class mechanics for less money. The board recommended that those helpers who had worked at the trade a sufficient time to qualify as mechanics, or nearly so, be admitted to the locals, and that a "vigorous law be . . . placed in our constitution, to eliminate for all time this dangerous menace to our trade and our Association."[29] The following section in the constitution was unanimously adopted: "No permits shall be given or issued to anyone . . . who is not a member of the United Association or who has not been accepted by the local union and is not paying an application fee for admittance to the Association."[30] The opposition of the national unions has been effective in curbing the growth of the permit-card system, and today it is of little importance.

EFFORTS OF EMPLOYERS TO PROTECT THEMSELVES AGAINST LABOR SHORTAGES DUE TO THE CLOSED SHOP

Some employers have embodied special provisions in closed-shop agreements for the purpose of protecting themselves against labor shortages. Many agreements of the pressmen's union have for some years provided that if the union failed to furnish a full crew for any press and the foreman could not obtain the required number of outsiders, such press might be run short-handed without the payment of any extra compensation to the men employed. Some agreements permit the employer to put on additional apprentices when the union is unable to furnish the required number of journeymen. Such, for example, was the provision in the agreement for 1926 of metal polishers' Local No. 28 of South Pittsburgh, Tennessee.[31] A similar provision is included in the agreement of the National Brotherhood of Operative Potters with the United

---

[29] The same.

[30] It should be noted that the board opposed the permit-helper system not only because the system created enemies of the union but also because it defeated the efforts of the union to regulate apprenticeship. Although the union apprenticeship laws limited the number of apprentices that employers might hire, there was no limit upon the number of helper permits which the local unions might issue.

[31] U. S. Bureau of Labor Statistics, *Trade Agreements, 1926,* Bulletin No. 448, p. 106.

States Potters' Association.[32] The agreement of electrical workers' Local No. 567 of Portland, Maine, effective May 1, 1927 to May 1, 1929, provided that if a sufficient number of union journeymen could not be furnished, apprentices who had worked four years or more at the trade might be permitted to perform journeymen's work till the union was able to furnish the contractor with the necessary number of journeymen. These apprentices, while performing journeymen's work, were to receive the journeymen's minimum scale. Some agreements permit employers to work men overtime at regular rather than penalty rates in case the union fails to furnish sufficient men.[33] Most important of all are the agreements in which the employer conditions his acceptance of the closed or preferential shop upon the union's willingness to maintain an open door and to keep its admission requirements reasonable. Thus the agreement in the Chicago men's clothing industry provides:

The provision for preference made herein requires that the doors of the union shall be kept open for the reception of non-union workers. Initiation fees and dues must be maintained at a reasonable rate and any applicant must be admitted who is not an offender against the union and who is eligible for membership under its rules. Provided, that if any rules be passed that impose unreasonable hardship, or that operate to bar desirable persons, the matter may be brought before the tribunal herein provided for, for such remedy as it may deem advisable.

An almost identical provision was written in the agreement of the same union in the Milwaukee market on May 1, 1925.[34] The agreement effective in the New York silk ribbon industry from April

---

[32] The same, pp. 114-15.

[33] The agreement between the Seattle local of the Typographical Union and the Seattle publishers, effective Dec. 14, 1936 to September 1937, provided:

". . . in no case shall the work week of an individual consist of more than five shifts except when for any reason the Union shall fail to furnish at straight time rates the number of journeymen called for by the office in which event, competent journeymen as needed shall work on their sixth day or sixth night at straight time rates."

The agreement between Local No. 3 of the International Brotherhood of Electrical Workers and the New York Electrical Contractors' Association, effective September 1937, after providing for a regular 6-hour day, stipulates:

"At such time that the joint Conference Committee decide that a general shortage of available labor of Local No. 3 of the International Brotherhood of Electrical Workers exists, then it is agreed that the members of the union shall work seven hours per day at the rate of wages specified in Rule 7 of this Agreement."

[34] *Monthly Labor Review*, October 1925, Vol. XXI, p. 756.

1920 to June 1923 gave the impartial chairman, who decided disputes between the union and the employers, authority to order variations in the amounts and dates of payment of initiation fees, assessments, and penalties when he thought that they would be unduly burdensome.[35] Perhaps the most interesting agreement of this sort is that between Equity, the actors' trade union, and the Managers' Protective Association, which was made in 1924. In return for the managers' agreement to employ, with certain permitted exceptions, only members of Equity, the union agreed, for a period of 25 years, not to refuse membership to any person of good character and of sufficient age to be allowed legally to be an actor and not to raise its initiation fee without the consent of the Managers' Protective Association.[36]

EFFECT OF THE CLOSED AND PREFERENTIAL SHOPS UPON THE QUALITY OF WORKERS EMPLOYED

Of greater practical importance than the possibility that union agreements will prevent employers from obtaining sufficient men is the possibility that these agreements will prevent employers from hiring the best available workers. The very fact that unions limit the freedom of employers to discharge or to lay off men makes the selection of new employees a far more important matter than ever before. Its importance is still further enhanced by the provisions in many agreements which require that furloughed employees shall be rehired, if qualified, in preference to persons who have never worked for the employer.

It is unlikely that the closed or preferential shop compels employers to accept inferior men in appreciable numbers provided the doors of the unions are open to new members. The reason is ob-

[35] Margaret Gadsby, *Trade Agreements in the Silk Ribbon Industry of New York City*, U. S. Bureau of Labor Statistics, Bulletin No. 341, p. 38.

[36] P. F. Gemmill, "Equity: The Actors' Trade Union," *Quarterly Journal of Economics*, November 1926, Vol. XLI, p. 144. Similar agreements are that of the terrazzo workers in Cleveland, signed Apr. 2, 1928, in which the union agreed to admit to membership workers whose competency is vouched for by two journeymen members, that of printing pressmen's Local No. 18 of Memphis, Tenn., stipulating that non-unionists who are competent and capable will be admitted to the union provided they have not broken any union laws, and that of the bricklayers' local in Cleveland providing that the union will admit to full membership within 30 days all competent bricklayers or masons who are citizens of the United States, upon payment of the regular initiation fee.

vious. A union which is strong enough to gain the closed or the preferential shop in many plants in the community is also likely to attract most of the best mechanics in the trade. Men may be reluctant to join a labor organization when they fear that membership may hinder them in finding employment, but they are usually eager to join when membership helps them to obtain work. Consequently, the very success of a union in establishing the closed or preferential shop in an appreciable part of the industry helps it to attract the best and fastest workers in the trade. In the cities where the building trades unions are strongest, for example, employers testify that the best mechanics are union members. Those on the outside consist largely of men who for one reason or another find difficulty in commanding the union scale or who work in branches of the trade which the union does not control.[37]

Even a union which pursues a restrictive admission policy may not seriously limit the ability of employers to find good men because labor shortages produced by the restrictive admission policy will attract union men from other cities. The local, however, may attempt to discourage such transfers, and if it succeeds, employers may have difficulty in finding good men. The effort of locals to discourage movement and to gain preference for local workers will be discussed in the next section. A few unions compel employers to do their hiring through the union office or through union-controlled hiring halls. Such an arrangement, of course, seriously interferes with the opportunity of employers to compare and select men and, therefore, to pick the best available men.[38]

Since trade and aptitude tests are still so undeveloped that employers need to test the efficiency and adaptability of men on the job, restrictions on the employer's freedom to hire are less important

[37] A person prominent on the employers' side of the job printing industry comments on this point as follows: "My general judgment is that with an effective foreman and an aggressive and forceful plant management just as efficient a force can be built up under union conditions as under open shop conditions both in the New York and Chicago markets. In as highly unionized centers as New York and Chicago, I am inclined to believe that the majority of plants can build up more efficient forces under union conditions since most of the higher skilled men are members of the union. This isn't true of centers like Detroit, Cincinnati, Cleveland, Los Angeles, etc. which have a very definite non-union or open-shop background. In these cities, I think the reverse is true."

[38] See pp. 85-86 below.

than restrictions on his freedom to drop men who, after a trial, do not seem to be well suited to the work. A trial or probationary period, therefore, within which the management may drop a man for any reason or no reason is important to employers and is becoming more important. The existence of a probationary period does not mean that the employer may not drop men after the period has expired.[39] A probationary period is provided in 90 out of the 400 agreements included in the table on pages 60-61.

The length of the period varies greatly. In some of the agreements of the printing trade it is only four hours; in other cases it is several months. The length in 90 cases is as follows:

1 week or less	3
1 to 2 weeks	17
2 weeks to 1 month	34
1 month to 3 months	18
3 months to 6 months	12
Over 6 months	1
Special combination	5

The probationary period required is likely to be much shorter in the case of skilled tradesmen than in the case of semi-skilled specialists. When an employer hires a man in a trade for which an apprenticeship is customary (a blacksmith, a compositor, a toolmaker), he can usually determine within several days whether the man knows his trade and is a good workman. On the other hand, when the employer hires a man for a semi-skilled operation which requires several months to learn, he may not be able to judge within several months whether the man will turn out to be an excellent workman, a good one, or a fair one.[40] There is some tendency among unions to press for shorter probationary periods. It is doubtful, however, whether the union gains by a shorter period because, if the period is too short, the employer plays safe by dropping any new employee whose fitness is still in doubt. Furthermore, the better selected the workers, the greater is the bargaining power of the union for the simple reason that a well-selected force is less easily duplicated. In view of the restrictions placed upon the per-

[39] But workers discharged after serving the probationary period may challenge the employer's decision and require him to show cause.

[40] Of course, the man who is plainly a poor worker can usually be identified as such quite promptly.

manent layoff of regular employees, most probationary periods are too short.[41] In several industries the union may prefer a probationary period long enough to prevent workers hired for the peak demand from becoming members of the regular force.

Some unions recognize a definite responsibility for seeing that their members are well qualified to perform their work, and the number may be expected to increase. These organizations realize that they themselves benefit from having in their ranks the best qualified journeymen in the trade. The point of view of these organizations is well expressed in an agreement between Local No. 134 of the International Brotherhood of Electrical Workers and the Electrical Contractors' Association of Chicago:

An obligation imposed upon and accepted by the Union, as being properly its own, is the furnishing at all times during the life of this contract of sufficient skilled workmen, capable of performing the work of this trade, and to constantly endeavor to improve the ability of such workmen, and further to have in the making, through apprenticeship training, workmen who can enter this trade properly equipped to perform the work.

Of course, such a declaration of principle means nothing unless the union does something to carry out the policy. A number of unions have done effective work in informing their members of new developments in the trade, in providing them with facilities for becoming familiar with new equipment and new processes, and in encouraging them to avail themselves of these facilities. Noteworthy among these organizations are the printing pressmen, the photo-engravers' union, and the electrical workers.

The facilities of the apprentice school in the New York printing industry have been open to journeymen pressmen at certain hours during the week in order to give them an opportunity to learn to operate the new and fast presses which have been coming into the trade. The photo-engravers' union has sent men to lecture to its members on the new processes in that trade and recently, as pointed out in the previous chapter, has established a research department to give service to both its members and their employers

[41] The length of the period needed depends partly upon the number of trials a new employee will be given before he is finally dropped as unsatisfactory.

on new developments and problems connected with them. The electrical workers' union in various cities has organized special classes for journeymen. These classes furnish an opportunity to study the work in new branches of this rapidly developing trade. The Milwaukee local went so far as to embody in its 1930 agreement a clause requiring its members to "attend evening school at least one night each week equivalent to two hours' time each week, except such members as qualify to the satisfaction of both the employers and the union." This clause was included in the agreement because the expansion of the union had recently brought into it a number of men from former non-union shops who had not served the regular apprenticeship.

ATTEMPTS OF LOCAL UNIONS TO ENFORCE PREFERENCE FOR LOCAL MEN

Efforts of local unions to obtain preference for local men, as against even union members from other cities, are by no means uncommon. The agreement of the stereotypers and electrotypers' Local No. 48 with the newspapers of Portland, Oregon, effective September 1, 1928 to September 1, 1933, provided that members of Local No. 48 should be hired first, then members of the international, and then non-members. At one time (1925) the agreement of Local No. 705 of the teamsters, chauffeurs, and stablemen with the Cartage Exchange of Chicago provided that the employers employ members of Local No. 705 "and under no circumstances will members of the International Brotherhood of Teamsters, Chauffeurs, Stablemen and Helpers of America be allowed to go to work when there are members of Local 705, I. B. of T. to be had." Locals in the building trades sometimes require that outside contractors coming into the jurisdiction of a local shall hire a certain proportion of local men. The Youngstown, Ohio, local of the bricklayers' union incorporated a clause in its constitution requiring that 50 per cent of the members on all jobs in its jurisdiction should be local members, provided they could be secured.[42] In order to secure the foremanship positions for its members, the same local required

[42] *Fourth Biennial and Fifty-sixth Report of the President and Secretary of the Bricklayers, Masons, and Plasterers' International Union*, 1926, p. 165.

that a foreman must have been a member of the local for one year unless he came into the city with an outside company.[43]

These restrictions on the employment of outside men mean little, if the local union is willing to admit union members who transfer from other cities. Some unions, such as the painters, definitely provide that any member holding a card in the international organization may go to work in any locality. Others, such as the plumbers, require that a member deposit a working card within a stipulated period and impose a fine upon men who fail to do this. The plumbers' union allows 48 hours. Some locals attempt to take matters into their own hands by requiring that members see the shop committee before seeking work. This has been done by a number of locals in the molders' union. At the 1921 conference between the molders' union and the employers in the stove industry, the employers protested against local rules of this sort. They said they could not afford to have a local union select the men that they were to employ as was the case under a rule requiring that members seek work through the business agent or the shop committee. The national officers of the molders' union have opposed such rules. A local refuses to accept transfer cards as long as some of its own members are unemployed. Some locals of the electrical workers' union do not accept "travelers" if 10 per cent or more of the local men are out of work.[44]

The issue was raised at the 1929 national convention of the Brotherhood of Painters, Decorators, and Paperhangers of America in the form of several resolutions which would authorize local unions to institute permit systems designed to give preference to local members. Resolution No. 29, submitted by Local No. 194 of Chicago, would have authorized district councils "to establish a

---

[43] The same, p. 167.

[44] Occasionally a local union will accept a transfer card on condition that the transferee give up his position as soon as a local man becomes available. For example, a man was sent for to fill an engagement as a string bass player at a theater because no local member was available. His transfer card was accepted by the local union and his dues were paid. After working two and a half weeks, he was given notice to vacate the engagement because a local member who had been laid off by another theater wished the job. The national union vetoed this action of the local on the ground that the local had no right to condition its acceptance of the transfer card with the provision that the transferee must give up his position to a local member as soon as one became available. *International Musician*, June 1925, Vol. XXIII, p. 21.

permit system that will give preference, during periods when work is scarce, to members who are permanent residents of the district and who, through years of continuous membership, have helped to build up the organization."[45]

The shortage of work produced by the depression has stimulated locals to impose conditions upon traveling members—sometimes in violation of the constitution of the national union. W. J. McSorley, president of the lathers' union, complained of such restrictions in *The Lather* for February 1931: "These impositions consisted of refusing transfers, the placing of unreasonable and unjust fines, as well as the levying of unfair and unjust assessments against members who have entered their [the local's] jurisdiction with clear transfers."[46] Local No. 46 in New York required the payment of $100 by a member coming into the local on transfer. Also it required that the member be three years in good standing, and collected a $2 permit fee under the caption "secretary's services." The local officers agreed to strike from their constitution and by-laws all provisions which were held to be in conflict with the constitution of the international union.

Although the refusal of a local union to accept transfers may not deprive employers of an adequate supply of labor when the policy itself is provoked by a local surplus of men, it may prevent employers from filling vacancies with the best possible men because the least efficient 10 or 15 per cent of a local are likely to be quite inferior to most traveling members.

The refusal of some locals to accept traveling members presents a difficult problem for the national unions and their influence is almost invariably against local restrictions on freedom to transfer. The very locals which refuse to accept transfers expect their members to be accepted by other locals in the national union.

---

[45] Brotherhood of Painters, Decorators, and Paperhangers of America, *Proceedings of the Fourteenth General Assembly*, 1929, p. 57. A similar resolution was submitted by Local No. 273, also of Chicago. This resolution stated that traveling members were coming into cities and localities during the season and leaving as soon as work slacked up, thereby shortening the season for the home members. It proposed that the locals or the district councils be allowed to inaugurate a permit system and that the permits to traveling members be revokable at the discretion of the district council or the local union of the locality. The same, p. 60.

[46] Vol. XXXI, p. 4.

At the 1924 convention of the plumbers' union, the general executive board reported:

We are again calling to your attention, that in the last three years, and even recently, we have had some serious complaints from our members and some of our local unions concerning the refusal of the clearance cards from our traveling members, even in jurisdictions where there was plenty of work, and no troubles in progress or any contemplated.[47]

Some cases had been adjusted by correspondence or by sending an international representative, but the board pointed out that the constitution did not empower the national union to enforce the acceptance of clearance cards.[48] The board said that the "violations complained of have reached a most serious aspect and . . . are endangering the very life of our International Organization . . . it will be the imperative duty of this convention to take determined and conclusive action."[49]

An excellent discussion of the problem of the traveling member is contained in the report of the general executive board of the plumbers' union to the convention in September 1938.[50] Continued difficulty led the general executive board in September 1940 to adopt another strong statement directed especially against locals which charge traveling members an assessment for the privilege of working.[51]

The national union which has taken the strongest stand in protecting traveling members against restrictions imposed by the locals

[47] *Plumbers, Gas and Steam Fitters' Journal*, November 1924, Vol. XXXIX, p. 77.
[48] The same.
[49] The committee on officers' reports, however, merely made the somewhat meaningless recommendation that "on account of the serious aspect that complaints have assumed . . . we recommend that the General Executive Board and Officers drastically enforce the constitution on violators." The same, pp. 77, 148.
[50] The report says: "The old perennial question of the non-acceptance of clearance cards by some locals is just as prevalent today as it has been in the past. . . . During the severe period of the panic, there were very few complaints because there was no work. Just as soon as work picked up a couple of years ago, these complaints from our members and from some of our local unions assumed the character of very vigorous protests, not only against the refusal to accept clearance cards in violation of the Constitution, but on account of the jungle attitude and discourteous treatment assumed towards our members by the officers or others in charge of the affairs of the local unions to the members seeking to have their cards accepted. This subject is growing more aggravated in this tremendous competitive age and is one of the most serious questions that we have to contend with." *Journeymen Plumbers and Steam Fitters' Journal*, December 1938, Vol. LIII, p. 50.
[51] The same, October 1940, Vol. LV, pp. 3-5.

is the printing pressmen's. As early as 1924 this union amended its constitution specifically to require the acceptance of traveling cards upon presentation to the secretary of the local union and the issuance of working cards granting authority to the member to work in the jurisdiction of the local. Failure to comply with the rule automatically suspends the local secretary from the international union and, in addition, subjects the local union to a fine of $50 in the first instance and to suspension by the board of directors of the international union in the second instance.[52]

The problem of traveling members has been particularly acute in the musicians' union because not only individual members but entire orchestras or bands travel. President Weber of the union has said: "Of all the developments to which our organization in the more than thirty years of its existence has had to adapt itself, none has presented such serious problems as did the development of the traveling orchestra."[53] Many local members believe that all local engagements belong to the local members and that the international should prohibit traveling orchestras. Indeed, the first attempt to form a national union of musicians was wrecked by the attempt to restrict musicians to their own towns.[54]

[52] International Printing Pressmen and Assistants' Union of North America, *Constitution and Laws*, revised and adopted by referendum February 1929 and July 1933, Art. VII, sec. 19, p. 32.
  In discussing the problem of the traveling member in his report to the convention of 1924, President Berry used the following strong language:
  "There has . . . been permitted to grow up in some localities a condition where traveling cards are not accepted upon presentation, but the secretary or the president of these unions advise the traveling members that they will be required to appear before the Executive Board, to appear before the meeting, or to do one or many perfectly silly and illegal things which quite often is to require the passage of time numbered in many instances by several days and sometimes weeks. By such a process the traveling member is placed in further embarrassment because of his inability to deposit his card and secure work in order that he and his dependents may live." International Printing Pressmen's and Assistants' Union, *Reports of Officers to the Thirtieth Biennial Convention*, 1924, pp. 105-06.
[53] *International Musician*, July 1926, Vol. XXIV, p. 19.
[54] The same, May 1929, Vol. XXVI, No. 11, p. 18. At this time there were many traveling bands. The local musicians' unions opposed these bands and succeeded in having the national prohibit the acceptance of engagements by bands in the jurisdiction of locals without the consent of the local. But the members resented the union's attempt to control the engagements which they might or might not accept. The locals were soon defying the very law which they had demanded, and the second largest local in the union defended its members who violated the law and was expelled because it refused to agree to discipline its members in the future. (The same, June 1926, Vol. XXIII, p. 25.)

The rise of jazz greatly accentuated the problem of traveling orchestras. In the beginning only a few orchestras played jazz, and the public came to believe that outside orchestras must be superior. The local unions endeavored to discourage traveling orchestras by requiring that outside orchestras charge 30 per cent over the local price plus the cost of their transportation. This rule did little to bring about the desired results. Orchestras of reputation received 30 per cent more than most local scales anyway, and many inferior orchestras simply violated the law.[55] The national officers realized that drastic restrictions would simply cause the traveling orchestras to become non-union.[56]

At present, the union imposes a tax of 10 per cent of the local's price on engagements by traveling orchestras. The tax money is divided into three parts: 4 per cent goes to the local in whose jurisdiction the engagement occurs, 3 per cent to the international, and 3 per cent to the members of the traveling orchestra.[57] In addition, various restrictions are placed on traveling orchestras to limit their competition with local orchestras. For example, traveling dance orchestras which have regular engagements in a locality may not play miscellaneous engagements of any sort during the contract period.[58]

[55] On account of the difficulty of controlling traveling orchestras, it was decided that whenever an employer was found in collusion with an orchestra to circumvent the laws of the union, an order would issue making the employer's establishment forbidden territory for all traveling orchestras, unless consent of the local union was secured. The prohibition remained in force for one year. The international president reported to the Baltimore convention in 1927 that this disciplinary action had been applied once to employers in Chicago, Cleveland, and Philadelphia, and twice against employers in Detroit. (*International Musician,* July 1927, Vol. XXV, p. 19.)

The union requires that the contracting member or leader submit his contract to the officers of the local union in whose jurisdiction the engagement is played. In the absence of a written contract he must submit a sworn affidavit fully explaining the conditions under which the engagement is played.

[56] Report of President Weber to the thirty-fourth annual convention, *International Musician,* May 1929, Vol. XXVI, p. 3.

[57] American Federation of Musicians of the United States and Canada, *Constitution, By-laws and Standing Resolutions, 1939,* By-Laws, Art. XIII, pp. 118, 121, 136-37.

[58] The same, p. 144; Art. XIV, p. 158.

ATTEMPTS OF UNIONS TO REQUIRE HIRING THROUGH
THE UNION OFFICE

Most unions do not require employers to hire through the union office. Many employers, however, particularly in trades where the enterprise is too small to have its own employment department, find it convenient to call the union office when in need of men; and the union is always glad to receive such calls. Some trade agreements require the employer to notify the union office when he needs men but permit him to seek men from other sources also. For example, the agreement made October 10, 1935 between the Jewelry Manufacturers of Philadelphia and Local No. 5 of the International Jewelry Workers' Union provides: "Before engaging new workers the employer will notify the union of such needs. The union in turn will furnish the employer with a list of competent available workers." The agreement adds: "The final choice of new employees, however, rests with the employer." The agreement between the Milwaukee Electric Railway and Light Company and Local No. 494 of the International Brotherhood of Electrical Workers, effective December 14, 1934, provided:

The company agrees that when its electric distribution department is in need of additional electrical workers it will notify the business representative of said union of the need of such men so that the union may have an opportunity to present candidates. This, however, shall not prejudice the right of the company to at the same time seek other candidates for any positions that may be open.

The demand that employers do all their hiring through the union office and the union office alone is usually provoked by special conditions. It may be a result of abuses in the labor market. In industries where shops are small and employers do not hire through central employment departments, jobs are often obtained through knowing people in the shop, through pull, and even through bribery. The workers may demand hiring through the union office in the hope that it will remove pull and favoritism. During the depression many unions in the building trades permitted their members to work below the union scale. With the improvement in business the unions have sought to enforce the scale, at least on large projects. When this has proved difficult, some locals have required contractors who were caught paying less than the scale to hire all of their men through the union office. This reduces the danger of special deals.

In trades where employment is intermittent, the union may seek to compel employers to hire through the union office in order to limit the control of employers over the speed of work. If the union determines the order in which workers get jobs, the employer cannot reward the fastest workers by giving them preference when he hires. The union may also seek to control placements in order to protect the unemployed from spending hours of waiting around shops in the hope of picking up a few hours' work.[59]

Where work is intermittent, as in the building trades, in longshoring, or in shipping, the requirement that all men be hired from the union office is about the only way the union has of equalizing the opportunity to work and of seeing that each man gets a fair share of the work. Under these conditions the rule is equivalent to a rule within a shop requiring equal division of work. The requirement has been imposed by some locals in the building trades for this purpose—for example, the electricians, the bricklayers, and the plumbers in New York. In August 1936, the painters in New York struck in support of a demand that the employers hire half of the workmen direct from the union office. The strike was settled by an agreement that the employers would hire 25 per cent of their men through the union office.

Occasionally a union may seek to compel an employer to divide the work by hiring from a list of unemployed workers maintained by the union, despite the fact that the agreement itself imposes no such obligation on the employer.[60] When men work in widely scattered crews with a high turnover within each crew (as in the case of sailors and maritime workers), it is not easy to maintain their interest in the union. The National Maritime Union has fought hard for union-controlled hiring halls partly in order

[59] The pressmen in New York have endeavored, outside the terms of the agreement, to enforce a house of call by fining members who accept employment directly. The union claimed this was a union matter, not the business of the employers.

[60] At various times some locals of the United Mine Workers, working under regional agreements which impose no restrictions on the employer's hiring, have compelled employers to hire from a list. This practice has given rise to debate at some conventions of the union.

to equalize employment opportunities but partly to make the men more dependent on the union and to prevent companies from developing more or less permanent crews which are loyal to the company.

Although a rule that employers must hire through a union office may eliminate some abuses from the labor market, such as favoritism by foremen and buying of jobs, it is likely to replace these abuses with others equally serious. It is almost certain, for example, to lead to discrimination by the local against traveling members. It gives the local union officers an opportunity to show favoritism, and they may use the control of hiring to build up a political machine.[61] The rank and file may seek to protect themselves against this by requiring that the union office send unemployed workers to jobs in the order of the duration of their unemployment. Such a rule is, of course, bound to make it difficult for employers to build up forces of well-selected men.

The employer may seek to avoid hiring poorly qualified workers by rejecting the applicant that the union sends and asking the union to send another and another until a satisfactory worker is sent. Some unions make it a point of policy that the employer must be absolutely free to reject any applicant and as many applicants as he sees fit. Other unions do not like to have the employers be too "choosy" and seek to prevent them from discriminating against the less competent members of the union. For example the agreement of the Bohemian bakers' Local No. 39 of Cleveland, expiring on May 1, 1930, not only required employers to hire men through the union office, but stipulated that in case the employer rejected three members in consecutive order "without reason" he should have no right to ask for another workman for a period of two months.

Not always does a rule of "first off, first hired" work out satisfactorily even to the members of the union. For some years such

[61] On the other hand, an officer of the teamsters' union in New England, who is opposed to union hiring halls, argues that the hall becomes a center for dissatisfied members of the union—the least competent and desirable men in the trade who have trouble in getting and holding jobs. With plenty of time on their hands they convert the hiring hall into a center where policies that are embarrassing to the officers and contrary to the interests of most of the members are planned.

a rule was enforced by the Milwaukee local of the electrical workers, but it was abolished in 1930 by a representative of the international office sent in to reorganize the local and to eliminate abuses. The abolition of the rule was welcomed by most of the members who, with the pick-up of building each spring, had been accustomed to seeing the first jobs go to the least competent, reliable, and industrious members of the union simply because these members had been the first ones dropped at the close of the last building season.[62] In trades where employment is intermittent and where men may be hired by the same employer several times in the course of the year or by several employers in the course of the year (as in the building trades), a requirement that an employer hire through the union office seriously interferes with efficiency on the job. When employers are free to do their own hiring, they naturally reward efficiency by rehiring the best men first. Union control of hiring destroys this reward for efficiency. This is why union control of hiring is likely to be particularly disastrous to efficiency in the building trades—as experience with several crafts in the New York market in 1938 and 1939 indicates.[63]

In time of national emergency the requirement that employers hire solely through the union office or hiring hall would seriously complicate the problem of preventing sabotage. Obviously the rule that employers must hire only men sent to them by the union would be a most convenient arrangement for Communists or Nazis who might obtain office in a local.

Although unions which compel employers to hire exclusively

---

[62] As a matter of fact, the rule greatly weakened the union because it gave non-union contractors a great advantage over union contractors and because some of the best workmen refused to join the union since they could get steadier work as non-union workers. When this rule (along with other hampering rules) was abolished in 1931, the membership of the union took a great jump.

[63] In the summer of 1940 the steamship companies obtained a modification of the hiring hall provision in their agreement with the Marine Cooks' and Stewards' Association of the Pacific Coast. This provides that the union shall make up a list of men all of whom must fulfill qualifications stipulated in the agreement. After such list is compiled, "any objections the employers may have against any persons being on the list shall be taken up through the Port Committee." The port committee is a joint committee which settles grievances. *Agreement between Marine Cooks' and Stewards' Association of the Pacific Coast and Steamship Companies in the Intercoastal and Offshore Trade and the Alaska Lines*, effective July 5, 1940, sec. 2.

through the union offices are likely to give poor employment service, there are exceptions to this rule. A conspicuous one is the employment department of the Amalgamated Clothing Workers in Chicago. The problem which confronted this employment office was unusually complex. At the time it was established there were about 500 firms in the market. The work was minutely subdivided —over 100 operations going into the making of a suit. There were important differences in the nature of the work in the various factories—some were in the ready-made business, some in the made-to-order business, some were large, some were small. The plants were located in different parts of the city and the workers naturally preferred employment in plants near their homes. The employees were of various races—Jews, Poles, Italians, Czechs, and others—and the employment in some factories was regarded as belonging to this or that racial group. The union was not at first well equipped to deal with the placement problems of such a complex labor market. As a result, the employment department received criticism from both union members and employers, and in negotiations for renewal of the trade agreement in 1922, the employers demanded that "the power to select and allocate labor in all branches of the industry must be restored to the employers." The union refused this demand, but it took immediate steps to improve its employment service by engaging Mr. Bryce M. Stewart, head of the Canadian Public Employment Offices, to reorganize the Chicago office. In 1925, the system in effect in Chicago was extended to the Rochester market, where the union had been unable to win from the employers the concession of the preferential shop. Partly because the reorganized employment exchange gave the employers good service and partly because the union brought direct pressure on employers who did not use it, more than 98 per cent of the hiring in the Rochester market was soon done through the union employment exchange.

Because control of placements by employers is often unsatisfactory to workers and because the control of placements by the union is unsatisfactory to employers, employment exchanges under joint supervision of employers and the union have been suggested. In many situations, it is true, such an arrangement would be impracticable because the volume of placement work is not sufficient to warrant the overhead of an office. Provision for joint employment offices was included in the national agreement negotiated in September 1931 between the Full Fashioned Hosiery Manufacturers of America and the American Federation of Full Fashioned Hosiery Workers, but such offices were not established. The agreement of the International Ladies' Garment Workers' Union in the New York cloak and suit industry, effective between 1937 and 1940, also provides that an employment bureau is to be established under impartial direction and that placements and replacements are to be made through it. The bureau, however, has not been created.[64]

Several notable attempts to establish joint control of employment have occurred in the maritime industry. Hiring halls under joint control of unions and employers have existed for longshore labor in British ports for some years. The first joint hiring hall for longshore labor in the United States was established in Seattle in 1921, but, although the longshoremen were represented, they were not organized into an independent union. Hiring halls in which labor had some representation were established in Los Angeles in 1922 and in Portland in 1923.[65]

In San Francisco there was no hiring hall and, during the depression in particular, great dissatisfaction developed among the men because of preference shown certain favored gangs known as "star gangs."[66] When the longshoremen of San Francisco in 1933 and 1934 organized the local that was the nucleus of the Inter-

---

[64] A letter from a representative of the union says: "The clause represents a compromise on the original demand of the union that such a labor bureau be placed under its sole supervision and was accepted in order to avert a strike in the industry. It was adopted with the understanding that both parties—the union and the employers—would contribute toward the maintenance of such a bureau, to be supervised by the impartial chairman in the industry. However, owing to the fact that certain elements in the union opposed the establishment of a labor bureau under *joint* auspices, *it was never set up.*"

[65] See U. S. Bureau of Labor Statistics, *Cargo Handling and Longshore Labor Conditions,* Bulletin No. 550, pp. 70-103.

[66] These men numbered about a thousand out of the three or four thousand men attached to the industry in San Francisco, and worked for less than a dozen contractors or steamship companies. Because of the preference shown to them, they had fairly steady work even during bad times. The local union in San Francisco, known as the "Blue Book Union," failed to protect its members against the hiring methods of the contractors and steamship companies.

national Longshoremen's and Warehousemen's Union (a CIO affiliate), one of their principal demands was that all hiring be done from a union hiring hall. The award of the National Longshoremen's Board, after the strike of 1934, attempted to compromise the issue by providing for hiring halls to be operated by joint committees of employers and workers with the costs borne half by the employers and half by the union. The award permitted the employer to select gangs and also to select individual men. However, the award also provided that the dispatchers (the men in the hiring halls who send workers in response to employer requests) were to be union members. This provision (in combination with some "direct action") practically enabled the union to take over control of the hiring halls. The dispatchers disregarded the requests of employers for men from given gangs and sent out men in rotation. If an employer refused to accept a gang of men or an individual, the dispatchers sent replacements, but the replacements did not show up for work.

SOME QUESTIONS OF LAW AND PUBLIC POLICY RAISED BY THE CLOSED SHOP

The closed shop is illegal on the railroads under the Railway Labor Act because it is a form of discrimination. It is permitted under the Wagner Act when a majority in the bargaining unit belong to the union. This is not the place to discuss the many legal questions raised by the closed shop. Several of the questions, however, should be indicated. Suppose, for example, that a factional fight within a local leads one faction, fearful of being defeated, to expel a large number of workers. Apparently the employer must discharge them from his service. Or suppose that the national intervenes in the fight and expels a majority of the local. In that case the employer may lose most of his force. Or suppose that the local union itself decides to leave the national or is expelled by it and the national organizes a new local with the same number as the old one. Must the employer now discharge his entire force and use only members of the new local? Apparently not in case the other party to the agreement is the original local. But in some cases the national as well as the local is a party to the agreement and underwrites its performance by the local in return for the employer's agreement to employ only members of the national. In that case the difficulty might be settled by holding that the national and the local made the agreement simply as representatives of the workers and that the agreement really belongs to them. There are difficulties, however, in holding that a closed-shop agreement belongs to the workers rather than the union.[67]

The closed shop also raises a number of questions of public policy. Should the law, for example, require that unions which make closed-shop contracts keep their membership requirements reasonable? Should unions which exclude negroes be permitted to negotiate closed-shop contracts? Should local unions be permitted to make closed-shop contracts if their members are not permitted to vote for their own officers? Obviously it may be necessary for the national union to suspend the voting privileges of the members of a local for a limited period of time. Suppose, however, that the suspension lasts for many years. The Chicago pressmen's local has not been permitted to elect its officers for about twenty years. Should such a union be permitted by closed-shop contracts to compel men to join it or to remain in it? Many districts of the United Mine Workers have for a number of years operated under so-called "temporary" officers appointed by the national. These districts make contracts which by the checkoff compel men to pay dues to an organization in which they have no vote.

ATTITUDE OF UNIONS TOWARD THE PHYSICAL EXAMINATION OF APPLICANTS

It is now standard practice in nearly all large establishments to give applicants for employment who are provisionally hired a

---

[67] Some of these difficulties have recently been experienced by the Transformer Corporation of America, a small manufacturer of sound-track equipment in New York City. In 1939 the company signed a closed-shop contract with a local of the electrical workers' union in the AFL. In May 1940 the employees voted to withdraw and join the United Electrical Workers, affiliated with the CIO. The AFL union demanded that the two employees leading the revolt be discharged— as the closed-shop contract required. When the company complied, the rest of the workers struck. The company hired a new crew through the AFL union as the contract required. The former employees picketed the plant and the AFL teamsters' union refused to cross the picket line. In order to resume operations the company rehired its original employees and signed a closed-shop contract with the CIO electrical workers' union. As this is written, an attempt is being made to settle the dispute through an election conducted by the National Labor Relations Board.

physical examination before finally engaging them. Such examinations obviously assist the employer in making a better selection of workers. When properly administered, the examinations are also advantageous to most applicants for employment because they protect the applicant from being hired for work which might be injurious, even dangerous, to him.[68]

Nearly all unions, however, are opposed to medical examinations as given by most enterprises. This does not mean that unions oppose limited medical examinations under special circumstances where the health or safety of the public is involved, as in the case of food workers or some groups of railroad workers whose duties require good eyesight or hearing.[69] It does mean, however, that most unions are opposed to general physical examinations for ordinary employment, and a few trade agreements prohibit such examinations. For example, Rule No. 46 of the national agreement between the United States Railroad Administration and the shopcrafts limited the physical examination which the employer might require to eyesight and hearing tests and those only in case the position required the employee to distinguish signals or to do flagging. In Decision No. 222, the Railroad Labor Board modified the rule to permit physical examination at the expense of the carrier in order to determine the fitness of the applicant to perform the service. Some of the agreements between the railroads and the

---

[68] Some states require workers in certain trades (for example, where handling foodstuffs is required) to submit to physical examinations. North Carolina requires workers in certain trades to submit to pre-employment examination (Workmen's Compensation Act of 1935, sec. 50½, sub-sec. (i)). Under the Motor Carrier Act the Interstate Commerce Commission requires every motor carrier subject to the act to have on file a certificate of physical examination by a qualified physician for every driver hired after Jan. 1, 1940, attesting that the driver meets satisfactorily the qualifications set forth in the commission's rules.

[69] The point of view of organized labor was well expressed by Mr. John M. O'Hanlon, secretary-treasurer of the New York State Federation of Labor at the New York State Conference on Social Work in Rochester in November 1928: "Organized labor recognizes that physical examination of employees in the interest of their own and the public health and safety is desirable. Workers in direct contact with the preparing of food for consumption now undergo such examination, and this regulation was promoted by the unions of these occupations, which had always maintained such a requirement of their members. For the security of passengers, train crews submit most willingly to regular physical examination compulsory in the interest of the health and security of such employees and their fellow employees." New York State Federation of Labor, *Bulletin No. 18*, Nov. 15, 1928, p. 3.

shopcrafts retain the rule enunciated by the Railroad Labor Board. For example, the agreements with both the Baltimore and Ohio and the Chesapeake and Ohio state that applicants for employment may be required to take a physical examination at the expense of the carrier "to determine the fitness of the applicant to reasonably perform the service required in his craft or class." Other agreements, such as that on the Chicago, Milwaukee, St. Paul, and Pacific, prohibit physical examinations except with respect to eyesight and hearing for jobs which require the holder to distinguish figures or to do flagging. Recently the Granite Cutters' International Association of America amended its constitution to forbid its members to submit to physical examinations. Restrictions on physical examinations would be more numerous were it not for the fact that the issue is not of first importance to most unions.

The usual reason given by union leaders for their opposition to physical examinations is that the examination might be used as a means of blacklisting union men. This is not convincing, because employers can easily discriminate against union men without employing the device of physical examination. The real opposition of unions to physical examinations seems to boil down to the fact that they do not like the employers alone to set the standards of fitness and they object to men's being rejected without provision for them to make a living. The trade union view is well expressed by a prominent and broad-minded union leader, who states that he is "very much opposed to medical examination for employment." He explained his position in a personal interview thus:

There are a very large number of workers who are not physically average men but who have craft knowledge. These men do not see the employer at all. They see only the physician who is solely interested in selecting physically perfect men. Because of that these men are barred from the chance to make a living. Physical examination can be very beneficial, but to give the employer the right to make his own physical standards bars out many men from the chance to make a living. We feel that a man who isn't physically perfect has as much right to make a living and support his family as a man who is. If industry is to be carried on only by the physically perfect, the government will have to meet the needs of those who fail to meet the degree of physical perfection which employers demand.

This argument has great merit. Many companies, however, have recognized that the standards of physical fitness should vary for different jobs and that men should not be rejected for all jobs simply because they are not fitted for certain strenuous ones. Some companies, for example, divide accepted applicants into two or more principal classes—an unrestricted class, who may be used on any job in the plant, and a restricted class who may be used on some jobs but not on others. Scattered reports show that when men may be accepted for either restricted or unrestricted jobs, complete rejections do not ordinarily run more than 3 per cent.

An examination of 200 trade agreements reveals very little effort to meet the problems presented by physical examinations. In fact, physical examinations were mentioned in only 23 out of the 200 agreements and in only 18 of these was the reference to examination at the time of employment. None of the agreements undertake to specify the standards which shall govern the acceptance or rejection of employees. Three agreements permit examination under certain circumstances by the employees' physician, and five by an impartial physician.[70] An agreement made in January 1937 by the Federation of Flat Glass Workers of America with the Pittsburgh Plate Glass Company not only permits physical examination on hiring but also permits re-examination from time to time and transfer of workers from one department to another when the re-examination shows this to be desirable. The agreement stipulates that physical examinations shall not be used to discriminate against employees and permits an appeal by employees who believe that they have been discriminated against.[71]

[70] For example, the agreement between the oil field, gas well, and refinery workers' union and the Sinclair Refining Company states that employees are not required as a condition of employment other than in exceptional cases to submit to a physical examination by a physician in the employ of the company, but may furnish a certificate of current date from any reputable doctor of the employee's own choice.

[71] The provisions of the agreement relating to physical examinations are as follows:

"(a) Due to laws imposing compensation insurance upon industry, and because of the company's policy which provides group life and health and accident insurance, all new employees must pass a physical examination.

"(b) Physical examination of employees or groups of employees shall be made from time to time, and should such examination disclose that a transfer to another department would be beneficial from a health standpoint, the employee shall be consulted and the transfer made. A transfer for this reason is not to be con-

Particularly interesting is the agreement negotiated in 1940 between the National Maritime Union and the Atlantic and Gulf Shipowners' Association. It requires unlicensed personnel to submit to such medical examinations as may be required by the company. The company agrees to review carefully any case when the medical examiners of the union certify the member to be free from communicable disease and disabling defects. If a review fails to establish the facts to the mutual satisfaction of the company's and the union's medical examiners, the two shall agree upon an outside physician whose judgment will be determining.[72]

The fact that most labor organizations are opposed to medical examination of applicants for employment, except for special and limited purposes, does not mean that they are unwilling to co-operate in order to discover how the workers in industry are affected by various health hazards. A notable example of such co-operation occurred some years ago in the New York photo-engraving industry where the photo-engravers' union co-operated with the New York City Board of Health by encouraging its members to submit to physical examinations. Influenced by the union, over 1,600 members of the New York local submitted to examination by physicians assigned by the City Board of Health. The fine, close work in the industry and the acids and chemicals used produce many ills, such as defective eyes, throat and nose troubles, and decayed teeth.[73]

---

sidered a violation of the promotion schedule. Employees may obtain, upon request, copies of the reports of their physical examination.

"(c) The physical examination of employees following layoff and sickness shall not be used as a guise to discriminate against any employee. If any employee feels that he has been discriminated against as a result of an examination, the case shall be reviewed by the company and the Industrial Relations Committee in the manner hereinbefore set forth."

[72] *The Pilot*, Jan. 12, 1940, Vol. V, No. 1, p. 16. An agreement of federal Local No. 19,184, composed of flour, feed, and cereal workers in Buffalo, negotiated in 1934, provided for appeal in the case of old employees found unfit for service by the company physician. The agreement provided that such an employee had the right to be examined by a physician chosen by himself. In case this examination was in disagreement with the findings of the company doctor, a neutral doctor would be chosen by the two and the decision of the majority of the three would be final. *American Federationist*, September 1934, Vol. XLI, p. 969.

[73] For a report of the survey from the union point of view, see International Photo-Engravers' Union of North America, *Reports of Officers and Convention Proceedings*, 1926, p. 50.

SOME CONCLUSIONS CONCERNING UNION EFFORTS
TO CONTROL HIRING

In the minds of American employers the expression "closed shop" has been a symbol of union domination. This is a mistake. An assured status for the union is not a guarantee of successful union-employer relations but it is a prerequisite, and the closed shop or its equivalent is one way of assuring the status of the union. The employer is likely to have more freedom in shops where the status of the union is established than in one where its position is more or less precarious. Where the union is not secure, it is compelled to attempt to restrict the employer's discretion at every point where he may discriminate against union members in favor of non-members. In particular, as pointed out earlier in this chapter, the union must endeavor to restrict his control of layoffs. The union virtually has no choice but to treat the control of layoffs as a major issue. Where the closed shop exists, however, the union has less at stake in many decisions of management. Hence it is not in a position to insist upon controlling these decisions. This is why more managerial discretion may be permitted in a closed shop than in an open one. The comparison of the layoff provisions in closed-shop and open-shop agreements made earlier in this chapter bears out this conclusion.[74]

The closed shop as a rule has not prevented employers from obtaining the number of men needed. It is more likely to affect the quality of the men available to union employers. Even here, however, its effect has been less important than one might suppose because unions which are strong enough to obtain the closed shop are usually strong enough to attract the best workmen into the trade.

Although the closed shop has some tendency to encourage unions to pursue restrictive admission policies, these policies are usually adopted because the wage scale of the union has attracted a surplus of workers into the trade—and sometimes because it has produced a shrinkage of employment in union plants. Nevertheless, it is desirable for employers who grant the closed shop to guard against re-

---

[74] In 140, or 83 per cent, of the 169 open shop agreements in the table on pp. 60-61, some restriction was imposed on the employer's freedom to make layoffs. In 150, or 65 per cent, of the 231 closed and preferential shop agreements there were similar restrictions.

strictive admission requirements. They should do this despite the fact that the national union can usually be counted upon to use its influence against restrictive admission policies by locals. The simplest and most complete protection which the employer can have is that he be free to hire anyone he sees fit, whether a member of the union or not, on condition that the worker become a member after serving a probationary period, and that the union keep its doors open on reasonable terms to such persons. As a general rule, there is no necessity for employers' conceding a closed shop except on these terms. The concession that all regular employees must be members of the union is so important for the union that in return for it the employer can usually insist that he be free to hire anyone he sees fit. The interest of the community requires that union membership be open to all and that the closed shop shall not be permitted to create a class of privileged workers who, as a group, control jobs to which other workers have no access, however willing they may be to join the union. In the long run the interest of the unions themselves requires that the closed shop shall not be linked with closed unions or that it shall not interfere with the employer's freedom to hire men willing to join, because only on these conditions can the community afford to permit free trade unions. Any other policy by the unions would eventually require regulation of the unions by the government.[75]

The arrangements by which some local unions seek to discourage the employment of union members from other cities are uneconomic and impede the adjustment of the labor supply to changes in demand. Fortunately, the influence of most national unions is thrown against these restrictions. Little is known, however, concerning the nature and the extent of the restrictions on movement, and more information is needed.

The requirement that men be engaged through the union office is likely to result in a poor selection of workers for employers and to have disastrous political repercussions upon the union and in times of emergency to jeopardize national defense. In industries where employment is intermittent, however, a centralized hiring

---

[75] Information concerning the admission fees and admission policies of unions is scanty. Studies of these matters are needed.

agency may be needed in order to avoid such abuses as men's wasting many hours waiting for work or paying for jobs. In view of the fact that efforts to establish jointly controlled employment offices have thus far failed, the most promising solution seems to be through special arrangements with public employment offices.

The growing tendency of unions to require that properly qualified furloughed men be given preference when vacancies are filled greatly increases the importance of the original hiring. Particularly it makes necessary an adequate probationary period and, in addition, the actual use of the probationary period to determine carefully the suitability of new employees for their work.

CHAPTER IV

CONTROL OF LAYOFFS—UNION POLICIES

The strong interest of unions in the control of layoffs springs from the violent fluctuations in employment that characterize a large part of American industry. True, in some industries, such as public utilities, newspaper publishing, and petroleum refining, work in most departments is fairly steady the year round and from good years to bad. Even in the steady industries, however, many plants or departments experience substantial seasonal and cyclical fluctuations in employment. In many other industries it is not unusual for enterprises to have only half or one-third as many men in slack months as in busy ones, while in bad years forces often sink to a fifth or a tenth their size in good years.

Employers naturally wish a free hand in picking the men who are to be dropped. Not only does such freedom permit managements to drop the least competent and least industrious men, but the knowledge that such men will be the first to go is at all times a powerful stimulus to efficiency throughout the force. But both unions as organizations, and their members as individuals, frequently object to the employer's having freedom to lay off anyone he sees fit. If the union has no closed shop, restrictions on the employer's freedom to lay off may be a matter of self-preservation, because if union members are always the first to be dropped, the men will not remain in the organization. However, the interest of wage earners in controlling layoffs goes beyond their desire to preserve and strengthen their unions. Workers wish an equity in their jobs—that is, they desire rights of tenure which protect them against arbitrary layoff and discharge. Furthermore, workers wish certainty—they want to know where they stand. If they are reasonably sure of not being laid off, they want to know it. Likewise, if they are almost certain to be among the first dropped, they want to know that also. This is true of non-union as well as union workers.

To the plea of managers that they must be free to select the men who are to be dropped, the workers have four replies. In the first place, they insist that the freedom is almost certain to be abused, because foremen find it difficult to resist pressure to favor friends or members of certain social groups—racial, religious, and fraternal. In the second place, the men point out that the efforts of individuals and groups to gain the favor of foremen and other officials are injurious to shop morale and efficiency. In the third place, the men argue that it is harsh and inhuman to concentrate the burden of unemployment upon a few men simply because they happen to be less efficient than the others. Workers regard unemployment as a social misfortune which, in so far as it must fall on some one, should fall on all workers, fast and slow, more or less alike. Some workers are bound to be less efficient than others. To drop them first and hire them last amounts to treating their lower efficiency as a grave social offense. In the fourth place, the workers deny the right of managers to destroy security in order to promote efficiency. Security, in the view of the workers, is more important than efficiency. So long as each worker holds his job only at the pleasure of the management, there can be no real security. Hence workers insist that managements should find ways of promoting efficiency other than constantly holding over the heads of workers the threat that the slowest and least skillful will be dropped at the first lull in business. Finally, the workers see in rules governing layoffs a safeguard against excessive speeding because the employer is no longer able to use the threat of layoff to maintain rivalry in a perpetual race for greater speed. For these reasons control of layoffs is of great importance both to individual workers and to unions.

GROWING INTEREST IN CONTROL OF LAYOFFS

A prominent official of a union in the paper industry writes:

When we first began to sign agreements with pulp and paper manufacturers, seniority was not much of an issue. . . . However, since the depression and the struggle for life itself, this question of seniority seems to loom larger in the workers' minds than anything else.

A union official from the glass industry writes:

I have been in the glass industry for over fifty years and never once had to work under the seniority rule. That came into the Trade Union Movement after I had given up the active work in the glass factory; but in getting around the country . . . I find that is the paramount question in local meetings that seems to overshadow all other questions before the group and it has been the cause of many requests upon the national office for an officer to go to a place to adjust it. That's why I call it a headache.

These two statements illustrate the rising interest of wage earners in controlling layoffs. An examination of 388 trade agreements made between 1923 and 1929 revealed that only 145 contained restrictions on the employer's freedom to make layoffs. Of 400 trade agreements negotiated between 1933 and 1939, on the other hand, 290 contained such restrictions.[1]

The growing interest in job security is partly a result of long-term trends in the American labor market and partly a result of the depression. Until 1920, the American labor market was a market of movement, in which the behavior of men was dominated by the idea of opportunity—a market in which there was a considerable number of men ready to give up one job in the hope of getting a better one. Before the war, separations averaged about 100 per cent of the average working force per year and over two-thirds of these were resignations. Throughout the twenties, personnel administration endeavored to promote the idea of continuous service.[2] By 1929, the median separation rate in manufacturing industries was about 50 per cent a year. In a market of diminishing movement, and therefore diminishing hiring, a man once displaced has trouble in quickly finding a suitable opening. In such a market layoffs become matters of vital concern, and employees fight hard to keep their jobs.

The depression, quite naturally, has greatly increased interest in job security. This is reflected in the lower resignation rate which,

---

[1] See the tables on pp. 105 and 106-07. No agreements from the building trades were included in the groups examined because it is a matter of common knowledge that building trade agreements almost never limit the employer's freedom to drop men.

[2] Rights to group insurance, vacations with pay, and pensions were based upon length of service and increased as the years of service increased. Special service buttons were issued and service clubs of men with 25 years' service or more were started.

in 1929, seems to have been in excess of 30 per cent per year among factory workers and in 1936 and 1937 below 15 per cent. The drop in the resignation rate has compelled an increase in layoffs because employers have been less and less able to rely upon resignations to produce adjustments in the size of the working force. For example, although the year 1936 was one of expanding employment, the layoff rate in manufacturing seems to have been 50 per cent greater than in 1929, a year in which employment did not expand.[3] With the interest in job security growing and the layoff rate increasing, it is not surprising that unions are paying more and more attention to the regulation of layoffs.

WHY SOME UNIONS DO NOT ATTEMPT TO REGULATE LAYOFFS

In view of the increasing importance which wage earners have been attaching to job security, it is somewhat surprising to find that over three-fifths of a group of pre-depression agreements and more than a third of a group of post-depression agreements contained no restrictions on the employer's freedom to make layoffs.[4] Of course, absence of restrictions on layoffs in the agreement does not necessarily mean that none are enforced by the union. For example, no restrictions on layoffs are contained in the agreement between Local No. 25 of the teamsters and chauffeurs' union in Boston and the Employers' Group of Motor Freight Carriers, but seniority has been imposed by the union in many shops by the threat of shop strikes. Nevertheless, the proportion of agreements containing no restrictions on layoffs is impressive. One might suspect that it reflects weak bargaining power on the part of the unions. This explanation, however, is inadequate, because few of the agreements of the powerful photo-engravers' and printing pressmen's unions contain restrictions on layoffs.

Why do even powerful unions sometimes fail to limit the em-

---

[3] Comparisons between 1929 and subsequent years are difficult to make because the figures for 1929 and earlier years, collected by the Metropolitan Life Insurance Company, are unweighted median rates and those for 1930 and following years, collected by the Bureau of Labor Statistics, are weighted average rates. For 1930, however, the figures have been computed in both ways. Despite the fact that the sample from 1930 on is much larger than in 1929 and before, a rough comparison is possible.

[4] As noted above, there were excluded from both groups all agreements in the building trades where it is not ordinarily practicable for unions to regulate layoffs.

ployer's freedom to drop workers? Primarily because it is difficult to restrict layoffs without also restricting the worker's freedom of movement and his opportunity to obtain new jobs and, under some circumstances, without producing an unfair distribution of the burden of unemployment and jeopardizing the existence of the union itself. The nature of these conflicts will be explained presently in connection with the analysis of the ways in which unions regulate layoffs. At any rate, the worker's desire for an equity in his job sometimes comes in conflict with his other interests and with the interests of the union. It may even come in conflict with the worker's desire for security, because in industries where there are a large number of small employers with a violently fluctuating demand for labor (job-printing, photo-engraving, building) the worker's security may depend upon his freedom to move.

The conflict between the worker's desire for an equity in his job and his desire for freedom of movement is seen most clearly in the building trades, where work is so intermittent and jobs are of such brief duration that no one ever thinks of an equity in jobs. Suppose that building trades unions were to regulate layoffs by either of the devices usually employed—equal division of work or seniority. The former would simply spread unemployment (through short time) among all workers on the job after the peak period had passed. It would lead the most energetic, enterprising, and efficient workers to leave first in order to get full-time work elsewhere. By assuming the risk of complete unemployment for themselves, they would be creating more employment for the other workers on the job—which would not impress the more efficient men as fair. Equally unsatisfactory would be the seniority rule, by which the man hired last is dropped first. Since the contractors naturally hire their favorites first of all, the burden of unemployment would be borne in the main by the rest of the workers. To a great extent, of course, this situation actually exists, but it does so by decision of the employers rather than by a rule of the unions. If the building trades unions were to attempt to enforce seniority by rule, the short-service men who were bearing the burden of unemployment would revolt against the union rules and go out and get work under such conditions as they could. This would threaten the destruction of the unions themselves. Consequently, when building trades unions attempt to control employment opportunities, they usually do so by endeavoring to control hiring, as described in the preceding chapter.[5]

Unable to restrict the employer's freedom to make layoffs without limiting the worker's freedom of movement or causing an unfair distribution of the burden of unemployment, many unions find themselves compelled to insist upon the closed shop in order to reduce the employer's incentive to discriminate against their members in making layoffs. This aspect of the closed shop has been quite generally overlooked and yet it is one of great importance. It reveals the closed shop as a restriction which unions seek to impose on employers in lieu of greater restrictions which they find themselves unable or unwilling to impose because of conflicts in the interests of their members.

METHODS OF CONTROLLING LAYOFFS

The mildest restriction which unions impose on layoffs is the requirement that the employer give advance notice of his intention to drop some men. The employer, however, is still free to drop anyone he sees fit. Or the union may require that the employer rehire laid-off employees, if qualified, before engaging other workers. In a few cases unions require that non-members be dropped before any union member is dismissed. The two principal ways in which unions attempt to control layoffs are (1) by requiring that the work be divided equally, thus preventing layoffs, and (2) by requiring that men be dropped in order of their seniority. Often these two restrictions are combined in various ways, as when layoffs are permitted in order of seniority after the work has been divided down to a certain point. A few unions attempt to restrict layoffs by requiring a policy of guaranteed employment, and a few of them require the employer to pay a dismissal wage to men who are dropped through no fault of their own. As a general rule, however, provisions for a dismissal wage have not been included in trade agreements, but have been especially negotiated to meet particular situations.

---

[5] An interesting exception, the New York local of the electrical workers' union, is described below.

The tables on pages 105-07 present the results of an analysis of the equal-division-of-work and the seniority provisions in two groups of agreements. The table on page 105 covers 388 agreements negotiated between 1923 and 1929, and the table on pages 106-07 covers 400 agreements negotiated between 1933 and 1939.

Two conspicuous facts which stand out from examination of these agreements have already been mentioned, namely, the large proportion which contain no restrictions on layoffs and the great increase since the depression in the proportion containing restrictions. Another conspicuous fact about the agreements covered by these tables is that they restrict layoffs through the use of seniority rules far more frequently than through equal division of work. In this respect the tables are misleading. The samples contain relatively few agreements from the large and important unions in the needle trades, which make use of equal division of work rather than seniority. Furthermore, informal arrangements are often made to divide the work down to a certain point even where the agreement provides for layoff only through seniority. Consequently, it is safe to say that the equal-division-of-work principle is far more prevalent than these tables seem to indicate.

Advance notice of layoffs. An old shopman on the Baltimore and Ohio said to me: "Our boss was always afraid to tell you there was going to be a layoff. I have seen McSweeney write on the door with a piece of chalk, 'No work tomorrow.' He waited so long that he could not get around to tell the men in time."

The simplest and least ambitious of all the ways by which unions attempt to protect their members against layoffs is to require a minimum advance notice. The protection, of course, is not much, but it gives the men a little time to look for other jobs and enables them to begin husbanding their resources against the lean period which is likely to be ahead. From the employer's standpoint, the requirement that he give advance notice of layoffs has disadvantages, because nothing is so destructive of morale and efficiency as an announcement that the force will be cut—nothing, that is, except dropping men without giving them notice! The latter practice is so unfair, arouses so much resentment, and, in times of slack business when layoffs are anticipated, produces so much uncertainty

LAYOFF PROVISIONS IN 388 TRADE AGREEMENTS NEGOTIATED BETWEEN 1923 AND 1929

Industry or Trade	Total	No Restriction	Union Preference Only	Seniority	Seniority and Ability	Equal Division of Work	Union Preference, then Equal Division of Work	New Employees Laid Off then Equal Division of Work	Equal Division with Reorganization Privilege	Equal Division of Work, then Seniority
METAL TRADES	73	46	1	9	3	3		1	1	9
Blacksmiths	5	5								
Boilermakers	12	7	1	1	3					
Machinists	21	13		3		2			1	2
Molders	22	21				1				
Railway shopcrafts	13			5				1		7
NEEDLE TRADES	18	3	2			8	2		3	
Amalgamated Clothing Workers	2		1						1	
Amalgamated Textile Workers	1	1								
Cloth hat and cap workers	2	1				1				
Fur workers	2	1				1				
Glove workers	4					4				
Ladies' garment workers	7		1			2	2		2	
PRINTING TRADES	167	85		77	2	2				1
Bookbinders	18	18								
Photo-engravers	27	25			1	1				
Printing pressmen	43	42								1
Stereotypers and electrotypers	19			18		1				
Typographical Union	60			59	1					
OTHER UNIONS IN MANUFACTURING	49	42		4		3				
Bakery and confectionery workers	35	34		1						
Bottle blowers	3	3								
Brewery, cereal, flour, and soft drink workers	5	2		3						
Leather workers	2	1				1				
Shoe workers	1					1				
Tapestry carpet workers	1	1								
Upholstery weavers	2	1				1				
MISCELLANEOUS UNIONS	81	67		11	1	2				
Barbers	13	13								
Longshoremen	6	6								
Laundry workers	3	3								
Street railway employees	20	12		7	1					
Teamsters and chauffeurs	39	33		4		2				
GRAND TOTAL	388	243	3	101	6	18	2	1	4	10

Layoff Provisions in 400 Trade Agreements Negotiated between 1933 and 1939

Industry or Trade	Total	No Restriction	Seniority	Seniority and Ability	Equal Division of Work	Union Preference, then Equal Division of Work	Union Preference, then Seniority	New Employees Laid Off, then Equal Division of Work	Equal Division with Reorganization Privilege	Equal Division, then Seniority	New Employees Laid Off, then Equal Division, then Seniority
METAL AND STONE TRADES AND MACHINERY	56	9	6	21	2					9	9
Aluminum workers	1			1						1	1
Blacksmiths	1										
Brass workers	1										1
Die casters	1			1							
Farm equipment workers	1										1
Granite workers	2	2			1						
Jewelry workers	2	1	2								
Machinists	17	5	1	2						6	2
Metal polishers, buffers, etc.	4		2	1							1
Molders	4	1								1	
Silver workers	1		1								
Steel workers	21		1	16	1					1	3
MINING, QUARRYING, AND OIL	14	6	3	5							
Mine workers	3	3									
Oil field, gas well workers	9	1	3	5							
Quarry workers	2	2									
NEEDLE TRADES	33	5	4	2	8			8	4	1	1
Cloth hat, cap workers	2	1						1			
Hosiery workers	4	1			3						
Ladies' garment workers	8							4	4		
Ladies' handbag workers	3	2	1								
Men's clothing workers	6	1			5						
Tailors	2	1						1			
Textile workers	8		3	2				2		1	1
PAPER, PRINTING, AND BOOKBINDING	65	27	7	21	7		1				2
Bookbinders	2	2									
Machine printers	1						1				
Paper and paper mill workers	20	2	4	11	1						2
Photo- and copper-engravers	12	8	1	1	2						
Printing pressmen	17	14	1	1	1						
Stereotypers and electrotypers	4	1			3						
Typographical workers	9		1	8							
TRANSPORTATION AND COMMUNICATION	48	23	16	6	1		2				
Longshoremen and seamen	9	6	1	1	1						
Marine cooks and stewards	1	1									
Marine engineers and firemen	9	7	1	1							
Masters, mates, and pilots	1	1									
Railroad workers	8		8								
Teamsters and chauffeurs	8	3	2	2			1				
Telegraphers	5	2		2			1				
Transport workers	7	3	4								

	400	110	69	97	32	2	4	10	4	37	35
OTHER UNIONS IN MANUFACTURING...	123	11	20	32	11			2		27	20
Automobile workers........	19	2	3	5	1					2	9
Bakery and confectionery workers...	7	1	2	2	6					2	1
Brewery and cereal workers.....	10	1	1	1							
Carpet and linoleum workers.....	1										
Chemical workers..........	3	3	1	3						4	
Cork workers............	1		1	2						3	1
Electrical and radio workers.......	8	1	2							7	
Glass bottle blowers.........	10	3								4	3
Glass workers...........	12		1								
Leather workers..........	4	1									
Lumber workers..........	1										
Pottery workers..........	1		2							2	
Remington Rand workers........	1		1	1	1						1
Rubber workers..........	7	2	2	2				1		2	
Shoe workers............	4		1	1							
Sugar refinery workers........	2										1
Upholsterers and mattress workers....	1										
Workers' Protective Union.......	1	1	1	13						5	4
Miscellaneous federal labor unions....	30		6		3	2	1	1			3
MISCELLANEOUS..........	61	29	13	10	3						
Actors, radio artists, and theatrical employees..........	5	5									
Barbers...............	5	1	1								
Bottlers..............	1										
Building service employees......	6	5	1	1				1			
Cemetery workers.........	1	1									
Cleaners and pressers........	1										
Cooks and waitresses........	3	1									1
Department store workers.......	6	3	3	3							
Distillery workers.........	1		1								
Drug workers...........	2	1	1	1	1						
Gas station operators........	3										
Grain and mill workers........	3										
Grocery workers and warehouse workers...........	8	3	3	4							
Hospital workers..........	5	1	2								
Hotel and restaurant workers.....	1		1								1
Janitors and cleaners........	1										
Laundry workers..........	2										
Newspaper workers.........	7	6	1	1	2						1
Office and professional workers.....	4	1	1		1		1	1			
Packinghouse workers........	2										
GRAND TOTAL...........	400	110	69	97	32	2	4	10	4	37	35

that the managements of many non-union plants voluntarily give advance notice of all layoffs.

The period of notice required in agreements with trade unions varies as a rule from two days to two weeks. The agreement between the shopcraft unions and the United States Railroad Administration, for example, required five days' notice, and five days are still required by agreement between the shopcrafts and the Chicago and North Western Railway. On most union roads, however, the notice has been reduced to four days and on the Chicago, St. Paul, Minneapolis, and Omaha to 36 hours.[6] The Hebrew butcher workers of greater New York, in their agreement for 1929, required two weeks' notice.

The notice requirement may or may not be reciprocal—that is, workers who resign may or may not be required to notify the employer in advance. The notice rule in the railroad shopcrafts is not reciprocal. However, the agreement between the Commercial Telegraphers' Union of America and the International News Service, effective October 1, 1937, provides that the employer shall give at least 15 days' notice of layoffs and that operators intending to resign shall notify the district chief operator 15 days in advance or be fined or suspended or both by the union.[7] The agreement of the Window Glass Cutters' League of America with the Pittsburgh Plate Glass Company, effective December 15, 1936, required a reciprocal notice of 7 days.[8]

[6] Most of the railroads which broke off relations with the shopcraft unions after the strike of 1922 retained some notice in the agreements which they made with the company unions of their shopcraft employees. The notice was usually less than on union roads. The Missouri Pacific and the New York, New Haven, and Hartford agreed to four days' notice; but the Chicago, Burlington, and Quincy, the Chicago, Rock Island, and Pacific, the Delaware and Hudson, the Missouri, Kansas, and Texas, the Northern Pacific, the St. Louis and Southwestern, and the Kansas City Southern agreed to give only two days. No notice requirement at all was incorporated in the agreements negotiated with the company unions on the Atlantic Coast Line and the Lehigh Valley. The Southern Pacific (Pacific Lines) retained the five days' notice required by the old agreement with the United States Railroad Administration.

[7] The contract further provides that fines imposed by the union upon members for violation of this rule shall be used to reimburse employers for any reasonable expense incurred in covering the positions during the unfilled term of notice. *Commercial Telegraphers' Journal,* October 1937, Vol. XXXV, No. 7, p. 112.

[8] For many years the agreement between the National Brotherhood of Operative Potters and the United States Potters' Association, covering pipe, granite, and

Furloughed workers rehired before new workers engaged. An increasing number of unions seek to protect men who are dropped because of lack of work by the simple rule that the employer must offer employment to furloughed men before he adds other workers in the same occupation. This has the effect of converting many layoffs that would otherwise be permanent into temporary ones. Exactly half of a group of 400 agreements negotiated during the thirties made some provision for re-employment after layoff, as indicated by the table on pages 110-11.

Among the 242 agreements covered in the table on pages 106-07 which contain a seniority rule, 68 stipulate the length of the layoff period during which the employee retains his seniority.[9]

Preferential rehiring is a policy which is most likely to be adopted by a large local whose membership is confined to one employer. The policy then enables the workers in this plant to assure preferential treatment for themselves as against all outsiders. But preferential rehiring is less likely to be enforced by locals which contain members working for many small employers.

Non-union workers dropped before union members laid off. A

---

semi-porcelain work, required two weeks' notice when a workman desired to resign or an employer desired to lay off a man. The agreement contained the interesting provision that a workman who gave notice of his intention to resign "must actually work for said two weeks and not loaf without reasonable excuse" and that "if these conditions have been fulfilled, the said workman shall receive at the end of the two weeks a 'discharge' signed by his employer or proper representative." The failure of the workman to procure a regular "discharge" signed by the employer indicated that he was dropped for unsatisfactory work. The agreement was one-sided, however, in that when the employer notified the workman that he would be laid off, the employer was required to give the man a "discharge" at the end of the period regardless of whether the man loafed or not. The requirement of notice is no longer a part of the agreement in the pottery industry.

[9] The following are the number of agreements stipulating each period: three months, 2; four months, 1; six months, 6; nine months, 2; one year, 25; two years, 2; no limit, 19; miscellaneous, 11.

The agreements in the miscellaneous classification include those which provide that the employee shall retain his seniority status for half the duration of his service with the company or that the worker shall not lose his seniority status during a "temporary" layoff. Of course, the fact that workers do not lose their seniority status for a given period after being laid off does not mean that they *accumulate* seniority while laid off. On this latter point practices differ. Some companies permit workers to accumulate seniority during temporary layoffs.

PROVISIONS FOR RE-EMPLOYMENT AFTER LAYOFF IN 400 AGREEMENTS NEGOTIATED BETWEEN 1933 AND 1939

Industry or Trade	Total	No Preference	General Preference for Laid-Off Employees	Preference on Basis of Seniority and Other Factors	Special Cases of Preference	Ambiguous	Provision for Notification
METAL AND STONE TRADES AND MACHINERY	56	16	13	25	—	1	1
Aluminum workers	1	—	1	—	—	—	—
Blacksmiths	1	—	—	—	—	—	1
Brass workers	1	—	1	—	—	—	—
Die casters	1	—	—	1	—	—	—
Farm equipment workers	1	—	1	—	—	—	—
Granite workers	2	2	—	—	—	—	—
Jewelry workers	2	2	—	—	—	—	—
Machinists	17	6	7	4	—	—	—
Metal polishers, buffers, etc..	4	1	1	2	—	—	—
Molders	4	1	1	1	—	1	—
Silver workers	1	1	—	—	—	—	—
Steel workers	21	3	1	17	—	—	—
MINING, QUARRYING, AND OIL	14	6	4	3	—	—	1
Mine workers	3	3	—	—	—	—	—
Oil field, gas well workers	9	1	4	3	—	—	1
Quarry workers	2	2	—	—	—	—	—
NEEDLE TRADES	33	25	2	5	1	—	—
Cloth hat and cap workers	2	2	—	—	—	—	—
Hosiery workers	4	4	—	—	—	—	—
Ladies' garment workers	9	9	—	—	—	—	—
Ladies' handbag workers	3	2	1	—	—	—	—
Men's clothing workers	5	5	—	—	—	—	—
Tailors	2	1	—	—	1[a]	—	—
Textile workers	8	2	1	5	—	—	—
PAPER, PRINTING, AND BOOKBINDING	65	43	12	8	1	1	—
Bookbinders	2	2	—	—	—	—	—
Machine printers	1	1	—	—	—	—	—
Paper and paper mill workers	20	8	5	6	—	1	—
Photo- and copper-engravers	12	12	—	—	—	—	—
Printing pressmen	17	16	1	—	—	—	—
Stereotypers and electrotypers	4	3	1	—	—	—	—
Typographical workers	9	1	5	2	1[b]	—	—
TRANSPORTATION AND COMMUNICATION	48	26	14	3	—	5	—
Longshoremen and seamen	9	7	2	—	—	—	—
Marine cooks and stewards	1	1	—	—	—	—	—
Marine engineers and firemen	9	8	—	1	—	—	—
Masters, mates, and pilots	1	1	—	—	—	—	—
Railroad workers	8	—	7	—	—	1	—
Teamsters and chauffeurs	8	3	2	1	—	2	—
Telegraphers	5	2	1	—	—	2	—
Transport workers	7	4	2	1	—	—	—
OTHER UNIONS IN MANUFACTURING	123	44	48	26	1	4	—
Automobile workers	19	—	12	6	—	1	—
Bakery and confectionery workers	7	4	1	2	—	—	—
Brewery and cereal workers	10	8	2	—	—	—	—
Carpet and linoleum workers	1	1	—	—	—	—	—
Chemical workers	3	—	—	3	—	—	—
Cork workers	1	—	1	—	—	—	—
Electrical and radio workers	8	1	3	2	—	2	—
Glass bottle blowers	10	8	1	—	—	1	—
Glass workers	12	—	6	6	—	—	—
Leather workers	4	3	1	—	—	—	—

[a] Agreement between Journeymen Tailors' Union, Local No. 86, A.C.W., and The Labor Standards Association, Pittsburgh, Pa., June 1937, provides that when new machinery displaces men and no employment can be found, these men become preferred extras.

[b] Agreement between Seattle Typographical Union No. 202 and Seattle Newspaper Publishers, December 1936: "When engaging a substitute the regular holder shall employ that unemployed person who has been a member of that office-chapel the longest without interruption and who is competent to perform the work ordinarily performed by such regular situation holder."

PROVISIONS FOR RE-EMPLOYMENT AFTER LAYOFF IN 400 AGREEMENTS NEGOTIATED
BETWEEN 1933 AND 1939—*Continued*

Industry or Trade	Total	No Prefer- ence	General Prefer- ence for Laid-Off Employ- ees	Prefer- ence on Basis of Seniority and Other Factors	Special Cases of Pref- erence	Ambig- uous	Provi- sion for Notifi- cation
Lumber workers..............	1	1	—	—	—	—	—
Pottery workers..............	1	1	—	—	—	—	—
Remington Rand workers.......	1	1	—	—	—	—	—
Rubber workers..............	7	1	6	—	—	—	—
Shoe workers................	4	4	—	—	—	—	—
Sugar refinery workers..........	2	—	2	—	—	—	—
Upholstery workers............	1	—	1	—	—	—	—
Workers' Protective Union.......	1	—	—	1	—	—	—
Miscellaneous federal labor unions.	30	11	12	6	1[a]	—	—
MISCELLANEOUS................	61	40	12	8	**—**	1	**—**
Actors, radio artists, and theatrical employees.................	5	5	—	—	—	—	—
Barbers.....................	1	1	—	—	—	—	—
Bottlers.....................	1	—	1	—	—	—	—
Building service employees.......	6	6	—	—	—	—	—
Cemetery workers.............	1	1	—	—	—	—	—
Cleaners and pressers..........	1	1	—	—	—	—	—
Cooks and waitresses..........	1	1	—	—	—	—	—
Department store workers........	3	3	—	—	—	—	—
Distillery workers..............	6	1	2	2	—	1	—
Drug workers.................	1	1	—	—	—	—	—
Gas station operators...........	2	1	—	1	—	—	—
Grain and mill workers.........	3	1	—	2	—	—	—
Grocery and warehouse workers...	8	3	4	1	—	—	—
Hospital workers..............	5	4	—	1	—	—	—
Hotel and restaurant workers.....	1	1	—	—	—	—	—
Janitors and cleaners...........	1	—	1	—	—	—	—
Laundry workers..............	2	2	—	—	—	—	—
Newspaper workers............	7	6	1	—	—	—	—
Office and professional workers....	4	2	2	—	—	—	—
Packinghouse workers..........	2	—	1	1	—	—	—
GRAND TOTAL....................	400	200	105	78	3	12	2

[a] Agreement between Federal Labor Union No. 20935 and the Creamery Package Mfg. Co., Fort Atkinson, Wis., January 1938: "In rehiring the last man laid off shall be the first rehired. And in no case shall any new help be hired until all Union members laid off, eligible for re-employment, are reinstated, if they so desire."

union which has failed to obtain the closed shop is likely to demand that non-unionists be dropped before any union worker in the same occupation is laid off or deprived of full-time work. Here again we encounter the close relationship that exists between the rules governing hiring and those governing layoffs. In case the union can induce the employer to show preference to union members in making layoffs, it can counteract in large degree its failure to obtain the closed shop. The railroad unions, however, neither demand the closed shop, nor insist upon preference for their members when layoffs occur. Their agreements provide for layoff in accordance with seniority regardless of union membership. Under pressure of the depression, there have been several attempts by railroad unions to obtain preference for their members, but, with one or two exceptions, these efforts have failed.

Equal division of work. As explained above, adherence to the equal-division-of-work principle is far more prevalent than the figures in the tables on pages 105 and 106-07 indicate. The needle trades unions, the boot and shoe workers, the textile workers, and the brewery workers rely mainly upon this policy. Some piece-working unions, such as the leather workers, enforce a rough equal division of work by limiting the amount which pieceworkers may earn in a day.[10]

The policy of equal division of work is usually followed in industries characterized by short and sharp fluctuations in employment—highly seasonal industries such as the needle trades or the boot and shoe industry. In these industries a seniority rule would divide the union into two groups, the long-service employees who work steadily, and the short-service employees who bear the brunt of frequent periods of unemployment. The short-service employees would revolt against a union which discriminated against them so drastically. Although regulation of layoffs has generally been regarded as impracticable in the building industry, in 1938 an experiment in dividing work was undertaken in the New York electrical industry. After extended negotiations a joint committee composed of union and employer representatives was established. Discretion was given the committee to set up minimum work periods. The committee first stipulated a four-week period. This meant that men were assigned to work for four weeks after which they were dropped and replaced from the unemployed.[11]

Equal division of work may be adopted because there are other objections to seniority. In the women's garment industry, for example, business mortality is so high that only a small proportion of the workers would find it possible to accumulate an appreciable amount of seniority. Of 1,687 contractors in the dress industry in

[10] In the case of the leather workers, the limits are set by the workers in each shop. The practice is not officially sanctioned by the national union. In fact, the national union is somewhat concerned about the long-run effects of the limits. They may eventually result in the workers in non-union shops earning more than the workers in union shops.

[11] Later the great demand for men in connection with the World's Fair led the period to be lengthened.

Manhattan in the spring of 1925, 1,411, or 83.6 per cent, had discontinued by the spring of 1933.[12] Even these figures do not tell the whole story, for they take no account of the firms that entered and left the industry during the period. By the end of each year, about 20 per cent of the manufacturers and jobbers and about 33 per cent of the contractors who were in business at the beginning of the year have discontinued. As a result, large numbers of workers are forced to seek new employment at frequent intervals. Naturally, they would be opposed to a seniority rule.

A few unions have endeavored to enforce equal division of work among employees in a market or a large part of an industry—or at least to prevent extreme inequality in the division of work. In Chapter III,[13] reference is made to the efforts of a few building trade locals and the longshoremen to enforce equal division of work through the control of hiring. The anthracite coal miners have also wrestled with the problem of unequal division of work. During the great depression, the mining companies confined their operations as far as practicable to low-cost mines. This meant that the men in some mines had little or no work. There was mass picketing by the unemployed for the purpose of compelling some diversion of work from the low-cost mines and there was great pressure within the union that the organization insist upon some spreading of work between mines. In 1936, the union succeeded in obtaining a clause which provided that "the operating time allowed to the different collieries of any company shall not show a greater disparity over a year of more than 20 per cent."

For some time before its dissolution in 1928, the National Window Glass Workers sought to enforce division of work in the hand-process factories. The plan originated during the war in the latter part of 1917. Because window glass was not a war essential, the government limited the output of the hand-process plants during 1918 to half the production of the preceding year. The nature of the industry made it uneconomical to operate factories undermanned. In co-operation with the employers, therefore, it was decided to have the factories which were idle when the order

[12] Letter from the union.
[13] P. 84.

was issued remain idle until the other factories had produced their quota. The idle factories were then opened up and the others were closed. This plan, devised to meet a war emergency, was continued for six years after the war. The need for the two-period system was accentuated by the new sheet-drawing process which was driving the hand-process plants out of business. Note that the arrangement was intended to deal, not merely with a surplus of labor, but also with a surplus of productive capacity, and that the manufacturers were no less interested in it than their employees.[14] So great was the surplus of labor in the hand-process factories, however, that the union carried the principle of equal division of work a step further by substituting four shifts and a 6-hour day for three 8-hour shifts. The object, of course, was to give each member of the union a share in the steadily shrinking employment in the hand-process factories. As the volume of available employment gradually dropped, many members of the union came to feel that those who obtained work should be permitted to take all that they could get and that the others should leave the industry. After a controversy within the union, the two-period system was abandoned when the union signed a scale, September 15, 1924, which permitted all manufacturers to operate the entire year. As a result of the displacement of hand-process plants by machine plants, the union disbanded in 1928.

The experience of the window glass workers illustrates a problem that has been encountered by a number of organizations which seek to protect their members against layoffs by enforcing equal division of work. This policy may be satisfactory for meeting short periods of poor business, such as seasonal slumps or short depressions. It is not a satisfactory method of meeting prolonged periods of unemployment, particularly "permanent" drops in employment due to permanent shifts in markets or changes in the business of the enterprise. The fact that each employee shares in the work discourages resignations and helps to maintain an excessive force.

[14] The two-period plan was attacked by the government as a violation of the Sherman Antitrust Act. The federal district court held it to be in restraint of trade (287 Fed. 228-39). The Supreme Court, however, reversed the decision of the lower court on the ground that the agreement applied only to the hand-process branch of the industry and that the machine factories offered plenty of competition and really determined the price (263 U.S. 403).

Sooner or later some employees demand that part of the force be
dropped in order to make work for the rest. Consequently some
unions which demand equal division of work make a distinction
between "temporary" and "permanent" drops in business and demand equal division of work only when the decline is temporary.
The flint glass workers and the women's garment workers are
examples. The agreements of the flint glass workers' union with
the National Association of Manufacturers of Pressed and Blown
Glassware have for many years required that in the event of a
temporary drop in business the work shall be divided evenly
among the men, but have given the employer freedom to retain
"such men as he feels are best fitted to do the work," in the event
of a permanent reduction in staff. These provisions are still in
effect. They mean that the employer has practically a free hand
to make permanent reductions in his staff. The agreements in the
New York cloak and suit industry and in the New York dress
industry also distinguish between temporary and permanent drops
in business. The agreement in the cloak industry, effective July 12,
1937 to June 30, 1940, provided that work should be distributed
as equally as possible "among all the workers who are competent
to do the work" but permitted an employer to reduce his forces
when this was made necessary "by a permanent curtailment of his
business or a fundamental change in the character of his business."[15]
The agreement in the dress industry is similar. Controversies arise
from time to time as to whether a change in an employer's business
is a permanent one entitling him to drop some of his employees, and
a number of these cases have gone to arbitration. The depression
increased such controversies. Employers wished to reorganize their
businesses to meet competition but the union struggled to save some
of its members from being dropped.

Layoff in accordance with length of service. Of the 145 agreements covered by the table on page 105 which restrict the employer's freedom to make layoffs, 117 impose a seniority rule in some
form. Of the 290 agreements in the table on pages 106-07 which
restrict layoffs, 242 contain a seniority rule. The railroad unions,
the Typographical Union, the Commercial Telegraphers, and the

[15] Clauses 23 and 25.

Amalgamated Association of Street and Electric Railway Employees are the leading organizations which seek to control layoffs in accordance with seniority. The rule is that the men hired last shall be dismissed first.

The principle of seniority is simple, but systems of seniority exhibit great variations. The rule of seniority may be so-called "straight" seniority, that is, seniority unqualified by ability or efficiency. Or the rule may specifically state that ability, efficiency, experience, or other qualities shall be taken into account. Among the 107 agreements negotiated between 1923 and 1929 which restricted layoffs solely by a seniority clause, 101 provided for so-called "straight" seniority, that is, seniority not modified by ability. Among the 166 agreements negotiated between 1933 and 1939 which restricted layoffs solely by a seniority clause, only 69, or 42 per cent, contained a straight seniority clause. In the remaining 97, seniority was modified by ability and, in some cases, other considerations. This difference is partly explained by the fact that the first group of agreements came almost entirely from long-established unions and the second group contained many agreements from new unions. There is some tendency for unions to get any kind of seniority clause they can at the beginning and then to convert it gradually into straight seniority. The difference is partly explained also by the fact that the second group of agreements contained many made by industrial unions. These unions find it more difficult than craft unions to use straight seniority.

The unit of seniority may be the occupation, the department, the division, the plant, or even the company—that is, the men on a given seniority roster may be restricted to those in a given occupation or department or may include everyone in a plant. If seniority is counted by occupation or by department, men who transfer from one occupation or department to another may or may not take their accumulated seniority with them. Sometimes they may take it with them only after a given period of time. There may be combinations of occupational, department, or plant seniority. For example, men may have seniority only in their own departments, except that all men may have seniority in the labor or yard gang and, if laid off in their own department, may displace junior men in the labor gang; or men of a given occupation who are found in several departments may have seniority in that occupation wherever it extends, regardless of department lines. In concerns where department seniority is the rule, men of a given period of service (five or ten years) may be given plant seniority. When an enterprise has several plants or operating units (such as the shops or divisions of a railroad), occupational or craft seniority may be combined with plant seniority—that is, the machinists in each shop may have their own seniority roster. The variations and combinations which are possible in a system of seniority are almost infinite.

The table on pages 118-19 classifies with respect to the unit of seniority—the plant, the division, the department, the occupation, or combinations of these—the 242 agreements (included in the table on pages 107-08) which regulate layoffs by the seniority principle. Several things stand out in this table. One is the great variety of seniority units or combinations of units and the wide scattering of agreements among them; a second is the fact that the largest single group is the one in which no unit of seniority is specified, which means in most instances that the agreement simply requires that some attention be paid to the seniority principle; a third is that the unit most frequently specified is the department and the next most frequently specified is the plant.

Although the seniority principle is widely used, there are some situations to which it is not adapted. As indicated above, it is not well adapted to industries in which there are frequent and violent fluctuations in employment, because it tends to divide the union into two groups, those who get steady work and those who do not. Nevertheless, a large number of new unions in seasonal industries have recently written seniority rules into their agreements. They have done this partly because during the depression equal division of work had been carried too far and there was a revolt against it. Thus, seniority came to be a symbol for job security. The new unions were inexperienced and did not realize precisely what they were doing. They simply found themselves confronted with an imperative demand from their members for "seniority," as a reaction from excessive division of work. When the new unions discover that in some industries seniority interferes with the

UNIT OF SENIORITY IN 242 AGREEMENTS NEGOTIATED BETWEEN 1933 AND 1939

Industry or Trade	Total	No Mention of Unit	Job Occupation	Department	Department and/or Job Occupation	Division	Department and Division	Plant	Department and Plant	Job Occupation, Department, Plant	Department, Division, Plant	Regional	Specific Lists of Crafts or Groups	Indefinite
METAL AND STONE TRADES AND MACHINERY	45	21	1	12	4			3	2				1	1
Aluminum workers	1			1										
Blacksmiths	1			1										
Brass workers	1			1										
Die casters	1				1									
Farm equipment workers	12	3		5	1			1					1	1
Machinists	4	1		2				1						
Metal polishers	3	2		1										
Molders	3			1					2					
Steel workers	21	15	1		1			1						
MINING, QUARRYING, AND OIL	8	1						1	6					
Oil field, gas well workers	8	1						1	6					
NEEDLE TRADES	8	4		3				1						
Ladies' handbag workers	1							1						
Textile workers	7	4		3										
PAPER, PRINTING, AND BOOKBINDING	31	20	1	6				2						2
Paper and papermill workers	19	13		4				2						
Photo- and copper-engravers	2	2												
Stereotypers and electrotypers	1	1		1										
Typographical workers	9	4		2										2
TRANSPORTATION AND COMMUNICATION	24	7					1	1				12	2	1
Longshoremen and seamen	2	1											1	
Marine engineers	2	1											1	
Railroad workers	8											8		
Teamsters and chauffeurs	5	5												
Telegraphers	3						1					2[a]		
Transport workers	4							1				2[b]		1

118

	C1	C2	C3	C4	C5	C6	C7	C8	C9	C10	C11	C12	C13
OTHER UNIONS IN MANUFACTURING	99	35	1	29	10	1	2	8	1	1		3	6
Automobile workers	19	1	1	6	7[c]	1	1	1	1	1	1	1	1
Bakery and confectionery workers	4	2						1					
Brewery and cereal workers	3	2						1					
Chemical workers	3	2											
Cork workers	1	1		2				2					1
Electrical and radio workers	8	4		6			1	1					1
Glass bottle blowers	4	1		4									
Glass workers	12	4											
Leather workers	4												
Pottery workers	1	1											
Remington Rand workers	1	1		2									
Rubber workers	7	3		1								1	
Sugar refinery workers	2			2[d]	1		1				1		
Upholstery workers	1	1	1	1									
Workers' Protective Union	1												
Miscellaneous federal labor unions	28	12		6	2		1	2					2
MISCELLANEOUS	27	12	1	9				1				1	2
Bottlers	1			1									1
Building service employees	1			1									
Distillery workers	6	1	1	5									
Gas station operators	2	2											
Grain and mill workers	2	2		1									
Grocery and warehouse workers	8	4						1				1	1
Hospital workers	2	2											
Janitors and cleaners	1												
Office and professional workers	2			2							1		
Packinghouse workers	2	1											
GRAND TOTAL	242	100	4	59	14	1	3	17	1	1	13	7	12

[a] The agreement between the Postal Telegraph Co. and the American Communications Association (January 1939) provides that "system seniority shall be the basis for determining the length of vacations," etc., whereas "office seniority shall govern promotions; *layoffs*, *rehiring*," etc.

[b] An agreement between the Amalgamated Association of Street Electric Railway and Motor Coach Employees and a public utility company provides that "carhouse or station seniority shall prevail."

[c] In four of these agreements the unit of seniority, although ordinarily the department, job, or occupation, becomes the plant for those workers displaced by technological change.

[d] Agreement between the American Sugar Refinery Co. and the Sugar Refinery Workers' L.I.U. No. 4 (August 1938): "In ordinary routine seniority questions, departmental seniority shall be the established practice, but in special cases, by mutual agreement between the Company and the Union, plant seniority may control."

solidarity of the union, many of them will attempt to substitute equal division of work for seniority at least to a limited extent. Indeed, this happened in many plants late in 1937 and early in 1938 when the new unions experienced their first large layoffs. The workers in many plants objected to being dropped before there was any sharing of work. Consequently, some unions negotiated special arrangements by which work would be divided to a certain point before junior employees were laid off. This arrangement was particularly important to the unions which had their greatest strength among short-service employees.

In some industries technical difficulties have deterred unions from using the seniority principle. In the full-fashioned hosiery industry, for example, the union reports that there is no practice of seniority in layoffs because some of the older workers are unable to operate the finer-gauge and faster machines which have come in since these workers learned the trade. The desire of the knitters to move from mill to mill has also discouraged the use of seniority. In cases where permanent layoffs are necessary, however, the principle of seniority has been applied among a group of workers (usually about one-tenth) determined by the management and the local union to be the least efficient in the department. In the flint glass industry, the union reports that seniority would not be practicable because the older men are shifting to lighter work where they do not have to handle heavy dies. The practice of seniority might require that older men handle dies weighing several hundred pounds—work which they are not able to do.

The seniority rule may or may not require that men who are laid off shall be restored to service in order of their seniority. Most of the railroad agreements have such a provision. The provision may or may not be qualified by a time limit. From the standpoint of the employer, a time limit may be important because men who have not worked at their trade for a considerable period are likely to lose some of their proficiency. Furthermore a time limit improves the opportunity of employers to introduce new blood into the force. The constitution of the stereotypers' and electrotypers' union provides that "should there be an increase in the force within 60 days after a decrease, the member or members displaced through such cause shall be reinstated in the reverse order in which they were discharged before other help may be employed."[16] Many of the agreements made by new unions since 1933 stipulate that furloughed employees shall retain their seniority status for six months or twelve months. In some cases, however, no time limit is set, which means that a furloughed man retains his seniority status as long as he is available for work. For example, no time limit was set by the agreement of the shopcrafts on the Canadian National Railways, but in the spring of 1934 the unions and the management agreed that the limit should be two years. This meant that the men who had been dropped in the large furlough early in 1932 lost their seniority. The management agreed, however, to consult the unions in selecting the men to be rehired. The unions accepted the arrangement because among the furloughed men there were wide differences of experience and ability. Some were skilled craftsmen who had served an apprenticeship; others were specialists and promoted helpers who had stepped into mechanics' places when men were scarce during the war. The union leaders felt that their organizations would be strengthened if vacancies were filled with skilled mechanics.

Restrictions on the period of time that furloughed men may retain the right to be rehired in order of seniority may affect union policies. If a large number of furloughed employees are about to lose their seniority because of the duration of their layoff, the employer will experience great pressure to divide the work and to give them a few days' employment in order to introduce a break in their period of layoff. This happened during 1938 in the automobile industry where a number of agreements had been negotiated stipulating that furloughed men would retain seniority rights for only a year. As the end of the year approached, the union demanded that the work be divided in order to give a short period of employment to furloughed men before dropping them again.

A limit on the period during which furloughed men retain seniority may be in the interest of the public relations of the union, particularly in small towns where the bulk of the employment is

---

[16] International Stereotypers and Electrotypers' Union of North America, *Constitution and General Laws*, 1929, sec. 90, p. 70.

furnished by one plant. If the plant is not expanding and if the resignation rate is low, a rule which requires that furloughed employees be rehired in the order of seniority without a time limitation becomes a device by which the union controls the employment opportunities in the community. Such an agreement is likely to arouse resentment against the union among the young people in the community—a dangerous situation from the standpoint of the union's public relations.

Combination of equal division of work and layoffs based on seniority. Most unions have found that neither the policy of equal division of work nor the policy of layoffs in accordance with seniority *alone* is satisfactory. As explained above, the policy of equal division of work operates reasonably well when the drop in business is of short duration, but not when it is long and severe. The unqualified seniority rule also is often unsatisfactory because it is better adapted to meeting more or less permanent changes in the volume of employment than to meeting frequent, short-term fluctuations.

Because the equal-division-of-work rule is more satisfactory under some circumstances and the seniority rule more satisfactory under others, unions have a tendency to combine the two principles. Particularly in periods of long and severe depression, such as the recent one, no rule for controlling layoffs is entirely satisfactory, and any rule which is in effect is subject to attack. When the drop in business becomes so severe that men of 10 or 15 years' service are furloughed, the criticism is bound to be made that the work should be divided before men of such long service are dropped. Likewise, when equal division of work gives each man one or two days a week, the demand is inevitable that some short-service men be sacrificed in order that the older employees may obtain a reasonable amount of work.[17] Hence, the recent depression had the effect of greatly increasing the tendency of the unions to combine the seniority and equal-division-of-work principles. This is seen by comparing the table on page 105 with that on pages 106-07. Only 10 out of 145 pre-depression agreements regulating layoffs

---

[17] Relief standards in the community are likely to have considerable effect upon the point at which men resist further spreading of work.

provided for a combination of the seniority and the equal-division-of-work principles. But 72 of 290 post-depression agreements restricting layoffs combined the two principles.[18]

As a matter of fact, however, the combination of the two policies is far more prevalent than analysis of trade agreements indicates because many unions have entered into special arrangements with employers which are not embodied in their trade agreements. For example, during the great depression, many locals of the International Typographical Union, which relies in the main upon the seniority principle, restricted their members from working more than five days a week.[19] As the depression grew worse, the number of locals enforcing a five-day week steadily increased, but some locals refused to give this help to the unemployed. Consequently, a demand arose that the five-day week be enforced by national rule, and by a popular referendum late in 1932 such a rule was adopted.[20]

The railroad shopcrafts, though long committed to the principle of seniority, have in recent years shown a marked tendency to introduce limited division of work. For example, the Baltimore and Ohio Railroad and the shopcrafts union made an agreement in 1925 and again in 1927 and 1929 to close all backshops for a few months of slack business. The alternative would have been to drop some of the junior men. When the Canadian National System was formed by consolidating the Grand Trunk, the Canadian Northern, and several other lines, the new system found itself

---

[18] In counting the agreements which represent a combination of seniority and equal division of work, those agreements which provide that new or temporary employees shall be laid off before work-sharing is instituted were not included. They do not strictly embody the seniority principle because they do not require that temporary workers be laid off in order of seniority.

[19] This was not an entirely new arrangement. For some years the union had permitted its locals "in times of stress" to enforce a five-day week for a period of eight weeks. The enforcement of such a rule did not mean that operation of the shops was limited to five days a week. They continued to run six or seven days, but no union man was permitted to work more than five—which meant that he was compelled to furnish a substitute for the days that he was off.

[20] The national officers opposed a national five-day rule, partly because they feared that it would involve the union in an untimely and expensive strike, and partly because they feared it would work hardships in many small cities where the union scale was not high and where there was little unemployment among union members and hence little need for spreading work.

with an excessive number of shopmen. The unions agreed to permit some of the shops to operate five days a week in order to avoid dropping junior men. It was expected that normal labor turnover would soon reduce the forces to a point where a full 48-hour week could be worked without any layoffs.[21] The Railway Employees' Department of the American Federation of Labor has been sponsoring a form of agreement which would permit weekly hours to be reduced to 40 before the application of the seniority rule. Such agreements have been made with the Chicago, Milwaukee, St. Paul, and Pacific Railway, the New York Central, the Buffalo, Rochester, and Pittsburgh, the Alton, the Chicago Great Western, the Chicago, St. Paul, Minneapolis, and Omaha, the Erie, and others. There has been some difference of opinion among the shopmen in regard to how periods of slack business should be met. The men in the backshops, who do the heavy repairs, prefer a reduction in hours; the men in the roundhouses, who do running repairs, usually prefer reducing the forces. The reason is that the work in the roundhouses is by nature continuous. Men must be on hand every hour the seven days of the week. Furthermore, many of the men specialize on certain repair operations and other men are not able to do their work satisfactorily. Consequently, it is difficult to reduce the weekly hours of the roundhouse workers and at the same time to rotate men so as to protect every job every hour of the week.

The severe unemployment produced among railroad employees by the depression and by the competition of trucks and buses forced some railroad unions to abandon strict adherence to the seniority rule. On many roads the shopcrafts consented to operating the shops four days a week in order to save the jobs of the junior men. The clerks and the maintenance-of-way employees also agreed on some roads to a five-day week or a four-day week—in a few cases even less. The firemen and the trainmen enforced a limited division of work by restricting the monthly mileage of their mem-

---

[21] This expectation was realized only in part because the rapid improvement in shop efficiency reduced the number of men needed. After several years of the five-day week, the older men demanded application of the seniority rule. In 1927, therefore, forces were finally reduced by layoffs and the 48-hour week was restored.

bers.[22] At the convention of the Brotherhood of Locomotive Firemen and Enginemen in June 1931, the most important subject of discussion was mileage limitation. The convention approved the principle of limitation, but left the application to be worked out by the divisions or seniority districts. As a result, the limits differ greatly. The convention of the Brotherhood of Railroad Trainmen, held in May and June 1931, voted that the president of the union direct all general committees (of which there is one on each railroad system) immediately to make effective a limit of 26 days or 208 hours a month in regular yard service, of 3,500 miles or its equivalent in days (an 8-hour day is considered equivalent to 100 miles in freight service) in regular freight service, and of 5,500 miles or its equivalent (an 8-hour day is considered equivalent to 150 miles in the passenger service) in regular passenger service. These limits were expected to give work to nearly 11,000 men.[23]

Some of the agreements to spread employment were made reluctantly by the unions under pressure from railroad managements. The long-service men, who were sure of their jobs, opposed spreading the work and favored strict adherence to the seniority rule. They argued that they had borne the burden of unemployment in earlier depressions when they were junior men and that they were now entitled to steady work. This was especially true of the locomotive engineers and the conductors, who were affected by the drop in traffic less than the firemen and trainmen because the junior engineers and conductors did not lose their jobs—they displaced the senior firemen and trainmen.[24]

There are three ways in which the principles of seniority and equal division of work may be combined. One is simply to provide that short-service or temporary employees shall be dropped before

[22] Limits on mileage had been in existence for some time but their purpose was not to compel the spreading of work but rather to define the normal month's work and thus to regulate the number of regular and extra employees. The limits adopted during the depression were for the purpose of spreading work.

[23] For a more detailed statement of the limits, see Circular No. W-50 of the Brotherhood of Railroad Trainmen. An attempt to repeal the limits early in 1932 failed by a vote of 474 to 415. *The Railroad Trainman,* July 1932, Vol. XLIX, p. 393.

[24] A special situation existed in the maintenance-of-way union. The rates of pay of the section hands were so low that the union found many of its members unwilling to pay dues when working less than four days.

work is divided. This arrangement is common in the garment trades where temporary workers are quite often hired to meet the peak demand at the height of the season. Many of these temporary workers are women who have married and left the trade. They do not wish steady work but are glad to obtain employment for a few weeks each year. The agreements in the needle trades often provide for the use of such workers.[25]

A second method of combining equal division of work and seniority is to stipulate that work may (or shall) be divided down to a given number of days or hours per week before the seniority principle is applied. The agreements of the shopcraft unions on the railroads are an example.

A third method of combining the two principles is a combination of the first two methods. The first step is to drop the short-service employees—those of 90 days or six months' service or less. The second step is to divide the work down to a certain point—four days or three days a week. The third step is to make subsequent reductions in employment by dropping junior employees.[26] This third arrangement is the one which may be expected to develop ultimately in most industries.

Guaranteed employment. During recent years, there has been a rapidly growing interest in the possibility of guaranteed employment. Three principal proposals have been made: (1) a guarantee of steady work to a minimum number of men; (2) a minimum

---

[25] The agreement of the International Ladies' Garment Workers' Union in Cleveland permits the employment of temporary workers for a period not to exceed four weeks once in each of two busy seasons. The number of temporary workers which an employer may hire may be limited. In the Cleveland garment industry the limit is 20 per cent of the employees in the department. The agreement requires that temporary workers be dropped before the work is divided among the regular employees. The agreement in the New York fur industry for the three years ending Jan. 31, 1932 provided that during the slack seasons (June, November, and December) there might be equal division of work among employees in the service of the firm for not less than seven consecutive weeks.

[26] The agreement in force several years ago in the Philco Radio and Television Company and the United Electric and Radio Employees' Union is an example. It stipulated that when it was necessary to reduce forces, employees of less than 90 days' service would be laid off in the reverse order in which they were hired. If further reduction in man-hours were necessary, there would be division of work in the department where a lack of work existed until hours were reduced to 20 per week. If still further reduction in hours were necessary, employees would be laid off in accordance with seniority.

number of weeks' employment to the regular force; or (3) an annual wage to regular employees.

At its convention in 1930 the Railway Employes' Department of the American Federation of Labor adopted as a part of its employment stabilization program a demand that steady, year-round employment be guaranteed to a minimum number of men in the railroad shops and roundhouses. The department proposed that the minimum force be established at the beginning of the calendar year in the light of business prospects for that year. The general committee of the unions and the representatives of the management would confer on this matter between November 1 and December 1 of the preceding year. No member of the minimum force would be laid off or obliged to work short time during the course of the year. The railroad, of course, might add additional men, but the model agreement proposed by the Railway Employes' Department provides that the company will not increase its force more than 5 per cent above the agreed minimum until the matter has been discussed with the union and an agreement reached with its general committee.[27]

The department has not negotiated such an agreement in all details with any railroad, but in 1927 an agreement embodying the principle of the minimum stabilized force was signed with the Seaboard Air Line. The road agreed (subject to certain exceptions) that during the year 1928 a minimum force of 2,170 mechanics, apprentices, helpers, and coach cleaners would be employed in the maintenance-of-equipment department. This was approximately two-thirds the normal force of the road. In 1928 the agreement was renewed for the year 1929, with the minimum force increased to 2,235. The agreement is still in effect in 1940, but the size of the guaranteed force has been reduced.

The national agreement of the United Wall Paper Crafts for a number of years required that print cutters be guaranteed 50 weeks' employment a year at full pay and machine printers and color mixers 45 weeks at full pay and 5 weeks at half pay. Most notable of all employment guarantee plans is that which prevailed in the

[27] American Federation of Labor, Railway Employes' Department, *Official Proceedings, Eighth Convention,* 1930, pp. 126-34.

Cleveland women's garment industry from 1921 to 1931. The original guarantee was for 41 weeks' employment a year—about 5 or 6 weeks more than the normal amount. The plan was modified from time to time in details and the guarantee was reduced to 40 weeks. The depression finally led to its abandonment. Workers who failed to receive 40 weeks' work were compensated at half their regular wages. The payment of this amount was assured by a guarantee fund to which each employer contributed 7.5 per cent of his direct labor pay roll. Each employer recaptured any part of his contribution that remained after the claims of his workers had been satisfied. So successful were employers in stabilizing their employment that they recaptured on the average over 80 per cent of their contributions.

An important feature of the Cleveland plan is its adaptability to a wide variety of industries. The guarantee need not be 40 weeks a year. It could be set above or below that amount depending upon the steadiness of work in the industry and the ability of employers to increase the steadiness of employment. Likewise the benefits paid for failure to give the guaranteed amount of work may be set above or below half the regular wages, depending upon the competitive position of employers and the amount of the pay-roll tax which they can afford. The most important feature of the Cleveland plan is the incentive that it gives employers to increase the amount of work given to their men. Unions which have been using their bargaining power to obtain a shorter working week or vacations with pay would do well to consider the advisability of shifting their efforts to obtaining an employment guarantee that would give employers an incentive to increase the amount and the steadiness of work.[28]

[28] There have been a few unsuccessful attempts by unions to negotiate an annual wage or an employment guarantee. In the negotiations which preceded the strike beginning July 1, 1924 in the New York cloak and suit industry, the union made an unsuccessful attempt to obtain the guarantee of a minimum number of weeks' employment. During 1935 some of the newly formed locals in the automobile industry began to agitate for an annual wage. The automobile industry is one in which a limited guarantee, such as was used in the Cleveland garment industry, might be applied, but it is obviously unsuitable for an annual wage. President Rieve of the American Federation of Hosiery Workers, in his report to the convention in 1935, suggested that a guaranteed annual wage might be made an objective of the union in the full-fashioned branch of the industry, but the annual

A guarantee of employment or an annual wage is likely to divide the employees into two groups—those who have the guarantee and are secure and those who do not have it and are not secure. Whether or not the arrangement is satisfactory will depend upon whether the employees who do not receive the guarantee or the annual wage see a reasonably good prospect of soon becoming members of the preferred group. This will depend upon the turnover in the group. But the very security of employment is likely to keep the rate of turnover down. If a union sponsors a guarantee plan and if the short-service employees see little chance of soon becoming members of the preferred group, they are likely to be hostile to the union. On the other hand, if the employer sponsors a guarantee plan for the purpose of discouraging organization among his employees, the workers excluded from the plan may form a union for the purpose of fighting it and getting a larger share of the work.[29]

A dismissal wage. When a seasonal or cyclical decline in business compels an enterprise to drop men, it usually makes the layoffs among short-service employees. This is true even when no strict seniority rule exists. The reabsorption of fairly young workers in other parts of industry presents no special problem.

Quite different is the situation when the men are dropped because a plant or department or process is being abandoned or because there has been severe and permanent shrinkage in the business of the enterprise or such improvement in methods of production that the need for men is heavily and permanently reduced. Under these circumstances, the men laid off may be long-service employees whose age makes it difficult for them to find re-employment.[30] These layoffs represent a problem quite differ-

---

wage has not yet become a matter of negotiation in the hosiery industry. The union, however, has been compelled to devote its attention principally to problems of southern competition. So long as non-union mills are a serious competitive threat, an annual wage or an employment guarantee is out of the question.

[29] It was pointed out above that organization among the longshoremen of San Francisco was stimulated by the "star gang" system under which members of certain preferred gangs were given preference in employment. The other men got whatever work was left. The men outside the star gangs were organized by the promise that the union would enforce a fair division of employment.

[30] There are several reasons for the increasing reluctance of business enterprises to hire men above 45 or 50 years of age, despite the fact that these men are recognized to be equal in efficiency to younger men for a large proportion of

ent from that presented by seasonal or cyclical declines in business.

A number of companies have attempted to meet the problem by paying special dismissal compensation where long-service employees have been permanently dropped. The payment of dismissal compensation has been encouraged by the rapid spread of industrial pension plans. In fact, it is a short and logical step from the payment of pensions to the payment of dismissal compensation, because if employees who reach 65 or 70 after 30 or 40 years of service are entitled to pensions, it is difficult for managements to drop men of 55 or 60 who have served 20 or 25 years and to give them nothing. Since 1920 over three hundred companies have paid dismissal compensation to long-service employees who have been dropped because of technological changes or abandonment of plants.[31]

Few of these companies had dealings with trade unions and the dismissal compensation was given as a gratuity—not as the result of bargaining. Trade unions, however, have become interested in dismissal compensation. The agreement of the International Ladies' Garment Workers' Union in the New York dress industry, effective February 3, 1927 to January 31, 1928, permitted employers to make permanent reductions in staff for two reasons: (1) because of the installation of new machinery and other labor-saving devices; (2) because of permanent curtailment of business. In each case, the employers were permitted to make reductions only at the beginning of the season—when the workers have the best opportunity to find other jobs in the industry—and workers who were dropped because of the introduction of machinery or labor-saving devices were to receive not less than two weeks' wages. Pattern makers or cutters who were dropped because of permanent curtailment of

---

jobs. Perhaps the principal reason is the growing sense of responsibility of business enterprises for older workers. This has led managements to go much farther than they previously had done in protecting the long-service employees from layoff, in rehiring them after layoff, and in providing for them on retirement. The first two policies have produced a considerable increase in the percentage of employees in the higher age brackets. Because of the growing proportion of older workers on their staffs, enterprises have given preference in hiring to younger workers.

[31] Everett D. Hawkins, *Dismissal Competition*, p. 19. Mr. Hawkins' comprehensive book is an authoritative treatment of the dismissal wage.

business received from one week's to not more than four weeks' salary depending upon their length of service. An agreement effective December 1, 1939 between the Inland Boatmen's Union of the Pacific and the Boat Operators of the Columbia River District provided that any employee whose employment was discontinued as the result of the introduction of labor-saving devices should be paid compensation during any subsequent unemployment for a period of three months at the rate of $15 per week of actual unemployment.[32] In 1940 the Textile Workers' Union negotiated contracts with Sidney Blumenthal and Company and with the Celanese Corporation providing for the payment of dismissal compensation to workers displaced by machines.

The Amalgamated Clothing Workers has not written a dismissal compensation rule in any of its agreements, but it has obtained compensation for its members through special negotiations. This union, in common with others in the needle trades, has enforced equal division of work during slack periods. Dismissal compensation is a logical outgrowth of equal division of work because, when every worker has a right to his share of the work, it is difficult to lay off anyone without compensating him for the loss of his job. The first case in which the Amalgamated Clothing Workers negotiated compensation for dismissed workers occurred in the plant of Hart, Schaffner, and Marx in Chicago. Changes in the methods of cutting created an excess of cutters. The workers wished the force reduced sufficiently to give a full day's work to each employee. Negotiations between the union and the firm resulted in the company's offering a fund of $50,000 to which the Hart, Schaffner, and Marx cutters agreed to add $25,000 from their unemployment insurance fund, making a total of $75,000 to be used in paying 150 cutters $500 each as a condition of their resigning from their jobs.[33] This reduction occurred in the spring of 1926 and included all non-union men and cutters who had been hired since

---

[32] However, no such compensation was to be paid to any person who failed to accept suitable employment at which his earnings would be in excess of $15 per week.

[33] Amalgamated Clothing Workers of America, *Report of the General Executive Board and Proceedings of the Seventh Biennial Convention,* 1924-26, p. 102.

1919. The cut proved insufficient, and in the fall of 1926 a second cut was made—bringing the total layoffs up to 236.[34]

After the establishment of a precedent in the shop of Hart, Schaffner, and Marx, the custom of compensating men who were permanently laid off was extended in the clothing industry. A firm in New York found that it could give full-time work to only 300 of its 380 employees. The union agreed to the layoff of the superfluous workers provided some financial provision could be made to help them until they could obtain new jobs. The firm advanced $3,000, and the other workers in the shop each contributed two days' earnings. A committee of the dismissed men was appointed to determine how the money should be divided. It was decided to distribute it on the basis of the financial needs of the individual workers, but to limit the amount which any worker would receive to a minimum of $50 and a maximum of $200. A second New York firm found itself with 25 superfluous employees. It contributed $500, and the other workers in the shop contributed a substantially larger amount. Each discharged worker received an indemnity of $120.58.[35] A decrease of employment in the cutting room of the Nash firm in Cincinnati led the Amalgamated Clothing Workers to arrange with the firm that any cutter who volunteered to seek other employment would be paid $300 by the company, and on June 15, 1928, 16 men took advantage of this offer.[36]

Dismissal compensation has recently been obtained by negotiation for displaced railroad employees. Late in 1934 the Baltimore and Ohio Railroad arranged to route certain trains through Pittsburgh over the tracks of the Pittsburgh and Lake Erie Railroad. As a result, a number of train crews were dismissed from service. After negotiations with the train service unions, the railroad agreed to allow the displaced workers a year's pay. In 1935 the Union

[34] R. J. Myers in *Journal of Political Economy*, August 1929, Vol. XXXVII, p. 481. Conditions in the Chicago clothing industry were such that the cutters who left Hart, Schaffner, and Marx were practically leaving the trade. Those who wished to obtain employment were put at the bottom of the union's waiting list but employers in Chicago were hiring few cutters.

[35] "American Trade-Unions and the Problem of Unemployment," *Monthly Labor Review*, March 1928, Vol. XXVI, p. 483.

[36] Amalgamated Clothing Workers of America, *Report of the General Executive Board and Proceedings of the Ninth Biennial Convention*, 1928-30, p. 77.

Pacific Railroad consolidated the general and accounting offices of four of its subsidiaries with its own offices in Omaha. Approximately 475 men were employed in these offices of whom 273 were needed in the consolidated office. An agreement negotiated with the Brotherhood of Railway Clerks provided that the displaced men would receive a year's pay with the first chance for future jobs on the road if they were competent to hold them.[37] A large proportion of the clerks preferred to accept the dismissal allowance rather than the transfer with the result that only 167 applied for the positions open at Omaha and 288 received dismissal allowances.[38]

Of particular interest is the agreement for dismissal compensation signed on May 21, 1936 after five months of negotiation between the 21 railroad labor organizations and the railroads of the country except several in the East and South.[39] The agreement

[37] Similar in general principle to compensation of employees for loss of their jobs is compensation for losses suffered because of the removal of the plant of the employer to a new location. Such a case arose in 1929 on the Texas and Pacific Railroad, as a result of the company's decision to abandon Longview Junction and Marshall as freight terminals and to establish a new freight terminal at Mineola, Texas. Longview was a town of about 6,000 or 7,000. It was estimated that the transfer of the train and engine service employees and their families from Longview to Mineola would produce an immediate loss of approximately 1,000 in the population of Longview. The result would be a serious depreciation in the value of the property owned and occupied by the employees affected. The employees demanded compensation for these losses. After a refusal of the employees to accept the railroad company's offer to arbitrate, President Hoover, on Mar. 29, 1929, created an Emergency Board, under sec. 10 of the Railway Labor Act. The Emergency Board held: "The change from Longview Junction to Mineola and from Marshall to Shreveport will result in a substantial saving for the carrier. It is not fair, we think, that the carrier reap the entire benefit and that the employees be compelled to bear the entire loss." The Board held that the loss should be borne equally by the carrier and the employees. The loss, according to the Board, would be the difference in the market value of the property just before it became generally known that the terminal would be moved, and the market value immediately after removal. (*Report of the Emergency Board, Transmitting its Findings upon the Dispute between Texas and Pacific Railway Company and Certain Engine and Train Service Employees.*)
Limited compensation has been obtained by other railroad organizations in connection with the removal of work. The agreements in the above-mentioned case of transfer of offices of the Union Pacific provided that the railroad would buy the homes of the transferred employees or make good any loss suffered by them if they were compelled to sell their homes for less than value.
[38] In addition, 13 were pensioned, and 7 were transferred to other jurisdictions, died, or resigned.
[39] The following railroads did not become parties to the agreement: Atlantic Coast Line, Delaware and Hudson, Florida East Coast, Kansas City Southern, Louisville and Nashville, and Southern.

applies only to employees affected by "co-ordination," which is defined as "joint action by two or more carriers whereby they would unify, consolidate, merge, or pool, in whole or in part, their separate railroad facilities or any operations or services, previously performed by them through separate facilities." Nevertheless, the agreement may be expected to form a precedent that will apply to employees who lose their jobs by economies effected within a single railroad system.

The men base their claim to dismissal compensation upon the fact that the economies of merging or pooling facilities or services are achieved in the main at the expense of labor. They argue, therefore, that these savings should be partly devoted to compensating the men at whose expense they are made. The agreement requires each carrier contemplating co-ordination to give 90 days' notice to the employees affected. Within 10 days a conference between the employers and the employees must be arranged and these conferences must begin within 30 days of the date of original notification. A displaced employee who receives work paying less than his former position must be paid the difference by the carrier for a period not exceeding five years or until, through promotion, he receives his previous compensation. An employee who loses his job through co-ordination and who has been in the service of the carrier for not less than one year is given the option of a monthly allowance or a lump-sum settlement. The monthly allowance is equal to 60 per cent of the employee's average monthly compensation during the preceding twelve months. Its duration depends upon the employee's years of service. The lump-sum settlement also depends upon the employee's length of service.[40] Men who retain their jobs, but are compelled to move, will be compensated for

[40] The schedule of allowances is as follows:

Years of Service	Number of Months Co-ordination Allowance Is Paid	Number of Months' Pay in Lump-Sum Settlement
1 year and less than 2	6	3
2 years and less than 3	12	6
3 years and less than 5	18	9
5 years and less than 10	36	12
10 years and less than 15	48	12
Over 15	60	12

moving expenses and property losses caused by the change. The spokesmen of the workers claim that even with the allowances agreed upon the railroads after the third year of a merger of facilities or service would receive 60 per cent of the savings accomplished.

It remains to be seen how important this agreement will be. When it was first negotiated, the expectation was that it would remove the opposition of unions to co-ordination and that it would lead to a number of co-ordination projects. The projects have not materialized. The principal reason seems to be indifference or opposition of managements. Nevertheless, the agreement does not seem to have accomplished the purpose of removing the opposition of unions to co-ordination. This is made clear by a strong statement by President Whitney of the trainmen's union in the *Railroad Trainman* for July 1936.[41]

The union which has shown the greatest interest in embodying dismissal wage clauses in its agreements is the Newspaper Guild. Nearly all of the contracts of this union contain a dismissal wage clause. Some of those which provide for no dismissal wage prohibit dismissals for any cause except gross misconduct. The dismissal wage provisions among 98 guild contracts may be summarized as follows:

One week's pay for each 6 months' service .... 8 contracts
One week's pay for each 30 weeks' service .... 12 contracts
One week's pay for each 8 months' service .... 17 contracts
One week's pay for each 40 weeks' service .... 3 contracts
One week's pay for each 12 months' service .... 22 contracts
Other ratios of pay to service or mixed ratios .... 36 contracts

Over one-third of the guild's contracts provide for the payment of a death benefit if the employee dies in service. Over half of the

---

[41] "I want to emphasize that so far as the Brotherhood of Railroad Trainmen is concerned, the agreement with the carriers relative to consolidation and co-ordination can in no sense be interpreted to mean that the way is clear for railroad consolidation and co-ordination. This Brotherhood will continue to fight as vigorously as it always has, such efforts to economize at the expense of humanity" (p. 386).

For an excellent discussion of the co-ordination agreement and the obstacles to co-ordination, see G. P. Baker, "Possibilities of Economies by Railroad Consolidation and Co-ordination," *American Economic Review*, Pt. 2, Supplement, March 1940, Vol. XXX, pp. 140-57. Mr. Baker quotes the significant statement of President Whitney.

contracts provide that no dismissal wage shall be paid if the employee is dropped for gross neglect of duty, gross misconduct, gross insubordination, dishonesty, or other serious fault, but the others do not have this qualification.

SUMMARY

Through the devices of notice, preferential rehiring, equal division of work, seniority, employment guarantees, and the dismissal wage, unions have developed comprehensive arrangements for dealing with layoffs. Trends in the labor market are greatly increasing the interest of workers in layoffs and raising the proportion of agreements which contain some restrictions on the employer's freedom to make them and special protection for the employees who are dropped.

Examination of the particular types of control reveals that certain types are particularly adapted to certain conditions and others to other conditions. Equal division of work, for example, is better adapted to meeting short-term drops in business; seniority to meeting permanent drops. Where permanent changes in the business necessitate dropping long-service men, there is a strong case for a dismissal wage. When a severe depression produces a substantial and prolonged shrinkage in employment, unions tend to combine the principles of seniority and equal division of work. In fact, the long-run tendency seems to be in the direction of relying not upon a single principle, but upon a combination of principles. The most usual combination seems to be first to drop short-service employees (usually those with less than six months' or a year's service), then to divide work down to a certain point (usually down to three or four days a week), and finally to make layoffs in accordance with seniority, possibly modified by ability. Particular conditions in particular industries, however, produce variations in this pattern.

The widespread and increasing efforts of unions to regulate layoffs produce many problems and are bound to have important repercussions upon the labor market and upon relations between employers and unions. These problems and the principal consequences of unions' efforts to regulate layoffs are the subject matter of the next chapter.

CHAPTER V

CONTROL OF LAYOFFS—PROBLEMS AND RESULTS OF MAJOR UNION POLICIES

Since the equal-division-of-work and the seniority rule are by far the most important methods employed by unions to control layoffs, this chapter will deal mainly with the problems raised by these policies and some of the effects of the policies.

SOME PROBLEMS CREATED BY THE EQUAL DIVISION OF WORK

The equal-division-of-work policy has the advantage, under ordinary circumstances, that it preserves the solidarity of the union, because it applies alike to all workers in an occupational group and distributes the burden of unemployment equally. The principal limitation of the policy, as pointed out on pages 114-15, is that it fails to provide a satisfactory way of meeting permanent changes in employment—changes produced by technological improvements, by market shifts, and by competition. When the drop in employment is permanent, equal division of work simply forces the retention of an excessive number of men. Unless the excess is soon eliminated by resignations, it becomes necessary to abandon the equal-division-of-work policy. Sometimes there is difficulty in deciding whether the drop in employment is permanent. If the issue is raised during a time of severe depression, the union, under pressure from its members to prevent layoffs, may argue that the drop in employment is mainly a result of the depression, and that no reduction in the working force is necessary. If it admits that a permanent drop in the employer's business has occurred, the decision as to who shall be dropped may split the union. To avoid favoring some of its members at the expense of others, the union may feel compelled to insist upon a continuation of division of of work—in other words, to attempt to enforce the policy under conditions to which it is not well adapted.[1] If an industry is feeling the impact of advancing technology upon a stationary or slowly increasing market or if the market is actually shrinking, it is easy for a union, by enforcing equal division of work, to become an agency for imposing a lower and lower standard of living upon its members. This danger is faced today by the bituminous coal miners and the leather workers. In the New York live poultry industry, the application of equal division of work to a declining industry has plainly converted the union into an instrument for reducing the standard of living of its members.[2]

Use of the equal-division-of-work policy in some industries is limited by technical difficulties. In the coal industry, for example, work-sharing is usually accomplished only by alternating groups of workers. Half of the miners may work for a two-week period and another half for the next two-week period. If the men finishing a two-week period leave timbering to be done by the next group or fail to shoot down enough coal, they may delay the new group a day's time. Since the men are paid by the ton, such delays cause friction. If the relationships between the union and the management are good, the union will be a valuable help in controlling the situation. In the Rocky Mountain Fuel Company, the union has done valuable work by requiring its members to leave the working places in proper shape. Even here considerable difficulty was experienced in some years.

In the textile industry the usual rule governing work-sharing has been that a weaver gets all the work that comes to his loom and that the work on the spare looms is equally divided. In some mills, however, the so-called rotary system of layoff has been

[1] In case the employer wishes to change the nature of his business (for example, to shift from the manufacture of cloaks and suits to the manufacture of dresses or from the manufacture of high-grade dresses to the manufacture of cheap dresses), a controversy may develop between him and the union over his right to drop his present workers and to hire new ones rather than train present employees for the new work.

[2] See U. S. Department of Agriculture, *Economic Survey of the Live Poultry Industry in New York City*, Miscellaneous Publication No. 283, 1937, pp. 10, 108-11. The live poultry industry has been losing out to the dressed poultry industry. The investigators of the Department of Agriculture conclude: "The policy of the labor unions to maintain their membership on a share-the-work basis has resulted in much-reduced incomes for individual laborers." The same, p. 109.

employed. Under this plan all the work is divided among the weavers. The plan has certain disadvantages from the standpoint of the employers because the weavers are not equally competent to do all jobs. On the other hand, it does tend to develop more all-round weavers.[3]

Since the policy of dividing the work eliminates layoffs, except in the case of shop reorganizations, it creates the need for particular care on the part of employers in selecting new employees. Once a worker has been added to the force, it is impossible for the employer to drop him except for unsatisfactory work or infraction of shop rules. If the seniority rule requires that furloughed workers be given preference in filling vacancies, it restricts the employer's freedom to drop less desirable workers. At any rate, the equal-division-of-work principle and, in some cases, the seniority principle make the hiring of a new worker a far more important event than it has usually been considered and make it imperative for employers to insist upon an adequate probationary period in which to try out new employees before adding them to the regular staff.

SOME PROBLEMS OF SENIORITY RULES

The operation of seniority rules introduces many problems. The following discussion is not exhaustive. It touches only briefly upon a few of the most important problems.

1. What constitutes continuous service? A man may work for a company more or less regularly for 15 or 20 years. This service, however, may have been interrupted several times for various reasons. If the man definitely quit of his own accord and then came back, there is likely to be no dispute over the fact that continuous service has been interrupted. If the break occurred many years in the past, however, the record of the cause of separation may be lacking. Strikes are likely to be causes of dispute. The men deny that strikes cause breaks in service records. The companies usually contend that they do. Temporary layoffs are not ordinarily regarded as interrupting the service record. If, however, a man who is laid off permanently or indefinitely, without any expectation that

[3] For an excellent discussion of the problem of work-sharing in several branches of the textile industry, see Gladys Palmer's *Union Tactics and Economic Change*, pp. 33-34, 55-56.

he will ever again be rehired, returns to the company's service after a few months, does he carry seniority from his previous service?

Some companies with seasonal peaks may have men working for them for a few months each year at the peak. After several years these men may be kept as members of the permanent force. Will their previous service as peak workers entitle them to any seniority? If business is slack and the plant is operating one week with half the force and another week with the other half, should seniority accumulate at the same rate as if the men were working full time? If some departments are working full time and others part time, do the men all accumulate seniority at the same rate? A boy finishes an apprenticeship course of four or five years and becomes a mechanic. Do his four or five years as an apprentice give him any seniority as a mechanic? If so, he may displace a mechanic with several years' service. If not, the completion of his apprenticeship course may terminate his employment. Most unions allow apprentices to accumulate no seniority as mechanics, but some allow each two years of apprenticeship to equal a year of seniority as a mechanic. These are some of the many questions which arise in connection with seniority record-keeping.

2. What should be the basis of reckoning seniority—the job, the occupation, the department, the plant, or the company? There have been many controversies during the last few years over the basic unit of seniority, and no unit is entirely satisfactory either to managements or to workers.

Company or plant seniority has the objection, from the standpoint of men and management alike, that one layoff may produce a number of displacements. For example, suppose a man of ten years' service is dropped because his work is no longer necessary. He is able to do a job performed in another department by a man of nine years' service. Consequently, the ten-year man replaces the nine-year man. The nine-year man finds a job which he can do in another department and displaces a five-year man from it who, in turn, is given a job performed by a three-year man. Thus, in order to make one layoff, four men may be displaced from their regular jobs. Each is more or less dissatisfied by the change, and the management, of course, has been caused considerable trouble and inconvenience. An inevitable result of plant seniority is that no one knows exactly where he stands because he does not know who may be able to displace him. To that extent it makes for uncertainty rather than certainty.

Practical obstacles to the operation of plant seniority have led unions and employers to use the department as a unit more often than the plant. Among 142 agreements which specified a unit of seniority and which are classified in the table on pages 118-19, 59 specified only the department as a unit, and 29 specified the department in conjunction with some other unit, whereas 17 specified the plant alone and 12 specified the plant in conjunction with other units. Even department seniority raises many difficulties. Sometimes there is a question as to what is or should be the definition of "department."[4] It is not uncommon to find occupations crossing department lines and for dissatisfaction to arise because men in the same occupation are being dropped in one department but kept in another.

It is not clear that the basis of seniority should be the same for all types of layoff. If a company with several plants curtails operations because of a depression, it is usually taken for granted that layoffs in each plant will be made entirely independently of layoffs in the other plants. In other words, long-service men in one plant will not be permitted to displace shorter service men in the other. Quite different is the situation, however, in the case of a permanent shutting down of a department in one of several plants. In that case there is strong feeling that the men in the department or plant which is being discontinued have some claim, on the basis of seniority, in the other departments or plants. The agreement entered into on June 24, 1940 between the General Motors Corporation and the United Automobile Workers provides that seniority shall be by non-interchangeable occupational groups within departments, or plant-wide, as may be negotiated locally, except that "when changes in methods, products, or policies would otherwise

[4] A new union in a middle western public utility insisted that the department be the unit. The company had linemen in both its construction and its maintenance departments. At the end of the season it laid off some linemen in the construction department. They objected that it was not fair to drop them while linemen of shorter service in the maintenance department were being kept. They argued that all linemen should be regarded as on one seniority list regardless of the department in which they worked.

require the permanent laying off of employees, the seniority of the displaced employees shall become plant-wide and they shall be transferred out of the group in line with their seniority, to work they are capable of doing."[5] As indicated in Chapter IV,[6] in a few cases where department seniority is the rule, employees may acquire plant seniority after a given period of service, such as ten years.

3. How do seniority rules affect the right of management to transfer work from one occupation, department, or plant to another and of the men to follow their work when it is transferred? Does the establishment of certain units of seniority give the men property rights in the work that they have been doing or in all work that in the future may be given to them or brought into the department or the plant?

Through two decisions of the National Railroad Adjustment Board[7] the railroad transportation brotherhoods have established the principle that seniority rules establish a form of property right in work, and at points where yards have been established and a seniority list for men in yard service created, yard work may not be transferred to men in road service. This amazing interpretation of the seniority rule was probably brought about partly by the fact that the agreements between the railroads and the unions contained no provision giving the men the right to follow their work. The Railway Employes' Department of the American Federation of Labor, which represents the shopcrafts, has not in general opposed the transfer of work from one roundhouse or repair shop to another, but it has supported the principle that when a roundhouse or a back shop closes and the work is transferred elsewhere, the men in the abandoned roundhouse or shop have a right to follow the work to the extent that new jobs are created in other roundhouses or back shops.[8]

[5] *Agreement between General Motors Corporation and the International Union United Automobile Workers of America*, p. 21.
[6] P. 117.
[7] The Caldwell, Kans., case, Award No. 1842, Docket No. 3467, decided Apr. 2, 1937, and the Haileyville, Okla., case, Award No. 1843, Docket 3468, decided at the same time.
[8] Some of the system federations do not accept the national policy. In the practical application of the policy, difficulty has been experienced in determining just where the work has gone and in what quantities. Shops may be abandoned as

The national defense program, which requires many enterprises to make drastic adjustments in their operations and to shift work from one plant to another, has made more important than ever the question of the effect of seniority rules upon the right of managements to transfer work and of men to follow their work without loss of their seniority position. If employers wish to avoid a repetition of the decisions of the Railroad Adjustment Board, they should guard against it by specific language in their agreements.[9]

4. Should certain employees of long service be entirely exempt from layoff? Occasionally an agreement is found which stipulates that no one of 15 years' service or more shall be laid off. As a rule, however, unions do not like this arrangement. Often the longest service employees are those least interested in the union, and the union in consequence is less interested in them than in the junior employees.

5. How far should the seniority principle be qualified by efficiency, ability, or other requirements? Where the unit of seniority is the occupation and all men in the seniority group do the same work (as among locomotive engineers), the rule may say nothing about ability or efficiency. But where the unit is a department rather than an occupation, some requirement that ability be taken into account is necessary. It is important from the standpoint of management in order to avoid an intolerable amount of transferring and retraining in times of general layoff. If a milling machine operator of 20 years' service can escape layoff by replacing a boring mill operator who has only 15 years' service, the management will be put to considerable trouble and no small expense because some time will be required for the milling machine operator (assuming that

---

economy measures in slack times with the result that no new jobs are created anywhere at the moment.

[9] Failure to provide in the seniority rule for the transfer of men either because their work has moved or because they are no longer able to do their customary work may result in distressing situations. A metal working plant in Pennsylvania with three plants and two foundries decided to close one foundry and to concentrate work in the other. The management wished to transfer the senior men. The local union in the foundry that was being kept in operation objected to dovetailing the seniority lists—despite the fact that the men in both foundries belonged to the union. As a result, one man of 37 years' service and another of 35 years' service were placed well toward the bottom of the seniority list in the second foundry.

he is not an all-round machinist) to learn to operate the boring mill. The men themselves would object to such indiscriminate replacement of junior men by senior men regardless of experience and ability.

Some agreements, usually known as "straight" seniority agreements, stipulate that "ability and efficiency being *sufficient,* seniority shall govern." Others provide that ability and efficiency being *equal,* seniority shall govern. Most of the agreements of new unions in the manufacturing industries are of the latter type,[10] while the old agreements, such as those among the shopcrafts of the railroads, are straight seniority agreements. As a matter of fact, in a great majority of cases the differences in the ability and efficiency of the workers are so small that competent observers will differ in their ranking of the workers. In only a few cases, from 10 to 15 per cent, would there be general agreement that certain men are definitely superior. There would also be general agreement about a similar proportion who are definitely inferior. In other words, under good personnel administration straight seniority will govern in two-thirds of the cases among men doing the same work.

Whether the new unions will press strongly for a change to straight seniority probably depends largely upon how the rule is administered. If seniority is permitted to govern in the great majority of the cases where differences in ability and efficiency are small and not readily distinguishable, pressure from unions for a change in the rule will probably not be strong. Such pressure is bound to occur, however, in case managements go to extremes in ignoring seniority and in retaining junior men who are not clearly and definitely superior to men who are laid off. Pressure will also develop even when the differences in ability and efficiency are clear, provided the man who is dropped has far more seniority than the man who is retained. It is dangerous, for example, for the management to drop a really long-service man (20 or 25 years) and to keep a short-service man of three or four years even though the short-service man is definitely better. When seniority is ignored, differences in seniority must not be so great that the men's sense of justice is outraged. The operation of seniority makes particularly

[10] See pp. 105-07.

important the development of definite standards of performance by which men may be judged. This topic is discussed below.[11]

6. When the seniority rule states that seniority shall prevail, ability and efficiency being equal or sufficient, precisely what is meant by "ability" and "efficiency"? Ability seems generally to be interpreted as referring to the variety of jobs that a man can do at a satisfactory efficiency. Efficiency is usually interpreted to mean the relative efficiency of several men at a given job. But when a man claims that he is able to do a job, does he mean that he is able to do it at once or that he is able to learn it within a very short time? Managements usually take the position that ability to do a job means ability to do it at once, not ability to learn it even within a rather short time. Allowance is, of course, usually made for time required to become familiar with the details of the particular machine and to acquire speed at the particular operation. There are, however, difficulties in a rigid and narrow interpretation of the word "ability," and managements may feel disposed to interpret it one way in some cases and another way in others. In the great majority of instances, managements may be expected to insist that a man is able to do a job only when he can do it at once without training. Suppose, however, the management has to choose between dropping an employee of 25 years' service who has an excellent record and an employee of only two years' service who performs an operation which the long-service man is not "able" to do in the narrow sense, but which he could easily learn within a few days. In this case the management might be disposed to give a broad interpretation to the word "ability," and yet it would not care to have this interpretation stand as a precedent. A rubber company permitted men with five years' service who had "versatility" (which was defined as being able to do several jobs) three days to learn a new job. In this way it was able to avoid dropping some especially valuable employees. In short, where no great differences in seniority are involved, a narrow interpretation of ability

[11] A full-fashioned hosiery mill has worked out an arrangement with the union under which men are laid off (and promoted) in accordance with seniority if they are above the average in efficiency and on the basis of ability if they are below the average. Such an arrangement, of course, presupposes that efficiency can be easily and accurately measured.

seems to be indicated. Where differences in seniority are great, there is a strong case for a broad interpretation of the word.

7. If the agreement provides that seniority shall govern, ability and efficiency being equal or sufficient, how are ability and efficiency determined? Who shall be the judge? A few agreements state that "management shall be the sole judge in all cases." Such an arrangement can never be satisfactory to the union. At the other extreme are the agreements which permit "bumping." By bumping is meant the right of a senior man on his own initiative to displace a junior man. It is not found in most of the newer agreements, but it is an established practice in railroading. It means that the man who is being displaced, rather than the management, selects a job which he is able (or thinks he is able) to fill. A few of the new agreements permit bumping by men of long service. The agreement in one rubber company, for example, permits men of five or more years' service to bump.

Some agreements state that ability and efficiency shall be jointly determined by a committee of the management and the union. In several instances this arrangement has worked very satisfactorily to both sides. It is cumbersome, however, and it imposes responsibility upon union officers or committeemen which they are not in a good position to exercise. The best arrangement for determining ability and efficiency seems to be to let management make the original decision subject to challenge by the union and to review in the event of challenge. This arrangement conserves the essential interests of all parties and involves a minimum of "red tape."

When a management departs from straight seniority in order to keep a junior man of superior ability or efficiency, it must be able to justify its decision. In order to do this, it needs two things: (1) definite standards of accepted performance on various jobs, and (2) definite information concerning the qualifications of employees. The latter can be provided only through a rating system under which every employee's qualities are periodically rated by those familiar with his work. Under this system, the layoff decision is based, not upon a single judgment, but upon a series of ratings (usually seniority included) made over a period of years. The management is further protected in case it informs each employee of his rating on those qualities on which he is low. This gives him an opportunity to correct his weak points and puts him on notice that he may be dropped unless he does so.

It may be stated as a general principle that the rise of collective bargaining, giving the employees, as it does, an opportunity to challenge a wide variety of decisions of management, requires that these decisions be made more carefully than ever before and that they be based upon more accurate and complete records than have heretofore been customary. The administration of an "ability and efficiency" clause is naturally easier when payment is by the piece, because men are more cautious at demanding transfers.[12]

8. If under a straight seniority rule a worker who is transferred to another job in order to save him from layoff fails to qualify on the new job, what is his status? Under most agreements he would be simply taken from the new job and furloughed, with the same rights to re-employment enjoyed by other furloughed men. Quite different, however, is the situation if the agreement permits bumping and if the man bumps another worker and then proves unable to do the job. He has claimed competency which he does not possess and under some agreements he is discharged for incompetency with loss of all rights as an employee of the company.[13]

9. In enterprises with seasonal fluctuations in employment or with several lines of goods, employment may be stabilized by transferring men back and forth between departments. In automobile plants, for example, tool workers are busy before the season and early in the season, but later on their work is slack. Some of them may be transferred to production work. As a rule it is agreed that workers accumulate seniority at their regular jobs or in their regular departments while transferred to other work, but some question on this point may arise.

10. In the expansion of a company many men are transferred from one department to another. Indeed new departments or new

---

[12] The prevalence of piecework has probably been important in discouraging the growth of layoffs in accordance with seniority in some industries, such as flint glass or pottery.

[13] This is the rule of the Typographical Union and of some of the railroad unions. Other unions follow a rule that is less harsh. They simply transfer the man to the end of the furloughed list, which means that all other furloughed men have prior claim to being rehired.

sections in departments are likely to be started with a skeleton crew of especially reliable and skillful employees from other departments. Thus the company may have men who have been in its service 15 or 20 years, but who have not been in their present departments for more than four or five. When a man is transferred from one department to another, does he take his seniority with him? If he does, his transfer will be objectionable to all junior men in the department which he enters. If he does not, he will object to being transferred and the way up will also be the way out. It is obviously important that management be able to preserve flexibility of operations by making interdepartmental transfers. Some transfer of seniority from one department to another, therefore, seems to be necessary. A compromise which has worked fairly satisfactorily is to permit transferred employees to transfer their seniority to the new department only after a given period. Some agreements specify six months, but a more usual period is a year. In the meantime, the employee retains his seniority in the original department. This arrangement makes men willing to be transferred and yet does not arouse extreme hostility among the junior men in the department which the transferees enter.

The principle of the transfer of seniority may cause difficulty when it is applied to transfers from one job to another and when one man acts as the teacher of the man who is transferred. Suppose, for example, that a plant has a welder who has five years' seniority. It needs another welder. The management selects for the promotion a handyman who works in the department and has seven years' service. The first man teaches the second how to weld, and the second gradually becomes proficient at the work. After several years a slump in business requires the dropping of one of the two welders. Regardless of which is dropped, there is bound to be acute dissatisfaction. If the original welder is dropped and the former handyman retained on the ground that the latter has more seniority, the original welder will be keenly resentful. He will say: "I was welding around here for five years before that chap knew anything about it and I taught him all he knows. Now he has my job." On the other hand, if the original welder is retained and the former handyman dropped, promotion is penalized. There is really no satisfactory solution to this case other than adherence to the rule of being careful to select a junior man to be taught whenever a promotion is to be made.

11. Should seniority rules be applicable to all employees? It is not unusual to confine seniority rights to employees who have served a minimum period or to exempt from seniority a few exceptionally able or qualified employees. In the settlement of the automobile strike of March 1934, only employees of one year's service or over were given seniority status and it was provided that

employees whose work in the judgment of the management is essential to the operation of the plant and production, or who have received special training or who have exceptional ability may be hired, retained, or returned to work notwithstanding the provisions of Clauses A, B, and C, and of Paragraph 2 below.[14]

The agreement of the International Association of Oil Field, Gas Well, and Refinery Workers of America with the Sinclair Refining Company provides a deviation from the strict seniority rule in not more than 2 per cent of the number of permanent job changes. Each deviation, however, must be made the subject of conference with the workmen's committee. The agreement of the Amalgamated Clothing Workers with Hart, Schaffner, and Marx provides for an equal division of work, but permits layoffs when permanent reductions in the force are necessary. Non-union workers are laid off first and then union workers in order of seniority, up to six months' service with the company. But the agreement also provides that "any exceptionally efficient worker or any especially valuable member of the union may be exempt from the rule of seniority." This provision is interesting because it is reciprocal. The union, as well as the employer, is granted exemption for workers who are particularly valuable to it.[15] A number of recent agreements

[14] These clauses are the seniority clauses in the agreement.

[15] A similar reciprocal arrangement is found in the agreement entered into on June 24, 1940 between General Motors Corporation and United Automobile Workers. It exempts from the seniority provisions on the one hand "exceptional employees" (defined as "employees who have a skill needed in facilitating the start of a new model or at times working forces are reduced") and also provides that "district and alternate committeemen shall head the seniority lists in their respective districts" and that "members of the Shop Committee shall head the seniority list of the plant." *Agreement between General Motors Corporation and the International Union United Automobile Workers of America*, pp. 23-24.

provide that union grievance committeemen or shop stewards shall head the seniority list as long as there is work which they are capable of doing.[16] Some unions, however, are opposed as a matter of policy to preferential seniority for their committeemen or stewards.[17]

Any special list of exempt employees, such as those established in the automobile industry, is almost certain to be under fire from the union and, unless the making of lists is carefully controlled by top management, it will be difficult for the management to defend. For example, it may be found that managements in some plants or departments are placing a much larger proportion of the employees on the exempt list than managements in other plants or departments. If the agreement provides that seniority shall govern only when ability and efficiency are equal or satisfactory, the need for special exemptions is obviated.

12. Should the seniority principle be applied to promotions as well as to layoffs? Certainly the case for seniority in promotions is much weaker than the case for seniority in layoffs. When applied to layoffs, it gives job security at least to the extent of letting each employee know more or less definitely where he stands and whether his turn to be laid off is likely to come soon or late. But seniority applied to promotions does not give job security. It simply regiments employees and takes away the opportunity for the abler ones to make their ability count. Furthermore, the very application of seniority to layoffs makes it important that it shall not be applied to promotions. The application of seniority to layoffs inevitably weakens the incentives to efficiency because superior efficiency is no longer necessarily a protection against layoff. With the fear of layoff weakening as an incentive to efficiency, it is all the more important that the hope of promotion be retained as an incentive.[18]

---

[16] Preferential seniority status for union committeemen, stewards, or officers was found in 61 out of a sample of 350 agreements studied.

[17] These unions believe that such preference is resented by the rank and file.

[18] Among 400 agreements negotiated between 1933 and 1939 in a wide variety of industries, 238 contained no provisions regulating promotions. The provisions in the remaining 162 may be classified as follows:

Promotion shall be by seniority 30
Seniority shall govern promotion if the worker is competent to hold the
vacancy 64

SOME EFFECTS OF SENIORITY RULES

The seniority rule has many repercussions important both to employers and to unions. One of the most obvious and most important effects is to discourage the voluntary movement of men from shop to shop. When a man resigns his position, he loses, of course, the seniority which he has accumulated. When he accepts a position in another shop, he is a junior man and in danger, therefore, of being laid off at the first lull in business. If the rule requires each employer to rehire men whom he has dropped before adding other men in the same occupation, a man who leaves one shop may have to wait a long time time before he obtains another job. Such loss of mobility is a handicap to the men in industries where there are numerous small plants in which fluctuations of employment are violent. It is also disadvantageous in industries where individual skill is important and where the better workers have an opportunity by individual bargaining to obtain premium wages for themselves. This explains why some unions do not adopt the seniority rule or are even opposed to it. The New York local of the Typographical Union, known as "Big Six," for many years opposed the seniority rule of the national union and, in 1908, succeeded in having the question of repealing the rule submitted to a national referendum.[19] The adverse effect of the seniority rule upon the individual

---

If the ability of several employees is equal, seniority shall govern promotion 42
Promotion is based solely on ability 1
Union employees are given preference in promotion 6
The company has the sole right to decide questions of promotion 4
Miscellaneous provisions 15

[19] The rule was retained in the union constitution by a close vote. Severe unemployment in the summer of 1924 led Big Six to reverse its attitude and to vote to extend the seniority (or priority) rule to the job and book shops in New York. The employers, with considerable reluctance, agreed to the change. They hoped that the seniority rule would enable them to eliminate the premium wages which had become prevalent among the compositors. This did not mean that the men already receiving premium wages would be reduced, but rather that new men would not be hired above the scale and that differentials of men already receiving premium wages would not be preserved when general wage increases were given. But the expectation that premium wages would be eliminated was not realized. Employers found that if they did not pay the premiums, they did not get the output. In short, it is not easy to take away from men premiums to which they have become accustomed. In the case of the machine compositors, there was some increase in the proportion receiving no more than the scale. A survey by the New York Employing Printers in 1922 indicated that among 633 machine

bargaining power of the workmen explains the opposition to the rule by the pressmen's union in the New York job printing industry. These workers are employed in the same shops as the compositors who in 1924 established the seniority rule. The pressmen, however, have refused to demand it. In fact, the president of the union a few years ago frankly told the employers that he did not believe in such a rule. In an interview with the writer he said: "If such a rule were established, the individuality of the men would be lost. We believe that the individuality of a man is of primary interest. For his special knowledge and ability he is often paid extra. The men do not wish to be put on a common basis so that they are all alike."[20]

A seniority rule which requires that furloughed workers be rehired, if qualified, in order of seniority is likely to increase the labor reserve attached to an industry. Men who do not have work, but who have claims to jobs when work picks up, are less likely to move to new localities in search of work and to be drawn away by a rise of employment in other industries. Many furloughed

---

compositors 10.9 per cent were receiving no more than the scale. Another survey made in 1926, about two years after the priority rule took effect, showed that out of 427 machine compositors, 22.3 per cent were receiving no more than the scale. Among the hand compositors, on the other hand, the percentage receiving no more than the scale decreased from 62.5 to 57.0. During the depression, however, there was a great drop in the payment of premium wages. This experience of the Typographical Union suggests that the priority rule may not reduce the individual bargaining power of wage earners as much as has been supposed.

[20] The 1926 survey by the Employing Printers' Association showed that 33.6 per cent of the cylinder pressmen, 36.5 per cent of the job pressmen and feeders, and 24.0 per cent of the cylinder press feeders were receiving premium wages. The pressman is in a strong position to bargain for a premium because he is able to save or to cause the employer great expense. The mistakes of the compositor can usually be caught in the proofroom. The pressman, however, has the final job. If he does poor work, either the job must be done over or the employer is in danger of losing the customer. Especially must the pressman who does color work (a three-, four-, five-, or six-color job) be highly competent. After he has several colors on the pages, he can still spoil the entire job. And the highly glazed paper which is used in color printing is expensive. All of these things help the pressman who is exceptionally competent to obtain premium wages, and the union wishes to assist rather than to hinder him. It is true that the standard wage scales of the pressmen's union provide differentials for different kinds of work. In the scale in the New York printing industry, for example, there is a spread of $10 a week between the lowest and the highest rate. There is a differential of $3 a week on close register color work, a differential for running a web press, and a differential for each of the attachments used. But in addition to all of the differentials allowed by the scale, the extra-competent man can obtain something because of his own superior ability.

railroad shopmen, for example, remained idle in the railroad shop towns during the brisk business in 1937 rather than take advantage of the shortage of metal workers in the automobile centers. Whether the increase in the size of the labor reserve induced by a seniority rule is to be regarded as "excessive" depends upon the criteria used in determining the proper labor reserve.

Seniority may promote or discourage the movement of men from department to department or from job to job within the department. This depends upon the nature of the seniority rule and the manner in which it is administered. A plant seniority rule, of course, tends to encourage movement from department to department and thus to develop a more flexible and versatile force. However, a plant seniority rule may be so administered that little interdepartmental movement results. A narrow interpretation of the meaning of the word "ability" will have this effect.

As indicated above, departmental seniority tends to discourage movement between departments but may encourage it within the department. Here again the effect depends upon the nature of the rule and its administration. A departmental rule which permits no transfer of seniority is bound, of course, to reduce transfers to a minimum and is likely to produce a dangerous lack of flexibility and versatility in the force. On the other hand, although a department seniority rule which allows transfer of seniority between departments will enable the management to develop a flexible working force, the actual result will depend upon whether the management takes care to arrange a sufficient number of interdepartmental transfers.[21] There has been some tendency among large plants to

---

[21] One company, however, reports some difficulty in persuading men to accept transfer despite the fact that after a year in the new department a man has full seniority and, in the meantime, retains seniority in the old department.

"We find it difficult to persuade a man who has a seniority standing to move to another department where he might serve us better, because we cannot assure him of as much security as he feels his regular job gives him. This lack of security on the new job is not necessarily an actuality because, when the transfer is not self-requested, he is returned to his residence department if the new job plays out before he has been on it a year. However, there is a natural fear that if he doesn't have his hands on his old job, it may slip away from him. In this sense, flexibility of the working force is impaired, although not yet to an alarming extent."

The difficulty which this company experiences is probably a temporary one which will pass away after seniority is better understood.

establish a zoning system whereby several departments with similar work are grouped for seniority purposes. This increases the number of interchangeable jobs to which men can be shifted without any appreciable break in training. Within the range of jobs found in a department, seniority by departments tends to develop versatility and flexibility provided management does not insist upon too narrow an interpretation of the "ability" requirement.

Seniority is likely to tie the whole organization together in such a way as to increase the number of men affected by technological changes and hence to strengthen the opposition to them. For example, a change in process which displaces a few men near the top of the seniority list may cause them to displace other men and those to displace others until a large part of the department has been affected. Hence the opposition, instead of being confined to a few men, may extend throughout the department. The tendency of seniority rules to tie the whole organization together may increase the interest in make-work rules because a large number of men will benefit. The strong interest of the railroad running crafts in laws limiting the length of trains is partly a result of the fact that an increase in the number of trains would give a large proportion of the membership an opportunity to move up to better runs.

The seniority rule makes discharge a more severe penalty than ever because the man who is discharged, like the man who resigns, loses his accumulated seniority and, when he obtains a new position in another shop operating under the seniority rule, is in great danger of being laid off. For this reason, unions which operate under the seniority rule fight most discharge cases stubbornly. At the same time nearly all men who work under the seniority rule are likely to join the union in order to gain the protection of the union grievance committee. In other words, the seniority rule is practically a substitute for the closed shop.

The seniority rule makes men less willing to strike and makes strikes more difficult to settle. When a man has acquired a number of years' seniority and has, therefore, become fairly certain of steady work, good years and bad, his job becomes to all intents and purposes a highly valuable piece of property. Such a man is reluctant to jeopardize this equity by going on a strike. He knows that if the strike is lost, the men hired to break it will hold seniority over the men who went out and that the strikers will be rehired as new employees with seniority standing dating from the time of their re-employment. At the same time, the seniority rule is likely to complicate the settlement of strikes, if the employer attempts to run his plant with strikebreakers. In order to attract them, he promises permanent jobs to the men who prove competent. He also promises that they shall have seniority over any strikers who later return to work. It is obvious that an issue is thus created which is bound to be difficult to settle. The employer feels it necessary to stand by the promises that he made to the strikebreakers. The men are determined not to lose their seniority standing. Consequently the two sides may be able to agree on every other issue and yet the strike may continue because they are deadlocked on the seniority question. A notable instance is the railroad shopmen's strike in 1922.[22]

[22] That strike would undoubtedly have been settled within a month or six weeks had the railroads and the unions been able to agree concerning the restoration of seniority rights. On July 11, ten days after the beginning of the strike, the Railroad Labor Board asked the leaders of both sides to meet in order to discuss the possibility of settlement. The Association of Railway Executives refused to consider a peace conference, but some railway executives attended as individuals. The conference agreed to a memorandum of five points to be used as a basis for further negotiations. Among the five was the provision that all strikers were to be returned to their former positions with seniority rights unimpaired. The Association of Railway Executives refused, however, to negotiate and on July 20, Chairman Hooper of the Railroad Labor Board announced that his effort to settle the strike had failed, primarily because employers and the shopmen were unable to agree on the seniority issue. (*Railway Age*, July 22, 1922, Vol. LXXVIII, pp. 142, 161.)

The next effort to settle was made by President Harding, who submitted a plan for settlement which provided that all strikers were to be returned to work without impairment of seniority rights. This plan was accepted by the unions but rejected by the Association of Railway Executives on the ground that to take back the men without loss of seniority would be "contrary to the highest considerations of expediency from the standpoint not only of the railways, but also of the public, because in the case of future railway strikes it would have furnished everybody an incentive to strike and nobody an incentive to work." (Railway Employes' Department, American Federation of Labor, *Official Proceedings, Seventh Convention*, pp. 45-49; *Railway Age*, Aug. 5, 1922, Vol. LXXIII, p. 233.)

During August an attempt to settle the strike was made by the four transportation brotherhoods. On August 21, the chiefs of the brotherhoods, acting as mediators, met in New York with representatives of the shopcraft unions and 258 railway executives. The transportation brotherhoods suggested that all men be reinstated in the position of the class held by them on June 30. As many men as possible were to be put to work on September 1 and all employees who had been

Perhaps the most serious drawback to the seniority rule from the standpoint of unions is its tendency to create dissension within union ranks. There is obviously a difference of interest between long-service and short-service men.[23] In the case of severe and prolonged unemployment, this takes the form of a demand by junior men that working hours be limited and the work shared. Depression may make this conflict acute, as the recent experience of the railroad unions shows.[24] So also may technological changes. For example, the introduction of machinery for finishing leather and the introduction of teletype have had this effect.[25] At the very beginning, employees on the old process may not be interested in obtaining jobs on the new process. Consequently, the new process is performed by new workers. As it more and more displaces the old process, the workers on the old process may desire to displace workers on the new. This may cause trouble, particularly when workers on the old process have much to learn before they are proficient on the new and are, therefore, less able to do the work than the younger workers who have mastered the new process. Another illustration of the conflict introduced by technological change between short-service and long-service workers is furnished by the partial shift from street cars to buses in some cities. This

---

on strike were to be put back to work by October 1, except such men as might be proved guilty of destroying railroad property or convicted of crime. Disputes concerning the seniority of any employee which could not be adjusted by the employer and the employee were to be referred to the Railroad Labor Board. The Association of Railway Executives rejected this proposal by a vote of 254 to 4. After further conferences on August 24 and 25 between the brotherhood executives and 52 members of the Railway Executives' Association, the railroads offered to take back all strikers and to refer disputes over seniority to a conference of five chiefs. This proposal was rejected by the shopmen on the ground that it did not adequately guarantee the seniority rights of their members.

The strike was finally settled on some roads in September by an agreement even less favorable to the shopcraft unions than that which they had rejected in the conferences called by the transportation brotherhoods. The men agreed, under the so-called Baltimore agreement, to go back with the seniority issue unsettled. Disputes over seniority were to be referred to a joint commission of railroad executives and representatives of the shopcrafts. This commission never settled this issue. On some roads individual settlements were eventually negotiated. Many other roads made the strike the occasion for ceasing to deal with the shopcraft organizations.

[23] See p. 112 above.
[24] See pp. 124-25 above.
[25] See Chap. IX, pp. 257, 276-79.

has raised the question as to whether the bus drivers are on the same seniority list as the street-car motormen and conductors. The motormen and conductors are usually longer-service men than the bus drivers. Hence, if the two groups are on one seniority list, the motormen and conductors may displace the bus drivers in times of a reduction of forces. The bus drivers naturally fight for their own seniority list. A case in which this was the essential issue went from the Detroit local of the union to the National Labor Relations Board.

Many conflicts between short-service and long-service men under the seniority rule have been produced by mergers of plants and facilities or by the transfer of work from one plant to another. In the newspaper industry, where the Typographical Union enforces a seniority rule, there have been many cases of papers merging or of one paper buying out another. In the railroad industry the lengthening of locomotive runs during the last ten years has led to the concentration of running repairs in fewer roundhouses. There has also been a tendency to concentrate the heavy repairs of locomotives and cars in the larger and better-equipped shops.

The position of the Typographical Union is that when two newspapers are merged, the length of service of each man on his paper shall establish his priority (seniority) under the new conditions. This means that the priority lists are dovetailed until the required number of men are obtained. The remainder have the opportunity to act as substitutes. When one paper buys another, the entire staff of the purchasing paper holds priority over the staff of the purchased paper. Frequently there is sharp difference of opinion as to whether the consolidation of two papers has been accomplished by purchase or by merger. The railroad unions hold that when work is transferred, the men shall be transferred with their work and shall have seniority in the new shop on the basis of their length of service in the old one. The practical administration of this rule may be complicated by a difference of opinion over how much work has been transferred and over how many men, therefore, should be permitted to move with it.

The seniority rules which give rehiring preference tend to convert permanent layoffs into temporary layoffs and to increase the proportion of layoffs which are temporary.

EFFECT OF MAJOR LAYOFF-CONTROL POLICIES UPON THE EFFICIENCY AND PRODUCTIVITY OF LABOR

Both the equal-division-of-work rule and the seniority rule tend in some ways to increase and in other ways to diminish the efficiency and productivity of labor. Their effects differ with circumstances, and it is impossible to measure the net result.

The rules may diminish the productivity of labor in two principal ways. In the first place, they may handicap the employer in finding the men who are best adapted to his work. In the absence of tests which enable employers to judge a man's fitness before he is hired, the employer must select his staff by a process of trial and error—that is, he must try men and drop those who do not seem well suited to the work. The equal-division-of-work rule and the seniority rule both interfere with this process of trial and error—unless they are limited by a probationary period during which the employer is free to drop the newly hired worker. In the second place, the rules prevent employers from dropping the slowest and least efficient men at the first lull in business—one of the principal methods used for stimulating efficiency. Where the worker's wages are based on his output, the effect may not be of great importance, but the combination of timework and either equal division of work or seniority (especially straight seniority) may substantially reduce the efficiency of the whole force because it removes virtually all incentive for each worker to avoid being among the low producers.

In the men's clothing industry, for example, where equal division of work has been combined in most plants with payment by the piece, one finds that the rule provokes little complaint from employers. In some branches of the women's garment industry and in the cap industry, where equal division of work has been enforced on day or week workers, it has aroused strong opposition from employers. In the New York cloth hat and cap industry, the employers complained not only that the week-work system prevented them from laying off their least efficient workers, but that it frequently caused them to lose their best workers. Some employers succeeded in obtaining enough business to make additional workers necessary while other employers were able to operate only part time. The best workers left to take jobs in the shops which were operating full time.[26] In the New York cloak and suit industry, where the union in 1920 had succeeded in replacing piecework with timework, employers found that the equal-division-of-work rule seriously interfered with efficiency. In 1926, they succeeded in forcing the union to concede them the right to reorganize their shops at the end of each season by dropping 10 per cent of the workers. The so-called "reorganization right" was a subject of keen controversy in the industry until 1933, when the union finally succeeded in eliminating it from the agreement.[27] The employers, however, have

[26] Dr. Abelson, arbitrator, in a decision on May 21, 1921, said: "In the opinion of the Board of Arbitration, the arrangement for the division of work which, by previous agreement and practice was inflexible and haphazard, has been the most potent cause of justifying the dissatisfaction on the part of employers with the working of the week-work system." In 1924 the cap workers' union, which had abandoned piecework in 1919, returned to it.

[27] The employers in 1924 demanded the restoration of piecework and greater freedom in getting rid of the slowest and least efficient workers. A strike on this and other issues was averted by a commission appointed by Governor Smith. The commission, which became known as the Governor's Advisory Commission, persuaded the two sides to sign an agreement for another year with the understanding that the problems of the industry would be settled under the direction of the commission. In the hearings before the commission, the employers demanded the reintroduction of piecework and freedom to discharge a certain proportion of their workers at given times. The report of the commission pointed out that the so-called "inside" shops, which had their own designers, did their own manufacturing, and sold directly to the retail trade, were losing out rapidly in competition with small sub-manufacturers who worked on contract for jobbers. Between 1916 and 1924, the number of workers in the inside shops dropped nearly two-thirds, and in 1926, the inside shops handled only one-fourth of the production in New York City. (Governor's Advisory Commission, Final Recommendations, May 20, 1926, p. 8.) In order to encourage the growth of larger and more responsible employers, the commission recommended that all establishments with a regular force of 35 or more be given the right to reorganize once a year at the beginning of the season provided: (1) that in any one year not more than 10 per cent of the workers in the shop were displaced; (2) that the workers affected be given either a week's notice or a week's pay; (3) that there be no unfair discrimination; and (4) that any workers displaced should be replaced through an employers' bureau, which the commission recommended be established under joint control of the employers and the union.

President Sigman advised the union to accept these recommendations, but the Communists, who at this time controlled the local in New York City, rejected Sigman's advice. The result was a long strike, which the union lost and which was eventually settled by giving the reorganization right to all "inside" manufacturers regardless of size. The right was made contingent, however, upon the employers' giving 32 weeks of employment or its equivalent during the year. An arbitration decision extended the reorganization right to the sub-manufacturers.

The union fought the reorganization right on the ground that employers used it to discharge workers for union activity and to eliminate premium wages. The joint employment bureau through which laid-off workers were to be replaced

succeeded in restoring piecework. In the job printing industry the combination of timework and seniority creates a difficult problem for employers.

In several important respects union control of layoffs tends to promote efficiency. In the first place, it tends to promote improvements in employment practice. As long as the employer can drop any man at any time for any reason, he may tolerate inefficient hiring practices, but when it is difficult for him to drop men, he is likely to exercise greater care in selecting them. Some employers have been slow to improve their hiring methods. In particular, they have been slow in insisting upon an adequate probationary period and in making use of it in selecting men.

In the second place, the union restriction of layoffs helps to prevent the development of demoralizing cliques and groups which receive or attempt to obtain favored treatment from foremen. It makes employment a matter of rule rather than the personal whim of foremen. In the third place, it tends to preserve the efficiency of some of the poorer workers by preventing the concentration of layoffs among them. When employers are free to hire and fire as they please, they naturally attempt to get rid of the least desirable men by dropping them at the first opportunity. Undoubtedly this practice causes some men to improve their efficiency and causes others to leave work for which they are unsuited. But the concentration of turnover and unemployment among a few men is discouraging and demoralizing to many of these men and injures rather than improves their efficiency. And certainly it is not good

---

was never established. Before the agreement expired in 1929, the union demanded that the new agreement give workers who lost their jobs in a shop reorganization first claim on jobs when the firm re-engaged help—an arrangement that would have defeated the purpose of the reorganization right. The union also demanded that all workers be engaged only through union-operated employment bureaus. (*Justice*, Dec. 14, 1928, Vol. X, p. 4.) The employers again demanded, as they had done almost continuously since 1919, the restoration of piecework. After a short strike, a settlement was made in which the employers lost their demand for piecework and the union its demand that workers dismissed under the reorganization clause be given first claim upon new positions. The reorganization clause, however, was qualified in several ways to prevent its abuse. (See *Justice*, July 19, 1929, Vol. XI, pp. 6-7, and Report of the General Executive Board of the Twentieth Convention, 1929, pp. 54-57.) In 1933, when the union consented to the restoration of piecework, the reorganization right was eliminated except in those cases where a permanent change in the business necessitates a reorganization.

for their families and for the next generation of workers.[28] In the fourth place, both the equal-division-of-work rule and the seniority rule tend to increase the productivity of men by prolonging their working lives. When the employer is free to drop anyone he sees fit, he is likely to select a number of the older and slower men. Later when the force is increased, some of the older men are not taken back. But these men are far more effective in their regular occupation than in any other. Consequently, when they are pushed out of their regular work, there is a permanent drop in their productivity. Furthermore, with the multiplication of hiring restrictions, most of these older men are never again able to obtain steady work. Layoff condemns them to intermittent employment. From the standpoint of employers it is often a hardship for them to be compelled to retain older men when more efficient younger men are available. This is particularly true of enterprises which in the course of time find their staffs composed of a large proportion of men of 50 or more and which are in competition with newly established enterprises manned with younger workers. From the standpoint of the community, however, prolonging the effective working life of employees is desirable because the important thing is not how much a man produces per *hour* or *day*, but how much he produces in a *lifetime*.

OTHER EFFECTS OF MAJOR LAYOFF-CONTROL POLICIES

Both equal division of work and seniority increase the importance of incentive methods of payment. For example, the cloak and suit industry found that the combination of equal division of work and day work placed union employers at considerable disadvantage. After 15 years' experiment with day work, the union part of the industry returned to piecework.

Both seniority rules and equal-division-of-work rules tend to make the cost curve of the individual plant more horizontal—that is, reduction in the working force does not lead to as great a reduction in operating costs as it would if the employer were free to drop

---

[28] It may be argued that the seniority rule also has the effect of concentrating layoffs among a few men, but this is only partly true. The concentration is temporary because as a worker's length of service increases, he is laid off less and less frequently.

the least efficient workers. The effect upon the slope of the cost curve has interesting implications for economic theory.

Both the seniority rule and the equal-division-of-work rule accentuate the problem of defining superannuation and of providing regular employment when men who reach a certain age or who fail to meet certain tests of efficiency are to be permanently retired. It is obviously dangerous for an employer to accept either the seniority rule or the equal-division-of-work rule without providing a pension plan supplemented by the dismissal wage to facilitate the retirement of superannuated employees.

Rules which compel employers to retain the older men tend to increase the volume of employment, because the retention of the older men in their customary occupations does not simply represent a transfer of employment from younger men to older men. Industry can afford to hire more efficient younger men for wages which it could not afford to pay less efficient older men. But when employers are compelled to retain older men, wage rates in general tend to be held down, particularly in establishments which do not pay by the piece, because there are frequently administrative difficulties in paying different wage rates to men performing the same operations.[29] Consequently, the rules which compel employers to keep older men tend to retard the advance in wage rates and thereby tend to increase the number of men which enterprises can afford to hire.

Of considerable importance is the question of how the methods of meeting reductions in employment affect the interest that unions take in the relation between their policies and the volume of employment. Since unions are democratic organizations, are they not bound to be devices by which the majority advances its interests quite regardless of the effect upon the minority?[30] Whether the union is divided between a majority that is indifferent to the effects of union policies upon employment and a minority that bears the

---

[29] Progress has been made in overcoming these difficulties, as the premium wages in some industries indicate, but the difficulties remain and in many plants are still important.

[30] In other words, whose income is the union intended to maximize, the income of all members regarded as an entity, or simply the incomes of the controlling majority?

burden of unemployment is likely to depend upon how employment is distributed among its members. The equal-division-of-work rule, by spreading unemployment among all members of the union, tends to increase the capacity of the union to be concerned about even a moderate amount of unemployment. This is less true of the seniority rule, which concentrates unemployment among the junior members. It was pointed out above, however,[31] that even the seniority rule sometimes ties a whole department together so that displacements at any one point produce a succession of displacements that affect a large part of the force. When this is true, even a union operating under a seniority rule may be greatly interested in the problem of employment.

[31] P. 154.

CHAPTER VI

MAKE-WORK RULES AND POLICIES

The efforts of unions to "make work" by various methods, direct and indirect, may be attributed primarily to the insecurity of employment in modern industry. The wage earner lives in a world in which the demand for labor is constantly changing in quantity, in kind, and in location. The proportion of workers who work for more than one employer in the course of a year is not known, but it is probably about one-fourth.[1]

Even the workers who are attached to one employer may not have full employment throughout the entire year. Seasonal fluctuations of employment in the United States are very great, both because the extremes in climate are great and because the level of income is high enough to introduce many style goods into the standard of living. Seasonal fluctuations in demand cause even regular employees to lose many days' work and to work part time on many other days. Considerable unemployment is caused even in good times by technological innovations, changes in demand, and geographical shifts in industry. Some intermittency of employment is the result of personnel policies by which employers endeavor to hold a labor reserve for use in peak periods. The competition for jobs is often intensified by the high wages established by collective bargaining. Since workers are inclined to be influenced more by the hourly rate of compensation than by annual earnings, the union wage scale often attracts more men to an industry than are required except in peak periods. The surplus workers remain, picking up such employment as they can, because they hope to obtain a regular job at the union rate.[2]

[1] For a discussion of this point, see Sumner H. Slichter, "The Impact of Social Security Legislation upon Mobility and Enterprise," *The American Economic Review*, Pt. 2, Supplement, March 1940, Vol. XXX, pp. 45-46.

[2] At this point it is desirable to warn the reader against the popular belief that a higher rate of unemployment means that industry has lost its capacity to increase the number of jobs. As a matter of fact, a high rate of unemployment may be associated with a rapid increase in the number of jobs because the very influences

Since employment is uncertain and fluctuating and much of it for a short term, it is not surprising that wage earners, both organized and unorganized, seek to increase their employment by controlling the pace of work. In addition, union workers seek to create and extend employment by various make-work rules and policies. Employers have been well aware of the workers' fear of unemployment and have often tried to foster it for managerial purposes —in order to step up the speed of work and to maintain discipline.[3] The very efforts to use the fear of unemployment, however, only strengthen the attempts of the men to make work.

It is not merely to increase or protect immediate employment opportunities that unions impose make-work rules. An important purpose may be to prolong trade life. This is accomplished by controlling speed.

Occasionally employers have some direct responsibility for make-work rules. When a machine is controlled by one employer, his competitors may seek protection from it by encouraging the union to limit its output.[4]

It is not always easy to determine when a union is "making work." There are some clear cases, such as those in which the union requires that the work be done twice. But the mere fact that the union limits the output of men, or controls the quality of the work (with effects upon output), regulates the size of crew or the number of machines per man, or prohibits the use of labor-saving devices does not in itself mean that the union is "making work." In such cases it is necessary to apply a rule of reason and to determine whether the limits are unreasonable. Opinions as to

which produce a rapid growth in the number of jobs produce a large amount of dislocation and hence a large amount of unemployment. The history of the United States illustrates this effectively—the number of jobs has usually been growing rapidly, but at all times the amount of unemployment here has been large. From this follows the important conclusion that even in rapidly growing societies, workers do not escape the hazard of unemployment.

[3] The superintendent of a large coal mine located several miles from a town in southern Illinois was asked: "When you don't need men why don't you put up a sign in town 'No men wanted'?" He replied: "Don't you know why those men are walking out there? We want the men going to work to see how many men are after their jobs."

[4] For an early instance of this in the glass industry, see U. S. Department of Commerce and Labor, *Regulation and Restriction of Output*, Eleventh Special Report of the Commissioner of Labor, 1904, p. 644.

what is reasonable are bound to differ, but failure to apply a rule of reason would be to accept the employers' requirements, no matter how harsh and extreme, as the proper standard.[5]

The efforts of unions to make work for their members fall into nine principal groups: (1) limiting daily or weekly output; (2) indirectly limiting the speed of work; (3) controlling the quality of work; (4) requiring time-consuming methods of doing the work; (5) requiring that unnecessary work be done or that work be done more than once; (6) regulating the number of men in a crew or on a machine or requiring the employment of unnecessary men; (7) requiring that the work be done by members of a given skilled craft or occupation; (8) prohibiting employers or foremen from working at the trade; (9) retarding or prohibiting the use of machines and labor-saving devices.

The policies pursued by unions toward machines will be discussed in Chapters VII-IX. All of the other make-work policies mentioned above will be discussed in this chapter.

LIMITS ON DAILY OR WEEKLY OUTPUT

One of the simplest ways of compelling employers to provide more employment is to limit the amount which union members are permitted to produce. *Formal* limits upon output are not especially common in trade agreements or even in union rules, but informal limits are not unusual. They are found more frequently among pieceworkers than among timeworkers.[6] At their *incep-*

---

[5] The physiological knowledge needed for informed judgments of the proper speed of work is not available. If one could determine the speed which would yield the maximum output *per lifetime* among a group representative of the men who do the work, one would know the maximum speed that should be permitted for these men. But perhaps the type of man selected for the work should be changed. And the speed that gives the most output per lifetime is not necessarily the optimum speed. Suppose that if men produce at a given rate, they are not compelled to retire until they are 65 years of age and that they then have the normal life expectancy for that age, which is about 12 years. Suppose, however, that if these same men produced at a 15 per cent higher rate, they would be compelled to retire at 62 and that, as a result of the faster speed of work, their life expectancy would be only 6 years. If work in each case began at 20 years of age, the faster rate of output would yield 7.3 per cent more product per lifetime but the men would live on the average 9 years less. Is 7.3 per cent more output worth 9 years of life? That is the type of question that must be answered in order to determine the optimum speed of work.

[6] The limits among pieceworkers are often in the form of limits on daily earnings rather than direct restrictions on the number of pieces that may be produced on each separate operation.

tion the purpose of limits applying to pieceworkers is not primarily to make work but partly to protect the union from being weakened by jealousies and dissensions arising from the fact that some workers receive better jobs than others, partly to prevent foremen from playing favorites in assigning jobs, and partly to prevent employers from cutting liberal piece rates or from using the high earnings of some workers as an argument against a general increase in piece rates.[7] Such limits have in the past been common among the glass bottle blowers, the flint glass workers, the potters, the stove molders, and in 1940 are being imposed by the leather workers in Massachusetts.[8]

Limits which are imposed by unions on pieceworkers are likely to be reasonable at the time they are adopted, for the pieceworkers want the limits to be high enough to permit good earnings. It is an important characteristic of limits on output, however, that they quickly become obsolete. Improvements in machinery, jigs and fixtures, raw materials, factory layout, and organization of the work are constantly being made by the management. In addition, the workmen themselves discover many short cuts. In the course of a few years, it often becomes possible for most of the workers easily to produce far more than the limit—sometimes twice as much.[9]

[7] It is always difficult to determine the time that should be allowed on new jobs. This was particularly true before the use of time and motion studies. But it is true even when a time and motion study has been made, if radical changes have occurred in process, equipment, or other working conditions.

[8] The limits in the leather industry are informally imposed by the workers in each shop without the official sanction of the national union. In fact, the national leaders are somewhat concerned over the long-run effects of the limits which may eventually permit workers in non-union shops to earn more than the union workers. That would create an obstacle to spreading the organization. The main purpose of the limits in the leather industry is to enforce a rough equal-division-of-work policy and to spread work among more people.

[9] The convention proceedings of the flint glass workers' union furnish much information concerning the problems which arise when limits become out of date. After the men have made all that the limit permits, they are naturally anxious to go home. But if they do go home, they simply advertise the fact that the limit is unreasonably low. The Detroit convention in 1908 enacted the "four-hour law," which provided that "no department working on a limited basis be permitted to make more than one turn's work in four and one-half hours," and recommended that "all shops use discretion in making their move on all wares and as far as possible work up to the full time of their turn." It also stipulated that "under no consideration shall any member leave the factory in less than four hours." (*Proceedings of the Forty-first Convention*, 1917, p. 29.) A turn's work is one-half day's work. A move was the amount of work which a shop was expected to do for one-half day's pay. Where output was limited it was also the maximum amount

But the very fact that a limit has become seriously restrictive creates both a demand for its removal and opposition to its removal. The demand originates from the obvious fact that some workmen find their earning power seriously restricted. The opposition arises from the fact that the size of the force has become adjusted to the per capita output which the limit permits and the men know that the removal of the limit would mean a reduction in the number of jobs. Although some of the younger and faster piece-workers, anxious to make more money, may be eager to raise the limit or even to abolish it, the older and slower men are opposed. One may compare the situation with that created by a protective tariff which is unnecessarily high. After a few years the duty brings into existence high-cost plants which need all the protection it gives. The more out of date a limit becomes, the larger the number of men who would lose their jobs if it were increased or removed and the greater the opposition to changing it.[10]

In industries where the output of each workman is easily measured, unions may seek to protect the slower men from discharge by establishing standards of competency. Such protection is particularly needed by the slower men when payment is by the hour rather

---

which the shop was expected to do. At the New Bedford convention in 1917, President Clarke said: "We are constantly receiving complaints about members violating the 'Four-Hour law.'" (The same.) Speaking on the limits in the paste mold department at the Toledo convention in 1918, President Clarke said that some men "will produce a turn's work in from 1 hour to 2½ hours' time. In some instances . . . we know of shops making their turn's work in two hours, then going home, and permitting other shops to come in and make their turn in the succeeding two hours. In other words, we know where two turns' work have been produced on a Saturday morning between the hours of 7 and 11 o'clock, and by two different crews, all in violation of our rules." *Proceedings of the Forty-second Convention,* 1918, p. 138.

[10] Direct limits have certain effects which are more or less peculiar to themselves and which do not follow from most other restrictions. Particularly disastrous in the long run are likely to be the consequences to the union. Not only do they undermine the solidarity of the union by creating conflict between the fast and slow men but they destroy the incentive of union employers to introduce the latest labor-saving devices and to make their plants more efficient. Under these conditions control of the market is likely to gravitate quickly into the hands of non-union plants. Perhaps the most illuminating example is furnished by the experience of the lamp chimney department of the American Flint Glass Workers' Union. But the discussion of these effects of direct limits on output can be advantageously deferred to Chap. XIII, which will analyze the general problem of abolishing restrictions.

than by the piece and when all workers, both fast and slow, receive about the same standard rate.

The most widespread example of standards of competency is the "deadline" clause found in many of the agreements of the Typographical Union with the newspapers. Any worker who on ordinary work sets the amount specified in the deadline is assumed to be competent. For example, in 1926 the deadline in thirteen cities ranged from 4,000 ems per hour in Cincinnati to an average of 8,000 ems per hour for seven and a half hours in Memphis.[11]

Although standards of competency define the *minimum* amount of work which an employee must do in order to be esteemed competent, they tend in practice to become limitations on production. If the fast workmen produce too much more than the minimum, the union has difficulty in preventing an increase in the minimum, which would be disadvantageous to the slower and older men. So shop opinion may be hostile to output that is far above the deadline. Occasionally an attempt is made to convert the deadline into a maximum. Since no worker *must* produce more than the minimum in order to hold his job, anyone who does so reduces the number of jobs in the plant and thus deprives fellow workers of employment.

The Hot Slug, a union paper published for several years by the Chicago Linotype Operators' Society, printed in each issue a table called "Our Speedometer" which stated: "For the benefit of operators who desire to regulate their output in accordance with the principles of unionism as well as fairness to the employer, we are printing a table showing the amount of type in a galley." This was followed by an extract from the agreement with the employers: "To be deemed a competent operator an average of not less than 3,000 ems solid on type larger than Brevier, or 3,500 ems solid an hour on Brevier or smaller type must be produced." The issues of the journal contain exhortations such as the following:

[11] Cincinnati, 4,000 ems per hour; Buffalo, 4,100; Chattanooga, 4,100; New York, 4,500; Birmingham, 5,000; San Francisco, 5,000 (not on piecework); Burlington, Vt., 4,375 (average for 8 hours); Boston, 4,500; Chicago, 4,500, with a bonus thereafter of 1 per cent per 100 ems; Nashville, 5,200 (piecework); Charleston, S.C., 5,300; Salt Lake City, 6,000 (not on piecework); Memphis, 8,000 average for 7½ hours (no piecework).

MR. OPERATOR

When you sit down to the linotype to begin your day's work, do you remember that you are a union man?

Do you remember that the union has established a deadline—the amount of type that is a fair day's work?

Do you realize that when you produce a much larger amount than the deadline you are forcing some brother member to walk the streets who should be receiving pay for doing the work that you are doing for nothing?[12]

EGGS

When a linotype operator orders a dozen eggs at the grocery store, how many does he receive?

Does the grocer count out 15, 18, or 24 eggs, simply because he has a good stock on hand?

Yes he does, —NOT!

He counts out exactly the number that are paid for.

But the operator considers that all right and is satisfied.

Then perhaps he goes to the print shop and hands out to the boss two days' work for the price of one.

The Intelligent Printer![13]

In some instances trade agreements, instead of specifying a minimum standard of competency, define a fair day's work. This is true of many agreements of the lathers' union. An agreement of the Chicago lathers' union stated: "It is conceded by both parties to this agreement that 100 yards of wood lathing on ordinary work is a fair day's work. . . . It is agreed that 90 yards of plaster board is considered a fair day's work when nailed on wood or ordinary construction."[14] Although the men are not specifically forbidden to do more, the intention plainly is to impose a limit. Indeed, the conditions of the trade are such that the workers keenly feel the need for some control over speed. Because jobs are short and men are constantly being hired and let go, the contractors have an excellent opportunity to discriminate in favor of the faster men. Were no check placed on this, many men would be compelled to leave the trade at an earlier age than they now do, simply because of their inability to obtain enough work to yield a decent living, and an

---

[12] *The Hot Slug*, February 1926, Vol. VIII, No. 2, p. 4.

[13] The same, April 1926, Vol. VIII, No. 4, p. 4.

[14] U. S. Bureau of Labor Statistics, *Trade Agreements, 1923 and 1924*, Bulletin No. 393, p. 33.

unnecessarily large number of young men would be drawn into the industry.

Restrictions may be created for the purpose of equalizing the opportunity to work. Such a restriction is illustrated by Grievance 1171, heard by the Anthracite Board of Conciliation. A local union had passed a rule forbidding any member miner from loading more than three cars daily when working alone, and five when working with a laborer. A miner was fined for loading more than the limit. He refused to pay the fine and the members of the local refused to work until he did. When the case was heard by the Board of Conciliation, the miners defended their stand on the ground that it was customary to fix tonnage rates on the assumption that three or five cars was a day's work and that the miner, by using more cars, had deprived others of their fair share of cars. The umpire refused to uphold the men's stand, on the ground that they had not proved their second point.[15]

An interesting case of the limitation of output is found in the restrictions on "double heading" (that is, the use of two locomotives to pull a train) which were forced on the western railways in 1903 by threat of a strike of the conductors and trainmen and which are still in effect. The railroads of the East and South have never had such rules.[16] The double-header rule in effect prior to 1924 forbade hauling more than 30 cars in one train with two engines. Exceptions to the general restrictions permitted the use of helper engines, without limit on the number of cars in the train, in certain heavy gradient districts. These exceptions enabled the roads to avoid breaking trains to get them over steep grades. In 1924, the railroads sought the elimination of the double-header rule. The unions re-

---

[15] A peculiar type of limitation is found in some agreements of the milk drivers. For example, the Chicago Milk Drivers' Union recently reduced its limit from 400 to 250 quarts of milk a day. In this case, however, the limit affects, not the speed of the work, but the length of the working day. The driver's day is measured, not by the hours he must work, but by the number of quarts he must deliver. Reducing the number of quarts is equivalent to reducing the number of hours—a reduction in the length of the working day, rather than in the speed of the work. Close examination of the limits in other industries will reveal that some are of this character. It is often not possible to draw a sharp line between regulating the hours of work and regulating the amount of work which a man may do.

[16] Double heading tends to reduce the number of trains and hence the need for conductors and trainmen. It is of little interest to the engineers' and firemen's unions.

fused, but some relief was given the roads by raising the number of cars permitted in double-header trains from 30 to 40 and by increasing the number of helper districts.[17]

It was pointed out above that formal limits on production are not frequent among union rules. The most important way in which limits are imposed is through tacit understandings and shop customs. These exist in unorganized, as well as in union shops, but the presence of a union helps the men to enforce them more effectively.[18] Furthermore, men hesitate to limit their output unless each feels that the other men in the shop will do likewise. The existence of a union gives each worker greater confidence that limits will be generally observed and, therefore, makes each man more willing to observe them himself.

An interesting case of informal restriction occurred a number of years ago in the cutting rooms in the Chicago men's garment industry. Although the official policy of the national union is to oppose arbitrary limits, various shop groups agreed not to earn more than the middle of five rates of pay provided for by the established standards of production. In some shops almost no cutters earned either of the two higher rates of pay. They justified the limit on the ground that the market contained more cutters than were needed and that it was desirable, therefore, to distribute the work as widely as possible.

During the building boom in the twenties, the painters' union in New York carried on a campaign against rushing. On much of the cheap, speculative work, men were employed as painters who could not in any other occupation have commanded the union scale of $10 and later $12 a day. This fact enabled employers to use the threat of discharge with great effectiveness to speed up the men;

---

[17] In 1928, the roads again sought the elimination of the rule. Upon the refusal of the unions to arbitrate, President Coolidge appointed an emergency board to arbitrate the rule. The board recommended that several proposals be submitted to the employees for their election. Among them was a 6½ per cent wage increase without change of rules or a 7½ per cent increase and the elimination of the double-header and other restrictive rules. On Nov. 23, 1928, the controversy was settled by a 6½ per cent wage increase with no change in working rules. *Railway Age*, Dec. 1, 1928, Vol. LXXXV, p. 1084.

[18] The buffers in some of the Massachusetts tanneries are now limiting their earnings to about $7.00 a day. A heavy snowstorm in February 1940 caused the men to lose a day, and some of the buffers made as much as $15 the next day. The local union threatened to fine them.

and the higher wages rose, the more effective the threat became. In order to keep their well-paying jobs, the workers were willing to meet almost any pace demanded by the contractor. Some contractors used pace-setters who received a little more than the usual wage rate, and some paid a bonus to the foreman at the end of the job, based on the number of labor days which he saved from the contractor's original estimate.[19] Mr. Alfred E. Joy, secretary of the Association of Master Painters, wrote: "The so-called 'rushing system' is the most serious evil of the painting trade. Few interested in the trade or dependent upon it in any way escape the harmful effects."[20]

The original proposal of the union was to establish standards of production. It recognized, of course, that the standards would necessarily differ with the nature and conditions of work. This proposal met favor among some contractors, especially those doing quality work, because the practice of driving the men had introduced cutthroat competition among employers. No contractor in estimating a job knew what speed of work and what standards of quality his competitors would assume in making their bids.[21] Some contractors, however, feared that the administration of standards

[19] A large painting contractor in New York, who was also a prominent official in the painting contractors' association, said to me: "There is plenty of ground for the feeling that the union has about rushing men, particularly in the Bronx and on uptown speculative work, but everything they have brought up as a method of regulating rushing has involved unsound principles. We gasped when we heard the output some contractors were getting on speculative work. The union would say: 'You are getting eighteen rooms per day.' The contractor would say: 'No, only fourteen.' They are getting twice as much as on regular commission work, and three or four times as much as on regular quality work. We are not depending on the union for our information. We have it from the mouths of our members."

[20] Brotherhood of Painters, Paperhangers, and Decorators of America, District Council, No. 9, The Painters' Bulletin, September 1924, p. 1.

[21] In favor of experimenting with standards, Mr. Joy wrote: "If we want high standards of workmanship, we must first take away from the contractor the right to demand that his men do as much as six or seven rooms a day. Then, we must cease to tolerate the so-called mechanics who cannot come up to the standards of the sort of men my firm has been employing. Standards of production are not impossible. Some contractors and some mechanics are observing standards of production voluntarily even at present. Why not enforce those standards in the whole trade?" (The Painters' Bulletin, September 1924, p. 3.) Mr. C. L. Dabelstein, a contractor, said: "A principle of checking quantity production would be advisable based on quality, also having in mind the standard of efficiency. In establishing a standard it will be difficult to apply any hard-and-fast rules as conditions alter cases. . . . A well defined system of standards derived through the

would be impracticable or that it would at least lead to graft. The union was compelled, therefore, to confine itself to urging its members to resist rushing.

Between 1933 and 1938, the longshoremen of the Pacific coast, according to the claims of the Waterfront Employers' Association of the Pacific Coast, have reduced tons handled per man-hour 33.3 per cent in San Francisco, 19.5 per cent in Los Angeles and Long Beach, 12.0 per cent in Portland and Columbia River ports, and 10.6 per cent in Seattle and Puget Sound ports.[22] The technique of slowdown is very elaborate.[23] The union denies these charges and on October 26, 1939 sent a letter to all its locals on the coast pointing out that the practices charged were not only violations of the agreement but in some cases violation of union rules and "against the best interest of the majority of the members of the union." The employers report that since the circulation of this letter output has not increased.

---

medium of a joint committee or board from the employers and organized labor, should do much to form a basis upon which the trade could depend for proper comparison to establish both a unit of production and a unit of efficiency, and thereby eliminate considerable of the doubt that now exists in the method of estimating, and will tend to aid the estimator in intelligently checking his work." (The same, p. 2.)

[22] Total tons of cargo were taken from the ships' manifests and the total man-hours worked from stevedore pay rolls. The investigation was made by Price, Waterhouse, and Co. For each period the results are based on samples. The tonnage per man-hour handled in the several ports changed as follows:

	San Francisco and San Francisco Bay	Los Angeles and Long Beach	Portland and Columbia River	Seattle and Puget Sound
Last quarter of 1933	1.588	1.452	1.876	1.847
Last quarter of 1934	1.421	1.236	1.702	1.640
Last quarter of 1938	.948	.995	1.522	1.444

[23] According to the employers, the technique includes the following:

Winch drivers time hoists and if they get ahead of their set schedule, they stop the winches; if they get behind, there is no effort to make up the loss.

Jitney drivers time their trips, going to the extent of fastening their watches in sight to be sure they do not take a load ahead of schedule. No one will relieve jitney drivers and jitneys will not haul loads out of "turn." All work stops if the jitney driver is off for any reason.

Hatchtender deliberately delays signals.

On commodities requiring extensive sorting, hold men purposely mix marks in building loads to slow down the dock work.

With different conditions prevailing in different hatches, gang stewards slow operations to rate of slowest hatch.

Hold men fail to leave wings to "meet the hook" promptly.

INDIRECT LIMITS ON THE SPEED OF WORK

The rules by which unions *indirectly* endeavor to limit the speed of work are numerous. The longshoremen's union, on the Pacific coast regulates the size of the sling load. Some unions specifically forbid their members to take extra pay for pacesetting. Such rules are common among the building trades unions. Furthermore, trade unions usually provide that members may be disciplined for actions inimical to the "good and welfare" of the union, and this clause is broad enough to cover extra pay for pacesetting. The International Typographical Union specifically forbids its members from engaging in speed contests. The fear that any wage above the standard rate may be a reward for pacesetting leads a few unions to prohibit members from accepting more than the standard rate *under any conditions*.[24] For example, the agreement between the Commercial Telegraphers' Union and the United Press Association and the International News Service, effective July 1, 1927 to June 30, 1929, provided that "bonuses shall not be paid and both parties to this agreement shall adhere rigidly to the scale accepted herewith."[25] Although such a prohibition is not ordinarily found in trade agreements in the construction industry, it is a well-established tradition, accepted by both employers and employees, that the rates prescribed in the agreements in this industry are both maximum and minimum rates.

The stop watch in its early days was so indelibly associated in the minds of many workers with speeding that some unions adopted resolutions against its use.[26] Most unions, however, have lost their

[24] But when the nature of the work is such that the union has no serious fear of speeding and when premium wages are paid to reward skill rather than speed, the union may take an active interest in helping its members obtain and retain wages above the standard rate. A large proportion of the members of the photo-engravers' union receive premium wages, and the organization does what it can to protect and increase the premium rates. In fact, it is the contention of the union that premiums attach to the position as well as to the workman and that once an employer pays more than the standard rate to the holder of a given position he must pay the same premium to all subsequent holders of the position, even though they may possess less experience and skill.

[25] P. 8.

[26] At the convention of the Glass Bottle Blowers' Association in 1915 there was a discussion of the spread of the stop watch in the industry. Pres. Denis Hayes reported: "We have protested at our conferences against the installing of this system and in the majority of cases the manufacturers have discontinued its use,

fear of the stop watch and some of them, such as the International Ladies' Garment Workers and the hosiery workers, use it themselves.[27]

Workmen are suspicious of attempts on the part of management to keep close track of the time which they spend on different operations. The International Photo-Engravers' Union has been eager to have the employers install reliable cost accounting systems, but it has insisted that the system shall not be used to keep track of how long each worker spends on each job. Other unions prohibit the use of detailed time sheets which would enable the employer to keep track of the time spent on different parts of the job. The Chicago painters' union has enforced such a prohibition.[28] The Cleveland plumbers' local and carpenters' local have gone so far as to forbid any member to punch a time clock.[29]

Some organizations object to payment by the piece on the ground that under the piecework system men will work faster. When the officers of the International Ladies' Garment Workers' Union in 1916, against strong opposition from many of the rank and file, sought to replace piecework with timework in the New York cloak and suit industry, one of their hopes was that the drop in speed would prolong the season as much as two months.[30] The unemployment created by the introduction of the linotype machine in the middle of the nineties led the Typographical Union to oppose the extension of piecework in the printing industry. The union definitely prohibited its members from working at piecework on the new machines.

---

but we regret to say that in some places it is still in effect." (*Minutes of Proceedings of the Thirty-ninth Annual Convention*, 1915, p. 71). The convention adopted a resolution forbidding any member of the association to work in factories where the stop watch, or speeding-up, system was in operation.

[27] In *The Hosiery Worker* of Jan. 31, 1930, Vol. VI, p. 2, appeared a statement by William Smith, secretary of the American Federation of Full Fashioned Hosiery Workers, entitled "Why Union Workers Should Co-operate with Time-and-Effort Studies." Nevertheless, the union-sponsored law forbidding the use of stop watches in the arsenals and navy yards of the government still remains on the books.

[28] R. E. Montgomery, *Industrial Relations in the Chicago Building Trades*, pp. 163-64.

[29] Cleveland Chamber of Commerce, *The Causes of High Building Costs in Cleveland*, p. 19.

[30] Louis Levine, *The Women's Garment Workers*, p. 325.

CONTROLLING THE QUALITY OF WORK

Another indirect method by which unions make work is to insist upon better quality than the employer requires. The more carefully and thoroughly the work is done, the more time, as a rule, is required to do it. Efforts to enforce standards of quality occur most frequently among the building trades unions. The tendency of some contractors to skimp on quality is in large measure an inevitable result of the practice of letting contracts to the lowest bidder. Not infrequently a bidder is low simply because he made a mistake in estimating and he may seek to avoid loss by skimping the work. This evil has been most prevalent in the so-called "speculative" construction. In painting, for example, unless a close check is kept, it is impossible to know whether or not the contractor mixed his paints of the materials specified or whether he put on the number of coats specified. A prominent painting contractor in New York said to me:

Everybody in the painting industry smiles at the specifications. I tell you that nobody figures on a specification in the painting game, and you can put that down in writing. The poor boobs who do that have been eliminated long ago. A fundamental difference between the building industry and most trades is that in most trades you bargain for what you see. In building you bargain first and get it afterwards.

Efforts of unions to raise the quality of work take three principal forms. The union may attempt to compel the contractor to live up to the specifications in his contract with the owner of the building or with the general contractor; it may attempt to compel him to observe the provisions of the city building code or the fire underwriters' code; or it may seek to enforce its own standards of quality. The agreement of Local No. 41 of the Brotherhood of Painters, Decorators, and Paperhangers of America, approved February 1925, required: "Where specifications are furnished on a job, the foreman must live up to the specifications as pertains to the number of coats required. The foreman will be held responsible for violations." The agreement of the Chicago lathers' local, effective July 23, 1923, required that plaster board "be nailed to each joist, stud or bearing with approved large-headed nails not to exceed 6 inches apart."[31] In 1924, the painters' local of New York, in connection with its campaign against "rushing," endeavored to interest the employers in fighting poor quality work and in compelling the observance of specifications. The union proposed that inspectors be employed jointly by the union and the employers for the enforcement of specifications, but the suggestion was not adopted. The Chicago electrical workers' union requires that

all electrical work put in or constructed by journeymen shall be done in accordance with the ordinance of the City of Chicago, or the rules of the Electrical Inspection Department governing the same. All journeymen shall be held responsible for having their work done in accordance with the above mentioned rules, and in a workmanlike manner. Any member of either party hereto found guilty of wilfully violating this rule shall be fined or suspended.[32]

Many building trades unions have a rule requiring that all work be done in a "thorough and workmanlike manner." The phrase "workmanlike manner" means many things. The New York electrical workers' local, for example, recently listed the following practices which it has been fighting:

Cramming wires into conduits not large enough to hold them.
Making long runs with numerous bends without any pull boxes.
Installing armored cable without any fittings or connectors at boxes.
Making long runs in cable with little or no strapping or supports.
Hanging fixtures insecurely, making poor connections with no soldering or rubber taping.[33]

This union once attempted to have bell risers, buzzer, and other low tension systems installed in conduit. Formerly these systems were operated by batteries. Now many of them are connected to electric lines of 110 volts. The New York Board of Fire Underwriters and the municipal Department of Water, Gas, and Electricity do not require low tension systems to be installed in conduit.

Too much importance must not be attached to the efforts of unions to compel the observance of specifications, building codes, or even the union's own standard. The union business agents are likely

---

[31] U. S. Bureau of Labor Statistics, *Trade Agreements, 1923 and 1924,* Bulletin No. 393, p. 33.

[32] *By-laws and Working Rules of Local No. 134,* I. B. of E. W., revised and adopted to take effect May 15, 1926, p. 36.

[33] Local Union No. 3, I. B. of E. W., *Union Progress in New York,* pp. 53-54.

to have more important matters demanding their attention than the enforcement of specifications or building codes. In fact, rules requiring the observance of specifications and codes have probably been more important as sources of graft to union officials than as sources of employment to union members.

REQUIRING TIME-CONSUMING METHODS OF WORK

The agreement in effect in 1939 between Painters' District Council No. 14 and the Chicago contractors prohibits the use of brushes more than four and a half inches wide in oil painting. This limit is enforced by the union in many cities. The Cleveland plumbers have prohibited preparing joints by means of sandpaper or what is commonly called scratch cloth; the Cleveland carpenters the use of door-fitting machines; and the plasterers have forbidden the practice of having one journeyman do all the gauging and have required that gauging be done with hawk and trowel.[34] The Boston cement, asphalt, and terrazzo finishers' union charges 12½ cents more per hour when material is used that contains quick sets or any matter to hasten the undue hardening or setting of cement.[35]

Rules prohibiting or discouraging the performance of certain operations in the shops rather than on the job are prevalent among building trade unions. Naturally it is often much easier and quicker to perform many operations in shops where special machines and equipment are available than on the job, and for many years there has been a tendency to transfer work from the job to the shop. The sharp advances in building trade wages after 1920 accelerated the tendency, but the efforts of the building trades unions to discourage the movement of work into the shops go back years.[36] The New

[34] Cleveland Chamber of Commerce, *The Causes of High Building Costs in Cleveland*, pp. 19, 30.

[35] Boston Cement, Asphalt, and Terrazzo Finishers' Union, Local No. 534, *Rates of Wages*, p. 2. The union formerly prohibited the use of any accelerating material. *Constitution and By-Laws*, Art. 15, sec. 6. The union still prohibits the use of any accelerating material that "unduly hastens the set of cement."

[36] The agreements of the Chicago plumbers' union between 1911 and 1921 prohibited iron pipe of specified diameter (⅛ to 2 inches) from being cut, measured, or threaded in the shop. (Montgomery, *Industrial Relations in the Chicago Building Trades*, p. 168.) The by-laws of the New York district council of the carpenters' union in effect in 1918 prohibited inside men or shopmen from cutting or mortising for locks, striking plates, hinges, or letter boxes or from

York plasterers have required that all plain moldings be run on the wall although they could be made more economically in the shops. The painters in Chicago have required that all sash frames and screens be primed, painted, and glazed on the job. The metal lathers in New York do not permit the bending of steel for concrete re-enforcement by machine in the shop. They insist that steel be bent only by hand on the job. Stirrups for re-enforcing concrete may not be bent by machinery, although the cost of this method is a small fraction of the cost of bending by hand. The Cleveland plumbers' local has required all the lead work to be prepared and wiped on the job.[37] The New York plumbers have prohibited the cutting and threading of pipe between certain sizes in the shop and have refused to install toilet, lavatory, and other fixtures that have been assembled at the factory where assembling can be most economically done. Not unusual today are rules against the installation of factory-glazed windows or of factory-painted kitchen cabinets. The Typographical Union has sought legislation in Congress to require the printing of tariffs for railroads and interstate buses by the letterpress process. This demand is aimed against the photographic process.[38]

REQUIRING THAT UNNECESSARY WORK BE DONE OR THAT WORK BE DONE MORE THAN ONCE

The New York plasterers' local has required that stock models be destroyed in order to provide work for the molders. In October 1940 in the construction of the Social Security building the Washington Painters' local refused to apply a resinol base paint that requires only two coats instead of the usual four coats of lead and oil paints.[39] Some unions require that work be done more than once. This demand may arise because changes in methods are causing one group of workers to lose work to another group. The first group may attempt to keep the work by demanding that it be done over

---

putting any hardware whatever on trim (movable fixtures, show cases, and furniture excepted) or from doing certain other work. *By-Laws and Working Rules of the District Council of New York of the United Brotherhood of Carpenters and Joiners of America*, approved May 29, 1918, p. 23.

[37] Cleveland Chamber of Commerce, *The Causes of High Building Costs in Cleveland*, p. 19.

[38] *Typographical Journal*, August 1936, Supplement, Vol. LXXXIX, p. 17.

[39] *Engineering-News Record*, Oct. 31, 1940, Vol. CXXV, p. 11.

again by its members. At one time the wiring of switchboards and much electrical apparatus was done on the job. The trend, however, has been to build and wire in factories switchboards and other self-contained electrical units which have a motor and electrically driven apparatus such as laundry machines. The New York local and others have refused to install switchboards or other electrical apparatus unless the wiring done in the manufacturing plant was torn out and union members were permitted to rewire the apparatus. The issue was arbitrated by the Council of Industrial Relations of the Electrical Industry, a body consisting of an equal number of employers and union representatives for the purpose of adjusting disputes in the industry. The council unanimously disapproved of the position of the New York local, saying: "It is uneconomical and contrary to the public interest to take down or disassemble parts of a manufactured unit in order that these parts may be restored by union mechanics."[40]

Most famous of all the rules requiring that work be done twice is that of the International Typographical Union on the interchange of plate matter or the papier-mâché matrices from which plates are made. The union requires that, when plates or papier-mâché matrices are exchanged, as they frequently are, the matter be reset, read, and corrected within a stipulated period and that proof be submitted to the union chairman in the office. The restriction applies to the interchange of matter not only between plants owned by different individuals or corporations, but also to those which, though conducted as separate institutions with separate composing rooms, are owned by the same individual or corporation.[41] The time limit within which borrowed or purchased matter must be re-set is regulated by agreement between the employer and the local union.

Strangely enough, this famous rule was not originally passed merely to make work. It dates from the time when compositors were paid by the piece, and its principal purpose was to protect the com-

---

[40] The Electrical Board of Trade of New York, Inc., *Service Letter*, Nov. 30, 1927, Vol. IV, No. 48, p. 2.

[41] International Typographical Union, *Book of Laws*, in effect Jan. 1, 1938, Art. IX, secs. 1 and 2, p. 103. The union has interpreted the rule to apply only to matter exchanged between newspapers in the same city. This interpretation exempts much plate matter, cuts, and matrices for national advertisements. But some local agreements require the re-setting of plates, etc. received from outside the city.

positors against loss of the most profitable piecework jobs.[42] Piece-work has now been almost entirely eliminated from the news-paper shops, but the abandonment of the rule would cause some drop in employment. Hence the union today is interested in it as a device for making work.[43]

It is difficult to estimate the amount of employment which the rule actually makes. Even if it were not necessary to re-set bor-rowed matter, most of the men on the "ad" room force would have to be retained to take care of the peak demand which often comes shortly before the paper goes to press. However, as a result of the variation in the volume of advertising from day to day the rule may produce some extra employment. On certain days of the week (such as Friday and Sunday) the newspapers regularly carry more advertising than on others. They meet these peaks by employing extra men. The smaller forces on the "light" days may not be able to re-set all of the exchanged matter that originates on the "heavy" days, and the papers may be compelled to use a few more "extras" on light days than would otherwise be necessary.

The opportunity of the newspapers to "re-set" exchanged matter without hiring additional men depends partly upon the length of time within which matter must be re-set. This period is left

[42] The measure used in setting piece rates was the "em"—the amount of space occupied by the piece of type for the letter *m*. The price on any job was determined by the number of ems which it represented. Naturally advertisements containing large type or blank spaces could be set more rapidly than ordinary matter. Conse-quently, the men could earn much more per hour when setting advertisements than when setting ordinary matter. In the parlance of the composition room, the "ads" were known as "fat." In order to equalize the earnings of the men in the shop it was the practice to auction off the "fat" to the highest bidder and to distribute the amount paid by the successful bidder among all the force. It is evident, however, that matter for advertisements might often exchange among newspapers. Identical news stories would not appear in several papers in the same town, but retail stores often run the same advertisement in several papers. By exchanging plates and matrices the newspapers would save money, but they would also deprive the workers of the most lucrative jobs, and this would amount to a cut in piece rates.

[43] The union is also interested in the rule because of the fear that exchange of plates and matrices would cause advertisements to be set up in specially equipped offices and furnished in the form of plates or matrices to newspapers. These offices might be located in communities where wages are low or where the union is weak or non-existent. Some publishers are also opposed to having the setting of ad-vertisements pass into the hands of special shops. Consequently, they have not been disposed to oppose the union rule requiring the reproduction of exchanged matter as strongly as they otherwise would.

to be regulated by local agreements. Professor Barnett, who made a thorough study of the subject, concluded that if several days were allowed for reproducing the plates or matrices, the men gained little employment.[44] A survey by the American Newspaper Publishers' Association in 1940 covering 256 contracts showed that only 47, or 18.3 per cent, allowed less than one week to re-set exchanged matter and 97, or 37.9 per cent, allowed at least 30 days.[45] Newspapers have not made an effort to determine how many additional men they require because of the rule. The time spent in re-setting exchanged matter and the amount paid for this can, of course, be readily ascertained, but as a considerable part of this time would have to be paid for anyway, the figures are not significant.[46]

REGULATING THE NUMBER OF MEN IN A CREW OR ON A MACHINE OR REQUIRING THE EMPLOYMENT OF UNNECESSARY MEN

One of the simplest ways of creating employment is to require that an unnecessarily large number of men be employed to do a given task. The hoisting engineers in New York City insist that when steam for power is obtained from pipe lines under the streets, three shifts of engineers must be employed, although all they have to do is to watch the valve. This can be turned on just as well by someone else. Some locals of the electricians require that, when temporary lighting is used, an electrician be constantly on the job even though he has nothing more to do than turn off the lights when the other men are through work.[47] A coal mine in northern

---

[44] G. E. Barnett, "The Printers," *American Economic Association Quarterly*, 3d series, October 1909, Vol. X, No. 3, p. 191.

[45] In the large cities the time allowed seems to be shorter than in the small ones. In New York it is four days; in Boston and San Francisco, three days. In Seattle it is one week. Even three or four days gives the newspaper an excellent opportunity to get matter re-set by stand-by workers at no additional cost to the employer.

[46] Whatever additional employment is provided by the "re-set" rule goes to the "extras" or "substitutes" who are needed by the industry to meet the peak demand on the "heavy" days. The effect of the rule is that some of these men obtain a day or two more each week than they otherwise would. The rule, therefore, may be regarded as a form of unemployment insurance by which the industry gives a little more support to its peak load employees but provides it in the form of "made work" rather than unemployment benefits.

[47] The agreement, effective May 1, 1926, of the Newark, N.J., electrical workers' union provides that "temporary lights, motors, or any other electric appliance installed for the use of other workmen shall be maintained and supervised by a

West Virginia had an electric pump with an automatic switch which required attention two or three times a day. The mine committee demanded that an attendant be employed and that the foreman be forbidden to give occasional attention to the pump.[48] The agreement negotiated in the Chicago dress industry in the spring of 1939 requires a shop operating over 14 machines to employ at least two cutters, and one operating over 24 machines at least three cutters.

One of the best known union rules is that of the International Association of Machinists prohibiting members from operating more than one machine in shops where this practice is not established.[49] Although the rule of the union makes no other exception, the interpretations of the officers have at times been highly ambiguous. Some years ago President O'Connell was quoted as saying that the rule was not intended to apply to machines which are operated automatically and do not require any great amount of skill. But he used the lathe as an illustration of machines which demand skill and which, therefore, should be operated one to a man.[50] Whether or not the operation of a lathe requires skill depends upon the nature of the work: much lathe work demands little skill. Although the rule still remains in the constitution, the union has made little effort to enforce it.

The motion picture operators have been waging a struggle to require two picture operators for each machine. The printing pressmen's union regulates in its agreements the size of the crew on

---

member of this local union during the whole life of such temporary installations. If said temporary appliances are used after the regular working hours, a journeyman wireman must be held on the job to take care of said temporary equipment." U. S. Bureau of Labor Statistics, *Trade Agreements, 1926,* Bulletin No. 448, p. 42.

[48] Boris Emmet, *Labor Relations in the Fairmont, West Virginia, Bituminous Coal Field,* U. S. Bureau of Labor Statistics, Bulletin No. 361, p. 24.

[49] At one time the constitution of the union made any member running two machines subject to expulsion, but in 1901 the prohibition was limited to shops where running more than one machine by one man was not the practice—in other words, the union determined to prohibit the spread of the practice rather than to require its abandonment where it had already become established.

[50] In the Eleventh Special Report of the Commissioner of Labor, *Regulation and Restriction of Output,* p. 106, Mr. O'Connell is quoted as follows: "We have in the machine shops of this country . . . machines that are operated automatically, which do not require any great amount of skill in their operation and to which machines we have no objection to any one man operating a number of them, as is now being done every day. We do object, however, to one man operating more than one lathe . . . and similar class of machinery requiring similar skill to operate."

large web presses, and this size varies from locality to locality according to the bargaining power of the union. Presses that have been operated with a crew of five in New York City have been moved to Chicago and other places and operated under union conditions with a crew of three. The press assistants' union in New York has been struggling for years to preserve the rule that there must be one pressmen's assistant to each automatic press feeder. There are two kinds of feeders. It is admitted by the employers that one man can operate only one cross or continuous feeder, but it is asserted that when pile-feeders are used, one man can run two feeders.[51] Furthermore, whether or not it is economical to have an assistant operate two feeders depends upon the length of the run. The press assistants' union (partly because it has not received support from the local pressmen's union) has been compelled gradually to accept the operation of two feeders by one assistant on a larger and larger proportion of the work, but the agreement still requires one assistant to a feeder on many jobs where an assistant could easily handle two feeders.

The intermittent and uncertain employment of stage hands and musicians has led these two unions to regulate the size of crews and orchestras in considerable detail. The musicians' union, for example, has been interested in regulating the minimum size of orchestras in motion picture theaters and in forcing radio stations to take on as many musicians as possible. The demand of the Chicago local that outlying theaters employ four-piece orchestras was one of the causes of a strike in the Chicago motion picture industry in September 1926. The theatrical price list of Local No. 9 of Boston, effective September 6, 1926, provided that in first-class vaudeville and picture houses "no less than ten musicians be employed in the regular orchestra during the regular season."[52] The agreement of Local

---

[51] In the case of the cross-feeder, men must climb up and put the paper on the feedboard and fan it. In the case of the pile-feeder, an automatic screw pushes the pile of paper up and a vacuum pipe flutters the sheets. There is no lifting and no climbing.

[52] U. S. Bureau of Labor Statistics, *Trade Agreements, 1926,* Bulletin No. 448, p. 112. The size of the orchestra required may vary with the seating capacity of the house and the price of admission. In some cities the locals forego the demand for a minimum number in the orchestra and follow the policy of maintaining a sliding scale in an effort to induce employers to use larger orchestras. The larger the orchestra, the lower the price per man. *International Musician,* May 1929, Vol. XXVI, p. 22.

No. 161 with the motion picture theaters of Washington, D.C., effective September 19, 1927, also stipulated the number of musicians to be employed.[53]

In 1937, 87 per cent of the 700 radio stations in the United States employed no musicians.[54] Since 1931 the American Federation of Musicians has been attempting to force radio stations to hire musicians. One device was to require a local station receiving remote control programs to employ a regular stand-by orchestra.[55] A few locals had a little success with this device, but on the whole it was a failure.

At the convention of June 1937, demand for action was so great that the national officers of the union were instructed to meet with the radio and recording industries and to work out a plan for more work for musicians.[56] Most of the stations affiliated with the three national networks organized a committee to negotiate. The employers' committee, however, had no authority to bind any station, but simply to recommend a settlement. After many conferences a plan of settlement was agreed upon in November 1937. It provided that the aggregate expenditures of the affiliated stations for musicians during the next two years should not be less than $1,500,000 per annum in excess of the amount so spent by them during the year ending August 31, 1937. The allocation of the increased expenditures among the affiliate stations was to be subject to the approval of the Federation. In no event was the aggregate expenditure for staff musicians by the affiliates as a group to be less than $3,000,000 per year. In addition, the National Broadcasting

[53] U. S. Bureau of Labor Statistics, *Trade Agreements, 1927*, Bulletin No. 468, p. 115.

[54] *Business Week*, Sept. 18, 1937, pp. 22-24. Although 55 per cent of all radio programs are of a musical nature, only about 800 musicians were employed by the broadcasting companies in 1937.

[55] A dozen resolutions were proposed in the conventions of the union between 1932 and 1937 requiring local stations to employ studio orchestras as they received music from remote control.

[56] *International Musician*, August 1937, Vol. XXXVI, p. 1. The Federation warned the broadcasting industry that members of the Federation would refuse to perform for stations "receiving network programs or using records or transcriptions unless such stations employ the number of musicians or expend an amount for compensation of station musicians satisfactory to the Federation." *Plan of Settlement between Representatives of Radio Stations Affiliated with National Networks and American Federation of Musicians.*

Company and the Columbia Broadcasting Company agreed to expend $60,000 additional for each of their key stations—a total of $480,000—and the Mutual Network agreed to spend $45,000.[57] The allocation of the $1,500,000 among the affiliate stations was a difficult task, but a formula derived by the accounting firm of Ernst and Ernst for the negotiating committee was accepted by the Federation. By April 1938, the union reported that 261 contracts had been signed, increasing the employment of musicians, according to President Weber of the union, by 1,000.[58] The union also is endeavoring to control the employment of musicians by recording companies.

One of the most ambitious efforts to make work by requiring excessive crews or the employment of unnecessary men is being made (with great success) by the train service unions on the railroads. These unions have been spurred to require the employment of unneeded men by the great drop in the employment of train service employees.[59] The train service unions have used three principal methods to make work: (1) support of legislation either requiring full crews or limiting the length of trains; (2) retaining obsolete rules which make work; and (3) enforcing the interpretations of rules so as to make work and to penalize the roads for using economical methods of operation.

As of August 1937, full-crew laws had been passed by 21 states[60] and train-limit laws by 4 states.[61] Typical of these laws is that passed by Indiana in 1937 requiring not less than four men on passenger trains of less than five cars, not less than six on freight trains of 50 cars or more, not less than five in yard crews, and not less than three on locomotives used on main lines for purposes other than

---

[57] American Federation of Musicians of the United States and Canada, *Official Proceedings of the Forty-third Annual Convention*, 1938, p. 158.

[58] *International Musician*, April 1938, Vol. XXXVI, p. 1; *New York Times*, Jan. 15, 1938, p. 18.

[59] The reports of the Interstate Commerce Commission show that between 1899 and 1925 the ton-miles of revenue freight increased 237.5 per cent, but the number of freight-train miles by only 18.7 per cent. Between 1925 and 1937, ton-miles of revenue freight decreased by 12.9 per cent and the number of freight-train miles by 15.2 per cent. Between 1925 and 1937, the number of employees directly engaged in conducting transportation dropped from 544,598 to 411,062, or 24.6 per cent.

[60] Ariz., Ark., Calif., Conn., Ind., Maine, Md., Mass., Miss., Neb., Nev., N.J., N.Y., N.D., Ohio, Ore., Pa., S.C., Tex., Wash., Wis.

[61] Ariz., La., Nev., Okla.

carrying freight or passengers.[62] It is estimated that the Indiana law costs the New York Central about $270,000 a year, the New York law about $1,200,000 a year, and the Ohio law about $325,000 per year. Pennsylvania passed a full-crew law in 1937 which required the railroad to put an extra brakeman on every passenger train having more than five cars, and on every freight train of more than 50 cars. Enforcement of the law was enjoined by the courts and the supreme court of the state found it unconstitutional.[63] The Pennsylvania Railroad contended that the act would necessitate the employment of 2,182 men on its train crews and would cost more than $4,500,000 a year. Labor union officials put the cost to the Pennsylvania Railroad at slightly under $3,000,000 a year.[64] Several full-crew bills have been introduced in the United States Congress, but none has been passed.[65]

The first law limiting the length of trains was passed by Arizona in 1912. It limited freight trains to 70 cars exclusive of caboose and passenger trains to 14 cars.[66] The federal court which passed on the constitutionality of the law in 1931 found that "the law bears no reasonable relation to safety of persons or property."[67] It also found that, based on 1927 traffic, the law imposed a direct

---

[62] *Railway Age*, Mar. 13, 1937, Vol. CII, p. 453.

[63] *Pennsylvania Railroad* v. *Driscoll*, Nov. 27, 1939, *United States Law Week*, Dec. 12, 1939, p. 689.

[64] *New York Times*, Nov. 28, 1939, p. 14.

[65] A bill sponsored by the railroad brotherhoods was introduced in January 1935 by Senator Wheeler. This bill would have required a crew of four men for passenger trains of less than five cars and an additional man for trains of five cars or more, any of which carried passengers, or trains of ten cars not carrying passengers. It would have required a crew of five for freight trains of less than 50 cars, and an extra brakeman for trains of over 50 cars. The railroads contended that this bill, if in effect in 1934, would have added 70 million dollars to their expenses. (*Railway Age*, June 29, 1935, Vol. XCVIII, p. 1054.) Another full-crew bill was introduced by Senator Neely in January 1937.

[66] After being passed by the legislature, the Arizona law was submitted to referendum and approved. Consequently, the state legislature has no power to repeal or amend it. At the time the law was passed, it imposed no hardship in the operation of freight trains as neither the locomotives nor the sidings and passing tracks permitted the operation of trains of more than 70 cars. After about 1923, the law became a hardship, and its constitutionality was eventually challenged. The law was held unconstitutional by the federal court (*Atchison, Topeka, and Santa Fe Railway Company* v. *LaPrade*, 2 Fed. Supp. 855), but the decision was reversed by the Supreme Court of the United States on a technicality without considering the validity of the statute.

[67] 2 Fed. Supp. 855, 862.

increase of $600,000 per year on the operating expenses of the Santa Fe within the state of Arizona and of $400,000 a year on one main line of the Southern Pacific.[68]

Nevada passed a train-limit law in 1935, Lousiana in 1936, and Oklahoma in 1937.[69] Train-limit laws were introduced in the Senate in 1934 and 1935, but were not favorably reported by the Senate Committee on Interstate Commerce. A bill supported as a safety measure by the Brotherhood of Locomotive Engineers, the Order of Railroad Conductors, and the Brotherhood of Railroad Train-men was introduced by Senator McCarran in January 1937. It prohibited the operation of more than 70 cars, exclusive of the caboose. The bill passed the Senate, but on March 31, 1938, the House Committee on Interstate and Foreign Commerce voted against reporting the bill.[70] The additional costs that would be imposed by a 70-car limit on freight trains are difficult to estimate. That they would be large, however, is indicated by a survey of freight train operations for four months in 1936, which showed that 42.7 per cent of the total freight car miles were handled in trains of more than 70 cars.[71]

[68] The same.
[69] These laws differed in minor respects but all of them limited freight trains to 70 cars exclusive of caboose. The enforcement of each was enjoined on the ground of unconstitutionality by federal courts. A Special Master who held extended hearings on the Nevada law concluded that it would increase rather than diminish the hazards of railroad operation.
[70] *Railway Age*, Apr. 2, 1938, Vol. CIV, p. 627.
[71] Mr. J. H. Parmelee, in a statement before the House Committee on Interstate and Foreign Commerce on Mar. 1 and 2, 1938, estimated that the direct costs of a 70-car limit law with a 1937 volume of traffic would be in excess of 100 million dollars a year. On the basis of a special survey for four months in 1936, he estimated that approximately 1,167,000 freight trains of more than 70 cars were operated in 1937, and that these trains averaged 23 cars per train over the 70-car limit. Consequently, a 70-car limit would have required that 26,841,000 cars be run in additional trains. The cost would depend upon the average number of cars in the additional trains—a matter of considerable uncertainty. The movement of the cars could not be delayed long enough to make each additional train 70 cars long. Mr. Parmelee estimated an average of 45 cars for the additional trains, which would have meant 596,000 additional freight trains in 1937, and 63,176,000 additional freight train miles. He estimated an "out-of-pocket" cost of moving a freight train one mile at $1.37. This includes the wages of the crew; the cost of fuel, water, lubricants, and other supplies for the locomotive; locomotive repairs; and engine house expense. To run 63,176,000 additional freight train miles at $1.37 per train mile would cost $86,551,000. This figure does not include other direct costs such as the additional yard costs of

The transportation unions have succeeded in creating a few unnecessary jobs by insisting on the employment of firemen on Diesel locomotives. When the locomotives are used in fast passenger service (as in the streamliners) two men are needed in order to check signals. Diesel engines used in switching service, however, and in slow branch-line service require only an engineer and for several years were operated without a second man. On February 28, 1937, the Association of American Railroads signed an agreement with the Brotherhood of Locomotive Firemen and Enginemen to employ a helper on all Diesel locomotives. It was estimated that this agreement meant the employment of 700 additional "firemen" or helpers on locomotives being operated at that time with only an engineer.[72]

Probably the most important make-work rule of all is the dual method of compensation in the train service. A day's work is defined as so many hours or so many miles. For example, in freight service a day's work for an engineer or fireman is either 100 miles or 8 hours and in passenger service 150 miles or 8 hours. This means that a freight engineer or fireman who runs 100 miles receives a day's pay regardless of how short the time he takes for the run. Likewise if he works 8 hours, he receives a day's pay even though he does not run 100 miles.

---

making up more trains at initial terminals and breaking them up at final terminals, and the maintenance, signaling, dispatching, handling, accident, and operating costs which follow an increase in the number of trains on the road. These costs are obviously very difficult to estimate. Mr. Parmelee put them at 18 million dollars, which he termed "a conservative figure."

In addition to the direct costs imposed by a 70-car limit, there would be additional capital costs. These are even more difficult to estimate than the direct costs. Because the railroads now have considerable reserve capacity, some of the additional capital costs might not be felt for a number of years. A considerable number of additional locomotive and caboose cars would be immediately required. If the additional freight trains reduced road speeds, additional freight cars would be needed. It is, of course, possible that the reduction in road speeds could be avoided. On many stretches of track, however, this could not be accomplished without adding a second, third, or fourth main track, or rearranging yard facilities. In addition, considerable expenditures on new and larger engine houses and repair shops would be necessary. Mr. Parmelee estimated that a 70-car limit would require immediate capital expenditures of close to half a billion dollars.

[72] *Brotherhood of Locomotive Firemen and Enginemen's Magazine*, March 1937, Vol. CII, pp. 147-50. Of course in the long run, as the use of Diesel locomotives in switching service increases, the agreement will force the employment of more than 700 unnecessary men. Some of the full-crew laws require a two-man crew on Diesel locomotives even when engaged in yard service.

The dual method of payment was not intended to be a make-work rule. On the contrary, it was introduced by the railroad managements in order to encourage efficiency and stimulate the crews to get the trains over the road faster. The rule has been converted into a make-work rule by technological progress which has made obsolete the definition of the day's work in terms of miles.[73] As the roads have been improved by double tracking, reduction of curves and grades, heavier rail, better ballast, and automatic signals, and as the locomotives have increased in power, it has become possible to move trains, particularly freight trains, with speeds that were undreamed of a generation ago. Some fast freights now run at what used to be passenger train speeds—500 miles in 12 to 15 hours. It is not unusual for a freight to cover a division in 3 hours or less— for which the engineer and fireman receive a full day's pay. This is the familiar case of changed conditions making piece rates obsolete. If the unions were to consent to a redefinition of the day's work in freight service so that men ran 150 instead of 100 miles for a day's pay (a reasonable change in view of the revolutionary changes in operating conditions), the number of men required in transportation service would be substantially reduced. That is precisely why the transportation unions vigorously oppose a change. The obsolete definition of a day's work of fifty years ago keeps in railroad service many thousands of men who are not needed there.

REQUIRING THAT WORK BE DONE BY MEMBERS OF A GIVEN SKILLED CRAFT

An easy way to create employment for members of a craft is to require that skilled men be used to do work which semi-skilled or unskilled workmen might do. Many skilled crafts attempt to do this. Controversies over what work should be done by mechanics and what by semi-skilled specialists and laborers are rendered more numerous and more acute by the fact that employers are constantly

[73] The unions have endeavored to get the day's work changed in terms of *hours*. Originally a day's work was 10 hours. By passage of the Adamson Act in 1916, the unions succeeded in getting the day in hours reduced to 8. The roads failed to take advantage of the opportunity to trade a reduction of the day in hours for an increase in the day in miles. The speeding up of freight service had not yet started and railroad managements were not aware of its possibilities. Indeed, they were exceedingly doubtful of their ability to run freight trains 100 miles in less than 8 hours and thus to avoid overtime payments.

searching for ways of having work performed by unskilled or semi-skilled men instead of by skilled mechanics—at least this is true when the men are paid by the time instead of by the piece.[74] Rules which require that skilled men perform operations of which unskilled or semi-skilled workers are capable do not necessarily limit output, but they do, nevertheless, raise costs, and for this reason should be noticed.[75]

Some locals of the plumbers' union require that distribution of plumbing materials above the first floor shall be made by union plumbers. Structural steel workers require that steel be brought from the unloading point to the building site by their members and that re-enforced steel for concrete be placed by them, though laborers could do the work. Bricklayers demand that only bricklayers wash down and point brick. The carpenters in many cities demand that stripping forms from concrete be done by their members. Rule 55 in the national agreement between the United States Railroad Administration and the shopcraft unions provided that the dismantling or scrapping of engines, boilers, tanks, cars, or other machinery should be done by mechanics of the respective crafts. Decision No. 222 of the Railroad Labor Board changed the rule to permit this work to be done by "crews" under the direction of a mechanic, thus allowing the use of common or semi-skilled labor.

The printing pressmen's union of New York City requires that two members of the crew on the large web presses be full-fledged pressmen, but the employers insist that only one man of the crew need be a pressman. This has been an acute issue in New York. In Chicago and elsewhere web presses are operated with only one pressman in the crew. When the presses used in printing the *Cos-*

---

[74] The different situation which prevails when men are paid by the piece will be discussed in Chap. XI.

[75] Not all of the rules defining journeymen's work and prohibiting helpers from doing it are intended to make more employment for the journeymen. Indeed, this may not be their principal purpose. Another important purpose is to protect the standard rate. If employers were able to get a large part of the work done by helpers at less than journeymen's pay, the journeymen, in order to obtain additional employment, would be tempted to enter into secret arrangements to do the work for less than the scale and the standard rate of pay could not be enforced. Still another purpose is to protect the apprenticeship requirements of the union and to prevent the trade from being flooded with "half-baked" journeymen who have literally "picked up" knowledge of the craft by working from time to time with journeymen's tools.

mopolitan, Good Housekeeping, and *Hearst's International* were shipped from New York to Chicago, there was a reduction in the size of the crew.

The agreement between the New York book and job printers and the Typographical Union requires that work set in the shops of the employers must have a first reading and be corrected and revised by members of the union before corrections emanating from outside the composing room may be made.[76] As the Typographical Union recognizes only two classes of labor in the composing room, journeymen and apprentices, this rule means that proofreading must be performed by practical printers.[77] The union's rule that all work-

---

[76] Sec. 29 of the agreement. This rule, however, does not apply to foreign languages when a member of the union competent to correct the proofs cannot be obtained.

[77] The constitution of the International Typographical Union specifically states that proofreaders shall be admitted to membership only when they are practical printers (*Book of Laws,* in effect Jan. 1, 1938, Art. I, sec. 1, p. 3).

In the old days it frequently happened that the proofreaders received more than the compositors. This had much to do with the union's interest in controlling the proofreading job. The rule requiring that proofreaders must be compositors is difficult to defend. A good compositor may not be a good proofreader. In the case of the newspapers there has been little opposition to the rule because proofreading on newspapers has become less and less important. The principal reason for this is the linotype machine. The correction of a single error necessitates resetting at least an entire line. Furthermore, the practice of getting out numerous editions increases the opposition of the management to corrections, because they delay the paper. Consequently, proofreaders on newspapers are not expected to make corrections in grammar or to maintain a uniform style as used to be the case. Even in the job shops proofreading is regarded by employers pretty much as a side issue. The fact that changes are expensive makes employers interested in keeping them down to a minimum. Hence they are not always anxious to have good proofreaders. The unsatisfactory state of proofreading led the New York local of the Typographical Union in 1925 to appoint a committee to investigate. The committee recommended the establishment of a class in proofreading in the school of apprenticeship which is jointly maintained by the union and the employers. This recommendation has been carried out. The class is not compulsory, but the apprentices may elect it in their fifth year. (Typographical Union No. 6, *Monthly Bulletin,* July 1925, Vol. XXV, p. 6, and May 1926, Vol. XXVI, p. 5.)

The union rule cannot be defended even on a humanitarian basis. It is true that the rule makes places for superannuated printers, but this is achieved by making a blind alley job out of copyholding. The copyholders are the logical workers from whom to recruit proofreaders, and the union rule closes this one and only avenue of advancement to the copyholders. Fortunately, the union rule is not always enforced. For example, the *Monthly Bulletin* of Typographical Union No. 6 quotes an editorial from *Printing* for Mar. 6, 1926 in which a Chicago employer is reported as saying: "Not one competent reader in ten in Chicago is a printer, and when we need help, we take one of the copyholders

ers in union shops must be either journeymen printers or apprentices has the effect of requiring that the work of distributing type must be done by skilled compositors. In the days when piecework was prevalent, the employers, of course, wished each journeyman to stay long enough at the close of the day to distribute his type. Now that piece rates are no longer important, the employers would like to use unskilled labor to distribute type, but the union holds fast to the old rule.

Not only do journeymen seek to regulate the dividing line between the work of journeymen and that of helpers and laborers, but each craft seeks to protect its work from encroachment by other crafts. These attempts to maintain sharply defined lines between crafts may compel the management to employ extra men or at least may create extra hours of employment in the form of additional overtime. The national agreement between the United States Railroad Administration and the shopcraft unions defined rather sharply the work of the different crafts. This made it necessary in some cases to use several men on a job which one man could easily do. A machinist or boilermaker, for example, might have to wait for a pipe fitter or an electrician to disconnect or connect pipe connections or wiring. On many roads the union did not take a technical stand and did not insist that journeymen from several crafts be used on jobs which could readily be done by one man.[78] In Decision No. 222 the Railroad Labor Board modified several rules in order to prevent jurisdictional lines from being used to make work,[79] but the problem still exists.

---

we have trained, even though the rule says it cannot be done. It is done by the back door process but should be done openly and on a test."

[78] An official of the Chicago and North Western Railway, a road which had had friendly relations with the shopcraft unions for many years, said that his road had not been troubled with the technical interpretations of which some other roads complained. The cases before Board of Adjustment No. 3 (which handled shopcraft matters) indicate that the unions were much more technical on some roads than on others.

[79] For example, the board expressly permitted machinists and boilermakers to connect or disconnect any wiring, coupling, or pipe connections when necessary to repair machinery or equipment. Rule 32 of the international agreement provided that "none but mechanics or apprentices regularly employed as such shall do mechanics' work as per special rule of each craft, except foremen at points where no mechanics are employed." This rule compelled the roads to maintain an unnecessary number of mechanics at certain small points in order to observe craft lines.

Recently the railroad unions, with the help of the National Railroad Adjustment Board, have been endeavoring to establish the principle that each and every piece of work in the operation of the railroad, no matter how minute, belongs to some particular class of employee and, in effect is *owned* by that class. The management has not the right to decide what class of labor could perform the particular job most expeditiously and economically under the particular circumstances; it must call a member of the craft which "owns" the work. If it fails to call a worker of the proper class, a furloughed worker of the class may claim a day's pay for not being called upon to do the work. Furthermore, the management acts at its peril in selecting an employee for the operation. If its interpretation of property rights in work fails to coincide with that of the Adjustment Board, the fact that the management acted in good faith does not relieve it of liability.

As indicated above, the agreements on the railroads do to some extent define the work belonging to different crafts. Nevertheless, on some types of work the agreements are indefinite. The Railroad Adjustment Board, however, has adopted the policy of reading property rights in work into the agreements, using as a basis of its decisions the seniority rule.[80] The severe decline in traffic during recent years has caused the roads to discontinue yard service at many small points and to have switching done by road crews. The unions have contested this change and have demanded an extra day's pay

---

Addendum No. 6 to Decision No. 222 amended the rule to read that in outlying points "where there is not sufficient work to justify employing a mechanic of each craft, the mechanic or mechanics at such points will, so far as capable, perform the work of any craft that may be necessary." Rule 65 of the national agreement did not permit machinists assigned to running repairs to do dead work at points where dead work forces were maintained. Dead work was defined to mean work on an engine which could not be handled within 24 hours by the regular running repair forces. Addendum No. 3 to Decision No. 222 modified this rule to permit running repair machinists to do dead work when there were not sufficient running repairs to keep the running repair force busy. These modifications of jurisdictional rules were not unwelcome to many leaders of the shopcraft workers. Speaking of the old rules, one of these leaders said to me: "They [the jurisdictional rules changed by the Railroad Labor Board] have been a big nuisance to the Railway Employees' Department, because they became such an object of propaganda."

[80] The board, which is virtually a court with authority to compel the railroads to pay large sums in back pay, operates in secrecy, with neither public nor reporters admitted to its hearings. Some of its decisions are among the strangest in the annals of industrial relations.

for laid-off yard crews for each time a road crew has done any switching. The board has upheld these claims. The seniority of the yardmen, according to the board's view, gives them the right to do all the yard work that will ever be done at that yard, regardless of whether there is enough switching to warrant the retention of a full-time yard crew. This conclusion is reached despite the fact that agreements make provision for the payment of road crews for doing yard work. In other words, the board holds that once a yard has regularly been established it can be abolished only with the consent of the union and that in the meantime the holders of seniority rights in the yard crew are entitled to compensation for all yard work done there. As a result, the roads are now required to retain many yard crews which are not needed.[81] It logically follows, of course, from these decisions that in the event of an *increase* in traffic, the roads could not establish yards and start yard crews at new points without the consent of the unions because that would be depriving road men of part of their work!

PROHIBITING EMPLOYERS OR FOREMEN FROM DOING JOURNEYMEN'S WORK

A firm with six workers in the New York fur industry called three of them foremen: one was foreman over the cutters, one over the operators, and one over the finishers. The agreements between the firm and these three "foremen" provided that they were to work until the shop was closed at night, and, when necessary, on Saturdays, Sundays, and holidays.[82] Obviously this was simply a device to avoid the observance of the union agreement limiting the length of the working day and the payment for overtime.

This case illustrates why unions need to restrict foremen or employers from engaging in journeymen's work. Such prohibitions are especially numerous in industries such as building construction and the needle trades where there are numerous small contractors and manufacturers. Although the restrictions are necessary in order to enforce union standards of hours and overtime payment, they are also intended to create employment for union members (1) by preventing journeymen from being laid off and replaced by mem-

---

[81] See the Caldwell, Kansas, case, Award No. 1842, Docket No. 3467, decided Apr. 2, 1937, and the Haileyville, Oklahoma, case, Award No. 1843, Docket 3468, decided at the same time.

[82] *The Fur Worker*, November-December 1925, Vol. IX, p. 10.

bers of the firm or by foremen and (2) by preventing foremen or employers from reducing the number of jobs by speeding up the pace. Employers or foremen are most likely to do journeymen's work during a slack year or a slack season when their time is not all required for supervising the force. It is precisely at such times, however, that unions are most anxious to prevent employers from increasing unemployment by working at the trade themselves or by having the foremen work and by speeding up the pace. The issue was very acute in many recently organized plants during the depression of 1937-38.

SOME CONCLUSIONS CONCERNING MAKE-WORK RULES

1. Some regulation of the speed of work or size of crew is often needed in the interest of health and safety. It should be remembered, however, that the most reasonable regulations quickly become obsolete with changes in equipment and working conditions. Hence, they need to be revised from time to time. Prompt and frequent revision is particularly important because the more obsolete a limit becomes, the greater difficulty the unions and employers will find in changing it. The reason is that the more obsolete the limit, the more the men who would be thrown out of work if it were removed or raised.

2. Make-work rules are likely to be paid for by wages lower than the union could otherwise obtain, because the disadvantages which the union can afford to impose on employers are limited.[83] Hence a union in deciding whether or not to impose a make-work rule should consider whether it would prefer a wage increase.[84] For example, the Boston newspapers have among the largest crews per press in the country (partly because of physical conditions in the press rooms), but the Boston wage scale for pressmen is one of the lowest among the large cities. The failure of the longshoremen of San Francisco to obtain a wage increase between 1934 and 1940 seems to be attributable to the rapid drop in man-hour output.

3. Limits on production are likely to be particularly dangerous to the union and union employers if payment is by the piece. As the

[83] The ability of unions to impose disadvantages on employers is examined in Chap. XIII.

[84] There may be a few cases where a make-work rule will actually raise the bargaining power of the union by depriving non-union firms of a source of skilled labor, but such effects are likely to be temporary.

limits become more and more obsolete, the earnings of union workers shrink relatively to those of non-union workers and in the course of time may drop below them. When this happens, the limits on production become a serious obstacle to the union in spreading its organization to non-union plants. The flint glass workers at one time suffered seriously from this difficulty in certain departments. Their experience will be discussed in Chapter XII.

4. From the standpoint of the community, make-work rules are a wasteful way of dealing with the unemployment caused by intermittent work, technological change, and market shifts. In the building industry and among musicians or stage hands, make-work rules do not eliminate the intermittency of employment or the unemployment caused by it. They simply draw into the industry more men than are needed and thereby reduce the capacity of the industry to give a high standard of living to its employees. What is needed in order to deal with the unemployment caused by intermittent demand for labor is a scheme of unemployment compensation.[85]

Make-work rules are not a satisfactory arrangement for dealing with the displacement of labor by technological changes because these rules are permanent in their effects. All that is needed when technological change threatens men with displacement is a temporary arrangement to give men work pending the time when the natural attrition of the working force will eliminate the excessive numbers. It is not necessary to reduce permanently the capacity of the industry to pay high wages.

Make-work rules are a dangerous expedient for dealing with the unemployment which occurs in declining industries or as a result of market shifts. When an industry is declining, it might seem a rational policy for the union to attempt, by make-work rules, to create jobs faster than the decline of the industry destroys them. If the industry's demand for labor happens to be inelastic, make-work rules may give temporary relief from unemployment. If the demand for labor in the industry is elastic, however, the make-work policy, by raising labor costs, only makes a bad situation worse. Even when the immediate demand is inelastic, the demand over a period of two to three years (the time required for employers and

---

[85] If accompanied by experience rating, unemployment compensation will cause employers to plan work so as to convert some temporary jobs into steady ones.

their customers and competitors to make various adjustments in their operations) is likely to be elastic. Consequently, in the case of declining industries or market shifts, make-work rules are almost certain to aggravate the very problem that they are intended to alleviate.

5. The Department of Justice has taken the position that forcing an employer to hire unnecessary labor may be a restraint of trade under the Sherman Act.[86] There may be some clearly definable cases, such as the requirement that work be done twice, which might safely be regarded as violations of the act, but there are bound to be many cases in which courts of law would be compelled to pass upon technical engineering and production problems. If a union is charged with requiring the employment of an unnecessarily large crew on a machine or unreasonably limiting the number of pieces that a man may produce or the number of machines that he may run, how can "reasonableness" be determined? If a union were charged with forcing the employment of an excessive number of men on a new printing press, the court would have to decide the technical question of how many men the press really requires. This number will differ for the same press in different press rooms or under different working conditions. Likewise, the courts might be compelled to decide how many looms a weaver should operate (and the number would differ with a multitude of conditions, such as the nature of the work, the nature of the machines, the kind and amount of help provided), what is a reasonable sling load under different conditions in loading and unloading ships, what are reasonable limits on the daily output of workmen in hundreds of occupations. The public policy of seeking to regulate such technical matters by law is open to grave doubts. These doubts are increased by the fact that there is a possibility of regulating them through the bargaining power of employers.

6. Attention has been called to the fact that many of the make-work rules and policies of trade unions are not embodied in the terms of trade agreements, but are enforced in ex parte manner by a decision of the local or by informal arrangements within the shop which receive the support of the local. Some employers have been

---

[86] "The Antitrust Laws and Labor," an address by Thurman Arnold before the American Labor Club, Jan. 27, 1940, *New York Times*, Jan. 28, 1940, p. 1.

tolerant of these arrangements, partly because the effect upon costs, at least at the outset, was not great, and partly because the restrictions were first imposed at a time when the enterprise was busy and making money and when it could not risk a strike. Although in some cases the direct action of the men in limiting output applies to pieceworkers, in a majority of cases, it originates with timeworkers. In these cases it may spring fundamentally from the nature of the labor contract. It is an important characteristic of the labor contract when payment is by the hour or day that the amount of work to be done is not specified. This may be regarded as a serious imperfection in the terms of the contract because it leaves the amount of work to be determined by a struggle. The management tries to get as much out of the men as possible and the men try to give as little in return as possible.

This raises the question of how the speed or quantity of output should be determined, particularly when men are paid by the day. Payment by the hour or day is usually employed where the amount of output cannot be readily measured, or where, if measurable, it does not accurately reflect the worker's accomplishments. In fact where output can be easily measured and where it accurately reflects accomplishments, piecework or some other form of payment by results is used. Consequently, definite determination of the amount of output by timeworkers is usually impracticable, despite the fact that failure to specify it leaves one of the terms of the contract indefinite.

The most satisfactory arrangement for day workers seems to be for the rate of output to be worked out by department management and the workers from day to day and in the light of changing conditions, subject to the right of the union to make a grievance of speeding or of the management to make a grievance of organized restriction or "slowdowns" whenever the facts seem to warrant it. But when the question is one, not of daily output, but of the complement of men on new machines or the number of machines per man, joint decision between the management and the union is necessary. This means that these questions become matters for collective bargaining. Resort to time studies may be helpful in substantially narrowing the difference of opinion between the union and the management, but it cannot be expected to eliminate differences altogether.

CHAPTER VII

TECHNOLOGICAL CHANGE—THE POLICY OF OBSTRUCTION

In no previous age has the search for new methods of production and new products been so vigorously and universally pursued, so generously financed, and so efficiently conducted. Trade unions themselves, through their pressure for higher wages, have been one of the influences stimulating the search for new methods. It is true that not all technological changes create problems for trade unions. Some increase the number of jobs for the members of a given craft, raise the skill required (as in the case of many recent developments in printing presses), reduce the physical strain of the work, or help the workers at one process compete with workers on other processes or in other industries.[1] Changes which are confined to particular union plants may assist union employers to compete with non-union. Hence there are some technological changes which unions encourage —sometimes against more or less opposition from employers.[2]

A great many technological changes, however, have the effect of (1) increasing the hazard or onerousness of the work, (2) reducing the skill required, or (3) reducing, at least temporarily, the number of men required. In any of these cases the union is confronted with a problem of policy. It has three principal alternatives: it may attempt to prevent the introduction of the new machine into union shops (the policy of obstruction); it may attempt to compete with the new machine (the policy of competition, which may be regarded simply as a special form of the policy of obstruction); or it may permit the new machine to be introduced but seek to control the men who operate it and possibly to control the rate at which it is introduced (the policy of control).

[1] For example, lighter and faster trucks, introduced at a time when the trucking industry was young and growing rapidly, have not displaced truck drivers. On the contrary, they have increased employment opportunity in that industry by helping it make greater inroads upon the business of the railroads.
[2] For example, the locomotive firemen's union for years has been pressing for equipment of locomotives with automatic stokers.

Almost every union at some time in its life has been confronted with the problem of adjusting itself to a major change in technique. The boot and shoe workers in the early days had the problem of adjusting themselves to the MacKay sewing machine and later to the lasting machine and the heeler; the window glass workers had to adjust themselves first to the cylinder machine and later to the sheet drawing machine; the glass bottle blowers to the semi-automatic and the feed and flow device; the stone cutters to the planer; the granite cutters to the hand surfacer; the cigar makers to the bunch-breaking and roll-up process and later to the cigar-making machine; the potters to the casting process; the telegraphers to the teletype; the street railwaymen to the one-man car; the miners to coal-cutting machinery and later to the loader; the clothing workers to pressing machines and electric cutters; the painters to the spray gun; the musicians to mechanical music; the steel workers to the continuous-strip mill.

Indeed, in view of the large number of important technological changes in the last several generations, it may seem surprising that unions have not been concerned far more than has been the case with the problems of technological change. The reason seems to be that changes occurred at a time of rapid economic expansion which minimized the displacement caused by any given change and helped displaced workmen find new jobs. Between 1880 and 1890, the number of those gainfully employed in the United States increased 33.9 per cent; between 1890 and 1900, 24.9 per cent; between 1900 and 1910, 27.8 per cent; but between 1920 and 1930, only 15.9 per cent. The rapid expansion of industry encouraged men to move from one plant to another in hopes of improving their condition. Before the war, the resignation rate among manual workers in factories seems to have averaged about 67 per cent.[3] Such a high resignation rate obviously facilitated the adjustment of the size of the working force to technological changes. As was pointed out in Chapter IV, however, the resignation rate gradually fell during the twenties and by 1929 was about half of the prewar rate. The great depression caused a further drop, and by 1937 the resignation rate

[3] That is, resignations in the course of a year were about 67 per cent of the average number of men on the pay roll. The rate, of course, fluctuates cyclically. It is higher in good years and lower in depressed years.

in manufacturing averaged about 15 per cent. Now that growth of employment is much slower and the resignation rate much lower, adjustments to technological change are made less readily, and the problems presented by it may be expected to be more important to unions than ever before.

Several years may be required for a union to determine its policy toward a new machine or proceess. Time is needed for the scattered members of the union to learn that they are confronted with a problem, particularly in view of the fact that machines in the early stages of their development are crude and inefficient. Hence the union members often refuse to regard the machine as a serious menace.[4] Even when they realize the need for action, there may be sharp differences of opinion among the members as to the policy that is desirable—as the history of the cigar makers and the window glass workers well illustrates. After a decision has been reached, so much precious time may have been lost that the union has difficulty in making its policy effective. The history of the attempts of unions to adjust themselves to technological changes suggests that they have a strong tendency to do the right thing too late.

As a general rule, unions adopt a national policy toward a machine or new process. Sometimes, however, the policy may be made a matter of local option—as in the case of the policy of the painters toward the spray machine. The fact that a union has a national policy does not mean that it is accepted by all locals, for some locals may rebel against it. Some locals of the cigar makers' union have refused to follow the national policy of accepting the machine. Nor does a national policy mean that a uniform policy is pursued by the national in all localities or in all branches of the industry. Not infrequently the national policy is a mixture of the policies of obstruction and competition, of competition and control, or even of ob-

---

[4] At the 1911 convention of the Glass Bottle Blowers' Association, President Denis A. Hayes said: "It has been difficult to convince members that a machine has been invented which is successfully making bottles without the aid of any skilled glass workers. This is especially true where men have not had a chance to see it in operation. As the Convention has received an invitation from the American Bottle Company to visit its factories at Newark next Saturday and see the automatics in operation, I hope the delegates will avail themselves of this opportunity to observe just what this invention is doing." Glass Bottle Blowers' Association of the United States and Canada, *Proceedings of the Thirty-fifth Annual Convention*, 1911, p. 41.

struction and control. For example, the union may do everything in its power to keep a new machine out of union shops and at the same time make concessions on the old process in order to help it hold its own with the new. Or the union may make concessions on the old process and at the same time insist that when the new machine or process is used, union members must do the work. Indeed, in a few cases, a union may pursue some of the milder forms of the policy of obstruction simultaneously with the policy of control—trying to prevent the use of the new machine by methods short of strike and insisting that, when it is used, union members shall operate it.

Not infrequently a union adopts different policies at different stages in the development of a machine. At the beginning the union may do little more than attempt to keep the machine out of union shops—the policy of obstruction. As the use of the machine in non-union shops spreads, the union often finds it necessary to make concessions for the purpose of assisting union plants to compete with the machine. As the machine is gradually perfected and becomes more and more superior to hand methods, the union is likely to find itself obliged to permit the use of the machine in union shops and to shift to the policy of attempting to control it.

Naturally the policies which unions adopt toward technological changes and the results which they achieve depend upon circumstances. This chapter will discuss the policy of obstruction to technological changes; the next chapter, the policy of competition; and the following chapter, the policy of control.

PRESENT STATUS OF THE POLICY OF OBSTRUCTION

Opposition to labor-saving devices and technological changes is by no means confined to labor organizations. The railroads fought the Panama Canal, which among other things was a labor-saving device; existing retail outlets oppose new methods of distribution, such as chain stores and super-markets; glass bottle manufacturers seek to prevent the use of paper milk bottles (and have succeeded in some markets); the basing point system had among its several purposes the discouragement of the erection of new and more conveniently located plants; stockyard and commission men have tried by legislative action to restrict direct buying of hogs by packers; small bankers fight branch banking; the NRA codes were full of restrictions on the introduction of new equipment. Business, if permitted to organize for the purpose, would erect high barriers against innovations—a protective tariff, so to speak, in favor of the existing against the new. Employers sometimes use unions to fight technological innovations. The flint glass workers' union, for example, was encouraged in 1899 by lamp chimney manufacturers to fight the lamp chimney machine in the plant of the MacBeth-Evans Company. The operators of thin-vein mines supported the efforts of the United Mine Workers to restrict the use of coal cutters by the thick-vein mines. Indeed, one of the dangers of national agreements between unions and associations of employers is that the agreements will be used by the less progressive employers to retard technological changes by progressive employers.[5]

The leading spokesmen of organized labor, until very recently at least, have been careful to disavow the policy of opposition to technological change. In fact, no stronger statements on the unwisdom and futility of opposing labor-saving devices can be found anywhere than those made by the leaders of organized labor themselves. Through bitter experience they have learned that the policy of obstruction is likely to involve the union in hopeless fights from which it emerges defeated and weakened.

Thus, at the 1923 convention of the cigar makers' union, Samuel Gompers argued that it is "absolutely futile for workmen to protest against or go on strike against the introduction of a new machine, a new device or a new tool,"[6] and George W. Perkins, then president of the cigar makers' union, said:

No power on earth can stop the at least gradual introduction and use of improved machinery and progressive methods of production. Any effort in that direction will react against those that attempt it. Our own condition proves that our efforts at restriction were futile, and ineffective, and injurious. Without an exception, every organization, since the beginning

---

[5] This statement does not mean that national or regional agreements are undesirable. Indeed it is difficult to see how collective bargaining could operate in the coal industry unless the cost differentials between mines were set by a blanket agreement. But provisions in national or regional agreements which prohibit technological innovation should be held contrary to the antitrust laws.

[6] *Cigar Makers' Official Journal*, October 1923, Vol. XLVII, p. 4.

of the factory system, that has attempted to restrict the use of improved methods of production has met with defeat.[7]

Speaking before the Bond Club of New York in March 1929, President Green of the American Federation of Labor said that "the American labor movement *welcomes* the installation and extension of the use of machinery in industry."[8] Matthew Woll, one of the most influential men in the American Federation of Labor, has said: "It is not a function of the labor movement to resist the machine. It is the function of the labor movement to turn the installation of machinery to the good of the worker."[9]

The persistent and severe unemployment since 1929 has altered the attitude of leaders toward machines. They do not advocate opposing the introduction of new machine processes. Nevertheless, one can search the *American Federationist* and other publications of labor in vain for a repetition of President Green's statement in 1929 that the American labor movement "welcomes" the installation of new machinery. Today union leaders, instead of emphasizing the futility of opposing new machines, stress the necessity of doing something about technological unemployment. The American Federation of Labor passed a resolution at its convention in San Francisco in 1934 calling for an investigation of displacement of labor by machines.[10] The Federation has supported bills in Congress calling for an investigation of labor-saving devices. The report of

---

[7] The same, August 1923, Vol. XLVII, p. 4.

[8] Address reprinted in the *Bridge Men's Magazine*, April 1929, Vol. XXIX, p. 228. Italics added.

[9] The *American Photo-Engraver*, March 1929, Vol. XXI, p. 325. An editorial in the *Shoe Workers' Journal* for March 1928 (Vol. XXIX, p. 15) said: "Experience should have taught us the folly of opposing new things. If they are poor our opposition is not necessary, and if they are good they will succeed, in spite of any opposition we can offer."

Mr. James O'Connell, late president of the Metal Trades Department of the American Federation of Labor, in his annual report for the year 1928 said: "Our trade union movement for a number of years has been committed to a policy of thoroughgoing co-operation with management. Instead of opposing the introduction of newer methods of machinery, we have declared our purpose to co-operate with the management. This policy is sound. To oppose improved methods of production would be as unjust and impracticable as to oppose the extension of education or the development of our civilization." American Federation of Labor, *Bulletin of the Metal Trades Department*, February 1929, Vol. XI, p. 7.

[10] Resolution No. 118.

the executive council to the Tampa convention in 1936 contains an extended discussion of technological changes which concludes with the statement: "Organized labor is determined to make sure that technological unemployment is not dealt with blindly in the years to come."[11] An extended discussion of the displacement of men by machines is contained in the report of John L. Lewis to the convention of the CIO in San Francisco in 1939.[12]

Despite the fact that the outstanding leaders of organized labor condemn opposition to labor-saving devices in emphatic terms, the policy is still practiced.[13] It is easy for leaders to generalize in sweeping terms about the futility of resisting labor-saving methods, but when a new device threatens to destroy the jobs of specific workers, it is difficult for those workers and their union to avoid fighting to keep their jobs in existence as long as possible. The lasters' union fought the lasting machine, the flint glass workers the lamp chimney machine, the stone cutters the stone planer, the granite cutters the hand-surfacing machine, the painters the paint-spraying machine, the street railway workers the one-man car, the cigar makers the leaf stripping machines,[14] and the musicians mechanical music devices.

Nor has the policy of opposition always been futile and unsuccessful. A large number of cases can be found, especially in the building trades, where the unions have succeeded over a period of years

[11] American Federation of Labor, *Report of the Proceedings of the Fifty-sixth Annual Convention,* 1936, pp. 169-73.

[12] See pp. 26-27. At the 1940 convention of the United Mine Workers, Mr. Philip Murray, a vice-president of the CIO, expressed himself as follows on the subject of machinery:

"I offer no argument against new machinery. I am wholly for the introduction of every known kind of new device that will speed up production and give more production. I am for it and for it wholeheartedly. . . . We think it should be the bounden duty of American industry to see to it that when a machine is put into an industry, no man or no woman is laid off." United Mine Workers of America, *Proceedings of the Thirty-sixth Constitutional Convention,* 1940, Vol. I, p. 287.

[13] Although union leaders may regard it as a mistake for unions to keep machines out of union shops by collective bargaining, they may be willing to support efforts to keep machines out of *all* shops by law. Strong support by the American Federation of Labor is reported for the ill-conceived bill introduced by Senator O'Mahoney in March 1940 to discourage the use of labor-saving machinery by taxation.

[14] There was a long strike against the stripping machine in the Tampa district in 1918-19. R. H. Mack, *Factors of Instability Affecting Production and Employment in the Cigar Manufacturing Industry,* p. 83.

in preventing or greatly restricting the use of various labor-saving machines and methods. Certainly the granite cutters have greatly restricted the use of the hand surfacer (and performed a public service in so doing);[15] the steamfitters have successfully resisted the use of pipe-cutting and threading machines on the job and also the assembling of plumbing fixtures in the shop instead of on the job; the stone cutters' union succeeded in keeping the stone planer out of St. Louis until 1915; the pocket-book workers' union for many years kept section work out of New York shops; and the painters are still successfully preventing the use of the spray gun on union jobs in many cities.

Even though a national union does not adopt the policy of opposing a new machine, many of its locals may fight the machine on their own initiative; or, in fact, they may do so in violation of definitely enunciated national policy. Indeed, as we shall see presently, one of the principal problems of national unions in making a policy of control effective is to prevent some locals from adhering to a policy of opposition and doing everything in their power to keep the new device out of union shops.

METHODS OF OPPOSITION

How does the policy of opposition express itself? It may take several forms. The union may:

1. Refuse to make the operation of the machine or new process a direct issue between itself and the employers but simply give encouragement and moral support to individual workers who refuse to operate the machine or who restrict production on it.
2. Refuse to permit its members to operate the machine but permit the employer to use non-members on it.
3. Attempt to restrict the use of the machine by demanding very high piece rates for operations on it or by limiting production on it.
4. Strike or threaten to strike if employers use the machine, and seek an agreement explicitly binding the employer not to use it.
5. Seek to prohibit the use of the machine by law.
6. Appeal to public opinion.

The first two policies—encouraging individual opposition to the machine without letting it become an issue between the union and the employer, or forbidding union members to operate the ma-

---

[15] This device was an extreme health hazard.

chine without striking against the use of it by employers—are likely to be pursued when the union is too weak to adopt a stronger policy or when a local union is pursuing a policy of opposition on its own initiative in conflict with the national union which is favoring a policy of control. Likewise the third policy—obstructing the use of the machine by organized restriction of output or by insisting upon very high piece rates—may be employed by local unions which wish to pursue a policy of opposition on their own responsibility but find their national union sponsoring a policy of control. Under these circumstances the locals may be unable to obtain authority from the national to strike against the machine and must content themselves with lesser obstructions. For example, after the cigar makers' union had decided as a national policy to accept the bunch-breaking and roll-up process (as will be explained later), some of the locals wished to continue the policy of obstruction and did so by the simple device of refusing to negotiate new piece rates for the process. As a result, it was necessary to amend the constitution in order to authorize the national officials to intervene in such cases and negotiate a scale for the local.

The national union itself, however, may in some cases prefer to oppose a machine by the indirect method of restricting output on it or insisting upon very high piece rates rather than by striking against its introduction. For example, if the union has an agreement extending to all union employers in the industry and if the new machine is being introduced by only a few employers, a strike against all union plants would be a clumsy and expensive weapon to employ. By standing out for very high piece rates on the machine or by insisting on limits on its output, the union may make the machine so unprofitable that employers cannot afford to use it. The flint glass workers' union discouraged the use of one of the earliest bottle-making machines by limiting the output so that the cost would be the same as by hand methods.[16] The flint glass workers also attempted to discourage the use of lamp chimney machines by demanding rates that would equalize the cost of chimneys produced by machinery and by hand.[17]

[16] G. E. Barnett, *Chapters on Machinery and Labor*, pp. 73-74.
[17] U. S. Department of Commerce and Labor, *Regulation and Restriction of Output*, Eleventh Special Report of the Commissioner of Labor, 1904, pp. 643-47.

The most direct form of opposition to a new machine or process is for a union to forbid its use by union members or threaten to strike against any employer who uses it. The old Lasters' Protective Union attempted to keep out the lasting machine by striking against its use.[18] Some years ago the stone cutters' union sought by rule to prohibit its members from using the stone pick—a heavy tool which enabled the men to do two or three times as much work as with a point and hammer.[19] When the stone planer was introduced, the union sought to prevent its use by strikes and embodied its policy of opposition in its constitution by a provision directing that "branches shall make every effort possible to prevent the introduction in their jurisdiction."[20] When the first window glass blowing machines came in about 1908, the window glass workers' union refused to make agreements with manufacturers who attempted to make window glass by both machine and hand methods and prohibited its members from accepting work in machine plants.[21]

The International Ladies' Garment Workers' Union first attempted to secure a provision in the trade agreement prohibiting the use of pressing machines in the New York cloak and suit industry. Unable to do so, the union sought to exclude the machines by shop strikes. Such strikes were contrary to the agreement, however, and their limited success led the union to attempt to confine the use of the machines to one for every five hand pressers.

A few unions seek to keep out labor-saving devices by law. A number of locals of the United Mine Workers at the 1936 convention proposed special taxes on loading machines, but the national union rejected the suggestion. The union may appeal to the public on the ground that a health hazard or an accident hazard is involved. Thus the painters' union has sought laws prohibiting the use of lead or other poisonous materials in paint sprayers, and the street railwaymen's union has sought ordinances prohibiting opera-

---

[18] A. E. Galster, *The Labor Movement in the Shoe Industry*, p. 137. See also *Shoe Workers' Journal*, January 1903, Vol. IV, pp. 13-17.

[19] Eleventh Special Report of the Commissioner of Labor, p. 344.

[20] Barnett, *Chapters on Machinery and Labor*, p. 40.

[21] A member who violated this rule was automatically suspended and, before he could return to membership and employment in a hand plant, was compelled to pay a fine and a reinstatement fee. "The Passing of the National Window Glass Workers," *Monthly Labor Review*, October 1929, Vol. XXIX, p. 779.

tion of the one-man car. The claim of the union that the new device creates a health or an accident hazard may or may not have merit: the real interest of the union is likely to be in the effect of the new device upon the number of jobs. The painters have had practically no success in obtaining legal prohibitions upon the use of paint sprayers, but the street railwaymen have succeeded in having one-man cars forbidden in a few communities.[22] In some cases, where the union has been unable to gain the complete prohibition of the one-man car, it has obtained ordinances limiting its use to short feeder lines in suburban districts where no heavy traffic exists. Many of such ordinances have now been repealed, and the rise of bus competition has compelled the union itself in many places to modify its attitude toward the one-man car.

A unique but unsuccessful method of opposing machinery was the appeal to public opinion by the American Federation of Musicians. Sound recording began to loom as a serious menace to movie orchestras in the summer of 1928. By the spring of 1929, about 4,000 of the 23,000 members employed in theaters had lost their jobs.[23] In some cities, notably Chicago and San Francisco, the union sought, by strikes or threats of strikes, to compel the employment of a given number of musicians. The union realized, however, that under most conditions strikes would be futile. Furthermore, it was aware of the danger of arousing public opposition by appearing

---

[22] In Detroit, for example, Division No. 26 of the street railwaymen's union obtained the passage of an ordinance forbidding the operation of one-man cars and buses that have a seating capacity of more than 40 passengers. (*The Motorman, Conductor and Motor Coach Operator*, February 1931, Vol. XXXIX, p. 12.) But such ordinances have not been confined to municipally owned street railway lines.

Despite the opposition of the union, the one-man car has spread with great rapidity. For example, in most cities the one-man car was not started until after 1919 or 1920. In 1932, however, the percentage of one-man car operation in certain leading cities was as follows: Buffalo, 100; Kansas City, Missouri, 100; Jersey City, 100; Newark, 100; Bridgeport, Connecticut, 100; Seattle, 97; Milwaukee, 92.3; Brooklyn, 71; Pittsburgh, 58.6; Louisville, 58; Indianapolis, 48; Portland, Oregon, 46; Philadelphia, 36; Baltimore, 26.6.

Evidence is lacking that one-man car operation is more hazardous than two-man car operation. Some statistical compilations indicate that accident frequency is less on one-man cars than on two-man cars. The comparison is misleading, however, because one-man car lines are usually the less congested ones where accidents may be expected to be less frequent than on two-man car lines. I know of no effort to correct for the difference in conditions.

[23] Letter from Pres. Joseph N. Weber, Mar. 29, 1929.

"in the role of rule-or-ruin partisans ready to attack and destroy something which the public might want."[24] Consequently, the union endeavored to create public aversion to machine-made music and a demand for hand-made music. In other words, it sought to raise a cultural issue.[25] Its essential position was that the machines "threaten the art of music with debasement." In support of this position the union advanced three principal contentions: (1) that despite any improvement in the mechanical means of production, synchronized music is bound to be frequently obtrusive or inane because it lacks the essential for real artistic quality—the interplay of conditions of the moment upon the mood of the artist; (2) that synchronized music tends to corrupt the public taste and hence to undermine the demand for good music;[26] (3) that the displacement of musicians would discourage young talent from entering the profession and would thus limit the number of outstanding musicians.

The union sought to reach the public in a variety of ways. Local unions were supplied with material to assist them in writing letters to editors of local papers; the national union issued special news releases to the press; direct appeals were made by letters to state federations of musical clubs, individual clubs, club leaders, and musical critics; and the president of the union visited large cities and endeavored to enlist the aid of civic organizations in the fight against "canned music." Most important of all, perhaps, was the national advertising campaign of the union against mechanical music. The campaign was supported by a special 2 per cent tax based on the minimum wage of each local.[27] The advertisements of the

[24] *International Musician*, February 1929, Vol. XXVI, p. 1.
[25] The strategy of the union is well summarized in the following statement from the official journal: "The agitation against synchronized music . . . had to be based upon a cultural premise, where it really belongs. Had we placed same merely on a protest against machine music because it threatened employment opportunities the result would have been nil, as protests of wage workers against development of machines have forever been in vain and, no doubt, will continue to be so." *International Musician*, May 1929, Vol. XXVI, p. 18.
[26] When "jazz" had become popular a few years earlier, the union had shown no concern for the public taste.
[27] The tax was authorized by the thirty-third annual convention of the union which met in Louisville in May 1928. The fund created by the tax was known as the "Theater Defense Fund."

union appeared in a large number of newspapers and magazines, but they had little effect in discouraging the spread of mechanical music. Undoubtedly the union was handicapped in its effort to raise the artistic issue by the fact that the programs displaced by mechanical music had little or no artistic appeal, whereas the music reproduced was that of outstanding orchestras and bands.

CONDITIONS THAT LEAD UNIONS TO OPPOSE TECHNOLOGICAL CHANGES

Opposition to technological change is such a natural reaction of those who are immediately injured by the change that considerable foresight and a careful weighing of consequences are necessary in order to induce a union to refrain from adopting the obvious and natural policy of obstruction. And yet it is important to observe that if the policy of obstruction is not adopted and if the supply of labor is permitted to adjust itself gradually to the change, the opposition will pass away. The structural ironworkers originally opposed the pneumatic hammer; now the iron workers would not think of opposing it—in fact, most of them do not know how to pound rivets by hand. When match plates first came into the foundry industry there was opposition to them from many members of the molders' union. Now the men ask for them.[28] Likewise there was great opposition among the molders to pneumatic rammers. Some shops wished to strike against them. Now they are preferred because they eliminate heavy work. Pouring the molten metal in foundries is hot and heavy work and sometimes hazardous. When this work was first transferred from molders to helpers, the molders strongly objected because the change meant less employment for them. Now that the labor supply has adjusted itself, the molders would object strongly to a return to the old methods.

The policy of obstruction is more likely to be practiced by craft unions than by industrial unions. The reason is obvious. When a union includes only the members of a single occupation, a machine or process which displaces men or reduces the required skill injures every member of the union. When the union includes all occupations in the industry, however, too few of its members are affected by most technological changes to permit the union to make a major

[28] The match plate reduces the work of finishing the mold by hand.

issue of the change. An official of the rubber workers' union explained its failure to oppose technological changes thus: "We couldn't afford to. There are too many small changes affecting too few of our people." This does not mean that industrial unions never oppose labor-saving devices, for sometimes a large proportion of the members may be affected. The opposition of the United Mine Workers to coal-cutting machinery and of some locals to the coal loaders is in point. On the other hand, the membership of the clothing workers' union has been unwilling to give strong support to the cutters in their opposition to labor-saving devices.

There are two principal occasions on which unions are likely to pursue a policy of obstruction toward new machines or processes: (1) when the policy seems to have a good chance of success, and (2) when there is nothing else to do. Certainly if a new machine or process is objectionable to a union and the chances of successful opposition are good, the union is quite certain to oppose it.

The building trades unions have probably had the greatest success in opposing labor-saving changes. One reason is that most of the changes opposed by these unions affect only a small part of the work done by the skilled craftsmen. The employer needs these men for other parts of the work. A second reason is that no single restriction imposed by these unions on labor-saving methods greatly increases the *total* labor cost of building. The percentage increase in the cost of performing *the particular operation* may be large, but if the operation is only a small part of the work, the effect upon total cost is small. This means that employers cannot afford to incur large expenses in order to prevent the restriction. Unfortunately, in the course of time a number of restrictions, each insisted upon and accepted because it was not important, may make an appreciable difference in cost. A third reason why building trades unions have been successful in their opposition to labor-saving methods is the fact that the areas of competition are so small that the unions are able to impose restrictions upon all employers in the area. Hence the competition of non-union employees does not compel the unions to give up their prohibitions upon labor-saving methods.

Sometimes the opposition of a union to a new machine or process may stimulate experimentation with another new machine or process that is even more objectionable to the union. In that event the union may be compelled to abandon its opposition to the first machine. The street railwaymen's union, for example, originally opposed the one-man car and endeavored to prevent its use. When the union found, however, that this opposition was accelerating the introduction of buses, it abandoned its opposition and used the one-man car to discourage the introduction of buses.

A union may oppose a new machine or process simply because no other policy serves its purpose. Such is the case, for example, when a new machine threatens to displace a very high proportion of hand workers. Control of the new process would mean jobs for such a small proportion of the displaced men that it would be of little help to the union. Or if the new machine or process requires a very different type of labor from that used on the old —a much lower degree of skill, for example—workers on the old process may not wish employment on the new. Under these circumstances also, a policy of control does not serve the interests of the union members.

In some cases the union will have difficulty in deciding between a policy of obstruction and a policy of control toward a new machine or process. The relative amount of labor displaced by any two machines is not the same; likewise there are differences in the attractiveness of jobs on the new process relative to jobs on the old. The members of the union must decide whether the displacement of labor and the drop in the attractiveness of the jobs are great enough to indicate a policy of obstruction rather than one of control. The members of the union may also wish to consider whether displacement produced by a new machine is temporary or permanent. Moreover, the reduction in costs and prices brought about by the new process may so increase the sales of the industry that there is no permanent drop in employment.[29] Almost never, however, do unions reject a policy of obstruction simply because, after carefully exploring the probable effects of a machine, they

[29] In 1935, for example, employment in the glass bottle industry was almost as large as in 1899. Technological changes had so reduced the costs of production and selling prices that the industry was able to increase its output from 1.1 billion units to almost 6 billion. *Investigation of Concentration of Economic Power,* Hearings before the Temporary National Economic Committee, Pt. II, "Patents: Automobile Industry, Glass Container Industry," p. 755.

decide that it will displace labor only temporarily and that ultimately it will increase employment. The long-run effects of a
machine are too uncertain and conjectural to be given much weight
against its immediate effects.

The union members may also wish to consider whether a policy
of obstruction helps to preserve their jobs on the old process indefinitely or only for a very limited number of years. Even if the
policy of obstruction enables the union to keep the new process
out of union shops, the old process may be gradually supplanted
if the new one enables non-union plants gradually to drive the
union plants out of business. The union members, however, may
insist on opposing a new process even though it is clear that the
policy of obstruction will only delay rather than prevent the ultimate supplanting of the old process by the new and even though
the policy may eventually bring about the destruction of the union
itself.[30] Nor are the union members necessarily irrational in supporting a policy which will eventually fail and which may destroy
their organization. Unions are composed of men who have a
limited time to live and who are primarily interested, therefore,
not in perpetuating their organization, but in obtaining within
their lifetime a return on the money they pay as monthly dues. If,
by insisting upon policies that eventually destroy the union, they
can protect their jobs from destruction for a few years, they may
prefer to sacrifice the union in order to prolong their jobs. This is
more likely to be true in case union policies are determined by the
rank and file rather than by the officers, because the latter are usually
more concerned than the rank and file with perpetuating the organization and building up its strength.

EXAMPLES OF SUICIDAL POLICIES OF OBSTRUCTION

A striking and illuminating illustration of suicidal opposition to
new methods by an exceedingly democratic organization is furnished by the cigar makers' union. The experience of the union
is significant, partly because the policy of obstruction was stubbornly

---

[30] The union may be destroyed because the union plants which are prevented
from using the new process are driven out of business and because the workers
in the non-union plants are unwilling to join an organization which is fighting
the machine or process by which they make their living.

pursued over a long period of time, and partly because the policy was enforced by the rank and file in the face of vigorous opposition from the officers. At the 1912 convention the membership of the union was reported to be 44,432 out of an estimated total of 107,000 persons in the cigar-making industry.[31] At the 1923 convention of the union, the membership was reported as only 23,155 although the number of persons in the industry had increased to about 114,500.[32] The president explained the drop in membership as follows:

The real cause of the present condition of the union is the restrictive rules in our Constitution, which in themselves drove men and especially women into the great non-union shops and were a potential force in helping to build them into large going concerns. These restrictions of all kinds, including the use of union label should be removed. They will have to be before we can be entirely successful.[33]

There are three principal steps in making a cigar: preparing the filler, putting on the binder, and cutting and putting on the wrapper. One man, performing all three operations, can turn out about 300 cigars a day.[34] Some years ago, however, specialization was introduced into the making of cigars. The cigar, when ready for the wrapper, is known as the bunch. One class of specialists, known as bunch breakers, did nothing but make bunches, that is, put the filler in the binder and roll on the binder. Other specialists, known as rollers, put on the wrapper. As a fast bunch breaker can keep two rollers busy, the workers were organized into teams consisting of one bunch breaker and two rollers. A fairly fast team can turn out 1,500 cigars in an eight-hour day. The specialization of labor prepared the way for mechanical aids, such as the moving belt and the suction table, which can be used to greatest advantage only when each operation is performed continuously.[35]

---

[31] *Cigar Makers' Official Journal*, September 1912, Vol. XXXVI, p. 14.
[32] The same, August 1923, Vol. XLVII, p. 5.
[33] The same, p. 3.
[34] There was one union member in New England with a national reputation who was able to make 700.
[35] The moving belt is used by the bunch breaker in making the bunch. The operator lays the binder flat on the belt, lays the filler in the binder, steps on a lever with her foot, and the movement of the belt rolls the binder around the filler. The suction table is used in cutting and rolling the wrappers. Perforations in the suction table make it possible to hold the wrapper by suction while it is

When the bunch-breaking and rolling-up system was introduced, practically all of the locals of the cigar makers barred the methods from the shops which they controlled and refused to take in persons who worked under the system. The national union did not prohibit the use of the new methods in union shops, but the constitution permitted the local unions to reject such methods, and most of them did so.[36]

By 1912 it was apparent to the leaders of the union that this policy was causing the manufacture of cigars to pass into the hands of non-union enterprises. The international president of the union strongly recommended to the convention which met in that year "removal of all unnecessary restrictions which are calculated to act as an impediment in the successful development of the union manufacturers' business under advancing modern methods of production."[37] As the initiation fee and the monthly dues of the union were high for the lower-paid specialists who worked at the new methods, the president recommended the creation of a special class of membership, known as Class A, for these workers, with an initiation fee of $1.00 and weekly dues of 15 cents.[38] The mere establishment of a special class of membership would do little good if the local unions refused to admit bunch breakers and rollers. The convention, therefore, adopted another amendment depriving local unions of the option of accepting or rejecting bunch breakers and rollers.[39] But changes in the constitution proposed by the convention did not become effective unless approved by a referendum

---

cut with a die. The suction also holds the wrapper in place while the operator rolls it around the bunch.

[36] The clause in the national constitution read: "The acceptance of rollers and filler breakers as members by initiation or by card, shall be optional with local union, except in places where the system has been already introduced." (*Cigar Makers' Official Journal*, October 1896, Vol. XXII, p. 7.) At the twenty-first convention of the union in October 1896, an unsuccessful attempt was made to tighten the restrictions against rollers and bunch breakers by adding the following clause to the constitution: "Rollers and filler breakers shall not be eligible to membership . . . except in places where the system has already been introduced." The same, "Proceedings," p. 34.

[37] *Cigar Makers' Official Journal*, September 1912, Vol. XXXVI, p. 16.

[38] The same, p. 13. These were half the regular dues of the union, and it was proposed that the members paying half dues should receive half benefits only under the union's various insurance and benefit plans.

[39] The same, January 1913, Vol. XXXVII, p. 3.

vote of the membership, and both the proposal to establish a special class of membership and the proposal to repeal the optional clause were rejected.[40] After two unsuccessful attempts to amend the constitution by the initiative, the membership in 1915 was finally persuaded to authorize the creation of Class A membership.[41]

The provision for a special Class A membership did not prove a success. The bunch breakers and rollers did not like to be graded and put in a special class, particularly one which marked them as inferior to the all-round hand cigar maker. "I am a cigar maker; why classify me?" was the attitude. Furthermore, the creation of a special class of membership did not go to the heart of the difficulty because it did not compel any local of the union to permit the bunch-breaking and roll-up system in its shops or to admit bunch breakers or rollers who came from other cities. The employers pointed out to the bunch breakers and rollers that even if they joined the union, they still could not work in most union shops. "That is the argument they used," said the president, "and by gosh it was a darned good one."[42]

At the 1920 convention of the union the president recommended that the Class A classification be abolished *on condition* that the optional clause (permitting locals to decide whether they would take in bunch breakers and roll-up workers) be eliminated.[43] Mr. Gompers, who was vice-president of the union, made a strong speech in favor of repealing the optional clause. "One of the greatest difficulties in organizing our trade," he said, "is the fact that a man or a woman may be a member in good standing in one locality and in good standing in our International Union, and still have his card disregarded and be recognized as a non-union member when

[40] The former was rejected by a vote of 4,574 to 5,535 and the latter by a vote of 4,106 to 5,565. The same, p. 25.
[41] Amendment of the constitution by initiative required a two-thirds vote. In May 1913, the Lancaster, Pa., local proposed an amendment creating Class A membership, but although there was a majority vote in its favor, it fell far short of receiving the necessary two-thirds majority. Another vote on the question was obtained at the initiative of the Syracuse local in February 1915, but again the proposal failed to receive the necessary two-thirds vote. The same, September 1913, Vol. XXXVII, p. 21; April 1915, Vol. XXXIX, p. 19; and October 1915, Vol. XXXIX, p. 23.
[42] Interview with the writer.
[43] *Cigar Makers' Official Journal*, April 1920, Vol. XLIV, p. 3.

he goes into another locality."[44] He called attention to the fact that three of the largest cigar manufacturers in Boston had transferred their plants to other places in order to use the bunch-breaking and roll-up system.[45]

The proposal to abolish the Class A membership was accepted by the convention and ratified by an overwhelming vote,[46] but the convention refused to repeal the optional clause,[47] which was, however, altered to read: "It shall be optional with local unions to permit the introduction of the roller and bunch-breaking system under their respective jurisdictions wherever this system does not exist at the present time."[48] This amendment was interpreted by President Perkins to mean that when the bunch-breaking and roll-up system already existed within the jurisdiction of a local union, the local would be bound to take in bunch breakers and rollers. The modification was approved by a large vote[49] but its practical significance was slight because there was no authority to compel a local union to admit bunch breakers or rollers.

The union constitution required that workers serve an apprenticeship of three years to be eligible for regular membership in the union and of six months to be eligible for Class A membership. One effect of abolishing the Class A membership, therefore, was to render ineligible for membership any person who had less than three years' experience at cigar making. As men can become proficient bunch breakers and rollers in a few months, the three-year requirement would prevent the union from admitting many competent workers. The leaders understood this, and the president recommended to the 1920 convention that, if the Class A membership were abolished, the term of apprenticeship be shortened. The convention, however, rejected a proposal to admit bunch breakers and rollers with two years' experience.[50] At the next convention, in 1923, President Perkins again recommended that the appren-

---

[44] The same, pp. 52-53.
[45] The same, p. 53.
[46] The same, August 1920, Vol. XLIV, p. 15.
[47] The same, May 1920, Vol. XLIV, p. 48.
[48] The same.
[49] The same, August 1920, Vol. XLIV, p. 15.
[50] The same, May 1920, Vol. XLIV, p. 92.

ticeship requirement be amended. The convention adopted, and the membership ratified, an amendment reducing the apprenticeship requirement one year in the case of bunch breakers and rollers.

At the 1923 convention the union finally repealed the optional clause. This meant that any employer who cared to change to machines or to the bunch-breaking and roll-up system might do so. But the action of the union had come at least fifteen years too late. The organization was but a shell of its former self. The manufacture of cigars had largely passed into the hands of non-union workers, and the restrictive policies of the union had made these workers either indifferent or positively hostile to it.

But though employers now had the right, under the laws of the union, to use the newer methods of manufacture, many locals continued to exclude these methods from the shops. They were able to do this because the universal method of wage payment in the industry was piecework. Hence the local unions were able to keep out the new methods by refusing to agree to rates which would make the new methods profitable. Some locals even demanded more for making cigars by the new labor-saving methods than by the old ones. The unwillingness of some locals to negotiate scales which permitted new methods led the 1925 convention of the union to authorize the general executive board to intervene in such cases and to negotiate a scale for the local union.

By the middle of the twenties the main problem of the cigar makers' union had ceased to be the bunch-breaking and roll-up system and had become the machine.[51] From 2.6 per cent of the national production in 1919, machine-made cigars had increased to 13.8 per cent in 1925. In 1929, 35.1 per cent of cigars were machine-made and in 1933, more than half, or 52.3 per cent.[52] The union,

---

[51] The so-called long filler machine was patented in 1917. It makes the complete cigar and requires four persons to operate: one to feed at the filler, one to lay the binder leaf, one to handle the wrapper, and a fourth to inspect and do patch work on the finished cigar. The machine turns out from 4,000 to 6,000 cigars a day. See "Technological Changes in the Cigar Industry and Their Effects on Labor," *Monthly Labor Review*, December 1931, Vol. XXXIII, pp. 1275 ff.

[52] Donald Creamer and Gladys V. Swackhamer, *Cigar Makers—After the Layoff*, WPA National Research Project, Studies of the Effects of Industrial Change on Labor Markets, Report No. L-1, p. 8.

weakened by its long opposition to the bunch-breaking and roll-up system, was now ready to accept the advice of national officers and to adopt the policy of accepting and controlling the machine. The changes made in the membership requirements of the union for the purpose of taking in workers under the bunch-breaking and roll-up system opened the doors to machine workers also.[53] In modifying the apprenticeship requirements in 1923, the union set a term of six months for machine operators. There was, however, much stubborn and bitter opposition to the machine from some local unions. Not only was the displacement of labor by the machines severe, but since the machines were operated almost entirely by women, they offered no employment opportunities to men, who comprised a majority of most locals. Nevertheless, under pressure from the national officers of the union, the convention of 1927 amended the constitution to permit the use of the union label by employers whose shops were mechanized.[54] The union did not find it easy to organize the machine workers and between 1925 and 1934, its membership fell from 23,400 to 7,000.[55] By November 1939, the membership had recovered to 12,487, roughly one-fifth of the workers in the industry.[56]

Another extreme case of union opposition to new machinery in the face of almost certain destruction of the organization is furnished by the window glass workers. The craft tradition in the union had always been strong—for example, the union had refused to admit snappers on the ground that their work was not skilled.[57]

[53] Although the policy of the national officers toward the machine did not differ from their traditional attitude toward new machines, they were probably influenced by the competition of cigarettes and by the need for a five-cent cigar to meet that competition. The machine made possible such a cigar. Cigar production reached its all-time peak in 1920 (although per capita consumption had been declining since about 1907). By 1925, production had declined over 20 per cent.

[54] It is interesting to note, however, that of twelve amendments to the constitution submitted by local unions between 1930 and 1939, four proposed that a separate union label be established for machine-made cigars. *Cigar Makers' Journal*, January 1940, Vol. LXIV, pp. 14-15.

[55] Leo Wolman, *Ebb and Flow in Trade Unionism*, pp. 184-85.

[56] *Cigar Makers' Journal*, January 1940, Vol. LXIV, p. 3.

[57] As a matter of fact, there was considerable skill in it. The snapper was a helper who, after the gatherer had collected a lump of glass at the end of his pipe, carried it to the blower and, after the cylinder was blown, cracked open the cylinder, removed it from the "swing-hole" near the tank (where the blowing was done), squared each end, and split it on one side.

When the first window glass making machines were introduced about 1908, the union adopted a strong policy of obstruction. When the sheet-drawing machine became important after the war, some members of the union favored taking in machine operators and making agreements with machine plants. A referendum was held, and the proposal was decisively defeated. Not until 1927 was the union willing to authorize its members to accept work in machine plants and to attempt to organize these plants. By that time, however, it was too late. The 1927 convention, which adopted the change in policy, also authorized the disbanding of the union, if, after a year's experiment, sufficient progress in organizing the machine plants were not made. Acting under this resolution, the union was formally disbanded on June 30, 1928.[58]

RESULTS OF THE POLICY OF OBSTRUCTION

To what extent has the opposition of unions to technological changes prevented the use of new machines and new methods? As we have seen, in the cigar industry and in the window glass industry, the union succeeded in keeping a machine out of union shops for some years. The building trades also have succeeded over a considerable period of time in compelling some types of work to be done on the job rather than in the shop. Were union control of industry quite complete, unions might be able to hinder seriously the use of new machines and processes. The unions, however, are not able to prevent the use of new machines and new processes in non-union shops. If the innovation gives non-union employers an important competitive advantage, the policy of obstruction may cause the union shops gradually to be driven out of business—as in the window glass and the cigar industries. The resulting expansion of the non-union part of the industry represents a wasteful duplication of capital.

Does retarding the introduction of technological change into union shops cause the rate of change to approximate more or less closely the optimum rate?[59] Pigou has expressed the opinion that

---

[58] "The Passing of the National Window Glass Workers," *Monthly Labor Review*, October 1929, Vol. XXIX, pp. 776-87.

[59] The optimum rate may be defined as the rate which permits the most rapid growth of the national net income.

under conditions of competition the actual rate of change corresponds to the optimum rate because any losses to displaced productive factors are offset by gains to consumers.[60] An old process will not be abandoned for a new one so long as the direct labor and the repair costs are less than the *total* costs (including the return on the investment) of the new process. Hence every unit produced by the new process is sold to consumers at a price which is less than the prime costs of production at the old process.

Pigou, however, considers only whether the losses to the owners of the old machines are offset by gains to the consumers. He overlooks the fact that the change may involve costs to wage earners and to others in the community. For example, a railroad which decides to abandon a division point in order to achieve certain savings in operating trains and maintaining equipment treats those savings as a net amount. It takes no account of costs which fall on its employees and the inhabitants of the division point—the amount of housing and business property which will be rendered useless by the change and the cost of moving people and furniture to different towns. Likewise, when an employer decides to abandon a process because the total costs on a new process would be less than the direct labor costs on the old one, he takes no account of the fact that the saving in labor costs to him may be partly offset by costs to the displaced workers—the cost of moving and possibly of learning a new occupation and, in the case of large displacements of labor occurring in small communities, the losses on property that is made idle by a drop in population. Under conditions of competition, therefore, it is probably true that the actual rate of change exceeds the optimum rate.[61] It does not follow, however, that trade unions by retarding the rate of change cause it to approach more closely to the optimum rate. They may cause it to be as much less than the optimum rate as it was formerly above it.[62]

---

[60] A. C. Pigou, *The Economics of Welfare,* 3d ed., pp. 190-91.

[61] At this point it is important to keep clearly in mind the distinction between the rate of discovery and the rate at which new discoveries are put into use. The preceding discussion of the optimum rate relates simply to the rate at which discoveries are put into use. The rate of discovery that is needed is determined by the propensity of the community to save—that is, the discoveries must be sufficient to put the current savings of the community promptly to work.

[62] In so far as unions stand firmly against accepting wage cuts on the old

The policy of obstruction is likely to hamper the union in organizing non-union plants in which the new process is used. Workers in these plants naturally do not wish to join a union which opposes the machine or methods by which they make their living. The experience of the window glass workers and cigar makers on this point is illuminating. Indeed the attitude of hostility toward the union is likely to persist long after the union has abandoned its policy of opposition to the labor-saving device.

The opposition of unions to a machine or new method and their organized and persistent criticism of its shortcomings are likely to stimulate efforts to improve the machine and to remove its defects. The one-man car illustrates the point. The street railwaymen's union severely criticized the one-man car and sought ordinances to prohibit its use on the ground that it was unsafe. This criticism led to important improvements. One is the "dead-man control," which automatically shuts off the power, applies the brakes, and balances the doors (so that they can be opened by hand from within or outside the car) in the event that the operator ceases to control the car by having his hand on the control handle or his foot on the control valve. Another safety feature is an interlocking device which prevents the operator from starting the car when the doors are open or from opening the doors while the car is in motion. Thus the union's policy of opposition (1) has performed a substantial public service by promoting improvement of the car and (2) has tended to defeat itself by stimulating changes which weakened the union's case against the one-man car.

When the policy of obstruction merely postpones the introduction of a machine or process until the machine has been perfected and until the union has been weakened by depression, it increases the displacement of labor by the new machine and causes such displacement to occur precisely when the men have the least chance to obtain other employment promptly. From the standpoint of the whole community, however, the postponement of the installation of new machines until a period of depression is desirable. A de-

---

process, they tend to accelerate rather than retard the rate at which new machines and processes are put into use. This matter will be discussed briefly in the next chapter in connection with the policy of competition.

pression is a time when too little new machinery is being purchased. Since the labor required to make a machine is much more than the labor it displaces in the course of a year, postponement of machine installations to periods of depression raises the total volume of employment precisely when that will do the most good.

In a large number of cases, the policy of obstruction proves to be temporary. One reason is that the interest of the union in opposing the machine diminishes as the use of the machine spreads. For example, in the early days of a machine, when the number of hand workers is still large and the number of jobs on the machine is still small, the opportunity to transfer to the machine may mean little to the hand workers. As more and more hand workers die, retire, or are displaced and leave the trade, and as the use of the machine spreads and the number of jobs connected with it increases, the opportunity to work on the machine becomes more and more important to the hand workers.[63]

A second reason why the policy of opposition often proves temporary is that in the early days of a new machine its superiorities over the old process may not be sufficient to warrant employers in making a long and expensive fight in order to introduce it into

---

[63] At the convention of the painters' union in September 1929 an effort was made to change the union policy from local option, which in effect meant opposition, to one of acceptance and control. Speaking in support of a resolution submitted by nine New York locals Mr. Philip Zausner said that the delegation from New York had changed its attitude on the spray painting machine from "unalterable opposition" to "that of accepting a situation as it is and trying to remedy it." "The spraying machine," said Mr. Zausner, "whether we like it or not, is making inroads into our industry every day . . . we cannot prohibit its use, but must accept its use and provide regulatory measures for the lives and health of our men." (Brotherhood of Painters, Decorators, and Paperhangers of America, *Proceedings of the Fourteenth General Assembly*, 1929, pp. 193-94.) Strong opposition to abandoning the policy of local option led to the appointment of a commission to study the spray machine. (The same, p. 210.) The commission, however, did not confine itself to a study of facts; it reached conclusions and made recommendations. The commission found that the solution of the spray gun problem "is not a local but a national one," that the health hazards associated with spray painting are subject to control and in fact were already being controlled, that with proper regulation "the adoption of the spraying machine as a tool of the trade will materially benefit our members." Behind these conclusions was the fact, pointed out by the commission, that the work lost to the union members was "enormous" as it consisted not only of the loss in spray operation but also of the loss of brush work on jobs obtained by non-union contractors. Hence the conclusion that the policy of regulation would open up a new field to union members and increase the membership of the painters' union.

union shops. As the machine is improved and the savings to be achieved from its use become greater, employers can afford to make a more expensive fight to win the opportunity to use the machine. They are likely to take advantage of a period of depression when unemployment is great and the union is weak in order to enforce a change.[64]

The fact that the policy of obstruction tends to be a temporary one leads to its supplementation or replacement by the policies of competition or control. These policies are discussed in the next two chapters.

[64] The employers in the women's garment industry, for example, greatly extended their use of pressing machines when the union was weakened by the great depression following the collapse of 1929.

CHAPTER VIII

TECHNOLOGICAL CHANGE—THE POLICY
OF COMPETITION

Unless the union is able to control all employees in a particular competitive area, the purely negative policy of seeking to prevent the use of new machines or new methods will eventually become unsatisfactory to the union members. Non-union employers, as has been shown, will gradually obtain a growing share of the business, and unemployment among union members will steadily increase. Consequently, the union will sooner or later find itself compelled (1) to make concessions to union employers for the purpose of helping them to compete with non-union plants, (2) to permit union employers to use the new machine or process, subject to such restrictions as the union may be able to impose, or (3) to adopt a combination of the two. The first is the policy of competition; the second is the policy of control; and the third, of course, is competition supplemented by control. Thus the policies of competition and control very often are outgrowths of an original policy of opposition. Notable instances of the policy of competition are the efforts of the glass bottle blowers to compete with the Owens automatic, of the telegraphers to compete with the teletype in the brokerage field, and of the street railwaymen to compete with buses.

REASONS FOR THE POLICY OF COMPETITION

What determines whether a union decides to adopt either a policy of competition or a policy of competition supplemented by control? In the main, union policy is determined by three considerations.

1. The union is influenced by whether concessions in the form of wage reductions or changes in working rules will prevent, at least for some years, the displacement of a considerable number of men. If the superiority of the machine is too great, the union will

not attempt to compete with it.[1] Even though the machine may be far cheaper than the hand process on some types of work or under certain conditions, it may possess little or no superiority on other types of work or under other conditions. The first bottle-making machines, for example, were adapted to making wide-mouthed ware and only gradually were improved so that they could make other types of bottles. Hence, for some years, there was an area in which the hand process could compete with the machine. Coal-cutting machines were cheaper than pick mining where veins were thick and reasonably horizontal. But only gradually was the machine developed so that it could displace pick mining in mines where veins were thin and inclined. The size of the order is usually important in determining the relative advantages of machine and hand processes. A machine which has great superiority on large orders may have little or none on small orders, particularly when there are variations in the specifications for individual orders which require that the machine be reset and tools and dies changed.

2. The union is influenced by whether the competition of the machine can be met without the necessity of concessions by too many members of the union. This is why a policy of competition is more readily pursued by unions containing mainly pieceworkers than by unions composed largely of hourly workers. Pieceworkers can accept reductions in the rates on the particular operations which are most threatened by the machine and on which concessions might preserve work for the hand process. A union of hour workers, how-ever, has difficulty in managing a reduction because it must either accept two hourly rates (which means keeping track of the time of each man to be paid at each rate) or accept a general wage reduction (which is not likely to be satisfactory to the members).[2]

---

[1] The commercial telegraphers' union, for example, did not attempt to compete with the teletype in the commercial and news fields, where its superiority was great, but did attempt to compete in the brokerage field, where the superiority was much less. When automatic machinery began to invade the iron mold department of the flint glass industry, the union refused to consider a wage reduction on the ground "that no wage reduction would remedy that situation." American Flint Glass Workers' Union, *Proceedings of the Fifty-first Convention,* 1927, p. 93.

[2] This is a special case of the general proposition mentioned in the first chapter, that unions, being democratic organizations, are not able to consider the effect of their policies upon employment unless the employment of a large proportion of the members is affected.

3. The union is influenced by the amount of displacement caused by the machine and the kind of jobs provided by it. If the machine provides very few jobs in relation to the number that it destroys and if the new jobs require much less skill than the old, the union is less interested in controlling the machine and the jobs which go with it. This means that it is more likely to be interested in attempting to preserve and prolong the jobs of its members on the old process by the policy of competition.

At no time, however, do unions easily bring themselves to adopt the policy of competition. The reason is that the policy runs counter to deeply established traditions of trade unions. Nearly all unions take it for granted that the demand for labor is inelastic and that the volume of employment and the incomes of their members would not be maintained or increased by making concessions in wages or working conditions. This is an understandable error because, if *very brief* periods of time are considered, demand for most types of labor by a plant or industry is inelastic. It rapidly rises in elasticity, however, as the period of time increases. At any rate, the fact that most unions have been in the habit of underestimating the elasticity of the demand for their labor greatly increases the difficulty of the leaders in persuading the rank and file to consider a policy of competition toward new machines and processes.

The willingness of a union to pursue a policy of competition may depend upon the willingness of employers to pursue the same policy. This is well illustrated by the case of the railroads. The substantial encroachments of trucks, buses, airplanes, and private automobiles upon railroad traffic and employment might seem to call for a policy of competition—an offer to accept changes in wage rates and working rules on condition that the railroads pass on the concessions in the form of lower rates and more modern service— more frequent, faster, and lighter trains, particularly in freight service. Railroad managements, however, have not been convinced of the desirability of reducing freight rates and of developing new forms of service for the purpose of meeting competition. In fact, the roads have elected in the main to pursue a policy of compensation rather than a policy of competition—that is, to seek compensation for their loss of business by endeavoring to obtain higher rates on certain products. The unions have pursued the same policy: they have attempted to gain compensation for the loss of jobs by a shorter working day without a reduction in pay.

It is important to observe that the organization of the railroad industry is well adapted to discourage any experimentation with a policy of competition by individual roads or unions. The exchange of traffic places the roads in an ideal position to penalize any road that experiments with a rate or service policy which the others disapprove. On the labor side, there are five unions involved in the actual conduct of transportation. Changes in rules and wage rates applying to this service must receive the acceptance of all five unions before the road can take advantage of them. Probably in no other industry in the country are the cards stacked so heavily in favor of the *status quo* and against change and experimentation.

SOME CASES OF THE POLICY OF COMPETITION

An illustration of successful pursuit of the policy of competition is furnished by the cloth cap industry of Chicago. In April 1922, the employers sought to change the methods of work by subdividing the sewing operations and specializing the operators. Until this time each operator had made the entire cap. The method of wage payment in the industry was standards of production—that is, workers were paid by the hour, but the hourly rate of each worker was determined by his average hourly output over a period of time. Since the new methods of production would enable the workers to increase their output, the employers believed that new standards of production were needed. In fact, unless the standards were changed, the new methods of work would have the principal effect of raising earnings of the workers rather than reducing costs of production. The union was strongly opposed to subdividing the work because this would eventually mean the displacement of all-round operators by narrow specialists. Consequently, it objected to changes in the standards. The dispute was submitted to an umpire, who decided in favor of the employers and held that the greater productivity of the new methods warranted an increase of about 15 per cent in the standards of production which determined hourly wages. The union refused to accept the decision and struck. After a week a settlement was made which provided that the union would accept a 5 per cent reduction in wages in return for a promise on the part of the employers not to adopt the new methods of work during the life of the agreement.

Particularly useful in shedding light on the conditions which govern union policy toward new methods and machines is the experience of the glass bottle blowers' union. The first machines were introduced in the bottle industry in the closing decade of the last century. These machines are known as "semi-automatics" in contrast with the Owens machine introduced about 1905 and known as the "automatic." The semi-automatic required that the glass be gathered from the tank by hand; the Owens automatic withdrew the glass by suction. When the semi-automatics were first introduced, the union made a brief but unsuccessful effort to compete with them by accepting a 45 per cent reduction in the hand price on fruit jars (the principal machine-made product at that time) and by removing the limits on the daily output of handworkers making fruit jars. These concessions proved insufficient, especially in view of the fact that the machines made more uniform ware than the hand methods, and the union soon abandoned the policy of competition for one of control. Its efforts to control the semi-automatics will be discussed in the next chapter.

Quite different was the policy of the union toward the Owens automatics. The semi-automatics required skilled workers, but the automatics required only semi-skilled attendants. Furthermore, the Owens machine displaced so many men that even if the hand blowers and semi-automatic operators had been willing to accept employment on the automatics, few of them could have obtained it. Consequently, although the union endeavored to control the Owens machine (that is, to have it manned with union members), it directed its main efforts toward competing with the machine. President Hayes stated the position of the union clearly at the 1911 convention. After pointing out that the general policy of labor was to control machinery, he said:

. . . in this respect we are at a greater disadvantage than any other union in the country. We cannot get control of the automatic nor meet it on our own terms, because it does not employ any glass workers. Therefore our object must be to create conditions that will enable us to keep our members employed and at the same time maintain the strength, discipline and usefulness of our organization.[3]

The union hoped that the semi-automatic machines would enable its members to compete with the Owens machine. It soon became evident, however, that drastic concessions would be necessary if the union was to keep its members employed. Accordingly, the union gave up its summer stop, permitted employers to operate three shifts, and, most important of all, accepted drastic cuts in piece rates on certain types of ware.

From early days in all branches of the glass industry it had been customary for factories to shut down during July and August and sometimes longer. The Owens automatics, however, had from the outset operated the year around. In 1908, the union permitted the semi-automatic machines to operate all summer; in 1912, it consented to a summer stop of one month for hand manufacturers and of two weeks for machine plants; and in 1917 it gave up the summer stop altogether, with the provision, however, that each blower take a compulsory vacation of four weeks and each machine operator one of two weeks.

In permitting three shifts instead of the customary two shifts of eight and a half hours each, the union was more interested in creating jobs for displaced men than in helping employers reduce their costs. Nevertheless, for the employers whose plants were adapted for continuous operation, three shifts would mean a reduction of costs. Opposition was encountered from some manufacturers whose plants could not be operated continuously without expensive changes.[4] In the 1911 agreement, however, the union obtained a rule regulating the operation of semi-automatic machines with three shifts, and in 1912 a rule applicable to hand blowers was obtained stipulating that "where there are a sufficient number of idle com-

---

[3] Glass Bottle Blowers' Association of the United States and Canada, *Proceedings of the Thirty-fifth Annual Convention*, 1911, p. 44.

[4] This is a point of considerable importance because it sheds light on one side of the problem that develops when collective bargaining on the employer side is conducted through an association of employers. Such associations have many advantages, but they sometimes become instruments by which some employers throttle technological change by other employers.

petent men and the branch so requests, every effort shall be made by the manufacturers to employ three shifts."

The big concession of the union to the automatic machine took the form of drastic reductions in certain piece rates. It was not easy for the union members or even their leaders to see any advantage in accepting rate cuts, for they believed that lower rates would do little to retard the spread of the machine. Nevertheless on small orders and on certain types of bottles the superiority of the automatic was relatively small and a reduction in rates might determine the ability of employers to compete. In 1909, the employers asked for a general reduction of 15 per cent on piece rates, urging that it would discourage the adaptation of the machine to new lines of work. The union refused to concede any reductions on ware which the machine was not then making, but accepted a 20 per cent reduction on certain classes of bottles—beers and sodas of 10 ounce weight or over, and brandies and catsups of 8 ounce weight or over—and a 10 per cent reduction on liquor ovals of 6 ounces or over. These classes included wares which the machine had been making successfully, or which it was beginning to produce.[5] In 1912 the union agreed to a discount of 20 per cent on piece rates for all ware made on the automatic and, in 1914, a 20 per cent cut on small sizes which the Owens machines were then beginning to make. Union officials believed that these cuts helped to retard the spread of the machine and to maintain employment for union workers.

Shortly after the acceptance of these cuts the position of the union was radically transformed by the introduction of a new device known as the "feed and flow." As this device produced bottles at much lower cost than the semi-automatics and as it employed considerably more labor than the Owens machine, the union was anxious to control it and to use it for the purpose of competing with the automatic. The activities of the union in connection with the feed and flow device illustrate the policy of control and will, therefore, be discussed in the next chapter.

Interesting because of the unusual methods employed is the attempt of the commercial telegraphers' union to compete with the

[5] G. E. Barnett, *Chapters on Machinery and Labor*, p. 102.

telegraphic printer in the brokerage field. The printer or "telegraphic typewriter," as it is sometimes called, dispenses with the Morse operator. At the sending end of the line an operator types the message on a keyboard similar to that of a typewriter and at the receiving end the message is recorded. For more than 25 years the printer has been displacing Morse in the general commercial and newspaper fields. Both Western Union and Postal use the machines for most of their business and so do the newspaper services —the Associated Press and the United Press.

Until the late twenties, however, the printer was little used in the brokerage field. One reason was doubt whether the printer was as fast as Morse. More important was the belief that the printer was less accurate than Morse. Errors of single letters are not usually serious in ordinary messages because a mistake is self-evident. In the brokerage business, however, where symbols and abbreviations are used, an error in a letter may cause the wrong security to be bought or sold, and an error in a figure may alter the price offered or asked. In most instances such errors would probably be detected before the order was executed, but there is always the possibility that they might not be, particularly in the case of errors in symbols in orders to buy or sell "at the market" or small errors in price.[6]

In the commercial and news-service fields, where the superiority of the printer is clear and substantial, the basic policy of the union was to control the machine rather than to compete with it. These efforts will be described in the next chapter. On the brokerage wires, where the Morse operator held his own until recently and where the superiority of the printer was not at first evident, the union attempted to compete with the machine.

When it became clear that a determined effort would be made to introduce the printer into the brokerage field, the 1928 convention of the union established a "Broker Printer Policy Committee" with the function of determining the union policy in dealing with the machine. The committee concluded "that the printer is not sufficiently accurate, flexible or efficient for this most technical and

---

[6] Accurate transmission of messages by the telegraphic printer depends upon the functioning of the electrical apparatus. A five-unit code signal system is used. The signals are of uniform length sent at different intervals of time. There are 32 different signals. These can all be sent by dividing a given unit of time into

important branch of telegraphy."[7] It concluded that brokers were being deceived by printer salesmen concerning the adaptability of the machine to brokers' work. In an attempt to counteract the selling talk of the printer salesmen, the committee prepared a brief, outlining the union's case. This was printed under the title of "Your Wire Room" and was distributed widely to brokers, chief operators, and operators.

About this time the firm of Logan and Bryan was considering the advisability of replacing Morse with printers. The firm argued that 50 per cent more wire traffic could be handled on a printerized circuit than on a Morse circuit. At the suggestion of union officials a test of the relative speed of Morse operators and the printers was agreed upon. Two New York—Chicago circuits were set up and a plan was arranged whereby the business handled on both systems would be identical.[8] The results, according to the union, showed that the Morse was actually faster than the printer. The average production for the four-day test was as follows:

	Number of Messages per Hour	
	Sent	Received
Morse	225	231
Printer	219	228

Despite the results of this test, negotiations between Logan and Bryan and the union were broken off on March 12, 1929, when the firm announced its refusal to use Morse operators on the New York—Chicago printer unless they were better qualified than the

---

five intervals, during each of which current may or may not be transmitted. If the electrical impulses are molested by any interference as they travel over the wire, the intervals may be shortened or lengthened and the result may be a wrong combination at the receiving station. Then the letter recorded at the receiving station will not be the letter pressed on the keyboard at the sending station.

Accurate transmission also requires that the motors on all machines on a circuit be in absolute synchronism at all times. If motors are thrown out of synchronism by fluctuations in the current supplied or by improper adjustments in a machine, the trouble is usually evident because the machine brings in a jumble of characters, but momentary interferences caused by storms or other factors may cause errors in single letters or figures.

[7] *Commercial Telegraphers' Journal*, February 1929, Vol. XXVII, No. 2, p. 22.

[8] One day the printer handled the live business and the Morse operator handled the duplicates of the same messages. The next day Morse men handled the live business and the printer the duplicates. The test covered four days. The Morse contestants were two of Logan and Bryan's employees. The printer operators were among the best in New York and Chicago.

printer operators and unless they were willing to work on the "printer scale," which would amount to a cut of $30 a week in wages.[9] The result was a strike which the union lost.[10]

As the speed and accuracy of the printer have been improved and as printer operators themselves have developed more speed and proficiency, the union has had to face the fact that the Morse operators could not hold their own against the printer even in the brokerage field. Hence the union was compelled to place less emphasis upon competition with the printer and to concentrate upon controlling it.

The window glass workers accompanied their uncompromising opposition to the machines with a vigorous effort to compete with them. The first window glass making machine was a cylinder-drawing machine. It displaced the gatherers (who collected a lump of glass from the tank at the end of a pipe) and the blowers (who blew out the cylinder from the lump of glass). The cylinders still had to be flattened and cut, exactly as in the hand plants. The machines were introduced shortly after the turn of the century and were first used by the American Window Glass Company. At this time the window glass workers were split into three unions. One union, whose members worked in the plants of the American Window Glass Company, accepted the machine; the other two, the Window Glass Workers' Association and Local Assembly No. 300, adopted a policy of uncompromising opposition. But both of the unions opposing the machine recognized the necessity of protecting the union manufacturers and their employees against competition from the machine. The agreement of the Window Glass Workers' Association for the blast of October 1, 1902 to June 30, 1903 provided

that if any window-glass blowing machine or machines is operated to a sufficient extent to affect the market by reason of their cost of production being lower than this scale, at which time and under such circumstances this scale shall be subject to revision upon demand of the manufacturers so affected by such machine or machines, the said conditions to be determined by the wage committee.[11]

---

[9] *Commercial Telegraphers' Journal*, March 1929, Vol. XXVII, No. 3, p. 45.
[10] The same, p. 46.
[11] "The Passing of the National Window Glass Workers," *Monthly Labor Review*, October 1929, Vol. XXIX, p. 777.

Local Assembly No. 300 also provided for the re-opening of the wage scale in the event that the machine-made glass affected the selling price of window glass.

In 1910 a price war broke out between the American Window Glass Company and the non-machine manufacturers. By this time the Window Glass Workers' Association and Local No. 300 had united to form the National Window Glass Workers' Association. Shortly before this, the union and the non-machine manufacturers had signed a scale for the blast of 1910-11 raising wage rates 40 per cent. The price war required a prompt reduction in wages to save the hand manufacturers from ruin. Not only were wages cut, but it was agreed that the wage committee would consider further reductions in case the American Window Glass Company further reduced its prices. The 1911-12 agreement reduced wages in the hand plants still more and in addition established a sliding scale by which wages would automatically fall when the price of glass was reduced. This, however, was not enough. The workers were forced to accept another cut of 30 per cent, which brought weekly earnings down to about $15.[12] With the ending of the price war in February 1912, wages were substantially increased.

By 1919 a new machine, the sheet-drawing machine, had become a competitive menace. This machine makes the glass in a flat piece instead of the cylinder and thus eliminates a third skilled craft, the flattener. In an attempt to meet the competition of this machine the union in its agreement for 1924-25 accepted a wage reduction of 25 per cent and gave the manufacturers the right to operate the year around.[13] The union also attempted to provide employment for its members by leasing a window glass plant in Huntington, West Virginia, in 1924. Labor organizations do not go into business themselves until their situation and that of their members have become desperate. The conclusion of the union's losing fight against the machine has been summarized in the previous chapter.[14] As it became more and more evident that the policy of competition in combination with opposition was a failure, some

[12] The same, p. 780.
[13] The machine plants did not observe the customary summer shut-down of two months or more.
[14] See pp. 222-23.

members of the union began to urge a policy of control. This policy, at first decisively rejected by the rank and file, was at last accepted, but too late to save the union.

RESULTS OF THE POLICY OF COMPETITION

The policy of competition must not be expected to halt the introduction of a labor-saving device or even greatly to restrict the field of its use. The very use of a new machine or device leads to great improvements in its construction and to the gradual elimination of defects which limit the field of its superiority. Consequently, although the union by a policy of concessions may be successful at first in greatly restricting the use of the machine, the area of the machine's superiority will steadily increase[15] and the efforts of the workers at the old technique to compete with the new will become steadily more hopeless.

This does not mean, however, that the policy of competition is a mistake and a total failure. If the concessions substantially retard the displacement of labor by the new technique, they will enable many workers to reach the normal retiring age without being displaced. In fact, if the policy of competition prevents the new technique from displacing labor faster than the attrition rate in the industry, it may prevent any displacement of labor whatever.[16] The extent to which it pays workers to make concessions for the purpose of keeping their old jobs depends, of course, upon what they would be able to earn in other employments. For workers who have reached middle age this is likely to be considerably less than they have been accustomed to earn in the occupation in which they are skilled. At the same time that the displacement of workers is being retarded, the retirement of old equipment is being postponed. Thus the depreciation allowances and the savings of the community are kept available for new uses, and investment funds are economized.

If the policy of competition does not lead to the ultimate extinc-

---

[15] The development of the molding machine, the Owens machine in the bottle industry, automatic feeders in the printing industry, the coal cutting machines, the one-man car illustrate the point.

[16] Assuming, of course, that new workers do not enter the declining trade. Sometimes temporary spurts of seasonal or cyclical activity draw them in.

tion of the union, as it did in the case of the window glass workers, it is almost certain to be superseded eventually by the policy of attempting to control the new machine. Obviously, if the union is to exist within the field affected by the new technique, it must include the workers who operate the new machine or device. Hence the ultimate adoption of a policy of control is almost a foregone conclusion. The workers at the old process may oppose the policy; they may be unwilling to learn the new technique themselves and reluctant to have the union admit workers who know it; but eventually the inescapable choice must be faced: "Will the union cease to exist, or will it attempt to control the new technique?" Even the window glass workers, strong as was their craft tradition and uncompromising as was their opposition to the machine, made a last futile effort, before going out of existence, to organize the machine workers. The officers of a union are likely to see the necessity of supplementing the policy of competition with one of control long before the rank and file; and the fate of the union is likely to depend upon the ability of the officers to persuade the rank and file to adopt the policy of control soon enough for it to be effective.

CHAPTER IX

TECHNOLOGICAL CHANGE—THE POLICY OF CONTROL

Our discussion of the policies of opposition and competition has shown that in the overwhelming majority of cases these policies are temporary. As a new machine or process is perfected and becomes more and more superior to the old methods, the union must either gain control of the jobs that go with the new machine or process and of the men who hold these jobs or else go out of existence—as did the old window glass workers' union. Consequently, the policy of accepting a new machine or process and attempting to control its operation is by far the most important of the several policies of unions toward technological change.

NATURE OF THE POLICY OF CONTROL

In general terms, the policy of control simply means that the union seeks to make working conditions and wages on the jobs created by the new technique a matter of agreement between employers and the union. The policy, however, is pursued under widely different circumstances and its specific objectives may vary greatly. In some cases, for example, employers may be quite ready to use union men on the new machine—as in the case of the one-man car, the spray gun in the painting business, the pressing machine in the women's garment industry. Under these circumstances the adoption of the policy of control may represent a concession by the union to employers—a withdrawal of opposition and obstruction to the machine or process. In other cases, employers may have more or less strong objections to the use of union men on the machine or process and to making agreements governing their employment on the machine—as in the case of the molding machine, some of the granite-cutting machines, and the teletype printers in commercial telegraphy. The employers may believe that the machines should be operated by less skilled men than the union has been willing to accept as members. Under these circumstances the adoption of the policy of control is the opposite of a concession by the union to employers. It represents an attempt by the union to impose conditions to which employers are vigorously opposed— possibly to compel employers to transfer to the new machines men whom employers prefer not to use there, to pay rates on the machines which employers are reluctant to concede, to regulate the size of crews on the new machines, the hours of work, the method of wage payment, or the rate at which the machines are introduced, or, in short, to make all labor questions that may arise in connection with the new machines or processes matters of negotiation and agreement with the union.

CONDITIONS THAT INFLUENCE UNIONS TO ADOPT THE POLICY OF CONTROL

The willingness of unions to seek control of the jobs on new machines or processes depends in the main upon six circumstances:

1. Whether the union is a craft or an industrial union.

2. Whether the machine or new process is useful in helping union employers to meet the competition of non-union employers or of other industries.

3. Whether the number of jobs created by the new technique is large in relation to the number that it destroys.

4. Whether the jobs created by the new technique require much of the skill and knowledge possessed by workers on the old technique and are readily learned by those workers.

5. Whether, in the event that new jobs do not appeal to workers on the old technique, the union is willing to admit the men who are used on the new jobs.

6. Whether control of the new jobs would materially assist the union in retarding the displacement of men from the old jobs.

Just as craft unions are more likely than industrial unions to adopt a policy of opposition to technological change,[1] industrial unions are more likely than craft unions to adopt a policy of control. A new machine or process which displaces men in a given craft or occupation usually helps the men in other occupations in the plant because, by reducing the cost of production, it is likely to increase

---

[1] See p. 213.

the market for the goods of the plant. Obviously, the proportion of the union membership which is helped rather than hurt by labor-saving changes is likely to be far greater in industrial unions than in craft unions.

The granite cutters, the potters, the street railway workers, the painters, and the miners have all been greatly influenced in adopting a policy of control by the knowledge that the new process or machine would help the union shops meet competition either from other products or from non-union employers. The granite cutters, for example, are keenly aware that granite suffers certain disadvantages in competition with softer stones. This made the union ready to accept saws and surfacing machines—provided members of the union operated them.[2] The potters have seen in various new machines a much needed help against foreign competition—the great problem of the union—and also a help against the competition of glassware and the growing competition of domestic non-union plants. The street railway workers, after experimenting with the policy of opposition to the one-man car, have seen in it a help to the street railways in their struggle to survive against the competition of private automobiles. For the same reason, this union has accepted the bus—subject to the provision that union men (preferably ex-street railwaymen) operate it. The painters' union, despite the advice of its national officers, has not adopted a national policy of accepting and controlling the spray gun, but a number of locals have seen that refusal to pursue this policy would give to non-union contractors a large market where the superiority of the gun over the brush is great. The miners' union has been influenced in its policy toward cutting machines, loaders, and other new machines by the competition of coal with fuel oil and water power and until 1933 was influenced by the competition of union mines with non-union. There can be no doubt that if unions could achieve a strongly

---

[2] In the *Granite Cutters' Journal* for December 1928, Vol. LII, the New York correspondent of the union discusses the relative cost of granite and limestone, and quotes a contractor as follows: "Give the right kind of machinery its proper place and it will not be long before the builders will insist on no other than the genuine material" (p. 11). An authoritative statement of union policy toward machines was made by the president, Sam Squibb, in an address before the New York State Memorial Craftsmen on Jan. 22, 1929. See the same, February 1929, Vol. LII, p. 15.

entrenched monopolistic position, they would be much less inclined to pursue a policy of control.

The more severe the displacement of men by the machine or new process, the less the interest of the union will be in a policy of control, for the simple reason that the machine does not provide enough jobs to be worth a fight. Of course, a union may *claim* control of new positions and hence may *appear* to be practicing a policy of control when in fact it is not. For example, at the 1921 convention of the flint glass workers' union, President W. P. Clarke directed attention to the rapid spread of machinery in the making of table tumblers, jelly glasses, beef jars, mixing bowls, sherbet cups, butter boxes, and various other pressed ware, and urged the union to "take some action that will encourage our members to the end that they will endeavor in the future to find employment in conjunction with the machine wherever it is possible to do so."[3] After a similar appeal by President Clarke the next year to the press ware branch of the union, the convention adopted a general resolution to the effect that "all operators of automatic glass-making machines, making glassware that comes under the jurisdiction of the American Flint Glass Workers' Union, shall be members of said union."[4] As a matter of fact, however, the policy of controlling the machines in the press ware department was not vigorously pursued because the number and character of the jobs did not create active interest in the policy. But as a machine continues to displace hand workers and as the number of machine jobs increases relative to the number of hand jobs, the policy of control becomes more attractive to the union. Consequently, as was pointed out in Chapter VII, a union which originally adopted a policy of obstruction to a machine may be led, after a large proportion of its members have been displaced, to adopt a policy of control.

If the skill and experience on the old technique are of use on the new machine or process, the objections of the old craftsmen toward the new process are likely to be softened and the workers on the old process more willing to accept employment on the new. This means

---

[3] American Flint Glass Workers' Union, *Proceedings of the Forty-fifth Convention*, 1921, p. 44.

[4] The same, *Proceedings of the Forty-sixth Convention*, 1922, pp. 64, 182.

that they are interested in controlling the new machines or process. But if the new jobs require little skill and involve little responsibility, the old craftsmen may look upon them with contempt and refuse to have anything to do with them. In that case the willingness of the union to pursue a policy of control will depend upon the willingness of the members to admit into the union the semi-skilled men who work on the new process. The union may be reluctant to do this because the skilled men may fear that the semi-skilled will eventually acquire control of the union. The window glass workers, as we have seen, were unable to practice a policy of control because they were unwilling either to accept jobs on the machines or to admit to the union the men who did operate the machines.

The officers of the glass bottle blowers' union, however, succeeded in persuading the members to seek a broadening of its charter from the American Federation of Labor, authorizing it to admit not only glass bottle blowers, but all men employed in the glass bottle industry who were not subject to other international unions.[5] This was done in order to put the union in position to demand control over the operators of the Owens automatics regardless of whether they were skilled glass workers.[6] At the next convention, in 1915, President Hayes recommended that the branches be authorized, when a company installed automatic machines, immediately to send a committee to request that the displaced blowers be employed on such machines. In case the blowers or machine operators did not desire to work on the automatics, an effort should be made to organize the men working on the automatics. In case of failure, the local should notify the national office immediately.[7] This recommendation of the president was unanimously adopted.[8]

By admitting semi-skilled workers on a new process and helping them increase their wages, the union raises the cost of operating the new technique and hence diminishes its superiority over the

---

[5] Glass Bottle Blowers' Association of the United States and Canada, *Minutes of Proceedings of the Thirty-eighth Annual Convention*, 1914, p. 87.

[6] See address of Pres. D. A. Hayes at the Rochester convention in 1914. The same, p. 34.

[7] The same, *Minutes of Proceedings of the Thirty-ninth Annual Convention*, 1915, p. 67.

[8] The same, pp. 226-27.

old process.[9] Hence a union may seek control over the workers on a new process, not primarily for the purpose of helping them, but for the purpose of retarding the displacement of hand workers by reducing the superiority of the competing process. Here we encounter the difficulty, mentioned in Chapter VII, of drawing a sharp distinction between the policy of obstruction, the policy of competition, and the policy of control. Control may be the means of making the policies of obstruction and competition more effective, and vice versa.

CONTROL OF THE NEW JOBS FOR DISPLACED WORKERS: FACTORS DETERMINING SUCCESS

When unions seek control over the jobs created by a new laborsaving machine or device, they are usually interested primarily in obtaining these jobs for the men displaced by the new technique. Their success in achieving this purpose depends in the main upon five conditions: (1) the usefulness of skill and experience acquired under the old technique to holders of jobs under the new; (2) the bargaining position of the union; (3) the willingness of the union to make concessions to obtain control of new jobs; (4) the relations between the union and the employers; (5) the willingness of the displaced men to learn the new technique promptly and to do their best at it.

1. Naturally a union has a far better chance of controlling the jobs created by a new technique when skill and experience acquired under the old technique are helpful under the new. Indeed in many cases of technological change there is no problem at all because the new process renders obsolete only a small part of the skill and experience of workers at the old technique. Hence, no one questions that the displaced workers are the proper persons to hold the new jobs. The substitution of electric or Diesel locomotives for steam is in point. Steam locomotive engineers must be taught to operate the new locomotives, but most of the skill, experience, and knowledge which they acquired as steam locomotive engineers is needed in operating electrics or Diesels. In other cases, however, there

---

[9] One of the unpredictable elements, however, is whether the pressure to raise wages of the workers on the new technique will not accelerate the improvement of the new methods.

may be considerable doubt whether the skill and experience on the old technique is advantageous on the new. Employers may even regard it as disadvantageous. Doubts as to the desirability of using displaced workers on the new jobs may be implanted by salesmen for the new equipment who represent that it makes unnecessary the highly paid skilled workers employed on the old equipment. Under these circumstances employers may object to giving the displaced workers a fair chance at the new jobs. The union is then confronted with the problem of convincing employers that the skill and experience of the displaced workers is valuable on the new jobs.

The success of the Typographical Union in controlling the linotype—the classic instance of the successful pursuit of the policy of control—is largely explained by the fact that employers early discovered that the compositor's knowledge and training made him a more satisfactory operator than workers who lacked experience in setting newspaper matter. The compositor had simply to learn how to manipulate the keys rapidly instead of picking type from the case boxes. Even non-union shops found it advantageous to develop machine operators from the ranks of hand compositors.

In some instances, considerable time (even years) may be required before employers discover what kind of labor is most satisfactory on the new jobs. An extreme case is furnished by the stove industry. When molding machines were first introduced, the stove manufacturers demanded the right to put unskilled or semi-skilled workers on them. Some foundries built separate shops in which machines were installed. Cheap semi-skilled labor was employed in these shops and molders were not permitted to go near the machines. Experience gradually revealed, however, that in the stove industry skilled molders were more satisfactory machine operators on most work than semi-skilled specialists. Part of the skill of the stove molder is in finishing the molds so that they will produce castings (stove plates) with a smooth, satiny finish.[10] Another part of the stove molder's skill is pouring the molten iron. Stove plates are broad and thin and unless the metal is skillfully poured, its weight expands the mold and produces a casting that

---

[10] This skill, however, is not required of molders in the machinery and jobbing foundries where, as we shall see, the union was not able to control the machine.

is too thick and heavy.[11] After several years' experience with semi-skilled operators, the stove manufacturers found it advantageous to concede the union's demand that molders operate the machines.

2. When the new jobs require far less skill than the old, a demand that employers give preference to displaced workers in filling the new jobs is certain to encounter strong opposition. The success of the union in compelling employers to use skilled men on the new jobs will then depend upon its bargaining power. Its bargaining position is strongest, of course, when the new technique affects a relatively small part of the work performed by its members. The success of the granite cutters' union in enforcing its constitutional provision that all machines in union shops be operated by journeymen granite cutters is largely attributable to the fact that most granite cutting must be done by hand. Through its control of the hand work, the union has won for its members the opportunity to operate the surfacing machines, saws, polishing machines, lathes, and other machines used in the industry. The union asserts that skilled men make more satisfactory machine operators, but employers deny this and non-union shops use unskilled men on the machines at wages far below the rate for journeymen.

Even where men experienced at the old technique make the most satisfactory workmen on the new, the bargaining power of the union may be important in gaining for the displaced employees an opportunity to show what they can do. At the time the new technique is introduced, employers may not know whether experience at the old process is valuable at the new. Certainly the Typographical Union was greatly helped in preventing employers from embarking on attempts to train specialists for the linotype by the fact that many jobs, such as the setting of advertisements, were not affected by the machine. No less important was the fact that linotypes were first introduced in newspaper offices, where the union has been strongest.[12] Strikes are peculiarly costly to newspapers because the failure of a paper to appear inflicts on it an irretrievable loss of advertising revenue. And if the paper is produced by strikebreakers,

[11] In the machinery and jobbing foundries pouring is usually an unskilled operation and is done by the molder's helper.

[12] In 1900, over four-fifths of the machines were in newspaper offices. G. E. Barnett, *Chapters on Machinery and Labor*, p. 19.

many advertisers refuse to patronize it for fear of incurring the enmity of the strikers and their sympathizers. Newspapers, too, are peculiarly vulnerable to boycotts. Since the circulation depends upon popularity, newspapers are reluctant to offend the wage earners of the community by becoming involved in serious labor trouble. Finally, the expense of setting the type for a large edition of a newspaper is too small a part of the cost of production to warrant an expensive battle. These factors, by strengthening the bargaining power of the Typographical Union, helped it forestall the move to train specialists for the linotype.

3. If the union is not in a strong bargaining position and if the new technique requires considerably less skill than the old, the ability of the union to gain preference for the displaced workers on the new jobs will depend upon its willingness to accept a much lower scale on the new jobs than on the old. The commercial telegraphers' union was greatly hampered in its efforts to have Morse operators transferred to the teletype by their strong demand that the Morse scale be paid on the new jobs, despite the fact that this scale was far above the rate at which workers suitable for the new jobs could be hired. The classic instance of a union which accepted severe wage cuts in order to control new jobs is furnished by the glass bottle blowers in their fight to gain control of the semi-automatic machines during the nineties and of the feed and flow device after 1915.

A few years after the semi-automatic machines were introduced, the glass blowers accepted the same piece-rate scale on the machines as was paid by non-union plants. In making this concession the union was influenced by the fact that a rival union, the flint glass workers, also claimed control of the machine.[13] When the machine

---

[13] The claim of the flint glass workers was based on the fact that the machine did pressing, and this union claimed jurisdiction over all pressed ware. The bottle blowers based their claim on the fact that the machine made bottles.

The first reaction of both the glass bottle blowers and the flint glass workers had been to oppose the machine. As early as 1892, the glass bottle blowers adopted a rule prohibiting any member from operating a bottle-blowing machine. In 1891, when a machine was introduced into the factory of D. C. Ripley of Pittsburgh, a plant controlled by the flint glass workers, the union insisted that the output of the machine be limited so that the cost of production on it would be no less than by hand methods. (Barnett, *Chapters on Machinery and Labor*, p. 73.)

was introduced into the factory of Ball Brothers in 1898, where the glass bottle blowers had an agreement, the union agreed to accept the non-union piece rates on the semi-automatic, but demanded that displaced workers be given a chance to operate the machines. Since the early semi-automatic machines made only wide-mouthed ware such as fruit jars, the union was able to use its control of the hand workers on small-mouthed ware to enforce control of the machine. The union's control of the hand workers and its willingness to accept non-union rates on the machines led the employers to operate the machines with union men. The union did not suffer long for its concessions on piece rates, because improvements in the machines and in the skill of the workers so increased the yield of the piece rates that within a few years semi-automatic operators were earning as much as non-machine workers.[14]

More than a decade later, when the "feed and flow" device, or the feeders,[15] as they are now called, came into the bottle industry, the union again accepted heavy wage reductions in order to control the machine. In the case of the feeders, as the name suggests, the glass flows from the tank into the molds. Since the operator does not have to gather glass, his main task is to see that the machine works properly and therefore he does not need to be a skilled workman.[16]

When the feeders were introduced, the union was struggling desperately to mitigate the displacement of its members by the

---

As a result, Mr. Ripley ceased to use the machine in his own factory but licensed non-union manufacturers to use it. This led the flint glass workers' union to approve more favorable piece rates for machine-made bottles. (The same, pp. 74-75.)

[14] This experience illustrates the important fact that, when a new machine is first introduced, it is exceedingly difficult to determine accurately what hourly earnings will be yielded by given piece rates. Two things, however, are virtually certain—that the skill of the men will improve rapidly during the first year or two on the new machine and that the machine itself will be improved in many respects. Consequently, rates which seem entirely too low at the beginning will often, after a year or two, yield very high earnings. The union which seems to be accepting a decrease on the new jobs may actually be winning an increase. This was the experience with the new heeling machines in the shoe industry.

[15] The feeders made an appearance during the season of 1915. At the close of the season of 1916 ten or twelve firms were making bottles by that method, but the feeder was still largely in an experimental stage. About 1920 and 1921, however, installation of the feeders was extremely rapid. By 1922 about 188 feeders were in operation.

[16] The early feeders produced twice as much as the semi-automatics and made a more uniform product.

Owens automatic machine. Although the feeders produced displacement, they used far more labor (and less capital) than the Owens machine. Hence the union was anxious to control them and to use them to compete more effectively with the Owens machines. By this time the displacement of hand workers had gone so far that the union was no longer able to use its control of them to force recognition of its claims over the feeders. It did not threaten to withdraw men from plants in which non-unionists were employed on the feeders, but it sought to use the good will and confidence which it had built up over many years with the employers to gain recognition for its claims. Because of the small amount of skill needed to operate the feeders, the union was compelled to accept a scale far below the rates on semi-automatics. The first agreements, made in 1918, provided for an hourly rate of 50 cents. Semi-automatic operators at this time were making from $6 to $8 per day at piecework.

Many plants were unwilling even at this low rate to give the union control of the machine. The union, however, persisted in its attempts to secure agreements covering the feeder in all plants. At the 1924 convention, President Voll reported that during the year jurisdiction was secured over automatic methods of production at 13 plants, thus extending its jurisdiction to 42 plants operating in whole or part under the new methods of production. Twenty-five plants had refused to concede the union's jurisdiction.[17] At the 1927 convention President Maloney reported that of 300 feeders installed 270 were operated by union men.[18] By this time more members of the union were employed on the feeders than at blowing or on the semi-automatics.[19] The problem of the feeder operators was

---

[17] Glass Bottle Blowers' Association of the United States and Canada, *Minutes of Proceedings of the Forty-eighth Annual Convention*, 1924, p. 27. "This does not mean," the president added, "that all these latter firms are hostile to or are fighting the Association. The fact is quite the contrary with most of the companies." Professor Barnett estimated that the union in 1924 controlled roughly two-thirds of the feed and flow devices in use. (*Chapters on Machinery and Labor*, p. 110.)

[18] Glass Bottle Blowers' Association of the United States and Canada, *Minutes of Proceedings, Fiftieth Convention*, 1927, p. 66.

[19] The figures were 375 blowers, 93 operators of semi-automatics, and 831 feeder operators. (The same, pp. 65-66.)

Having accepted a low rate on the feeders, the union was naturally eager to get the rate increased. The war boom enabled the union to raise the wages for feed and flow operators by 1920 to 66 cents an hour, but the organization was hampered by

eventually solved for the union by the repeal of prohibition in 1933. So important was the demand for union-made beer bottles that the union was able, without opposition from employers, to organize virtually all feeder operators and to obtain agreements covering them.

4. The success of a union in obtaining transfer of displaced workers to the new technique is much affected by the relations between employers and the union. If there are serious unsettled differences and an acute contest for power between the two, the employers may welcome the new machine as a weapon against the union. In that event they will be unyielding in their refusal to transfer displaced workers to the new jobs. The failure of the molders' union and the founders to reach an agreement over the molding machine in the jobbing and machinery foundries is illuminating.

The machine became important about the turn of the century. At first the union ignored the machine. Rarely did the local unions attempt to exclude it from the foundries or to regulate its use, but their members refused to work on it.[20] As the use of the ma-

---

the fact that it did not control the feed and flow machines in all factories. In the depression of 1921 the manufacturers demanded a reduction to 50 cents again. As a result the agreements covering the feeders were not renewed in that year. The union, however, did not withdraw its members from the factories, and in August 1922 obtained an agreement from the employers to pay 60 cents an hour. (Glass Bottle Blowers' Association of the United States and Canada, *Proceedings of the Forty-seventh Annual Convention,* 1923, p. 31.)

The problem of obtaining agreements covering all feeder operators and of winning higher wages for the men led the union to make an interesting attempt to introduce skill into the work by changing the nature of the machine tender's job. The union leaders advocated that part of the repair and maintenance of the machines be done by the operators and urged the operators to study the construction and repair of the machines and to make small repairs and adjustments on their own initiative without calling for the upkeep men. (Glass Bottle Blowers' Association of the United States and Canada, *Minutes of Proceedings, Forty-eighth Annual Convention,* 1924, pp. 232-40.) At the wage conference of 1924, the union urged the employers to transfer part of the maintenance to the feed and flow operators. One representative of the union said: "What we want is more wages. Now how can that be secured without increasing costs to the manufacturer? I would suggest that the operators be given full control over their units and be expected by you to do all the upkeep work, also to be the persons responsible for production. You can dispense with some or nearly all of your upkeep men and by doing so you can pay our people a much greater wage than 60 cents per hour on the feeders; and I believe you will get better results and save money." (*Workers' Report of the Sessions of the Final Wage Conference between the Employers and the Glass Bottle Blowers' Association,* 1924, p. 52.) This policy was abandoned when the repeal of prohibition greatly strengthened the position of the union.

[20] F. T. Stockton, *The International Molders' Union of North America,* p. 190.

chine spread, however, the national officers became convinced of the necessity of establishing control over it. At the 1899 convention, President Fox urged that the members operate the machines and bring out their best possibilities, and the convention adopted a resolution to this effect.[21] But the policy proved difficult to carry out.

The first several years of the century were a period of great boom in the metal trades. Employers complained of the scarcity of skilled molders. Molding machines were sold on the claim that they did not require skilled labor, and employers bought them for the purpose of overcoming the shortage of journeymen molders. At this time, also, the jobbing and machinery foundrymen were involved in many serious clashes with the union, which had been growing rapidly and had recently established itself in many shops. In many of these newly organized shops, relations were strained. Furthermore, an important issue had developed over the right of foundrymen to employ semi-skilled molders at wages below the journeymen's scale. The boom in the industry and the scarcity of skilled men led managements to study ways and means of organizing the work so that much of it could be done by semi-skilled specialists. Indeed the dispute over the machine was simply one aspect of this broader controversy. The employers demanded the right to pay a certain proportion of their molders less than the standard rate for skilled workers.

A number of conferences between the union and the National Founders' Association failed to settle the issue. In 1899, a general agreement, known as the New York Agreement, had been made between the National Founders' Association and the molders' union for the purpose of providing machinery to adjust disputes between the molders and the foundrymen. Unfortunately, this agreement, instead of preserving peace, itself became a source of discord, for it led the union to dispute the right of foundrymen to make changes in their shops which affected the workmen without securing the consent of the men or handling the matter through machinery created by the New York Agreement. This interpretation was rejected by the foundrymen.

Numerous controversies over this and other issues soon con-

[21] The same, p. 191.

vinced the foundrymen that the possibility of using semi-skilled men on the machines was an important weapon to them in their dealings with the union. In other words, the state of industrial relations in the industry made the foundrymen alive to the importance of keeping control of the machine away from the union. The employers were using the machine to defeat the union, and they could not afford to give up this weapon. The union has never succeeded (except in the stove industry) in inducing employers to use skilled molders on the machines. And although it has made several special efforts to organize the machine molders (at one time creating a special class of membership for them), it has never acquired a large membership among them.[22]

5. Even willingness of the union and the employers to go far in making concessions for assuring preference to displaced men on new jobs does not assure that the policy will succeed. It may shatter because of unwillingness of the workers at the old process to accept jobs on the new, at least promptly enough, or to do their best at the new jobs. It is natural for workers to feel hostile toward a machine or process which renders much of their skill obsolete. The skilled mechanic is likely to regard it as beneath his dignity to become a machine tender. And even if he is willing to operate the machine, he may show little zeal or ingenuity in overcoming difficulties and in getting the best out of the machine. On the contrary, he may be delighted to have the employer discover that the new method has its shortcomings. One of the most troublesome problems of unions in pursuing the policy of controlling the jobs on new machines or processes has been to gain the co-operation of their own members.

The Typographical Union was fortunate in escaping this difficulty when the linotype was introduced—despite the fact that the members of the union were at first bitterly hostile to the machine and punished the president who initiated the policy of control by refusing to re-elect him. The linotype was first introduced on a

---

[22] The skilled molders have not been too eager to organize the machine molders because a large influx of machine molders would shift control of the union from the skilled men to the machine operators. And the machine molders have not been too eager to join the union because they have regarded it as an organization run by and for the skilled workers.

considerable scale during the severe depression between 1893 and 1897. Since the machines were new and rapidly increasing in number, there was a scarcity of linotype operators. Consequently, ability to operate a linotype meant steady work in a period of great unemployment. It is not surprising that compositors were soon willing to learn linotype operation and do their best at it.

Quite different was the experience of the molders' union. The molding machine was introduced, it will be recalled, just after the turn of the century at a time of brisk business in the metal trades. The molders did not like to operate the machines and regarded assignment to them as a demotion. Consequently, skilled workmen assigned to machines quit or refused to do their best. Foundry laborers or handymen, on the contrary, regarded machine jobs as a promotion and were eager to make good at them. Employers (except in the stove branch of the industry) quickly discovered that the way to get the best results from the machines was to operate them with semi-skilled specialists rather than journeymen molders. Thus the persistently hostile attitude of union members toward the machine defeated the efforts of the union to control the new jobs.

If the union must accept large wage reductions on the new jobs in order to control them, its difficulty in getting displaced workers trained to accept the new jobs or to do their best at them is much aggravated. The breakdown of national collective bargaining in the sanitary ware branch of the pottery industry in 1921 was partly caused by the insistence of the union that piece rates on the new process of casting yield as high earnings as rates on the old process of pressing which required a higher degree of skill than the new process.[23] When the glass bottle blowers' union accepted the non-union scale on the semi-automatic machines, the operators of these machines could earn only about half as much as the hand blowers, and many displaced workers refused to accept work on the machines. President Hayes, reviewing the experience of the union in his report to the 1915 convention, said: "Quite a number availed themselves of the chance and have done well, giving entire satisfaction to their employers; but an equally large number refused,

[23] See pp. 364-65, and D. A. McCabe, *National Collective Bargaining in the Pottery Industry*, pp. 381-438.

hence, we had to secure machine operators from outside the trade."[24] As pointed out above, however, payment was by the piece, and as the semi-automatics were improved and as the operators gained skill, the earnings of machine operators rose until, by 1905, the machine workers were making as much as the hand workers.[25]

The great reduction in the wage scale that was necessary for the union to gain control of the feed and flow device has been discussed. President Maloney said to the 1927 convention that for years after 1918, when the union made its first agreement governing the feeders,

many employers were fearful of giving a displaced blower or machine worker an opportunity to work on this machine. . . . They seemed to think it required a new man, one who had not been an active glassworker, accustomed to older methods of making bottles. . . . I am satisfied that the great majority of employers now using this method have changed their minds. . . . The blower and machine worker too realize that when drastic changes in methods of production are introduced in a factory, and displace them, the old method has gone forever, and naturally do their very best when given a chance with the new process.[26]

The policy of transferring men from the old technique to the new may be defeated, at least in part, because the workers are not willing to transfer promptly enough.[27] Sometimes the success of a new machine cannot be accurately foreseen. Its productivity and adaptability are uncertain, and hence the extent to which it is likely to encroach on the old process. Employees on the old process may be quite confident that there will always be enough work for them. After a year or two, when the machine has taken over most of the work and drastically reduced the earnings of the hand workers, some of them may wish to transfer to the machine at the expense of the new workers. This has happened in connection with the introduction of large new buffing machines in the leather industry since

[24] Glass Bottle Blowers' Association of the United States and Canada, *Minutes of Proceedings of the Thirty-ninth Annual Convention*, 1915, p. 52.

[25] Barnett, *Chapters on Machinery and Labor*, p. 83.

[26] Glass Bottle Blowers' Association of the United States and Canada, *Minutes of Proceedings of the Fiftieth Convention*, 1927, p. 59.

[27] The management may not be entirely free of responsibility. It may make no particular effort to persuade the workers to transfer, particularly if it prefers to use new workers rather than the old ones on the new jobs.

1936. Most of the buffing in the industry had been done on the Buzzell buffers, which have a cylinder about 12 inches long.[28] The new machines have a cylinder from 24 to 50 inches long and have other advantages. When the new machine first appeared, the union told the operators on the Buzzell buffer that if they wished to transfer to the new machine, they should so state. Many at first showed no interest in transferring. They thought that the plants would always do Buzzell buffing. Indeed, some of them were told this by the management. They were also influenced by the fact that piece rates had not been set for the new machines and that they could earn considerably more than the day work minimum at piecework on the Buzzell buffers. Within a few months, however, some managements entirely replaced the Buzzell buffers with the new machines, and younger men who had held unskilled positions learned to operate them. The old buffers wished to replace the newly promoted employees. Under the circumstances, however, the union was obviously not in a strong position to support the claim of the operators of the old machines.

This brief survey shows wide variation in the success of unions in gaining control of new jobs for displaced workers. The Typographical Union had a high degree of success, but the molders' union very little, except in the stove foundries. The glass bottle blowers had considerable success when the first semi-automatic machines were introduced and also when the feed and flow device came into the industry. The survey shows also that the problems confronting unions vary widely. Sometimes, as in the case of the linotype, employers are quite willing to give the displaced men a chance at the new machine; at other times, as in the case of the molding machine, the employers are strongly opposed to transferring the displaced workers. The union may be in a strong bargaining position or a weak one; it may be willing to make substantial concessions in order to control the new jobs, or perhaps no concessions at all. It may be assisted by good relations with the employers, or hampered by bad relations; the displaced men

---

[28] Some buffing had been done on the overshot machine, but it was practically obsolete by 1936.

may be willing to do their best at the new jobs or, as in the case of the molders, they may themselves defeat the efforts of the union to help them by refusing to do their best at the machine.

CONTROLLING THE NEW JOBS BY TRAINING UNION MEMBERS FOR THEM

Occasionally a union undertakes to obtain control of a new type of work by promptly training its members to do the work or by helping them to obtain training. If the union has the most competent labor, it is obviously in a strong position to control the new jobs.

The union which has gone farthest in providing technical training to gain control of new types of work is the photo-engravers' union.[29] One of the first attempts of the union to provide its members with special help occurred when the photo-offset process came in. The union was anxious to control the new process, and it knew that in order to do so it must be able to supply competent workmen. The lead was taken by the New York local, which published a 50-page pamphlet on the photo-offset process. The president of the New York local, who was also vice-president of the national union, was sent on a nation-wide trip by the national for the purpose of explaining the new process to members of various locals and of interesting them in learning it. More recently the Chicago local has introduced training courses through which members may become familiar with that process. As early as 1924, the president of the union recommended that it consider forming an advisory agency to draft a plan for the technical education of the members.[30] At the

---

[29] Other unions, such as the electrical workers and the printing pressmen, have provided training for journeymen, but their purpose has not been primarily to gain control of new types of work, but rather to help their members keep up with new developments in the trade. For example, the electrician who served his apprenticeship before 1920 might know very little about radio or movietone work. Consequently, the electricians' union has started evening classes in a number of cities. The development of small high-speed presses has created a demand for skill which many pressmen trained before 1920 do not possess. The movement of magazine work out of New York City left the pressmen's union with many journeymen who were skilled in running large web presses, but who were unfamiliar with the high speed automatics. The pressmen's union in the New York book and job industry instituted short evening courses for the training of journeymen. See *Bulletin of New York Printing Pressmen's Union*, No. 51, April 1929, for a statement about these classes by the president of the local.

[30] International Photo-Engravers' Union of North America, *Reports of Officers and Convention Proceedings*, 1924, p. 30.

1936 convention the president pointed out that new processes and methods were being introduced into the industry and that it would be wise for members of the union to keep informed in regard to all of them.

The desire of the union to control offset lithographing was perhaps primarily responsible for its decision at the 1937 convention to establish the office of technical director. The services of the technical director are at the disposal, not only of members of the union, but also of employers who are interested in enlarging their activities by the addition of new departments or who are confronted with production problems of a technical nature.[31] In his first annual report, the technical director reported a large correspondence with members and employers in which requests for information on offset lithography were by far the most numerous.[32] He made visits to 69 plants, some at the request of the employees, others at the request of employers.

CONTROLLING THE NEW JOBS BY ORGANIZING THE WORKERS ON THEM

Although many unions attempt to secure the jobs at the new technique for their old members, they may find this impossible either because a large proportion of the displaced men refuse to transfer to the new jobs or because many employers are unwilling to use displaced men at terms which the men are willing to accept. In either event, the policy of control may take the form of organizing the employees on the new jobs. If the union is an industrial one, there is usually no question concerning its willingness to organize the workers. Craft unions, however, may be unable to take in the new workers without altering their admission requirements, and they may be unwilling to do this. Not until 1907, about ten years after the appearance of the molding machine, did the molders' union open its doors to molding machine operators who are not journeyman molders. When the teletype or printer began to invade the brokerage field about 1929, the original policy of the

---

[31] *American Photo-Engraver*, December 1937, Vol. XXIX, p. 1014.
[32] He reported many requests for textbooks, not only on photo-engraving, but also on chemistry, optics, and other subjects, and inquiries on new developments, such as the Kodachrome and the rolling-up process of etching. International Photo-Engravers' Union, *Officers' Reports and Convention Proceedings*, 1938, pp. 127-32.

commercial telegraphers' union was to ignore the printer operators and to make every effort to procure the printer jobs for Morse operators. After about a year, however, the union changed its policy to one of organizing the printer operators.[33]

There are several reasons why the workers at the old technique may object to taking in the workers at the new. One reason is that they may wish the new jobs for themselves. A second reason is that the journeymen may fear that the machine operators will become competitors for the journeymen's jobs at the old technique. A third reason is craft pride and union tradition. If a union has always been an organization of highly skilled men, the members are likely to be reluctant to take in semi-skilled workers. This is particularly true if the workers on the new jobs are numerous, because admitting them may mean turning over control of the union to them.[34]

Experience with the policy of control, however, may induce the union to admit workers on the new process. The molders' union decided to admit machine operators after it became evident that journeymen molders could not be persuaded to operate the machines in the jobbing and machinery foundries.[35] The commercial telegraphers were led early in 1930 to modify their policy toward the admission of printer operators in brokerage houses. They found that they could not win strikes for the control of the printer without the printer operators and also that they needed the help of the

---

[33] When the teletype was introduced into the newspaper and commercial telegraphers' field a few years earlier, the policy of the union was very different. During the early stages of the introduction, the union was not interested in gaining for the Morse operators the opportunity to transfer to the printers. It was interested, however, in organizing the printer operators and in raising their wages in order to diminish the advantage of the printers over Morse. This matter is discussed in a subsequent section of this chapter.

[34] There are instances, however, in which semi-skilled workers have been taken into the union for the express purpose of imposing union discipline on them and controlling them. The molders' union took in the core makers, for example, to prevent them from interrupting production by unnecessary strikes.

[35] The admission of the machine operators required a change in the union's constitution, which provided that members must have served an apprenticeship of four years or its equivalent. In 1907, the constitution was amended to admit "any molder competent to operate any machine, squeezer, or other mechanical device used for the purpose of molding castings in sand." (Art. VIII, sec. 7.) As will be indicated below, however, restrictions were placed upon the work which members admitted as machine operators might do.

operators in establishing one standard scale for Morse and printer operation in the brokerage houses.[36]

If the journeymen fear that the workers on the new technique may become competitors for jobs customarily held by journeymen, the union may place special restrictions upon the new members. It has been pointed out in Chapter VII[37] that when the cigar-makers' union first embarked upon the policy of admitting bunch breakers and rollers, it created for these workers a special membership known as Class A. These members were permitted to work only as specialists under the bunch-breaking and roll-up system. When the molders' union in 1907 decided to admit machine operators, the constitutional amendment provided that "members admitted under this section must be designated as machine operators on their cards and bluebooks," and that such members "should not be permitted to work on the bench or floor without having served the regular apprenticeship." Special classes of membership have not proved a success because workers do not like to be graded and put into a special class. Class A membership, established by the cigar makers in 1912, was repealed in 1920. The requirement of the molders that workers admitted as machine operators be designated as such and given special cards was abolished in 1928 on the earnest recommendation of President Keough.[38]

METHODS OF LIMITING TECHNOLOGICAL DISPLACEMENT OF MEN

Since the new technique usually fails to provide enough jobs to

[36] In 1929, the commercial telegraphers lost a strike against Logan and Bryan over the installation of automatic printers. In 1930, the union lost a strike against C. F. Childs and Co. on the same issue. The Morse operators of the company had struck 100 per cent, but the printer operators, whom the union had not attempted to organize, continued to work. The executive board of the eastern brokerage division of the union was informed that the Childs printer operators would be willing to join the strike if they were given cards by the union and treated as equals with Morse members. After the loss of the Childs strike, Mr. Frank Powers, president of the union, recommended that its policy be broadened to include the organization of the printer operators in the brokerage field. The revised policy was placed before the membership of the various brokerage divisions for ratification and was accepted by the Eastern, the Michigan, the Pacific Coast, the New England, the Western Middle Atlantic, and the Eastern Canada divisions and rejected by the Western and Southern. *Commercial Telegraphers' Journal*, September-October 1930, Vol. XXVIII, pp. 197-98.

[37] Pp. 218-19.

[38] *International Molders' Journal*, November 1928, Vol. LXIV, Supplement, pp. 5, 246.

absorb all of the men that it displaces, unions which adopt the policy of control are likely to demand rules for the purpose of limiting the displacement of men by new machines and methods. There are seven principal ways in which unions seek to accomplish this purpose: (1) by limiting the influx of workers into the shrinking occupation; (2) by regulating the size of crews under the new technique; (3) by limiting the number of new machines that a plant may install; (4) by requiring that operations, previously done by non-unionists, be performed by displaced workers; (5) by requiring that the men employed on the new process be compensated at a substantially higher rate than men on the old technique; (6) by requiring that men displaced by the new technique be given other jobs or be paid a dismissal wage; (7) by reducing the hours of work.

1. Control of entrance into the declining occupation presupposes that a union exercises control over hiring in the form of either apprentice regulations or their equivalent. It may seem strange that unions should find it necessary to discourage workers from entering a shrinking occupation. These occupations, however, are subject to seasonal and cyclical bulges, and at such times employers may prefer to hire new workers rather than rehire men displaced by the new technique. The glass bottle blowers' union was compelled to restrict entrance to the trade for the purpose of prolonging the employment of its members. By 1909 it was clear that the Owens automatic machines would ultimately cause a drastic displacement of bottle blowers, but employers were still taking apprentices and training glass bottle blowers. In the contracts for the years 1909 and 1912, however, the union induced the employers to take no apprentices during the ensuing year. In 1913, the union altered its tactics. It insisted on an increase in the wages of apprentices to three-fourths of the rates paid to journeymen. This effectively restricted the number of apprentices by making it unprofitable for employers to train them.[39] The displacement of press assistants by automatic press-feeding devices led the New York local of press assistants (No. 23) to cease admitting new members.[40]

---

[39] Barnett, *Chapters on Machinery and Labor*, pp. 98-99.
[40] "American Trade-Unions and the Problem of Unemployment," *Monthly Labor Review*, March 1928, Vol. XXVI, p. 485.

2. Unions may attempt to limit the displacement of men by demanding that excessively large crews be employed at the new process. Indeed, as was pointed out in Chapter VI, every technological change which causes severe displacement is likely to produce a crop of make-work rules. When the automatic nail-making machines were introduced nearly fifty years ago, the iron and steel workers attempted to check the displacement of men by limiting the number of machines which a man might operate. The operation of four machines was defined as a job and the union constitution was amended to prohibit a member from holding more than one job. The very severity of the displacement, however, produced such competition for jobs that the union was unable to enforce its rule.[41]

The introduction of automatic press feeders into printing press rooms has produced disputes over the complement of men required on the new equipment. When presses were all hand fed, a feeder was used on every press. On many kinds of work, automatic feeding devices enable one feeder to feed two presses. The first automatic feeding attachments were applied to the large cylinder presses used on long-run jobs such as magazine printing. When these devices were first introduced about 1900, the pressmen's union, of which the feeders are members, sought to prevent displacement of the feeders by adopting a rule which prohibits a pressman from feeding his own cylinder press, operating an automatic feeding machine when attached to a press, or making ready a press without an assistant.[42] At the convention in 1924 an effort was made to repeal this rule. President Berry recommended its repeal, provided adequate safeguards against unemployment could be secured.[43] The

[41] J. S. Robinson, *The Amalgamated Association of Iron, Steel, and Tin Workers,* pp. 126-27. As pointed out in Chap. VI, some locals of the musicians' union have endeavored to limit displacement by movietone devices by demanding that theaters which install movietone equipment employ a specified number of musicians. The demand of train service employees on the railroads for "full-crew laws" was stimulated by the displacement of men as heavier power and better road beds made possible the hauling of heavier trains.

[42] In 1920, a paragraph was added to the rule requiring that an assistant be employed where two or more Kelly or automatic cylinder presses were in operation. This meant that on the small automatics one assistant might be used to two or more presses. International Printing Pressmen and Assistants' Union of North America, *Constitution and Laws,* revised and adopted by referendum February 1929 and July 1933, Art. XXX, sec. 32, pp. 86-87.

[43] The same, *Reports of Officers to the Thirtieth Biennial Convention,* 1924, pp. 92-93. Mr. Berry said: "We find ourselves in this position . . . that to maintain as a

convention, however, instead of repealing the rule, authorized the
board of directors to call conferences to study the problem.[44] No
action resulted, and the rule is still on the books, though not in all
cases strictly enforced.

Although the press assistants have demanded that one feeder be
employed to each press—just as in the days of hand feeding—
regardless of whether the press is equipped with an automatic feeding device, they have been compelled during recent years to accept
one assistant to two feeders on some types of work. The assistants
made this concession because the pressmen were willing to operate
some types of presses without assistants. In 1925 the pressmen's
local in the New York job printing industry agreed to operate
automatic cylinder presses up to and including 42 inches either with
one pressman and one assistant to two presses or with one pressman to a press without an assistant.[45]

3. A union may attempt to limit the displacement of labor by
restricting the number of machines which an employer may use.
The Chicago stone cutters' union in 1898 demanded that the contractor employ at least four stone cutters for every planer. This
led to a strike, which was settled by the contractors' agreeing to
employ two hand cutters for every single planer and four hand cutters for every double planer.[46] When pressing machines were introduced into the New York cloak and suit industry about 1920, the
union, after failing to exclude the machines entirely, attempted to
limit the machines to one for every six hand pressers and later to

set policy one man to a feeding machine . . . we would be engaged in a program
that would be economically unsound. It is infinitely more important that the assistant in charge of the feeding machine be given additional responsibility, and
for it be given adequate compensation, than it is to force upon the industry
persons that are not now in the industry and are totally unnecessary in its conduct.
Obviously the pursuance of such a course minimizes the possibility of increasing
our own compensation."

[44] The same, *Proceedings of the Thirtieth Convention*, 1924, Friday afternoon
session, p. 21.

[45] To the extent that employers adopted the latter alternative, there would
be more for the pressmen and less for the assistants. On some work, particularly
high-quality work, it is more economical for employers to use a pressman to
each press rather than one pressman and one assistant to two presses. The convention
of the union in 1940 adopted a resolution against the practice of using pressmen
instead of assistants on presses, but it is doubtful whether all of the delegates realized what they were voting for.

[46] Barnett, *Chapters on Machinery and Labor*, p. 37.

one for every four hand pressers.[47] The union preferred not to write any provision regarding the machines into its contracts, since that would be "legalizing" the use of the machines. The efforts of the union to enforce the rule failed.

4. The union may create work for its displaced members by demanding that certain operations previously done by non-members be assigned to displaced workers. This method, of course, simply *shifts* the displacing effect of the machine; it does not reduce the effect. For example, the Typographical Union, in order to provide jobs for compositors displaced by the linotype, adopted a rule at its convention of 1898 requiring that after January 1, 1900 all proofreaders in union shops be members of the organization. Although employers had drawn a considerable number of proofreaders from the ranks of compositors, this was by no means a universal practice.[48]

5. Unions may retard the introduction of labor-saving methods by requiring that men employed on them be compensated at substantially higher rates than men employed on the old technique. Of course, not all the wage scales which call for higher compensation on the new equipment than on the old are intended to affect the rate at which the new methods are introduced. Some differentials are intended merely to give the workers a share in the savings or to compensate them for the additional responsibility which the new equipment imposes upon them. Into this classification fall the small differentials in favor of the operators of one-man street cars; the scales of the locomotive firemen and engineers, which rise as the weight of the locomotives on the drivers increases; and some of the scales of the printing pressmen. At the other extreme are cases where the policy of control becomes indistinguishable from the policy of obstruction, because the differentials demanded

[47] Pressing machines had long been used in the men's clothing industry, but in 1920 not more than 50 shops in the New York women's garment industry had them. The simpler styles and the shift to cheap and medium-grade coats and suits has facilitated their use. At present practically every shop making cheap or medium-grade garments uses the machine. On some types of work a machine operator can do two and a half or three times as much as a hand presser.

[48] G. E. Barnett, "The Printers," *American Economic Association Quarterly*, 3d series, October 1909, Vol. X, No. 3, p. 247. In order to avoid depriving non-compositor proofreaders of their jobs, the union stipulated a limited period during which such workers would be entitled to join the union.

by the union are prohibitively expensive. Between the extremes are a considerable number of instances in which the primary purpose of the union in demanding a differential has been to retard the rate at which the new technique is introduced. After the New York locals of the women's garment workers failed to enforce a ratio of one pressing machine to six and later to four hand pressers, they endeavored to discourage use of the machine by demanding a minimum of $65 a week for machine pressers in contrast with $50 for hand pressers.[49] The differential rate, however, seems to have had little effect upon the use of machines.

A notable use of wage differentials to limit the adoption of labor-saving methods is furnished by the policy of the United Mine Workers toward coal-cutting machines. Both pick mining and machine mining are paid by the ton. The union retarded the spread of the machine by allowing in the machine tonnage rate only a small differential below the pick mining rate. The union has been most successful in enforcing a small differential in Illinois, where the machine rate in 1898 was set only 7 cents below the pick mining rate as against 11 cents in Indiana and 17 cents in western Pennsylvania. The union was assisted in keeping the differential small by the operators of thin-vein mines, who could not profitably use the machines and who wished protection against the competition of the thick-vein mines. By accepting a high differential the union would have permitted a few large mines to close down several hundred smaller ones and to throw many men out of work.

Improvement in coal-cutting machinery has led employers to demand new and lower piece rates. In some cases the union has attempted to retard the use of the latest and best machinery by delaying the agreement on the new rates. When the operators of the northern West Virginia district attempted to introduce the "arc-wall" machine, the labor commissioner of the operators and the sub-district presidents of the union failed to agree on piece rates. The matter was referred to the joint board of the district, which ordered an investigation of the matter. Tests showed that the machine cut about twice as rapidly as the old type. The union insisted that the loaders' earnings were reduced by the new machine and

---

[49] The union claimed that the machine work was heavier and more skilled than hand work, but this does not seem to be true.

refused to accept a change in the cutting rate unless adjustment were also made in the loading rate. The operators contended that any adjustments in the loaders' rates should be made in individual mines rather than for the district as a whole. In April 1921 the two sides agreed to submit the case to an umpire for decision, but they could not agree on an umpire. Finally, in the spring of 1923, nearly three years after the dispute had arisen, the rate was settled by an agreement.[50]

The policy of retarding the introduction of labor-saving devices by high piece rates is likely in the long run to produce serious trouble for the union. The holders of the new jobs earn substantially more than men of equal skill on other jobs. This introduces jealousies and dissension into the ranks of the union, particularly if some disappointed members feel that the union officers have tolerated favoritism by management in making assignments to lucrative jobs. Furthermore, if the new jobs are fairly numerous, the high rate may place union employers at a serious disadvantage in competition with non-union plants and substantially limit employment in the union plants.

6. Sometimes unions take the position that the employer may introduce labor-saving devices and methods as fast as he wishes, provided he gives a new job to every man displaced by the new technique or pays a dismissal wage. The dismissal wage was discussed in Chapter IV. As a general rule, provisions for a dismissal wage have been especially negotiated rather than embodied in agreements. An agreement which provides for a dismissal wage for employees displaced by labor-saving devices was negotiated between the Columbia River Boat Operators and the Inland Boatmen's Union on December 12, 1939. It provides that any worker whose employment is discontinued as the result of introduction of labor-saving devices will "by voluntary action of the company be paid compensation during any subsequent unemployment within a period of three months at the rate of $15 a week of actual unemployment."[51]

[50] Boris Emmet, *Labor Relations in the Fairmont, West Virginia, Bituminous Coal Field*, U. S. Bureau of Labor Statistics, Bulletin No. 361, pp. 31-33.
[51] The agreement adds that no such compensation shall be paid to any person who has failed to accept suitable employment for which his earnings would be in excess of $15 a week.

Provisions or arrangements that other work will be found for men displaced by labor-saving devices are not unusual. When the union demands that displaced workers be given new jobs, it may or may not insist that they receive their previous rate of pay. The potters' union requires that the new jobs pay no less than the old ones. For some years this was the policy of the Amalgamated Clothing Workers[52] and at times of the International Ladies' Garment Workers. During recent years, however, the former, while insisting that there be no displacements, has not required that previous earnings be maintained.[53] At the instance of the railroad unions, section 7b was written into the Emergency Transportation Act of 1933. The unions feared that co-ordination projects initiated by the Co-ordinator of Transportation might displace workers. Section 7b provided that no employee might, as a result of co-ordination projects, be ousted or shifted to a job paying less money than the one he held in May 1933, and that the total number of employees could not be reduced by co-ordination projects more than 5 per cent a year under the level of May 1933.[54]

In arbitrating the complement of men on new web-rotary presses in the New York printing industry in 1928, Dr. W. M. Leiserson ruled that the employer was justified in removing the utility men from the presses, but that he was not justified in discharging them from his employment.[55] Thus the employers were free to introduce the more efficient presses and to operate them without utility men, provided jobs could be found for the displaced workers. When the United Textile Workers' Union co-operated with the management of the Naumkeag Steam Cotton Company in introducing the "stretch-out,"[56] part of the union policy was that the new job assignments be introduced so gradually that no worker would be displaced who was in the service of the company at the time the union con-

[52] Amalgamated Clothing Workers of America, *The Clothing Workers of Chicago, 1910-1922*, p. 291. The policy of the union is expressed in its Rochester agreement in the following language: "The right of the employer to make changes in shop management and methods of manufacturing is recognized, such changes to be made without loss to the employee directly affected." E. W. Morehouse, "The Development of Industrial Law in the Rochester Clothing Market," *Quarterly Journal of Economics*, February 1923, Vol. XXXVII, pp. 269-70.

[53] The policy of the Amalgamated Clothing Workers is discussed in Chap. XVII.

[54] 48 Stat. L. 211, 214.

[55] E. F. Baker, *Displacement of Men by Machines*, pp. 153-54.

[56] The Naumkeag experiment is discussed in Chap. XVIII.

sented to the stretch-out.[57] The agreement of the women's garment workers' union with the Affiliated Dress Manufacturers of
New York, effective February 20, 1936, provided that the administrative board and/or administrator should adopt rules and regulations in connection with the introduction of new machinery in the
industry, in order that workers might not suffer any undue hardships.[58]

7. One of the most usual ways by which unions attempt to limit
the displacing effect of labor-saving devices is by reducing the
length of the working day. If the shorter working day were confined to jobs on the new technique and were accompanied by an
offsetting increase in the price of labor per hour, the introduction
of the new technique would be retarded and, hence, the displacement of labor by it would be reduced. Ordinarily, however, it is
not practicable to apply the shorter working day solely to the new
jobs. Furthermore, unions are equally interested in reducing the
hours of work on the old jobs. Whether a reduction in the length
of the working day for *both* old jobs and new will reduce the displacement of men depends upon: (1) whether the shorter work
day is accompanied by an increase in either hourly or piece rates
and, if it is, (2) whether the reduction in the working day more
than offsets the effect of higher wage rates upon the number of
hours of labor purchased by employers. If the demand for the particular type of labor is elastic, a reduction in hours accompanied by
a compensating increase in rates will diminish rather than increase
employment in the plant. Unfortunately most unions assume rather
uncritically that the demand for their labor is inelastic. Hence movements for shorter hours of work with offsetting increases in hourly
rates often follow the introduction of important labor-saving methods. If the demand for the particular type of labor happens to be
elastic, the result is unfavorable to the union.

When the stone planer was introduced, the Chicago stone cutters' union demanded that the plane be operated only eight hours

[57] See p. 542-44.

[58] In 1940 a manufacturer of automobile springs and bumpers installed some
new buffing machines which displaced 27 men. The union (SWOC) persuaded
the company to keep the displaced men at work around the plant and to add
their wages to the cost of the machine, thus treating them as a capital expenditure rather than a current expense. At the end of five months all of the
27 men had been absorbed at regular jobs, and the extra expense ceased.

a day and six days a week.[59] There was a close connection between the struggle of the Typographical Union for the 8-hour day and the introduction of the linotype. The committee which reported to the convention of 1891 on the problem of machine policy recommended that the hours of labor on the machines be restricted to eight per day, and this was adopted by the convention. Some locals objected to the restriction, however, on the ground that it interfered with their freedom of action, and the rule was repealed by the convention of 1893. Most local unions continued to limit the machines to eight hours a day wherever possible, and the great majority of early agreements covering linotype operators provided for an 8-hour day.[60] The business depression prevented the union from gaining the 8-hour day throughout the trade at the time when the machine was spreading most rapidly and when the short day would have done the most good in limiting displacements. With the return of prosperity the union made vigorous efforts to gain the 8-hour day on all work. By 1902 the issue had become acute. As newspaper contracts were renewed, the 8-hour day was gradually extended in the newspaper industry and after a long and bitter strike in 1906 it was achieved.

The union has a particularly keen interest in a shorter working day when it feels the impact of labor-saving methods upon a stationary or declining demand for the production of the industry. Thus the railroad unions, confronted by the encroachment of trucks and buses and by economies made possible by heavier rails, more powerful locomotives, and a multitude of labor-saving devices, are demanding the 6-hour day. Between 1920 and 1927, the number of Class I railway employees declined by 288,000, or 14.2 per cent. Indeed, the railroads of the country had 24,000 fewer employees in 1927 than in 1913. In April 1929, the Railway Labor Executives' Association adopted a program for dealing with the unemployment problem among railroad workers. Four of seven items in the program involved reduction in the hours of work. In 1931, the Railway Labor Executives' Association decided to demand the basic 6-hour day.

The miners' union, caught between a non-expanding market for

---

[59] Barnett, *Chapters on Machinery and Labor*, p. 37.
[60] The same, pp. 10-11.

coal and technological progress (particularly the spread of the loading machines), is also demanding the 6-hour day. Even in 1929 the volume of bituminous coal mined in this country was 5.9 per cent below 1920, and in 1937 it was 17.3 per cent below 1929.[61] The most important technological development in the coal industry since the first world war has been the loader. The first loaders were introduced in 1923. By 1929, 7.4 per cent of the deep-mined bituminous coal production was handled by loaders, and by 1938, about 25 per cent.[62]

The loading machine does not involve a change in the type of labor employed, but it does produce considerable displacement. Over half of the underground workers in coal mines have been hand loaders.[63] Dr. Walter N. Polakov, the expert of the United Mine Workers, has estimated that 46 men working with mobile loaders can do the work of 100 hand loaders.[64] Producing a substantial displacement at a time when markets and employment were declining, the loader has presented difficult problems for the union.

The policy of the United Mine Workers has long been one of accepting machines and attempting to obtain a large share in the benefits. The union has adhered to this policy toward the loader, despite the fact that many locals have favored obstructing the use of the machine. At the convention of the union in 1934, the committee on resolutions, in reporting on a resolution asking that the union work for actual removal of mechanization from the mines, recommended that

rather than object to mechanization of industry, we should devote our

---

[61] In 1920, the tonnage was 568,667 thousand; in 1929, 534,989 thousand; and in 1937, 442,455 thousand. Employment in the industry declined from 639,547 in 1920 to 502,993 in 1929, and 491,864 in 1937. *Statistical Abstract of the United States*, 1937, pp. 721-22, and *Minerals Yearbook*, 1938, pp. 696, 708; 1939, p. 787.

[62] "Employment in Relation to Mechanization in the Bituminous-Coal Industry," *Monthly Labor Review*, February 1933, Vol. XXXVI, p. 265, and *Minerals Yearbook*, 1939, p. 767.

[63] The United States Coal Commission found in 1921 that 58.5 per cent of all underground workers in 1,900 mines were loaders. *Monthly Labor Review*, February 1933, Vol. XXXVI, p. 265.

[64] United Mine Workers of America, *Proceedings of the Thirty-fifth Constitutional Convention*, 1938, Vol. I, p. 23. Studies of the Bureau of Labor Statistics yield substantially the same result. *Monthly Labor Review*, February 1933, Vol. XXXVI, p. 268.

efforts toward a shorter work day and work week, toward a greater participation in the blessings of invention, of science, of progress, with the fundamental objectives of making mankind the masters of their destiny and subjecting machines, science, and modern developments of industry to human kind.[65]

This resolution was adopted.

At the next convention of the union in 1936 there were more resolutions than ever concerning the loader. Most of these resolutions proposed that taxes be imposed on loaders, and two of them asked that the convention reconsider the action of the previous convention in accepting the loading machine.[66] A provision was incorporated in the Appalachian agreement for 1937 providing for a joint operator-miner commission to study the problems arising from the mechanization of coal mining. But the report of the officers to the convention of 1938 indicated that the operators were non-co-operative.[67] The union, however, hired an expert to study the problem. Again at the convention in 1938 many resolutions proposed taxes on labor-saving equipment, and at the convention of 1940 no less than 29 resolutions on machinery were introduced, most of them proposing a special tax on it. The officers of the union opposed these proposals and advocated accepting mechanization and attempting to extract benefits from it.[68]

[65] United Mine Workers of America, *Proceedings of the Thirty-third Constitutional Convention,* 1934, Vol. I, p. 188. There was a long discussion of the original resolution and also considerable discussion of the substitute resolution of the committee on resolutions during which Mr. John L. Lewis made a strong statement concerning the futility of opposing mechanical change. During the course of his remarks, Mr. Lewis said: "There is no other modern solution to the machine problem of our present day and age than to increase the wages, shorten the working hours and shorten the working week to any degree necessary to let the machine do the work for mankind, but at the same time give to the workers in industry a wage produced by the machine that will maintain them and their families in comfort and with a provision for old age." (The same, p. 204.)

[66] Resolutions 725 and 816 from locals at Holden, W.Va., United Mine Workers of America, *Proceedings of the Thirty-fourth Constitutional Convention,* 1936, Vol. IV, pp. 247-48, 278. The resolutions came particularly from locals in West Virginia where mechanization was proceeding most rapidly.

[67] United Mine Workers of America, *Proceedings of the Thirty-fifth Constitutional Convention,* 1938, Vol. I, p. 87.

[68] The committee on resolutions at the convention of 1938 introduced a substitute resolution for the various proposals to tax the machine which provided that the federal government make a survey of technological displacement and that it pass legislation providing for a 6-hour day and a 30-hour week in coal mining. (The same, p. 309.) At the convention of 1940 another substitute resolution was adopted which simply referred the machine problem to the international

In the steel industry, the Steel Workers' Organizing Committee has been confronted with problems of displacement from the introduction of the continuous strip mill. It is not clear by how much, if at all, the new mills have reduced employment in the steel industry because they have stimulated increases in the use of steel.[69] It is certain, however, that considerable dislocation of labor has been produced, with many men in the old hot mills losing their jobs. The union has made some effort to get displaced employees transferred to the new strip mills, but with little success. At the first national convention of the SWOC December 14-16, 1937, the establishment of a 6-hour day and a 30-hour week as a national law was recommended as a means of offsetting the inroads of technological improvements upon employment.[70]

This survey shows that unions have many ways to limit the displacement of labor by technological change. In analyzing these methods, one should distinguish between those policies which temporarily retard the introduction of labor-saving devices (such as requiring that new machines be introduced no faster than jobs can be found for all displaced men) and policies which more or less

---

executive board for study with broad authority to initiate appropriate legislative action. (*Proceedings of the Thirty-sixth Constitutional Convention*, 1940, Vol. I, pp. 151-52.)

[69] The construction of the continuous strip mills has undoubtedly substantially increased the amount of employment in the country as a whole—as distinguished from employment in the making of steel itself—because much labor has been needed to construct the new mills and the equipment in them. For example, the Irwin works of the Carnegie-Illinois Steel Corp. cost approximately $60,000,000, of which labor received about $40,000,000. It would take many years of operation for the Irwin works to save as much labor as was used in building the plant. In addition, there must be considerable indirect employment afforded by an investment of $60,000,000. As indicated below (p. 274), if one-fourth of any additional income were saved, an increase of one dollar in investment would generate three dollars of additional income. On this assumption, an investment of $60,000,000 would generate an increase of about $240,000,000 in national income, of which labor would receive roughly $180,000,000. Some time would be required to generate this increase in income, but most of it would be realized within two or three years.

[70] *Steel Labor*, Nov. 25, 1938, Vol. III, p. 3. At the instance of Philip Murray of the SWOC, the convention of the CIO at San Francisco in 1939 unanimously adopted a resolution recommending "a further shortening of the number of hours of work per day and the total number of hours per week, without any decrease in established wages . . . until the goal of a 6-hour day and a 30-hour week is reached," as a method of dealing with the problem of technological unemployment. Congress of Industrial Organizations, *Daily Proceedings of the Second Constitutional Convention*, 1939, pp. 110-13.

indefinitely deprive the community of part of the benefits of new inventions (such as requiring the employment of an excessive crew at the new machines). Somewhat ambiguous in its effects is the policy of cutting the hours of work, such as introducing a 6-hour day. If it happens that the community prefers additional leisure to additional income, a 6-hour day is, of course, an ideal way both (1) of reducing displacement by new machines, and (2) of causing the kind of benefits which the workers most desire. But if more income is preferred to more leisure (or if, as is most likely, a mixture of additional leisure and additional income is desired), drastic reductions in the hours of work on new machines go far to deprive the community of the benefits of technological advance. Obviously there is little good in limiting the output of new machines by shorter hours if the principal desire of the community is for more income rather than more leisure.

Even if a union succeeds in protecting the workers immediately affected by a labor-saving device from losing their employment, it does not follow that the union has increased the total amount of employment in the community. It is well established that the general level of employment depends among other things upon the volume of investment. A dollar increase or decrease in investment will ordinarily produce a considerably greater rise or fall in the national income (and hence, in employment). The change in the national income will be large or small depending upon whether a small or a large proportion of income at the margin is saved.[71] Unless, therefore, there is already full employment, retarding the introduction of labor-saving devices will reduce rather than increase the volume of employment.

EFFORTS OF THE MORSE OPERATORS TO APPLY THE POLICY OF CONTROL

In order to illustrate the many issues which may be precipitated by the policy of control, let us review briefly the efforts of the Morse operators to follow their work as Morse was replaced by the teletypewriter or the printer. The commercial telegraphers' union

[71] If the marginal propensity to save is one-fourth (which means that one out of every four additional dollars of income will be saved), an increase of one dollar in investment, not produced by a decrease in consumption, will produce an increase of four dollars in income. On the other hand, a decrease of one dollar in investment will produce a decrease of four dollars in income.

had no agreements with either the Western Union or the Postal at the time the printer was introduced, but the union was recognized by the Canadian National Telegraph. It was with this company that the issues arose.

The introduction of the teletype began shortly before the first World War. The principal advantage of the apparatus is that it makes possible a great increase in the carrying capacity of the wires. Consequently its superiority over Morse is greatest on the main trunk lines (which handle messages from branch lines), especially those on which the traffic is heaviest and the distance between traffic centers is greatest. The teletypewriter was introduced gradually, first on the busiest and longest trunk lines, and then on those less busy and shorter. Subsequent to the war, the simplex printer (as distinguished from the multi-plex printer used on trunk lines) was perfected and was introduced on branch lines where the traffic was light.[72]

The growth of the telegraph business was so rapid and the introduction of the teletype so gradual that for many years no serious displacement problem was created for Morse operators. Displacements were scarcely greater than the normal attrition rate. Under these circumstances the telegraphers' union was not particularly interested in gaining for the Morse operators the opportunity to transfer to the printer on a satisfactory basis. It did attempt to organize the printer operators and to raise their wages—in large part, as stated above, to diminish the advantage of the printers over Morse and thus to retard the displacement of Morse. But the spread of the printers to branch lines created a displacement problem which was greatly aggravated when the depression brought a falling off in business. The union then became keenly interested in gaining for the Morse operators the right to follow their work to the new jobs. It demanded:

1. That the men receive reasonable notice of the company's intention to replace Morse with printers.

2. That the men be permitted to use company facilities for learning printer operation.

[72] In 1931, 90 per cent of one company's and 80 per cent of another company's messages were handled by printers. "Displacement of Morse Operators in Commercial Telegraph Offices," *Monthly Labor Review*, March 1932, Vol. XXXIV, p. 506.

3. That the men be permitted to learn printer operation on company time.

4. That the Morse operators transfer to printer operation without a reduction in pay.

5. That the men retain their seniority standing gained in Morse operation after transferring to printer operation.

6. That senior Morse operators be given the first chance to transfer to printer work.

The first two demands—for reasonable notice and an opportunity to use company facilities for learning printer operation—caused no difficulty, and agreement on these was reached early in the negotiations. The third demand was not important. The union supported it by pointing to the practice of Western Union, which maintained a school to teach printer operation to Morse operators and paid them, in the large centers, half their wages for time spent learning printer operation and, in small places, all expenses for three months. The union, however, was not insistent that men be paid while learning, and the Canadian National Telegraphs refused to grant the point.

The last three demands were the most important. The wage issue was aggravated by the great disparity in the compensation of Morse operators and printer operators. Morse operators earned from $160 to $180 a month. Any good typist could learn the printer, and printer operators were paid from $90 to $135 a month. Naturally the Morse operators were not anxious to follow their work at a substantial reduction in pay. At the same time, the company argued that it would be unfair and demoralizing to pay ex-Morse operators substantially more than other printer operators who were no less skillful and were more experienced at printer work than the ex-Morse operators.

Most difficult of all were the last two demands—those provoked by the problems of seniority created by the displacement of Morse by the teletype. The fifth demand—that Morse operators retain their Morse seniority after transferring to printer operation—involved a sharp conflict between the Morse operators and the automatic operators. If the Morse operators thus retained their Morse seniority, many of them, in times of seasonal layoffs, would be able to hold their jobs at the expense of printer operators who actually possessed much more experience at printer operation. The last issue

—the right of the senior Morse operators to have the first opportunity to transfer to printer operation—would be important only in the event that the Morse operators did not carry their accumulated seniority to printer operation and had to begin to accumulate seniority anew as printer operators. If the seniority rule were permitted to work in its normal fashion, a displacement of Morse by printers would cause the junior Morse operators to lose their jobs. If given the opportunity to follow their work, the junior Morse operators would become printer operators and begin to accumulate seniority as such. Further displacement of Morse by printers would compel more Morse operators to shift to printer operation. As *Morse* operators, this second group of transferees would be senior to the first group, but as *printer* operators, they would be junior to the first group. Hence, unless the Morse operators carried their seniority with them to printer operation, or unless the senior Morse operators were given the first chance to transfer, the displacement of Morse operation by the printer would reverse the seniority standing of the Morse operators, putting the junior men at the top of the seniority list and the senior men at the bottom!

Late in 1930, the officers of the union and the company reached a tentative agreement. The company conceded the first two demands of the union (reasonable notice and opportunity to use company facilities for learning the printer), rejected the third (pay while learning), and granted the important fourth demand that Morse operators be permitted to transfer to printer operation without reduction in pay. In order to secure this last demand, however, the union negotiators sacrificed the demand that Morse operators carry their Morse seniority with them into the printer department and accepted the company's proposal that Morse operators working as printer operators should accumulate seniority only in the printer department. Mainly because of this concession, the rank and file of the union rejected the proposed agreement.

The negotiations were then carried up to Sir Henry Thornton, president of the Canadian National Railways, which controlled the telegraph company. Sir Henry accepted the principle of the men's following their work to new jobs at no reduction in pay and agreed that senior employees should have the first chance to qualify for the printers if they desired to do so. He was impressed with the demoralizing influence of the job-fear that had developed among the Morse operators as a result of the rapid spread of the printer, and he sought a way of eliminating it. Officials of the company estimated that 60 per cent of the Morse operators in the central offices could reasonably look forward to permanent work as Morse operators. Sir Henry expressed interest in the idea of guaranteeing employment to 60 per cent of the Morse operators.[73] The directors of the company and high operating officials did not share all of the views of Sir Henry. Consequently, the agreement ultimately negotiated on March 1, 1932 did not provide for an employment guarantee. It embodied the first two demands of the union but not the third. On the important issue of the rate of pay, it provided that Morse operators in trunk line offices might transfer to printer operators at a moderate reduction in pay.[74] Morse operators in city, branch, and district offices, if properly qualified, might transfer to printer operation at no reduction in pay. The company conceded this because the Morse scale in the branch line offices was less than in the trunk line offices.

Particularly interesting is the compromise on the seniority issue. The agreement provided that Morse operators, while working in the printer department, might accumulate seniority in that department separate and distinct from their Morse seniority. Senior Morse operators, however, were given the first opportunity to transfer to the printer department. If a staff reduction in the printer department displaced Morse operators who had transferred to that department, they might exercise their *Morse* seniority to transfer back to Morse operation. In the event of a subsequent restoration of employment in the printer department, the men who had transferred back to Morse would be recalled to printer operation in accordance with their *printer* seniority. These arrangements permitted Morse operators to retain *as against other Morse operators* the benefits of the seniority which they had accumulated as Morse operators. They were not permitted, however, to use Morse seniority to displace

---

[73] For an account of the president's position, see *Commercial Telegraphers' Journal*, June 1931, Vol. XXIX, p. 90.

[74] The provisions are too complicated to reproduce here, but in practice they meant that Morse operators in trunk line offices might transfer to printer work at a salary of $148 against $170 and $175, which most of them received as Morse operators, and $105, which was the standard rate paid beginning printer operators.

printer operators. In this way the conflicting seniority interests of two groups of union members, the Morse operators and the printer operators, were reconciled.

The experience of the commercial telegraphers is a significant illustration of the complications which may arise when important technological changes occur in enterprises which have seniority rules. If trade agreements are held to be enforceable by the courts, as is the tendency, and seniority rules are interpreted by the courts, managements may find that the present carelessly worded seniority clauses may be interpreted not only to restrict seriously management's freedom to make technological changes but also to require the payment of heavy damages to men whose seniority has been disturbed.

RESULTS OF THE POLICY OF CONTROL

The policy of control tends to promote a more effective utilization of the nation's labor force by requiring employers to transfer and train old employees who otherwise would be laid off. In so far as it does this, it tends to increase the volume of employment. For example, if the union had not required that Morse operators be given a chance to follow their work, many of them would not have had that opportunity. Likewise it was the street railwaymen's union which obtained for electric car operators the opportunity to qualify as bus drivers. But why is this a net gain? If industry had not trained employees from the old technique for the new jobs, it would have trained young men just entering industry. Does the policy of control, therefore, simply produce a *shift* in opportunity rather than a gain in employment—better jobs and more work for the displaced men at the expense of young people trying to get into industry? The answer is "No." Industry finds it more advantageous to hire and train young people than to retrain the old employees whom the unions protect under a policy of control. Hence when the unions require the retention and retraining of old employees, they compel industry to make a larger investment in training men, for it is still worth while at existing wage levels for industry to hire and train almost as many young people as it otherwise would. Hence the policy of control becomes a method of making a larger number of people worth a given wage scale and thus of increasing the volume of employment.

Is it not wasteful to compel industry to retrain older workers whom it does not regard as worth training? If the return were sufficient, would not industry provide the training without compulsion? By no means. In fact the return on the cost of retraining may be very high. The alternative to not retraining displaced workers is to pay them relief, at least for a large part of their lives. Since the cost of relief falls on no particular enterprise, no employer is willing to bear the cost of retraining in order to escape the cost of relief. That is one reason why industry spends less on training than is economically desirable.[75]

In some cases the policy of control compels employers to use skilled men where semi-skilled would do—as when the granite cutters require all machines to be operated by skilled granite cutters. Training costs money. Is it not wasteful to compel industry to train more skilled men than it needs? Possibly. There is much to be said, however, for the view that the amount of training which is desirable from the standpoint of the community is greater than is commercially profitable. Training does more than merely increase the economic value of men; it develops them as men.

In a few instances the policy of control may establish such high rates on the new jobs, or may surround the new technique with so many restrictions, that union employers are at a serious disadvantage compared with non-union. Consequently, there may be a substantial shrinkage of employment in the union plants. It is possible, therefore, that the displacement of labor *caused* by the policy of control may exceed the displacement *prevented* by it. For example, the efforts of the railroad unions, through full-crew laws to reduce the displacement of men by increasing the length of trains have aggravated the very tendency which they were intended to counteract. Furthermore, by discouraging the roads from running faster and more frequent trains, the full-crew laws may have reduced rather than increased the number of jobs. To the extent that the policy of control increases the cost differentials between union and non-union plants, it stimulates expansion of non-union

[75] If wages were free to adjust themselves to increases in the supply of labor, there would, of course, be no need to force industry to increase the number of men whom it trains.

plants and brings about a wasteful duplication of capital.[76]

When unions permit employers to introduce technological changes only so fast as can be done without laying off men, they accentuate the tendency for machines to be introduced in periods of prosperity. Thus they accentuate the instability of business and intensify both booms and depressions—an unfavorable result of the policy of control.

The requirement that technological changes produce no layoffs also reduces the rate of change. In Chapter VII it was pointed out that under conditions of competition the rate at which discoveries are put into effect may exceed the optimum rate. This assumes that investment opportunities in the community are sufficient to satisfy the desire to save. Hence there is a possibility that the policy of control (like the policy of obstruction) by retarding the rate of change will cause the actual rate to approximate more closely the optimum rate. As pointed out in Chapter VII, however, there is no assurance that the actual rate of change may not thus be reduced as much below the optimum rate as it was formerly above that rate. The policy of control is to be distinguished from the policy of obstruction, however, in that it does not seek to prevent changes but only to retard them sufficiently to prevent layoffs. Its effect on the rate of change, therefore, is likely to be small. Consequently, the probability is great that it will cause the actual rate of change to be closer to the optimum rate than it otherwise would be.

If it happens that investment opportunities are not sufficient to absorb the savings of the community, the policy of control, in so far as it retards the introduction of new equipment, will limit the total volume of employment. During recent years, investment opportunities have been too small relative to the community's propensity to save. Under these conditions, more rapid technological change is needed, and the policy of control, to the extent that it reduces the rate of change, is particularly harmful.

---

[76] Put in another way, it produces unemployment of capital in the union plants.

CHAPTER X

UNION ATTITUDES TOWARD BASIC SYSTEMS OF WAGE PAYMENT

The two basic methods of paying labor are by the time worked and by the piece produced. As pointed out in Chapter VI, payment by time leaves an important item of the labor contract undetermined, namely, how much the worker is expected to do in a given time. Nevertheless, more than half of the workers in manufacturing and a much larger proportion in non-manufacturing industries are paid by the hour, the week, or the month.[1] It is also true that payment by the piece leaves an important item of the labor contract undetermined, namely, how long the worker is expected to take to produce a given amount. Consequently, workers who are paid by the piece often seek a time rate guarantee.

One finds numerous variations and combinations of piecework and timework. Workers may be paid so much an hour, but earn a bonus or premium for all output produced over a given amount—the premium or bonus system. Most premium or bonus plans do

[1] A survey undertaken late in 1924 showed that out of 220,536 wage earners employed by 175 manufacturing establishments, 113,526, or 51.5 per cent, were paid by the time spent; 78,837, or 35.8 per cent, by the piece; and 28,173, or 12.7 per cent, by a bonus or premium. (Sumner H. Slichter, "Competitive Exchange as a Method of Interesting Workmen in Output and Costs," *American Economic Review*, March 1925, Vol. XV, No. 1, Supplement, pp. 94-95.)

A survey made by the Wisconsin Industrial Commission showed that the proportion of annual workers paid on a time basis in the public utility and transportation industries was 61.7 per cent; in personal and professional service, 83.2; in retail stores, 85.5; in the construction industry, 99.3; and in manufacturing, 59.4. (*Wisconsin Labor Statistics*, November 1924, Vol. II, p. 8.)

Two studies by the National Industrial Conference Board of wage payment methods in factories (see *Financial Incentives*, Study No. 217, p. 17), one in 1924 and the other in 1935, show that during the eleven-year period the proportion of workers paid time rates scarcely changed. In 1924 it was 56.1 per cent and in 1935, 56.3 per cent. Among those on incentive plans, however, there was a pronounced shift from piecework to premium and bonus systems. The proportion of employees paid by the piece dropped from 36.6 per cent to 22.1 per cent and those working under premium or bonus plans increased from 7.3 to 21.6 per cent. In view of the unfairness of nearly all premium and bonus plans in comparison with piecework, this must be regarded as a serious backward step.

not compensate workers in proportion to their additional output and for that reason are strongly opposed by nearly all unions.[2] Workers may be paid by the time, but may be paid according to standard times assigned to the work rather than by the time actually consumed. This is really a form of piecework, but it may be called standards of production. It was so called when used in the Cleveland women's garment industry.[3] Standards of production may also take the form of establishing different hourly or weekly rates of pay for different rates of output and determining the hourly rate of each worker every few weeks on the basis of his performance during the immediately preceding period. This type of payment has been used in some cutting rooms in the men's clothing industry.

In most industries, unions and employers are in agreement as to the form of wage payment—either both wish piecework or both wish timework, or occasionally both wish standards of production. Not infrequently, however, there is a clash, the union desiring day work and the employers piecework, or occasionally the union desiring piecework and the employers preferring timework. It is important to ascertain the reasons which govern the preferences of unions for different wage payment systems under different conditions. That topic will be examined in this chapter. Payment by the piece creates a large number of special problems and produces many distinctive union policies which are not found when payment is on a time basis. These special problems and policies will be discussed in the next chapter.

DIVERGENT ATTITUDES OF UNIONS TOWARD INCENTIVE SYSTEMS

The man in the street believes that virtually all unions are opposed to incentive methods of payment. It is true, as explained above, that almost all unions are opposed to premium or bonus plans because these plans are essentially devices by which the fast workers are compelled automatically to cut their own piece rates. From the workers' point of view, piecework has a number of ad-

[2] An exception is the Glass Bottle Blowers' Association, which has pressed for bonuses on the feed and flow device.

[3] The experience with this method of wage payment in Cleveland will be discussed in Chap. XIV.

vantages and a number of disadvantages. Also it works differently under different conditions. Advantages which may be important in some industries may be unimportant or totally lacking in others, and disadvantages which may be serious in some instances may be unimportant or absent in others. Consequently, it is not surprising that unions are much divided in their attitude toward piecework.

Some unions (such as the miners, the textile workers, the men's clothing workers, the hosiery workers, the cigar makers, the shoe workers, the iron and steel workers, the potters, and the flint glass workers) either prefer piecework or accept it willingly; others (such as the printers, the building trades, and the railroad shopcrafts) strongly oppose it.[4] Some unions favor piecework in one industry or branch of an industry and oppose it in others. For example, the molders' union, which has struggled hard to drive piecework out of the jobbing foundries, accepts it willingly in the stove and furnace industry, and the women's garment workers' union, while opposing piecework generally in the cloak and suit industry, accepted it for the buttonhole makers. The fur workers forbid piecework in the fur manufacturing branch of the industry, but prefer it for certain types of work in the fur dressing and dyeing section.

Some unions may change their attitude toward piecework in the course of time. About 1916, the women's garment workers' union, which had until then accepted piecework in the cloak and suit industry, changed its policy to strong opposition. In recent years the union has been inclined to let the question of piecework or timework be a local issue. For some years the cloth hat and cap workers' union opposed piecework and in 1919 it succeeded in replacing piecework with timework in New York, the principal market. Experience with timework, however, led the union to reverse its stand and since 1924 it has preferred piecework.[5] There is some tendency for workers to prefer the system of wage payment under which they work and to which, in consequence, they are adjusted. In some

---

[4] In 1938 the International Typographical Union amended its constitution to prohibit local unions from renewing existing piece or bonus scales beyond Jan. 1, 1941. Until 1938, the union had prohibited the making of new piecework or bonus scales and had "discouraged" the extension of existing scales.

[5] But the president of the union writes: "No labor union, certainly not ours, makes of the system of payment a fetish."

industries, therefore, one finds some locals preferring piecework and some preferring timework.

There is often a difference between the official and the actual attitude of unions toward piecework. Years ago the United Garment Workers took an official stand against piecework, and this action has never been repealed. Nevertheless, piecework is the prevailing method of payment in the plants where this union is recognized, and it is accepted willingly by the rank and file. The metal polishers' union is officially opposed to piecework, but an officer, writing in 1940, says: "Quite a large number of our members work on a piecework basis . . . and it seems that when the question is put to them plainly, they don't voice any objection to it." Although the official policy of railroad shop unions is to oppose piecework, many members in shops which pay by the piece like it and are glad to keep it.[6] Years ago the machinists' union adopted a provision in its constitution forbidding the introduction or acceptance of piecework in shops where it did not already exist. This provision is still in the constitution, but an officer of the union writes: "In actual practice, however, little heed is given the provision. Many thousands of I. A. of M. members are working under piecework systems provided for in agreements negotiated by their own representatives and shop committees."

In 1908 Professor McCabe classified unions according to their attitude toward piecework and timework. Some of the unions which he included are no longer in existence, and many in existence today have been organized since 1908. Consequently, the proportions of unions and the several classifications which Professor McCabe found would not necessarily hold true today. A check of those in existence in 1908 and still in existence today indicates, however, that the McCabe classification holds good for all but three or four. The table on page 286 summarizes his classification. It will be observed that in the case of only eight unions, with 4.1 per cent of the 1908 membership, was piecework an acute issue; that is, it was the pre-

[6] A large minority voted in favor of piecework among the New York Central shopmen in 1923. Out of 13,549 voting, 3,849 favored piecework, and 9,601 opposed it. There were 102 ballots defaced and not counted. *International Brotherhood of Blacksmiths, Drop Forgers, and Helpers' Monthly Journal*, October 1923, Vol. XXV, p. 15.

vailing method of payment, and the unions were opposed to it. In the case of 18 unions, with 14.6 per cent of the members, it was something of an issue: it was not the prevailing method of payment, but the unions favored its total elimination.

ATTITUDE OF UNIONS TOWARD PIECEWORK[a]

Method of Payment	Number of Unions	Members of the Unions	
		Number	Percentage
Piecework is the prevailing system of payment and is accepted willingly................................	24	399,500	*23.6*
Piecework is not the prevailing system of payment, but is accepted by a considerable number of local unions without opposition and without discouragement from the national unions..............	9	110,900	*6.5*
Payment is by time and is not an issue...........	58	864,600	*51.2*
Piecework is the prevailing system of payment and is opposed by the unions.....................	8	65,900	*4.1*
Piecework is not the prevailing method of payment, but its total elimination is favored by the unions..	18	246,400	*14.6*
Total................................	117	1,687,300	*100.0*

[a] D. A. McCabe, *The Standard Rate in American Trade Unions* (1912), pp. 187–99.

The eight unions for which piecework was a more or less acute issue were: the cloth hat and cap workers, the fur workers, the United Garment Workers, the glove workers, the leather workers on horse goods, the metal polishers, buffers, and platers, the piano and organ workers, the travelers' goods and leather novelty workers. Of these unions, the cloth hat and cap workers and the glove workers no longer oppose piecework, and the United Garment Workers nominally oppose it but do not actually make an issue of it. The fur workers, as indicated above, continue to oppose piecework except in the fur dressing and dyeing section. The unions of leather workers on horse goods and of travelers' and leather novelty workers no longer exist. Of the existing leather workers' unions, the United Leather Workers' International Union (AFL), which absorbed the leather workers on horse goods, takes no stand on piecework. The leather workers' division of the International Fur and Leather Workers' Union (CIO) took no official stand until

1940, when it decided to oppose piecework.[7] It has been impossible to obtain information concerning the piano and organ workers.

Some of the important new unions oppose piecework. This has been true of many of the locals of the United Automobile Workers. This union has greatly reduced the use of piecework in the automobile industry. In some plants where employers have corrected the abuses associated with piecework, the automobile workers have abandoned their opposition.

BASIC REASONS FOR THE PREFERENCE OF SOME UNIONS FOR PIECEWORK OVER TIMEWORK

The satisfactory operation of piecework from the standpoint of the workers requires (1) that the unit of output or accomplishment be definable with precision, and (2) that conditions of work be maintained with substantial uniformity over periods of time.[8] Where both of these conditions cannot be fulfilled, the union is likely to oppose piecework. There are occasional exceptions to these generalizations, as is proved by the ready acceptance of piecework by the United Mine Workers. The working conditions of the mines are by no means uniform over a period of time and the operation of piecework in mines is full of problems. So difficult is supervision of the individual miner, however, that day work would be even more impracticable than piecework. Indeed, the union could scarcely afford to oppose the employers on an issue where they have so much at stake. Consequently, it accepts piecework and attempts to protect its members against special handicaps by requiring payment for "dead" work, special rates for narrow rooms, and compensation for other unfavorable conditions.

Given the prerequisites of a measurable performance and fairly constant conditions of production through time, there are four principal factors which lead unions to prefer piecework to timework: (1) certain bargaining advantages which it gives to the men in dealing with individual employers; (2) its adaptability to the operation of national trade agreements (or agreements covering a

[7] The union, however, does not make an active issue of piecework. Most of its members are paid by the piece, but by limiting output they have practically converted piecework into timework.

[8] In pre-union days in the coal industry many mines paid by the car instead of by the ton. This enabled the employer to cut the rate by buying larger cars.

competitive area); (3) the protection which it gives both union employees and employers against non-union competition; and (4), a closely related factor, the opportunity which a shift to piecework gives a union to raise the earnings of its members without raising the employer's labor costs.

1. The bargaining advantage which piecework confers on the employees, particularly when there is a union in the shop, are fairly obvious. The worker who improves his output does not have to ask the employer for a raise—and possibly bargain with him over the amount. He gets it instantly, automatically, and in exact proportion to the increase in his output. The unusually fast and competent worker who knows that he is producing more than other employees and who knows that he is entitled to higher pay than they receive is not dependent upon the fairness or whim of the foreman for his reward. His earnings are automatically greater in proportion to his production. Most important of all, piecework protects the employees against a form of exploitation which is almost inevitable when payment is by the hour and the employer is able to keep accurate track of the output of each worker. The employer is quite certain to reward the very fast workers (though not necessarily in proportion to their superior output) and to penalize the slowest. Thus he generates a rivalry which slowly but steadily raises the output of the force. If they are paid by the hour, the employer obtains the additional output for nothing. Piecework protects employees against such exploitation because it makes their earnings rise in proportion to their output.

2. The superior adaptability of piecework over timework in the operation of national (or competitive-area) agreements takes several forms. It is necessary to point out first that, in general, unions are eager to make national agreements covering their industries or at least agreements covering competitive areas. Such agreements have two principal advantages from the union point of view: (1) they prevent weak locals from holding back increases in wages and improvements in working conditions—or, put differently, they prevent the strong locals from endangering the solvency of their employers and the jobs of their members by pushing wages too high; and (2) they reduce the resistance of employers to union demands because

the demands apply to all union employers alike. Most, though not all, national (or competitive-area) agreements are piecework agreements, because piecework greatly facilitates the making of such agreements.[9] The principal problem in making national agreements is fixing the labor cost differentials between competing plants. Both the union and the high-cost manufacturers may desire to keep labor costs uniform between plants. Uniformity of hourly rates does not accomplish this because the labor and the equipment in some plants may be more efficient than in others. Uniform piece rates, however, assure uniformity of direct labor costs. The desire to obtain uniformity of labor costs among competing plants was the principal reason which led the cloth hat and cap workers, after five years' experience with timework, to favor piecework in 1924.[10]

In some cases union leaders may find themselves confronted with two conflicting demands from their rank and file. Some members may desire that the wage rates in all plants under the national agreement be the same. Other members, who live in high-cost communities, may demand differentials to compensate them for their higher cost of living. Piece rates are a convenient compromise. When they are made uniform for all plants, the workers who oppose rate differentials are satisfied. At the same time the workers in high-cost communities are given the opportunity to meet the higher cost of living by producing a little more, if they so desire. No such compromise could be accomplished with hourly rates.

In industries where there are great differences in freight rates and in operating conditions, such as the coal industry, uniform labor costs would put many employers out of business. Consequently,

[9] For example, those in the stove, pottery, flint glass, hosiery, and bituminous coal industries. This was true of the window glass workers' union and, until recently, of the glass bottle blowers.

In the railroad industry wage negotiations are usually on a national scale despite the fact that most of the rates are not piece rates. The railroads are a special case because government regulation of rates prevents operating costs from having a close relationship to the charges for railroad service.

[10] The union reports that timework gave the larger units in the industry an advantage in labor cost because they were able to introduce machinery which gave them a greater production or were able to sectionalize their work so that the individual operative turned out more work for the same wage. The smaller shops did not have enough workers to sectionalize their work. The reversion to piecework removed labor costs from the field of competition.

neither the union nor the employers wish uniform labor costs. But neither do they wish arbitrary or uncontrolled labor-cost differentials such as hourly rates would entail. When they seek to compensate some employer for unfavorable operating conditions or higher freight rates, they wish to know precisely how much of a concession they are giving him. Piece-rate agreements enable the negotiators to know and permit the size of the differentials to be precisely controlled—an important advantage in the operation of national agreements.

3. In highly competitive industries in which there is considerable non-union competition, piecework may be an important protection to union employees and employers from such competition. The cost differential which union plants can stand without losing business to non-union plants is limited. If union plants were to abandon piece-work while non-union plants kept it, the cost differential between union and non-union plants would be intolerably large. This would certainly be true in the coal industry.

4. The Amalgamated Clothing Workers has probably been as aggressive as any trade union in encouraging the spread of piece-work. It has organized many plants in which a considerable fraction of the workers were not paid by the piece, and it has encouraged these employers to install piecework in all departments.[11] In the process of organization of the Chicago market in 1919, the union found that a large portion of the workers were paid by the hour. The union co-operated with employers in spreading piecework and in some instances urged the employers to make the change. It did the same in Rochester, Indianapolis, Cincinnati, and other markets. Most notable of all was the gradual introduction of piece-work into the New York market in the face of strong rank and file prejudice against it.[12]

The leaders of the Amalgamated encouraged the spread of piece-work because this enabled them to raise the earnings of the workers without appreciably increasing labor costs. The union leaders realized that in an industry as competitive as men's clothing, increases in the price of union labor accomplished by raising labor costs in

[11] With a few exceptions such as cutting and trimming.
[12] Within a ten-year period New York was transformed from a day work to a piecework market.

union shops would be of only temporary benefit to the workers, and the men would lose in unemployment what they gained in higher wages.[13] The leaders of the union realized also that hour work, when combined with trade unionism, might result in a substantial drop in labor efficiency and dangerous increases in labor costs.

In the main, it will be noted, these four primary reasons for unions' preferences for piecework constitute bargaining advantages for labor.

SECONDARY FACTORS INFLUENCING UNIONS TO FAVOR PIECEWORK

Wherever a union shows a distinct preference for piecework, it is likely to be influenced by one or more of the basic reasons discussed in the preceding section. There are, however, additional advantages to piecework from the standpoint of wage earners, though they are not ordinarily decisive in determining union policy.

In some industries piecework tends to increase the proportion of the work done in the plants of the larger and more responsible employers and to discourage the growth of small contract shops which unions usually find difficult to control. In the men's clothing industry the contract shops which make trousers or vests for other manufacturers are likely to have something closely akin to uncontrolled piecework, though payment is nominally by the hour. The success of the employer in getting contracts depends upon the price he quotes and, under timework, this price depends upon the output of his workers. The employees know this. The employer may even tell his people that he can get a contract at such and such a price, but that he cannot quote it unless they turn out a certain amount. The absence of piecework, therefore, encourages the manufacturers to play contractor against contractor and thus to develop in the contract shop a high speed of work and a low level of labor costs that the manufacturer cannot match.[14] Under piecework, faster work by the employees in the contract shops means higher earnings for the

---

[13] As it was, the union had an extremely difficult time in keeping the cost differential between union and non-union plants from becoming disastrously high.

[14] The manufacturer also tries with some success to speed up his people by threatening to send more work out to contract shops if costs in his plant do not come down.

workers, not lower labor costs for the employer. Thus, growth of contract shops in the men's clothing industry is at least not encouraged under the piecework system.[15]

Piecework may help unions and union employers to adjust themselves to changed business and market conditions. For example, during a business depression or under formidable non-union competition a union employer who thought it desirable to bring out a cheaper line of goods would have less difficulty in securing concessions from the union if the workers were on piecework than if they were on a time basis. In either case, concessions are politically difficult for union leaders to grant. If payment is by the hour, concessions in labor costs can be made by the union only by reductions in the hourly rate of pay. If payment is by the piece, the union can make concessions by consenting to lower piece rates, which may be yielding very high earnings, or by accepting, for new operations, piece rates which are quite favorable to the employer. This is possible because such concessions do not necessarily mean corresponding reductions in hourly earnings or they affect only part of the employees. Through such devices as these the Amalgamated Clothing Workers was able to do much to help its employers meet the non-union competition which became very formidable after 1920. More recently, through conceding special piece rates on sports trousers, the union helped some of its employers meet the competition from the manufacturers of work clothes, who began to invade the sports field about 1936. And even when business or competitive conditions require a general reduction of piece rates, the resulting dissatisfaction among workers is likely to be less than would be provoked by a corresponding reduction in hourly rates, because the pieceworkers have the opportunity to maintain their earnings by increasing their output. For example, when the Amalgamated Clothing Workers accepted a cut of 8 or 9 per cent in the Chicago market on May 1, 1921, and another cut of 7 or 8 per cent a year later, the hourly earnings of the pieceworkers dropped scarcely at all.[16]

[15] On the other hand, as noted in footnote 10 on p. 289, conditions in the cloth hat and cap industry were such that timework favored the large shops rather than the small. If the union in this industry had not changed its policy, it would probably have lost its members in the small shops.

[16] The hourly earnings of operators in a Chicago shop, by six-month periods, were as follows:

An advantage that might well be regarded as of primary importance is that piecework helps the employees profit from improvements that are constantly being made in management, technique, equipment, and raw materials. At least this is true when there is a union in the plant to prevent arbitrary cuts in piece rates. Most of these improvements are too small to justify changes in piece rates. Some of them are made by the men and are not known to the management. In the course of a few years, however, these improvements have an appreciable effect upon the earnings of pieceworkers.

For example, in 1894 the earnings of glass bottle blowers averaged about $4.94 a day. Because of the depression, piece rates were reduced about 15 per cent. In 1900, when the men were still working under the reduced rates, their average earnings were $5.46 per day.[17] In 1910 there were widespread complaints among the men that the piece rates for the newly invented narrow-mouth bottle machines were too low. As the men learned how to run the machines and as small improvements in the machine and in management were made, earnings increased. By 1914 the daily wages of machine operators were about equal to those of handblowers and by 1917 somewhat larger.

Studies of wage rates and earnings in the pottery industry reveal that between 1911 and 1924, although most union piece rates had increased less than 60 per cent, the hourly earnings of the workers had doubled.[18] The increase in earnings was partly due to speeding

July-December 1920	82	cents
January-June 1921	80	"
July-December 1921	77	"
January-June 1922	76	"
July-December 1922	76	"
January-June 1923	78	"

On May 1, 1923, an increase of 10 per cent went into effect. From July to December 1923, piece rate earnings were 84 cents and from January to March 1924, 83 cents. Poor flow of work affected earnings in the first quarter of 1924.

[17] G. E. Barnett, *Chapters on Machinery and Labor*, p. 82.

[18] U. S. Bureau of Labor Statistics, *Wages, Hours, and Productivity in the Pottery Industry, 1925*, Bulletin No. 412, pp. 23-29.

Although the jiggermen's earnings per hour increased 98 per cent, the rate for jiggering a 7-inch plate increased only 61 per cent. Although the average rate of the bisque kiln placers increased 68 per cent (allowing for the change from 212 to 200 cubic feet of kiln space per kiln day), the hourly earnings of kiln placers increased 120 per cent. The piece rate for turning ordinary thin tea cups was increased from 3.5 cents per dozen to 4.935, or 41 per cent, but

up during the war, but it was also due to changes in equipment and arrangements that made work easier.

In the Rochester clothing industry the earnings of pieceworkers increased about 164 per cent between 1916 and 1920. *General* wage increases amounted to 71 per cent and special increases brought the total advance in piece rates up to over 100 per cent. The remainder of the increase, in the opinion of Dr. W. M. Leiserson, who was arbitrator in the industry in 1921, must be explained by increased production.[19]

A specific instance of how pieceworkers profit from improvements in equipment is furnished by the introduction of steam irons into the clothing industry in place of the gas iron. In pressing with gas irons it was necessary for the presser to use a sponge cloth. The steam pressing machine makes this unnecessary. With the gas iron there was danger that the worker would scorch the cloth. This made it necessary for the operator to watch the heat of his iron carefully. The steam iron relieved him of this responsibility and enabled him to produce more work. When steam irons were introduced into the Chicago market, the firm which put them in attempted to have the piece price reduced because the handling of the sponge cloth was eliminated. The union claimed that this gain was offset by the fact that the presser had to spend more time drying out the cloth. No change in the rate was made, and the balance of advantage was with the workers.

Furnaces were first made by stove foundries as a side line. The stove foundrymen did not foresee how important the furnace work would become and were less careful than they otherwise would have been in bargaining for rates. Furthermore, the fact that the work was new and different made it difficult to determine how long the jobs would take. In the course of time the molders discovered many short cuts and by the late twenties their earnings came to be far out of line with those of men of similar skill making stoves in the same foundries. Some men made as high as $18 or $20 a day, and

---

average earnings of turners increased from 49.87 cents per hour to 94.2 cents, or 88 per cent. The piece rate for casting 24-size jugs increased 41 per cent between 1911 and 1924, but the earnings of casters on semi-vitreous ware increased from 38.91 to 90.3 cents, or 155 per cent.

[19] Labor Adjustment Board, the Rochester Clothing Industry, *Case No. 4G*, Wage Adjustment, Fall Season, 1921, p. 7.

the average of the men on furnace work was about $12 a day—several dollars more than the stove molders.

The cloth hat and cap workers report that piecework has largely eliminated the problem of superannuated workers. Under timework, employers sought to get rid of the older workers who produced less than the younger workers but who received substantially the same wage as the younger men. Under piecework the employer has no strong incentive to rid himself of older workers because he pays them only for what they produce. His loss is confined to overhead. The president of the union writes:

In our industry we do not have the problem of superannuation to any considerable degree. Because we have the piecework system we have men of 65 and even 70 still working at our trade and earning a living by it. True, they may not be earning as much as younger and faster men, but they can make their living at the trade.

A minor advantage of piecework is the freedom from minute supervision which it gives the workers. A pieceworker in a New York Central shop—a man who was also a member of the shop committee of the union—said on this point: "If you want to rest half an hour or fifteen minutes, the time is yours. They don't openly stand for it, but the foreman or nobody bothers you." The freedom from minute supervision conferred by piecework is said to be one of the reasons why it is liked by union workers in the Swedish building trades. Of course, if a pieceworker, by taking a few minutes off, delays other pieceworkers, he is likely to hear from them.

These five secondary factors which influence some unions in favor of piecework—its tendency to discourage outside contracting; the fact that it facilitates adjustment to changes in business and market conditions; the opportunity that it gives to workers to profit from small improvements in management, technique, equipment, and raw materials; the protection that it gives older workers; and the fact that it gives workers freedom from supervision—would bulk large if they appeared together. Indeed, in that case they might have a pronounced effect on union policy. As a matter of fact, they do not usually occur together. The influence of two of these factors is limited by the fact that their effects, though important, are easily overlooked. It is not apparent to the union rank and file that piece rates diminish the political difficulties of adjusting the union wage scale to market changes. Nor are the substantial gains in earnings which gradually accrue to pieceworkers over a period of years as a result of many small improvements in management and methods easily foreseen.

BASIC REASONS FOR UNION OPPOSITION TO PIECEWORK

Just as the unions which prefer piecework or accept it willingly are influenced in the main by the bargaining advantages it gives them, so the unions which oppose piecework are influenced largely by bargaining considerations. Unions are at a bargaining disadvantage under piecework (1) when the unit of performance is difficult to define or to measure; (2) when operations in various shops are very different and when new operations are numerous and not closely comparable with the old ones; or (3) when it is difficult to compel the employer to maintain standard working conditions. When these disadvantages are marked, the union is likely to oppose piecework.

1. Building construction, railroad repair shops, and women's garment manufacturing are good examples of industries in which it is difficult to define or to measure the volume of performance. In the building industry, work is done under such dissimilar conditions that it is difficult to measure the amount of time and effort that different jobs will require.[20] In the women's garment industry changes in styles and materials[21] make it difficult to judge the amount of work involved. In some industries, such as building, the standards of quality required are indefinite and subject to change. The molders' union occasionally has experienced trouble of this sort in the stove industry, where it willingly accepts piecework. An employer might obtain low piece rates on a special stove brought out to meet cheap competition and then might gradually become stricter and stricter in his inspection until he was requiring the same standard of quality on the special stove as on his regular line.[22]

---

[20] The obstacles are not insurmountable, as the fairly satisfactory operation of piecework in the Swedish building trades testifies. Nevertheless, the difficulties are sufficiently serious that the building trades unions are strongly opposed to piecework.

[21] Some materials are much more difficult to handle than others.

[22] The men's clothing workers' union has encountered the same problem, but it has not been particularly serious.

A radical change in method, such as the introduction of a new machine, may make it difficult to judge the proper output or to measure performance and thus may lead the union to demand that timework be substituted for piecework. This happened when the linotype was introduced in the nineties, and today the miners' union is demanding that the men on the new coal loading machines be paid by the hour instead of the ton.[23]

2. Unions can use piece rates to control the relative labor costs in different shops only when the operations in the several shops are the same or quite similar, so that either the same piece rates can be used in all shops or new rates in a given shop can be based upon similar operations in other shops. In virtually all industries where the union prefers piecework these conditions are present. When the products of several shops are so different from each other that rates cannot be accurately compared, piecework is likely to lead to competition among the workers in the various shops, which the union finds very difficult to control. Workers in one shop may attempt to enlarge their employers' share of the business, and thus to increase their own employment, by consenting to piece rates that are slightly lower than rates in other shops. The workers in the other shops attempt to meet this competition, with the result that the union finds the downward pressure on piece rates extremely difficult to resist.

The ability of the union to control inter-shop competition among pieceworkers depends to a great extent upon whether changes in the

---

[23] Until the introduction of the linotype not only were nearly all compositors paid by the piece but there had never been opposition in the union to piecework. When the linotype appeared, the national union advised the locals to adopt a time scale for the machines. This was done, not because of opposition to piecework but because of the difficulty of estimating the output. (G. E. Barnett, "The Printers," *American Economic Association Quarterly*, 3d series, October 1909, Vol. X, No. 3, pp. 131-32.) In the course of time the scale gradually became a make-work arrangement because abolishing it would have produced layoffs.

Concerning the demand of the miners for timework on the loaders, the union expert writes (in a personal letter): "Labor productivity with power-driven machines is a variable of the design, of the management, of the planning and so on. Therefore to set a tonnage rate for mechanized mining is a task that can hardly satisfy either labor or stockholders. If management is lax, conditions will reduce a man's output and he will suffer through no fault of his own (lack of supplies, interrupted power, unprepared working place, etc.)." Of course, a guarantee of a minimum hourly rate could meet some of these difficulties.

employer's line require large numbers of new operations to be priced each season or each year and upon whether the new operations are closely comparable with the old ones. If the number of new rates to be set each season is not large, the union can be represented in dealing with all employers by two or three bargaining experts (as in the case of the men's clothing workers) who can keep piece rates in the several shops closely in line. But when changes in the employer's line require large numbers of new operations to be priced each season, the union is compelled to leave most of the bargaining of rates to committees in each shop. Under these conditions inter-shop competition is not easy to control. The difficulty is particularly great when the new operations are not closely comparable with the old ones, because the union officials have trouble in checking the work of the shop committees. In years of depression, when work is scarce, the committees are under strong temptation to make concessions on new rates in order to help employers get business. However desirable this may be from the standpoint of its effect upon the general economic situation, unions are afraid of uncontrolled inter-shop competition.

The job foundry industry illustrates this difficulty in operating piecework. Since separate rates must be negotiated in each shop and rates cannot be easily compared, inter-shop competition has been hard to control.[24]

The best example of the bargaining difficulties that we have been discussing is furnished by the women's garment industry. The ordinary cloak and suit or dress house has from 50 to 150 models in a season. There are two seasons in a year—sometimes three. Separate rates must be set for each model. Because the seasons are short and deliveries must be made promptly, the rates must be set without delay. Hence the union must bargain with employers through shop committees. Styles and materials change from season to season so that the rates set in one season are of little use in those of future seasons.

The bargaining difficulties created for the union by this combination of circumstances have been accentuated by the large num-

---

[24] This largely explains why (as stated at the beginning of this chapter) the molders' union opposes piecework in the job foundries, although it prefers piecework in the stove industry.

ber of contract shops which work for jobbers and also for manufacturers. The presence of the contract shop affects the bargaining of piece rates in the manufacturing shops (called inside shops) because the employer threatens to send the garment out unless he gets a favorable piece rate. The costs of the contract shops are almost entirely labor costs, because the jobber or manufacturer supplies the designs and the material. Hence the piece rates are of decisive importance in determining the success of the shop in getting contracts, and inter-shop competition is keen.[25]

It was this combination of circumstances which caused Mr. Morris Sigman, then manager of the New York joint board and later international president, to lead a fight about 1916 to change the union policy from acceptance of piecework to opposition to it. The change was made, and about 1920 the union succeeded in eliminating piecework from the cloak and suit industry.[26] The union hoped that timework would lessen inter-shop competition in labor costs, make for greater equality in labor costs, and halt the growth in the number of outside shops. It overlooked the fact that uniformity in time rates did not necessarily mean uniformity of labor costs. Inter-shop competition now took the form of employers' trying to get more output for a given hourly wage and, as the contract shops were better able to drive the workers than were the larger manufacturing shops, they continued to increase in number. As stated above, the union later (during the great depression) changed its policy and began to treat piecework as a local issue.[27] When the New York cloak makers, the most influential group in the union, in renewing their agreement in 1933, agreed to restore piecework, after having enforced timework for nearly fifteen years, the acceptance of piecework may be said to have become the national policy of the union.

The New York cloak makers were willing to restore piecework

[25] For further details of the competition between inside and outside shops, see p. 395, footnote 4.

[26] Its policy was to eliminate piecework from the dress industry also, but the union was not strong enough there to raise the issue.

[27] Only the Cleveland local refused to attempt to deal with the complicated problem of inter-shop competition by the crude and simple method of eliminating piecework. It attempted to draw on the resources of time study and scientific management. This experiment will be discussed in detail in Chap. XIV.

largely because certain safeguards came with it. The most important of these were the limitation of the number of contractors who might work for any jobber, and jobber responsibility for wages and for the equitable division of work among the designated contracting shops. The policy of accepting piecework has led the union to concentrate upon developing methods of controlling its operation. For example, when the cloak and suit agreement in New York was renewed in 1935, the new agreement provided that piece rate settlements must be made simultaneously, on the premises of the jobber, with all contractors manufacturing the same style and type of garment. The most highly developed control is in the New York dress industry, where garments are now priced in large measure on the basis of standard times for various operations. These times have been established by time studies. The plan in its fundamentals is similar to the scheme of standards of production which existed in the Cleveland market from 1920 to 1931, and which will be discussed in Chapter XIV.[28]

3. Finally, a union which accepts piecework is at a serious bargaining disadvantage when it is unable to compel employers to maintain reasonably standard working conditions over a period of time. Almost all pieceworking unions have trouble with this problem and are compelled to give considerable attention to it. Their efforts to deal with different phases of it will be discussed in the next chapter. When the difficulty of maintaining standard working conditions becomes too great, and the earnings of the men are subject to violent fluctuations which cannot be foreseen and which are beyond their control, the union is likely to turn against piecework. The opposition of the automobile workers' union to piecework in the body plants was mainly due to the peaks and valleys in earnings produced by changes in models, fluctuations in production schedules, material shortages, and other causes beyond the men's control.

The experience of the molders' union with piecework in the jobbing foundries also illustrates the problem of maintaining standard working conditions. For instance, in a jobbing shop where a heavy

---

[28] The machinery for price settlement in the New York dress industry is centralized in the office of the impartial chairman. In Cleveland each house had its own time-study man. This proved to involve too much overhead.

casting is being made, a molder may need the crane two or three times a day. The crane, however, may be giving service to another molder and the first one may be compelled to wait some time for it. In shops where the work is repetitive and where large quantities of one casting are made, flasks well adapted to each job are provided. But when the jobs are constantly changing, the worker may to-day have a flask well adapted to the casting, while the next time he makes the same piece, he may have to use a flask which is not adapted to it. Today he may use a certain flask and match plate which are in good repair, so that he is able to turn out a good day's work. A year later the foundry receives another order for the same casting. In the meantime the flask and the match plate have become more or less out of repair. Perhaps the flask has been stored in the yard and has been banged around and is out of shape. On the second job, therefore, the molder has difficulty in making a fair day's wage. The very fact that payment is by the piece diminishes the interest of the management in keeping equipment in good repair. In other words, the management is least interested in keeping equipment in repair when the molder is most interested in having it in perfect condition. In short, the inherent economic interest of management under the piecework system may tend to make this type of variable working conditions chronic and thus to accentuate the union's opposition to the system.

The ability of pieceworkers to earn is also greatly affected by the run of work. In a jobbing foundry the size of the order differs greatly. A rate may be set on a pattern when it first comes in. A year or so later the foundry may obtain a much smaller order for the same casting. A piece rate which was fair in the first case may be unfair in the second.

SECONDARY OBJECTIONS OF UNIONS TO PIECEWORK

In the same way that the unions which prefer piecework find a number of advantages in it which are not of decisive importance in determining their attitude, so unions that oppose it find a number of disadvantages in piecework which, though important, reenforce rather than determine their attitude. Many of these objections would not exist in well-managed plants. Some of the more important of them are:

1. Piecework is too powerful and continuous an incentive and may cause men to injure themselves by excessive speeding. This result may occur in industries where the union is in a weak bargaining position. It may occur also in highly seasonal industries in case the union is unable to enforce equal division of work effectively, because when there is not a full day's work for everyone the employees may race to obtain a larger share of it. "The race for the bundle" was one of the problems that piecework gave the women's garment workers' union. When the union is able to control the division of work and to prevent arbitrary reductions in piece rates, piecework is not likely to lead to excessive speeding because the short cuts which the workers discover, and small improvements in equipment and in raw materials, make it constantly easier for the workers to earn a given wage.

2. Some unions object to piecework because in their judgment it increases unemployment by causing workers to produce more than they would turn out under day work. The unemployment argument was important in determining the opposition of the Typographical Union to piecework after having accepted it for many years on hand composition. At the time that expansion of the industry began to slow up, important labor-saving devices were introduced into the industry. The union accepted the linotype but, quite naturally under the circumstances, pursued a make-work policy. It insisted on an 8-hour day on the linotype and forbade piecework on the machines. In general, this objection to piecework is obviously of a make-work nature and may be regarded as a form of make-work policy.

3. Piecework creates many opportunities for employers to show favoritism to certain workers. Some jobs are bound to be more liberally priced than others. The foreman, if he chooses, can give the best jobs to his friends and the least desirable ones to men whom he wishes to punish for union activity, insubordination, or other reasons. Some locations may be better than others because of better lighting or differences in other conditions. The foreman can put his favorites in the best locations.[29] He can also take care that his

---

[29] This may happen under timework also, but is less important because the employees' earnings are not affected.

favorites do not lose time because equipment is out of repair, because they have to wait for work, or because of bad material. When such delays do occur, the foreman can be generous or stingy in granting a time allowance at the hourly base rate. Moreover transfers to new jobs usually cause pieceworkers to lose earnings. A little time is required to get the equipment and material for the new job ready; then there is a warming-up period before the worker has attained normal speed. Here again the foreman has an opportunity to discriminate.

Many managements are scrupulously careful to show no favoritism in the operation of piecework. The fact remains that the opportunity is there and the management can use it, if it desires, in an attempt to keep the union weak by penalizing its most aggressive and loyal members. If the management does this, it should not be surprised to find the union fighting hard to get rid of piecework.[30]

4. Piecework sometimes creates the problem of preventing dissension within the ranks of the union and preserving its solidarity. Naturally, if the management is showing favoritism, jealousies are bound to arise inside the union. Furthermore, some members may feel that the union's shop committee is showing more zeal in pushing the claims of some members for extra compensation to make up for unavoidable delays, bad material, or out-of-order equipment (essentially piecework grievances) than in pushing the claims of others. Finally, the very fact that under piecework some workers earn much more than others may arouse jealousy and division in the ranks. For example, the highest earners in the union may be quite reluctant to support demands for higher wages. They may be satisfied with their earnings and unwilling to risk having them interrupted by a strike. If piecework seems thus to be causing

[30] It would be interesting to make a catalogue of the ways in which unions at various times have attempted to deal with the problem of some jobs' being more liberally priced than others. The auctioning off of "the fat" in the newspaper offices (see p. 182, note 42) is one of the most interesting. Another effort to equalize piecework earnings occurred in the stove industry. In the early days of the industry, before the work had become highly specialized, three to five molders might make all of the castings in a stove. The foreman would call the men together and tell them to divide the castings. None of the men knew which lot of castings he would make. After the division, the foreman assigned a lot to each man.

serious division in the union ranks, the union may attempt to get rid of it.

5. Some craft unions object to piecework on the ground that it tends to destroy the craft by encouraging excessive specialization. One encounters this objection among railroad shopcraft unions. It is something of a paradox that, although the individual craftsman usually prefers to specialize himself, he is fearful that the employment of all-round craftsmen will be greatly narrowed by increased specialization, and therefore dreads its spread. This is true even of men who are paid by the hour. After learning one or two jobs thoroughly, they find these jobs easier to do than any others and prefer to continue doing them. When payment is by the piece, the desire of the men to specialize is even stronger, because they make more money when each does a single job with which he is thoroughly familiar and loses no time in transferring from job to job. Union leaders are fearful that, if piecework makes the men themselves strongly disposed to specialize, employers will lose interest in training all-round craftsmen and will organize their shops so that nearly all of the work can be done by handymen trained to do one or two operations. Then the bargaining power of the union will be reduced.

6. Related to the above is the objection that piecework sometimes gives the management an opportunity to weaken the bargaining position of the workers by transferring part of the work to helpers. The pieceworkers themselves may be favorable to this, provided piece rates are left unchanged. In fact pieceworkers may demand that certain operations be transferred to helpers, or they may hire helpers out of their own wages.[31]

The effect of the use of helpers upon the bargaining power of the union depends upon the kind of work the helpers do. If it is strictly unskilled, the union's bargaining power may not be affected; if the helpers assist the journeymen in such a way that they learn to do the journeymen's jobs, a dangerous group of potential strikebreakers may be created, because a strike would give the helpers an excellent opportunity to get journeymen's jobs. In the foundry industry there formerly prevailed a system of work known

---

[31] For a discussion of this topic, see pp. 338-39.

as the "Berkshire system." A molder, with the aid of five or six helpers hired out of his earnings, would run five or six floors. His helpers would ram the pattern and he would draw the pattern and finish the mold. This system was made possible, of course, by piecework and was a potential threat to the union's bargaining power because it led to the training of helpers who could replace the journeymen. In order to keep the system out of union shops, the union for many years has prohibited its members from working with helpers when payment was by the piece. Only when payment is on a time basis is the molder permitted to work with helpers.[32]

AN EXAMPLE OF CONFLICT BETWEEN THE UNION'S AND THE WORKERS' ATTITUDE TOWARD PIECEWORK

Conditions in some industries or branches of an industry may cause a union to become strongly opposed to piecework. The union then may attempt to apply its official policy to other industries or branches of the industry where the employees prefer piecework. Such efforts to fight piecework against the wishes of the workers may seriously hinder the union in extending its organization.

The machinists' union is an illustration of this experience. When the piecework policy of the union was formulated, the organization was composed largely of skilled craftsmen employed in railroad shops and in plants making machine tools and industrial equipment. Their work was largely either by special order or on equipment turned out in small lots—in other words, non-repetitive work. Under these conditions the union was at a disadvantage in bargaining piece rates and the men were strongly opposed to payment by the piece. For many years the constitution of this union has contained a clause against piecework. About 1905, when the union was in the midst of its fight against piecework, the clause read:

Any member introducing or accepting piecework in any form whatever where it does not now exist, or any member running more than one machine in any shop where such is not now the practice, unless such introduction is upon the decision or advice of the local lodge and approved by the Grand Lodge, shall be expelled.

---

[32] In late years the union has made some exceptions to this rule in the furnace branch of the trade. The purpose was to help union furnace manufacturers meet non-union competition.

This and other sections gave the officers of the union discretion to accept or reject piecework, but the actual policy of the union for many years was vigorous opposition to piecework.

At the turn of the century, manufacturers of industrial equipment were reorganizing their operations so that a large part of the work could be done by specialists rather than all-round men. This involved standardizing various parts and manufacturing for inventory to a greater extent than formerly. Manufacturers were stimulated to make these changes by the acute shortage of skilled labor which developed during the boom of 1898-1901 as a result of failure to train mechanics during the long depression of the nineties. As a larger and larger part of the work was made repetitive and specialized, it became practicable to pay for it by the piece. Consequently, the spread of specialization was accompanied by extension of piecework.

The skilled machinists in the union were strongly opposed to specialization because it meant a loss of part of their work. Likewise, they were strongly opposed to piecework—partly because they identified it with specialization and partly because they did not realize that when work is repetitive, piecework operates more satisfactorily than when the work is non-repetitive. Efforts of the employers to subdivide and specialize operations, to make work repetitive, and to introduce piecework, involved the union in a large number of strikes and lockouts. At the 1901 convention, for example, the president reported that three-fifths of the difficulties with employers during the preceding two years had been over the question of piecework. He said that during the period the union had prevented the introduction of piecework into 114 shops affecting 2,800 machinists, but that it had been introduced into 49 shops affecting 3,653 machinists. His recommendation to the convention was that piecework be accepted in union shops and that it be controlled. He pointed out that the union was handicapped by the fact that the men often desired piecework.[33]

The convention, however, was not disposed to accept the advice

---

[33] *Machinists' Monthly Journal*, July 1901, Vol. XIII, p. 465. The president said: "The men of our trade, to a very great extent, are desirous of accepting piecework or premium plans, and refuse in a great number of instances to join our Association on account of our opposition to this method of performing work."

of the president.[34] The members were affected (1) by the fact that shortage of skilled men after the long depression put the union in a strong bargaining position and (2) by their intense opposition to specialization and their identification of piecework with it. Consequently, the convention took a stronger stand against piecework than ever: it amended the constitution to permit union men to accept piecework after August 1, 1903 only on condition that the employer agree to discontinue it on or before July 1, 1904. The national officers of the union saw that this amendment was certain to involve the union in many strikes. Consequently, they submitted the matter of enforcing the amendment to a referendum and succeeded in persuading the rank and file to vote against enforcement.

At the 1907 convention President O'Connell again pointed out that the union was facing difficulties because it was opposing a method of wage payment which a growing proportion of the workers found satisfactory.[35] The convention, however, went on record in support of a committee report "that the present policy of our association in regards to piecework be vigorously continued, and that our members be urged to fight this objectionable feature whenever and wherever possible until its abolition has been accomplished."[36]

By 1909, the continued failure of the union to halt the spread of piecework, and the obvious handicap to the union from the strong policy of opposition, led the president to plead for a more tolerant policy and greater discretion to the officers in dealing with the problem. "At least 50 per cent of the strikes in which our members are involved result from the attempt to establish piecework and 60 per cent, if not more, of our money expended on

[34] The same, August 1901, Supplement, Vol. XIII, pp. 650-52.
[35] "This subject, like Banquo's Ghost, is always with us. The persistent effort on the part of the employers to introduce piece work in all its multifarious phases keeps us constantly on the alert and almost continuously in trade disputes in many sections of our jurisdiction. . . . The great difficulty in handling this problem is the fact that many machinists are not opposed to piece work when conducted upon a fair and practicable basis. Therefore, it is difficult to induce men who are working under what they are pleased to term an honest system of piece work to vote for its abolition, or if necessary, to go on strike against it." *Machinists' Monthly Journal*, October 1907, Vol. XIX, p. 967.
[36] International Association of Machinists, *Proceedings of the Twelfth Biennial Convention*, 1907, p. 68.

benefits is the result of piecework strikes." He pointed out that
several of the largest branches of the metal working industry, such
as locomotive building, electrical equipment, and automobiles, were
largely piecework:

We have been unable to prevent its introduction or growth, and, worse
still, we have not succeeded in organizing these industries. . . . Other large
industries might be mentioned in which tens of thousands of men are
employed who are eligible to membership in our association, but the
fear that they may be compelled to strike against piecework is used as
an argument why they will not join with us.[37]

President Johnston, who succeeded Mr. O'Connell as president
of the machinists, continued to urge that the union modify its
piecework policy. His recommendation to the Baltimore convention
in 1916 produced no change in the constitution.[38] The actual policy
of the union, however, has gradually been changed. The constitution in 1940 still contained a strong clause against piecework, which
the union retained out of deference to old members, but the union
no longer wages a general fight against piecework.[39] Many thousands of its members work under piecework systems provided for
in agreements negotiated by the union.

One of the most influential officials of the union privately expressed the opinion in 1938 that its uncompromising opposition to
piecework was the greatest single mistake the organization ever
made. He believed that had the union attempted to regulate and
control piecework, the organization would be the largest one

---

[37] *Machinists' Monthly Journal*, October 1909, Vol. XXI, p. 928. The president added: "I am, therefore, of the opinion that more latitude should be given
the International President and General Executive Board in dealing with the
piece work and kindred questions, so that if opportunity presents itself for organizing
any of the industries where it is in existence, and an arrangement can be made to
properly regulate piece work as we now regulate the day rate, we would be in a
position to take advantage of these opportunities."

[38] "It is very evident to all who have had experience in organizing work that
if we are ever to organize the many manufacturing and railroad shops where
piecework is established, our attitude on this question must necessarily be modified."
Machinists' Monthly Journal, August 1916, Vol. XXVIII, p. 745.

[39] The clause in the constitution in 1940 was somewhat more temperate than the
one of 30 years earlier. It read: "In shops where it is not now in practice no member
is permitted to accept piecework or to operate more than one machine or to accept employment under tenure, merit, task, or contract systems. Members found
guilty of advocating or encouraging any of these systems in shops where they
are not in operation shall be liable to expulsion."

in the American Federation of Labor. Unquestionably the union's piecework policy was a blunder, but it was a very natural one. The skilled journeymen doing non-repetitive work could not appreciate the advantages which piecework brings to men doing repetitive work and did not realize the possibility of controlling it and guarding it from abuse under such conditions. By attempting to impose their ideas of policy upon men working under conditions different from their own, the skilled journeymen kept the union out of many shops.

SUMMARY AND CONCLUSIONS

1. Trade unions are much divided in their preference for timework and piecework. Their preferences are determined in the main by the precision with which it is possible to define the unit of accomplishment, the possibilities of maintaining standard conditions of work over periods of time, the bargaining advantages which piecework gives to the men in dealing with individual employers, the adaptability of piecework to national agreements, and the protection which piecework gives union members against non-union competition.

The attitudes of individual unions toward piecework and timework have undergone little change since McCabe made his study in 1908. However, as the proportion of semi-skilled productive workers in trade unions increases, the proportion of unions which prefer piecework or accept it willingly may be expected to increase. Although the Typographical Union has recently decreed the end of piecework in printing shops by 1941, this does not represent a real change in union policy. The building trades have shown no signs of adopting the Swedish policy of piecework, and the employers have not demanded it. Hence piecework is not an issue in building construction. The most important development in union policy toward timework and piecework is the final change of the International Ladies' Garment Workers' Union, after years of indecision, in favor of piecework. This change is partly a result of the experience of the union with timework and partly a result of its success in compelling jobbers to negotiate with it and to assume responsibility for rates. Almost equally important is the change of the cloth hat and cap workers in favor of piecework.

2. The division of trade unions on the subject of timework and piecework does not necessarily mean that there is a clash between employers and unions on the subject. In practically every case where the union prefers piecework, the employer also prefers it. And in a great majority of cases where the union prefers timework, the employer also prefers it. The number of cases where unions compel employers to use a method of payment which they would not voluntarily adopt is small. More than a generation ago union policy eliminated piecework from certain branches of the building trades, particularly carpentry and stone cutting. Recently, the automobile workers have eliminated piecework from a few plants in the automobile and automobile parts industries. Piecework would be used more extensively in the printing industry and railroad shops were it not for union opposition.

3. The tendency which employers have displayed during recent years to use premium and bonus systems in place of piecework is in conflict with union policy and is likely to be a source of dispute.

4. Although the cases of difference between unions and employers over piecework and timework are not numerous, there are frequent conflicts over the matter of combining a timework guarantee with piecework. These will be discussed in the next chapter.

5. The effect of piecework upon union policy is profound. It introduces many special problems into the relationship between the union and the employers. It makes many conditions which are matters of indifference to timeworkers the subject of grievances. It alters the interests of the men and the behavior of the management. The many special problems introduced by piecework and its effect upon union policies will be discussed in detail in the following chapter.

CHAPTER XI

PROBLEMS AND POLICIES CREATED
BY PIECEWORK

No better illustration of the molding of union policies by circumstances can be found than the effect that piecework has had upon the attitude of unions toward managerial efficiency and working conditions. Introduce piecework into a shop and many conditions which are a matter of indifference to timeworkers—breakdowns in machinery, inadequate or unsatisfactory equipment, poor materials, faulty routing or planning of the work which results in delays and idle time—become grievances. The timeworker may even welcome delays to work because they help him stretch the job over a longer period and diminish the immediate danger of unemployment, but to the pieceworker any condition which interferes with output reduces his earnings.

Perhaps the major problem created by piecework grows out of the effect of the system upon the interest of both workers and management in shop conditions. Curiously enough, the introduction of piecework very often diminishes the interest of managements in efficiency. Since the workmen earn only when they are producing, the management knows that no direct labor cost is entailed by keeping them waiting for work. And since the earnings of the men depend upon their output, the management also knows that when a machine is not working properly or when poorly prepared raw material is causing delays and trouble, the men will work a little harder in order to maintain their customary earnings. Consequently, managers of piecework shops are often lax in planning work in such a way as to avoid delays, in keeping machinery in the best of repair, and in seeing that raw material is uniformly of proper kind and quality. All of these shortcomings of management are costly to pieceworkers and, consequently, the agreements of unions in piecework plants usually contain rules designed to protect the employees against such shortcomings of the management and the resulting conditions which interfere with earning capacity.[1]

[1] An excellent statement of the interest in proper shop conditions manifested by

Not only does piecework cause unions to seek to protect their members against conditions which impede production, but it causes them to be interested in standards of quality and in the problem of spoiled work—matters that are not usually of importance to time-workers. In addition, it causes union policies on a number of matters to be the opposite of those which prevail under timework. For example, instead of attempting to keep as many men at work as possible, unions of pieceworkers are quite likely to make a grievance of the retention of more men in the shop than are actually needed. Indeed, it is not unusual for the managements of pieceworking shops to endeavor to keep as large a force as possible and for the union to combat this tendency. Instead of attempting to broaden the operations which are regarded as the skilled mechanics' work and opposing specialization, unions that serve pieceworkers often encourage specialization and seek to transfer as much work as possible from journeymen to helpers because the skilled workers can thus increase their production and earnings.

LIMITATION OF OUTPUT OF PIECEWORKERS BY THE UNION

Although unions composed largely of pieceworkers attempt, in general, to protect their members against obstacles to production, some of these unions have themselves imposed definite limits upon the output or the earnings of their members. These restrictions are caused by the desire of the workers to protect themselves against the tendency of employers to cut piece rates when the earnings of some workers become large; to avoid being handicapped in negotiating general wage increases by the large earnings of a few workers; to prevent wide disparities in the earnings of the members from arousing jealousy and dissension among them; and to force division of employment opportunities among as many workers as possible.

In the long run, limits on output are likely to become exceedingly

---

unions serving pieceworkers is found in an address entitled "The Golden Rule in Industry" delivered by William P. Clarke, then president of the American Flint Glass Workers' Union, before the National Association of Manufacturers of Pressed and Blown Glassware at Pittsburgh, Pa., on Apr. 22, 1920.

The labor manager of a prominent Chicago special order house in the men's clothing industry said to me: "Unquestionably there has been a great increase in the efficiency of shops since the market was organized, just because the union has insisted upon good production conditions."

expensive to the employer and disadvantageous also to the union. However reasonable at the beginning, they gradually become obsolete, as equipment, materials, conditions of work, and methods of work are improved. Since the restrictions prevent these improvements from resulting in higher individual output, the plant or department becomes overmanned. Although the employer may be at a serious competitive disadvantage, the union finds itself compelled to fight for the retention of restrictions because their removal would result in the layoff of some of its members. The more obsolete and burdensome limitations become, the harder the union fights to retain them, because the greater would be the displacement in case they were removed. As the problem of these restrictions was discussed in Chapter VI, it is unnecessary to consider them in detail at this point.

BLANKET PROTECTION AGAINST UNFAVORABLE WORKING CONDITIONS—A MINIMUM WAGE

One way of protecting pieceworkers against unfavorable working conditions and obstacles to production is a blanket guarantee of a wage which each worker receives no matter how much he produces. The guaranteed rate, of course, is somewhat less than the workers are expected to earn. A few employers give a guarantee voluntarily as a matter of good business. They believe that the guarantee more than pays for itself because it is an incentive to department heads to see that their workers earn at least the base rate.[2] Most employers, however, have been unwilling to give a blanket guarantee to pieceworkers. An examination of fifty agreements providing for piecework disclosed only ten with a blanket guarantee. Among these were the agreements of the International Ladies' Garment Workers' Union in the dress industry, and agreements between the Amalgamated Silver Workers and the Gorham Manufacturing Company, and the Doehler Die Casting Company and the Association of Die Casting Workers. The upholstery weavers' Local No. 25 of Philadelphia for some years had an understanding, not incorporated in its agreement but in effect none the

[2] For example, a guarantee of the hourly rate of its employers is one of the rules of the Merganthaler Linotype Company but is not provided for in the company's agreement with the union. The management states that make-up losses because of the guarantee provision are far less than 1 per cent of the pay roll.

less, that pieceworkers would be guaranteed 80 cents an hour.

The turn-work system, recently established in most departments of the flint glass industry, affords a limited guarantee. A "move" is the number of a given article which the workers are expected to make in a half-day turn (four hours). A price is set for each move. Regardless of whether or not the workers make the move, they receive this price for each turn they work. In case they make more than a move during a turn they are paid in proportion.[3] But in many instances it is easy for the workers to make much more than the move. In these cases the guarantee may not provide a great deal of protection. The glass bottle blowers have been attempting to get guaranteed minimum wages but thus far without success. At the 1937 conference between the union and the bottle manufacturers, the workers requested a minimum wage of a dollar per hour in the blown ware department, but the manufacturers declined to agree to the request.[4]

Sometimes a blanket guarantee is limited to new workers, as in the case of the agreement of a paper processing company with the printing pressmen's union. The agreement provides that "in event

[3] The history of turn work in the flint glass industry has been touched upon in the discussion of make-work rules in Chap. VI. Until 1893 the men worked "limited turn work," which meant that they were not permitted to make more than a move during a turn but received a turn's pay for every turn worked regardless of whether they made a move. Competition of non-union factories in 1893 led the union employers to demand introduction of straight piecework with no limits on production. Against the advice of its president the union refused the demand and a long and expensive strike followed. This resulted in the introduction of unlimited piecework into virtually all departments of the industry except the chimney and paste mold. During the war the limits were removed in the paste mold department and by 1924 in the chimney department. In 1937 the union at last achieved the restoration of turn work in virtually all departments of the industry—but turn work without limits on production. Hence most of the industry in 1938 was on unlimited turn work.

In the several departments where turn work has prevailed for some years, the guarantee afforded by the payment for a move regardless of whether or not the move was made has created the temptation for the men to take time off and go slowly. This has aroused considerable complaint from employers, because it often resulted in failure of the shops to reach the regular listed move. Nevertheless, the manufacturers were compelled to give them a full turn's pay. The union officials have condemned this practice strongly and have warned the members against it.

[4] Glass Bottle Blowers' Association, *Report of the Proceedings of the Final Wage Conference*, 1937, pp. 22, 23. This is an old demand of the glass blowers. For example, at the 1927 conference the union requested a guarantee of $6.50 a day in the blown ware department, but failed to secure the consent of the manufacturers. *Workers' Report of the Sessions of the Final Wage Conference*, 1927, pp. 11-17.

a new employee fails to attain the minimum time rate of 45 cents per hour, his pay will be adjusted to the minimum for a four weeks' period."[5] A question of some importance is whether the blanket guarantee is to be computed upon a daily or weekly (or pay-period) basis. Usually it is computed upon a daily basis, but occasionally it is computed upon a weekly or pay-period basis.[6] In the latter event, the guarantee may be of very limited practical significance because in a week's period the hours in which the employee earns above the base rate may more than offset the few hours in which he falls below the rate.

The guaranteed rate must, of course, always be somewhat below the usual piecework earnings of the employees, and in the case of fast workers it is likely to be considerably below. For this reason a blanket guarantee is never a complete protection (particularly for the more rapid workers) against the multitude of conditions which interfere with the earnings of pieceworkers. Consequently, unions seek to protect their pieceworkers in numerous more specific ways against impediments to production, as will now be shown.

PROTECTION OF PIECEWORKERS AGAINST SPECIFIC OBSTACLES TO PRODUCTION

The various conditions impeding production which have induced unions to seek specific forms of protection for pieceworkers may be classified as follows: (1) inadequate, obsolete, or poorly maintained equipment; (2) unsatisfactory working conditions; (3) insufficient or unsatisfactory raw materials; (4) faulty organization of the work and routing of material; (5) avoidable delays; (6) obstructions imposed by other workmen.

1. *Inadequate, obsolete, or poorly maintained equipment.* It was indicated in the preceding chapter that piecework creates the

---

[5] If, after four weeks, the employee consistently fails to meet the minimum rate, he will be transferred or discharged.

[6] The agreement between the Amalgamated Silver Workers and the Gorham Manufacturing Co., effective June 5, 1937, provides for a guarantee upon a weekly basis but adds: "It is, however, understood and agreed in case any employee shall fail to earn such guaranteed amount while performing piecework, which, on the basis of experience with such employee or with other employees, should have been reasonably possible, the matter of adjusting such employee's day rate to prevent his taking advantage of the guarantee provided in this section to the detriment of efficient operations shall be considered between the company and the union and appropriate action taken with respect thereto."

temptation for managements to limit expenditures for equipment and repairs of equipment and to let the workmen maintain output (and their earnings) by working a little harder. Hence, every union operating under piecework must be alert to require management to furnish more and better equipment, to replace old and worn out and obsolete equipment, and to keep equipment in proper repair. The coal miners' union is constantly exerting pressure to have the managements provide more cars and better car service.[7] A chronic complaint of the molders' union has been that some managements allow the flasks to become old and rickety and fail to renew them. In the flint glass industry the union complains of the frequent inadequacy of wind, hose, punties, molds, and snaps.[8]

[7] President Lewis of the union quotes the Report of the United States Coal Commission as follows: "As a matter of fact, the determination of the correct number of mine cars that should be available at any particular mine to transport the coal from the face to the tipple has been given extraordinarily small consideration from an engineering standpoint. It was with the greatest difficulty that the management of most of the mines visited could be induced to discuss or explain in concrete figures their method of determination of the proper number of mine cars for their own particular mine." *The Miners' Fight for American Standards,* p. 59.

[8] In making glass ware which is pressed in molds, the operator must have wind in order to make speed. The hose is used for conveying the wind to the molds. As soon as the article is pressed the operator directs the wind on it so that the article will keep the proper shape and so that he can release it from the mold more quickly. If the molds get too hot the glass sticks to them and the scale will make an impression on the next piece. Sometimes the management is stingy in supplying hose. The wind is made by a fan. Sometimes the fan is not large enough and sometimes it is set where it produces hot wind instead of cold.

The punty is the iron on which the men gather their glass from the pot or tank where it is heated. Punties get out of order and are sometimes not promptly repaired. (The union admits that the men are partly responsible. It has made some progress in influencing them to take proper care of tools and facilities.) The union also complains that very often an insufficient variety of punties is supplied. The glass for a 12-ounce article or a 7-ounce article can be gathered on the same punty, but the work can be done faster if a punty of the ideal size for each article is supplied.

If a man can make 450 pieces with two molds, frequently he could make 600 with three. The mold may cost $50 or $100. When a manufacturer starts a new article he does not know whether or not it is going to sell. If the worker gets a good production with one mold and does not seriously complain, the manufacturer may not supply a second one.

To finish articles it is necessary to reheat part of them. The small furnace in which this is done is called the "glory hole." The ware is held in the glory hole by a tool called a snap. If the supply of snaps is so limited that they do not have sufficient time to get cool, they leave a mark on the ware.

Because of the shortage of facilities in some factories, the workers formerly made a practice of getting down early to get their equipment and arrange it before beginning work—in some shops an hour and a half or two hours. Men living near the

Some unions seek to guard their pieceworkers against inadequate equipment by specific provisions in their trade agreements. Thus the agreements of the Window Glass Cutters' League stipulate that "proper facilities shall be provided for handling large sheets so that the cutter may not be unreasonably slowed up in his work or endangered." The standard agreement of the International Glove Workers' Union of America provides that all dies and mallets and cutting blocks in the cutting room shall be in good condition and that the employer shall supply solid cutting blocks. But it is easy for employers to find excuses for postponing repairs or replacements. An agreement of the Detroit local of the International Broom and Whisk-Makers' Union provided that when an operator was required to spend one hour or more in repairing his sewing machine he should be paid by the hour.[9]

In extreme cases a union may adopt a more drastic policy of penalization such as refusal to negotiate prices on new work until equipment is brought up to the standard. A vice-president of the molders' union refused on one occasion to negotiate prices on cores in a foundry at Aurora, Illinois, because there was a shortage of dryers and oven space and because the core room in other respects was insufficiently equipped. When the lamp chimney department of the flint glass workers' union abolished limits on the output of its members in 1923, the union expressly stipulated "that should any company refuse to equip their plants sufficiently or to the satisfaction of the workers, then such company shall not have the privilege of working the unlimited system in their plant until the same is properly equipped."[10]

2. *Unsatisfactory working conditions.* Closely related to the protection of pieceworkers from inadequate or poorly maintained machinery is their protection from hampering conditions of work. A good illustration of the usefulness of unions is furnished by an experience in the Chicago clothing industry. A company had moved

---

factory would go before breakfast and then go home to eat. To control this the union passed a rule fining anyone who attempts to get tools ready more than 30 minutes before starting time.

[9] U. S. Bureau of Labor Statistics, *Trade Agreements, 1926*, Bulletin No. 448, p. 25.

[10] American Flint Glass Workers' Union, *Proceedings of the Forty-seventh Convention*, 1923, p. 226.

its vest shop into a new building. Soon after it started working, the vest pressers claimed that the vacuum "was no good."[11] The union insisted upon an investigation, which disclosed that the steamfitters had put in too small a pipe from the vacuum pipe to the steam pressing machines. It was necessary to tear out the pipe and put in a new line and a new $2,500 pump. Despite the expense, it was definitely a benefit to the firm. But the labor manager explained that in the old days the foreman would not have dared report to the management that he needed a new vacuum pipe; he would have been the last person to recommend such expensive changes.

A frequent complaint of the coal miners' union is that a boulder or a low timber in a mine is preventing the miners from loading their cars full. Another more or less standing complaint of the miners has been poor ventilation. Air is sucked into mines through ventilating shafts which may become partially obstructed by rock falls or cave-ins. The air is deflected into the working rooms by curtains or swinging doors in the entries. The movement of the mine trains through these curtains causes them to become torn. Then the air, instead of going into the working rooms, continues down the entry, and the miners are compelled to work in hot, dusty, and ill-ventilated rooms. Because payment is by the ton, managements are likely to assume that the men will mine all the coal for which they can get cars. Hence the management may fail to maintain the timbers, to remove rock falls in the ventilating shafts, or to keep the curtains and swinging doors in proper condition. Sometimes conditions beyond the management's control may subject the employees to unsatisfactory working conditions, as when a working room in a mine becomes wet. In that case the agreement may provide that the employees shall be given other work.[12] Because of the tendency of piecework to reduce the interest of managements in

[11] On steam pressing, the iron must stand on the vacuum long enough to dry out the goods.

[12] The rule in the agreement effective in the Illinois district in 1928 provided: "The company shall keep the mine in as dry condition as practicable by keeping the water off the road and out of the working places. When a miner has to leave his working place on account of water, the company shall employ said miner when practicable to move the water or do company work, provided said miner is competent to do such work, or he will be given another working place equal to the average place of the mine, until such water is taken out of his place." Louis Bloch, *Labor Agreements in Coal Mines*, pp. 223-24.

shop efficiency, it is frequently only through pressure from the union that unfavorable working conditions can be overcome.

3. *Insufficient or unsatisfactory material.* Insufficient material or bad material may seriously limit the output and the earnings of pieceworkers. When this happens, the union business agent or shop committee is likely to complain. In an industry where operations are as highly subdivided as in the men's clothing industry, any lack of balance among the sections means too much work for some and too little for others. Lack of balance among the sections has been a frequent complaint of the union. Poor thread has been another frequent complaint, and, among the pressers, the amount or the quality of the steam supply. If there is not enough steam, or if the steam is too damp or not sufficiently hot, the output of the pressers is retarded.

Some unions seek by definite rules to protect their members against loss of earnings through insufficient or bad material. In the stove industry, for example, if the molder is not furnished enough iron to "pour off" his work, his earnings the next day will suffer because his space is limited. If part of the floor is occupied by molds made the preceding day, he will not be able to make the usual number of new ones. To protect the men against this, the agreement between the employers and the union provides that if the molders are not furnished sufficient iron to pour off their work, they shall be paid for the work remaining over at the regular price.[13] An exception was made of cases where failure to provide sufficient iron was the result of "break-down of machinery or other unavoidable accidents." This provoked a dispute over the meaning of "breakdown of machinery" and "unavoidable accidents."[14]

[13] *Conference Agreements in Force and Ruling between the International Molders' Union of North America and the Manufacturers' Protective and Development Association,* effective Jan. 1, 1937, clause 11½. This agreement was in effect without change in 1940.

[14] The union argued that breakage of the belt on the cupola fan or the cutting through of the cupola bottom should not be regarded as breakdowns or as unavoidable accidents. The cupola has a fan belted to a shaft. The fan furnishes the draft necessary to heat the iron. If the belt breaks and is not replaced, the iron cannot be heated sufficiently for pouring. In the bottom of the cupola are two cast iron doors held together by a pole. The doors are opened after each heat to release the slag. To prevent the doors from being melted by the molten metal, the cupola man covers them with a bed of sand. Sometimes the molten metal cuts through the sand and melts the doors and the metal escapes.

The tapestry carpet workers' union of Philadelphia exacted an extra price for weaving bad stock. The agreements of the Window Glass Cutters' League provide that, if the cutter has glass in his stall which he does not consider suitable for his orders and if he refers the matter to the chief preceptor and the boss cutter and his complaint is sustained, he will be compensated for time lost. In the flint glass industry the system of payment gives the men limited protection against loss of wages because of bad material. As described above, the men are paid so much per turn whether they make the move or not, and up to the number specified in the move they are paid for bad ware as well as good. But beyond the number specified in the move they are paid for good ware only.

For a number of years the workers in the glass bottle industry have demanded that they be paid for all "melted, bursted, and stony ware," or for loss of any ware for causes beyond their own control. This demand has been presented at many wage conferences between the union and the employers, but has not been obtained.[15] At the 1925 conference in the glass bottle industry, the stopper grinders complained that they were receiving stoppers which were too thick (or bottles with necks that were too small) with the result that an unusual amount of glass had to be ground off and the grinders, through no fault of their own, could not make a day's pay. The motion to change the piece rate was lost, but the firms agreed to correct the defective ware.[16]

In the stove industry the quality of materials gave rise to two prolonged disputes between the foundrymen and the union, one

---

The union contended that the firm should keep a spare belt on hand and that cutting through of the cupola bottom should be regarded as the fault of the cupola man. In 1922 the union succeeded in eliminating from the rule the phrase "or other unavoidable accidents" (thus making it clear that the men would not be put to loss by belts breaking) and in adding a clause specifically stating that the cutting-through of the cupola bottom would not be regarded as a breakdown of machinery.

[15] For an early discussion of this demand, see *Workers' Report of the Final Wage Conference between the Employers of the Glass Bottle Industry and the Glass Bottle Blowers' Association*, 1924, p. 21.

[16] The men wished the piece rate changed so that they could make not less than $6.50 a day. They said that it took twice as long as usual to grind this ware, but that they would not insist upon an increase if the firms would eliminate the cause of trouble. Glass Bottle Blowers' Association, *Workers' Report of the Final Wage Conference between the Employers of the Glass Bottle Industry and the Glass Bottle Blowers' Association*, 1925, p. 26.

over "dull" iron and the other over "dirty" iron. Dull iron is iron which is too cold to pour properly. The fault may be either the management's or the molder's. The iron may be too cold when it comes from the cupola, or it may become too cold because the molder does not pour it rapidly enough. Prior to 1896 the foundry-men as a rule did not pay for castings made with dull iron. In that year, however, the conference between the union and the foundrymen adopted the rule that payment was to be made for dull iron, when caused by a bad heat, only if poured by the fore-man's order.[17] In 1903, the dull-iron rule was changed to a per-centage basis intended to establish a test of responsibility for dull iron.[18]

The dirty iron dispute became important about 1906. By dirty iron is meant, not iron which has dirt in it, but iron which has chemical properties that produce defective castings. In 1906 the union representatives asked that their members be paid in full for work lost because of dirty iron. The foundrymen denied that there was such a thing as dirty iron and insisted that the losses of which molders complained were due to careless pouring. The issue came up for discussion each year thereafter and was regarded as of great importance by the molders. The 1910 conference decided that it would be unwise to adopt "any sweeping resolution," and that the best plan would be to adjust locally cases of abnormally dirty iron.[19] In 1922, however, the conference clause relating to loss from defective iron was entirely rewritten. The percentage test of dull iron was abandoned and the clause was altered to read: "It is agreed that the molder must exercise the skill of his trade and care in preparing the mold, skimming, handling, and pouring the iron. The molder having exercised the care and skill, if the casting is defec-tive in consequence of the condition of the iron, the work shall not

---

[17] F. T. Stockton, *The International Molders' Union of North America*, p. 142.

[18] The original percentage test was that if the loss of castings because of dull iron ran 4 per cent or more of the total value of work poured in any one heat, this would be accepted as evidence that the fault was the management's and not the molders, and all castings lost because of dull iron were to be paid for. In computing percentages, each cupola was to be considered separately. In 1906 the rule was altered to provide that, if the loss for the entire heat was less than 4 per cent but 10 per cent of the molders lost 10 per cent or more of their work, these molders were to be paid for all loss in excess of 4 per cent of their work. The same, p. 143.

[19] The same, p. 144.

be discounted."[20] This means that wherever the molder exercises proper care and skill he is paid in full for ware defective because of the condition of the iron. In 1924 the conference added a note to the clause which defined "the skill of the trade," and added that "it is required of the employer to furnish him (the molder) with iron in good condition throughout the melt to run the work, or stand loss due to such failure, whether the loss covers few or many castings." This rule was still in effect in 1940.

Castings may be lost because of the sand in the mold cutting or blowing. By cutting is meant that the sand does not hold when the iron is poured into the mold. Blowing occurs when the steam and gases from the molten iron cannot escape through the sand as rapidly as they should and must escape through the iron. They then form blow holes. Cutting and blowing may be caused by the molder's not ramming the sand properly; but they may also be due to sand that is too dry or too wet. At one time the molder had to stand all the loss from cutting or blowing. He still has to stand the loss if it is caused by him; but not if the sand was not in proper condition.

4. *Faulty organization of the work.* In some industries, such as the glass industry, the location of the workers in the shop materially affects their earnings. One of the complaints of the flint glass workers' union is carelessness on the part of the managements in placing the "shops."[21] If the shop making a small article, of which it can produce a great many, is placed at a pot with a shop making a large article, the shop making the small article is deprived of a fair opportunity to work. The men making the small article have to go to the pot for glass much more frequently than the men making the large article, but it takes the gatherer of the shop making the large article much longer to gather his glass. The result is that the men making the small article are kept waiting for the gatherers from the other shop to finish gathering their glass.

The union wishes the shops to be so placed that those at one pot will be making as nearly as possible the same number of articles

---

[20] *Conference Agreements in Force and Ruling between the International Molders' Union of North America and the Manufacturers' Protective and Development Association,* Jan. 1, 1937, cl. 11.

[21] A "shop" in the glass industry means a group of two or three men with their helpers, who work together in making an article.

per turn. The manufacturer says: "Our orders govern this." With better planning, however, the management could sometimes hold over certain work until the next day. At the conference of the chimney department of the flint glass industry in 1925, the workers proposed that shops employed on common bulbs that are the farthest distance from the tank should make 15 per cent less than the regular listed "move" and be paid the regular listed wages. This was rejected. A substitute was then offered by the workers providing that the manufacturers do all in their power to help the men farthest from the tank to reach normal production. This was agreed to.[22]

5. *Avoidable delays.* Since pieceworkers can earn only when they have the opportunity to work, unions seek to protect their pieceworkers against delays not due to the workers' fault. Delays may occur for a multitude of reasons—equipment that is out of order, lack of necessary facilities and equipment (particularly when the pieceworker is shifted from one job to another), lack of raw material, raw material that is not in proper condition to work. Some of the obstructions to production already discussed are included here, but these obstacles are of concern at this point only in so far as they cause loss of working time.

The agreements of many pieceworking unions contain provisions designed to compel management to compensate pieceworkers for time lost through no fault of their own. The agreement between the Doehler Die Casting Company and the Association of Die Casting Workers protects the workers against time lost by breakdowns of machinery by providing: "In the straight piecework departments, employees shall be paid their hourly rates for all time lost by breakdown of equipment or similar causes through no fault of theirs on that day." The agreement effective April 7, 1937 between the United Automobile Workers and the Reo Motor Car Company provides that time lost by reason of machine repair, die repair, and other delays will be compensated at the guaranteed rate for piecework.[23] The agreement effective November 30, 1935 between the women's garment workers' union of Cleveland and the Cleveland Dress Manufacturers' Association has a similar pro-

---

[22] American Flint Glass Workers' Union, *Circular No. 131*, Aug. 22, 1925, p. 2562.
[23] P. 13.

vision.[24] The agreement between the United Rubber Workers and the Sun Rubber Company, effective September 1939, provides for payment at the hourly base rate for all delays which exceed four minutes.[25]

The agreement in the machine department of the glass bottle industry provides that when a machine is not in proper working order or necessary facilities are not furnished, the operator shall report it promptly to the factory manager. If the machine is not put in order, or facilities not furnished within an hour, the manager shall notify the shop to operate by timework from the expiration of the hour, or to lay off until the next turn. The agreement also provides that if the shop loses over sixty minutes during the day for causes beyond its control, the men are to be paid for all time lost. Stops of five minutes or less, however, are not to be counted.[26] Before this rule was adopted the men would often wait nearly the whole day for a machine to be repaired. Many conferences were required before they obtained this rule.[27] The convention of the Glass Bottle Blowers' Association in 1917 adopted a resolution recommending that shops which lost time on account of burnt molds, bad plates, or other causes not the fault of the shop, should be paid at the rate of a dollar for each half-hour lost.[28] The union, however, has never succeeded in gaining this demand.

[24] "For idle time in the shop the workers shall be paid the minimum rates herein provided." Art. IV (F).

[25] Art. IV (E). The delays covered specifically include injuries requiring medical attention (first-aid within the factory).

[26] Sec. 4.

[27] At the 1927 conference in the glass bottle industry, the workmen made a strenuous effort to obtain the adoption of a rule providing that the men should not wait after starting time on account of bad glass or for any other cause. Should delay be occasioned by any cause, and the management fail to instruct the workmen to lay off, they were to be paid for the time worked. The union representatives insisted that the proposed change would not raise the manufacturers' costs, but would make for efficiency and economy. (Glass Bottle Blowers' Association, *Workers' Reports of the Sessions of the Final Wage Conference*, 1927, pp. 6-7.) The president of the union said the men complained that the factory foremen made no special effort to get a shop started because they knew that, under the existing agreement, the men were obliged to wait at least one hour without pay. If there were no waiting period, the union representative said, "the foremen will be more keen to have the snaps, moulds, etc. ready for the shop to start work." The manufacturers, however, declined to accept the proposal to abolish the waiting period. The same, p. 8.

[28] Glass Bottle Blowers' Association of United States and Canada, *Proceedings of Forty-first Annual Convention*, 1917, p. 66.

The tapestry carpet weavers' union in Philadelphia found that its workers in a large shop were being held back by delays in making repairs. The firm had no one in charge of its storeroom. When a machine broke down and a new part was needed, the weaver went into the storeroom and attempted to find his needed part. Naturally it often took him some time to find what he wished. In some cases he discovered that a mistake had been made in filling the orders and that the part was not the proper size. The union suggested that the firm hire someone to take charge of the storeroom. The firm was reluctant to do so because it did not believe that the saving would be worth the cost, but the union insisted. The man put in charge was a machinist, who acted as a buyer and helped out on the repair work. He kept track of spare parts so that he always had a supply on hand. When new stock came in, he checked it to see that it was the proper size and not defective. Where two or three hours had sometimes been lost in making a repair, under the later arrangement only a few minutes were required.

The molders in the stove industry complain that time is lost in starting new jobs because of the failure of the management to have proper facilities available. The agreement contains no mandatory rule, but it states:

Where a change of job is made, the molder often loses considerable time and is put to great inconvenience through the necessary clamps, bolts, and other facilities needed for the job not being supplied to him promptly. We believe that in well regulated shops that should be made a feature of the shop management and should be a subject of favorable recommendation to the members of the M.P. & D.A.[29]

One of the most frequent causes of delay is lack of raw material or of proper raw material. In the glass industry the men may lose time because the glass is too hot or too cold to work. The men also complain that the management does not always use care in assigning shops to pots and tanks—sometimes a shop which is making an article that requires hot glass is assigned to a cold pot, so that it is delayed while the pot is picking up heat. The agreements of the flint glass workers' union provide that

[29] *Conference Agreements in Force and Ruling between the International Molders' Union of North America, and the Manufacturers' Protective and Development Association*, effective Jan. 1, 1937, cl. 18.

if the men wait 30 minutes on glass to be placed in the proper working order at the beginning of the turn, and they commence work and after working a reasonable period of time find that the glass is not in working order, they shall report the same to the manager and the manager shall either instruct them to continue at work and pay them turn work or else knock them off for the remainder of the day.

Since pieceworkers may be delayed by innumerable causes, many unions seek to protect their members by a blanket rule that their members be compensated for idle time. The agreement between the Gorham Manufacturing Company and the silver workers' union provides that pieceworkers "shall be paid at the hourly rate when compelled to wait for work." When standards of production were adopted in the Cleveland women's garment industry, it was provided that manufacturers must pay workers for all idle time falling within each day that the workman is required to come to work. Idle time was compensated at 20 per cent below the worker's regular hourly rate. It is usual in union coal mines to compensate tonnage workers for time lost through no fault of their own, as when the company fails to supply a miner with timbers and powder or to lay switches and to provide cars within a stipulated time.

The Amalgamated Clothing Workers has taken the position that workers who are kept waiting for work through no fault of their own shall be paid for the time lost at the rate which they regularly earn per hour at piecework. This has been a powerful incentive to manufacturers to eliminate unnecessary delays. Some factories found that they were paying for so much idle time that they made radical changes in their managerial methods and established far more effective control over the flow of work from one section to another. As long as the workers were unorganized and it was not necessary for the management to pay for idle time, they felt no concern about the matter.

6. *Obstructions imposed by other workmen.* Piecework is an incentive for each workman to make as much as he can, regardless of the effect upon his fellow workmen.[30] In order to save time for himself he may do things which interfere with the ability of other workmen to produce. It is, therefore, often necessary for unions

[30] Except of course when payment is made to a gang or group rather than to each individual.

to protect their members as a group, not only against the faults of the management, but also against the faults of individual workmen. In doing this the union incidentally increases the output of the plant. Some of the agreements in the bituminous coal industry regulate the shooting time because powder smoke impedes the work of miners in their rooms in the entry.

The problems of protecting some pieceworkers against other pieceworkers are most likely to arise in industries where specialization of work routes the article through the hands of many different workers. In the men's clothing industry, for example, the union has found itself compelled to insist that the work come to each section in proper condition. The foreman may have a "pet" in one section and the workers in the next section may be expected to make up for the poor work done by the foreman's favorite. "We can't work on the edges" or "we can't work on these seams" are the complaints which may come to the union and lead it to require that the management obtain better quality from some workers.[31]

The rules of the tapestry carpet workers' union of Philadelphia provided that when a weaver cleaned his loom, he use a hand brush for waste and not fan the loom. Fanning saves a little time but it blows the dust and dirt into the air and causes some of it to settle on the near-by looms. To protect the looms of other weavers and thus save time for the group as a whole, the union prohibited fanning. Upholstery weavers' Local No. 25 of Philadelphia attempted to protect its members against loss of earnings from the careless handling of cards by other weavers.[32]

---

[31] Standards of production have the same effect as piecework upon the attitude of workmen toward the quality of the work of other employees. The replacement of straight timework with standards of production in the cutting rooms of the Chicago clothing industry led the cutters to insist on a number of improvements in the handling of cloth. For example, in one large house plaids had frequently come to the cutting room in bad shape. They should come up with stripe on stripe but, due to careless sponging, they sometimes came up with the stripes on a bias instead of straight across. This meant that the cutter was compelled to spend some time putting the cloth into shape before cutting it. The union insisted that the sponging room do its work properly.

[32] The rules of the local provided that "all cards must be properly cared for; repairs must be made when necessary and cards must be properly laced with card lace and the name of the weaver placed on the card when repairs are made or new cards are inserted. Weavers must not hammer card wires. All loose wires must be properly tied with wax ends." (*Uniform By-laws and Shop Rules of the Upholstery Weavers' Local No. 25, of the United Textile Workers of America*, pp. 20-21.)

QUALITY AND SPOILED WORK

Another major problem created by piecework is that of quality of output and responsibility for spoiled work. Payment by the piece penalizes the employee who produces better work than necessary to pass inspection, because it usually takes more time to produce good work than poor.[33] Consequently most pieceworkers are careful to do no better work than the management demands. In hewing so close to the line, naturally they sometimes go too far. But in some cases the failure to produce satisfactory work is due to causes beyond the control of the individual workman. And naturally there are many cases in which the blame for sub-standard work is difficult to assign. Consequently, wherever piecework exists, there is almost certain to be a controversy over who shall bear the loss for spoiled work. The management fears that if the workmen are given the benefit of the doubt, they will be encouraged to be careless; and the workmen fear that if the management does not pay for spoiled work, it will become lax in maintaining equipment and

---

The card is a piece of pasteboard with many holes. Each one of the holes represents part of the pattern in the cloth. The cards come up over a gantry and, as they come, they make the pattern in the cloth. Every time a needle hits a hole in the card it raises the hook. If it fails to strike a hole in the card, the hook does not go up. Since it is cut with so many holes, the card is pliable and easily broken. If it is bent out of shape some of the shots, instead of going into their proper places, will go half way across the figures. Then they must be cut out.

The cards are tied together and there is supposed to be a certain space between them. Otherwise the needle will not hit the cards properly. If the cards are not properly tied together—for example, if a round knot is used—the next worker is likely to have trouble with the cards' slipping. If it is tied with a flat knot, the more it pulls, the tighter the knot gets. In replacing one card with another, if the card lace is not properly laced, a hole will soon be torn in one of the cards and the right space will not be maintained between the cards, making trouble for the next weaver. These are some of the reasons why the union requires that "cards must be properly laced with card lace and the name of the weaver placed on the card when repairs are made or new cards inserted." If a new card is not tied in properly, the weaver whose name is on the back is held responsible.

There is a rack wide enough to hold the cards, and card wires extend about $1\frac{1}{2}$ inches over to hold the cards on the rack. If a wire gets loose, the cards may fall down and, being full of holes, are likely to break. There may be 5,000 cards in a pack and a large number of them may drop down. Hence the requirement that all loose wires must be properly tied with wax ends. The wax prevents the cord with which they are tied from slipping.

[33] The fastest workers are likely to be the most accurate and hence to produce the best work. This fact should not be confused with the one mentioned above that, for most workers, producing better quality requires more time and that piecework, therefore, penalizes the production of high standards of quality ware.

in seeing that proper materials are provided. In non-union plants the general rule is that the men are paid only for work which is satisfactory. Naturally such an arrangement does not make for efficiency, because it weakens the incentive of the management to keep down spoilage. When a union becomes established among piece-workers, it is likely to demand that the men be paid for spoiled work. A gradual nibbling process is likely to set in by which payment for more and more classes of spoiled work is required.[34]

Disputes over payment for imperfect work are particularly likely to arise when standards of quality become unusually high or the percentage of spoilage is very large. The bottle trade has developed a business in high-grade cologne and perfumery bottles. The output of these bottles is small (most firms do not make them at all), but they present something of a problem because they are difficult to make and they must be perfect. A speck of dirt in the glass or a tiny blister means that the bottle is destroyed, and does not go on the market. The unwillingness of the management to pass very small defects greatly increases the proportion of bottles rejected. In addition, on some of the fancy shapes the workers have found difficulty in avoiding a high percentage of breakage. In one instance the men claimed that breakage ran as high as 40 per cent. The union argued that a guaranteed minimum wage would be helpful to the manufacturers as well as to the blowers, because the factory managers and foremen, being held strictly accountable for all losses, would be more alert and efficient in looking after shop needs and in providing adequate working facilities. The union complained of the slight attention paid to blowers, molds, lehrs, and other facilities. The manufacturers replied that the blowers had time after time found ways of overcoming the difficulties in making certain bottles and that if a minimum wage were in effect, the incentive

---

[34] A good example is found in the history of the stove industry. At one time the molder was paid only for those castings used. If the stove mounter broke a casting, this gave him a chance to steal one from the molder by hiding the one which he broke. Later the union succeeded in getting payment when the castings were put on the shelves in the store room. Finally, the union secured the gangway count, which means that the molder is paid for the castings when they are stacked beside the gangway. This has meant a shift in responsibility from the molders to the management. It is now the management's responsibility to see that nothing happens to the castings after they leave the gangway.

for the men to use their ingenuity to solve production problems would be seriously weakened.

A special conference between the union and certain manufacturers largely engaged in producing high-grade cologne and perfumery bottles was held in 1924. This resulted in an agreement to pay by the time on some bottles and to increase the piece prices of other bottles by 10 to 30 per cent. These changes almost entirely eliminated appeals to the annual conference concerning the prices of these bottles. At the 1925 conference the men demanded a 10 per cent increase in the piece rate on a certain bottle which, they claimed, it was impossible to make without heavy breakage. It was agreed to give the increase for as long as the loss through breakage continued; then if a way of stopping the loss were developed, the increase was to be removed.[35] The problem of compensating workers for breakage of bottles that were particularly difficult to make was still unsolved as late as 1937 and received extended discussion at the annual conference of that year between the manufacturers and the union. The workers sought protection in a demand for a guaranteed minimum of a dollar an hour, but were unsuccessful in obtaining it.

Sometimes the union takes a greater interest than the employer in the quality of the production. An illustration is provided by the tapestry carpet workers' union of Philadelphia. One of the operations in carpet making is burling. After the carpet has been taken from the loom, the burlers sew in the ends of threads which have broken in weaving. They are paid by the piece. In a shop where there were only four burlers it appeared that the company was losing trade because the carpet was not being properly burled. Both the weavers and the firm were suffering. The union put a weaver in charge of the burling, the number of burlers was increased, and the inspection of the carpets was made stricter. Naturally, these changes were not welcome to the burlers, who were now compelled to burl carpets properly and, being paid by the piece, could not make as much as formerly. One burler had been making as much as $64 a week but, after inspection was tightened up, the burlers were lucky

[35] *Workers' Reports of the Sessions of the Final Wage Conference between the Employers in the Glass Bottle Industry and the Glass Bottle Blowers' Association,* 1925, p. 8.

to make $40 a week. Here the union's concern for the employment of its members led to improved quality of piecework and of the firm's output.

In the flint glass industry the union and the employers have been trying for years to find a satisfactory way of dealing with the problem of spoiled work. As explained above (p. 314, note 3), until 1893 the prevailing method of payment in most departments of the industry was "turn work," which gave the workers the protection of a guaranteed turn's pay even though they failed to make a move of good pieces. The shift to straight piecework in 1893 meant that the men were paid only for good ware produced. The men complained that much of the loss of ware was not their fault: the glass was bad—too hot, too cold, cordy, or seedy; the gas was bad; the mold oven was not hot; the carrying-in boy was at fault; or a poor workman behind the lehr lost the ware.

At its convention in 1923, a resolution was presented to the union asking that workers be paid for cracked ware on the ground that the loss could be largely eliminated by the manager's instructing those carrying the ware to take only a certain number of pieces each time.[36] The rule in effect in 1923 provided that the shop was responsible for cracked ware unless it promptly reported to the manager that the ware was cracked. This arrangement, however, was not satisfactory to the men. Some workmen were inclined to seek favor with the boss by not reporting their difficulties. Then, if a dispute arose over defective ware, the manager said that the men failed to report bad glass.

Several departments in the flint glass workers' union (the caster

---

[36] American Flint Glass Workers' Union, *Proceedings of the Forty-seventh Convention,* 1923, p. 165. It is necessary for someone to carry the ware to the lehrs for annealing. If a man is working close to the lehr, there is less danger of breakage because the workmen can watch the boy who carries the ware. But if the workmen cannot easily watch, the boy may take his time, or if he has some distance to go, the ware may get cold before it reaches the lehr. Then it is likely to crack. Or it may crack because the fire in the lehr is too low. Some ware is more susceptible to crackage than other.

The issue of responsibility for mistakes of the carrying-in boy produced an interesting difference of opinion between the union and the employers. The union contends that the boy is a facility furnished by the management and that the management should be responsible when this facility is at fault. The employers contend that the carrying-in boy is part of the shop and that the head of the shop should complain if the boy is inefficient.

place, the paste mold, and part of the iron mold) managed to keep turn work after 1893. Just as in the straight piecework departments the union complained that the men were not paid for ware bad through no fault of their own, so in the turn-work departments the employers complained that since they were compelled to pay for bad ware, the men became careless and the employer had to pay for bad ware which was the fault of the workers. Year after year the employers demanded that straight piecework be substituted for turn work. Repeatedly the officers of the union warned the members that a few careless or unscrupulous workers were jeopardizing the interests of all.

At the 1924 convention the president of the union quoted a circular he had sent to the members on the matter:

There is one phase of our relations with the employers that I find it necessary to dwell on, and that is the advantage that some of our members take when working turn work. Frequently your officers have sounded an alarm on this subject, but some of our indifferent members will not take heed and the final outcome will be that the turn work rule will be abolished, unless, perchance, something is done to punish the negligent. Members working turn work should be compelled to exercise just as much care as when working piece work. . . . If a few of our members do not exercise the necessary care, then the many members should condemn the acts of the few, thereby protecting the conscientious workmen who may need the protection of the turn work rule.[37]

This convention adopted a resolution condemning "the action of our members when working turn work in being careless in the marking of ware and wasting time on turn work jobs," and recommending that "local unions use their best efforts to have their members exercise more care."[38] The problem was discussed at the 1926 convention and a more emphatic resolution was adopted.[39] At the conventions of 1927, 1928, and 1931, the national officers of the union again warned the members.[40]

[37] American Flint Glass Workers' Union, *Proceedings of the Forty-eighth Convention*, 1924, p. 24.
[38] The same, p. 177.
[39] It read in part: ". . . we very emphatically condemn the actions of the careless and negligent men who are jeopardizing the best interests of the conscientious workmen. Therefore, we recommend that this matter be referred to the executive board of the various departments." The same, *Proceedings of the Fiftieth Convention*, 1926, pp. 72-74, 265.
[40] In 1927, the vice-president said: "Our efforts to impress upon our members employed on unlimited turn-work jobs the real situation that will sooner or later

At the convention of 1931 the vice-president warned the members of the paste-mold department on bad work. He stated that it had been called to the attention of the officers on several occasions that individual shops had sent in three-fourths of a turn of bad ware, and that the employers had strenuously objected to paying for such products. He informed the members that the employers were experiencing difficulty in keeping their plants in operation and that the workmen should exercise greater care in times of depression to see that nothing except first-class products were sent to the lehr.[41]

The difficulty of determining the responsibility for imperfect ware led to an interesting arrangement in the iron mold and part of the paste mold departments of the industry. The agreements provide that the shops working unlimited turn work shall not stand a loss to exceed 5 per cent. This means that the shop shall be paid for all ware made over a move, less 5 per cent of the total made.[42] This 5 per cent is expected to take care of the defective ware. The 5 per cent dockage rule was suggested by the manufacturers, but it has proved unsatisfactory to them and they have been trying to get rid of it.[43] When the rule was adopted, it was part of the understanding that ware obviously bad would not be turned in by the workmen. The rule was intended to cover only legitimate defects which might pass unnoticed. Such an arrangement is open to abuse, and in some cases the men have turned in and obtained pay for what they knew to be imperfect work. This violates the spirit of the rule and has caused much resentment among employers.

At the 1923 conference in the paste mold department, the com-

come to this organization due to bad ware being made as a result of neglect or indifference on the part of some workmen, seem to be treated lightly in many respects. It is needless to try to sidestep this issue. It is constantly before your National Officers and Executive Board members in the various departments where this system of work prevails." The same, *Proceedings of the Fifty-first Convention*, 1927, p. 69. See also *Proceedings of the Fifty-second Convention*, 1928, pp. 91-92.

[41] The same, *Proceedings of the Fifty-fifth Convention*, 1931, p. 126.

[42] The agreements, however, provide that "shops failing to report imperfect metal or molds to one designated to receive reports, shall be responsible for imperfect goods made thereby."

[43] The 5 per cent dockage rule was proposed during the war. The paste mold illuminating department and part of the press ware department had been working limited turn work, which meant that the shops produced only a move in a turn. In return for an agreement by the men to produce up to 50 per cent more than the move, the employers agreed to pay for all ware produced, less 5 per cent.

plaints of the manufacturers led to the adoption of a resolution by the representatives of the two sides, condemning the attitude of some workmen who "seem to think they are privileged to send in 5 per cent bad work." President Clarke referred to this resolution at the next convention of the union, stating:

I cannot too strongly emphasize the wisdom of greater care being exercised in the production of good ware. It seems to me a great mistake is being made by men who will take advantage of a situation about which the manufacturers frequently complain.[44]

At virtually every conference the manufacturers proposed that the dockage rule be abolished, but the workers' representatives argued that practically all defective ware was the fault of the manufacturer because it was due to bad glass, and stated that the men had been warned during the last several years not to take advantage of the dockage rule and that some progress had been made. In 1926, however, the conference in the iron mold department adopted a rule providing that

when a shop, or shops, employed on jobs that are now worked on an unlimited turn-work basis, lose ware through carelessness, or neglect of work, and the same is admitted by the shop, shops, factory committee, or National Officers, to be the fault of the workmen, they shall not be paid.[45]

This modification has not been obtained in the paste mold illuminating department.

As pointed out above, the union in 1937, after a fight of over 40 years, succeeded in substituting turn work for straight piecework in virtually all of the straight piecework departments—this despite the difficulties that turn work had given. The union attempted also to extend the 5 per cent dockage rule to the new turnwork departments but failed. The new agreement provided that, regardless of the change, "the relative responsibility for producing salable glass is not shifted in any way. Both manufacturers and workers are expected to co-operate fully in getting proper production in both quantity and quality."[46] The necessity of guaran-

[44] American Flint Glass Workers' Union, *Proceedings of the Forty-eighth Convention,* 1924, pp. 42-43.

[45] The same, *Proceedings of the Fifty-first Convention,* 1927, p. 93.

[46] The agreement went on to interpret the new rule to mean that "under ordinary conditions" the workers would receive the guaranteed wages for the turn in case

teeing the workers a turn's wages, according to union officials, has led the managements to apply themselves to guarding against bad glass and eliminating the bulk of the lehr breakage. As a result, the earnings of the men in nine shops increased from 15 to 20 per cent upon transfer to turn work—and quite apart from the increase gained from a 10 per cent advance in piece rates which the men also won in 1937.

In 1938 the union was again pressing for a 5 per cent dockage rule in virtually all turn-work departments. Their argument to the employers was that since the responsibility for bad ware was not changed, the workers had not really gained anything by the new turn-work rule.[47] The employers oppose the dockage rule because it creates too much of a temptation for the workers to attempt to pass wavy or cordy glass which the foreman cannot be expected to see and which the men should report to the management. To counter the union's demand for a 5 per cent dockage rule, the employers in 1938 asked a return to straight piecework. A compromise is likely to be worked out eventually which will establish a certain percentage of loss of ware (probably 10 per cent) beyond which the workers will not be held responsible. If the shop is losing more than, say, 10 per cent, the foreman should tell it to knock off. If he lets it continue despite the large loss, the loss should fall on the management.

The problem of payment for spoiled work is largely one of ascertaining responsibility, but responsibility is often difficult to locate. The management may be at fault, but in some instances it may be other workers. Many of the union rules which we considered in preceding sections are intended to prevent disputes by preventing spoiled work. This is particularly true of the rules relating to materials. Despite the efforts of unions to prevent disputes, cases of spoiled work are bound to arise where the responsibility is in doubt. The attempt of the flint glass workers to settle these cases by a 5 per cent dockage rule and the molders to dispose of them by a similar

---

they worked a full turn, but that "in unusual cases where carelessness or neglect of work is shown and unsalable wares are produced by the shop, on account of such carelessness or neglect of work, the shop should be docked for such defective wares."

[47] This argument, however, conflicts with the fact that greater care by the managements has increased earnings up to 15 or 20 per cent.

rule have not been widely imitated. In the vast majority of industries, the problem remains one of determining in each individual case whether or not the responsibility is the worker's.

AVOIDANCE OF DISPUTES OVER QUALITY

The disputes over quality which are an inevitable accompaniment of piecework are often embarrassing to the union shop committee because it is called upon to present cases in which the claim of the men is weak. The committee does not wish to decline to represent aggrieved workers, but if it frequently goes to the employer with weak cases, its ability to get settlements in other cases may be impaired. Union shop committees get the best results when the employer is willing to give them the benefit of the doubt in disputes over facts because he knows that they are careful to press only grievances which they honestly feel to be just.

To protect shop committees against being compelled to handle weak cases, some unions serving pieceworkers have rules forbidding practices which are likely to produce defective work. For example, it is usual in the textile industry for the local unions to forbid weavers to read while their looms are in motion. Such provision is found in the rules of the upholstery weavers' Local No. 25 of Philadelphia and the tapestry carpet workers' union. Though advantageous to the employer, it was not to benefit him that the rule was adopted, but rather to protect the committee from having to attempt to collect pay for bad work which the employer might claim resulted from the weaver's reading. Another rule of the upholstery weavers' Local No. 25 provided: "Working before starting time or during the noon hour is strictly prohibited; any weaver failing to keep his loom properly oiled shall be subject to a fine. . . ."[48] There were several reasons for this rule, but one of them was to prevent disputes over bad work. If a thread breaks, it is necessary to tie it, and in order to produce the best quality of goods, it should be tied at once. The weavers, being pieceworkers, are tempted to let some threads go until the noon hour in order to avoid stopping the loom to tie them. By letting the loose ends go, however, they make seconds and this is likely to involve them in a

---

[48] *Uniform By-Laws and Shop Rules*, Upholstery Weavers' Local No. 25, United Textile Workers of America, p. 21.

dispute with the management. In order to prevent disputes arising from this cause, the union prohibited its members from working at noon. If the men cannot work at noon or before hours, there is danger that they may fail to keep their looms properly oiled. Consequently, at the manufacturers' request, the union provided that any weaver failing to keep his loom properly oiled would be subject to a fine.

Rule No. 9 of the upholstery weavers' Local No. 25 provided:

Pulling yarn off bad cops or bobbins makes waste; cutting yarn off bobbins injures the bobbins; these things must not be done. It is part of your job to prevent waste. All bad windings must be given to the winding boss in order that the trouble may be corrected.

Sometimes the yarn is not wound on the bobbin with uniform tightness. When a soft spot occurs, the yarn is likely to break. Bobbins or cops with soft spots should be removed and given to the winding boss to be rewound. It is quicker, however, for the weaver to pull off the yarn until he is past the soft spot. This, of course, means that the yarn is wasted. Rule No. 9 protected the shop committee from being requested to handle disputes between weavers and the management over the practice of pulling yarn off bad cops or bobbins.[49] It also protected the employer and the workers in general because a soft spot in the winding indicates that there is something wrong with the frame or spindle. If the worker simply pulls off the yarn, the source of the trouble will not be promptly discovered and corrected.

SOME FURTHER EFFECTS OF PIECEWORK ON UNION ATTITUDES AND POLICIES

The piecework system alters union attitudes and policies in other important ways. Three of these effects of piecework will be noted.

1. *Efforts to restrict the size of the force.* Unions of timeworkers usually do what they can to keep as many employed as possible, but, as pointed out at the beginning of this chapter, unions composed largely of pieceworkers often do the opposite. Since, in the

---

[49] The employer, of course, could include in his shop rules a regulation against pulling yarn off a bad cop or bobbin, but if it were his rule only, his foreman would be the only one responsible for enforcing it. When the union also has a rule the union shop committee helps enforce it.

absence of a guaranteed minimum, employers pay pieceworkers only for what they do, managers are usually glad to have more piece-workers in the plant than are really needed. Then the plant is able to meet temporary peaks in demand without adding inexperienced workers. But the earnings of each pieceworker are limited by the amount of material he receives and, the more workers there are, the less material each one receives. This is why unions resist the tendency of managers to maintain an unnecessarily large force of pieceworkers—keeping down the size of the force is simply one way of keeping up earnings.

The coal miners, in order to protect the earnings of the loaders, limit the number to each undercutting machine. Some of the agree-ments of the miners' union specify that overcrowding is a definite subject of grievance.[50] Overcrowding of sections has been a frequent complaint of the union in the men's clothing industry. As indicated above in connection with delays to production, the union has at-tempted to guard against overcrowding by requiring the employer to pay for idle time. In a Cincinnati clothing factory it had been the custom of the management to keep the pieceworkers in the shop whether there was work for them or not. After the shop was organized, the union demanded that the workers have the right to go home after waiting for work one hour. This caused the man-agement to allow the sizes of the sections to drop and led to an improvement in the flow of work and in the earnings of the workers.

2. *Efforts to limit the operations of skilled men.* When pay-ment is by the time, employers are careful to have as many opera-tions as possible done by cheap, unskilled laborers or helpers. The skilled journeymen, in an attempt to protect themselves against unemployment, adopt rules specifying what operations belong to the skilled men and forbidding laborers and helpers from doing them. When payment is by the piece, however, the management seeks to require the pieceworkers to do as many operations as possible while the unions seek to transfer work to laborers and helpers.[51]

[50] This was true, for example, of the Wyoming agreement, 1922-23, and the Western Kentucky agreement, 1920-22.

[51] There are some exceptions to this general rule, especially when the helper is likely to acquire the journeyman's skill and bcome a competitor for his job and a

For if the skilled worker can gain a slight reduction in his responsibilities without an offsetting reduction in the piece rate, he can increase his earnings. The jiggermen in the pottery industry have demanded that clay be delivered to them at their benches by the employers free of charge; the flint glass workers demand that the factory have a man to take care of snaps, punties, and plugs and to see that these are furnished the workmen before starting time.

In the stove industry the skilled pieceworkers over a period of years have brought about the transfer of a considerable part of the work to unskilled laborers who are paid by the company on a time basis. In the early days the molder brought in his flasks from the yard and obtained the clamps with which the top and bottom of the mold are held together. As the result of pressure from the union the firms now deliver the flasks, clamps, and other facilities such as gates, chaplets, cores, etc. to the job. The molders' union has also been successful in getting the firms to supply laborers to shift weights and sleeves.[52] An important achievement of this union in the stove industry was the transfer of the work of wetting and cutting sand and dumping out and trimming castings from the molders to laborers paid by the employers—obviously work which an unskilled laborer could do.[53] This occurred in 1919.

---

potential strikebreaker. This is one reason why the full-fashioned hosiery workers oppose the two-machine system, which involves the operation of two machines by a knitter and a helper instead of one machine by a knitter.

[52] In some cases when a mold is rammed up in the flask, the flask is taken away from the mold, leaving only the sand, and used to make another mold. This is cheaper because it saves flasks. When the flask is removed, however, there is nothing to keep the iron when it is poured from bursting the sand apart. To avoid this a cast iron brace, called a sleeve, is set down over the sand. It takes the place of the flask. On top of the sleeve is placed a weight. The molder may have four or five sleeves and weights. When the iron in the mold has had a chance to cool, the weight and sleeve are removed and placed on an unpoured mold.

[53] When the molders were responsible for this work, they might hire laborers to do it. The sand wetting and cutting agreement illustrates well some of the difficulties which are encountered in operating a collective agreement successfully. The superintendents and foremen were strenuously opposed to the change because they did not wish to have the responsibility of seeing that the work was properly done. The foremen objected also because they had to stay in the foundries longer getting the system started. Many of them did what they could to convince their employers that the arrangement was not workable. In some cases managers complained that, when the castings were shaken out by laborers who did not use the flasks, the damage and breakage of flasks was greatly increased.

3. Attitudes toward labor-saving devices. Piecework has diverse effects upon the attitude of unions toward technological improvements. Toward changes which are relatively *small* and which will not disturb existing piece rates, but which will increase production and hence the earning power of the workers, the unions are friendly. In fact, they may encourage the adoption of such changes. This is illustrated by the stove industry. Originally the molders carried iron from the cupolas to the floor. As some foundries became large, the men began to demand that the firms put in overhead carriers for delivering iron to the molders' floor.

Similarly, unions operating under piecework are friendly toward changes which increase earning power by reducing spoiled work. Castings may be lost because the gate is not properly planned. (The gate is the opening through which the metal is poured into the mold.) If there is a dispute because of frequent losses of a certain casting, the molder or the union representative may be able to suggest a better location for the gate. In fact, bargaining over piece rates or settling disputes over lost work may often afford the union representative opportunity to suggest and encourage improvements of various kinds. A foreman, for example, in planning a job may have decided to make one casting only in a flask. The

---

On the other hand, the molders in some shops took advantage of the new arrangement. In some cases, they did not instruct the laborers how to prepare the sand and, sometimes, on arriving at work and not finding the sand to their liking, they would go home, using the condition of the sand as an excuse for taking a day off. The disposition of the molders to withhold co-operation was naturally strongest in shops where relations between the men and the firm were strained. In such cases the molders were rather tickled that the firm was having trouble. In other words, the new agreement gave them a chance to even some old scores and they took advantage of it. In other shops, where relations between the firm and the molders were good and where neither side was constantly searching for an opportunity to hang something on the other, the molders put themselves out to help the firm.

At the first annual conference after the adoption of the new rule the employers complained bitterly about the way it was working. The representatives of the molders admitted that their members were not in all cases giving proper co-operation and consented to changes in the rule which imposed an obligation upon the molders to notify the foremen immediately if they did not find the sand in proper condition and also to put the sand in condition if requested by the firm. For doing this the molder was to be paid at the rate per hour which he earned during the molding period of the previous day. The union conferees agreed that if the sand needed a little more water, the molder was to throw it on without compensation. They further agreed to present the subject to their members and to promote co-operation between the molders and the sand cutters and shakers out.

union may object that the proposed piece rate on the new operation is too low, but the management may be firm in its refusal to pay more. As a solution, the union representative may point out the possibility of making two castings in a flask so that the men can make more money at a lower rate.

In the case of major technological changes, however, the union's attitude is likely to be quite the reverse. Where new machines or new methods upset piece rates, displace many men, and threaten to create serious unemployment, unions operating under piecework are pretty certain to oppose them, just as would unions operating under timework. Furthermore, as was pointed out in Chapter VII, unions of pieceworkers may delay the introduction of labor-saving equipment by refusing to agree to piece rates on the new machines or by holding out for rates which are almost prohibitively high.

THE INTEREST OF UNIONS IN METHODS OF FIXING PIECE RATES

Sometimes piece rates are set by the employer and go into effect subject only to the right of the unions to challenge them if it desires. Many unions, however, require that all rates be submitted to a price committee for approval and, if necessary, negotiation. Submission to a price committee or a price expert of the union is required by the unions in the needle trades and in the boot and shoe industry. In the New York neckwear industry the process is reversed. The agreement requires that each member of the employers' association send to the union each new style or shape for the purpose of having the price fixed by the price board of the union. Within a week the price board is required to fix the price and return to the president of the employers' association the style or shape with the price attached. If the association fails to notify the union within two weeks that it is dissatisfied with the price so fixed, the price is to be final. If the association notifies the union that it is dissatisfied with the price, the matter is referred to a conference committee for adjustment.[54]

The adjustment of rates between employers and union price committees naturally leads to a great deal of bargaining. The em-

---

[54] Agreement between the New York Joint Board of Neckwear Workers and the Men's Neckwear Manufacturers' Association, effective September 1938, Art. 16.

ployer is likely to set the price in the expectation that it will be bargained. Much time may be consumed and resulting rates may be unsatisfactory—some liberal and others too low. This means that some rates yield considerably higher earnings than others which pertain to the same grade of work. Such a result is satisfactory to neither the union nor the employer because it produces jealousies and hard feelings in the shop. Consequently, a number of efforts have been made by unions and employers to get piece rates set more scientifically.

In the early days of time study, many unions were opposed to having their workers timed by stop watches. When the union undertakes to improve the setting of piece rates, it is likely to find itself accepting time study and attempting to improve and regulate its operation. The reason is that time study is the most accurate way of determining how much time an operation requires. Consequently, a few unions even insist upon time studies as a right. For example, the agreement between the Cleveland Metal Trades Council and the F. H. Lawson Company, effective 1937, provides:

Piecework rates shall not be changed unless a change in the method of operation takes place, or machine methods, in which event a time study shall be made, and the rate of such job or jobs shall be established by mutual agreement between the shop committee and the management. Unsatisfactory rates set on new operations shall be adjusted in the same manner.[55]

Likewise, the agreement between District 50 of the United Mine Workers and the American Agricultural Chemical Company provides: "The employees shall have the right to have time studies made of any job they feel to be improperly timed. The company agrees to make such study within three days after request therefor."[56]

Occasionally, the unions undertake to regulate the making of time studies either in specific respects or in general. The agreement between the United Automobile Workers and the Willys-Overland Company, effective April 15, 1937, specified the percentage to be added to times for contingencies. The hosiery workers' union concerns itself with the technique of time studies and, when important

[55] Art. 9.
[56] Art. 4, sec. 9.

rates are being set, insists on timing during three days of the week and at various times of the day. The broadest attempts to regulate the use of time studies have been those in the International Ladies' Garment Workers' Union in the Cleveland market and of the United Textile Workers in the Naumkeag Steam Cotton Company discussed in Chapters XIV and XVIII. In Cleveland the time study men were subject to joint control by the union and employers. At the Naumkeag plant the union had one of its representatives trained to make time studies, and he participated in accumulating the data for new job assignments.

In the New York dress industry, samples of dresses are submitted by jobbers or other employers to the price settlement department of the union. This department has a staff of experts who analyze each garment in detail. For the guidance of its experts in bargaining piece rates, the union hired industrial engineers to reduce the various jobs in making dresses to measurable units and to determine the average time required for certain operations that are common to all garments. With the aid of these standard times, the experts of the union estimate a piece rate for the garment. Then they meet with representatives of the jobber or manufacturer. If agreement is reached, the matter is settled. Otherwise, the office of the impartial chairman is requested to assign an experienced impartial adjuster to study the garment and decide on the piece price. Either the employer or the union may appeal from the adjuster to the deputy in charge of settlements or to the impartial chairman. In the great majority of cases, however, the expert adjuster's settlement is regarded as final.

Perhaps the most highly developed method of setting piece rates that has been used in American collective bargaining was that employed in the Cleveland women's garment industry from 1920 to 1931.[57] It involved classifying the operation of making garments into "elements," that is, the parts into which the operation naturally breaks up, and obtaining times for each element from numerous stop watch studies. This method of setting times did not eliminate bargaining, but it did achieve the remarkable result that the workers' committees accepted without bargaining from two-thirds to three-fourths or even more of the times each season.

[57] See Chap. XIV.

The collection of element times is slow and expensive. Indeed, it was too expensive for most of the small shops in the Cleveland garment industry. The method has important advantages to both unions and employers, however, and it shows some signs of spreading.[58] Particularly important is the fact that the construction of piece rates from element times reduces the range of bargaining when changes occur in products or methods. An analysis of the new operation usually reveals that very few of the elements are totally new. This means that, for all of the others, times can be set from assembled data. Only on the new elements for which data are not available is there likely to be serious dispute between the union and the employer. Consequently, the area of bargaining is greatly narrowed. Not only does this diminish the seriousness of conflicts between the union and the employer, but it greatly reduces the probability that deadlocks over new piece rates will retard the introduction of technological changes.

In industries where national piecework scales have been negotiated, special problems of administration exist. It is particularly important that it be easy for managements to obtain new piece rates when changes in conditions warrant this. Otherwise the managements will be discouraged from making every possible effort to increase production by improving shop conditions. Where the machinery for setting new piece rates is national, it may be slow, cumbersome, and inflexible, with the result that the progressive employer who improves conditions may have trouble in getting an adjustment in piece rates.[59] The fact that the machinery for approving new piece rates is likely to be partly in the hands of the unprogressive employers does not make it function more promptly and effectively when an employer asks for an adjustment in rates because of an improvement in working conditions. Consequently, unless the danger is realized and guarded against, national setting of piece rates is likely to discourage managerial initiative and efficiency. And this may also be true of local setting of piece rates if it is too difficult for managements to get rates changed when conditions change.

---

[58] It has recently been adopted by an important manufacturer of automobile parts who has contractual relations with the United Automobile Workers.

[59] Such adjustments, even though applicable only in one shop at a time, are not incompatible with a national piecework scale, because any employer who provided the improved conditions would be entitled to the new piece rate.

CHAPTER XII

RESULTS OF COMPETITION BETWEEN UNION AND NON-UNION PLANTS

One of the principal purposes of the system of industrial juris-prudence built up by trade unions is to increase the security of their members. This purpose runs through their efforts to control entrance to the trade, to regulate hiring and layoffs, to make work, and to prohibit or to regulate the use of new machinery. And yet there is danger that union policies will defeat their purpose and produce not security but insecurity for union members. When unions by their working rules and their wage scales raise costs in union plants above those in non-union plants, they limit the amount of goods which union employers can sell. Employment shrinks in the union plants and expands in non-union plants. As non-union plants are then ordinarily producing beyond their planned capacity, the short-run supply price of the product rises and con-sequently the market price advances. There is a temporary and par-tial recovery of employment in the union plants. This is the primary adjustment to the introduction of union conditions. The higher market price attracts new capital into the industry. The output of each non-union plant then gradually shrinks to the planned capacity, the supply of the commodity increases, and the price falls to virtually the original amount. In the course of this secondary adjustment, union plants again find it necessary to reduce their employment.

The contraction of employment in union plants results in their working at less than their planned capacity, and this in turn means that (subject to certain exceptions to be noted presently) their average costs exceed their selling prices. Now it is true that plants will remain in operation for years at a loss either because manage-ments hope for a change for the better or because one way of re-covering part of the investment in an unprofitable enterprise is to continue operations so long as gross revenues are sufficient to yield some depreciation allowance over and above other costs. Indeed some small items of equipment may be replaced in order to make it possible to wear out large items more completely. But obviously no business can operate indefinitely if it is selling below its average cost. Does not the differential in costs between union and non-union plants, therefore, eventually force all union employers out of business?

Some union employers are, of course, forced out of business after running their plants long enough to wear out most of their equipment and not earning enough to replace it. A considerable number of union employers, however, may survive indefinitely. Their volume of output is less than it would be if their labor costs were lower, but they are able to stay in business. There are four principal reasons for this. One is that union plants may have managements of unusual efficiency and, therefore, costs below those of the average plant.[1] In the exceptionally well-managed plant there can be a rise in labor costs without raising average costs above selling prices. A second is that under the spur of necessity the managements of some union plants may improve their efficiency and discover ways and means of cutting expenses so that, despite the higher costs imposed by the union, average costs do not remain above selling prices.[2] A third is that the competition of non-union plants may lead the management to invent ways of increasing the differentiation of its product from competing products and enable it thereby to raise the price to average costs.

A fourth reason is that the rate of return necessary to cause a perpetual renewal of the capital in an industry is less than the rate necessary to attract additional capital into the industry. The explanation is that some loss is involved in moving capital out of an industry. The rate of profit necessary to attract additional capital may be called "the attraction rate" and the rate necessary to assure the indefinite replacement of equipment as it wears out "the re-

---

[1] In a "normal" or average plant the rate of production under competitive conditions tends to be such that the average cost is at a minimum. When the management is unusually efficient and has costs below those of the average plant, production is greater than the amount which gives the lowest average cost. Thus there is leeway for an increase in labor costs, which may merely reduce output toward the point at which average cost is lowest.

[2] If collective bargaining compels managements to work harder for the same compensation, does it constitute a method by which labor exploits management?

tention rate." Depending upon circumstances the difference between the two rates may be large or small. Cost of production,
as the economist uses the term, includes the necessary compensation of capital. Since the compensation necessary to attract capital
is greater than the compensation necessary to retain it, there are
two cost curves—one based on the attraction rate and the other
on the retention rate. So long as unions do not raise costs so
much that the selling prices of union plants are less than average
costs *based on the retention rate,* these plants will remain in business. If the union rules or wage scales, however, reduce the return
on capital below the retention rate, the union plants will eventually
disappear—except as new plants replace those going out of business.

Since any differential in costs between union and non-union
plants imposes some loss of employment on union members, the
unions must consider how far it is in their interest to impose disadvantages on their employers. In this chapter we shall examine
the results of competition between union and non-union plants in
several industries and analyze the conditions which determine the
effect that differences in labor cost will have upon employment in
union plants. In the next chapter we shall examine some of the
questions of policy for trade unions which arise from the fact that
their wage scales and some of their working rules create differentials in labor costs and thus limit the employment of union workers.

EXAMPLES OF ENCROACHMENT OF NON-UNION UPON UNION PRODUCTION

If the organizing power of unions were equal to their bargaining
power, there would be no problem of cost differentials between
union and non-union plants from the standpoint of the union. The
union would maintain the balance between union and non-union
parts of the industry by organizing plants of non-union employers
as fast as they took business from union employers. The organizing power of trade unions fluctuates violently with business conditions. Although there are a few strategically situated groups whose
organizing power is always high (moving picture operators, compositors in newspaper offices, photo-engravers, and others), most
unions are able to increase their membership rapidly only under
exceptionally favorable conditions. This is why the growth of the

American labor movement has been exceedingly jerky. In fact about three-quarters of the membership has been acquired in four sellers' markets—1897-1903; 1916-20; July 1933-April 1934; and July 1936-September 1937.[3] The history of most unionized industries, therefore, has consisted of long periods during which the proportion of business done by union employers slowly declined and unemployment remained high among union members, punctuated every now and then by great increases in the unionized area as labor organizations seized a favorable opportunity to extend their membership. Let us review briefly this experience in a few industries.

The lamp chimney industry. In 1904, all lamp chimneys made in the United States were produced by union workers. About that time a machine was invented for making chimneys. Control of the machine passed into the hands of the MacBeth-Evans Glass Company. In order to protect its members against displacement, the union so restricted output on the machine that the cost of production was substantially the same as the cost by hand methods. A break between the union and the MacBeth-Evans Company resulted. After a long and bitter strike in 1904 the union was defeated and the company operated "non-union." Other non-union factories sprang up, licensed to use the machine, and some union factories went non-union.

The growth of non-union competition was greatly stimulated by the limitation of output and other restrictions which were enforced in the union shops. The limits took the form of a maximum number of chimneys (known as a "move") which a "shop"—that is, several men and their helpers—might produce in half a day.[4] At the Toledo convention of the flint glass workers' union in 1918, a report showed that the moves in union plants were only about 60 per cent as large as the moves in the MacBeth-Evans plants. The price per hundred chimneys in the non-union plants was usually one-

---

[3] In the first of these four sellers' markets, which followed the long depression of the nineties, the AFL increased its membership from 272,000 in 1897 to 1,556,000 in 1903; in the second, the period of the war and postwar booms, from 2,124,000 in 1916 to 4,039,000 in 1920; in the third, the period of the NRA, unions gained about a million members; in the fourth, the boom that began in the summer of 1936, the AFL and CIO together gained about three million members.

[4] See footnote 9, pp. 167-68.

fourth to one-third below the union scale. The union also enforced other restrictions, such as a summer stop of six weeks, which were not found in the non-union plants.[5]

In the summer of 1904, when all the lamp chimneys produced in the United States were still made by members of the flint glass workers' union, there were 1,728 members of the chimney department. By 1907 the membership had dropped to 1,603, by 1910 to 1,411, by 1913 to 1,292, and by August 31, 1922 to 1,124. By this time about 51.5 per cent of all chimneys were produced in non-union plants.[6]

The leaders of the union, especially President Clarke, seeing the passing of chimney manufacturing to non-union plants, pleaded with the chimney workers to give up their restrictions, particularly the limits upon daily output.[7] As a result of the menace of non-union competition a special conference of the chimney department was held in Pittsburgh in October 1922. It recommended that the limits on output be abandoned, but, despite the vigorous support of the officers of the union, the rank and file rejected the proposal in the referendum vote by 332 to 211.[8] In 1923 the efforts of

[5] American Flint Glass Workers' Union, *Proceedings of the Forty-second Convention,* 1918, pp. 72-78.

[6] The same, *Proceedings of the Forty-first Convention,* 1917, p. 46, and *Proceedings of the Forty-seventh Convention,* 1923, p. 58.

[7] So earnestly and continuously did the president plead that something of a breach grew up between him and the chimney workers. In reporting to the New Bedford convention in 1917 the president said: "The unlimited system is one of the subjects that has widened the breach between the writer and members of this department. . . . Let it be known that I did not become a convert to the unlimited system since I have assumed the position of president. I proposed this to the chimney department on December 5, 1905, and as time has passed and I witnessed the decline of this department, so much firmer have I become convinced that it will require radical changes in order to preserve this department." (The same, *Proceedings of the Forty-first Convention,* 1917, p. 49.) The president called attention to the fact that men left jobs in union plants to work in non-union where, though the rate of pay was lower, they could make more money because their output was not limited. "On April 17 there were 149 men employed in Sand Springs and Tulsa, and 56 of the 149 were former members of our union." (The same, p. 47.) President Clarke also asserted that a large part of the chimney workers did not want the long summer stop of six weeks. This was proven by the fact that during the summer stop many chimney-makers found employment in other branches of the flint glass industry. The same, p. 50.

[8] The same, *Proceedings of the Forty-seventh Convention,* 1923, p. 62. The Alexandria, Ind., local asked that the recommendation be resubmitted to the members for a vote by secret ballot, and a new appeal for its acceptance was made by the president; but the recommendation was again rejected, this time by a vote of 310 to 228. The same, p. 68.

the officers to get a relaxation of restrictions began to bear fruit. The chimney department agreed to increase moves 15 per cent in return for a wage increase of 10 per cent.[9] This small concession did little good. Locals 27 and 61, recognizing the seriousness of the situation, proposed removal of limits on output and a 10 per cent reduction in piece rates. This was submitted to a vote of the department and rejected.[10] "Conditions," in the words of the president, "went from bad to worse. All the union chimney workers, practically speaking, were in idleness, while the non-union plants were in some instances flourishing."[11]

In April 1924, the national officers called another meeting. "The attitude assumed by some of our members, contrasted with the position they formerly took, was startling," the president reported. He suggested a 25 per cent reduction in piece rates, the unlimited system, and suspension of the summer stop, but he reported that "many representatives declared that my suggestion was not agreeable, because the reduction in wages I had proposed was not sufficient."[12] Finally, it was unanimously agreed to reduce blowers and gatherers 42 per cent, paste mold and chimney workmen 35 per cent, to adopt the unlimited system, and to suspend the summer stop for 1924. These concessions were made with the understanding that the union manufacturers would reduce their selling prices on all chimneys to a point that would enable them to compete with non-union production. But even these concessions proved insufficient, for the non-union factories met the reduction in union plants by reducing wages also. Consequently, at the 1925 convention, the committee of the chimney department made the unprecedented recommendation that the chimney executive board be authorized to accept further reductions, but that the chimney workmen be compensated for the additional loss from the national treasury of the union. This plan was unanimously adopted.[13]

[9] The same, *Proceedings of the Forty-eighth Convention,* 1924, p. 38.
[10] The same, pp. 38-39.
[11] The same, p. 39.
[12] The same.
[13] The same, *Proceedings of the Forty-ninth Convention,* 1925, pp. 183-85.
The proposal of the members of the chimney department that they be compensated for additional wage concessions out of the union treasury was not accepted by the rest of the union. The efforts to save the jobs of the members of the chimney department came too late to succeed. On May 31, 1935, the membership

Carpet and upholstery weaving in Philadelphia. Between 1913 and 1920, the tapestry carpet weavers in Philadelphia acquired control of that labor market. Between 1915 and 1920 wages were advanced 165 per cent. The union secured, after 1918, the requirement that new employees be hired through the union office, the right to transfer workers from one shop to another, and the right to name foremen from the seniority list of union weavers. Union control was exercised through shop committees appointed by the general officers of the union. This control weakened discipline in the mills and restricted the ability of managements to make economies. For example, the Philadelphia mills were slow compared with their competitors in installing the broad loom for making seamless rugs. In spite of these three disadvantages the union believed that the Philadelphia mills, because of the superior skill of the experienced union labor, could stand a 10 to 15 per cent wage differential above the non-union mills in New York and New England. Prior to 1910, the differential, according to union estimates, was 10 to 20 per cent. Between 1910 and 1920, the differential rose to 25 per cent. Wage reductions in mills outside Philadelphia after 1921 increased the differential. By 1926, it was nearly 50 per cent.

Union membership reached its peak about 1920 when there were 1,800 members in 11 mills. By 1926, the union had only 800 working members, and more than half of the union mills had ceased operating. Philadelphia's share of the carpet output, which had been nearly 50 per cent before the war, had declined to a little more than 20 per cent. No important organizing work outside of Philadelphia was attempted by the union until 1920 and this effort failed. In 1926, employers took advantage of a factional split in the union to revolt against union domination. Several long and costly strikes followed, and by 1929 the Phildelphia industry was open shop. The disadvantages imposed by the union on the employers were so great that the employers could afford an indefinite shutdown rather than continue under union conditions.[14]

---

of the chimney department, which had been 833 on May 31, 1924 and 661 on May 31, 1925, was 486, of whom only 195 were employed at the trade. *Proceedings of the Fifty-ninth Convention,* 1935, pp. 226-27.

[14] For a more complete account of the experience of the tapestry carpet weavers, see Gladys L. Palmer's excellent study, *Union Tactics and Economic Change.* I have drawn heavily on her analyses of both the tapestry carpet weavers and the upholstery weavers.

Prior to 1914 the upholstery textile industry was largely concentrated in Philadelphia. In that year the union secured a trade
agreement covering the Philadelphia mills. Between 1911 and
1921 wage rates more than doubled. A reduction of 8 or 9 per
cent made in the depression of 1921 was restored when business
improved. Business was good during the next several years, and
wages in Philadelphia were still further increased. A serious disadvantage to the Philadelphia mills was the union limit of one
loom to a weaver. In non-union mills outside Philadelphia, weavers
operated two or three looms and sometimes even four. As in the
case of the tapestry carpet weavers, union control was exercised by
shop committees, but in the upholstery weavers' union the committees were elected in the shop, not appointed by the general officers. In fact the business agent and general officers had little power.
Their terms were for only six months. Negotiations for new agreements were controlled by mass meetings.

Rapid expansion of the demand for upholsterers produced an increase in the Philadelphia business until 1925, despite the fact that
outside production was increasing even more rapidly. The union
membership increased from 1,600 members in 16 mills in 1920
to 2,000 members in 26 mills in 1926. After 1925, however, demand ceased to expand and the non-union mills began to cut
heavily into the markets of the union mills. Efforts of the union
to organize outside mills had some temporary success in New
Jersey, but on the whole were a failure. Unemployment in the
Philadelphia mills rapidly increased, but the union was slow in
recognizing the situation as serious—partly because it failed to
distinguish the new chronic unemployment from the seasonal
unemployment which had always been characteristic of the industry. After 1927, however, not more than one-third of the union
membership was working. In 1930 the employers asked for a
15 per cent reduction in wages. The issue went to arbitration. When
the arbitrator awarded a 14 per cent cut pending a final award
based on a survey of the industry, the union struck. As a result
the United Textile Workers, with which the upholstery weavers
were affiliated, revoked the charter of the Philadelphia union,
which continued as an independent. In May 1931 the union settled

the strike by accepting a wage reduction somewhat greater than that awarded by the arbitrator and also accepting the two-loom system. During the strike two mills left Philadelphia. Other mills have since left or shut down. Cost differentials between Philadelphia and other places have almost completely destroyed the Philadelphia industry.

The full-fashioned hosiery industry. In 1922 the hosiery workers' union controlled about 90 per cent of the industry. The output of hosiery was growing by leaps and bounds. Between 1919 and 1923 the output of women's full-fashioned hosiery increased nearly 50 per cent; between 1923 and 1929 it more than trebled. This rapidly expanding and highly profitable business attracted new capital and several hundred new hosiery mills sprang up during the twenties, starting out as non-union. The union made vigorous efforts to organize these mills. But they could afford to pay high wages —far above other industries in their communities—and the new employees did not care to jeopardize their good jobs by joining a union. Hence the union's organizing efforts met only limited success. The rapid growth of the industry and the scarcity of skilled men put the union in a strong bargaining position and it rapidly advanced the wages of its members. Union wages rose to roughly double those of non-unionists. Many union knitters made as much as $5,000 a year. Another advantage possessed by non-union mills was that they customarily used the two-machine system—that is, a knitter and a helper to two machines. About 25 per cent of the union knitters worked under the two-machine system in 1929, but the union was strongly opposed to it and prevented its extension in union mills during the twenties. The great fear of the union was that the helpers would become aspirants for the knitters' jobs and potential strikebreakers in case of trouble.[15]

The hosiery industry is one in which machine costs are a large

[15] The two-machine system in the non-union plants was an obstacle to the union's organizing efforts. Some non-union mills operated by paying the knitters virtually as much as the union scale, but by paying the helpers very little. Their high wages made the knitters indifferent to organization. Furthermore, fear that the helpers would take their jobs if they joined the union or struck made the knitters hold aloof from the union. By 1939, the two-machine issue had virtually disappeared because the introduction of longer, faster, and finer-gauge machines had made single machine operation more economical than two-machine.

and labor costs a small part of total costs. Furthermore, the union mills during the twenties had the more experienced and therefore the more skillful workers. This was important because it meant a lower production of "seconds." In the late twenties it was estimated that the proportion of seconds produced in union mills was less than half that in the new non-union mills. Moreover, most of the old established mills selling branded hose were union controlled. These conditions in conjunction with the rapid expansion of demand prevented the union mills from being seriously inconvenienced by the non-union competition until 1927 and later. About that year, however, seasons began to appear in the union mills. The union then recognized the threat of non-union competition by instituting a program of waste elimination which was intended to interest the members in the reduction of seconds. By 1929, however, the rapid growth of non-union mills had reduced union control of the industry to 30 per cent.

The depression brought a moderate shrinkage in consumption of full-fashioned hosiery. Output in 1931, the low year, was 7.7 per cent below 1929. Small as this was in comparison with the drop in other industries, it was serious for the high-cost union mills because the bulk of the shrinkage was concentrated on them. It was estimated at the 1930 convention of the union that non-union mills enjoyed a labor-cost advantage of $1.00 to $1.50 per dozen pairs. Labor costs in union mills at this time were about $3.30 per dozen pairs, in northern non-union mills about $2.14, and in southern mills (all non-union) about $1.60. Non-union mills were reported as operating on the average at about 80 per cent of capacity as against 60 per cent for union mills.[16] Mills were beginning to move out of the union territory.[17] As the depression continued, the

[16] Branch 1 of the Philadelphia local, then comprising half the membership of the national union, reported to the 1930 convention: "It is safe to say that less than 25 per cent of our Philadelphia membership has worked steadily during the past six months. Of the remaining 75 per cent, at least half have not worked 50 per cent during this period and the remainder have just been out and have been eating up their savings."

[17] President Rieve of the national union told the convention of 1930: "At the present time, if every mill would start working full time in the city of Philadelphia, we estimate about 1,500 full-fashioned hosiery workers would be out of employment. There would be no jobs for them due to the fact that the mills have moved out."

advantages of non-union mills increased because they were free to cut wages. Pressure of competition led the non-union mills also to go into two-shift operation. In view of the heavy overhead, the savings from two-shift operation were important.[18]

The officers of the hosiery workers' union, in contrast with the officers of the tapestry carpet workers and the upholstery weavers, were very prompt in appreciating the competitive position of the union. Late in 1929 the union, at the recommendation of its officers, agreed to permit the employers to "double" one-fourth of their equipment (that is, to operate two knitting machines with one knitter and a helper instead of one machine to a knitter) and conceded a number of rate reductions on "extras"—that is, on special operations caused by style features. In the summer of 1930 the union, after a close referendum vote, made additional concessions. Piece rate reductions ranging from 11 to 23 per cent (averaging about 15 per cent) were conceded and the employers, subject to certain restrictions, were permitted to double all 18- and 20-section legging equipment. The doubling did not prove a success and after several months the union consented to additional reductions in piece rates in return for single operation.

The rate reductions of 1929 and 1930 did little to reduce the differentials between union and non-union mills because they were met by the non-union employers. By the summer of 1931, therefore, the union employees were in desperate condition. Half of the Philadelphia membership was unemployed. Bankruptcy of some union employers threatened some union members with permanent loss of their jobs. Union control in the industry had dropped to about 25 per cent. It was evident to the national officers that the union must do something drastic and decisive to meet non-union competition. They proposed, therefore, a wage reduction of 35 to 40 per cent. The intention was to make the cut so large that non-union mills could not meet it without provoking a revolt of their workers

---

[18] In order to operate two shifts it was necessary for many employers to purchase some new equipment, particularly footers. Women are employed as helpers on footers. The laws of most states prohibit night work for women. In order to obtain enough production from the footers in one shift to operate the leggers two shifts, it was necessary to double the number of footers. Even after this expenditure for new equipment the savings were great. A few manufacturers endeavored to operate footers two shifts by using boys as helpers.

—which would give the union an opportunity to organize them. Not until a futile effort had been made to call an organization strike in Reading, the largest non-union center, were the rank and file ready to accept this drastic cut. Even then there were several short-lived revolts against the new scale. This wage cut was undoubtedly the salvation of the union. The non-union mills dared not meet it. Several union brands were able for the first time to get into the large mail order catalogues, and employment in the union mills made substantial gains. Without the help of the wage cut of September 1931, it is doubtful whether the union would have survived with sufficient strength to take advantage of the organizing opportunity presented by the NRA in 1933. The union was quick to seize this opportunity. Reading was organized in the summer of 1933 and within a few months most of the workers in the northern mills were in the union. Union strength was up to 70 per cent—the highest in ten years.

Despite the substantial gains made possible by the NRA the position of the union was far from secure. In the first place, there was virtually no union organization in the South. True, wages in the South, which in 1929 had been half the union scale or even less, had been greatly increased, but in 1935 hourly earnings in the southern mills were approximately 30 per cent below Philadelphia and about 25 per cent below other union centers.[19] In the second

---

[19] A survey by the U. S. Bureau of Labor Statistics, based in the main upon a pay-roll period during September 1938 (after some relief had been given union employers, as indicated below), showed the following hourly earnings in union and non-union full-fashioned hosiery mills: 51 northern union mills, 74.3 cents; 27 northern non-union mills, 60.5 cents; 27 southern mills (all non-union except one), 58.1 cents. (*Monthly Labor Review*, May 1939, Vol. XLVIII, pp. 1153, 1161.)

The South had other advantages in addition to lower labor costs. The southern mills got their silk thrown for less than the northern mills, despite the fact that even in the north silk-throwing is a very low-paid industry. The absence of union rules gave the southern mills various small advantages. The employers did not object to a knitter's coming to the mill on Saturday morning to clean his machine or to his pliering a few needles during the noon hour. The employees would work a few hours overtime to get out an order without insisting on penalty rates. The South also has some disadvantages. It has never been able to get the efficiency from the women workers (toppers, loopers, and seamers) that most northern mills obtain. In some branches of the industry the South has a marketing disadvantage.

place, the union scale contained many very high rates for operations which had been introduced as "extras" and which had been carelessly and liberally priced because they were not expected to remain long or to become important. Then, as often happens, these extras became standard operations, the workers with practice acquired skill at them that no one had foreseen, and improvements in operating conditions and appliances greatly reduced the time required to do them.[20] Nevertheless, the original rates remained— a handicap to union mills. Finally, the piece rate scale had been so constructed that employers had only a limited incentive to install longer, faster, and finer-gauge machines.[21]

The disadvantages of the union plants led to a great shrinkage

[20] One of these extras (substantially reduced in the arbitration of 1938) was the extra for three-carrier knitting. Knitting first from one carrier, then from a second, then from a third instead of from one carrier constantly averages out yarn conditions and prevents variations in the thickness of the yarn from making bands. When three-carrier knitting was first introduced, a liberal extra was allowed on the assumption that three carriers would slow up production considerably and greatly increase the frequency of "smash ups." Improvements in the apparatus, higher standards of maintenance of equipment, and experience with three-carrier knitting greatly reduced the additional time required and made the extra piece rate allowance excessive.

Another extra that became excessive was the differential for thread weights. This differential had been established at a time when light weights were being handled in very limited quantities. As experience with lighter threads increased and changes in fashion caused greater and greater quantities of them to be used, the art of making and handling them developed. The preparation of the thread improved, improved twists reduced the danger of breaking or kinking, improvements in the shape of the cone reduced the danger of catching. These changes all made the original differentials excessive and caused the earnings of knitters on lighter threads to be out of line. Other extras that had become obsolete and excessive because of improvements in mechanism, higher standards for maintenance, or increased experience of the knitters were those for French heels and for picots.

[21] The union piece rate scale provided for some reduction in the rate per dozen on the more productive machines (more sections and faster speed), but only up to a given point. Beyond this point the employer who installed a longer or faster machine got no benefit in a lower piece rate. For example, the deduction for increases in sections above 18 on 20-, 22-, and 24-section machines was $.0162 per dozen. No additional deduction was specified for 26- or 28-section machines. This deduction, by giving most of the gain to the workers, reduced the incentive of the employer to install larger machines. The agreement permitted a limited deduction for speed—½ cent per dozen for each four courses per minute over 52 for each section over 18—but limited the total deduction for speed to 4.87 cents per dozen. Had this limit not been in effect the rule would have given a rate of 10 cents less per dozen on a 28-section machine running 60 courses per minute or 9 cents less per dozen on a 24-section machine running 64 courses per minute.

of the business in the Philadelphia area and a rapid expansion in the South. At the beginning of 1937, there were more than a thousand fewer knitting machines in the Philadelphia area than in 1929. Not less than 58 firms since 1929 had sold their equipment and moved from Philadelphia or its immediate environs. New England, New York, and New Jersey districts had barely held their own. There had been a good increase in the West, but Milwaukee, the chief union center in the West, had lost one-seventh of its machines. In the South, however, the number of machines had increased over three-fold. In fact, of the 4,505 machines added between 1929 and 1937, 2,177 had gone into the South. Of the increase of 360 machines between July 15, 1933 and April 15, 1935, 301 had gone into the South. The proportion of machines in the South increased from 7 per cent in 1929 to 18 per cent in 1937.[22]

The competitive problems of the union employers led to an arbitration award in February 1938 reducing or abolishing many of the "extra" rates and altering the piece-rate scale so as to give union employers a greater incentive to install modern equipment.[23] The union, however, recognized that these concessions were not enough to meet the competition of southern non-union mills. The national piece-rate scale which prevailed in most of the union plants, while producing uniform labor costs in the several plants, was a discouragement to managerial ingenuity and efficiency because an employer could not obtain a reduction in a given rate by providing the workers with unusually favorable conditions which increased their earning power. The union leaders saw that managerial efficiency needed to be rewarded and stimulated and also that union employers needed to be further encouraged to install a large number of up-to-date machines. To achieve these two purposes the union decided in the summer of 1938 to abandon its national wage scale and to negotiate wages with employers individually. This gave any employer an opportunity to obtain special reductions in piece rates

---

[22] *Brief Presented to Wage Tribunal by Full-fashioned Hosiery Manufacturers of America, Inc.*, Feb. 7, 1938, pp. 7, 18.

[23] For example, the award permitted a deduction in the rate on legging of 1 cent per dozen for each section over 18. On a 24-section legger this meant a deduction of 6 cents per dozen. The award also continued the deduction of ½ cent per dozen for each four courses per minute over 52 for each section over 18, and abolished the limit of 4.87 cents in the deductions for speed.

provided he was able to furnish unusually favorable working conditions or provided the nature of his business justified them. It also gave employers an opportunity to obtain concessions by agreeing to buy new equipment. The more or less standard bargain was that in return for the purchase of 10 per cent new equipment, the union would concede piece rate reductions of about 15 per cent.

In the year following the adoption of the new policy, union hosiery manufacturers placed orders for about 525 machines. These would increase the capacity of the northern mills about 11 per cent and of the entire industry about 7.5 per cent.[24] The average piece-rate reduction granted by the union was about 13 per cent, but the drop in hourly earnings was only approximately 6 per cent. There were several brief flurries of rebellion against the concessions by the rank and file of the union, partly the result of the fact that the officers made the new policy on their own responsibility. Southern mills did not meet the northern cuts. Although the union has made little headway in organizing the South, it has kept southern employers worried by constant agitation. The difference in labor cost between the North and the South in 1939 was about 25 cents per dozen or 13 per cent.[25]

A year after the new policy was initiated, the South was still operating at a slightly higher rate than the North, but it had suffered a curtailment—except that of the great depression, the first in its history. Purchases of new machines by the South for a short time virtually ceased. Not enough of the 525 new machines contracted for by the union mills had been put in operation to judge their effect upon the competitive situation. That the expansion in capacity would itself be a cause for cutthroat competition, however, appeared unlikely. Much of the expansion represented replacements of machines which were scarcely worth operating. The style trend was toward lighter-weight hose with a shorter life. The long-term demand for full-fashioned hosiery was still expanding and the immediate demand was aided by business recovery.

An awkward problem in connection with the union's policy was

[24] The new machines were virtually all leggers, as most mills had spare footers.
[25] The labor cost is about $1.90 per dozen in the South and $2.15 in the North. There are great differences between the wage scales of the southern mills. These may turn out to be a weakness to the mills in resisting union organization.

created by the rise in the price of silk during 1939.[26] This increased the need of the mills for working capital, particularly in view of the fact that there was no corresponding increase in the price of hosiery.[27] A few of the least prosperous mills which had been granted concessions by the union found themselves unable to fulfill their promises to purchase new machines because they lacked credit and hence needed the funds they had expected to spend on machinery for working capital.[28]

Eventually the union may find itself compelled to abandon individual bargains with employers and revert to a uniform national wage scale modified perhaps by special allowances where conditions warrant them.[29] For the time being, however, the union has successfully employed the device of separate bargains with employers to stimulate managerial efficiency and plant modernization and substantially to narrow the margin of labor costs between union and non-union mills. Whether the differential has been sufficiently reduced, however, is doubtful.[30]

The bituminous coal industry. When the first agreements for the central competitive area (Illinois, Indiana, Ohio, and Penn-

---

[26] Between January 1939 and January 1940, the price more than doubled.

[27] This situation presents an interesting problem in economic theory.

[28] The Philadelphia branch of the union brought several cases before the impartial chairman in the industry charging bad faith and violation of the agreement. In each instance the impartial chairman ordered a restoration of the piece rates in effect before the negotiation of the special agreements of 1938 and imposed a monetary penalty on the companies. As a consequence, each of the mills went out of business. The international executive board of the union decided to give the local branches discretion as to whether or not to bring similar cases before the impartial chairman. American Federation of Hosiery Workers, *Report of the Officers and Executive Board, Twenty-eighth Annual Convention,* 1939, p. 16.

[29] One might ask why a union, which is interested in maximizing the incomes of its members, should negotiate uniform wage scales. Why should it not treat the demand of each employer separately and impose the price which in his particular case would yield maximum pay rolls—at least the maximum pay rolls possible without permitting an increase in employment beyond the present membership of the union? In other words, why should the union not practice price discrimination?

This question has not been adequately explored by students of labor problems. The fact of the matter seems to be that most, but not all, unions find it advantageous to impose uniform wage scales. The reasons are partly political rather than economic. Nevertheless, uniform wage scales have some economic advantages to unions.

[30] One of the interesting by-products of the union policy was the improvement in employee efficiency in some plants. Knitters hoped to win assignment to the new machines that were being installed by improving the quantity and quality of their production.

sylvania) were signed in the bituminous coal industry about the beginning of the century, the union controlled almost 100 per cent of the production of bituminous coal in that area. Non-union production, however, immediately began to expand rapidly in West Virginia and Kentucky. Between 1900 and 1920, the output of these two states increased by 349 per cent—from 27,976 thousand tons to 125,662 thousand. The union tried vigorously to organize these states, but its successes were only limited and temporary. The accompanying table shows the course of production in the two groups of states.

COAL PRODUCTION IN THE CENTRAL COMPETITIVE FIELD, 1900–37[a]
(In thousands of short tons)

Area	1900	1910	1920	1929	1932	1937
Illinois..........	25,768	45,900	88,725	60,658	33,475	51,602
Indiana..........	6,484	18,390	29,351	18,344	13,324	17,765
Ohio............	18,988	34,210	45,878	23,689	13,909	25,178
Pennsylvania.....	79,842	150,522	170,608	143,516	74,776	111,002
West Virginia....	22,647	61,671	89,971	138,519	85,609	118,646
Kentucky........	5,329	14,623	35,691	60,462	35,300	47,086
United States....	212,514	417,111	568,667	534,989	309,710	445,531

[a] U. S. Department of Interior, *Mineral Resources of the United States*, 1900, 1910 1921, p. 28*A*; *Minerals Yearbook*, 1939, p. 780.

So long as the coal production of the nation was rising rapidly, as it did from 1900 to 1920, the output of the union districts continued to expand, though at a slower rate than the output of the non-union districts.[31] In 1900, the four predominantly union states of Illinois, Indiana, Ohio, and Pennsylvania produced 131,082 thousand tons of bituminous; in 1920, 334,562 thousand—an increase of 155 per cent. Following 1920 the situation changed radically. Economies in the consumption of coal and shifts to substitutes stopped the expansion in demand. Despite a large increase in industrial production between 1920 and 1929, the output of bituminous coal in 1929 was 6 per cent below 1920. During the war and postwar booms, the union had raised the common labor rate to $7.50 a day. The non-union rates also rose rapidly between 1916 and 1920. In the depression of 1921, however, the non-union

[31] Between 1900 and 1920 the output of bituminous coal more than doubled— from 212,514 thousand tons to 568,667 thousand.

rates were reduced, while the union held fast to the wartime rates. Non-union rates were now 30 to 50 per cent below the union scale. As labor represented over half of the cost of the coal at the mouth of the mine, the differential in labor cost was of great importance.

With the total market for coal contracting, the higher costs of the union mines became a far more serious disadvantage than in the days of expanding markets. The output of the non-union states of West Virginia and Kentucky continued to expand rapidly: in 1929, it was more than 50 per cent above 1920. The production of the four predominantly union states, however, dropped during this period from 334,562 thousand tons to 246,207 thousand. The inroads of non-union competition became so serious that before the expiration of the three-year agreement signed in 1924 some union operators refused to pay the scale. When the agreement expired in 1927, the union operators, hard pressed by competition, demanded wage cuts. The union refused, and a long strike followed which the union lost. Some district settlements were made at greatly reduced rates and operations in other districts were resumed on a non-union basis.

After the strike of 1927, wages in the union and former-union mines were only moderately above non-union rates. From then on, the union territory held its own fairly well in competition with Kentucky and West Virginia. The depression brought a great drop in production, but the drop of 45 per cent in the area composed of Illinois, Indiana, Ohio, and Pennsylvania was only moderately above the drop of 39 per cent in West Virginia and Kentucky. The NRA brought the union a new organizing opportunity, which it was quick to seize. The severe competition, greatly intensified by the depression, made the workers and many of the operators eager for an organization to enforce a wage scale and to prevent competition from taking the form of wage cutting.[32] At the convention of the United Mine Workers in 1936 the officers reported that 95 per cent of the industry was organized.[33] With union scales estab-

[32] Some of the employers who had operated under union conditions for a generation prior to 1927 found that they did not know how to operate "non-union." They missed the union machinery through which many grievances had been handled and many problems settled.

[33] The problems of the industry and of the union, however, are far from settled. Economies in coal consumption and the encroachments of substitutes continue to

lished and enforced in virtually all mines, West Virgina and Kentucky have no longer been able to encroach upon the markets of Illinois, Indiana, Ohio, and Pennsylvania. In fact, recovery of production between 1932 and 1937 was considerably greater in the old union territory than in recently organized West Virginia and Kentucky—52 per cent as against 37 per cent.

The men's shoe industry. In 1919, 41.7 per cent of men's shoes were manufactured in Massachusetts; ten years later, only 22.8 per cent. Between 1919 and 1929, the output of men's shoes in the United States increased slightly, but the output in Massachusetts declined 46.2 per cent.[34] The men's shoe factories in Massachusetts nearly all operated under union contracts.[35]

The shoe industry is almost unique in that virtually all manufacturers obtain their machinery on lease from the same source— the United Shoe Machinery Corporation—and pay the same rates for it. Investment in fixed capital is small. This leaves leather and labor as principal sources of differences in costs. Since leather prices vary little between sections of the country, differences in labor costs become of great importance. In 1919 wage rates in Massachusetts were about 15 per cent above New York and the Middle West. When wages in general began to decline in 1921, the employers of Brockton, the principal center of men's shoe manufacture, asked for a 20 per cent wage reduction. A deadlock occurred and the controversy was referred to the state board of arbitration, which awarded a reduction of 10 per cent in March

---

produce a shrinkage in the market for coal. The operators attempt to meet the lower demand (and low prices) for coal by cutting costs through mechanization. The union has attempted to offset the displacement produced by mechanization by pressing for a shorter work day. In 1934 it obtained the 7-hour day and in 1937 it pressed without success for the 6-hour day. Reducing the hours of work, however, seems to aggravate the very ills that it is intended to cure because it stimulates mechanization and attaches to the industry a larger number of part-time workers to meet peaks in demand. A good living cannot be realized in the coal industry without a substantial reduction in the number of workers in the industry and without a flexible working week which will permit the peaks to be met by the regular workers, not part-time workers.

[34] T. L. Norton, *Trade-Union Policies in the Massachusetts Shoe Industry, 1919-1929*, p. 105. In 1920, about 35.8 per cent of shoe workers of the country and 66.7 per cent of the shoe workers of Massachusetts were organized. The same, pp. 114-15.

[35] Higher labor costs, it is true, were not the only reason for the decline in Massachusetts. The shift of demand to cheaper shoes was one.

1922. In May 1923, the Brockton locals, against the orders of the national union, struck for restoration of the cut. The strike failed, but in October 1923 the national union obtained a restoration of the cut for a year. Not until the fall of 1924 were permanent wage reductions made in Brockton to meet the cuts made in other markets in 1921. This cut did not make the differential between Brockton and the Middle West any less than it had been before 1920; it simply restored roughly the differentials of 1920. Non-union output continued to encroach upon union.

The great depression was particularly hard on the union plants. The freedom of non-union plants to make wage cuts promptly permitted them to obtain an even larger share of the shrinking market. Furthermore, the depression intensified the shift in demand toward cheap shoes, which the non-union plants made but which the Brockton plants had not been able to make. Between 1929 and 1933 the percentage of the national output of men's shoes produced in Massachusetts dropped from 22.8 to 20.9. When it became apparent to the national leaders that rate cuts were needed to assist Brockton employers to meet competition, a break occurred between the national union and the Brockton locals which led the Brockton locals to withdraw from the national.

Other examples. The loss of business by the union women's shoe factories of Brooklyn to St. Louis and the West is similar to the story of Brockton.

The ladies' handbag industry in 1929 produced 90 per cent of its output in New York City where the industry was almost entirely union. The New York scale was substantially above the non-union scale. Furthermore, the union in New York prevented the use of section work, which permitted handbags to be made by semi-skilled workers, mostly women.[36] By 1939, only 2,000 out of the 16,000 workers in the industry were employed in New York City.

The breakdown of the national agreement in the sanitary branch of the pottery industry in 1922 was caused by the inability of the union to meet non-union competition. The growth of non-union plants was stimulated by the introduction about 1910 of the casting

---

[36] In 1939, three-fifths of the workers in New York were male and two-fifths female; outside New York, 28 per cent were male and 72 per cent female.

process in the sanitary branch,[37] by the insistence of the union on piece rates in casting high enough to make the job attractive to pressers, and by the enforcement of informal limits to production in casting.[38] The competition of non-union plants during the depression of 1921 caused a rapid shift from pressing to casting in union plants and led the manufacturers in 1922 to demand half-pressing piece rates for casting. It was the strike over this demand and the defeat of the union which led to the termination of the national agreement.[39]

The potters' union, with a national agreement in the general ware branch of the industry, finds its employment restricted by the rise of non-union concerns, particularly a large plant in Michigan which produces especially for the chain store trade and pays no more than half of the union scale. Union capacity in semi-porcelain dinner ware manufacturing showed no growth between the first half of 1931 and the second half of 1938 (being about 32 million dozen per year in each period), but non-union capacity more than doubled, increasing about 3.4 million dozen to about 8.5 million dozen.

During the twenties the union clothing markets lost heavily to the markets of Cincinnati and Philadelphia, at that time non-union. The union in this industry solved its problem by successfully organizing non-union centers—not, however, until they had encroached heavily upon union markets.[40] The manufacture of men's street clothing is over 90 per cent organized. Nevertheless, the union is experiencing competition from non-union manufacturers of work clothing, who take advantage of their low labor costs to embark upon the manufacture of sports clothing. The NRA enabled the International Ladies' Garment Workers' Union to establish almost complete organization in the women's dress industry and to maintain a fairly high wage scale. This scale has given the non-union factories in the house dress industry an opportunity to offer

[37] The old process was pressing.
[38] The limits were an obstacle to reducing the piece rates to the levels required by non-union competition.
[39] For an excellent account of this episode see D. A. McCabe, *National Collective Bargaining in the Pottery Industry*, pp. 381-438.
[40] Philadelphia was not organized until 1929. Cincinnati was organized in 1924.

styled street dresses at prices which the union manufacturer cannot meet. The union estimates that between 1935 and 1939 it lost nearly 10,000 jobs in the New York market to non-union house dress manufacturers.[41]

Many other examples of the encroachment of non-union production upon union markets might be given. These are sufficient, however, to show that, except when conditions are exceptionally favorable for organization, the bargaining power of most unions is greater than their organizing power. This is especially true of unions which operate in national markets, as in the cases illustrated above. Unions usually have sufficient bargaining power to undermine the security of their members by making it impossible for their employers to hold their own in competition with non-union employers.

HOW UNION RULES CREATE DANGEROUS COST DIFFERENTIALS

The serious cost differentials imposed upon employers through the bargaining power of unions result not only directly from union wage scales but indirectly from make-work and other rules. In the rapidly changing world of modern industry, union rules easily become obsolete. As they do, the disadvantage which they impose on union plants increases.

Rules limiting the number of pieces a man may make in a day or regulating the size of crew on a machine or the number of machines a man may run are almost certain soon to be rendered obsolete by improvements in the skill of the men, in the machines, in the raw material, or in operating conditions. When the various departments of the flint glass workers' union first imposed limitations on output, the limits were for the most part quite reasonable because the men were paid by the piece and the restrictions did not limit their earnings too severely. In the course of time the men developed many little short cuts. In the non-union shops the invention of short cuts led to increases in output so that the

---

[41] International Ladies' Garment Workers' Union, *Report of the General Executive Board to the Twenty-fourth Convention*, 1940, p. 53. In Chicago the union suffered similar losses. Carsel, in his excellent history of the Chicago union, says, that in 1938 the local dress production was practically limited to the better grades of silk dresses priced at $10.75 and up. The cheaper grades, he says, had been largely lost to the cotton dress and out-of-town shops. Wilfred Carsel, *A History of the Chicago Ladies' Garment Workers' Union*, p. 229.

non-union workers were soon producing half again to twice as much as the union workers. In the union shops the development of short cuts made it possible for the men to finish their work early and led the union to pass rules forbidding its members to leave the shop early. Improvements in presses have rendered obsolete the rules of the pressmen's union specifying the size of crews; the development of Diesel switchers has made the fireman unnecessary in switching service, although he is still required; the air brake and modern signalling reduced the number of brakemen needed on through freight trains; the improvement of looms and better control of raw material (reducing end breakage) have greatly increased the number of machines a weaver can tend. The replacement of pots by tanks in the glass industry, making possible continuous operation, greatly increased the disadvantage imposed by union restrictions on night work.

Changes, not only in operating conditions and technology, but in competitive conditions, are likely to render rules obsolete. The heavy extra payments required under the agreements of the railroad unions when passenger trains pick up freight or when road crews do yard work were not onerous so long as the railroads did not have to meet truck competition. Now they are a serious obstacle to much-needed speed in freight service.

Thus the impact of changing conditions upon union rules may in the course of time cause these rules to produce cost differentials that union employers cannot tolerate in competition with non-union plants.

WHEN DIFFERENTIALS IN LABOR COST BECOME SERIOUS

Differentials in labor cost above the non-union plants are more disadvantageous to union plants (1) when the proportion of labor cost to the total cost of production is large; (2) when the differentiation between the products of the several plants is small; (3) when costs other than labor costs are uniform between plants and not easily altered; (4) when it is easy to start new plants in the industry; (5) when the capital demands created by technological change are large; (6) when the industry is contracting; and (7) during periods of severe depression.

Bituminous coal is a good example of an industry in which differences in labor cost are important partly because wages constitute such a large part of the cost of the product. But even when wages represent a small part of total costs, differences in them may be important when there is little or no real or apparent difference between the products of the various producers and when buying is done very closely on a price basis. The rise of large retailers, such as chain stores, mail order houses, or department stores, and of large manufacturers, such as the automobile companies, which buy large quantities of goods made to their own specifications, makes small differences in cost of vital importance in many branches of industry. Each manufacturer is bidding on an identical product, and if he is only slightly higher he loses the business. This is one reason why small differences in labor cost are of great importance in the hosiery industry—an industry in which wages are only a small fraction of total expenses.

In the shoe industry, differences in labor cost are important (1) because all plants pay the same rent for machines so that high labor costs cannot be counterbalanced by other costs, and (2) because the system of leasing rather than selling machines makes it easy to start new enterprises in the industry. The relatively small amount of capital necessary to enter the garment industry causes non-union competition to grow rapidly there at the expense of the union plants. The ease with which capital enters an industry depends partly upon the ease of marketing the product of new plants. The chain stores, mail order houses, and department stores increase the mobility of capital by making it easier for new concerns to find outlets for their products without building up elaborate marketing organizations and gradually acquiring hundreds of accounts.

High-cost plants are likely to have difficulty in keeping pace with technological change because their funds are insufficient to permit them to replace old machinery as promptly as they otherwise would. The most transferable of all forms of capital, and therefore the quickest to leave unprofitable enterprises, is working capital. The banks, which usually supply a substantial part of it, are quick to reduce their line of credit once the profit outlook for the enterprise becomes unfavorable. Reduction of bank loans forces the management to use part of its depreciation allowance for work-

ing capital and thus compels it to postpone the replacing of obsolete equipment with new.[42] The faster the rate of technological
change, the greater are the difficulties of high-cost enterprises.

Even though costs in union plants are substantially above non-
union costs, the union part of the industry may flourish and expand
provided the entire industry is rapidly growing. This is vividly
illustrated by the experience of bituminous coal prior to 1920, of
upholstery weaving until 1925, and of full-fashioned hosiery until
about 1927. But let the rate of expansion slacken substantially or
let expansion change to contraction, and the situation of the union
plants changes suddenly and dramatically. Union employers and
union officials should not, therefore, judge the differential in costs
which union plants can stand by the success of union enterprises in
holding or gaining business in times of expansion. The fact that
contraction always occurs mainly at the expense of high-cost producers explains also why differentials in cost are particularly serious
to union plants in times of depression. The losses of markets suffered by high-cost plants at such times may produce a permanent
contraction in their business by causing the banks to curtail their
credit. Sometimes it takes a depression to bring home to a union
that cost differentials between union and non-union plants have
become dangerously large.[43]

[42] The experience (described above) of the union plants in the Philadelphia
carpet industry is closely parallel to this. In the northern hosiery mills also,
the special inducements offered the employers in 1938 to purchase improved equipment illustrate the same general situation.

[43] It was the failure of business in the organized men's clothing plants to show
much revival from the depression of 1924 that aroused the Amalgamated Clothing Workers to the necessity of doing something to bring down costs in union
plants.

CHAPTER XIII

CONTROL OF COST DIFFERENTIALS BETWEEN UNION AND NON-UNION PLANTS

Since any differential in costs between union and non-union plants limits the employment of union members and since the unemployment created by a given differential is likely to increase in the course of time, trade unions must consider: (1) how much unemployment it is worth while to incur in order to improve conditions for the employed; (2) how far it is desirable to achieve present advantages at the cost of future insecurity and unemployment; and (3) what form the disadvantages imposed on employers should take. Since the disadvantages which the union can impose on employers are limited, a disadvantage in the form of a working rule limits the ability of the union to achieve wage increases. This means that the cost of working rules falls in large measure upon the members of the union.

These considerations lead to the necessity of specific attention by unions to the following questions of policy or administration:

1. How the bargaining power of the union can be economized by getting the maximum benefit for union members with the least handicap to union employers.[1]

2. How responsibility and authority within the union can be distributed in such a way as to insure that all available and relevant facts will receive consideration and that the short-run and the long-run effects of union policies will each be given a weight satisfactory to the members.[2]

---

[1] The bargaining power of A is measured by the cost to him of securing concessions from B. When a union at little cost to its members can impose heavy costs on employers, its capacity to extract concessions (and hence its bargaining power) is great. The greater the cost which the union attempts to impose on employers, the more employers can afford to spend on resistance.

[2] More precisely, that the union representatives judge accurately the rates of discount which the various members accept in judging the present importance of future gains and losses. Since each member attaches an importance to future gains and losses different from that attached by every other member, judging the average rate of discount in a group is obviously a difficult matter and accuracy cannot be expected.

The problem of making policies reflect the rate of discount in the group has political aspects that have been little explored. Men who attach great importance

3. How the union can get rid of restrictive rules that impose more indirect disadvantages than direct benefits on union members.

4. Under what circumstances and by what methods unions may advantageously help employers offset the disadvantages imposed by union wage scales and working rules.

In this chapter we shall consider the first three of these questions.[3] The six chapters immediately following will explore the possibilities and problems of union co-operation with management to keep down costs in union plants.

GENERAL POLICIES LIMITING THE DISADVANTAGES IMPOSED UPON EMPLOYERS

Each union must determine for itself how much unemployment to impose on some members in order to obtain benefits for other members and how far to insist upon present advantages for its members at the expense of future security for them.[4] But since every disadvantage to a union employer necessarily limits, even though very slightly, his ability to give employment, unions have an interest in obtaining maximum protection for their members with minimum disadvantage to the employer. Furthermore, unions must consider the fact that every expansion in the proportion of employment in non-union shops reduces the bargaining power of

---

to the present are likely to rate present losses high in relation to the past gains which were responsible for the losses. Such a rank and file may at one period require its officers to insist upon immediate gains which eventually mean large losses and later, when the losses have materialized, turn against the leaders for pursuing the policies that produced them.

[3] Here we encounter a little-explored aspect of collective bargaining—the question of how unions make decisions and whose interests their decisions are supposed to represent. Are trade unions, being democratic organizations, politically capable of taking account of the effect of their policies on employment so long as only a minority of members are unemployed? What rights have minorities to consideration by majorities? How can the interests of minorities be protected against being overridden by majorities? A theory of collective bargaining needs to be constructed on the foundation of realistic assumptions concerning the interests which trade unions are trying to promote, but the work necessary to construct realistic assumptions has not been done.

[4] Would it not be rational for every union to increase its demands on its employers fast enough to reduce employment in union shops as fast as union membership shrinks because of retirement and death? In some situations (some types of public utilities) where non-union firms cannot spring up, this policy would maximize the incomes of the union members. But when it is possible for non-union firms to enter the industry, unions must take account of the fact that the growth of non-union plants reduces the bargaining power of the union because it increases the elasticity of the demand for the output of union shops.

the union because it makes the demand for output from union shops more sensitive to any increase in price of the firm's line. Hence, when unions seek to get the maximum immediate gains for their members with the least possible disadvantage to the employer, they are conserving their own bargaining power.

There are several general policies which help unions to economize their bargaining power and to obtain large gains for their members with a minimum of loss to employers. Quite frequently full protection to union members can be achieved by imposing only a temporary disadvantage on union employers, and yet the union may, quite unnecessarily, impose a permanent restriction. In order to protect union membership from displacement by a new machine, it is not necessary for the union to seek a rule limiting the output of the machine or stipulating the number of men who must be employed on it or restricting the number of machines which a worker may operate. Any one of these rules would impose a permanent disadvantage on union employers—a disadvantage that would grow in the course of time as the facility of workers increased and the machine was improved. The essential interests of the union members would be preserved by a simple rule stipulating that no workers might be displaced by the introduction of machines. This rule would impose a disadvantage on union employers, but it would be a temporary one. For a short time after the introduction of the new machine, the employer might be compelled to keep an excessive number of men, but as resignations and retirements occurred, his force would drop to the number really needed.

Ingenuity will often develop ways of giving union members the protection they desire without imposing serious restrictions on employers. It has been pointed out that make-work rules are a crude and expensive way of protecting union members against unemployment and that by handicapping union employers they are likely to create as much unemployment as they prevent. More effective protection to the workers with less burden on employers may be provided by an employment guarantee which furnishes employers an incentive to give more employment. Such a scheme existed in the Cleveland women's garment industry from 1921 to 1931. The employers guaranteed 40 weeks' employment a year with unemployment benefits at two-thirds the regular rate of pay for any unemployment in excess of 12 weeks a year. In order to provide for the payment of benefits, the employers paid a percentage of the amount of each pay roll into a guarantee fund. At the end of the year each employer recovered whatever part of his guarantee fund was not needed for paying unemployment benefits. During the life of the agreement the employers succeeded in recapturing about 85 per cent of their contributions. The union was thus able to obtain considerable protection for its members at very little expense to employers. This result was largely achieved because the plan was so drawn that the employers could save themselves expense by giving employment.[5]

Professor R. F. Hoxie, one of the most careful students of trade unionism, believed that unions can function successfully only through the maintenance of fixed industrial conditions and through the establishment of definite rules and restraints governing the use of new processes.[6] In his view trade unions were bound to oppose change. Now the internal political difficulties which unions experience in accepting changes are great. But Hoxie was most certainly wrong. In a world so full of changes as ours, the ability of unions to survive depends upon willingness and capacity to adjust themselves to new conditions. Adherence to fixed rules that have become obsolete and are producing unintended consequences threatens the existence of unions in two ways. In the first place, it threatens the ability of the union employers to survive. In the second place, it gives the employers an important issue for which they can afford to make great sacrifices.

Since detailed and elaborate rules are likely to become obsolete and to produce unintended results, a few unions as a matter of definite policy attempt to keep their agreements short and simple and free of elaborate provision. These unions endeavor to protect their members against arbitrary management by the administrative method of settling individual cases as they arise in the light of the particular facts rather than by the legislative method of spelling out rules in advance. This means that the unions are less interested in the terms of the agreement (beyond a few general provisions

---

[5] The employers took advantage of the weakness of the union during the depression following 1929 to terminate the plan.

[6] See R. F. Hoxie, *Trade Unionism in the United States*, pp. 341-42.

governing wages and hours) than in machinery for adjusting disputes. But one reason for elaborate and detailed rules is the fear of unions that employers will weaken or destroy them by discriminating against their most active members. Because of this fear, unions will not rely upon the methods of administration rather than those of legislation unless they feel that their position is secure. Furthermore, they will not use the administrative method unless they find that it yields good results—that is, unless they find employers willing to consider cases on their merits and to make reasonable adjustments in the light of the facts.

DISTRIBUTION OF AUTHORITY WITHIN THE UNION—THE POWER OF OFFICERS TO NEGOTIATE FINAL SETTLEMENTS WITH EMPLOYERS

Since the effect of cost differentials between union and non-union plants on the employment of union men is felt only slowly and over a period of years, unions are likely to underestimate it.[7] To the extent that unions do underestimate this effect, they fail to achieve the maximum possible income for their membership. There is less danger that the results of cost differentials will be underestimated and that the long-run effects of union policies will not be taken into account (1) when agreements with employers are negotiated by officers of the union with full power to settle them than when the agreements must be submitted to a referendum vote by the rank and file, and (2) when agreements are negotiated by national officers or with their assistance rather than by local officers.

The rank and file can easily visualize the benefits that will come to them from a wage increase or from certain changes in working rules. These advantages are definite and immediate, whereas the possibility of some loss in employment is remote, uncertain, and conjectural. Even more difficult for the rank and file to appreciate is the loss in the union's bargaining power from the growth of non-

---

[7] This means that unions tend to underestimate the elasticity of the demand for labor, particularly over a period of time. This tendency of unions appears to be a consistent and almost universal bias in their calculations. A similar bias exists among business men who sell goods at "administered prices." The disposition to underestimate the elasticity of demand for the product causes many prices to be set too high to yield maximum profits to the enterprise in the long run.

union plants. The union members are eager to enjoy the immediate benefits that concessions by employers will yield and they are likely to be impatient with anyone who counsels that they consider the consequences of a larger differential between union and non-union plants. The ordinary worker believes that the employer is quite able to look out for himself; that he can always afford to give more than he does give or than the union can compel him to give; and that the union need never worry about getting too much.[8] Least of all is the ordinary member of the union concerned with the possible or even probable consequences of union policies three, four, or five years hence. Too much may happen in that time for such distant results to be worth considering.

The union officers, particularly the national officers, have a different point of view. They gain nothing from concessions made by employers except the political credit of having negotiated concessions. Hence their point of view is somewhat detached. They know something about market conditions; they observe the growth of non-union competition; they are often familiar with the problems of union employers in meeting non-union competition; they know that the financial resources of union employers are limited and that some union employers are distinctly "hard up."[9] The union officers also know that the growth of non-union competition weakens the bargaining power of the union and makes it more difficult to obtain concessions from employers tomorrow—which means that it will make the jobs of the union officers more difficult. They also know that unemployment within the union ranks creates political difficulties for the union officers.

All of these comments on the point of view of union officers apply much more to the national than to the local officers. The national officers are men of longer experience—usually a man is a local officer before he becomes a national one. And the national officers naturally have a far better opportunity than the local officers to become acquainted with conditions in the trade, to observe

---

[8] The rank and file are not accustomed to think in terms of *how many* men the employer can afford to hire at different rates of pay. He can often afford to pay considerably higher rates than he does, *but to considerably fewer men.*

[9] Even in such a prosperous year as 1929 over 40 per cent of American corporations lost money. In 1937, the best year of the recovery, three out of five corporations had deficits.

business conditions, to meet employers and learn something of their competitive problems. Finally, the national officers usually have more prestige with the rank and file than the local officers and consequently are able to show more political independence. Union members are often willing to take advice from them which they would not accept from local officers. In short, the national officers are likely to be real leaders rather than messenger boys.

Because the officers of unions are both more willing and better able than the rank and file to take account of the consequences of union policies and because they attach less importance than the rank and file to immediate effects and more importance to long-run results, unions are more successful in adjusting themselves to technological and market changes when the officers are permitted to make policies and negotiate agreements without ratification by the rank and file. The power to settle, as it is called (which means without ratification), is far more important in the case of national agreements than in the case of local ones. When a local agreement is negotiated, it is possible for the officers to call a meeting of the rank and file and explain to them exactly what was done and why and to answer objections from the floor. When the agreement is national (or regional) in scope, however, it is impossible for the officers to appear before each local to explain their action. Under these circumstances ratification is often difficult to obtain. The decision of the hosiery workers' union in 1938 to abandon the national wage scale and to make concessions to individual employers in return for an undertaking to install new machinery was made by the officers on their own responsibility. Had the proposal been submitted to the rank and file, it is doubtful whether they would have approved it.[10] The reasons behind the policy could scarcely have been presented in sufficient detail to convince the workers of the need for it. Yet the policy has greatly improved the security of the union workers, with little or no loss in annual earnings.

In contrast, the cigar makers' union and some departments of the flint glass workers have been sadly handicapped in meeting economic changes by restrictions on the authority of the officers to make union policy or to negotiate agreements without a referendum

---

[10] As pointed out in Chap. XII, there were a few strikes against it.

by the rank and file. The efforts of the cigar makers to deal with the bunch-breaking and roll-up system have been discussed in Chapter VII. The constitution of the cigar makers' union required that all action of the convention be approved by a popular vote before becoming the law of the union.[11] Experience proved that the union officers could convince the delegates assembled in convention that changes in the rules were desirable, but persuading the rank and file was quite a different matter. Had the conventions possessed authority to amend the constitution, the rules of the union would undoubtedly have been adapted to changes in the industry with relatively little lag. In the words of a former president of the organization, the union was "cursed with the referendum. Now that is strong language," he added, "but it's the truth."[12]

At the convention of 1927, when little was left of this once powerful organization, the principal issue was the recommendation of President Ornburn that actions taken by the convention become laws of the union without going to popular vote.[13] The president's recommendation was adopted by the convention and the necessary popular vote. "So far as I know," wrote President Ornburn, "this is the first case in history where the membership at large voluntarily and by popular vote gave up the initiative and referendum."[14] He added that the initiative and referendum are "more responsible for stunting the growth of the International Union than all other causes combined."

CONTRASTING EXPERIENCES OF THE GLASS BOTTLE BLOWERS AND THE FLINT GLASS WORKERS WITH THE RIGHT OF CONFEREES TO SETTLE

Particularly illuminating are the contrasting experiences of the glass bottle blowers' and the flint glass workers' unions with the power of their negotiating committees to make final settlements.

[11] To amend the constitution required the approval of two-thirds of those voting.
[12] Interview with the writer.
[13] Commenting on the union's experience with the initiative and referendum President Ornburn said: "The initiative and referendum system, as we now have it and apply it, may have served a certain purpose in the early bygone days. But, owing to the extraordinary economic revolutionary changes in the industry, it no longer serves any useful purpose." *American Federationist*, February 1928, Vol. XXXV, p. 237.
[14] The same.

Each union negotiates national agreements. No union in the American labor movement has a more brilliant record of adjusting itself to great technological and market changes than the glass bottle blowers. Some of its experiences with the semi-automatic machines which came in about 1900, the Owens machine which was introduced about 1910, and the feed and flow device which became important during the war have been described in Chapters VII, VIII, and IX. In addition, the union had to meet the problem of prohibition, which destroyed one of the largest markets for its product. In order to adjust itself to these changes, the union on several occasions had to make drastic concessions, part of which were later recovered. It is safe to say, however, that the union would never have made these concessions had the officers not possessed the power to make settlements.

From the very beginning it was the tradition of the glass bottle blowers that the officers had full authority to negotiate agreements without submission to the rank and file. On several occasions an effort has been made to deprive the officers of this power, but these attempts have invariably failed. For example, in the depression of 1894, it was proposed at the convention of the glass bottle blowers to deprive the conferees of the power to settle anything relating to price lists or apprentice laws, but the proposal was defeated.[15] Again in 1906, shortly after the introduction of the Owens automatic machines, when the members feared that their representatives might accept a wage cut, it was proposed to instruct them not to do so. This action, however, was averted, and the convention simply passed a resolution stating "that we do not deem it advisable to accept a reduction for the coming session."[16] Finally, at the 1922 convention of the Glass Bottle Blowers' Association, as a result of the fact that the conferees had accepted wage reductions in 1921 in the face of instructions from the convention of 1921 to seek a 10 per cent increase, there was a discussion of the power of the officers to make settlement. But the power was not withdrawn.[17]

---

[15] Leo Wolman, "Collective Bargaining in the Glass Bottle Industry," *American Economic Review*, September 1916, Vol. VI, p. 559.

[16] The same.

[17] Glass Bottle Blowers' Association of the United States and Canada, *Proceedings of the Forty-sixth Annual Convention*, 1922, pp. 139-44.

The flint glass workers' union has had, on the whole, an unusually successful experience with collective bargaining. The early practice in this union, however, was not to give the officers power to settle, and they had to fight in order to get it. Each of the several departments of the union negotiates its own national agreement. Several of the departments were very slow in giving their conferees authority to make settlements and suffered as a result from their failure to adjust themselves to changing conditions.

In 1905 only three departments of the flint glass workers' union gave their negotiators power to make agreements without a referendum approval by the rank and file. In this year trade conditions were bad. The general executive board of the union, fearing difficulty in concluding satisfactory agreements, passed a resolution by a vote of 25 to 5 stating:

Whereas many of our present trade troubles are directly due to . . . our conference committees being denied power to settle . . . resolved, that we earnestly implore all departments to clothe their newly elected conference committees with power to settle.[18]

This power, however, was not to include acceptance of a general reduction in wages or a general change in the system of working. Such concessions could be made only with the approval of the rank and file. Following this recommendation by the executive board, department after department decided to give its representatives authority to make agreements. By 1921 there were only a few departments which did not confer this authority.

These departments suffered severely because the rank and file, against the advice of the national officers, were unwilling to meet the competition of new machines by giving up limits on daily output, prohibitions of three-shift operation, and other restrictions. Removal of these restrictions, it is true, would not have prevented the ultimate replacement of hand work by machines, but it would have prolonged the jobs of the hand workers.[19] Despite the de-

[18] American Flint Glass Workers' Union, *Proceedings of the Forty-fifth Convention*, 1921, p. 29.

[19] Speaking of the failure of the officers to get their recommendations accepted by the bulb and tube departments, President Clarke of the union said: "The referendum and too much democracy were, to a great extent, responsible for the rapid decline of the Bulb Department. Those who were guiding the association could see the danger signal years before it crossed the vision of the men more directly

velopment of machinery, the bulb department did not give up its limits on output until 1922. In this same year, however, the president reported to the convention that there was little chance for many of the men in this branch of the industry to secure again the opportunity of working at their trade;[20] and at the 1924 convention the president reported that the department was practically extinct:

It is to be regretted that our bulb workmen failed to heed the advice of the officers of this organization during the past twelve years. Former President Rowe did his best to prevail upon them to see the mistake they were making, and the record is replete with the efforts put forth by the present president in his endeavor to avert the calamity that finally overtook the members of this department.[21]

The depression of 1921 led the president of the union to make a strong effort to get the remaining departments to authorize their representatives to make settlements:

We are now in the midst of another depression. Within the past few years we narrowly averted trouble because the conference committees were denied the power granted to all other departments. It appears to me that we should make the law universal, and we should do it before we are involved in trouble.[22]

He called attention to the frequency with which the rank and file in these departments rejected the agreements made by their representatives. For example, in the chimney department, reports of the conferees were rejected in 1916, in 1917, twice in 1919, and in 1920; in the paste mold department, in every year from 1916 to 1920 inclusive; in the shade and globe department in 1916 and 1918; and in the press ware department twice in 1919. Attention was called to the fact that only a small fraction of the membership was

---

affected, yet because of our democratic form of government it was impossible to have plans adopted that would have averted the great havoc that has been wrought on that department.

"When the inevitable began its destructive march on the Tube Department, the alarm was sounded by those in a position to see the danger, but the alarm was not heeded. I do not want to infer in this instance that the disaster could have been avoided, but it could have been lessened if our men had changed their method of working and husbanded their resources." The same, *Proceedings of the Forty-seventh Convention,* 1923, p. 40.

[20] The same, *Proceedings of the Forty-sixth Convention,* 1922, p. 69.

[21] The same, *Proceedings of the Forty-eighth Convention,* 1924, pp. 41-42.

[22] The same, *Proceedings of the Forty-fifth Convention,* 1921, pp. 40-41.

in the habit of voting.[23] The convention decided that the authority of the conferees to settle should be submitted to a vote in each of the four departments.

The National Bottle Manufacturers' Association, which dealt with the union, realizing that the rank and file would probably reject any agreement making concessions to the employers, announced in 1921 that it would refuse to meet any conference committee which lacked power to settle. As a result, the representatives of the mold-making department submitted the proposition to a referendum, asking that the conferees be given full power to act, and by a vote of 228 to 180 the authority was given.[24] After the mold-making conference it was necessary to decide the power of the conferees of two other departments,[25] in which the National Bottle Manufacturers' Association was interested. The officers of the union apparently did not dare submit the question to a vote of these departments, but simply assumed the power to act.[26] Each of the other four departments which had been asked by the 1922 convention to vote on the authority of their conferees to settle rejected the proposal.[27]

The refusal of these four departments to give their conferees power to settle led President Clarke to concentrate in 1922 upon getting authority for the conferees to concede the three-shift system. The inroads of machine competition had some years before caused the officers of the union to recommend that the rank and file consider adoption of three shifts. Fearing that the officers might make this concession, the Tiffin convention of the union in 1916 had

[23] In the elections rejecting the conferees' reports, the percentage of the total membership of each department voting ranged from 23 to 56 per cent. It was more than 50 per cent in only three instances. The same, pp. 42-43.

[24] The same, *Proceedings of the Forty-sixth Convention*, 1922, p. 42.

[25] Press prescription and perfume cutting.

[26] President Clarke reported their action to the Fairmont convention as follows: "After giving serious consideration to the situation in which these committees [the conference committees of the two other departments] were placed, that of having the question raised as to their power to act finally in the pending negotiations, it was universally agreed that the conditions confronting the departments in question, the history of their development, as well as the unusual conditions confronting our organization made it the part of wisdom that your officers assume the responsibility of advising that the representatives in these two departments would have full power to act." The same, *Proceedings of the Forty-sixth Convention*, 1922, pp. 42-43.

[27] The same, p. 51.

resolved "that no officer, National or otherwise, or Local Union of the A.F.G.W.U. shall have authority to grant the concession of the three shift system to any manufacturer."[28] President Clarke told the 1922 convention:

When the foregoing resolution was adopted automatic machines had not invaded our trade to the extent they have today. These machines are now being worked 24 hours a day and, in many instances, producing ware that is either glazed or fully fire polished, requiring the services of a person doing the work that a finisher should do. Furthermore, this new method of production is depriving our members of an opportunity to secure employment at their trade.[29]

The president called attention to the fact that the large non-union enterprises were operating three shifts and that the factories under the jurisdiction of the Glass Bottle Blowers' Association would compete to a considerable extent with the factories in the flint glass industry. As a result of the president's efforts the convention agreed to repeal the Tiffin resolution prohibiting the concession of the three-shift system.[30]

At the 1922 convention President Clarke also made an effort to

[28] American Flint Glass Workers' Union, *Proceedings of the Fortieth Convention,* 1916, p. 156.

[29] The same, *Proceedings of the Forty-sixth Convention,* 1922, p. 47.

[30] *Proceedings of the Forty-sixth Annual Convention,* 1922, p. 174. This action, however, did not mean that the officers had authority to concede the three-shift plan without submitting the question to a popular referendum. According to the terms of the Toledo resolution of 1905 even the conferees who had authority to make settlements without a referendum vote possessed this authority only in so far as they did not concede general reductions in wages or general changes in working conditions. The three-shift system would be a general change in working conditions and would necessarily be submitted to vote of the rank and file.

At the 1923 convention a special report on machine-made articles was submitted to the convention by Assistant Secretary Cook, and many articles produced by the machine were exhibited and figures were supplied showing the rate at which the machines produced them.

The president urged: "The three-shift system is a question that you will have to meet if you are going to have finishers work on these machines. . . . They operate 24 hours each day, while we only permit our members to finish on these machines 16 hours out of the 24. At Sapulpa, Oklahoma, our men worked only two shifts, and the firm has installed a machine to take the place of the men on the third shift. But I ask you to open your minds. Set aside your prejudices. See how the situation is affecting you and your families. Sit down and realize fully that we are telling you the truth, and don't wait until you are removed from your position and then say, 'The national officers did not tell us or make us acquainted with the real facts.' " The same, *Proceedings of the Forty-seventh Convention,* 1923, pp. 163-65.

have secret ballots used in the referendum votes on the conferees' settlements.

In voting on conference settlements we have had to meet much opposition, which we believe could be overcome if a secret ballot were authorized. There is no denying the fact that many members will not vote their honest convictions when their views are in opposition to those of other men who may censure them for the position they may take. During the year we tried out the secret ballot in the Bulb Department, and it is my belief that had not the secret ballot been used we would have failed in getting the ratification of the membership for the work of the conference committee.[31]

The president's proposal that secret ballots be used was approved.[32]

The rank and file know that the officers often view the union's problems differently from the men in the shop. They fear that their officers have lost contact with the man in overalls. To be sure that the views of the man in the shop are understood and fully represented (and also that negotiations are better reported to the rank and file), many unions include working members of the union on the negotiating committee. This is done by the potters, the molders, the flint glass workers, and the glass bottle blowers. The negotiations in the northwestern paper industry are conducted before a large audience of rank and file representatives.[33]

DISTRIBUTION OF AUTHORITY WITHIN THE UNION—THE CONTROL OF THE POLICIES OF LOCAL UNIONS BY NATIONAL OFFICERS

Since local unions usually take a shorter-run view of the interests of their members than do the national officers, some national unions impose restrictions on the passage of working rules by local unions or reserve the right to intervene when the local union goes too far. In this way the union obtains an adjustment of the conflict between the short-run and long-run interests of the members that gives greater weight to long-run interests.

---

[31] The same, *Proceedings of the Forty-sixth Annual Convention*, 1922, p. 51.

[32] The same, p. 229.

[33] Much needs to be done in most unions to give the rank and file more complete and informative reports of negotiations. Such reports are one of the best ways of keeping the rank and file informed of conditions in the trade. Unless they know such conditions, they do not know what demands the union may wisely make of employers.

The flint glass workers' union which, as we have seen, has national agreements with employers in the industry, found that some of its local unions were passing and enforcing working rules not contained in the national agreement. The manufacturers complained, and in 1922 nearly all departments of the union, with the exception of the chimney department, passed restrictions on the imposition of working rules by the locals. As adopted in the press ware department, the rule reads: "The Press Ware Department shall be governed only by the rules adopted by the manufacturers and workers in conference, and mutually accepted factory rules."[34]

If a business enterprise finds that its district sales manager in a given territory is doing a poor job of selling, the management does not hesitate to replace him with another man. The democratic traditions of unions do not usually permit the national officers to have similar authority to remove local officers who are doing a poor job of selling the labor of the members. A few unions, however, give the national officers authority to "reorganize" locals in extreme cases. The International Union of Operating Engineers and the International Brotherhood of Electrical Workers have each taken this step. The electrical workers adopted a constitution conferring great authority upon the national officials in 1930.[35]

A typical case is the reorganization of the Milwaukee local of the

[34] American Flint Glass Workers' Union, *Proceedings of the Forty-seventh Convention*, 1923, p. 31.

[35] Among the powers conferred by the new constitution was authority to the international president:

1. To suspend card and membership of any member who, in the judgment of the president, is working against the welfare of the IBEW in the interest of any group or organization detrimental to the IBEW or creating dissensions among members or local unions.

2. To suspend or revoke the charter of any local union that fails or refuses to observe the laws and rules of the IBEW.

3. To take charge of the affairs of any local union when, in his judgment, such is necessary to protect or advance the interests of its members or the IBEW or to suspend any local officer or member who offers interference in such cases.

4. To remove or suspend any local officer, representative, appointee, or agent for incompetency, non-performance of duties, or failure to carry out provisions of the laws of the IBEW.

Other provisions stipulated that when a local union does not organize or protect a jurisdiction awarded it, its charter may be suspended or revoked by the international union and a new local established; and that all by-laws, amendments, rules, and agreements shall be submitted to the international for approval. No local shall put into effect any by-laws, rules, or agreements without

IBEW. This union had been gradually losing control of work in its territory. In 1922, out of 171 contractors, 68 were union; in 1930, out of 257, only 32 were union. About 90 per cent of the apartment buildings were being done in 1930 by non-union firms; membership had dropped from 580 at its peak to 384. The union had hampered itself by a number of rules. One of them established the city limits as the deadline beyond which a contractor must pay transportation expenses.[36] Men were not allowed to drive their cars between 8 A.M. and 4:30 P.M. Another union rule required that the foreman be paid $2 more than the scale if there were more than five men on the job. This tended to limit the number of men on the jobs and to retard their completion. One of the most detrimental rules was one requiring that all men be hired through the union office on a first-off-first-on basis. This rule was mentioned in Chapter III.[37] As pointed out there, it handicapped the union contractors because the poorest men were the first to be dropped in the fall. Hence in the following spring, when employment increased, the union employers were required to take the worst men first. Naturally this rule was unpopular with the best workmen and tended to drive them out of the union. The rules had also been administered in an inflexible manner. For example, the restrictions on working hours in the agreement were under no circumstances relaxed. For this reason union contractors had lost nearly all of the factory repair work which could be done only outside of regular hours.

When the international union entered the situation in May 1930, it decided that no one among the union officers was fitted to carry out the reforms needed. A business agent was appointed from the outside. A new agreement was written, and the restrictive rules were abolished. The union retained the closed shop, but employers were given freedom to select their own men. The requirement that

---

first securing such approval. *The Journal of Electrical Workers and Operators,* August 1930, Vol. XXXIX, pp. 440-45. See also *Constitution of the International Brotherhood of Electrical Workers,* revised July 1930 and amended by referendum submitted Jan. 30, 1931 and May 6, 1935, Art. IV, sec. 3; Art. XVI, sec. 4 and sec. 7.

[36] Union members were not allowed to leave the city limits before 8 A.M. or to drive their cars across at any time. At 8 A.M. the contractor had to pick them up with his own conveyance or else pay their fare by bus or trolley.

[37] P. 86.

employers must pay transportation beyond city limits was abolished. Union men were permitted to use their cars to go from job to job. Within 18 months, despite rapidly declining business, membership increased from 384 to 560. The union expanded in the repair and maintenance fields and emerged from the depression in virtually complete control of the market.

Although as a general rule the national officers of unions are more willing than either local officers or the rank and file to help union employers to meet competition, this generalization is open to a few exceptions. Occasionally, the national officers believe that certain conditions can be maintained in the great bulk of union plants despite the fact that these conditions either drive marginal plants out of business or force them drastically to curtail employment. Special concessions to assist these employers would create precedents that would embarrass the union leaders in maintaining conditions in the majority of union plants. Under these circumstances national leaders may oppose special concessions despite the fact that the rank and file whose jobs are at stake and the local officers may favor them. The national officers of the railroad transportation brotherhoods have opposed special concessions to certain weak roads (or special trip rates on branch lines), although these concessions would have assisted in limiting the shrinkage of railroad employment. They feared that concessions made on weak roads would spread to strong ones.

OBSTACLES AND AIDS TO REMOVAL OF RESTRICTIVE RULES

We have seen that in the course of time the disadvantages imposed by the union on union employers may increase to such a point as to threaten the survival of union shops and the security of employment in them. Consequently, unions must often consider the advisability of abandoning some of their restrictive rules. The union officers and the employers are likely to find great difficulty in persuading the rank and file to give up long-established rules. To begin with, the discovery that drastic concessions are necessary to help union employers meet competition all too often is made too late. Even the employers themselves may not realize the seriousness of their disadvantage. It may be concealed by the expansion of the industry or by a boom. Not until a depression comes and the shrinkage of employment occurs mainly in the union plants may the seriousness of the situation become apparent.[38]

The abandonment of restrictive rules is likely to mean some displacement of labor—as when limits on output, limits on the number of machines a man may run, or regulation of the size of crews, are abandoned. In the midst of depressions, when jobs are difficult to find, unions are reluctant to make such concessions. The more obsolete the rule and the greater, therefore, the number of jobs temporarily created by it (in other words, the more burdensome the rule), the greater is the opposition within the union to its abandonment. A long-established rule tends to be regarded by the workers as sacred. The rank and file do not stop to ask whether it is beneficial or harmful to them. It is simply a rule which they fought hard to obtain, which has become a cherished right, and which, therefore, they resent giving up.[39]

This attitude may even arise in connection with rules which originally were imposed against the will of a large minority of the union. The summer stop rule of the glass bottle blowers is a case in point. The competition of glass factories using Owens machines, often with non-union operators, eventually caused the other employers to demand that the summer stop be abandoned, and with great reluctance the union gradually gave up the rule.[40] It is interesting to observe, however, that this much-cherished rule was not originally adopted with enthusiasm by the union.[41]

[38] The importance of the cost differentials in the bituminous coal industry did not become apparent until the industry began to decline after 1920. The disadvantage of the union hosiery mills did not become apparent until the growth of the industry began to slow up after 1927, and it did not become fully apparent until the depression. It took the great depression to convince the upholstery weavers of the severe handicap that they were imposing on their employers.

[39] When the employers were attempting to get the several departments of the flint glass workers' union to abandon the summer stop, some workers argued that the rule must be kept because they could not stand the heat in the glass works during the hot months. These same workers, however, did not cease working when their own departments shut down but sought employment in departments where the summer stop had not been abandoned. This fact was no small embarrassment to the union negotiators in meeting the employers' arguments. American Flint Glass Workers' Union, *Proceedings of the Forty-second Convention,* 1918, pp. 42-43.

[40] See p. 233.

[41] The proposal was discussed at the second convention of the union in 1879, but failed to carry. In 1881, a stop during July and August was approved for the

Ordinarily union restrictions are only some out of many conditions which handicap union employers. If the growth of the industry has been occurring mainly in non-union areas, the non-union plants will be more modern and better equipped than the union ones and, in many cases, directed by younger, more aggressive, and more progressive managements. Under these circumstances the union may feel that abandonment of certain rules would be futile, that the union plants are eventually doomed anyway unless the non-union part of the industry can be organized, and that the union might as well keep its rules and get such good as it can out of them.

Despite the difficulties, obsolete rules have been repealed. The cigar makers (all too late) dropped their restrictions on the bunch-breaking and roll-up system; the flint glass workers (too late in some departments) dropped their limits on production, their prohibition on three shifts, and the enforcement of the summer stop; the stove molders dropped their limits on output; some of the textile workers' unions have permitted substantial increases in the number of looms per weaver; the men's clothing workers have given up limitation of the height of lay in the cutting room and many other restrictions. How have these abandonments of restrictive rules been accomplished?

An essential first step has been that the employers convinced the union leaders, and the union leaders in some cases convinced the rank and file, that the cost differentials between union and non-union plants must be reduced in the interest of employment of the union members. Unfortunately in some cases the evidence did not become convincing to the union leaders until a large portion of the union plants had been driven out of business.

No restrictive rule, however burdensome to employers and even injurious in the long run to the union members, is purely an arbitrary obstruction. It is a device for protecting the union members against real dangers. Consequently the willingness of the union to

---

prescription bottle factories, but a motion to apply it to all branches of the industry was defeated. The next convention, in 1882, passed a summer stop rule for all branches, but the convention of 1884 repealed it. Sentiment of the men in favor of summer closing grew, and in 1885 the union re-enacted the summer stop rule. U. S. Department of Commerce and Labor, *Regulation and Restriction of Output,* Eleventh Special Report of the Commissioner of Labor, pp. 627-28.

abandon the restriction may depend upon the willingness of the employers to offer the union an alternative form of protection from the danger against which the rule is directed. The purpose of the limits imposed by the molders' union in the stove industry was to prevent piece rates from being cut when the men made large earnings. In 1886, the national union voted that pieceworkers should not be permitted to make over $3.50 a day.[42] The unwillingness of a number of the locals to enforce the rule rendered it a dead letter, and in 1888 it was abolished.[43] Many of the local unions, however, continued to impose limits of their own. At the 1902 conference of the union with the Stove Founders' National Defense Association, the employers asked that all limits to output be removed. It appeared evident to the representatives of the molders, however, that some guarantee should be given which would eliminate the belief that large earnings would tend to reduce piece prices. This guarantee was given by incorporating in the agreement provision "that the earnings of a molder should exercise no influence upon the molding price of work, which is set according to well-established precedent and rule of conference agreements, *by comparison with*[44] other work of a like kind."[45] In return for this method of pricing work it was agreed that limits upon the earnings of molders should be discontinued in the shops of the members of the Stove Founders' National Defense Association. What this provision means is that the negotiation of new piece rates is largely bargaining over the differential which should exist between a new job and an old one. It is assumed that the price on the old casting is right, no matter how much the molders may have earned in making it.[46]

Similarly when abandonment of a restrictive rule is likely to

[42] F. T. Stockton, *The International Molders' Union of North America*, p. 148. The name of the employers' association has been changed to the Manufacturers' Protective and Development Association.

[43] The same.

[44] Italics added.

[45] *Iron Molders' Journal*, April 1902, Vol. XXXVIII, p. 204.

[46] This solution of the problem of limits on output, however, must be regarded as far from ideal because it perpetuates and even spreads rates which for one reason or another are out of line. A periodic review (say every three years) of out-of-line rates by time-study analysis would be preferable. This would give the union an opportunity to obtain a review of low rates and employers a review of high ones.

mean displacement of men, the union may refuse to give up the rule unless the employer agrees to provide protection either by avoiding the dropping of men or by compensating those who are dropped. When the union agreed to an increase in job assignments in the Naumkeag Steam Cotton Company, a plan was worked out that would avoid the dropping (though not the demotion) of regular employees in service when the plan was adopted.[47]

If the union can get something in exchange for abandoning a burdensome rule, it will naturally do so. Likewise the best opportunity for employers to insist that a restrictive rule be dropped is when the union wants something—a wage increase, a reduction in hours, or something else. In 1905 the Chicago local of the Typographical Union agreed not to require the resetting of matrices in the Sunday editions of the Chicago *Examiner* and *American* in return for an agreement that the working day would be shorter and the pay higher on these papers than on any other Chicago newspaper.[48] As a means of increasing production during the war when there was a labor shortage, the employers in the flint glass industry in 1918 gave the paste mold and illuminating departments a 5 per cent dockage rule which meant that the employers would pay for that proportion of spoiled work. The men in return agreed to raise the limits on their production by 50 per cent. In 1919 the union agreed to remove all limits on production in these departments in return for a 12.5 per cent wage increase. When the women's garment workers' union in 1932 finally gave up its long-continued efforts to limit the use of pressing machines in the New York market, it demanded a differential of $15 a week for machine pressers over the hand pressers.[49] The newspaper publishers and job printers have been gradually bargaining down the size of crews on the presses. It has been a slow process, but some progress has been made. In 1939, there was a reduction in the size of crews on newspaper presses in Evansville, Indiana, in return for a wage increase and other concessions including an increase in the size of the crew under certain conditions.

[47] The Naumkeag experiment is discussed in Chap. XVIII.
[48] G. E. Barnett, "The Printers," *American Economic Association Quarterly*, 3rd series, Vol. X, No. 3, p. 193.
[49] See p. 266.

If the union waits too long before giving up burdensome restrictions, so that drastic action is necessary to keep the union employers in business, it not only may receive nothing in return for dropping the restriction but may be compelled to accept severe wage cuts as well. The chimney department of the flint glass workers' union kept limits on output so long that, when it finally dropped them in 1924, it was compelled to accept a severe wage cut at the same time. The upholstery weavers of Philadelphia failed to take advantage of the expansion of the industry in the early twenties to give up the one-loom system. When the union finally accepted two looms in 1931, it was compelled to accept a wage cut of 15 per cent as well. Consequently, as a general rule, it is to the interest of union and employer alike to take advantage of every general wage increase (or other important concession to the union) to eliminate or modify obsolete restrictive rules.

THE CASE FOR UNION-MANAGEMENT CO-OPERATION

Although unions by taking care to economize their bargaining power (and organizing the distribution of authority within the union so as to promote this result) may reduce the limitation on the employment of their members to a minimum, some restriction of the employment opportunities of the union men is almost inevitable because union wage scales are usually higher than non-union.[50] A union suffering from shrinkage of employment among its members may seek to force their absorption by imposing even more numerous and more severe make-work rules upon employers. This policy, we have seen, has recently been attempted by the musicians' union and by the railroad brotherhoods, among others. It is, however, short-sighted indeed because it aggravates the disadvantage of the union employers. Hence the very remedy creates the need for still more remedy.

The alternative plan is for unions to pursue an active policy of co-operating with management for the purpose of keeping down costs. Obviously, the greater the efficiency of labor in union shops,

---

[50] In seasonal industries the seasons in high-cost plants (whether union or non-union) will be shorter than in the low-cost plants. The high-cost plants with higher price lines will usually be slower in getting orders at the beginning of the season, and at the end of the season they will be able to pick up less low-price business for post-season sales.

the higher the union can raise wages without reducing the employment of its members. The very fact that the men have in their union an organization which (usually) commands their confidence and loyalty means that there is the possibility of more effective co-operation between workers and management than exists in unorganized plants. The experience with union-management co-operation in several industries will form the subject matter of the next five chapters.

CHAPTER XIV

UNION-MANAGEMENT CO-OPERATION IN THE CLEVELAND WOMEN'S GARMENT INDUSTRY

Although scattered unions had from time to time manifested concern over the cost differentials between union and non-union plants, formal schemes of union-management co-operation for increasing production, improving quality, or reducing costs date from the postwar period. This may be partly because union-management co-operation presupposes a certain maturity of the labor movement and a high development of collective bargaining. But the specific origin of most of the experiments in union-management co-operation seems to be explained by the peculiar problems which confronted unions after the war and during the decade of the twenties.

When the postwar boom collapsed in 1920, the unions were confronted with problems of great difficulty. The war had enabled labor organizations to make enormous membership gains and to establish themselves in many plants where unions had never before been tolerated. Now that the sellers' market had changed to a buyers' market, many of the new unions found themselves confronted with hostile managements eager to seize the first good opportunity to destroy them. They badly needed better relations with employers. Co-operation in eliminating waste and increasing production was one way of developing better relations with management. The co-operative movement among the railroad shopcrafts is an example.

But it was not only the new unions which faced difficulties because of the change in the business situation. All unions were affected by the severe drop of 36.8 per cent in average wholesale prices from 1920 to 1921—the largest decline within such a short period in the history of our price statistics.[1] This severe drop in

[1] The annual index of the U. S. Bureau of Labor Statistics dropped from 154.4 to 97.6. Between 1893 and 1894, wholesale prices dropped 10.3 per cent; between 1873 and 1879, 29.8 per cent; between 1865 and 1867, 20.6 per cent; between 1836 and 1838, 5 per cent; between 1814 and 1816, 33.1 per cent. U. S. Bureau

prices led employers to seek wage cuts, which the unions endeavored to prevent.[2] Most unions were compelled to accept some cuts, but usually much smaller ones than those accepted by non-union plants.

The very success of the unions in maintaining wages at or close to war levels brought about a greater degree of non-union competition. Differentials between union and non-union plants became larger than ever. The problem of the union plants was further accentuated by the fact that for the first time in a generation the secular trend of prices was downward.[3] Several experiments in union-management co-operation which sprang up during the twenties were designed to help the unions cope with problems created by the great drop in prices following 1920 or by the difficulties in meeting non-union competition after cost differentials between union and non-union plants had widened.

Four significant cases of union-management co-operation are found in the Cleveland women's garment industry, the railroad shopcrafts (and to a less extent among the maintenance-of-way men), the Amalgamated Clothing Workers, and the Naumkeag Steam Cotton Company. These will be discussed in this and the four succeeding chapters.

BACKGROUND OF STANDARDS OF PRODUCTION IN THE CLEVELAND WOMEN'S GARMENT INDUSTRY

The first of these experiments was the joint introduction of standards of production in the Cleveland women's garment industry. The agreement to introduce a system of standards was made in December 1919, shortly after the Cleveland market had

---

of Labor Statistics, *Handbook of Labor Statistics: 1936 Edition*, Bulletin No. 616, p. 673.

The annual figures, of course, understate the magnitude of the drop. For example, from a peak of 131 (1834-42 = 100) in February 1837, wholesale commodity price fell to 98 in September 1837 (W. B. Smith and A. H. Cole, *Fluctuations in American Business, 1790-1860*, p. 158). Smith and Cole's index of commodity prices for this period is superior to that quoted by the Bureau of Labor Statistics and shows a drop of 13.4 per cent between 1836 and 1838.

[2] A few unions whose wages had lagged during the war, such as those in printing and the building trades, were generally successful in preventing cuts. Even the mine workers, despite the rapid rise in their wages during the war, were able to prevent cuts until 1927.

[3] High-cost plants usually fare worse in a period of falling prices. When prices are rising, old plants are helped by fixed costs that are low because equipment was acquired at an earlier and lower price level; when prices are falling, new plants start up with new equipment purchased at low price levels.

been organized. The decision sprang indirectly from the efforts of the international union in the women's garment industry to substitute timework for piecework. For many years the industry had used piecework in nearly all departments, but at the Boston convention in May 1918, the international union adopted the policy of replacing piecework with timework.[4]

[4] This decision was not taken without serious controversy within the ranks of the union. A large part of the members preferred piecework because they believed that it increased their earning power. There was division among the leaders. Even the international president, Mr. Schlesinger, was opposed to timework for some years after it had been adopted in the principal markets.

The opponents of piecework urged four principal objections to it. One was that it tended to produce division and dissension among the union members in each shop. Toward the end of the season when there were not enough bundles to keep everyone busy throughout the day, the employees had a strong incentive "to race for the bundle" in order to get a larger share of the work. Differences in the liberality of rates—an inevitable result of the rule-of-thumb methods of setting piece rates—were another source of jealousy and dissension. The workers who got the lower paying garments were envious of those who got the higher paying ones.

A second objection of the union to piecework was that it shortened the seasons and reduced employment by producing extreme speeding. Without the piecework incentive to produce a race for work at the end of the season, the employees would stretch the work and thus increase their incomes.

A third objection was that piece rates, being set each season, depended too much on the state of business and fluctuated too much from good years to bad. In good years, when the manufacturer was particularly anxious to get into production and was able to get good prices for his line, the union committees would be able to bargain high rates. In depressed years, of course, the result was quite otherwise.

The fourth and most important objection of the union to piecework was that it encouraged the diversion of work from the so-called "inside shops" to contract shops or sub-manufacturers. (By an "inside shop" is meant a manufacturer who has his own designer and line, sells directly to the trade, and cuts his garments in his own shop. He may or may not have all of the garments completed in his own shop. The sub-manufacturer does not deal with the trade, but simply makes garments on contract for a jobber or an inside manufacturer. He does not supply the material and often he does not cut the garments.) The opponents of piecework argued that it diverted work to the contract shops because the worker in the latter, being partly dependent for employment upon work from the inside shops, consented to lower piece rates than were bargained in the inside shops. The majority of the union leaders believed that timework would equalize competition between inside and outside shops because it would eliminate shop bargaining and would give the same rates of pay to the workers in all shops. Other leaders, including some in the Cleveland market, were skeptical of this reasoning. Timework, they argued, would make competition between inside and outside shops a matter of the employer's ability to drive the workers, and the sub-manufacturer would be far better able to do this than the inside manufacturer, for the simple reason that the employees in each outside shop were competing with those in the inside shops for work and also with the employees in other outside shops for contracts.

In the summer of 1919, general strikes for timework, wage increases, and the 44-hour week occurred in the cloak and suit industry in most of the principal producing centers. As a result, timework was established in New York, Chicago, Boston, Montreal, Baltimore, and San Francisco. In the spring of 1919, the Cleveland union had also presented a demand for timework, wage increases, and other concessions. In Cleveland a strike was averted by an arbitration award which was to run for six months, to December 24, 1919. The award gave the workers a wage increase, but did not abolish piecework. During the life of this award, the relations between the employers and the union, which had been severely strained, underwent a marked change for the better. As a result of this change, the union and the employers, on expiration of the award, entered into an agreement which provided for a system of standards of production as a substitute for both piecework and timework.

Leadership in persuading the union to accept standards of production as a substitute for timework and the employers to accept them as a substitute for piecework was assumed by the H. Black Company, the leading union employer in the Cleveland garment industry. For some years this company had been using standards of production, which it was anxious to retain.[5]

The employers accepted standards of production in order to avoid timework. Why did the union accept them? The leaders of the union realized that under timework it would be difficult for employers to know and to control their labor costs. This would be injurious to the Cleveland workers and the union in two ways. In the first place, it would impair the ability of the employers to compete with New York plants and would thus reduce the employment opportunities of Cleveland workers. The union leaders realized that the city, not being a style center, was at a disadvantage in competition with New York and less able than New York to stand higher costs. In addition, they knew that the prevalence of production in submanufacturing or contract shops in New York would prevent time-

---

[5] To the other employers the system seemed at first an unnecessarily complicated and expensive way of setting rates. Consequently it was not easy for the H. Black Co. to persuade the employers to give up piecework for standards of production.

work from affecting production costs as much in that market as in Cleveland, where most of the work was done in the so-called "inside shops."[6] In the second place, the inability of the outside shop manufacturers to control their costs under timework would encourage the movement of work from the inside shops to sub-manufacturers. This was a movement which the leaders of the union were anxious to prevent. Cleveland had always been a city of large shops, as shops in the women's garment industry go. About three-fourths of the Cleveland output in 1919 came from inside shops. For some years, however, throughout the industry as a whole the outside shops or sub-manufacturers had been gaining at the expense of the inside shops.[7] The union feared the growth of the sub-manufacturers because they intensified competition among employers and thus tended to keep down wages and to speed up the workers and because the union had difficulty in enforcing its agreements in the sub-manufacturing shops.[8] The leaders were persuaded that if the sub-manufacturers were to be prevented from invading the market, the inside manu-

[6] For explanation of an inside shop and a sub-manufacturer or outside shop, see footnote 4, p. 395.

[7] Precise figures on the increase in sub-manufacturing shops are not available, but the movement is indicated by the drop in the average size of the establishment. Between 1904 and 1919, the number of workers employed in the average establishment in the industry dropped from 35 to 21. In the same period, the number of shops employing 6 to 20 workers almost trebled, from 1,107 in 1904 to 3,284 in 1919. The number of shops employing from 51 to 100 workers decreased slightly, from 487 to 483; but the number with more than 100 declined from 294 to 196. Louis Levine, *The Women's Garment Workers*, p. 388.

[8] In order to understand the fears of the union leaders it is necessary to know how the sub-manufacturers operate. The supervision is usually supplied by the owner; no hired superintendent or foreman intervenes between him and the workers. The owner is not off in the front office seeing customers; he is in the shop constantly. As one manufacturer put it: "Nothing is more efficient than the vigilant supervision of the man who himself pays for what he gets."

The nature of competition between the sub-manufacturers creates a powerful incentive for them to cut costs to the bone. Competition between the inside shops and jobbers is to a considerable extent a matter of style and design. Between sub-manufacturers competition is almost entirely a matter of price. The reason is that they do not design the garments they make: they simply bid on the designs which the jobber or manufacturer wishes made. The intense competition between the sub-manufacturers leads the workers to connive in the violation of union standards in order to help their employers to get more orders and themselves to get more work. The difficulty of enforcing union standards is enhanced by the incompleteness of records. Although pay-roll figures exist, time clocks and time cards usually do not.

facturers must be helped to keep their costs low. The union leaders in Cleveland, therefore, accepted standards of production as a device which would eliminate the objectionable features of piece-work without making the market shoulder the disadvantages of timework.

Acceptance by the joint board of the International Ladies' Garment Workers' Union of the proposition that a compromise between piecework and straight timework was desirable led to their agreement of December 24, 1919 with the Cleveland Garment Manufacturers' Association. The agreement itself did not attempt to specify a detailed system of standards, but it provided that a system would be worked out and that standards would be subject to review by the Board of Referees—a board of three neutrals to whom disputes between the parties to the agreement could be appealed.[9]

Pursuant to this agreement, the union and the manufacturers' association engaged the engineering firm of Miller, Franklin, Basset, and Company to study the industry and to propose a system of standards of production. On March 27, 1920 the engineers submitted a report which suggested two plans. Plan A provided for grading the workers within each occupational group according to productivity and paying different time rates to workers in the different grades. Plan B, which the engineers recommended as preferable, provided for setting a standard time on each job by time studies and paying the workers at their regular hourly rates on the basis of the time value of each job. A guaranteed time wage of 90 per cent of each worker's hourly rate, irrespective of the amount he actually produced, was suggested. The standards were to be set and administered under the direction of a Bureau of Standards which would be maintained jointly by the manufacturers and the union and which would be responsible to the Board of Referees.

On June 23, 1920, the employers and the union agreed to adopt

[9] The agreement of December 1919 did pay lip service to the recently adopted policy of the international union in favor of timework and in opposition to piece-work, for it stated that the system of week work was approved. Nevertheless, the agreement provided for the establishment of a new method of payment by results which would "have due regard to the productive value of the individual worker based on fair and accurate standards."

Plan B, and in July the Bureau of Standards was established, the engineering firm furnishing the personnel. As the standard times were to be set by time study, each employer required a time-study man, but there were virtually no time-study men familiar with the needle trades. By the end of 1920, however, the engineers had trained a group of men and were ready to begin the installation of standards. The pressing department was selected as the starting point because it was small, because the work was much simpler than in the operating department, and because many of the pressers were paid by the hour rather than by the piece. Hence, there was reason to expect that standards of production would increase their earnings. On January 1, 1922 the scheme was extended to the operating department.

ORGANIZATION FOR INSTALLING AND OPERATING STANDARDS

The organization for installing and operating standards in the Cleveland market originally consisted of:

1. Time-study men—one in each plant
2. Joint plant approval committees—one in each plant
3. The Bureau of Standards
4. The supervisory committee on standards

The immediate responsibility for gathering the data for setting standards and for constructing tentative standards was in the hands of time-study men—usually one in each plant.[10] It is important to notice that the time-study men, in theory at least, were not considered employees of the plants in which they worked. They were hired and supervised by the Bureau of Standards and were presumed to be impartial representatives of both sides. Actually, the time-study man tended to regard himself as an employee of the manufacturer for whom he worked and by whom, until the end of 1922, his salary was paid.[11]

[10] At various times several of the larger plants had two time-study men, and some of the smaller plants tried the experiment of dividing the services of one time-study man. The latter arrangement, however, did not prove satisfactory.

[11] Any employer who wished to discharge a time-study man could doubtless do so. Certainly the Bureau of Standards would scarcely compel an employer to accept a time-study man who was objectionable to him. A case of an employer's discharging a time-study man occurred in August 1923. The time-study man and the union contested it, but the referees upheld the discharge.

After the time-study man had constructed tentative standards for operations from his data, he submitted them for criticism to a joint plant committee composed of representatives of the manufacturer and the workers in the shop. These meetings were known as "approval meetings." Either side might reject standards. In the case of a deadlock between the time-study man and the approval committee, the dispute was submitted to the Bureau of Standards.

The Bureau of Standards was charged with responsibility for the technical work of installing and setting standards. On it devolved the task of selecting and training the time-study men, of planning the collection of data, of standardizing the procedures of the time-study men, of deciding the technical questions which arose in the course of collecting and using the data, of seeing that standards worked out fairly in practice, of deciding disputes concerning standards, and of handling complaints concerning any aspect of the work of time-study men. Decisions of the bureau might be overruled by an agreement between the manufacturers and the union or by the Board of Referees, which was the supreme appeal body in the market. As a matter of fact, in all technical matters the bureau was given a free hand.

Until the end of 1922, the bureau consisted of a supervising engineer. The union, however, was not satisfied that one expert could take adequate account of the interests of both sides. In the agreement signed between the union and the manufacturers for the year 1923, the bureau was changed to consist of two supervising engineers, one chosen by the union and the other by the manufacturers, and the title was altered to the Joint Bureau of Standards. The two engineers had such great difficulty in settling questions that the bureau virtually ceased functioning during 1923. At the end of 1923, the union and the manufacturers decided to dispense with the technical experts and to make the Joint Bureau of Standards consist of the manager of the manufacturers' association and the manager of the union. These men had had considerable experience in dealing with each other and had demonstrated a capacity to reach agreements.

General direction and supervision of the entire standard-setting procedure was vested in a supervisory committee on standards, composed of five representatives of the union, five representatives of the employers, and the engineer in charge of the installation of standards. This committee, being composed almost entirely of non-technical men, was a policy-determining and supervising body. It was not expected to concern itself with technical matters, but to define in a broad way the policies which the Bureau of Standards and the time-study men were expected to pursue. For a short time during the early stages of the experiment, when basic policies were being formulated, the committee on standards held meetings. After this stage had passed, there were virtually no questions which could not be settled by the manager of the union and the manager of the manufacturers' association, and the committee became dormant.

METHOD OF SETTING STANDARDS

With the line of each manufacturer different, with many styles in each line, and with the lines changing several times a year, how could standards be set so as to provide some semblance of uniformity as between different shops and in the same shop over a period of time? This was made possible by basing standards upon "element times." As pointed out on page 343, the elements of an operation are the parts into which it naturally breaks up—different actions and motions with definite starting and stopping points. Although garments may differ, elements do not. Element times may be compared to bricks in houses; though the houses are not alike, they are composed of the same elements.

Elements may be divided into two groups: those with constant values and those with variable values. In the operation of hand pressing a skirt, certain elements—obtaining the skirt, examining it, removing the ticket—have constant values. Other elements—such as arranging the garment, arranging the press cloth, sponging, pressing—require different times depending upon the area involved; whether the area is plain, has seams, pockets, or pleats; the kind of cloth; and the quality of pressing expected. For these so-called variable elements, tables or curves were constructed showing the time required to arrange the press cloth or to sponge the garment when various areas were involved; for different kinds of cloth; for seams, pockets, or pleats. In the case of the operating department, it was possible to construct tables showing the time required to sew seams of different lengths in different kinds of cloth and under different conditions. For example, the time required to sew a seam in cloth with stripes or design which must be matched is different from the time required for sewing plain cloth.

The time-study man began the work of setting standards for a garment by carefully analyzing the garment into its operations and each operation into its elements. First he looked up the time for each element in his book of element times already determined. If he had times for each element in the operation, he could construct the standard simply by adding them, including in the total allowances for unavoidable delays and personal needs. Fortunately, in the great majority of cases standards could be completely constructed in this way.[12] Otherwise, the scheme could not have been operated in the women's garment industry, because new time studies for all garments at the opening of each season would have been impossible. But it was expected that some special time studies would always be necessary because garments would have new features not covered by previous time studies.

Setting standards required that the union and the manufacturers agree upon what was the proper speed of work and what was the proper method of work. As for the first, they agreed that standards should be based upon the average output of the average worker under pre-standard conditions. As to the second, they agreed that the method of doing the work should be neither the best nor the poorest in use, but one which occupied a midway position. The reasons for these conclusions are important because they indicate the problems involved in replacing the old wage system with the new one. Acceptance of the speed of the average worker, using a method midway between the fastest and the slowest, meant in effect that standards of production would reflect the success of the employers in speeding up work under bargaining conditions and that likewise they would represent the success of

---

[12] For example, during the second season of standards in the pressing department, practically 85 per cent of the pressing standards were set entirely by reference to data already in hand without making new time studies.

the union in preventing speeding up. The employers could scarcely consent to standards based upon a slower rate of work than managements had been able to require nor could the union agree that standards should call for more output than the men on the average had been compelled to give.

Equally important was selection of the method of doing the work. When efficiency engineers undertake to set standard times on jobs in non-union plants, it is usually their custom to work out the best possible method and to make it the basis of the standard times. The union, however, was unwilling to consent to this procedure. For one thing, it would have been unfair to base standard times on ideal methods unless the manufacturers were prepared to train the workers in the best methods. The union could not be sure that the manufacturers were prepared to do this. More important, however, was the fact that under pre-standard conditions the method of work was determined by the employees themselves. In an industry as unstandardized as the manufacture of women's garments, where the product is changing and where subdivision of labor has not reduced operations to simple routine acts, freedom to plan the work affords pieceworkers an exceptional opportunity to increase their earnings by contriving a quicker way of doing the work than was assumed by whoever set the piece price. Had the engineers and the time-study men made a special effort to devise the best possible method of work, the employees would have been deprived (in fact, if not in theory) of their traditional opportunity to increase their earnings by discovering short cuts. In other words, the union regarded the superior methods of work which some employees had discovered as the property of these employees and was unwilling for the employer to make the superior methods the standard methods without compensating the workers. In order to protect the superior employees, the union insisted that the time-study men make no efforts to change working methods and that they base standards upon methods more or less midway between the fastest and the slowest.

Once it was decided to base standard times upon average speed of performance and average methods of work, the question arose: "Should the averages be shop or market averages?" In the case of the speed of work, the practice at the outset was to base standards as much as possible upon market averages. This procedure in the long run would discourage innovations by individual employers but it also would tend to put different shops on an equal competitive basis. Furthermore, market averages would discourage manufacturers from speeding up their workers until their earnings greatly exceeded the standard rate and then seeking a revision of standards on the ground that the ability of their employees to beat the standard times indicated that the standards had been set too liberally. In the pressing department, the element times were averages derived from observations on hundreds of workers, both fast and slow, throughout the market. For example, in setting standards on pressing coats, 15,510 observations in 16 factories were taken to derive an average time for arranging the press cloth over areas of less than 110 square inches. In the operating department, the task of collecting the necessary data was formidable, and it was necessary to limit the work in order to save time and money. Hence the element times in the operating department were individual shop times and, in many instances, were based upon a very limited number of observations.

In selecting average methods of work, the shop rather than the market was the unit. This decision was largely dictated by practical considerations. To decide which method out of a great variety in use throughout the market was the average one would have been difficult in the extreme—in many cases impossible. This was particularly true in view of the fact that there were great differences in the organization of the work in the various shops. Some were sectionalized, others were not, and still others were partially sectionalized. Furthermore, there were great differences in shop customs and also differences in methods which were the result of differences in the quality and quantity of the goods manufactured.

In general the selection of methods of setting standards in the Cleveland garment industry was guided by three principal considerations: (1) the desire to base standards upon the speed and methods of work that had been achieved under bargaining; (2) the desire to equalize competitive conditions among the several shops; and (3) the need for a method that was largely independent of style changes and that could be quickly applied at the beginning of each season to new lines. It was the last consideration which led to the use of element times, probably the most distinctive and most important part of the Cleveland experiment. Indeed, it was the use of element times, which, more than anything else, gives permanent importance to the experiment.

PROBLEMS IN THE INTRODUCTION OF STANDARDS

Few serious problems were encountered in introducing standards in pressing. In the spring of 1921, the industry was busy and the flow of work was good. This helped the pressers to make good earnings on the standards. Some trouble was experienced in several houses where the pressers had been paid by the piece rather than by the hour. In the preceding years of prosperity, the piece-workers had bargained up their rates considerably. In these houses standards either reduced the earnings of many pressers or at least compelled the workers to speed up in order to maintain their previous earnings. In one piecework shop there was a short strike against standards.

The introduction of standards into shops where pressers had been paid by the hour raised problems of controlling the quality of the pressing. In two shops, it was necessary in the first season to reset the standards because the inspection requirements were changed. In several shops the workers attempted to force increases in standard times by restricting production. In one shop, for example, pressers started with an efficiency of 98 per cent. They held to this for several weeks. Then a presser was discharged and efficiency suddenly rose to 136 per cent. In a second shop, efficiency during the first week was 82 per cent. By the third week it had dropped to 50 per cent. Five pressers were then discharged for restricting output and there was a big jump in production.

Far more difficult than the introduction of standards in pressing was their introduction in operating. Most of the work of making garments is performed in the operating department. Hence, the number of standards to be set in this department was large. Since the operating department contained the great bulk of the workers in the industry, the union was necessarily very sensitive to any dissatisfaction with standards among the operators. Practically all of the operators were paid by the piece. During the wartime boom they had bargained up their piece rates so high that their earnings far exceeded the hourly scale provided in the agreement.[13] Since standards were based upon the time actually required to do the work, they had a tendency to bring the workers' earnings down to a wage scale which never had been effective. Naturally, the workers fought against this result. Frequently, workers who rejected standards in operating would admit that they could easily make the garments in the time allowed. A man might say: "Yes, I can make that, but I am a $9 a day man." It was something new for the workers to have their wage scale mean anything and to discuss the time for doing the work rather than the price for doing it.

The opposition of the operators to standards was increased by the fact that, in bargaining, the workers had endeavored to push piece rates high enough to offset the time lost waiting for work. In an industry as seasonal as women's garments, the flow of work is very irregular, and at the beginning and end of the season the employees have to wait for work. The standards, as explained above, allowed the workers no more time for making a garment than was really needed. It is true that the agreement providing for the introduction of standards stipulated that the workers would be paid for idle time in the factory at 90 per cent of the hourly base rate for the occupation—an important change from the previous practice.[14] But the payments which the workers might receive for waiting time were not, of course, reflected in the standards themselves. Consequently, when the workers translated the standards into dollars and cents, the resulting rates seemed low compared with the price they would expect to reach by bargaining.[15] In the spring of 1921, the union and the

---

[13] The agreement stipulated various hourly rates which the piece rates were expected to yield.

[14] For each occupation the agreement specified a base rate which normally the standards of production were expected to enable the workers to earn. In the days of piecework the piece rates were expected to yield hourly earnings not less than the base rates.

[15] At the beginning, the workers did not understand the payment for idle time and failed to take advantage of the agreement with the manufacturers. If a worker knew that he did not have enough work, he would drag the job out instead of making a high efficiency for which he would be paid accordingly and then creating idle time for which he would be paid 90 per cent of his base rate.

manufacturers had adopted an employment guarantee plan (effective January 1, 1922, when standards were first applied in the operating department) which guaranteed each worker not less than 40 weeks' employment each year or pay at one-half his minimum rate. In comparing standards with bargaining, the workers were inclined to overlook the money value of the employment guarantee.[16]

Opposition to standards arose also because they tended to disturb well-established earning differentials, particularly the spread between earnings of workers on the higher-priced garments and those of workers on the cheap garments. Under the bargaining system, managements had been more liberal in bargaining piece rates on the more expensive garments because a difference of 50 or 75 cents or even a dollar in the labor cost of an expensive garment made little difference to the manufacturer. In the case of the cheaper garments, however, labor cost was of great importance, and manufacturers bargained tighter rates on these garments. Indeed, there had been some tendency for manufacturers to accept high rates on expensive garments in order to obtain low rates on cheap ones. In setting standards no allowance was made for this customary liberality of rates on expensive garments.

Nor did standards take account of differences in the run of work. Naturally, the larger the lots in which garments came to employees and the longer an employee could work on a single number without changing, the faster he could produce. The cheaper garments came in larger lots than the expensive ones. An adjustment could have been made for this by establishing different unavoidable delay allowances for the cheap and the expensive garments. This, however, was not done. All in all, therefore, standards were more unfavorable to the operators on expensive garments than on cheap ones.

Finally, standards of production encountered difficulties in the operating department because they imposed responsibilities on employers which the managements were not prepared to assume.

---

[16] The precise gain to the workers from the guarantee is conjectural, but opinion in the market was that previous to the guarantee most regular workers had been receiving about 35 or 36 weeks' work a year. The original employment guarantee plan gave the worker two-thirds of his minimum rate in case he failed to receive 40 weeks' work. This was later changed to half the minimum.

The old piecework system had encouraged managements to shirk their responsibilities. As soon as the price was fixed on a garment, the employer lost all interest. He did not care whether or not an employee was delayed in doing his work. A leading representative of the employers said:

One result of the piecework system was an almost total loss of management in the shops. In the small shops, the men themselves have often been the managers. Since the manufacturer did not pay for idle time, he was unwilling to trouble about seeing that the employees were steadily supplied with work.

The manager of the union hoped that standards would compel the manufacturers to assume the proper responsibilities of management. The necessary transformation, for example, presupposed both standard methods of work and standard shop conditions. In the H. Black Company, which had had standards for several years, each new garment was analyzed by a member of the efficiency department, who standardized the method to be used in setting the time. But the other shops into which standards were now suddenly introduced were unprepared for them. Neither the methods of management nor the conditions of work had been adapted to standards.[17] Still more serious were the delays experienced by the operators for which allowance was not made in the standards. It was not uncommon for a worker to obtain a bundle which did not contain all of the parts or which contained parts that were not properly cut. The workers were not always given the class of work which they could do best, and they were not always kept busy on the same models. In one of the most efficient shops the management regularly tested the belts on the sewing machines in order to keep them tight. The usual practice, however, was not to fix the belts until the workers complained. The workers too, it must be remembered, did not know what their rights were or what to expect under standards. They might find difficulty in making the garments in the standard time without under-

---

[17] For example, it had been the custom in many shops for the operators to interrupt the pressers with parts which they wished pressed. The pressers, being paid by the hour, had not objected. When standards were installed, however, the pressers objected and it was necessary for the management to prevent the practice.

standing why they were being held back or wherein the management was failing to perform its duties.

Another factor which increased the opposition of the workers to standards was that earnings under the new plan were not as large as the workers were accustomed to. Part of the reduction was undoubtedly attributable to a wage reduction of about 12.1 per cent ordered by the Board of Referees in May 1921, just one season before standards were introduced.[18] But the workers did not draw fine distinctions: a large part of them knew that they were earning less under standards than formerly under piecework and they held standards responsible. Comprehensive figures on the drop in the hourly earnings of operators immediately following the introduction of standards are not available. In the first season (spring season of 1922) the average earnings of male operators on standards was 15 per cent above the standard rate and of women operators 7 per cent.[19] In several of the best managed shops, however, the increased efficiency of the management, under the stimulation of standards, went far to counteract the tendency of the system, in combination with the cut in wages, to reduce earnings.[20]

EARLY DIFFICULTIES REFLECTING DISSATISFACTION WITH STANDARDS

Fundamental problems in various phases of the operation of standards developed in the early stages of their introduction. These

[18] The gross cut was 15 per cent, but certain offsets permitted by the referees brought the net loss to the workers down to 12.1 per cent.

[19] This meant that the workers were doing 15 and 7 per cent more work in a given time than the standard time allowances called for. Had they only equalled the standard times their earnings would have only equalled the standard rate. In a cloak and suit house where the operators earned $1.49 per hour for the spring of 1921, they earned $1.24 an hour in the spring season of 1922. In another cloak and suit house the average earnings of operators dropped from $1.38 during the last season on piecework to $1.17 during the first season on standards. In a dress house the operators earned an average of 93.2 cents an hour during 1921 and 71.4 cents per hour during 1922.

[20] For example, in one large dress house, probably the best managed in the market, the average hourly earnings fell from $1.08 to 96 cents in 1922. About 10 cents of this was accounted for by the wage cut of 1921. At the same time there occurred an increase of about 34 per cent in production. In other words, increased efficiency in management, better facilities, and better organization of the work in this instance practically prevented any loss in earnings in excess of the wage reduction, despite the fact that under piecework the employees had bargained rates that yielded more than the regular hourly scale.

problems had their origin in the workers' dissatisfaction with their earnings under standards.

1. *Difficulties of approval meetings.* The intense dissatisfaction of the workers with the standards was reflected in the meetings of the joint plant committees for acceptance or rejection. There were three principal difficulties with the approval meetings: (1) they were regarded by the workers as an invitation to bargain; (2) the workers were not prepared to discuss standards in technical terms and to point out with precision where the standards were wrong; (3) the meetings occurred before garments had been put into production and the workers were reluctant to approve standards which they had not tested under production conditions.

It is easy to see why the workers interpreted the meetings as an invitation to bargain. Piece rates had always been set by a bargaining committee of employees and the management, and the workers regarded the committee for reviewing standards simply as the old bargaining committee under a new name. Of course each committee was under strong pressure from the workers in the shop. When it accepted standards, it was accused of "taking the bread out of the mouths of fellow workers—of 'selling out.'" It was natural for the committee to protect itself against such criticism by rejecting a large proportion of standards.[21]

The failure of the reviewing committees to justify their rejections of standards by making technical criticisms was partly a result of the inability of the committees to make such criticisms—at least in the early days. The original expectation had been that these committees would be a useful check upon the time-study man, pointing out where he had assumed conditions which did not exist, where he had assumed a method of work that was not used, or where he had omitted elements which it was necessary to include.[22] But few of the committee members knew enough about time study or the

---

[21] Some time-study men reported that the committees were easiest to deal with on the garments which the members themselves expected to make.

[22] Such criticism was expected to be of great value because, as the first engineer in charge of the Bureau of Standards pointed out in a circular letter to the employers on July 1, 1922, "it is very difficult to get a standard too high, as the tendency is all in the other direction, due to the omission of work."

method of constructing standards to criticize them effectively.[23]

Not only did the committee members know little about the technique of time study, but they were not given at the approval meeting the information which would have enabled them to criticize standards in a specific fashion. In other words, they were not given a list of the elements included in each standard and the time allowed for each element.[24]

The tendency of the committees to reject standards was accentuated by the fact that the standards were submitted to the shop committees as soon as the salesmen went on the road and before the house had made any stock. Not a worker in the factory knew how long it would take to make the garments. The best information which the reviewing committee had was derived from the experience of a few workers in making salesmen's duplicates.[25] Even after regular production started, it was difficult to tell at once

[23] When standards were first being introduced, a class on time study had been organized in the "Workers' University," which the union was then conducting. About 30 workers registered for the course, but the class dwindled quickly because the members lost interest. This may have been partly the fault of the instructors. The topic for the first two evenings was the history of the efficiency movement—perhaps not the best way of getting class-conscious socialist workers interested in time-study technique. The manager of the union hoped that eventually the workers' committees would learn how to make time studies themselves. The union never reached the point of actually encouraging this.

[24] When the committees rejected a standard, the time-study man often went over it with them element by element and asked the committee to point out where he was wrong. Sometimes the committees would refuse to do this. They were used to thinking not in terms of how long it takes to sew a seam or to join a sleeve but of how long it takes to make a garment. They had figured garments in terms of 3 or 4 or 3½ a day. Estimating in this crude fashion, they might be fairly close and yet estimate the time at 10 or 20 per cent above the standard. Another customary method of estimating, which had been used in the bargaining days and which the committees continued to use in checking standards, was the body-base method. The estimator would set what he considered a fair price for the body and to this he would add allowances for special features. These allowances had become more or less customary and standardized—10 cents for a pair of sleeve vents, 5 cents for curved pockets, 15 cents for double-breasted, notched lapels. Obviously such a rule-of-thumb method of estimating might give results substantially different from the standard.

[25] For these the workers were given a 20 per cent additional time allowance, which the engineer in charge of the Bureau of Standards considered insufficient except for skirts. There are various reasons why it takes longer to make the salesmen's duplicates. Not only is the work unfamiliar, but often it is found that the patterns are not cut exactly right and that the garments have not been simplified down to a production basis.

how long it would take to make a garment. The standard on a garment might be 4½ hours, but a worker might take 6 hours to make the first one. The workers knew, of course, that they gained speed by experience, but they had not been accustomed to taking times and they did not know definitely how much speed they might gain.[26] As the operators became more familiar with the garments, as the management solved its production problems, and as the flow of work improved, earnings increased.[27]

The experience of the time-study men with the approval meetings made them hostile toward the meetings. One of them said:

When you have an approval meeting you are inviting trouble. The meetings are a farce. The workers have nothing to base their arguments on; they have not worked on the garments yet. Also they are used to bargaining and you are not going to satisfy them with the first price.

The time-study man at another plant said that he had held but one meeting, that the meetings did not mean anything and he did not approve of them. He simply called in the operator and the chairman of the department, and they went over the garment together. The difficulties with the approval committees led some time-study men to delay in submitting standards and in resubmitting rejected ones. Many time-study men developed the practice of not holding

---

[26] On the basis of the standard time as 100 per cent, the operating department in one shop averaged 94 per cent efficiency in the first week of the season, 108 in the second, 124 in the third, and 135 in the fourth.

[27] The intense dissatisfaction with standards resulted in two weeks' stoppage in one of the largest cloak and suit houses in July 1922. This was a shop in which the union was particularly strong and which contained several of the most important union leaders. The workers had been good bargainers and had always come out exceptionally well in the bargaining days. Despite the fact that the shop had averaged 120 per cent efficiency under standards in the spring season of 1922, the workers felt that they were not earning enough. As a result, in July 1922, the reviewing committee approved the standards on only eight garments out of a line of 65. They said that the standards were hours off, despite the fact that the operating department had averaged 95 per cent efficiency during the first week of production—reasonably good for the first week. The time-study man checked his standards and made changes in seven instances. The committee accepted two of these, making a total of ten accepted. The other standards, it continued to insist, were still hours off. After two weeks the men returned to work and during the first week averaged 122 per cent efficiency. The union contended that this gain was partly the result of an accumulation of orders during the two weeks' stoppage, but the committee immediately accepted 54 more standards without change. Forty-six of these were standards which had previously been rejected. During the stoppage, the line had been increased from 65 to 85.

approval meetings until the shop had been in production for about a week, because they found that the committees were much more disposed to accept standards after the operators had tested them for a few days under production conditions. In several shops no approval meetings whatever were held.

Although the approval meetings failed to produce the technical criticism of standards that the drafters of the agreement had hoped for, they did prove of value in protecting the impartiality of the time-study men and in counteracting in some measure the day-to-day pressure which the time-study men were likely to feel from the employers. The engineer in charge of the Bureau of Standards stressed this aspect of the meetings.

2. Workers' suspicion of the time-study men. Only a few of the time-study men had had experience of any kind in the women's garment industry, and almost none of them had worked as operators. Their training consisted of a six weeks' course in time study as applied to the industry.[28] The workers and the union leaders had difficulty in believing that men so unfamiliar with the manufacture of garments could set reliable standards.[29]

The most important objection of the union, however, was that every time-study man tended to become the kind of man that the employer wished him to be. The manager of the union once said: "The majority become hirelings for advancement."[30] Some manufacturers did attempt to put pressure on the time-study men, and this created a serious problem—less because the time-study men were influenced and the standards affected than because the workers were aware of the pressure and their confidence in the fairness of the time-study men and of the standards was impaired.[31]

[28] They went through the course in three groups of eight or nine each.

[29] When one considers the importance of handling-time (the time spent in handling the cloth for each operation) in the operating department and the necessity for the time-study men to decide whether the handling-time in the particular case was reasonable, these doubts of the workers do not seem without foundation. Nevertheless, ability to time an operation is not so dependent upon ability to perform it as the workers imagined.

[30] Many of them undoubtedly did hope for advancement, but they were not consciously unfair in order to obtain it. Promotion was inevitable because the work of the time-study man prepared him admirably for the position of shop superintendent or production manager.

[31] Because the employers paid the time-study men, it was natural for them to regard them as employees rather than as impartial representatives of the Bureau

3. Workers' distrust of the basic data. The great dissatisfaction of the workers with the standards led them to doubt the reliability of the basic data. At no time had an agreement been reached between the union and the time-study men or the manufacturers concerning the validity of the element times. The position of the union was that such an agreement must be reached. The manager of the union admitted, however, that there were no shops in which the committees were able to analyze the garments element by element and to criticize the element times. In view of this situation, reaching an agreement on the basic data was out of the question. Nevertheless, dissatisfaction with the standards was bound to produce doubts about the element times.

It is undoubtedly true that, particularly in the early stages, much fault could be found with the data used in setting standards in the operating department. The engineer in charge of the Bureau of Standards admitted that standards had been introduced into the department too rapidly. One of his assistants expressed the opinion that ten years might easily be spent collecting data for the determination of element times in operating.[32] It had not always been possible to obtain data by timing a number of workers—not infrequently the time-study men were able to obtain times on some elements from one worker only. In such cases it was neces-

---

of Standards. Furthermore, the employers had been told that standards would lower their costs, and some of them did not hesitate to criticize the time-study men because the workers were earning too much money. One of the time-study men said that when he set a standard on a cheap coat which the workers accepted without protest, the manager became suspicious. "Why not knock off about one-fourth?" the manager asked the time-study man. The engineer in charge of the Bureau of Standards reported to the manufacturers that some time-study men had told him that "it takes real bravery on their part to raise a standard on which they had made an error, so great is the resistance of the manufacturer and payroll department to such changes." In some cases the management requested the time-study man not to take check studies which he thought necessary and, when check studies were taken, attempted to assist the time-study man in selecting the worker to be studied. In a few instances the manufacturer instructed the time-study man to get his approval on all standards before submitting them to the workers and in cases where the manufacturer regarded the standard as too high, he brought great pressure on the time-study man to get it reduced. In July 1922, the Bureau of Standards issued a strong statement to the manufacturers on the necessity of respecting the impartiality of the time-study men.

[32] When time studies had been made in the pressing department, the practice had been to continue taking readings on an element until the reading showed a normal curve of distribution.

sary for him to use his judgment in estimating the kind of performance which the worker had given. As stated above, differences in methods of work and in working conditions made it impracticable to set up many market element times for the operating department. Had there been more time, it would have been possible to do this to a greater extent, but the engineer in charge of the bureau and his assistant had their hands full.

The most important difficulties in applying standards seem to have arisen, however, not over obtaining element times, but over building up standards from these times. For example, there are many ways in which the workers lose time that cannot easily be detected by time studies unless a good many observations are taken.[33] An important element particularly difficult to standardize was handling-time. Arranging the garment or its parts for the operation consumed a large part of the worker's time. The number of arrangings and the time consumed by them varied greatly as between workers and with the same worker from time to time. A spread of from 7 to 20 arrangings in pressing was not unusual.[34] Closely related to the problem of handling-time was that of cloth classification—a matter of great difficulty.[35]

Another factor which made it difficult to set standards was that

[33] In working on bundles containing the parts for several garments, it is sometimes necessary for the operator to sort the work. All parts of a garment must come from the same piece of cloth, because mixing parts from several pieces of cloth will produce "shading"—that is, slight differences in the color of the several parts of the garment. To avoid mixing the parts, the operator must sometimes mark them with chalk.

[34] The engineer in charge of the Bureau of Standards thought that observations on at least ten operators were necessary in order to standardize handling-times for each operation on each type of material, but this number of observations was impossible, especially in the operating department.

[35] The original intention was to have a market classification of cloths, but this was not made in the operating department. In some coat and suit shops two classes of cloths were recognized, and in others three. The time-study men knew little about the cloth classifications in the several shops. One of them said: "I can see two classes of cloth: the hard and the easy. You can't catch the difference on the watch. We simply divide them into two classes." This shop arbitrarily allowed 5 per cent extra time for the difficult cloths. But there was no uniformity in the allowance. The engineer in charge of the Bureau of Standards said in December 1922 that the greatest difference between the easiest and hardest cloths was 10 per cent, but when asked how this was arrived at he said that "it had been picked out of the air." There had not been time to study the different cloths intensively.

when the time-study man set the standard, he did not know whether the garment would sell and consequently whether the workers would have an opportunity to make it in large quantity. Nor was there a satisfactory way of allowing for the frequency of style changes in setting standards. The fewer style changes a worker has in the course of a week, the more he is likely to produce, but it is extremely difficult to define a style change. Is every change from one model to another, regardless of how similar the two models may be, a style change, or do style changes include only changes from one model to a radically different one?[36] The method of work which an operator uses will be affected by whether he is making one garment or many. If he is making many, he will mark the different parts and do an operation requiring one color of thread on all parts before beginning an operation requiring another color of thread. The same thing applies to operations requiring special adjustment of the machine, such as putting cording on the bottom of a cuff, which requires a change in the foot of a machine.[37]

Garments with feature parts caused some difficulty at the beginning, because the time-study men were too busy to take time studies on these parts. Consequently, they were compelled to rely largely on their judgment in putting times on the feature parts. The difficulty was overcome to a great extent by having the time-study man notice which garments contained feature parts and then obtaining times on these parts when the salesmen's duplicates were being manufactured.[38]

[36] Suppose that the body of two garments is the same, but that they have different pockets. A change from one to the other would scarcely be regarded as a style change. It is not easy, however, to determine just when a change of models becomes a style change.

[37] There was little reason, however, for union complaint because of these differences in the methods of work, because the practice was to base standards upon the method which an operator used when making a single garment only. In other respects also it was the policy to make liberal assumptions as to methods. For example, time was allowed for the worker to pick up scissors and cut each thread after each sewing. As a matter of fact, some workers bite the thread, others break it. Often they clip it only after several sewings. Nor was it practicable to allow differentials for bundles of different sizes. One of the engineers expressed the opinion that the workers gained about 10 per cent because of receiving part of their work in large bundles.

[38] The result was a liberal time, perhaps too liberal, but that was not objection-

There was considerable complaint, as indicated above, that the standards did not allow sufficient difference between the times on the cheaper and the more expensive garments. The manager of the union complained that the quality of the work required was not adequately taken into account. The engineer in charge of the Bureau of Standards admitted that the most skilled workers were not earning proportionately as much as they did before the introduction of standards, but it was his opinion that the standards were too liberal on cheap garments rather than too tight on quality garments. The failure to make allowances for style changes or changes in methods of work were advantageous to the operators on the cheap garments because they frequently received big runs of work. In fact, the engineer expressed the opinion that the standards on the cheap garments were so liberal that only the employment guarantee prevented the manufacturers from having these numbers made in outside shops. The assistant engineer in charge of the bureau thought that labor costs on the cheaper garments were probably slightly higher under standards than they previously had been.[39] But the attitude of the workers was that the employers made a big profit on the expensive garments and that labor costs had little or nothing to do with sales of such garments; hence the workers felt that they were entitled to higher earnings than the standards permitted them to earn.[40]

CRISIS OF THE FALL OF 1922

At the end of the first season on standards in the operating department, the feeling of the operators against standards was very strong—despite the fact that the hourly earnings of the male op-

---

able because the data on the feature part would probably never be used again. In any case it would have been difficult to secure accurate times on feature parts because the time consumed in handling the garment and rearranging it was sometimes 75 per cent of the total time.

[39] Moreover, considered simply as time allowances, the standards on the more expensive garments were not unfair. The real source of dissatisfaction over the differential between the standards on cheaper and higher-priced garments arose from the fact that in the days of piecework the workers had always been able to bargain liberal rates on expensive garments.

[40] In one case a standard was rejected despite the fact that a 100 per cent performance was later made on it. The attitude of the workers was well summed up by one of the time-study men who said that "when a little cape is made of expensive material to sell at approximately $65, it is absurd to ask a tailor to operate it for $1.25."

erators had averaged 15 per cent above the base rates prescribed
in the agreement. The manager of the union said that he had never
seen such unanimity among his people on any matter before. The
union was unable to show the Joint Committee on Standards where
the standards should be more liberal, but it convinced the engineer
in charge of the Bureau of Standards that the workers should be
helped to earn more. In July 1922, he issued a strong letter of suggestions to the employers in which he said: "If the Association desires to have standards written into another agreement with the
union, the manufacturers must make every effort to see that the
standard scheme is as fair and attractive to the workers as possible."
In particular he stressed the need for managements to assume the
full responsibilities which standards imposed on employers but
which some of them were not prepared to assume. He recommended
that every manufacturer have his pay-roll department furnish him a
weekly report of the efficiency of each worker and that he investigate low earnings and undue fluctuations in the earnings of
individuals.

Despite the vigorous efforts of the bureau to improve the operation of standards, the dissatisfaction of the workers with them was
very intense at the end of the year 1922 when the agreement expired. As a matter of fact the standards were quite fair and the
earnings of the workers were well above the base rates, but the
earnings were less than they had been under the wartime piece
rates and the workers were bitter. The rank and file instructed
their leaders to sign no agreement which included standards. The
employers also took a strong stand. They were anxious to get rid
of the 40-week employment guarantee (although it had cost them
little) and to obtain the right to use piecework in small shops
where the overhead of a time-study man was burdensome. The
Board of Referees offered its services as mediator and its offer
was accepted.

The outstanding issue turned out to be whether standards of
production should be retained or the old system of bargaining piece
rates restored. Neither side was willing to arbitrate this issue. Despite the opposition to standards among the union rank and file,
the manager of the union still believed in the principle of stand-

ards, and finally, on December 27, 1922, a compromise agreement
was reached. It provided that standards of production and the
employment guarantee would be continued. In shops or departments where standards had not been introduced, the union conceded to employers the right to arrive at times or rates "either
by bargaining or over-all tests." The agreement specifically recognized that some shops were too small to have standards of production and permitted them to introduce piecework. Two concessions were made to the union. The first and more important was
the replacement of the one impartial engineer employed by the
Bureau of Standards by two engineers, one to be employed by the
manufacturers and the other by the union. With this change the
title of the bureau was changed to the Joint Bureau of Standards.
The second concession was a declaration that the time-study men
were to be solely and entirely responsible to the Joint Bureau and
a provision that their salaries would be paid by it rather than directly by the employers.

OPERATION OF JOINT CONTROL IN THE BUREAU OF STANDARDS

The changes in the Bureau of Standards and the method of paying time-study men failed to increase the confidence of the workers in the time-study men or the standards and failed to improve
the operation of standards of production. In fact, the new arrangement had the practical effect of preventing the Bureau of Standards from functioning. The relations between the two engineers
were so unsatisfactory that they held practically no staff meetings
of time-study men to compare methods and to discuss problems.
When a time-study man wished to consult an engineer about a
problem, he did not like to call in one engineer rather than the
other. Hence, he called in neither, with the result that the time-
study men received little help from the engineers.

Bipartisan control of the Bureau of Standards meant that the
bureau was virtually useless in settling disputes concerning standards in the various shops. The engineer who represented the union
was unfamiliar with the garment industry. He felt that the basic
data were unreliable and he made suggestions for improving them.
He was unwilling, however, to go out into the shops and adjust

disputes over standards.[41] But adjustment of cases in itself was one way of finding weak spots in the basic data and initiating improvements in them. On the rare occasions when the two engineers did attempt to settle disputes on standards, deadlocks almost invariably resulted. Each adopted the point of view that it was his duty to stand inflexibly for accurate standards. This, of course, made compromise impossible. The failure of the Joint Bureau of Standards to settle disputed standards compelled the managements and workers to fix the compensation on many garments by bargaining. This was contrary to the spirit of the agreement, but the manager of the union and the manager of the manufacturers' association winked at it because they knew that settlements had to be made.

Nor did the new method of paying the time-study men alter their attitude toward the Joint Bureau of Standards or the employers, or the attitude of the workers toward the time-study men. In fact, the new method of paying the time-study men was regarded as a farce by all concerned. The change was a mere technicality, for the fund from which the men were paid was provided by the employers and each employer contributed the exact amount received by his time-study man.[42]

The engineer representing the union, instead of endeavoring to improve the work of the time-study men and the actual administration of standards, spent most of his time compiling material for a report. This report was submitted to the union in the fall of 1923. It criticized existing conditions and practices in sweeping terms and recommended improvements in the basic data and changes in (1) the methods of gathering data; (2) the methods of working up data; (3) the methods of building standards; and (4) administra-

---

[41] In a sense this was a consistent attitude because if the basic data were unsatisfactory, they needed to be improved before cases could be settled. But logical or not, the attitude of the union engineer was obviously impractical. Production had to go on in the workers' interest as well as in the employers', and disputes over standards had to be adjusted. There was not time in a few weeks to revise all of the basic data.

[42] One of the time-study men said concerning it: "A man takes his employer's check down to the Bureau of Standards and gets another back. The new method of payment does not alter our attitude toward labor or the manufacturer one bit. It is foolish. We have to deal with the manufacturer to get a raise."

tive practices. The report, however, had no immediate influence upon union policy.[43]

LATER DEVELOPMENTS AND DIFFICULTIES

Since operation of the Joint Bureau of Standards by the two engineers, one representing the union and one the manufacturers, had the practical effect of preventing the bureau from functioning, the union and the manufacturers decided to dispense with the services of the engineers and to make the manager of the union and the

[43] 1. In criticizing the methods of gathering data, the engineer pointed out that the agreement required standards to be based upon the average speed of average workers, but that the "time-study men have no clear conception of what the term 'average' means and there has been no attempt to define it." He called attention to the fact that there had been substituted for the "average" worker an unwritten rule that 115 per cent efficiency was a fair average in the cloak and suit houses and something less in the dress houses. He offered the alternative suggestion that "the productivity of the normal worker at normal speed should be the standard measure of productivity." He said that "finding the 'normal' worker from a productivity viewpoint is simple," but neglected to explain how to do it. He suggested that time studies be confined to "normal" workers unless it were possible to study all workers in a department. He criticized what he declared was a tendency for time-study men to gather data from workers of high efficiency.

2. Although the time-study men attempted to correct for exceptional efficiency, the engineer suggested that the error would be greater in correcting for an efficiency of 160 per cent than for an efficiency of 115 or 120 per cent. He criticized the practice of deriving element times from the arithmetic average of the times observed in several observations and expressed the belief that "in an industry where the skill of the workers is the only significant variable and where the range of skill is 50 per cent or more on either side of the average, the mode instead of the arithmetic average should be used." He expressed the belief that the use of average times instead of modal times accentuated the differences in the results obtained in the different shops and rendered the development of market standards more difficult.

3. He criticized the disparities in the time allowances in the several shops, particularly the unavoidable-delay allowances. One shop had no unavoidable-delay allowances, another allowed 5 per cent, another 6 per cent, another 6.5 per cent, and still another from 5 to 10 per cent depending upon the class of work. He found wide disparity in four cloak and suit houses in the special allowances for the use of crepe in linings. He recommended that the unavoidable-delay allowances be restudied with special reference to so-called cloth and quality allowances and that these allowances be standardized in so far as this might prove feasible.

4. The most serious criticism by the union engineer related to the methods of administering standards of production. In a large proportion of the shops the approval meetings had been dispensed with. Furthermore, there were serious delays in settling disputed garments. "There is a tendency," the engineer stated, "to feel that such delay is good for its own sake; the opinion is frequently expressed that the grievance will die out if it is ignored. On such an excuse time-study men

manager of the manufacturers' association directly responsible for supervising the time-study men and for the operation of the standards. This change was effective January 1, 1924. In case of deadlock the question was referred to Mr. Morris L. Cooke, the well-known industrial engineer, who had recently become a member of the Board of Referees in the industry.

The new arrangement meant, of course, that the time-study men had no technical supervision. Of course, they had had little supervision during the year of joint engineering control of the Bureau of Standards.[44] The continued absence of technical supervision, however, was most unfortunate because dozens of technical problems were crying for attention. Standards of production had been introduced into the operating department with great haste and had been in use there only a year when central technical supervision of the work virtually ceased. No progress was being made in developing market element times out of shop element times.[45] Nothing was being done even to work out uniform definitions of elements—the first step in developing market element times. No one was checking whether the workers studied by the time-study men actually approximated the average worker. Some time-study men compiled

have refused to make check studies without definite joint instructions; and the management's representative has refused to join in such instructions because he insists that the time-study men's judgment in such particulars must be upheld."

The engineer complained that the union shop committees were supplied with inadequate information. He recommended that each time-study man draw up tables giving both the time value and the money value of the various standard parts of dresses or coats, that the tables be posted in the shop, and that copies be given to each member of the approval committee. He expressed the belief that such tables might enable the workers to offer valuable criticism of the time allowances set up for various operations. He also recommended that copies of the pay-roll report for each section (showing the efficiency attained) be given to the shop chairmen regularly, and that season efficiency records covering all workers in the section also be supplied the shop chairman at the end of each season. The engineer suggested that the workers' committee should be permitted to go over standards on garments in private before the regular approval meeting. "At the present time," he reported, "the committee is required to hold whispered conferences in the presence of management and time-study men and there is naturally a good deal of restraint when the workers are required to judge the fairness of the standard under those conditions."

[44] The employers' engineer, a time-study expert from the plant of H. Black and Company, had spent some time in shop helping the time-study men, but he was handicapped by the unwillingness of the union's engineer to co-operate.

[45] Market element times had been established for 133 elements mainly in pressing.

their data much more carefully than others; some kept it in better form than others; a few (as it turned out later) could not demonstrate how they arrived at their standard times. No one, however, had the responsibility of watching these matters, spreading good practices, and eliminating bad ones.

There were great differences in approval committee practice and many problems connected with these meetings. The union complained of delays in presenting standards to the committees and lack of detailed information about the derivation of standards. The time-study men complained of the unwillingness of the committees to discuss part times. The problems of the approval meetings urgently required attention, but there was no one to give it to them. The workers knew little or nothing about the methods of constructing standards. They did not know whether an allowance was made for different kinds of cloth or for joining on the bias or whether standards were constructed with sufficient liberality to allow for frequent style changes. Everything was a mystery and there was no one to see that the mystery was removed. The time-study men were under pressure from employers to keep down costs and equally subject to criticism from the union shop committees who, on discovering a mistake in a standard, suspected all standards. No wonder the morale of the time-study men was low and that, as some one in the market said, they felt like orphans. They needed an administrative superior to direct their work, help them with their problems, protect them against pressure from the employers and criticism from the union committees.

With the union members suspicious of the basic data and of the time-study men, with the scheme of standards of production lacking an administrative head and central direction, it was natural that traditional bargaining methods persisted. From time to time there were further wholesale rejections of standards. In the spring of 1924, the workers at the E. Sperling Company rejected practically the entire line of standards.[46] In the spring of 1925 the workers at

[46] The managers of the union and the manufacturers' association failed to adjust this case and it went to the impartial chairman, who, in his decision of April 5, 1924, said:

"Such a sweeping rejection of time-study work—presumably carried on in good faith—if made with a full understanding of its implications, would be

the S. C. Kline Company rejected the entire line of standards, and in another shop in 1925 the workers rejected 80 per cent of the line.

Mr. Cooke's experience in handling disputes under standards and his observation of the union's distrust of the data, the methods, and the time-study men convinced him that an investigation of the system of standards was needed. How good were the basic data? Were the union suspicions of them justified? Were the time-study men impartial? Were the approval meetings properly conducted? How could the operation of standards be improved? Mr. Cooke persuaded the manufacturers' association and the union to finance an investigation and, on his recommendation, Mr. Francis Goodell was retained to do the work. Mr. Goodell's report was submitted on October 1, 1925, and published later.

FINDINGS OF FRANCIS GOODELL AND UNION COMMENTS

Mr. Goodell's general conclusion was that "the market has no conception of the value of the work that has been done. . . . It is far better than is supposed."[47] But he also found serious shortcomings and he made several important recommendations. His report dealt with six principal matters: (1) the quality of the data; (2) the use of the data; (3) the approval procedure; (4) the complaints of the workers; (5) criticisms of the administration of standards; (6) constructive suggestions.

1. The quality of the basic data in the operating departments of eight shops was rated by Mr. Goodell as excellent in three cases,

---

the equivalent of rejecting standards. . . . As a result of a careful, if necessarily cursory, inspection of the data, as now being used in setting standards, your arbitrator is much impressed with the progress already made in securing dependable basic data in most of the shops operating under the agreement. . . . It would seem feasible, however, to bring more definition into this work and also to provide the workers more opportunity than they have had in the past to inspect and more particularly to understand the details of time-study practice." The impartial chairman found that the allowances for unavoidable delays in this shop was lower than the general market practice. He also found that there were "temporary and remediable delinquencies in certain phases of management in this shop," and for this reason decided that the allowance for unavoidable delays should be raised from 5 to 15 per cent.

[47] Francis Goodell, *A Report on the Production Standards Situation in the Ladies' Garment Industry of Cleveland*, p. 8.

good in two, and passable in three.[48] In appraising the quality of the data, three principal questions were asked: Were enough workers studied to approximate the average worker? Were studies carefully compiled? Were the over-all allowances convincing? Mr. Goodell found one plant in which an insufficient number of workers had been studied. Two plants he rated as only "passable" in this respect, another passable in one department and unsatisfactory in another, and four as good or excellent. With respect to whether the time studies were carefully compiled, the investigator rated all plants as either good or excellent and three as excellent. In two cases he found the over-all allowances unsatisfactory, in one case passable, and in five good or excellent.

2. On the question of the use of the data, or methods of building up standard times from them, Mr. Goodell found three plants where the time-study men were unable to show how they had arrived at the standard times and another plant in which this was true in one department. In other departments of this last plant the use of the data was rated as satisfactory. Among the other four plants the use of the data was rated excellent in two cases, good in one, and very bad in one.[49]

3. As to approval procedure, Mr. Goodell found that practically all time-study men had made an attempt to bring about a discussion of parts times—that is, the time allocated to specific parts of the garment as against the allowance for the entire garment. In all shops but one there were the beginnings of a discussion of parts, but in most cases it was only a bare beginning. The workers' committees felt unprepared and unqualified to discuss parts times.[50] In only one firm was the shop committee willing to discuss the garments part by part and to approve an allowance for the entire garment if the parts were correct and complete and added up correctly. Of course, discussing the entire garment gave the committee

---

[48] The same, p. 3.

[49] The last was a firm which, despite excellent data, had fallen into the habit of bargaining rates. For example, the time-study man had reduced the time allowance on feature parts below the amount he had estimated was fair in anticipation that the workers would expect to bargain. When they protested the allowance, he raised it to the correct figure.

[50] A typical attitude of the committees was: "We don't know about parts. We know only about the time for the whole garment."

a better opportunity to talk price rather than time and, therefore, to bargain. The time-study men and the employers could not escape all responsibility for the failure of the committees to talk parts because only two firms were furnishing the committee with basic data. Mr. Goodell found one concern in which the committee always rejected one-third of the standards. In four cases he concluded that the approval meetings seemed to widen the gap between the time-study men and the committee.[51]

4. The principal complaints of the workers which Mr. Goodell investigated were: (a) that there was unreasonable delay in settling standards; (b) that sub-normal workers had been excluded in computing the average shop efficiencies; (c) that in collecting figures for element times more fast workers had been timed than slow ones.

That there was delay in the adjustment of standards in some of the shops was beyond question. This was a result, Mr. Goodell found, of failure of the approval committees to function as intended. When a standard was protested, the easiest course for the time-study man was to wait until the operators had made a considerable number of the models. If the workers attained reasonable efficiency, the time-study men could take the position that experience had proved the standard to be fair. This procedure, however, was open to two objections. In some instances the workers might push themselves a little harder than usual in order to make their normal earnings, so that the verification of the standard would be more apparent than real. In others, they might hold back and attempt, by restricting production, to make the standard appear to be unfair. The former procedure might cause an unfair standard to be kept; the latter was expensive to both sides.

Mr. Goodell found that sub-normal workers had been excluded in computing average shop efficiencies. This was an error because it made the shop efficiency figures overstate the actual average efficiency of the workers in the industry in relation to the standard times.

In order to check the complaint that the basic data yielded inadequate time allowances because in collecting them more fast workers

---

[51] The same, p. 6.

had been timed than slow ones, Mr. Goodell selected six elements, noted the pay-roll numbers of the workers timed in collecting data, and compared their efficiency over a ten-week period with the average shop efficiency of the firm. The results were as follows:

Shop	Department	Efficiency of the Workers Timed	Efficiency of the Department
A	Operating	118.3	122.5
B	Operating	92.2	91.8
D	Operating	132.3	130.5
G	Operating	132.5	131.5
H	Operating	131.6	124.0

In one case the workers timed were distinctly less efficient than the department and in another case distinctly more efficient. In three shops there was little difference. In shop *H*, Mr. Goodell suggested a more comprehensive test. If the difference remained, he suggested that the element times be corrected.

5. Mr. Goodell made two principal criticisms of the administration of standards: (a) laxity in the use of data and (b) the failure of shop managements to maintain standard conditions. In one shop the time-study man had no element times for feature parts and was setting rates on feature parts in a rough way from such data as he had on hand. A second shop made no allowance for unavoidable delays.[52] In a third shop the time-study man allowed 5 per cent for unavoidable delays on jobs of two hours or less and 10 per cent on jobs longer than two hours. The supporting data, however, showed that unavoidable delays amounted to a little over 7 per cent on the shorter jobs. It was recommended that he change the allowance on the shorter jobs to 7.5 per cent.[53]

Mr. Goodell found that managements were still not accustomed to maintaining standard working conditions and that this constituted a serious problem. In finish pressing, for example, he found instances of garments coming to the pressers in badly wrinkled

[52] This omission was defended on the ground that the management furnished an unusual amount of service to the workers (for example, messenger service to bring parts to the workers and to take work from the operators to and from pressers), in consequence of which there were no delays. The time-study man, however, had no data with which to prove this contention.

[53] The same, p. 21. In a fourth shop the time-study man assumed that in pressing dresses three shifts in the position of the garment were necessary. Some dresses, however, required four shifts.

condition; tickets pinned in the wrong place; "shine" left on the garment by the parts pressers; lack of information on the part of the time-study man as to the number of arrangements needed on the press buck.

6. Mr. Goodell made several important constructive suggestions for improving the operation of standards. His inquiry showed vividly the need for central supervision of the administration of standards and for better procedure in setting standards each season. He suggested that the first need be met by holding regular and frequent meetings of the time-study men with the manager of the union and the manager of the manufacturers' association. These meetings would help build up an *esprit de corps* among the "orphaned" time-study men, subject to criticism and pressure from both sides, and create a sense of their being engaged in a cooperative effort. It would give them an opportunity to exchange ideas; to discuss mutual problems, and to enlist the help of the two managers. Mr. Goodell foresaw that regular meetings of the time-study men and the union and association managers might not be fruitful unless some one person were responsible for results, so he suggested that a time-study "boss" for the market might be needed at least for a limited period.

To eliminate the difficulties of the approval meetings and particularly to discourage bargaining and to eliminate the workers' distrust of the time-study men, Mr. Goodell suggested that the committees be given the information which they needed in order to make an informed and specific criticism of standards. He suggested posting on a bulletin board in each shop (a) the condition of service (sectional or entire garment work, the list of tools furnished, conditions of machines, lighting, etc.) understood to be in effect with the installation of standards and (b) times for all regular parts of garments with the elements. He recommended that each season's line of garments be figured so that the parts could be checked from the posted figures and that times for new feature parts be shown with the component element times. Copies of the sheets showing the build-up of the season's standards were to be given to the shop committee and also posted on the bulletin board in advance of the approval meeting.

RESULTS OF MR. GOODELL'S INVESTIGATION

Both the manager of the manufacturers' association and the manager of the union submitted letters of comment upon Mr. Goodell's report. Each manager expressed faith in the value and soundness of the system of standards and a desire to co-operate in improving its operation. Neither side was attracted by the proposal that the basic data be posted and the shop committees supplied with detailed computations of standards each season. The manager of the manufacturers' association emphasized that the time-study men were all overworked and that, if too much of their time were taken posting data, they would not have the time to make adequate studies. He pointed out that 80 per cent of the elements which go to make up any garment were standard and that the allowances for these elements were not in dispute when cases were appealed for adjustment by the manager of the union and the manager of the association. The disputes related to about 20 per cent of the element times involved in the feature parts that change with style changes from season to season. According to the manager of the association, solution of the difficulties with standards lay in better methods of compiling and checking times for feature parts.

The union manager expressed doubt concerning the feasibility of presenting the basic data to the committee in a form that would be sufficiently simple to be of use. He also feared that it would require more time than the time-study men could spare. As a substitute the union manager proposed a simple "Time-Study Manual" which would go to every committeeman and shop superintendent and tell how time studies are made, how the basic data are built up, to what extent methods and equipment should be standardized. Basic data might be included in the manual.[54]

The manager of the union approved the proposal of periodic meetings between the time-study men and the manager of the association and of the union. He expressed disappointment at the failure of the report to make specific recommendations for improv-

[54] This was true as far as market element times were concerned but probably not true with respect to the shop element times that prevailed in the operating department.

ing the basic data and recommended that a joint committee of the union and the manufacturers' association be established to supervise this job.[55]

The main concern of the union manager, however, was with certain constructive suggestions of his own. The most serious trouble with the standards system, he wrote, was the delay in setting standards at the beginning of the season. To reduce delays, he suggested that time-study men submit proposed standards to the committee in lots of one-third of the line beginning as soon as the first third had been figured. He also requested that the time-study men supply the committee with the following information in connection with each standard: (1) number of garments of the model on order; (2) character of material used; (3) specialty features; (4) operations by parts; (5) time allowances for operations by parts; (6) allowance for unavoidable delays; (7) allowance for personal needs; (8) total time for the garment. The information would also be posted on the shop bulletin board. Finally, the manager suggested that employees who were compelled to work on garments for which standards had not been set be paid by the hour at a rate determined by their last season's efficiency.

Neither the proposals of Mr. Goodell nor those of the union were adopted. The investigation by Mr. Goodell had the effect of bringing about improvements in the data and in the practices in several shops. It failed, however, to produce an improved organization for supervising and checking the work of the time-study men and the actual administration of standards or to bring about improvements in approval procedure.

DECLINE AND END OF STANDARDS

Standards of production lasted in the Cleveland market until the break between the union and the manufacturers in 1931. The importance of standards in the market, however, was steadily diminishing. The women's garment industry is one in which business mor-

---

[55] This was not quite fair to Mr. Goodell because he made many specific suggestions firm by firm for improving the data. His periodic meetings, however, would probably have been a less effective supervising agency than a joint committee with a specific mandate to bring the data in all shops up to the "reliable" level.

tality is high and the turnover among firms great. Almost every year one or two concerns using standards of production went out of business. New enterprises were springing up—although the business births did not offset the business deaths.[56] The way for the restoration of piecework was paved by the agreement made at the end of 1923 which provided that employees not under standards might be paid by the piece. Nearly all of the new firms, especially at the beginning, were too small to afford a time-study man. Had their bargaining position been unfavorable, some of them might have voluntarily adopted standards. The decline of employment in the Cleveland market, however, placed the new firms in a strong bargaining position.[57]

Fierce competition in the industry during 1930 and 1931 made it imperative that the employers have lower costs, particularly on the cheaper garments. Standards stood in the way of lower labor costs so long as the union refused to accept cuts in base rates. With unemployment severe and growing, employers were confident that they could bargain piece rates which would give them lower labor costs than standards of production. Furthermore, dropping the time-study man would save overhead. One after another of the manufacturers insisted on dropping standards and shifting to piecework. The union did not believe it advisable to call strikes against the abolition of standards and was compelled to acquiesce in every request made by the firms. By the end of 1931, when the garment manufacturers' association was dissolved and the employers broke with the union over the issue of a wage cut, standards of production were practically at an end in Cleveland. Thus the employers, who

[56] In 1921, there were 46 inside shops and 40 sub-manufacturers in the union part of the market. By 1928, the number of inside shops had dropped to 14 and the number of sub-manufacturers to 17. Bryce Stewart, *Unemployment Benefits in the United States*, p. 376.

[57] In 1921, there were about 3,000 workers in the shops controlled by the Cleveland union; in 1929, about 2,000. The Cleveland market was having difficulty in holding its own in competition with New York and with non-union markets such as Kansas City and Los Angeles. In New York the union for various reasons was unable effectively to maintain union conditions in the shops. New York was helped by greater frequency of style changes, which led many retailers to prefer to buy directly from New York jobbers, going to New York for that purpose, rather than from road salesmen through whom the Cleveland houses sold.

had taken the initiative in introducing standards, also took the lead in abolishing them.[58] And ironically enough, it was the fact that standards protected the compensation of the workers against fluctuations in bargaining power that led to their abolition. When the employers had attempted to persuade the union to accept standards, they had stressed this characteristic as an important advantage to labor. It turned out to be true that standards protected the compensation of the workers against fluctuations in bargaining power, but in so doing they impaired the ability of employers to hold their own in the fierce competition of the depression and thus standards eventually threatened the jobs of the workers.

PRESENT ATTITUDE OF THE UNION AND THE EMPLOYERS TOWARD STANDARDS

The NRA gave the union an opportunity to re-establish itself in the Cleveland market and it is now stronger than ever. Payment is by the piece. Rates are bargained with each shop committee but with a union business agent present.[59] The strength of the union is reflected in the fact that between the fall season of 1935 and that of 1937 the average hourly earnings of male operators in inside shops rose from $1.46 to $1.66. The manager of the union says that the possibility of restoring standards of production is an empty dream. Nevertheless, it is interesting to note the present attitude of the union and the manufacturers toward them.

The manager of the union says that it would not object to the restoration of standards because it found them a protection against hard bargains and shifts in bargaining power. The union would, however, insist upon two conditions: (1) application of the standards to outside shops and (2) an agreement to maintain standards for at least five years. The last time, the union manager says, the

---

[58] Today the union stresses the fact that no time-study man was dismissed at the request of the union. In fact under the conditions of 1930 and 1931 the union saw a great protection in standards.

[59] The influence of the sub-manufacturer upon rates in the inside shops is controlled by the following provisions: (1) rates paid by contractors to their employees are bargained by the union with the manufacturer or jobber for whom the contractor works; (2) no contractor may work for more than one manufacturer or jobber without the union's consent; (3) the manufacturer or jobber is responsible for the wages paid by the contractors who work for him and for maintaining an equal division of work between his employees and those of his contractors.

employers took the benefit of standards during the good years and when hard times came, they demanded the right to bargain.

Most employers now in the Cleveland industry have had no experience under standards. Despite the great strength of the union and the high hourly earnings of the workers, the manufacturers in the Cleveland industry are fairly well satisfied with bargaining. The leadership of the union is able and experienced and there is a real disposition on the part of the union leaders, according to an important manufacturer, to be fair about prices and to tell the shop committees to be fair.

The present manufacturers who have had experience under standards object to their restoration for the same fundamental reason that the union would not object—the manufacturers think that the union would have an easier time bargaining under standards. Bargaining would not be prevented, for it never was.[60] Standards would simply set a minimum below which the bargain could not go. In the past, standards were the minimum, not the average, and that would happen again. The employers would object particularly to the restoration of standards with the use of the old basic data. Manufacturing conditions and methods have changed, faster machinery has been introduced, work is sectionalized and specialized to a greater extent than formerly. Hence the old data are obsolete. This objection suggests a point of great importance. Although standards of production at first had the effect of compelling manufacturers to standardize and improve many conditions, standards over a period of time tended to weaken the incentive for employers to improve methods and machinery. Since the times for operations were standardized, the manufacturer had gained little from pressing for greater output because all of the saving, except that on overhead, went to the worker. Likewise the incentive to make changes in equipment and methods was diminished because many of the changes had too little effect to warrant changing the element times. This sort of thing happens under piecework also, as was pointed out in Chapter X. Nevertheless when

[60] But employers who say this overlook the fact that bargaining under standards of production occurred on a surprisingly small scale. Although occasionally an entire line was rejected, the rejections as a general rule were a small proportion of the line.

element times are used to set either the standards of production or piece rates, provision needs to be made to revise the data at proper intervals.[61]

SOME CONCLUSIONS CONCERNING THIS EXPERIMENT IN UNION-MANAGEMENT CO-OPERATION

1. Standards of production helped to bring about moderate reductions in the high labor costs that were the result of bargaining up piece rates during the war boom until they yielded far more than the union scale stipulated. Whether the reduction would have been as large under piece-rate bargaining and whether it could have been accomplished with as little friction no one knows. Since standards involved the payment of a guaranteed minimum by employers and since they presupposed that employers would maintain standard working conditions, they led to the introduction of many managerial improvements that would not have been made under piecework. Hence it is probable that reductions in labor cost were achieved with less reduction in average hourly earnings under standards than would have been true under piecework.

2. In so far as standards helped to reduce labor costs they helped the inside manufacturers hold their own against sub-manufacturers and helped the Cleveland market to hold its own against New York and other markets. The savings were not sufficient, however, to prevent Cleveland's output of women's garments from shrinking from 2.5 per cent of the national output in 1921 to 1.9 per cent in 1927. The inside shops lost a little ground but not much.

3. The Cleveland experience illustrates very plainly the difficulties encountered in defining, providing, and maintaining standard conditions of work, particularly when the use of piecework has made managements inefficient and irresponsible. It indicates also that, under conditions similar to those in the women's garment industry, time allowances can be accurate only as averages and over a period of time. The individual jobs are affected by such things as variations in the size of bundles, frequency of style changes, condition of materials. These conditions make the unavoidable-delay allowance important and also difficult to determine with accuracy.

4. The experience indicates the need for criticism of time studies

[61] The union manager in a conversation with me also insisted upon this necessity.

by the workers, especially in view of the danger that elements may be omitted. Time and again the workers' committees, handicapped though they were by lack of technical knowledge, were able to point out omissions and mistakes in the standards.

5. Although there is definite evidence that standards of production, particularly at the beginning, gave managements the benefit of many improvements in their efficiency, it developed in the course of time that standards had the effect of giving the benefit of many small improvements, such as faster machines or sectionalizing the work, almost or entirely to the employees. The reason was that each of these changes was not large enough in itself to warrant changing the element times.

6. Joint administration of rate setting, such as was tried in Cleveland during 1923, is likely to mean no effective administration at all. A neutral administrator might well be made responsible to a joint supervising committee, but two partisan administrators produce a stalemate.

7. Most important of all, the Cleveland experience illustrates the almost insuperable difficulty of changing well-established practices and deeply rooted propensities, such as bargaining over the speed of work. Indeed, the history of standards in the Cleveland market is largely an account of attempts to prevent bargaining from creeping into the setting of time allowances on individual jobs.[62] Employers bargained by the constant pressure which they put on the time-study men to reduce labor costs. The workers bargained by rejecting all or part of a line until some of the standards were raised—with or without reason. When the great depression occurred, employers found that standards interfered with their opportunity to bargain down labor costs—an opportunity which the employers had to seize or go out of business. While standards were in effect, employers were remarkably successful in keeping down bargaining over time allowances. Eventually, however, the

---

[62] It was not expected, of course, that standards would eliminate bargaining over base rates. Furthermore, the standards themselves were based upon a bargained speed of work and methods of performance. When it was decided to set standards in accordance with the speed of the "average worker," that was bargaining. Likewise, it was bargaining when it was decided that the standards should be based, not on the best method that the time-study man could devise or that he could find among the workers in the shop, but rather on the "average method."

old bargaining system triumphed and replaced the system of standards that had been introduced to replace it.

Although the method of basing the times for operation upon standard element times survived in the Cleveland women's garment industry for only eleven years, the Cleveland experience has permanent significance. The spread of collective bargaining makes the problem of determining time allowances for jobs under piecework or standards of production of increasing importance. Under certain circumstances the use of element times has great advantages for both employers and unions—as pointed out in Chapter XI, it reduces the range of bargaining when changes in products or methods occur.[63] But the use of element times is not always practicable and it raises difficult problems. Nowhere are the advantages, the limitations, and the technical and administrative problems associated with the use of element times under union conditions so abundantly illustrated as in the experience of the Cleveland women's garment industry.

[63] P. 344.

CHAPTER XV

UNION-MANAGEMENT CO-OPERATION ON THE RAILROADS—BENEFITS TO MEN AND MANAGEMENT

The union-management co-operative movement among the railroad shopcrafts began on the Baltimore and Ohio in 1923. The origins of the movement go back several years earlier. The father of the movement was O. S. Beyer, Jr., who during the war had developed a plan of union-management co-operation among the workers at the government's Rock Island arsenal. The success of the experiment led Mr. Beyer to suggest the idea to the leaders of the railroad shopcrafts while the roads were still under government operation. After their approval, he submitted it to the Director General of the Railroads, who in 1919 recommended its consideration by the mechanical departments of the roads. Further development of the idea was interrupted by the return of the roads to private operation in 1920.

Under government operation the shopcraft unions had made enormous gains in membership and had obtained recognition on many roads where they previously had had no members. In the agreements negotiated with them by the United States Railroad Administration they had obtained many provisions which the private managements were not prepared to concede. The return of the roads to private operation led, therefore, to a struggle in which some of the roads were plainly endeavoring to destroy the unions and others were seeking to change certain provisions introduced into the trade agreements during government operation— such as punitive overtime and the abolition of piecework. One of the principal issues between the unions and the roads was the "contracting out" of repair work to non-union shops. The roads contended that this contracting was necessary in order to get equipment repaired in time and to save money. The unions replied that the contracting was simply a device to evade union rules and that the work actually cost more than it would have cost in the railroad shops.

Relations between the shopcrafts and the roads were made worse by the depression of 1921, which led the roads to seek wage cuts and changes in the union rules. The demands of the roads were heard by the Railroad Labor Board. The carriers complained that the union rules were wasteful and uneconomical. The unions countered with an elaborate brief charging the railroads with uneconomical management and arguing that wage reductions would not be necessary if the wastes of management were eliminated. Thus the question of waste in the railroad industry was pushed into the limelight by both parties.

In view of the business situation in 1921, the leaders of the shopcraft unions regarded the strained relations between the organizations and some of the railroads as dangerous and, indeed, as a threat to the existence of the unions on some roads where the organizations were new. The idea of co-operation between the unions and the management to increase output and reduce costs appealed to several (though not all, at least in the beginning) of the union leaders as a way of improving industrial relations and as a method of discouraging the contracting out of work.

President Johnston of the machinists' union was particularly interested in the idea of co-operation. He and Mr. Beyer sought a railroad on which a demonstration could be made—a road willing to give the policy a trial.[1] In the spring of 1922, President Willard of the Baltimore and Ohio was approached. The plan had been virtually adopted for the Baltimore and Ohio when the shopmen's strike of 1922 occurred. This strike extended to almost all roads in the country, including the Baltimore and Ohio. Thus the showdown between the union and the railroads took place before union-management co-operation could be introduced to improve relations.

---

[1] A. H. Smith, president of the New York Central, was interested, but an obstacle was encountered in the existence of piecework on the New York Central. The unions wished to use union-management co-operation as a means of eliminating piecework, but the management was unwilling to give it up. The Southern Railroad was approached, but the management hesitated to accept the program because it foresaw the difficulty of measuring the gains from co-operation and, therefore, of dividing the savings.

The shopmen's strike did not alter the willingness of either the Baltimore and Ohio or the union to go ahead with the proposed experiment. It was decided to begin the program in the Glenwood shop in Pittsburgh. At Glenwood union-management relations had been unsatisfactory for a number of years—indeed, so bad following the strike that, after a short period of operation, the shop had been shut down because of low production and high costs. The union would have preferred a shop in which relations were good, but the management insisted that the experiment be made at Glenwood. Mr. Beyer went to Glenwood in February 1923. Before the plan was started, considerable preliminary work was done: physical conditions of work were improved; the storeroom was reorganized; meetings were held with the local management and the men, in which the proposed plan was outlined in detail. After a year's experiment in Glenwood, an agreement was reached between the management and the federated shopcrafts in February 1924 which provided for the extension of union-management co-operation throughout the roundhouses and repair shops of the road.

The success of the experiment at Glenwood led the executive council of the Railway Employes' Department of the American Federation of Labor formally to adopt union-management co-operation as part of its program and to engage Mr. Beyer as technical adviser in extending the policy. The original purpose of the unions in adopting the program had been, as stated above, to protect themselves against attacks by the companies through the development of better relations with managements, and against loss of employment due to the contracting-out of work. After the defeat of the shopcrafts in the strike of 1922 and their loss of recognition on a large number of roads, they saw in union-management co-operation a policy which would be useful in helping them win back lost ground.

In 1925, an agreement to introduce union-management co-operation was negotiated with the management of the Canadian National Railways. In the same year it was started in the Richmond shops of the Chesapeake and Ohio and also in the shops of the Chicago and North Western Railway. In 1926, it was adopted in the shops of the Chicago, Milwaukee, St. Paul, and

Pacific. In 1929, it was extended to the maintenance-of-way department of the Canadian National Railways.

Setting up the machinery for the co-operative plan and enlisting the active interest of men and management involved many difficulties. Additional problems were raised by the depression. The plan has survived on only two roads—the Baltimore and Ohio and the Canadian National. On the Chesapeake and Ohio, meetings were held for a few months at one shop. There was considerable interest in them among the leaders of the union, but the shop management was not interested because top management was not interested. On the Chicago, Milwaukee, St. Paul, and Pacific the co-operative plan was abandoned in 1929 and on the Chicago and North Western in 1930.

The plan, however, cannot be adjudged a failure. Although it has been abandoned on three roads where it lacked adequate support from top management, both the principal experiments with it have survived and were still in operation in 1940. Furthermore, while its benefits are difficult to measure, they have been substantial even on roads where the plan of union-management co-operation has been abandoned. This chapter considers the benefits yielded by the plan to men and management; the next chapter, some of the principal problems that the plan has encountered.

BENEFITS TO WORKERS

The gains which union-management co-operation on the railroads has brought to the shopmen (and, in the case of the Canadian National, to the maintenance-of-way men[2]) have been

---

[2] Although the gains achieved in the maintenance-of-way department on the Canadian National were substantial, limitations of space make it convenient to illustrate the benefits to the men from the experience of the shopcrafts, which extends to several roads and covers a longer period of time than in the maintenance-of-way department.

Careful analysis of the experience of the maintenance-of-way department and attendance at a number of their meetings indicate that the benefits to the men were of the same general nature as those achieved by the shopcrafts. Particularly noteworthy was the great improvement in the tools and in many working conditions. Because the maintenance-of-way forces are scattered along the entire line, their contact with their superiors is less close than that of the shopcrafts and they are less able to inform their superiors of conditions which need changing. Consequently, the point of contact furnished by the co-operative committee meetings in the maintenance-of-way department has been particularly valuable to both

greater than most of the men realize. This is partly because gains, once achieved, tend to be taken for granted. Another reason is that the men remember best the things which they have sought but not secured. As a general rule, the railroad officials and the union leaders, who are more fully acquainted than the men with the problems of both the unions and the railroads, have a better appreciation of the contribution which union-management co-operation has made.[3]

The principal benefits to the men have been: (1) better relations between the men and management; (2) reduction in the number of grievances; (3) improved methods of handling grievances; (4) improvement in working conditions; (5) improvement in apprentice training; (6) increase in union membership; (7) wage increases either earlier in date or larger in amount than would otherwise have been achieved; (8) elimination of the bonus system in a number of shops on the Canadian National (this being a form of wage payment which the shopcraft unions opposed); (9) stabilization and increase of employment; and (10) more complete information for the men concerning operations of the railroad.

1. *Better relations between the men and management.* Representatives both of the men and of the management agree that the greatest benefit produced by union-management co-operation to

---

men and management. Although the Brotherhood of Maintenance-of-Way Men has adopted union-management co-operation as an official policy of the union, only the Canadian National (and its subsidiaries) has seen fit to take advantage of this policy in the maintenance-of-way department.

[3] Comprehensive reviews of the gains to the shopcrafts from union-management co-operation are contained in the officers' reports to the conventions of the Railway Employes' Department of the American Federation of Labor in 1926 and 1930. Railway Employes' Department, *Official Proceedings of the Seventh Convention,* 1926, pp. 69-74, and *Official Proceedings of the Eighth Convention,* 1930, pp. 10-22.

"There can be no doubt but what this plan has been beneficial to our membership. While no grievances are to be discussed at the co-operative meetings, there can be no doubt but what the plan has improved our working conditions, and reduced the number of grievances. Since its inception, much additional work has been done in our own shops, such as reconditioning cars, building new cars, and rebuilding and remodeling locomotives, modernizing passenger cars and trains, fabricating material for building new cars, and repairing freight cars, and the manufacture of parts for locomotives and cars, and your committee is ever on the alert to seek more work to be done in our own shops." Report of the Officers of the Baltimore and Ohio System Federation to the convention held in May 1930.

each side is better relations with the other. Speaking in May 1940, the head of the Baltimore and Ohio system federation said: "Of course we get washrooms, pits repaired and so forth, but I really believe the biggest thing is the better relationship in the shop." Although it is true that the co-operative plan, at least in its early stages, created a few new points of friction in some shops, the evidence is overwhelming that in the long run the plan has substantially improved relations between men and management.[4] In general, the improvement springs from the willingness of each side to deal with the other in a spirit of greater tolerance and reasonableness and to approach problems in the spirit of give and take.

2. *Reduction in the number of grievances.* Statistical records of the number of grievances on roads pursuing union-management co-operation are not complete, but testimony is universal that the total number has been greatly reduced.[5] In addition, there is general agreement that a larger proportion of cases are settled locally, thus avoiding appeal. This is in itself an important gain because it means more prompt disposition of grievances.

The following table shows the sharp reduction in the number of appeal cases on the Baltimore and Ohio in the years just before and just after the introduction of union-management co-operation. Since the unions handle the grievances of members only, it is best to consider the cases in relation to the membership of the shop-craft unions. It will be observed that the number of appeal cases was diminishing even before union-management co-operation be-

---

[4] In talking with the men one encounters many references to particular supervisors who changed greatly after the co-operative plan was started. A worker on the Baltimore and Ohio, when asked what had been gained, replied: "Well, we got rid of old man grouch in the blacksmith shop." A machinist on the Canadian National, referring to his general foreman, said, "There is as much difference in that man as between day and night."

No less interesting and illuminating are the comments from supervisors on the change in the attitude of the men. A master mechanic at a Baltimore and Ohio shop said: "The men used to think the officials had horns. In the old days when you went through the shop they thought you were going to fire someone. They didn't figure that we are here to help someone."

[5] A master mechanic on the Baltimore and Ohio said: "When I first came here, I'd say that on the average of once a day some committee would come here with some grievance. Now I'm safe in saying I don't have a grievance to settle twice a month." A high official on the Canadian National estimated that the total number of grievances in the Canadian National shops was reduced by more than 75 per cent.

came general on the Baltimore and Ohio in 1924. This was partly due to the fact that the strike of 1922 produced many grievances,[6] after which the management and the workers settled down to learn how to live together. Some of the reduction, however, must be attributed to the better relations between the unions and the management which accompanied the trial of union-management co-operation in the Glenwood shops early in 1923.

SHOPCRAFT APPEAL CASES, BALTIMORE AND OHIO, 1922–39

Year	Average Membership of Shopcraft Unions	Total Number of Appeal Cases	Appeal Cases per 100 Union Members
1922.......	10,295	261	2.53
1923.......	5,799	117	2.02
1924.......	9,228	154	1.67
1925.......	10,083	146	1.45
1926.......	11,077	87	.79
1927.......	9,776	103	1.05
1928.......	8,966	85	.97
1928[a].......	8,026	35	.44
1929.......	8,835	68	.77
1930.......	8,630	65	.75
1931.......	6,158	50	.81
1932.......	3,564	28	.78
1933.......	3,056	56	1.83
1934.......	3,897	18	.46
1935.......	3,796	20	.53
1936.......	4,991	21	.42
1937.......	5,366	21	.39
1938.......	3,934	25	.64
1939.......	4,839	25	.52

[a] Ten-month period March 1 through December 31. Preceding figures apply to year ending February 28; those following to year ending December 31.

Although the contribution of union-management co-operation to the reduction of grievances cannot be precisely determined, it has been substantial. The policy has tended to make both managements and union leaders avoid the kind of behavior which produces grievances; it has given the men greater success in settling matters

[6] The very fact that the unions ceased to represent the men on over half the mileage of all roads made union leaders anxious to improve the relations of their organizations on the roads where the unions were recognized. Moreover, the process of settling cases gradually produced interpretations of the agreements, which removed uncertainties and hence reduced disputes. For these and other reasons the number of disputes dropped on all roads, whether they were pursuing the policy of union-management co-operation or not.

with their foremen; it has made managements more disposed to settle difficulties with the help of union committees before imposing discipline;[7] it has made union committees more discriminating in the cases they take up as grievances with the management;[8] and it has enabled the men to obtain things by making suggestions instead of making complaints.[9] Only on the Chicago and North Western did an unsatisfactory condition in relation to grievances persist despite the policy of union-management co-operation. The number of local grievances on this road dropped, but the disposition of appeal cases was unsatisfactory to the men largely because higher management seemed disposed to back up local officials without a proper fresh investigation.[10]

3. *Improved methods of handling grievances.* A grievance long delayed in settlement is likely to be a grievance substantially lost. The unions and the management on both the Baltimore and Ohio and the Canadian National realized that the union-management co-operative plan could not be expected to work satisfactorily unless grievances were expeditiously settled; consequently, the arrangements for handling grievances on both of these roads were subjected to re-examination and reconstruction.

On the Baltimore and Ohio two principal changes were made. The first was to reduce the number of appeal steps between the shop superintendent and the highest appeal authority. Under the

[7] A master mechanic on the Baltimore and Ohio said that he almost invariably leaves to the union committee the handling of men who are not producing. He said: "The committees are far more responsible than they used to be. Problems of unsatisfactory quality of work are also frequently handled by the method of calling the union committeeman and asking him to take up the matter with his members."

[8] This has not meant that they have been willing to wink at violations by management of the terms of the trade agreement. On the contrary, union officers express the opinion that the co-operative plan makes the local unions more vigilant in enforcing the agreement.

[9] Suppose, for example, that a drop pit needed cleaning, or that the management failed to give certain workers protection against heat. The old method was for the grievance committee to make a complaint. Under the co-operative plan the custom is for such matters to be taken up as suggestions.

[10] During the depression, after the plan of union-management co-operation on the Chicago and North Western had been abandoned, the accumulation of unsettled appeal cases grew so serious that a strike vote was taken among the shopmen. This led to the intervention of the president of the road and the disposal of many old cases.

previous arrangement there had been three intermediate appeals between the shop superintendent and the assistant to the vice-president who disposed of grievances. A case might be on appeal for a year or more. Under the new arrangements all grievances from the three large shops (Mt. Clare, Cumberland, and Glenwood) went directly from the shop superintendent to the assistant to the vice-president. For other (small) shops, there were two intermediate appeals in grievance cases and one intermediate appeal for non-discipline grievances.

The second innovation was to require on appeal a statement known as a joint submission of facts, which included a statement of the question at issue, a summary of the agreed-upon facts, a statement of the contention of the man and of the management, and the decision of the officer from which appeal was taken. It was signed jointly. The joint submission had several beneficial effects. The very statement of the issue helped the local representatives of the railroad and the union to clarify their minds and in some instances enabled them to settle cases on which they had disagreed; it discouraged "buck passing," because it made the appeal officer decide the case on the basis of facts rather than by simply backing up his subordinate right or wrong; it gave the general chairman of the union a chance to stop appeals which he did not approve (previously, he might permit appeals without being quite clear as to the precise issue involved); and, finally it saved much time by eliminating a flood of correspondence.

4. *Improvement in working conditions.* An analysis of a sample of 1,076 suggestions on the Baltimore and Ohio revealed that nearly one-fifth related to better working conditions. On the Canadian National, over one-sixth, or 4,542 out of 25,012 of the suggestions received up to the end of 1939, related to the conditions of shops and grounds, including heating, sanitation, and repairs. In addition, 4,146, or 16.6 per cent, related to safety and first aid, and 338, or 1.4 per cent, to lunch rooms, lockers, garages. In all, more than one-third of the suggestions, or 9,026 out of 25,012 (36.1 per cent), pertained to better working conditions. The depression increased the proportion of suggestions which related to working conditions. For one thing, it discouraged the men from suggesting

labor-saving methods and devices. Possibly it made them more critical of their working conditions. In the five years 1932 to 1936 inclusive, slightly more than half of the suggestions on the Canadian National (3,769 out of 6,954, or 54.2 per cent) related to conditions of shops and grounds, safety, lunch rooms, lockers, garages.

The union-management co-operative plan has made the managements more interested in improving working conditions. An official of one of the unions on the Canadian National said: "The management has become more pliable. They try to do everything they can instead of finding reasons for not doing things." Improvements in working conditions have been of the widest variety: roads in a car repair yard are oiled in order to reduce the dust raised by the tractor in hauling over them; the furnace near a 6,000-pound hammer is moved back six feet to reduce intense heat; 20 additional steel lockers are obtained for a blacksmith's shop at a cost of $200; a blower is installed in connection with a band saw so that men nearby will not have to stand in dust all the time; low places in a car yard are filled in at a cost of $364.

Better washroom facilities, cleaner shops, better ventilation, and better heating have been important accomplishments of the co-operative plan. At Weston, West Virginia, the men obtained a washroom costing $6,000. A washroom costing thousands of dollars was also obtained at Ivorydale as a result of one of the first suggestions made. Cleaner and drier locomotive pits have been a very common accomplishment.[11] At a large shop on the Baltimore and Ohio where the men had fought to get better ventilation for years, they got a new $100,000 roof, greatly improving ventilation and lighting. "Nothing could have done that," said the committee chairman, "except carrying that item along on the co-operative minutes." At Stratford on the Canadian National, the men got a new heating system that had been requested for years.[12]

[11] A typical comment is that of a Baltimore and Ohio committeeman, who said: "The managament has repaired the bottom of some pits which had been in bad condition for years. There were no drains in the light repair pits. The bottoms were uneven, water would lie there for a long time, and if you had to use a jack you had trouble getting it level. They put drains in and new cement bottoms."

[12] The blacksmiths at a western point on the Canadian National got their tool room moved inside. "We had to go outside," said the chairman, "when it was

Better tools have been an accomplishment which, while useful to the railroad, has meant much to the men.[13] Many of the labor-saving suggestions are intended to eliminate heavy work. Although they saved the company money, many of them should be counted as improvements in working conditions.[14]

On the Canadian National the management was dissatisfied with the safety record of the shops, and early in 1931 it decided to make the co-operative committees responsible for accident prevention. Immediately there was an enormous jump in the number of suggestions pertaining to safety. In 1931, they totalled 800, or over twice as many as in the preceding six years. The annual co-operative meetings on the Canadian National have discussed the most important safety problems of the shops. At the meetings of 1936, 1938, and 1940, there was considerable discussion of the problem of eye injuries, the most frequent kind of injury in the shops, and the problem of obtaining satisfactory goggles and of getting the men to use them.

5. *Improvement in apprenticeship training.* In 1925 the need of improving apprenticeship training was raised at the system union-management co-operative committee on the Baltimore and Ohio. A joint union-management committee was appointed to study the problem. It recommended that arrangements be made with the Railway Education Bureau to provide lessons for apprentices and, in order to assure personal help and attention for the apprentices, that traveling apprentice instructors be provided. It also suggested

---

twenty or thirty below and hunt around for tools. That is a dangerous thing, for a man who has been sweating at the fire."

[13] A committee chairman on the Baltimore and Ohio said: "We used to have the awfullest time getting tools. The first thing I went after when I got on the co-operative committee was tools. The fact that you didn't have tools didn't mean a thing to the management. I had to break my back all the time using old broken-jawed Stilson wrenches. I don't have a bit of trouble getting tools now."

[14] For example, at a Baltimore and Ohio shop the men suggested that they make a wagon to use in removing cylinder heads. The wagon is run up against the cylinder head, the head is held to the wagon by a stud in the center, a nut is placed on the outside of that, and the cylinder head is pulled off. One of the men said: "It saves a lot of lifting and is a safety measure." At a number of points the men asked for pipe threading and cutting machines in order to get rid of hard hand work. Contrast this with some of the steamfitters' agreements in the building trades which forbid cutting and threading pipe below certain sizes by machine.

that, at a number of shops, designated workmen give special attention to the boys and help them with their work. The report was accepted by the union-management co-operative committee of the system, and was put into effect. In order to insure that the boys would not be neglected and that the apprentice training would be conducted on a high plane of efficiency, the position of supervisor of apprentices was created, and a former general chairman of the machinists' union on the Baltimore and Ohio was appointed to the place. Reports on the operation of the apprentice plan were made at the regular meetings of the co-operative committee, and the supervisor of apprentices was a member of the committee. The necessity of curtailing expenses during the severe depression (combined with the fact that the company had large numbers of furloughed journeymen) led to the abandonment of the apprentice training plan in 1932.

On the Canadian National an apprentice training plan was in full operation before union-management co-operation was adopted. The co-operative committee meetings, however, have been a convenient device through which the men have been kept informed of apprentice training and have contributed to its improvement. Each year a detailed report on the operation of the apprentice plan is made to the system co-operative committee meeting. The outbreak of the war led the Canadian National to make a considerable increase in the number of apprentices. At the annual meeting of the union-management committee of the system in May 1940, there was an extended discussion of the need for enlarging the apprentice training program.

6. *Enlarging union membership.* Agreements on the railroads do not provide for the closed shop, and it is contrary to the policy of the railroad unions to seek the closed shop.[15] Consequently, the ability of the unions to maintain their organizations in railroad shops depends upon their own efforts and such informal help as they may obtain from the managements.

The union-management co-operative plan has been of substantial

---

[15] As a matter of fact, the Railway Labor Act makes the closed shop illegal on the railroads. Most of the shopcraft unions, however, do endeavor to obtain a closed shop in other industries.

assistance to the unions in building up their membership. On the Baltimore and Ohio in the year just prior to the shopmen's strike of 1922, the average membership of the shopcraft unions was 10,494. The effect of the strike is shown by a drop in the member-ship during the following year to 5,969. During the next three years the membership rose—to 8,998 in 1924; 10,230 in 1925; and 11,371 in 1926. Some rebound after the strike was, of course, to be expected, but in view of the fact that the unions had lost the strike, the rapid recovery in membership can only be explained by the improved status and prestige which the organizations acquired from the policy of union-management co-operation.

As a result of the Winnipeg general strike of 1919 and the One Big Union movement of the Canadian National, union membership in the western shops had fallen quite low at the time the co-operative plan was introduced. The membership of the affiliates of the American Federation of Labor in the Fort Rouge Shops in Winnipeg was about 35 per cent. The proportion of the membership at the Transcona shops near Winnipeg was greater than at Fort Rouge, but in some departments of the Transcona shops the AFL unions at one time had virtually no members. By late 1927 over 90 per cent of the workers in the western shops had joined.

The union-management co-operative plan assisted the unions in building up their membership (1) because it indicated more complete and whole-hearted recognition of the unions by the management and because it gave the unions an opportunity to claim credit for many improvements in working conditions;[16] (2) because it helped the union in getting grievances adjusted more promptly and satisfactorily; (3) because it reduced or limited opposition on the part of supervisors;[17] (4) because it led union men to be given

[16] This improvement in the status and prestige of the unions helped them interest the timid worker who thinks he stands in better with the boss by remaining outside the organization, the new worker who is likely to be cautious about joining, the indifferent worker, and even the selfish worker who sees no reason for paying union dues so long as he gets the benefit of union conditions.

[17] A superintendent on the Baltimore and Ohio agreed that he would send men to see a union committeeman before hiring them. Unless the committeeman recommended the man, he was not hired. The same arrangement applied to the boilermakers and the carmen at this point. The car foreman made it clear to his men that he wished them to belong to the organization and that he would be willing to do anything he could to get them to join.

some preference in layoffs,[18] transfers, and promotions.

7. *Increase in wages.* When the union-management co-operative plan was started, many of the union members had high hopes that their share in the savings would add appreciably to their wages. Both the men and the management hoped that the savings could be accurately measured. There were even suggestions of a direct financial reward on a percentage basis every three months calculated on the savings.[19] Although it proved impossible to give a direct financial reward for union-management co-operation,[20] the plan has helped the men in obtaining wage increases and other concessions.

The Baltimore and Ohio was the first road in trunk line territory to be approached for a wage increase in 1926 by the unions and was the first in that territory to give an advance and to restore time and a half for overtime.[21] The unions told the management

---

[18] In the spring of 1927, it was necessary to reduce forces at the Transcona and Fort Rouge shops of the Canadian National. The unions demanded that, in view of their co-operation, the layoffs be confined to non-members. The union committees were called to help decide who would be laid off. This produced a rush to join the organizations. Machinists at Fort Rouge soon had a 95 per cent organization and the other crafts about the same. At Transcona the figures were almost as high.

On the Baltimore and Ohio the co-operative program contributed to the solution in the union's favor of a troublesome seniority issue that developed from the shopmen's strike of 1922. The railroad had taken the usual position that the strike broke the service record of the strikers. The union argued that, regardless of events of 1922, it was not fair to discriminate against the men who were now co-operating with the company. For several years the management was able to avoid raising the seniority issue. This was done partly by not bulletining vacancies (when promotions were to be made) and partly by not carrying layoffs to the point where it was necessary to decide the relative seniority of the men who had struck and those who had worked during the strike. But the layoffs necessitated by the depression raised so many questions of seniority that it was decided to review all service records and to establish revised seniority rosters which would accurately represent the length of service. When the new service rosters were posted in 1934, the strike of 1922 was not treated as an interruption of service. Possibly this revision of the service records would have occurred quite regardless of union-management co-operation. Nevertheless, the improved status which the unions acquired on the Baltimore and Ohio was a favoring circumstance in helping their members win back the seniority lost during the strike of 1922.

[19] See O. S. Beyer, Jr., *Report Covering the Development of Union Management Cooperation in the Maintenance of Equipment Service of the Canadian National Railways,* Aug. 23, 1924, pp. 66-67. This report was made a few months before the plan was put into effect on the Canadian National.

[20] The reasons for this are explained on pp. 494 and 497.

[21] The first wage increases to shopmen in 1926, however, were given by the

of the railroad that they wished to take up the issue of a wage increase as a "co-operative grievance"—as something standing in the way of the co-operative spirit. The negotiations were long and difficult and the road did not readily yield.[22] The officers of the unions were convinced that the co-operative plan had much to do with helping them win their demands.[23]

In the wage negotiations of 1926 between the shopcrafts and the Canadian roads, the management of the Canadian National wished to reward its shopmen for their co-operative efforts by raising their rates 2 cents an hour above the Canadian Pacific. The officials of the latter road objected, however, and a uniform increase of 4 cents was the result.[24] However, some officials of the Canadian National expressed the opinion that in the absence of the union-management co-operative plan, the increase would have been less than 4 cents an hour. In 1928, a week's vacation with pay was given to all shopmen with two years' seniority on the Canadian National. This was done in lieu of the extra 2 cents an hour over the Canadian Pacific scale which the Canadian National had been unable to grant in 1926. The vacations, it will be noted, were confined to the shopcrafts which, in 1928, were the only unions participating in the co-operative program on the Canadian National. In 1940, the vacations with pay were still in effect among the shopcrafts, but they had never been extended to the maintenance-of-way employees.

The clearest case of the co-operative plan's helping the men obtain a wage increase is furnished by negotiations with the Chicago and North Western in 1926. The railroad at this time, like most of the granger roads, was in poor financial condition. No other road in western territory had granted a wage increase. In view of the unsatisfactory financial condition of the road, the management saw

---

prosperous coal roads and other roads to the Southeast, some of which had been helped by the Florida boom.

[22] See pp. 495-96.

[23] In 1929, when the shopcraft unions again considered starting a wage movement on the Baltimore and Ohio, the management pointed out that it was not fair for the unions to begin every wage movement on the roads most friendly to them. The unions were thus persuaded to begin the 1929 wage movement elsewhere.

[24] The complicated negotiations which led to this increase are explained on pp. 494-95.

difficulty in justifying an increase to the board of directors. The co-operative plan offered a way. Furthermore, it was agreed in the negotiations that the unions, through their co-operative activities, would endeavor to save the company as much of the wage increase as possible. A circular letter was sent by the men's conference committee to the local unions on the North Western urging them to do their best to prevent the wage increase from raising operating costs.[25] It was the firm belief of the officers of the shopcrafts on the North Western that the increase of 3 cents an hour was made possible by the co-operative plan.

8. *Elimination of bonus system on the Canadian National.* The shopcraft unions are opposed to piecework and bonus systems. When the co-operative plan was introduced on the Canadian National in 1925, a bonus system was in operation at a number of shops in the central region, and the management contemplated extending it to all shops on the road. The unions asked that the bonus plan be discontinued in four shops where it had recently been introduced; that in one of these a test be made of the co-operative plan; and if, after a fair trial, the co-operative plan justified itself to both management and men, that it be extended as a substitute for the bonus plan.

The suggestion that the bonus plan be immediately abandoned at certain shops was not adopted. Nevertheless, the men pressed steadily for its abandonment. Through the improvement in the efficiency of the non-bonus shops, for which the co-operative plan was partly responsible, the management was gradually convinced that the bonus system was not worth its cost and, late in 1926, agreed to its abandonment.

9. *Stabilization and increase of employment.* More stable employment is undoubtedly one of the chief benefits which the men

---

[25] The letter pointed out that the wage advance without a gain in efficiency would mean an increase of approximately $1,000,000 per year in pay rolls. The letter added: "We are confident those whom we represent realize that $1.00 increase in pay roll is not 100 cents increase in operating costs and that wages can be increased without necessarily increasing the cost of production provided the proper co-operative relations between management and employees exist. . . . We desire to urge each and every member of our organizations to have ever before them . . . that it be the recognized duty of each and every individual to contribute all possible consistent with our agreement to increase production and decrease the cost thereof. . . ."

have derived from union management co-operation. It is a benefit, however, which cannot be accurately measured.[26] Possibly almost as much would have been done to stabilize employment on the Baltimore and Ohio and other roads without the co-operative plan as with it—no one knows.[27] Three things, however, are clear: the co-operative program has made managements feel keenly the responsibility for doing everything possible to stabilize employment; it has given the men a chance to bring to the attention of management opportunities of various kinds to make work steadier; and it has encouraged the men to cut costs so that it is more economical for management to have work done in the shops than outside.

The problem of stabilizing employment in railroad shops has involved: (1) bringing into the railroad shops new work to offset the rapid progress that has been made in economizing in railroad maintenance; (2) planning work to offset seasonal fluctuations in the operation of the maintenance-of-equipment department;[28] (3) offsetting the cyclical drops in employment.

Railroad managements have used six principal methods of stabilizing employment: (1) planning work ahead on an annual budget basis; (2) transferring men between running repair work and back shops; (3) modernizing and rebuilding cars and locomotives in

[26] Roads which have not practiced union-management co-operation have found that it paid to stabilize employment in their shops. One of the roads which did most in this direction was the Delaware and Hudson, a railroad which for many years tolerated no unions among its shopmen. In 1926, the difference in employment between the best and the worst months in the Baltimore and Ohio shops was 12.2 per cent as compared with 9.7 per cent on the Pennsylvania and 11.3 on the New York Central. Neither of these roads had a co-operative policy and the Pennsylvania at that time had no unions in its shops.

[27] The management of the Chicago and North Western insists that stabilization of employment has been quite independent of the co-operative plan. The management of the Canadian National, on the other hand, admits that considerable impetus to stabilization of employment was received under the union-management co-operative policy. The management of the Baltimore and Ohio is non-committal. A high official said: "We've always felt it would bring about a much better condition if we could furnish a man with steady work. It is good business, but it is something that was always overlooked. I believe that a great deal of labor unrest has been due to the unsteady work. We started to stabilize employment before we started the co-operative plan."

[28] The business of all railroads is more or less seasonal, but that of the granger roads—such as the Chicago and North Western, the Chicago, Milwaukee, St. Paul, and Pacific, and the western branches of the Canadian National—is particularly seasonal. Traffic on the Baltimore and Ohio is sensitive to changing conditions in the coal and steel industries.

railroad shops; (4) building cars and locomotives in railroad shops during dull periods; (5) manufacturing railroad equipment in railroad shops; (6) using furloughed shopmen on other types of railroad work.[29]

The unions as well as management have had an opportunity to contribute to the stabilizing of employment. As a result of the union-management co-operative plan, the workers have been able (1) to spur the management to greater efforts because every major layoff is discussed and often criticized in the co-operative meeting; (2) to present their needs for work directly to the management; (3) to suggest many employment opportunities; (4) to influence the policy of the company by demonstrating that articles can be manufactured in the shops for less than the outside purchase price.[30]

The violent movements of business in the last decade have made fluctuations in railroad employment since 1929 more extreme than ever. Furthermore, the deterioration in the financial condition of the roads has made it increasingly difficult for them to fight fluctuations in employment by making expenditures charged to capital

---

[29] Each year at the annual union-management co-operative meeting, the management of the Canadian National presents an annual report on labor matters which includes a statement of the "factor of stabilization." By this is meant the percentage of hours actually worked to the total which would have been worked if every man on the pay roll had worked the standard number of hours (44 a week for 51 weeks a year—2,240 hours per year). Some of the hours missed may be the men's fault, as in the case of absenteeism, lateness, or sickness, and some the company's fault, as in the case of shop shutdowns or layoffs. The annual statement allocates the responsibility for time lost. This report of the management to the men is unique in industrial relations and does much to spur interest in stabilization of employment.

The report also includes a statement of the labor cost of articles manufactured in the shops each year and the proportion of pay roll represented by such articles. About 6 per cent of the pay roll in the mechanical department of the Canadian National is represented by the labor costs of articles manufactured in the shops.

[30] Illustrative of the efforts of the men to win work for themselves by keeping costs below the bids of outside contractors is a statement of a general foreman of a North Western car shop which, for the first time in history, was building an order of 600 new cars. The foreman said:

"When we started in building these cars, our men were determined they were going to build them just as cheap as the factory. Our workmen here seem to have the spirit that there ain't nobody going to beat them on this kind of a job. We had quite a time getting started. We started out making three or four cars a day. Now we are getting out eight cars a day. I know the carmen's organization has impressed upon the men that they must get results. I have heard the general chairman tell the men that they could not afford to fall down on this job."

account in bad years. This is plainly shown in the case of the Baltimore and Ohio. As the road's income declined, its cash position became so weak that it was compelled promptly to cut shop operations whenever business fell off and to concentrate the rebuilding of equipment and the production of new parts and equipment in good years. Under these conditions, the pressure of the men for the construction of more equipment in railroad shops has had the effect, not so much of stabilizing employment, as of giving temporary snatches of work to employees who had been furloughed because of the secular decline in railroad employment. For example, the improvement of business in the latter part of 1936 and early part of 1937 led the Baltimore and Ohio to build a considerable amount of new equipment, including some stream-line trains, in its shops. This was an important gain to the men despite the fact that it did not represent employment stabilization.

10. *More complete information for the men concerning operations of the railroad.* A master mechanic on the Baltimore and Ohio said to me:

You know, when I was a roundhouse foreman, I did not know half what those fellows know now. These meetings are educational to both sides. The road foreman of engines comes in and tells you things you didn't know and he offers a lot of suggestions about things he thinks should not occur.

A committeeman at Ivorydale on the Baltimore and Ohio said: "There are lots of things we never knew about before. We never knew how long an engine went from shopping to shopping. We know now what different work costs and what materials cost."

Statements such as these are encountered very frequently from representatives of both men and management. The men have valued the opportunity which the union-management co-operative meetings give them to learn about the work of the shops, the problems of the railroads, and particularly the plans of the management. They have been interested in information pertaining to the performance of the railroad—the record of engine failures, "federal defects,"[31] and locomotives ordered out of service by federal inspectors. Most of all they have been interested in reports on the future plans of

[31] See p. 471, footnote 49.

the management because these plans determine employment opportunities. It has been customary for the local management at many
shops to tell the men about work that was coming in.

It has been at the system co-operative meetings, however, that
the most important information concerning operating results and
plans has been given to the men. At these meetings, of course, the
representatives of the men are the system chairmen. They are even
more interested in obtaining information than are the local craft
chairmen. Furthermore, the general officers who represent the company at the system meetings are better able than are the local shop
officials to give information. More or less comprehensive reports are
regularly presented. These reports deal with operating results,
financial conditions, the business outlook, and employment prospects.
The management is likely to go into detail concerning the work
program for the near future.[32]

CONCLUSIONS CONCERNING BENEFITS TO THE MEN

The benefits which union-management co-operation has yielded
to the shopmen in the form of better relations with management,
fewer grievances, better working conditions, better training of apprentices, and more employment opportunities have been substantial. The benefits in the form of higher wages have been considerably less important. The improved status which the unions
derived from the co-operative plan was of great importance at the
time. Now that they are strongly established, it is less important.

At the present time the current gains which the men are obtaining
are less important than during the period 1924 to 1929. One reason
is that most of the big gains have been achieved—the methods of
handling grievances have been reformed; the most important improvements in shop conditions and in methods of training appren-

---

[32] For example, at the system meeting on the Baltimore and Ohio on Jan. 9,
1940, the chief of motive power announced that 100 cement cars would be started
when materials were obtained about Feb. 1, that it was planned to change 50
gondolas for containers, that authority had been granted to modernize one complete train for the National Limited at a cost of approximately $240,000,
that 350 box cars had been recommended for fast freight service which, if approved, would be built in the railroad's own shops, and that tools had been added
at one of the shops which would make possible the fabrication of freight car
parts.

tices have been made; the policy of stabilizing employment, in so far as the fluctuations in business and the financial condition of the road permit employment to be stabilized, has been well established. As a result, the opportunity to make changes is no longer what it used to be.

The benefits yielded by the co-operative plan to the men have been limited also by the poor financial condition of the roads since 1929. Many improvements in conditions which the men have suggested (and which ordinarily would have been accepted) have been postponed because of lack of funds. At the same time, however, the very decline in the railroad business has in some respects made the co-operative meetings more important to the men than ever. They have given the unions an excellent opportunity to discuss the employment problem with management and to press for more work in the shops, particularly work which might otherwise have been done on the outside. During the worst of the depression, co-operative committees discussed problems of dividing work and of giving relief to furloughed shopmen.

Although the greatest opportunities for improving working conditions have already been taken advantage of, new safety problems are constantly developing, and there are always opportunities for men to bring employment into the railroad shops by suggesting articles which could be manufactured there. Although the most important problems of apprenticeship training have been disposed of, the depression, and later the war, brought new problems. The co-operative committee meetings have given the unions an opportunity to discuss them with management. Consequently, although the heavy work has for the most part been done, the meetings continue to consider important items and to be a convenient and useful way by which the unions deal with all manner of problems which are of interest to the men, but which are not covered by the schedule and which cannot be disposed of by adding new rules to the schedule. Furthermore, the system co-operative meetings offer an excellent opportunity to review labor conditions in general on the road. This is particularly true of the annual meeting on the Canadian National at which reports on matters of special interest to the men are regularly presented.

SPECIFIC BENEFITS TO MANAGEMENT

The benefits of union-management co-operation to the railroads should be appraised in terms of its effect upon: (1) the volume of output; (2) the consumption of materials; (3) the quality of work. These effects may be classified as specific or general. The specific effects consist of the more or less clearly identifiable results of specific suggestions. The general effects include the influence of union-management co-operation as a whole, such as its influence upon the efficiency of management, the morale of the men, and the relations between the unions and the management. The general effects may actually be more important for shop efficiency than the specific suggestions, but it is difficult to trace a direct relationship between them and output, consumption of materials, or quality of work.

1. *Larger volume of output.* An appreciable number of foremen and other shop officials deny that union-management co-operation has increased output at all.[33] The statements of operating officials, however, must be taken with substantial quantities of salt because these officials (particularly the lower ones) are inclined to claim credit for nearly all the increase in production.

The difficulty of detecting the effects of union-management co-operation upon production is accentuated by the fact that it is only one among many influences raising shop efficiency. There have been changes in personnel, in equipment, in methods of work. The attraction of the war industries in 1917 and 1918 caused the railroads to lose many experienced men and compelled them to promote helpers to mechanics' jobs. The reconstruction of the force of skilled craftsmen required years. Supervisory personnel was grad-

---

[33] The general foreman in a western shop on the Baltimore and Ohio said: "I don't feel the co-operative plan has increased our output, but we get it easier than before." A high official in the mechanical department of the North Western said: "Personally I think that the change of policy on the North Western and the stabilization of employment will account for everything we have accomplished. [The change of policy referred to was the willingness of the new administration to spend money on new equipment in order to increase output and reduce expenses.] I think we would have had the same results if we hadn't had any co-operative committee. I don't think it amounts to a thing." The superintendent of a large Canadian shop said: "There may be an increase in output over 15 months ago, but I don't think it has been brought about by the co-operative plan. It is an awfully hard thing to say there has been any improvement from the co-operative plan as far as output is concerned."

ually changed and undoubtedly improved. Considerable sums have
been spent on new shop equipment. Old and poorly equipped shops
have been abandoned and work concentrated in the most modern
and best equipped shops. Important changes in methods of work
have been introduced.[34]

One possible way of judging the contribution of union-management co-operation to shop efficiency is to compare the gains in output in shops on roads practicing it with the gain in output on all
roads. There are difficulties in making such a comparison because
no two repairs of railroad equipment are exactly alike. This means
that railroad shops do not turn out a uniform product.[35] Furthermore, the quality of the work may vary. Standards of maintenance
may vary as between roads, so that it is not easy to compare the shop
efficiency of several roads. They may also vary from year to year.[36]
A rough measure of shop efficiency, however, can be obtained by
comparing gross ton-miles run by freight trains with man-hours
spent in keeping equipment in repair.

Gross ton-miles are obtained by multiplying the weight of freight
trains by the number of miles run by them. The resulting figure
roughly indicates the amount of work which the shops have to do.
Obviously the figure is affected by any change in the weight and size
of equipment and also by changes in the use of equipment. The
larger and heavier the equipment, the more work is required, as a
general rule, to keep it in repair. Likewise, the more miles that

[34] For example, after the introduction of the co-operative plan, the Baltimore
and Ohio radically altered its methods of repairing freight cars. The new "spot"
system was inspired by methods of assembling automobiles. Instead of having all
the work done on a car in one place as formerly, the cars are moved from spot
to spot (six in all) at each of which a given group of operations is performed
by a group of specialized workmen.

[35] It is customary in the United States to divide the heavy repairs of locomotives
into six classes, called "classified repairs." But even two repairs of a given class
are not necessarily identical because one locomotive may have some auxiliary
work done to it and the other may not. Furthermore, locomotives vary in size
and type and in equipment which they carry. Consequently, a Class 3 repair to
a locomotive of one size or type will involve a different amount of work than a
Class 3 repair to a larger or smaller engine. Over periods of time these changes
in equipment become quite important. The amount of work required in repairing
cars is likewise variable and the size and type of cars are constantly changing.

[36] A short period of bad business may produce a rise in standards of maintenance
because it releases equipment for repairs which cannot be easily spared in busier
times. A long period of bad business, on the other hand, may force a drop in
standards of maintenance, particularly on roads in weak financial condition.

GROSS TON-MILES, SERVICE HOURS EXPENDED IN THE MAINTENANCE OF EQUIPMENT, AND PERCENTAGE OF UNSERVICEABLE EQUIPMENT ON ROADS PRACTICING UNION-MANAGEMENT CO-OPERATION, 1923-39[a]

Year Ending December 31	Baltimore and Ohio Railroad				Chicago and North Western Railroad				Chicago, Milwaukee, St. Paul, and Pacific Railroad			
	Gross Ton-Miles per Shop Service Hour	Index of Ton-Miles per Shop Service Hour (1924=100)	Unserviceable Equipment		Gross Ton-Miles per Shop Service Hour	Index of Ton-Miles per Shop Service Hour (1925=100)	Unserviceable Equipment		Gross Ton-Miles per Shop Service Hour	Index of Ton-Miles per Shop Service Hour (1926=100)	Unserviceable Equipment	
			Freight Locomotives (Per cent)	Freight Cars (Per cent)			Freight Locomotives (Per cent)	Freight Cars (Per cent)			Freight Locomotives (Per cent)	Freight Cars (Per cent)
1923	755.0	94.6	16.9	6.2	718.6	86.7	19.3	7.1	803.1	89.0	17.2	7.9
1924	798.5	100.0	22.0	10.6	785.5	94.8	22.5	9.1	744.5	82.5	14.6	7.0
1925	832.3	104.2	21.8	8.6	828.5	100.0	22.3	9.8	767.7	85.1	16.1	7.8
1926	962.7	120.6	16.0	4.6	838.3	101.2	18.3	6.9	902.0	100.0	17.8	5.9
1927	1,111.4	139.2	17.9	4.8	841.5	101.6	15.5	7.0	1,019.0	113.0	16.9	5.6
1928	1,164.4	145.8	19.3	5.3	917.2	110.7	14.3	6.4	1,243.9	137.9	14.9	3.2
1929	1,189.3	148.9	16.1	5.7	959.9	115.9	11.1	6.7	1,269.4	140.7	15.3	2.9
1930	1,264.3	158.3	18.7	5.3	1,004.0	121.2	11.7	7.3	1,332.1	147.7	14.8	2.7
1931	1,365.4	171.0	24.0	5.7	1,075.8	129.9	16.3	8.3	1,569.3	174.0	15.8	2.4
1932	1,526.7	191.2	38.0	11.8	1,248.8	150.7	22.0	7.7	1,531.0	169.7	17.1	3.2
1933	1,743.4	218.3	44.8	18.0	1,313.9	158.6	28.6	10.0	1,678.4	186.1	25.4	4.1
1934	1,592.9	199.5	43.3	18.6	1,363.6	164.6	29.5	12.1	1,664.1	184.5	38.1	4.9
1935	1,737.3	217.6	45.7	18.8	1,324.3	159.8	31.8	10.1	1,610.1	178.5	25.7	2.9
1936	1,633.8	204.6	46.6	17.8	1,301.7	157.1	33.2	8.1	1,686.0	186.9	18.8	2.9
1937	1,635.5	205.8	39.8	13.0	1,168.3	141.0	30.5	7.3	1,565.9	173.6	16.5	2.6
1938	1,894.7	237.3	41.8	19.1	1,391.0	167.9	31.6	8.8	1,659.4	184.0	21.7	2.8
1939	1,685.5	211.1	38.9	16.5	1,429.6	172.6	42.3	9.7	1,713.4	190.0	23.9	2.6

[a] Freight service gross ton-miles: Bureau of Railway Economics, *Summary of Operating Statistics of Class I Steam Railways, January, 1923–December, 1935; Freight Train Performance, January, 1936–December, 1938.*
Service hours in maintenance of equipment and stores: *Annual Reports to the I. C. C., Form A.*
Unserviceable equipment: Interstate Commerce Commission, Bureau of Statistics, *Comparative Statement of Railway Operating Statistics* No. 3920o.

460

GROSS TON-MILES, SERVICE HOURS EXPENDED IN THE MAINTENANCE OF EQUIPMENT, AND PERCENTAGE OF UNSERVICEABLE EQUIPMENT ON ALL CLASS I STEAM RAILROADS, 1923–38[a]

Year Ending December 31	Freight Service Gross Ton-Miles, Including Locomotives and Tenders (In millions)	Total Service Hours in Maintenance of Equipment and Stores, Exclusive of Switching Terminal Companies (In millions)	Gross Ton-Miles per Service Hour	Index of Ton-Miles per Service Hour			Unserviceable Equipment		
				1924=100	1925=100	1926=100	Freight Locomotives (Per cent)	Passenger Locomotives (Per cent)	Freight Cars (Per cent)
1923	1,123,970	1,471	764.1	89.8	82.3	76.5	21.6	20.8	8.0
1924	1,085,860	1,276	851.0	100.0	91.7	85.2	18.8	18.4	7.8
1925	1,162,154	1,252	928.2	109.1	100.0	92.9	17.8	17.8	7.7
1926	1,246,532	1,248	998.8	116.2	107.6	100.0	16.4	17.0	6.5
1927	1,232,232	1,167	1,055.9	124.1	113.8	105.7	16.1	16.4	5.9
1928	1,252,138	1,096	1,142.5	134.3	123.1	114.4	16.3	16.4	6.2
1929	1,294,412	1,092	1,185.4	139.3	127.7	118.7	16.4	16.2	6.0
1930	1,142,943	914	1,250.5	146.9	134.7	125.2	17.5	17.0	6.2
1931	959,539	714	1,343.9	157.9	144.8	134.6	20.7	20.5	7.8
1932	758,011	542	1,398.5	164.3	150.7	140.0	26.6	24.9	10.6
1933	788,624	525	1,502.1	176.5	161.8	150.4	32.7	28.6	14.1
1934	855,576	583	1,467.5	172.4	158.1	146.9	33.9	29.4	14.6
1935	882,204	579	1,523.7	179.1	164.2	152.6	33.8	27.5	14.0
1936	1,029,486	676	1,522.6	178.9	164.0	152.4	30.5	23.3	12.8
1937	1,079,506	715	1,509.8	177.4	162.7	151.2	25.5	20.2	10.1
1938	907,027	534	1,698.6	199.6	183.0	170.1	29.4	23.3	11.9

[a] Interstate Commerce Commission, *Statistics of Railways in the United States, 1923-35* and *1938*; Bureau of Railway Economics, *Statistics of Class I Railways*, Summaries 12, 19, and 23.

equipment runs, the more is required to keep it in repair.[37] The
table on page 460 shows the gross ton-miles per shop service hour
on the Baltimore and Ohio, the Chicago and North Western, and
the Chicago, Milwaukee, St. Paul, and Pacific for the period 1923
to 1939, and the table on page 461 shows the same information for
all Class I railroads. As a check upon changes in standards of maintenance, the percentage of equipment out of service at the end of
each year is indicated.[38] The figures for the years subsequent to
1930 are less significant than the figures for earlier years because
of the sharp drop in the standards of maintenance induced by the
severe depression.

The tables on pages 460 and 461 indicate that between the inception of union-management co-operation (1924 on the Baltimore
and Ohio, 1925 on the Chicago and North Western, and 1926
on the Chicago, Milwaukee, St. Paul, and Pacific) and 1929,
ton-miles per shop service hour increased faster on the Baltimore
and Ohio and the Chicago, Milwaukee, St. Paul, and Pacific than
on all Class I roads and more slowly on the Chicago and North
Western.[39] In the years immediately following the dropping of
union-management co-operation on the Chicago, Milwaukee, St.
Paul, and Pacific, ton-miles per shop service hour continued to increase slightly faster than on all Class I roads.[40] On the Chicago
and North Western, the abandonment of union-management co-

---

[37] Annual gross ton-miles do not measure the use of passenger equipment. Nor
does there seem to be any satisfactory way of combining passenger train miles
or gross ton-miles into a single index. As passenger train mileage has tended to
drop faster than ton-miles of freight, gross ton mileage tends to exaggerate slightly
the amount of repair work required from railroad shops. Gross ton-miles are
affected, as a measure of shop output over the long period, by changes in the kind
of equipment.

[38] Figures for the Canadian National are not available.

[39] For example, between 1924 and 1929, ton-miles per shop hour increased 48.9
per cent on the Baltimore and Ohio against 39.3 per cent for all roads. Between
1926 and 1929, ton-miles per shop hour increased 40.7 per cent on the Chicago,
Milwaukee, St. Paul, and Pacific against 18.7 per cent on all roads. On the
Chicago and North Western, on the other hand, the increase in ton-miles per
shop hour between 1925 and 1929 was only 15.9 per cent against 27.7 per cent
for all roads. On the other hand the drop in the percentage of unserviceable
equipment was much greater on the Chicago and North Western than on all
Class I roads.

[40] Between 1929 (when union-management co-operation was abandoned on the
Chicago, Milwaukee, St. Paul, and Pacific) and 1932, gross ton-miles per shop
service hour increased 20.5 per cent against 18.0 per cent for all Class I roads.

operation was followed by a gain in ton-miles per shop service hour which considerably exceeded the gain on all Class I roads.[41]

The figures indicate that union-management co-operation may have been partly responsible for the superior record of the Baltimore and Ohio and the Chicago, Milwaukee, St. Paul, and Pacific in improving shop efficiency. The record of the Chicago and North Western, however, does not indicate that union-management co-operation was a help. It is, of course, possible that in the absence of the co-operative plan the improvement in shop efficiency on this road would have been slower. The safest and most important conclusion yielded by the figures is that union-management co-operation, however helpful, has not produced effects large enough to be clearly distinguishable in view of the other powerful influences playing upon shop efficiency.

Another way of attempting to measure the contribution of union-management co-operation to shop efficiency would be to analyze the thousands of suggestions one by one and to estimate the contribution of each. This procedure, however, would consume much time and the estimates would necessarily be exceedingly rough; for many suggestions, estimates would be out of the question. For example, a fairly common suggestion has been that locomotive pits should be cleaned, resurfaced, and drained. Certainly co-operation has done much to produce cleaner and dryer pits. Undoubtedly men move a little more rapidly and get more done in clean, dry pits, but it is not possible to measure the difference. Or it may be reported, as it was, that the grade of spelter received is poor and burns on the pipes before it runs, that the quality of brakeshoe iron is poor, or that the rivets are unsatisfactory because the heads pull off. All these suggestions undoubtedly help to improve efficiency, but no one could say how much. Furthermore, as indicated above, some of the most important effects of union-management co-operation are not reflected in any specific suggestion. The morale of the working force has undoubtedly been improved and this has undoubtedly increased output, but there is no way of measuring (1) how much co-operation

---

[41] Between 1930 (when union-management co-operation was abandoned on the Chicago and North Western) and 1932, gross ton-miles per shop service hour increased 24.4 per cent against 11.8 per cent on all roads.

has contributed to better morale or (2) how much better morale has increased production. Nor is there any way of measuring the effect of union-management co-operation upon managerial efficiency, although most observers agree that this effect has been important.[42]

The best that we can do, therefore, is to examine in realistic fashion the way in which the co-operative plan has affected production or the conditions upon which productivity depends. Several concrete ways in which the plan has increased output may be mentioned. The utilization of specific suggestions by workers for labor-saving methods, for improved organization or routing of work, for new machinery or equipment, for more adequate supplies of materials, and so forth, obviously enables workers to produce more for each unit of time. An examination of such suggestions together with the functioning of meetings of the co-operative committees leads inescapably to the conclusion that union-management co-operation has helped to increase output.

(1) Suggestions for labor-saving methods and devices. Analysis of 1,076 Baltimore and Ohio suggestions shows that 83, or 7.7 per cent, related to labor-saving methods or devices. On the Canadian National 3,592 of the 25,012 suggestions made up to December 31, 1939, or 14.4 per cent, related to shop methods or practices for the development of new devices. Most of the suggestions so classified are labor-saving. Many of the other suggestions, such as those relating to changes in the location of machinery or standardization of materials, undoubtedly contained labor-saving ideas.[43]

---

[42] The plan has caused local officials to feel that they are being watched. This intangible effect of co-operation is likely to be overlooked by the officials affected; yet its indirect influence upon volume of output has been a very real benefit from the plan.

[43] In a Canadian National car shop, the men recommended that a sleeve be made to top pipe flanges instead of their being chipped by hand. This would cut down the time from 20 minutes to 5 minutes. This was considered a good suggestion and it was decided to make the tool.

In a shop on the Baltimore and Ohio the machinists' representative stated that mistakes were being made in selecting sets of tires (for locomotive wheels) to be turned down. The tires were stacked in sets according to the type of engine to which they belong, but the sets might vary only ⅛ or ¼ inch in dimension. Hence a man without realizing it might get one or two tires of the wrong size. If a tire was too small, an extra cut would be necessary to turn it down. After considerable discussion, the storekeeper said he would stencil the tires in order to eliminate mistakes.

The great drop in employment produced by the depression and by the steady loss of business to trucks has discouraged labor-saving suggestions. By 1940, few were being offered on either the Baltimore and Ohio or the Canadian National. Thus out of 60 suggestions offered at 22 points on the Baltimore and Ohio in April 1940, none were of a strictly labor-saving nature (though some of them related to new tools or equipment that was needed). On the Canadian National, suggestions pertaining to shop methods and practices, which had been 381 in 1929 and 320 in 1930, had dropped to 96 in 1938 and 83 in 1939.

(2) Improvement in layout and routing of work. About 2.5 per cent out of the sample of 1,076 suggestions on the Baltimore and Ohio related to the organization, layout, and routing of work. At one of the car shops a committee member said: "Now we have a place to pile blocks. It used to be that the men in cleaning up would scrap them, or throw them outside. We would have to hunt around for half an hour for blocks. Now we have a place for them on the platform." At another Baltimore and Ohio shop the men suggested that the punching of larger boiler sets, which necessitated the use of the machine shop crane, be performed on the second trick, to avoid tying up the crane when required for work in the machine shop.

(3) New machinery and equipment. Wage earners are commonly assumed to be hostile to the introduction of new machinery. Nevertheless, 12.0 per cent of the 1,076 suggestions analyzed on the Baltimore and Ohio, and 6.4 per cent of the suggestions on the Canadian National (1,608 out of 25,012 down to the end of 1939) were recommendations for the use of new machinery and equipment. A large proportion of the machines suggested would eliminate heavy work and it is evident that the object of the men in many cases was

---

In connection with the manufacturing of frogs and switches at the Moncton shops on the Canadian National, the shop made riser plates which go under the frogs. One of the men suggested a tool which reduced the time of a machining operation on the riser plate to about one-sixth of the previous time.

A certain bolt on the Baltimore and Ohio cars tended to turn when the nut was being screwed on. In order to prevent this it was necessary to hold the head of the bolt with a monkey wrench. The head was so located that it was difficult to get a wrench in place. One of the men suggested that if T-head bolts were used instead of square head, the bolt would be unable to turn because the head would hit. This suggestion was adopted.

to get rid of hard and disagreeable jobs.[44] Even the most unskilled workers have been able to make valuable suggestions.[45]

(4) Obtaining money for additional equipment and facilities. The co-operative plan has helped local managements obtain machinery and equipment which they needed. Recommendations made in co-operative committee meetings often seemed to have more weight with the general officers than recommendations made merely by the local managements. When shop superintendents discovered this, some of them encouraged the men to ask for machinery or equipment in the co-operative meeting. The master mechanic of a Baltimore and Ohio roundhouse gives the co-operative plan credit for assisting him in obtaining many new machines:

Our conditions in this roundhouse are no more like those of two years ago than day is to night. We have been able to induce the management, through the co-operative plan, to spend money on new machines. An enormous amount has been spent. At the same time there is no question that the railroad has gained through this expenditure.

Part of the explanation of this rather curious situation is that some foremen and superintendents have been timid about asking for new equipment. They have feared they might be criticized by their superiors for not making a better record with existing facilities. Thus, unexpectedly, a rather important need has been met through the functioning of the co-operative program.

(5) More and better materials. The enormous variety of parts and materials required in the repair of locomotives and cars creates a difficult problem for the stores departments. On the one hand,

---

[44] At the shop the men suggested that a crane be put in for handling car wheels. It used to take eight or ten men a full day to load a car of wheels. With the crane two men load a car in five or six hours. A nut tightener for taking out and turning up large nuts, such as $1\frac{1}{2}$-inch, was suggested in a Baltimore and Ohio shop. One of the men said: "It eliminates very heavy work. It is a money saver and a life saver for the men too."

At another Baltimore and Ohio shop the machinists' representative suggested that a 15-ton Toledo crane be installed in the machine shop to eliminate delays in crane service. A 30-day check showed the delays totaled nearly three hours a day at a cost of $67.38 a month.

[45] At a large roundhouse, two laborers were employed splitting the old ties used for firing locomotives. They suggested that a buzz saw be installed and the ties cut before splitting. This enabled one man to do the work. The man released from the tie-splitting job was put to work wiping engines. Keeping the locomotives clean makes it easier to find defects and helps prevent engine failures.

work must not be delayed by lack of needed parts or materials; on the other hand, large amounts of capital must not be tied up in inventories which are not immediately needed. Stores departments have leaned in the direction of carrying low inventories, with the result that work was frequently held up by lack of materials; and the practice of "robbing" locomotives—that is, taking a part off one locomotive in order to put it on another—has been prevalent. The wastefulness of this practice is obvious.

Union-management co-operation has had an important effect upon the operations of the stores departments, for a large part of the suggestions relate to materials. On the Baltimore and Ohio 315, or 29.3 per cent, of the sample of 1,076 suggestions studied related to a shortage of either material or small tools and 36 were reports of poor grade or wrong kind of material. On the Canadian National 1,148 out of 25,012 suggestions made before the end of 1939 related to the storage and handling of materials and 639 to defective materials. Both workmen and the supervisors testify that the co-operative plan has led to a marked improvement in the efficiency of the stores department. A general foreman on the Canadian National said:

Everywhere the stores department has been on the carpet. There has been improvement in getting material and the efficiency of the stores department has been improved by the co-operative plan. Before, you got material when you got it. The purchasing department didn't bother. Now those departments have got to co-operate.

At several points on the Baltimore and Ohio the committee minutes have revealed rather general shortages of material. For example, the March 20, 1926 minutes at Garrett, Indiana, listed a shortage of 113 items; on May 13, 1925, the pipe fitters' representative at Newark, Ohio, brought in 11 shortage suggestions; on July 22, 1925, the general car foreman at the same point brought in 14 shortage suggestions.

Suggestions concerning unsatisfactory quality of material, though less numerous than those relating to material shortages, have been important. For example, the management of a Canadian National shop brought samples of wrought iron pipe to a meeting to show that it was of poor quality and that it failed to come up to specifications. The management said that the ¼-inch pipe split easily and the 1-inch pipe and 1½-inch pipe had prominent seams. Moreover the trade-mark on the pipe was so large that it interfered with the threading. At a local meeting on the Baltimore and Ohio the men reported that certain reamers were not properly tempered and were not giving good service. One of these was sent in for a test. At another shop it was reported that the rivets were unsatisfactory because the heads pulled off. Several rivets from which the heads had pulled off were sent to the engineer of tests for inspection.

On the Baltimore and Ohio the management of the mechanical department has gradually developed the policy of not encouraging suggestions relating to material shortages because another department (the stores department) is affected. Nevertheless, in 1940, some such suggestions are being received and a representative of the stores department attends each of the local meetings.[46]

(6) Improvements in the tool system. Reports by both supervisors and men concerning the tool situation at some shops on the Baltimore and Ohio and the Canadian National previous to the co-operative plan are almost unbelievable. The general foreman in a Canadian National car shop described the situation as follows:

Previous to the co-operative plan the tools were scattered over the shop. You had to hunt up the man who used the tool last. It was understood that when a man was through he would return the tools, but often he would not do so. When you get a tool out of there now, you know it is fit to use; and you don't have to spend half an hour in finding it.

A machinist in a Baltimore and Ohio roundhouse reported:

There has been a wonderful change in working conditions. Anyone can see that. It used to be if a man had a good special tool, he would put it in his box and raise hell if some one else tried to use it. But it was the company's tool. One man had the blacksmith make a couple of chisels which he never let anyone else use. At the suggestion of the men the toolroom system has been changed. I dare say we now have one of the best toolroom systems on the road.

At another Baltimore and Ohio roundhouse, a machinist said:

[46] Material shortages in 1940 are receiving more discussion than the minutes of the meetings indicate, because there is some tendency to keep these matters out of the minutes. The unsatisfactory financial position of the railroad, of course, makes the task of the stores department more difficult.

We are going to centralize the tools. Some fellows have kept tools which they would never use in a thousand years. I have been on the Baltimore and Ohio for twenty years and their toolroom system is rotten. There is no one to repair tools now; we are going to get someone. If anyone wants a 1¼-inch die, he has to come to me to get one. I have the only one in the shop. When the tool system is changed, it will be in the toolroom all the time. We have only one 5½-inch box wrench; you should see the men fight over that wrench. We are having one hung between every three stalls.

Although the precise effect of union-management co-operation upon output cannot be measured, this survey of specific suggestions leaves little doubt that the direct contribution of the co-operative plan to higher production has been important. Undoubtedly the contribution has been considerably less since 1929 than before, not only because the most obvious suggestions have been made but because the severe shrinkage of employment during the depression has made the men reluctant to offer labor-saving suggestions. In 1940 the contribution of the co-operative plan to higher production is in the main indirect through its effect upon morale and union-management relations.

2. *Savings in the consumption of materials.* There is very general testimony that the co-operative plan has helped to encourage economy in the use of material. Just how much it is impossible to say, because some conservation of material must be attributed to the fact that, about the time the co-operative plan was adopted, the mechanical departments of the Baltimore and Ohio and the Chicago and North Western were placed on budgets. Signs posted in Baltimore and Ohio shops read: "A dollar saved in material will be spent for labor. Save material!"

No doubt the desire of the men to gain employment helped to conserve material. The co-operative plan, however, contributed in several ways.

(1) It introduced a spirit which made the men more disposed to economize. A committeeman in a Baltimore and Ohio locomotive shop said:

If you see a fellow throwing away material, you speak to him about it. In the old days you would say, "To hell with economy—let the foreman worry about it." We do not do that any more because we know that a dollar saved on material is a dollar more for labor.

The electrician of a Chicago and North Western roundhouse made a special effort to interest the men in saving current. He said: "The men used to get by with murder on this floor. There would be ten or twenty cords with the plugs not pulled out when they went to lunch."

(2) The co-operative plan provided an opportunity for the men to suggest to the management ways of saving material. Out of 25,012 suggestions made on the Canadian National up to the end of 1939, 695 involved the reclamation or conservation of material.[47]

(3) The co-operative committee meetings have provided a convenient opportunity for shop superintendents to interest union officials in preventing waste of specific material. The superintendent of the Moncton locomotive shops on the Canadian National reported that the consumption of hacksaws was great and asked the committeemen to bring the matter up in their lodge meetings. In this instance the men replied that proper saws were not being provided. As a result a change was made in the type of saw used in pipe cutting. The superintendent of the Ivorydale shops of the Baltimore and Ohio called the attention of the committee to the fact that there had been a great increase in the use of small tools, and expressed the opinion that a large reduction could be made if the men would exercise more care. On another occasion he reported that costs were running about 64 per cent for labor and 36 per cent for material, and that they ought to run about 75 per cent for labor and 25

[47] At a large Canadian National car shop, union representatives made suggestions concerning the handling or use of material which, according to the superintendent, saved many hundreds of dollars a year.

The veneer used in passenger cars comes in crates. A worker would knock off one side of the crate and take out a few sheets of the veneer. Then some of the veneer would get dry and crinkle up, and it would have to be pressed down straight. The men suggested that racks be made to hold the crates. When a crate is opened now, a panel is put on top of the veneer to keep it flat, so that there is no waste to it.

At this shop white wood had been used for cores of veneer work. The men suggested that pine be used instead—a saving of $15 to $25 per thousand. The wood used for flooring had been purchased on the west coast at about $55 per thousand. The men suggested that it could be milled from common 3-inch plank. Rough planks cost about $25 per thousand, and the milling about $5 per thousand. The men also suggested that fir be used instead of ash for setbacks and headrests— a difference of $38 compared with $120 per thousand. Ash had been used for sash in cabooses. At the suggestion of the men, pine, costing less than half as much, was substituted.

per cent for material. The storekeeper explained to the committee which materials were running high.

3. *Improvement in the quality of work.* That the quality of work performed in the railroad shops substantially improved at least during the twenties is indicated by the increase in the locomotive miles per engine failure, the decrease in the proportion of engines found defective by federal inspectors, and the decrease in the number of defects per locomotive inspected.

From 1914 to 1921 inclusive, the locomotive miles per engine failure[48] on the Baltimore and Ohio averaged 13,125. There was a considerable drop in miles per engine failure in 1922, the result undoubtedly of the shopmen's strike in that year. In 1923, the year before the co-operative plan became general on the system, the mileage per engine failure was 15,107. This figure may have been slightly affected by the deterioration of equipment during the strike. In 1924, the first year of general operation of the co-operative plan, the mileage per engine failure was 21,503. Then the mileage gained rapidly as follows: 1925, 26,033; 1926, 26,810; 1927, 40,092.

The table on page 472 shows the drop in the proportion of locomotives found defective by federal inspectors and the drop in the number of federal defects per locomotive.[49] On all roads the improvement was considerable. During the period 1923 to 1939, the improvement on the roads practicing union-management co-operation was not substantially different from the improvement on railroads in general. It is more satisfactory, however, to confine the comparison to the period between the date when union-management co-operation started and 1929 because during the depression the financial conditions of the different roads affected their standards of maintenance. This comparison indicates that during the operation of the co-operative plan on the Chicago and North Western and the Chicago, Milwaukee, St. Paul, and Pacific, the percentage of locomotives found defective dropped faster than on

[48] An engine failure is a delay of more than a given length which is due to mechanical causes in the locomotive. There are variations in the definitions used by different roads. The Baltimore and Ohio defines the limit as 3 minutes in the case of passenger trains and 20 minutes in the case of freight trains.

[49] The Bureau of Locomotive Inspection of the Interstate Commerce Commission defines the conditions which its inspectors are instructed to report as defects. There are over 300 of these defects. They are known in the railroad industry as "federal defects."

I. PERCENTAGE OF INSPECTED LOCOMOTIVES FOUND DEFECTIVE

Year Ending June 30	All Roads	Baltimore and Ohio		Chicago and North Western	Chicago, Milwaukee, St. Paul, and Pacific	Canadian National
1923......	65	62		67	48	84
1924......	53	55[b]		38	27	45
1925......	46	52		35[c]	27	50
1926......	40	46		32	21[d]	57[e]
		East Lines	West Lines			
1927......	31	30	49	19	13	50
1928......	24	21	28	11	12	47
1929......	21	15	17	12	9[d]	34
1930......	16	8	8	8[e]	6	30
1931......	10	4.1	4.7	7	4.5	37
1932......	8	5	5	4.9	4.6	23
1933......	10	6	8	9	6	22
1934......	12	13	11	12	6	15
1935......	12	10	9	13	8	32
1936......	12	13	8	17	8	24
1937......	12	15	9	20	7	17
1938......	11	11	9	14	8	18
1939......	9	9	7	13	6	13

II. NUMBER OF DEFECTS PER LOCOMOTIVE INSPECTED

Year Ending June 30	All Roads	Baltimore and Ohio		Chicago and North Western	Chicago, Milwaukee, St. Paul, and Pacific	Canadian National
1923......	2.73	2.86		2.51	1.57	—
1924......	2.16	2.43[b]		1.21	.75	1.34
1925......	1.79	2.44		1.20[c]	.94	2.04
1926......	1.51	1.97		1.03	.58[d]	2.29[e]
		East Lines	West Lines			
1927......	1.15	1.36	2.09	.53	.39	2.01
1928......	.85	.75	1.05	.32	.34	1.95
1929......	.56	.57	.73	.37	.33[d]	1.27
1930......	.60	.25	.34	.25[c]	.22	1.50
1931......	.37	.16	.17	.21	.15	1.25
1932......	.29	.21	.17	.16	.17	.86
1933......	.37	.23	.33	.31	.23	.89
1934......	.48	.68	.45	.48	.21	.52
1935......	.47	.43	.35	.47	.30	.84
1936......	.49	.60	.30	.68	.30	1.00
1937......	.50	.74	.33	.88	.27	.55
1938......	.40	.47	.35	.52	.30	.51
1939......	.32	.40	.24	.48	.23	.52

[a] Interstate Commerce Commission, Bureau of Locomotive Inspection, *Report of Chief Inspector*, 1923–1939. For the period 1923–26 the figures pertain to all locomotives inspected; for the period 1927–39 to all steam locomotives inspected.

[b] Union-management co-operation became general in 1924.

[c] Union-management co-operation was started April 1925 and abandoned in 1930.

[d] Union-management co-operation was started in 1926 and abandoned in 1929.

[e] Union-management co-operation was started in the summer of 1926. Figures are available for United States lines only.

roads in general. During the first eight or nine years of union-management co-operation on the Baltimore and Ohio, the percentage of locomotives found defective dropped considerably more than on all roads—from slightly above the general average in 1924 to considerably below it in 1931, 1932, and 1933. Since 1933, however, the percentage on the Baltimore and Ohio has risen and is about the same as the average for all roads. On the Canadian National lines in the United States, the drop in locomotive defects has been considerably less than the average for all roads.

When one compares the decline in locomotive defects on the Baltimore and Ohio, the North Western, and the Milwaukee before and after the adoption of union-management co-operation and also in the case of the North Western and the Milwaukee during the operation of the co-operative plan and after its abandonment, one finds no striking change in the trend. Does this mean that union-management co-operation had little effect upon the quality of work? Not necessarily. The figures do suggest, however, that union-management co-operation was a secondary rather than a fundamental influence in the reduction of defective locomotives. So long as co-operative meetings were held, the managements used them to improve performance. The managements, however, were not satisfied to fall behind other roads. Consequently, when the meetings ceased, they found other ways of keeping up the improvement.

How did union-management co-operation produce improvements in the quality of work? One way was by producing a better spirit—more interest in doing good work and more willingness to respond co-operatively when the quality of work was criticized. In discussing this matter, a general officer of the Canadian National pointed out that the men, particularly those in the roundhouses, are more or less left to themselves as to the work which they do, and that the co-operative plan, by improving the spirit and morale of the men, had helped to make them feel their responsibility more keenly.[50]

[50] Things are often seen by the men which are not booked by the locomotive engineer and which affect the efficiency or safety of the engine. The man with an indifferent spirit says: "Oh, well, I wasn't supposed to see that! It wasn't booked. I'll let it go."

The pipe work in a large back shop on the Baltimore and Ohio was criticized in a letter from a high official. The superintendent posted the letter in the pipe shop. He said: "The men have responded to it. Each one is asking the foreman: 'What are they saying about our pipe work now?'"

In some cases the unions have contributed to better quality of work by checking bad practices of the foremen. Putting a car out without proper repairs is known as "shooting" it. If it passes, the foreman gets credit for production. If it is caught, he is likely to "pass the buck" to the carman. The union-management co-operative plan has encouraged the men to stand out against this sort of thing.

Closely related to the checking of supervisors is the backing of inspectors. Every now and then an inspector is under pressure from the supervisor to pass a locomotive or car which should not be passed. Of course, if he is caught, he is in trouble. Many an inspector has lost his job by doing a favor for a supervisor who needed to get a locomotive on the road in a hurry. The co-operation between the management and the unions to improve the quality of work has greatly helped the unions to control this situation because it has encouraged the local union officers to insist that inspectors pass no defects. It has helped the inspectors also because they have been able to point to the organized efforts of the unions and management to reduce federal defects.

Particularly important in improving the quality of work have been the discussions, in both local and system co-operative meetings, of engine failures and federal defects—and the efforts of the national and local officers of the unions to interest the rank and file in these matters. The local co-operative committee meetings have been a convenient occasion for the shop or roundhouse supervisors to discuss each locomotive failure with the men—particularly if the shop was having an unusual number of failures.[51]

[51] A typical report on the Baltimore and Ohio is as follows: "Chairman H——— also spoke of the number of engine failures we've had during the month of June as compared with our previous months and urged everyone to give the locomotive the proper attention when it is in the shop to avoid engine failures." The minutes of a Chicago and North Western shop report the master mechanic as saying: "We are having a time with engine failures at the present time and would like to ask your co-operation in seeing that the work is properly done in order to avoid these failures."

At the Baltimore and Ohio system co-operative meeting on Jan. 5, 1926, the inspection of locomotives was discussed. It was decided to have locomotive inspection regularly discussed in the local meetings, and for this purpose to furnish a statement of the defects found by federal inspectors. At a western shop on the Baltimore and Ohio the men became so interested in federal defects that they requested that each man be given a copy of the blueprint report on federal defects

Very early in the development of the co-operative plan the management of the Baltimore and Ohio sought to help the unions in reducing federal defects. President McGee of the Baltimore and Ohio System Federation in his report to the convention of the Federation in May 1924, only a few months after the co-operative plan had become general on the road, urged the members to do everything in their power to reduce the number of federal defects. He said:

These defects have been cause for considerable comment by the management while in conference with your committee. . . . It is the belief of some that such conditions exist by reason of carelessness on the part of the employees in inspecting, failing to detect these defects. . . . We, of course, resent the charge that our men are careless but it is really up to our people to disprove such belief as unwarranted by diligence in their work to the extent of seeing that equipment is thoroughly inspected and work properly done. . . . In the light of what we as shopmen are trying to accomplish in our co-operative program such a large percentage of federal defects is a good talking point for some of our competitive railroads, who do not enjoy as favorable conditions and relationships as we.

The effectiveness of the union in promoting better work was, of course, different in different shops. A general officer of the Canadian National reported spotty results from the efforts of the organizations to improve the quality of work, largely because of differences in the efficiency and interest of the local union officers.

SOME GENERAL BENEFITS OF THE CO-OPERATIVE PLAN

Intermingled with the more specific benefits of union-management co-operation discussed above, and helping to produce them, are certain more intangible effects of the plan.

1. *Help from the union in dealing with various secondary shop problems.* These problems are too numerous to classify or catalogue but the following examples indicate their character: jumping from the shop train while it is in motion; creating a fire hazard by leaving overalls in the shop at the end of the week's work; rough usage resulting in the breakage of many small tools; throwing hot tobacco ashes on the shop floor; lighting pipes on the way out or

---

issued by the mechanical department for the superintendents and master mechanics. It was impossible to furnish so many extra copies, but arrangements were made to have one posted in the union meeting hall.

smoking in the shop at the noon hour. The satisfactory solution of such shop problems has been much facilitated by the spirit that is fostered in the men through union-management co-operation, as well as by the help of the unions.

2. *Improvement in morale and relations between the unions and management.* Just as the union leaders regard better relations with management as the most important gain to the unions from union-management co-operation, so the managements regard better morale among the men and better relations with the unions as the chief gain to management. A high official in the mechanical department of the Baltimore and Ohio said in May 1940: "I think that the co-operative plan is the greatest thing ever done to bring the employer and organized labor closer together and to give them an opportunity to discuss their problems." He stressed particularly the opportunity afforded to explain to the union leaders the reasons for every reduction in force and to tell them in advance of prospective increases of employment through an enlarged maintenance and construction program. Obviously, the willingness of the men to make suggestions for improving operations or conserving material and their interest in raising the quality of work depends partly upon their relations with management.

3. *General stimulation of managerial efficiency.* This is perhaps the most important benefit which the union-management co-operative plan has conferred on the railroads. It has organized and systematized criticism of any managerial shortcoming. Naturally managements have striven to forestall suggestions by keeping conditions so satisfactory that the men would find it difficult to call attention to changes which needed to be made, to machines that were out of order, to tools that were lacking, or to any other deficiency in shop conditions. Local managements have been particularly desirous to keep items unfavorable to them from being brought up in co-operative committee meetings and included in the minutes. One of the general officers of the Canadian National Railway writes:

Our experience has been that the foremen in the shops have been more or less spurred on to look for undesirable conditions and have them remedied, rather than wait until recommendations were brought in to the co-operative committee. This, of course, you will realize is of considerable benefit to the management.

What applies to the foremen applies all the way to the top of the mechanical department. It has made the entire supervision more alert, more interested in removing sources of inefficiency and in keeping working conditions at their best. That the indirect effect of this increased efficiency upon operating results is very considerable cannot be doubted.

CONCLUSIONS CONCERNING BENEFITS TO MANAGEMENT

1. It is plain that the benefits of union-management co-operation to management cannot be measured with precision. The plan has been operating at a time when all railroads have been making remarkable progress in reducing the cost of keeping their equipment in repair through changes in the equipment itself, changes in methods of operation (such as longer locomotive runs), improvement in shop facilities, abandonment of old and poorly equipped shops and concentration of repair work in the shops best equipped, and improvements in methods of shop operation. When so many powerful influences are at work, it is difficult to isolate the effect of any single cause such as union-management co-operation. On the Baltimore and Ohio and the Chicago, Milwaukee, St. Paul, and Pacific there is circumstantial evidence that production was increased by the co-operative program. At least these two roads did distinctly better than the average in increasing the productivity of their shops and, in the case of the Chicago, Milwaukee, St. Paul, and Pacific, the increase in efficiency definitely slackened after the abandonment of the co-operative plan.[52] On the Chicago and North Western the operating statistics reveal no effect from union-management co-operation. Statistical evidence is lacking in the case of the Canadian National, but, even if available, it would mean little because the first four or five years of the co-operative plan on the Canadian National coincided with drastic and comprehensive changes in shop methods. That the officers of the railroad were satisfied that the plan contributed substantially to the increase in production is indicated by their willingness in 1926 to give the

[52] There were, however, important changes in personnel on this road.

Canadian National shopmen 2 cents an hour more than the Canadian Pacific paid and by their willingness in 1928 to give the shopmen a week's vacation with pay in recognition of their co-operative efforts.

2. The depression, with its severe and prolonged unemployment, has effectively destroyed any interest in increasing output which the men may once have possessed. Whatever influence the co-operative plan was having an output in 1940 was indirect—through its effect upon morale and managerial efficiency and through the opportunity which it gave the men to get better equipment, more favorable working conditions, and higher standards of maintenance.

3. Although the amount by which the co-operative program has raised production cannot be measured, the program undoubtedly has made it easier for management to achieve any given improvement in production.

4. The effect of union-management co-operation upon the conservation of material cannot be accurately measured. The specific suggestions, however, indicate that savings of some importance have been achieved.

5. Despite an abundance of specific evidence that the co-operative program has improved the quality of work, statistical support for this conclusion is far from satisfactory. Between 1924 and 1931 federal defects dropped on the Baltimore and Ohio considerably faster than on all roads. After that time the percentage of locomotives found defective on the Baltimore and Ohio rose and in 1939 was no less than the national average. On the Chicago, Milwaukee, St. Paul, and Pacific the cessation of union-management co-operation did not halt the drop in the percentage of defective locomotives nor did it prevent the road from keeping the percentage below any other road in the country. In the case of the Chicago and North Western the ending of the co-operative program did not prevent the percentage of defective locomotives from dropping two more years to the extremely low figure of 4.9 per cent in 1932. After that time the percentage on the North Western rose to a figure higher than the national average in 1935-39. On the Canadian National lines in the United States, the percentage of defective locomotives dropped by a large amount, but in 1939 was still well above

the national average. One is safe in concluding that the co-operative plan has made it easier for management to attain any given goal in the improvement of the quality of work, but it is impossible to say whether this has led managements to insist upon higher standards of quality than they would otherwise have demanded.

6. Clearest of all is the effect of union-management co-operation in improving morale and the relations between the men and their unions on the one hand and the management on the other. On these points the testimony of both sides is clear and emphatic. Furthermore, as the passage of time and the depression have produced a drop in the labor-saving suggestions, the effect of the co-operative program upon morale and upon management-employee relations has become the result most stressed by both union leaders and managers. In 1940 this was clearly the most important gain from union-management co-operation to both the Baltimore and Ohio and the Canadian National.

CHAPTER XVI

UNION-MANAGEMENT CO-OPERATION ON THE RAILROADS—PROBLEMS

The success of union-management co-operation, as practiced on the railroads, obviously depends in the last analysis upon the willingness and ability of the rank and file of shopmen to make suggestions. This willingness is affected by a great variety of circumstances—by the extent to which the rank and file understand the significance and the possibilities of the policy, by the interest which their own leaders show in it, by the attitude of the management toward the plan and toward specific suggestions which are offered, by the relations between the union and the management, and by other factors. This means that the plan is constantly being played upon by a multitude of conditions which directly or indirectly affect its operation.

FEAR ON THE PART OF WORKERS THAT THE PLAN WOULD REDUCE EMPLOYMENT

At the beginning, the rank and file possessed only scanty knowledge of the nature of the policy, why it was considered desirable by the leaders, just what gains might be expected from it, and how these gains were to be achieved. Indeed, it is probably safe to say that the plan was started on most roads with a large fraction of the shopmen, possibly even a majority, either opposed to it or frankly skeptical of it.

On the Canadian National and the Chicago and North Western, officials of the unions and of the railroad visited the principal points and explained the plan before the first meeting was held. On the Baltimore and Ohio, instructions concerning the nature of the plan and how to conduct meetings were issued by letters. Afterward, officials of the railroad and the unions visited the principal shops and roundhouses in person and straightened out difficulties. Important as such educational work undoubtedly was, it could not clear up all doubts and misunderstandings about the plan. The attitude of the workers could be changed only by the slow process of observing the operation of the plan and acquiring experience under it.[1]

Co-operation to increase output runs counter to long-established views of self-interest which have prevailed among wage earners. It directly challenges the idea, accepted by most workers, that more efficiency means less employment.[2] This belief is sufficiently valid as far as particular men are concerned, especially in the short run, to be a real influence.[3]

Although remarkable progress was made prior to 1929 in stabilizing employment on all of the roads experimenting with co-operation, layoffs and short time, as indicated in Chapter XV, were not entirely avoided even during the twenties.[4] The great depression and the loss of business to trucks and other forms of transportation produced a drop in employment with which managements were unable to cope. In 1933, the volume of employment in the Baltimore and Ohio shops and roundhouses, as measured in man-hours, was only 39 per cent as large as in 1929; in 1937, it was 42 per cent above 1933, but even so it was 45 per cent below 1929.[5] In

[1] A union leader at one of the large Baltimore and Ohio shops where the plan had been working with unusual success said, after the plan had been in operation for two years: "The percentage of the men who understand the co-operative plan is very small—almost confined to the members of the committee. Our committee man has quite a job when he goes out and tries to educate the men as to what co-operation really means. Fifty per cent of the men rarely attend the meetings of the lodge. They pay their dues and that is as far as it goes. There are fellows who feel that co-operation is purely and simply a movement to benefit the management."

[2] The president of one of the system federations, who has been an enthusiastic supporter of the plan, said that his first reaction was that the plan would mean more efficiency and that this would mean less employment. A committeeman at London, Ontario, said: "I was opposed to it at first in the worst way. I looked at it as something in the interest of management."

[3] The foreman of a Canadian National foundry said: "The old haunting fear that a man is going to lose his job keeps them from making suggestions. Mark you, as far as the foundry is concerned, the railroad is doing its best, but that fear remains."

[4] At the time the co-operative plan was started on the Canadian National, the shops were overmanned and were working only five days a week. This continued for several years. In the spring of 1927, largely at the request of the men, it was decided to make layoffs in order to give the other men full-time work. This led the sheet metal workers in the Winnipeg shops to withdraw their delegates from the co-operative committees for about a month.

[5] There was also a slow decline of nearly 20 per cent in employment in the Baltimore and Ohio shops between 1924 and 1929.

1938, employment in the Baltimore and Ohio shops dropped even below the level of 1933. There was also a substantial drop of employment on the Canadian National. The result was a great drop in labor-saving suggestions. By 1940, suggestions for new labor-saving methods had virtually ceased on the Baltimore and Ohio. On the Canadian National they dropped from 25.3 per cent of all suggestions (2,240 out of 8,861) prior to 1930, to 8.4 per cent (1,352 out of 16,151) during the period of 1930 to 1939 inclusive.[6]

DIFFICULTIES DUE TO WEAKNESSES OF THE SHOPCRAFT UNIONS

When the co-operative plan was introduced, the shopcraftsmen were very incompletely organized at several points and, in some cases, the unions were weakened either by factional conflicts or by attacks from outside organizations. These factors limited the ability of the unions to build up support for the co-operative plan.

1. *Incomplete organization.* The shopmen's strike of 1922 was largely responsible for the incomplete organization on co-operating roads in the United States upon the introduction of the plan. In western Canada the weakness of the AFL unions was particularly persistent. Even as late as 1926 the international unions did not have a single member in the Transcona blacksmith shop.

The unions have little influence with the men outside the organizations. Not only do these men refuse to make suggestions, but in many instances they lose no opportunity to ridicule the co-operative plan. As a member of the Transcona committee remarked: "We have no means of educating the men outside the organization. They are the hardest knockers we have. If we had a chance to talk to them we would make them see what we are doing."

2. *Factional conflicts within a union or between unions.* The operation of the co-operative plan is naturally impaired when factional conflicts arise either between two or more unions or within one union, and such conflicts are bound to arise from time to time. Many of the men who had withdrawn from the machinists' union during

---

[6] These figures are obtained by adding the suggestions for the development of new devices to the suggestions pertaining to shop methods and practices. Virtually all of the suggestions in the first class and a great majority of those in the second are labor-saving.

the general strike of 1919 to join the One Big Union returned later on and fought for control of the union. This factional struggle impaired interest in the co-operative plan.

A more general way in which factional fights have been a hindrance to the co-operative plan grows out of the dislike of a substantial number of men in every shop to the paying of union dues. Whenever a factional fight breaks out and two or more unions compete for the allegiance of the men, these men use the factional controversy as an excuse for staying out of all unions. They may say that they will join the union when the unions settle their own differences. It is also undoubtedly true that the co-operative plan at Winnipeg suffered for some time from the unpopularity which the international unions incurred from their opposition to the general strike of 1919. A leading company official said: "If the co-operative plan were divorced from the international unions, it would go over big." Probably this statement was an exaggeration, but it is true that, during the first year or so, many workmen in Winnipeg opposed the co-operative plan because it was the child of the international unions.

The co-operative plan has had also to meet persistent attacks of organized groups, such as Communists, Canadian Brotherhood of Railway Employees,[7] and the One Big Union, who do not believe in "class collaboration." It is probable, however, that these attacks upon the co-operative movement were more helpful than harmful to it. True, at points where the unions were weak, the attacks temporarily halted the progress of the plan and made it difficult for the leaders and management to arouse confidence in it. But the criticisms also prevented the co-operative plan from being regarded as something of little importance. They compelled the international unions to push the plan vigorously, and stimulated

---

[7] In 1925 the boilermakers' union adopted a compulsory insurance plan which substantially increased the union dues and was strongly opposed by a sizable minority of the membership, especially because of its compulsory feature. On the Baltimore and Ohio the average membership of the boilermakers dropped from 1,319 in 1925 to 1,043 in 1926, and there was a drop during the same period on the Canadian National. The Canadian Brotherhood of Railway Employees took advantage of the disaffection in the ranks of the boilermakers to start an organizing campaign among them. The conflict was intensified by the efforts of the firemen and oilers (an AFL affiliate) to extend their organization among the shop laborers, for whom the brotherhood had an agreement with the company.

them to obtain results under it, in order to justify their decision in adopting it.

OPPOSITION IN THE RANKS OF MANAGEMENT

The co-operative plan encountered considerable opposition in the lower ranks of officials among shop superintendents and master mechanics and above all among foremen, and the overcoming of this constituted a major problem. One reason for the opposition of local officials was the fear that the policy might restrict managerial authority. When the plan was introduced, there was considerable vagueness in the minds of both men and management concerning exactly what the plan was and what the men would be expected to do. A few of the men expected a revolution in management: they thought that they would have some choice in appointing foremen. In both Montreal and London, Ontario, they made a specific demand that they be so consulted. The fear of the supervisors was expressed by a superintendent who said: "It looked to me like handing over the reins to the men that you are boss of."[8]

Another reason for opposition of local officials was the fear of being "shown up" before their superiors. This fear manifested itself particularly in efforts on the part of superintendents and foremen to keep certain suggestions from being recorded in the minutes of committee meetings,[9] and in ridiculing the co-operative plan, discouraging men from making suggestions, and trying to kill such suggestions as the men's representatives offered.[10]

Of course, there were many local officials who saw the possibility of using the co-operative plan to improve the output of their shops and who were strongly in favor of it from the very start. At the shops managed by such men the plan has prospered most. The two

[8] At the first meeting of a large shop on the Chicago and North Western the representatives of the machinists brought in a list of over 30 suggestions. The superintendent was excitable and so was the committeeman. Each lost his head and there was a lively time. The superintendent thought the men were attempting to take over the running of the shop. It was necessary for one of the general chairmen of the machinists and someone from the office of the vice-president in charge of personnel to go to the shop and advise them how to conduct their meetings.

[9] See pp. 486-87 below.

[10] A high official of the mechanical department said: "There is no use shutting your eyes to the truth. The foremen are bucking the co-operative plan. You can see that because when a suggestion comes up, they sit on it."

places on the Baltimore and Ohio in which the interest of the men in the plan was greatest were places where the shop superintendents were strong backers of it.

The opposition of some officials to the union-management co-operative plan, as indicated above, took the form of objections to many suggestions made by the men. Though the record shows that over 80 per cent of the suggestions offered were adopted on the Baltimore and Ohio, the Canadian National, and the Chicago and North Western, this does not mean that all of the accepted suggestions were liked by the local managements.

One criticism frequently made of the men's suggestions was that too many related to better working conditions and not enough to direct improvements in efficiency.[11] The demand of the men for information concerning the cost of articles purchased on the outside has occasionally been a matter of dispute. Some managers have felt that, in seeking to determine what the railroad shall make and what it shall purchase, the men are stepping beyond their proper province.[12] Some suggestions are objected to on the ground that they are grievances and that the co-operative plan is not intended to deal with grievances. This objection has usually been employed to keep out of the minutes items which the management did not wish to appear. Most objectionable of all from the standpoint of local officials are the suggestions which reflect in one way or another upon the management—upon its efficiency or its observance of standards.

Experience has indicated that opposition to the co-operative program from within the ranks of management is almost certain to occur at the beginning of the plan. This opposition is not particularly difficult to deal with, provided top management makes it plain that the co-operative plan is not intended to undermine the au-

[11] The superintendent of an important Canadian National shop, a man who is friendly to the co-operative plan and has helped make it a success in his shop, said: "The committee seems to be particularly good at suggesting expenditures which do not increase production."

[12] The chairman of the committee at a Chicago and North Western shop said: "At the first meeting we had to fight to put through our suggestions. On one particular subject we fought for an hour. That was a proposal that we put on a test in the shop to estimate the cost in the shop and to compare it with outside firms."

thority of supervisors or "to show them up" and, most important of all, provided top management stands strongly behind the plan. On both the Baltimore and Ohio and the Canadian National, where top management was conspicuously and vigorously behind the plan, opposition from local superintendents disappeared, but on the Chicago and North Western and the Chicago, Milwaukee, St. Paul, and Pacific, where top management was either lukewarm or divided, the co-operative meetings were abandoned after several years.

OPERATING DISAGREEMENTS AND DISPUTES

The principal disagreements between workers and management that developed in connection with operation of the co-operative plan have been concerned with methods of operation and credit for the suggestions made. Further controversies have sometimes arisen over the time spent by workers in co-operative committee business.

1. *Disputes over methods of operating the co-operative plan.* There have been a few more or less serious disputes over methods of operating union-management co-operation. The most important causes for disputes have been the question of whether the men should notify the foreman of conditions in need of correction before reporting them to the co-operative committee, and whether certain items should be recorded in the minutes. These two causes of controversy are closely connected because managers have been reluctant to have recorded in the minutes items which they believe should first have been handled with the foreman.

It is quite natural, indeed inevitable, that the co-operative plan should lead the men to bring into the committee meeting many matters which under other circumstances they would have taken up directly with the foremen—such matters as a leaky roof, a floor in need of repairs, or even a machine out of order. The men may bring the matter before the committee because that is the easiest way to get quick and certain results or simply because their supply of suggestions is small and they wish to make a better showing in committee. Naturally also, the foreman and the superintendents often object to matters' being brought to the committee before being called to the attention of the foreman.

At nearly all shops there have been sharp disagreements over the inclusion of items in the minutes. At the Tenth Street, Pittsburgh, car yard of the Baltimore and Ohio, the men refused to attend co-operative committee meetings on two occasions because of disputes over the inclusion of items in the minutes. Sometimes a further controversy arises concerning how the minutes shall be worded.[13]

2. *Credit for suggestions.* The smooth operation of the co-operative plan has been interfered with occasionally by jealousy between the men and the management over credit for suggestions. In some instances, the superintendent and foremen resent having credit given to the men for ideas which really originated with management.[14] In other cases the men accuse the management of keeping suggestions out of the record by acting first, and in a few cases actually stealing the men's suggestions. At some shops the superintendents have urged the foremen to bring up every possible matter in the foremen's conferences. Then if any of the same matters are raised by the men at the co-operative meetings, the management can reply that they are being taken care of. This attempt of superintendents to forestall the men's suggestions is one of the ways in which the co-operative plan is expected to promote managerial efficiency, and, from the standpoint of the management, it is a desirable result. Nevertheless, it has aroused resentment among the men at a few points, and at a number of shops the men have protested against the holding of the foremen's meetings.

It should be emphasized, however, that the difficulties over credit for suggestions, though important in certain cases, were confined to a few shops and to the early years of the co-operative plan. As the

[13] At a shop where brass molding was done, the pattern for a certain casting did not allow a large enough hole. Consequently, it was necessary to bore out metal which could have been eliminated in making the casting. The men took measurements and suggested that the pattern be changed. The management objected to having this item in the minutes. Finally it was decided to include it, but to leave out the figures showing that there had been a mistake of $7/8$ of an inch in the pattern. The men's chairman said: "When a suggestion reflects on the shop, the management squeals like a stuck pig."

[14] At a car shop on the Chicago and North Western, a dry kiln was suggested by the employees. The superintendent said: "It was originally brought up by me. I have been asking for it for seven years. I think that we have been co-operating too damn much and have gotten ourselves in bad and should bring these things up ourselves instead of letting the men do it."

plan came to be better understood and more firmly established the matter of credit for suggestions has ceased to be an issue.

3. *Controversies over time consumed on committee business.* At a few shops, controversies have arisen between committee members and the management over the time spent by the union representatives on co-operative committee business. Obviously, there is danger that some committee members may abuse the privilege of leaving their work to go about committee business during working hours. Likewise it is understandable that some superintendents and foremen, especially those who are not very friendly to the co-operative plan, may believe that the men spend too much time on committee business. It is significant that most of these disputes have occurred in two shops where the management has been more or less hostile to the co-operative plan and where the plan at the time was not working too well.

UNSATISFACTORY PERSONAL OR INDUSTRIAL RELATIONS

Occasionally the success of the co-operative plan has been interfered with by having a chairman representing the men and a chairman representing the management who could not get on with each other. The shop superintendent and the machinist who was chairman of the men's section of the committee at a large Canadian National locomotive shop consumed most of the time of the committee in personal arguments.[15] In contrast to such merely personal frictions there have been a few scattered instances in which the relations between the men as a whole and the supervision have been unsatisfactory. In one car yard on the Baltimore and Ohio relations between the men and the supervisor became so bad that

---

[15] Arguments developed over trivial points which elsewhere would cause no trouble whatever. A foreman on the committee described the situation as follows: "We have a chairman for the men, who should have been a lawyer. You think you are sitting in a police court. 'You said this.' 'You said that!' The other committee members are all right. When he is not in the committee, everything goes smoothly. He wants to be the whole thing and he *will* be it. If you don't just say the things to suit him he starts an argument." A representative of one of the crafts said: "We have a chairman who would make a damn good man on a grievance committee. They argue too much about small points that don't do anyone any good." So much difficulty was exierenced in reaching agreement between the men's chairman and the superintendent concerning the proper wording of the minutes that a special meeting on the matter of minutes was held on Mar. 24, 1927.

the men on several occasions refused to attend the co-operative committee meetings.[16]

UNSATISFACTORY HANDLING OF SUGGESTIONS BY THE MANAGEMENT

In some cases the workers have been dissatisfied on account of delay in the handling of suggestions by officials. On the Baltimore and Ohio and the Canadian National, the authority of the local shop superintendents to make capital expenditures on the shop is limited to items costing not more than $100.[17] This means that a considerable proportion of the suggestions must be referred to regional or system officials for approval. Weeks or even months may pass before a decision from higher authority is obtained. Particularly in the early days of the co-operative plan the men did not appreciate the need of time for officials to investigate suggestions, and they attributed delays to indifference or hostility to the co-operative plan.[18]

[16] The supervisor said: "To put it in a few words, we have a bull-headed bunch of men to deal with down there. Unfortunately we have a bunch of men who think that co-operation was intended only to improve working conditions. In fact they don't know what co-operation means. I will say we have more trouble from those 100 men than from the hundreds of men at the roundhouse and back shop. They bring too much unionism into the co-operative meeting. They have allowed things to come into the co-operative meeting that were grievances."

A representative of the men said: "N—— is what I would call a slave-driver. He has all the men down on him. You know you can't get work done that way. He is always sneaking around through the cars trying to find out what he can get on you, he is such a goddam sneak. He is not going to get work done as it ought to be as long as he is around here because nobody likes him."

[17] On some roads the limit is as low as $25. The local officers may order expensive changes to locomotives. One master mechanic on the North Western put it this way: "I can put nothing into practice in the shop that will cost more than $25, but I can order a pair of cylinders on a locomotive that cost $1,400 or $1,600 and there is no question at all."

[18] In the Transcona minutes of Oct. 14, 1925, the following item appears: "On behalf of the employees, D. R. McKinnon raised the question of getting replies from the management with regard to different matters brought up through these meetings and asked that this complaint be recorded in the minutes and also requested that in the spirit of the co-operative principles, action should be forthcoming from the management in clearing up these several matters." At this time the records showed that out of 39 suggestions made at the Transcona shops, 33 had been accepted, 3 had been dropped, and only 3 were pending!

A few extreme delays in acting on suggestions have occurred. At one point on the Baltimore and Ohio a bank slid in along the west bound track so that car inspectors had to walk in the water in bad weather. The item was on the minutes

Sometimes delays occur because even after the suggestion has been approved the work must be done by another department, such as the bridge and building department. Before the department acts, the division engineer must approve the proposal. Both the division engineer and the bridge and building department have many duties and are inclined to give first attention to conditions which affect movement of trains and to postpone matters connected with repair shops and roundhouses.[19]

Sometimes the men's dissatisfaction grows out of failure to explain the rejection of suggestions. To important officials absorbed in major problems of railroad operation, most of the men's suggestions seem trivial and unimportant. Consequently, it is easy for the management, quite unintentionally, to cause offense by rejecting suggestions either too abruptly or without adequate explanation. A committeeman on the Canadian National said:

> One of the men devised a way of welding in booster crank pins. They had always come loose. E—— (the general superintendent of motive power) thought it O. K. and the mechanical officers approved it. A couple of weeks later we got a letter from B—— (the chief of motive power) saying not to weld any more booster crank pins. That is all there was to it. Some explanation is due us—they treat us like children.

A union leader on the Baltimore and Ohio, when asked how the co-operative plan could be improved, said: "Baltimore reports: 'This plan is not feasible,' or 'It is not feasible to do this now.' The reasons for rejecting suggestions given by Baltimore are too incomplete."

---

two years before action was finally taken. A photograph showing a car inspector in the water was finally sent to Baltimore and produced prompt action.

[19] On June 12, 1925, it was reported that four ventilators in the blacksmith shop at one point on the Baltimore and Ohio were in bad condition. Over a year later, on July 7, 1926, the item was still carried on the minutes as unsettled. On June 15, 1926, the superintendent wrote to the division engineer: "Summer season has now arrived and the men in both the spring plant and on the large furnaces are complaining bitterly about the heat. As these air ducts are used for ventilation in the summer as well as heating in the winter, we will not be able to overcome the complaints unless immediate action is taken to have the system overhauled. Will you kindly advise when you will be in a position to handle?" This matter had been referred to the division engineer on June 26, 1925 and followed up 23 times before action was obtained over a year later.

MISCELLANEOUS CONFLICTS AND STRAINED RELATIONS BETWEEN MEN AND MANAGEMENT

Seniority issues are likely to produce serious differences unless handled with skill and tact. At Cumberland, Maryland, where the co-operative plan on the whole has worked exceptionally well, there was a brief stoppage of meetings in 1925 because of a dispute over seniority. The men in the back shop belonged to the same local unions as the men in the roundhouse, but were on separate seniority lists. Some of the men, particularly those in the back shop, wished to combine the two seniority lists. During the summer of 1925, lack of work caused the back shop to be shut down several days each month for several months. The roundhouse, however, which was engaged in making running repairs, was not shut down. The senior men in the back shop felt that they should be permitted to "bump" the men in the roundhouse.

Seniority makes discharge an extremely serious matter to railroad shopmen. Consequently, discharges are likely to result in sharp clashes between the unions and the management. At a shop on the Chicago and North Western a machinist who had been employed for 18 or 19 years was discharged as a result of an engine failure caused by his forgetting to put a cotter pin in a locomotive. The machinists at the point announced that they would make no more suggestions until the man had been restored to work.

Considerable disturbance was caused in one of the Canadian National shops by the introduction of a "scheduling" system which was designed to get engines out on time without the usual rush and congestion. The union leaders were in favor of the plan. The management agreed that the union leaders would have a chance to explain the new system to the men before it was introduced, but through an oversight the plan was put into effect while the two leading members of the co-operative committee were away at a union convention. The One Big Union element in the shop undertook to show that the scheduling system was a speed-up device. Fortunately, the AFL unions had able leaders in this shop and on their return they were able to straighten out the difficulties.

The settlement of grievances has been a persistent sore spot in a few shops. A union leader on the Canadian National said: "The lower official says, 'My superior will have to decide that.' The superior says, 'I am not going to tell my subordinates what to do.' And they want us to co-operate. That is the bloody thing we are bucking all the time." On the Chicago and North Western, in the summer of 1927, the unsatisfactory method of handling grievances was the most serious obstacle which the co-operative plan was encountering.

Loss to outside concerns of work previously done in railroad shops has been a serious grievance at a few points and has temporarily hurt the co-operative plan. A foreman said: "We are buying Franklin automatic shoes and wedges when we could make them for one-third. The foundry here is doing nothing. It is pretty hard to tell these men this is co-operation."

Every now and then the men at some shops develop the idea that as part of the co-operative plan the management should submit proposed changes in methods of shop operation to the co-operative committee before adopting them. "They put something into effect and then consult you afterward—is that co-operation?" said the chairman of a Canadian National committee. Although the management can scarcely be expected to make the introduction of changed methods depend upon the committee's approval, much would be gained in shop good will and in avoiding friction if the local managements made a practice of explaining proposed changes to the shop committees, thus giving the committees a chance to criticize them.

Experience on the railroads shows that negotiations which develop serious differences between the unions and the management put the co-operative plan under severe strain and temporarily reduce its effectiveness. Suggestions drop off, the men threaten to discontinue attendance at meetings, and sometimes do discontinue for a short period, but, after the differences have been adjusted and the strain is over, the co-operative plan goes on very much as before.

On August 10, 1927, less than nine months after a 3-cent wage increase had gone into effect, the unions on the Chicago and North Western asked for an increase of 25 per cent. The management was surprised by the men's extraordinary request and undoubtedly feared that the co-operative plan was to be used to support extravagant demands. The road therefore countered with a proposal for a wage cut. In many shops the announcement produced little effect upon the number of suggestions offered, but in others the effect was quite pronounced. At Escanaba, Michigan, no new suggestions whatever were offered at the November meeting; at Council Bluffs, Iowa, only one suggestion was offered, and the meeting lasted only half an hour; at Adams, Wisconsin, there were only two new suggestions; at New Butler, only three suggestions were offered, including one from a foreman.

It is interesting and significant that the wage movement of 1938, when the railroads sought a 15 per cent wage reduction, had no effect on the operation of the co-operative plan on the Baltimore and Ohio, according to the head of the shopcrafts' federation. One reason was that the plan had by then become an accepted institution on the road; another was that the demand for a wage reduction was not confined to the Baltimore and Ohio, but extended to all railroads.

SHARING THE GAINS OF UNION-MANAGEMENT CO-OPERATION WITH THE WORKERS

The co-operative agreements between the unions and both the Baltimore and Ohio and the Canadian National stipulated that the gains of co-operation would be shared, but did not stipulate how the gains were to be measured or in what proportions they were to be divided. The agreements on the Chicago and North Western and on the Chicago, Milwaukee, St. Paul, and Pacific contained no provision concerning sharing the gains. Some moral obligation to share them, however, was obviously implied, as the officials on these roads admitted.

In the early years of union-management co-operation there was a more or less general feeling among the men that they were not receiving a proper share in the gains. They wanted a definite share in the money gains or savings—some additional dollars and cents in the pay envelope. At the time the plan was introduced, its possibilities were probably "oversold" to many of the rank and file, particularly in the case of the Baltimore and Ohio. Many of the men believed that it was saving the roads immense sums, larger sums undoubtedly than was the case.

There were several difficulties in giving the men a pecuniary reward from the gains of union-management co-operation. One was the difficulty of measuring the gains. In the spring of 1926, the unions on the Baltimore and Ohio asked the management to consent to the appointment of a "joint committee" to study the problem. An inquiry was made by the accounting department of the railroad and some estimates were made. Everyone conceded, however, that the estimates were necessarily exceedingly rough. On the Canadian National a committee was appointed in 1927 to study the savings achieved, and a report was made in the winter of 1928.

The second difficulty in rewarding the men arose from the unwillingness of roads which did not have the co-operative plan (or had just introduced it) to pay less than the roads on which the plan was well established. When the Chicago and North Western gave a wage increase of 3 cents an hour effective January 1, 1927, the Chicago, Milwaukee, St. Paul, and Pacific, a closely competing road, granted the same increase effective a month earlier than on the North Western. At this time the co-operative plan had not been adopted on the Milwaukee road. Although there could be no doubt that the co-operative plan had much to do with the wage increase on the North Western, the action of the Milwaukee in raising wages led many of the men on the North Western to question whether they were getting anything from union-management co-operation. Their doubts were increased by the fact that the Milwaukee was in even worse financial condition than the North Western, being at this time in the hands of a receiver.

In Canada, the Canadian Pacific was unwilling to pay lower wages than the Canadian National. The men on the two roads had been in the habit of negotiating a joint agreement with them through Division Four of the Railway Employes' Department of the American Federation of Labor with which the shopcraft federations on both roads were affiliated. In December 1926, however, the federation on the Canadian National negotiated a 2-cent advance in wages which, strictly speaking, was a wage redistribution rather than an increase.[20] At this time joint negotiations were be-

---

[20] It was a redistribution of the money saved by the discontinuance of the bonus system in several shops in the central region. See p. 452.

ing conducted between the shopmen of Canada and the two roads. The Canadian Pacific offered to give its shopmen an increase of 4 cents an hour provided the Canadian National counted the 2-cent advance already given as part of a similar 4-cent increase. Had the Canadian National unions negotiated separately, they could probably have obtained 3 or 4 cents *in addition* to the 2 cents already received. The Canadian Pacific unions, however, appealed to the Canadian National men not to break up the joint arrangement by negotiating separately. Consequently, the proposal of the Canadian Pacific management was accepted.

Many of the Canadian National shopmen then felt they had been tricked out of 2 cents an hour which they otherwise might have had. Moreover, they had regarded the first advance of 2 cents as a reward for co-operation, and when they failed to receive more than the Canadian Pacific shopmen, they felt that they were not getting any share of the gains after all. One of the union leaders in Winnipeg said: "The co-operative plan got a black eye in Winnipeg on account of having that 2-cent bonus taken away." Another leader said: "We figured that the $860,000 that was saved by the co-operative plan in the East should be distributed among the men. The distribution of that is the main issue."

The management of the Canadian National recognized that this feeling existed among the men. It appreciated the importance of rewarding co-operation. The president of the road appointed a committee to investigate the savings achieved and this committee made a report in the winter of 1928. As a result, it was decided to grant the men vacations with pay—an advantage which did not exist on the Canadian Pacific.

The feeling of the men that they were not sharing properly in the gains of union-management co-operation was strongest during periods of wage negotiations; it was quite natural for the men to interpret the company's resistance to their demands as unwillingness to reward their co-operative effort. This feeling became pronounced among the men on the Baltimore and Ohio during the negotiations of 1926. The roads in the southeastern territory, which were profiting from the Florida boom and the rapidly developing West Virginia coal traffic, had already given their men increases. The Baltimore and Ohio shopcrafts asked for an advance of 2 cents an hour and restoration of time and a half for Sunday work and overtime. The company was prospering, and in August 1926 the stock, for the first time in many years, went above par on the New York Stock Exchange.

The resistance of the company to the restoration of time and a half created much resentment among the men and provoked strong criticism of the management and of the co-operative plan. One man said:

My idea is that the management is getting about 80 per cent and the men about 20 per cent. The co-operative plan would be a swell thing if it would work out as Captain Beyer wanted it to work out—if you could get a 50-50 break. The company is making more money than ever this year, but we are not making any more.

The company argued that it received no more from the public for running its trains on Sunday and that it was unreasonable for the men to expect a higher rate for maintaining equipment. But other roads in the southeastern territory, some of them non-union roads, had conceded time and a half. Furthermore, time and a half had existed on the Baltimore and Ohio for many years prior to 1921 when it was taken away by the Railroad Labor Board. An old employee at the Glenwood shop said:

I have been working 39 years on the Baltimore and Ohio and was always paid overtime rates until the Labor Board took it away. But we can't get that now, after we have been co-operating three years. The men ain't going to be content without something we have always had.

When the committee reported in July 1926 that the management had offered a 2-cent increase without time and a half, a mass meeting was held by the men at Cumberland and a resolution to discontinue the co-operative plan was introduced. Two of the leaders, however, succeeded in getting it withdrawn. They said it would surely have carried had it been put to a vote.[21] In September the company conceded the restoration of time and a half.

---

[21] There is some evidence that the dissatisfaction which developed among the men during the course of negotiation affected the number of suggestions. Of course, the number of suggestions had been dropping throughout 1925, as it might be expected to do, because accumulated matters were being cleaned up. Nevertheless, between the first quarter of 1926 and the second, the drop was unusually large— from 1,286 to 699. In the third quarter, surprisingly enough, there was an increase

Sharing the gains of union-management co-operation has ceased to be an issue. It never was as serious on the Canadian National as on the Baltimore and Ohio, and it was pretty effectively eliminated on the former by the granting of vacations with pay in 1928. Even on the Baltimore and Ohio, sharing the gains was an acute issue only so long as the men were struggling to recover conditions which they formerly enjoyed. It has been the policy of the Railway Employes' Department to establish uniform wages and working rules on all railroads. An effort on the part of the men on the Baltimore and Ohio or on any other road to claim extra compensation as a reward for co-operation would have conflicted with the uniform wage policy of the department. Consequently, the union leaders gave no encouragement to the men on any road to use union-management co-operation as the basis for demanding differentials above rates paid on other roads. The men gradually came to regard their gains from co-operation as consisting in more employment, better working conditions, and better relations with management.

EFFECT OF THE DEPRESSION ON UNION-MANAGEMENT CO-OPERATION

Any disposition that there might have been to base claims for extra compensation upon union-management co-operation was destroyed by the depression and its effect upon the nature of the suggestions and the financial condition of the roads. Whatever savings the co-operative plan accomplished were more than needed to offset the losses from the great drop in business. On both roads the problem of the unions was to get as much employment for their men as possible and to limit the reduction in wage rates.[22]

---

in the number of suggestions to 783 and in the fourth quarter to 883. After the fourth quarter of 1926, the number of suggestions began to fall and the drop continued throughout the year 1927.

[22] The maintenance-of-equipment force on the Baltimore and Ohio dropped from an average of 17,237 in 1929 to 8,751 in 1933 and the average weekly hours from 40.8 in 1929 to 17.7 in 1932, 17.1 in 1933, and 19.6 in 1934. For a large part of the time in the latter years the shops were down to four days a week. In 1932, the men on the Baltimore and Ohio, together with all other railroad workers, took a 10 per cent reduction in wages. On the Canadian National, in addition to small layoffs, there was a large one in April 1932. The shops for many months operated only 16 days a month. The employees on the Canadian railroads received a 15 per cent reduction in pay.

The cuts in employment and pay were discouraging. They reduced morale, made both the men and the management highly conscious of their own troubles and concerned with these rather than with helping the other fellow, and they tended to engender a spirit of "What's the use?" With employment low and dropping, the men were naturally not in the mood to make labor-saving suggestions. They also knew that the company was operating on a severely curtailed budget and not in a position to purchase much new equipment or to make expensive improvements. This knowledge discouraged certain types of suggestions.[23] The local managements in many instances had a difficult time getting out production with drastically curtailed forces, and this made some of them irritable and more difficult to deal with—a situation not conducive to a co-operative attitude among the men.[24] A few local manage-

[23] Some evidence of the effect of the depression is given by the drop in the number of suggestions which, on the Baltimore and Ohio, decreased as follows for years ending about March 1:

1925	9,277	1929	1,659	1933	534	1937	812
1926	6,006	1930	1,444	1934	601	1938	598
1927	2,976	1931	1,038	1935	720	1939	544
1928	2,623	1932	647	1936	635	1940	790

The number of suggestions on the Baltimore and Ohio dropped each year prior to 1929, largely because bad conditions had been cleaned up and the accumulated ideas of the men had been exhausted. Consequently, it is impossible to know how much of the drop between 1929 and 1933 was due to the depression. The moderate recovery from 534 in 1932-33 to 812 in 1936-37 indicates that in part it was.

On the Canadian National the number of suggestions actually increased during the years of the depression—from 2,430 in 1929 to 3,018 in 1931 (after a small dip to 2,313 in 1930). It then fell, however, to a low point of 1,083 in 1938. In 1939 it recovered to 1,243. The increase between 1929 and 1931 was largely attributable to the policy of asking the men to make suggestions pertaining to safety-first and fire prevention—subjects which had received little special attention from the co-operative movement up to that time. This policy was part of an effort to maintain the number of suggestions during the depression by finding new fields of attention. One cannot assert that the drop after 1931 was entirely due to the depression, because it continued slowly after recovery began and, therefore, must have been influenced by the fact that the most obvious items had been suggested. Some significance, however, may be attached to the drop in the suggestions for labor-saving equipment and changes in methods from 666 in 1929 to 241 in 1932. Moreover, the men knew that the company had little money to spend on new shop equipment. Hence suggestions for this purpose on the Canadian National dropped from 320 in 1929 to 52 in 1932.

[24] One of the union leaders on the Baltimore and Ohio described the effect of the depression as follows: "Frankly it's been a bit dull. I don't mean that our relations have been changed to any extent but our conditions have been so doggone rotten—layoffs and short time—and of course our people have been in a very

ments, struggling to get out equipment, begrudged the time spent on co-operative committee meetings if held on company time, and tried to make them as brief as possible. When the management was obviously in a hurry to get the meeting over with, the men decided that it was not interested and this discouraged them from bringing up matters. One or two shops on the Baltimore and Ohio were caught sending in fake minutes—for meetings not held.

The hard-pressed managements in some cases used short cuts which violated the agreements with the union—such as disregarding jurisdictional lines. Such actions put temporarily under strain the excellent relations between the workers and the management which had played so important a part in the functioning of co-operation. In a few cases layoffs impaired the administrative efficiency of local unions by causing them to lose key men. An important carmen's local on the Canadian National lost through layoff its president, recording secretary, and financial secretary. The severe drop in business also provoked controversies among the men, which occupied their attention and created an atmosphere unfavorable to co-operation. For example, the men differed as to whether the decline in business should be met by dropping junior men or by dividing work.

The staff reductions at small points raised jurisdictional controversies between the unions. Where there was not enough work to keep an electrician, a sheet metal worker, a pipe fitter, or a blacksmith busy, the work of these crafts (the less numerous ones in railroad shops) would be done by the larger ones—the machinists, boilermakers, and carmen. The smaller crafts protested, but the management could not afford to employ a craftsman who would not be kept busy and the larger crafts did not object to the opportunity for their members to do some additional work.

Most serious of all, particularly on the Baltimore and Ohio, were the numerous controversies over the seniority standing of individual workmen. The drastic nature of the layoffs caused men who had twenty or more years' seniority to be dropped. Many

___

bad state of mind. They are more irritable and find fault with every little matter that ought not to be worth a darn. Also, you'll find the same attitude in the supervision. With layoffs and short time the foreman has one heck of a time getting an engine out."

long-service employees had paid little attention to the precise position of their names on the seniority rosters and errors had crept in. Consequently in the summer of 1934 the management and the unions decided to throw open the rosters to revision for a period of 60 days. During this period over 500 cases were settled.[25]

On the Canadian National the co-operative plan suffered to some extent during the depression from its association in the minds of the employees with the so-called "unit system." This was a plan for measuring output by assigning unit values to each operation performed in repairing equipment. When the management consented to abolishing the bonus system in certain shops, it took the position that it must have a way of measuring the output of the shops. As part of the general policy of co-operation, the unions assisted the management in installing the unit system. This system naturally tended to increase shop efficiency because each superintendent knew whether his costs were above or below those of other shops. The shop management with the highest cost per unit struggled to get out of that position. Some of the men felt that the unit system had led to speeding up and that it increased the number of layoffs.[26]

Although the depression created difficulties for the co-operative plan, it tended in several important ways to strengthen it. The very difficulties of the times made both sides appreciate the opportunity of meeting together regularly to discuss mutual problems. At some points on the Baltimore and Ohio the local committees handled

[25] See p. 450, note 18, for discussion of the restoration at this time of the original seniority status of the strikers of 1922.
[26] Union officials agree that while labor efficiency was increased, there was no real speeding. One of the leaders of the machinists said that an improvement in labor efficiency in the Canadian National shops had to come because those shops had not measured up to the Canadian Pacific. He added that although labor efficiency had improved somewhat, it was, in his judgment, still below the Canadian Pacific, and that the men were still working "fairly comfortably."

The management of the Canadian National states that the unit system aided the men by giving the management reliable evidence that labor efficiency was being maintained right through the depression. Without that measuring stick, the management says, it would have concluded that the men were restricting output because with smaller forces repair jobs took longer to finish. With definite evidence that the efficiency was holding up, the management felt justified in going farther than it would otherwise have done in bringing work into the shops and in trying to find work for them to do on capital account. Hence the management believes that the unit system helped the men gain employment.

relief for unemployed shopmen. The employment situation and employment prospects were naturally of unusual interest during the depression. The meetings gave the men a chance to press for more work, to suggest opportunities for doing work in the company shops instead of contracting it out, and to hear the management discuss the business outlook. Suggestions for doing company work in the company shops in the Canadian National increased from 24 in 1929 to 31 in 1932. The managements on their side felt that their efforts to provide the maximum possible employment were not always fully understood by the men. Hence they welcomed the opportunity presented by the meetings, especially system meetings, to describe their efforts, explain their difficulties, and discuss their plans. As a matter of fact, the very severity of the drop in employment made many of the men more appreciative of the efforts of the management to provide work.[27] Naturally this helped strengthen the men's interest in the co-operative plan.

In many other ways the co-operative plan proved adaptable to conditions of the depression, and its successful functioning under these conditions strengthened it. Although the small budgets of the companies discouraged suggestions for the purchase of new equipment, the co-operative meetings were useful in bringing about transfers of equipment to points where it would be most useful. The co-operative meetings gave the men a chance to question economy measures and to point out that some of them were not economy measures at all. At one point on the Baltimore and Ohio, for example, where the management had shut down a power plant and substituted a locomotive to furnish power, the men convinced the management that it would be more economical to use the power plant.

On the Canadian National in particular the unions were quick to see that the co-operative plan offered them a way of rendering some service to their members during a period when the unions

[27] A leader of the Canadian railwaymen said: "The thinking man realizes that the co-operative plan has meant more work in the shops. He knows that the management has made a determined effort to find work." Another Canadian leader, while bewailing the fact that the shops were then operating only sixteen days a month, said: "Some of us feel that without the co-operative plan we would not even be getting sixteen days."

were mainly engaged in making concessions. When they found their members losing jobs and working reduced hours at reduced pay, they endeavored through the co-operative plan to achieve some compensating advantages in better shop conditions. The number of suggestions pertaining to the condition of shops and grounds increased from 289 in 1929 to 472 in 1931. In 1932, however, it dropped to 296—probably because the most obvious things had been done. On the Baltimore and Ohio the unions were somewhat less aggressive in using the co-operative meetings to help their members. Nevertheless the plan did give them a chance to improve many shop conditions and to deal with such ever-present matters as locomotive pits in need of deepening and resurfacing and inspection tracks in need of better drainage.

On the Canadian National the difficulties of the depression led to a general re-examination of the purposes of the co-operative plan and of the ways in which it could be made useful. This was advantageous to both sides. The drop in the number of labor-saving suggestions from the men led the leaders of the union to point out at the annual meeting in 1933 that the value of the local meetings did not consist solely in the suggestions which the employees might offer. The meetings also gave the shop superintendents an opportunity to discuss with the men matters of mutual interest—conservation of materials, reduction in the number of engine failures, quality of workmanship, etc. Most important of all perhaps was the fact that the depression gave the managements and the unions opportunity to demonstrate that the co-operative plan could survive a depression of unusual duration and severity. Its very success in doing this was a source of strength to the plan after the depression was over.

SUMMARY

Union-management co-operation on the railroads has had its ups and downs. The number of obstacles that it has had to overcome is impressive. At the beginning its purpose was not clearly understood by a large part of the men and supervisors. It has suffered from the fact that a few officials on both sides were either indifferent to it or opposed to it, and it has also suffered from personal incompatibilities, from factional fights between unions and in unions, from negotiations which have temporarily strained relations between the unions and management, and finally from the depression. It is amazing that in spite of all these obstacles, the plan has survived on two of the principal roads which experimented with it.

Experience on the railroads seems to demonstrate clearly that whether the plan succeeds or fails depends, above everything else, upon how strongly it is supported by top management and by the principal leaders of the unions. There is no substitute for this support. If it is there, most obstacles will be overcome. Shop superintendents and master mechanics, however, will not display much interest in the plan if their superiors are not interested in it. If the local management is indifferent or hostile, it is virtually impossible to maintain interest among the union members of the committee. Equally important is the interest of the top leaders of the unions. Unless they give strong support to the plan as a matter of union policy, the interest of the local leaders is likely to lag. All of this amounts to saying that the success of the co-operative plan is fundamentally a matter of administration and that the effectiveness with which administrative policies are carried out depends, above everything else, upon the vigor and determination with which they are supported by top management and union leaders.

CHAPTER XVII

CO-OPERATIVE POLICY OF THE AMALGAMATED CLOTHING WORKERS

Co-operation with employers to help them meet the competition of non-union plants became a definite part of the policy of the Amalgamated Clothing Workers in 1924. At the peak of the postwar boom the union controlled about 50 per cent of the output of men's clothing. It was strongest in Chicago and Rochester, which manufactured mainly medium-grade and high-grade clothing. It was also strong (but less so) in New York and Baltimore, which in the main produced cheap clothing and boys' suits. The principal non-union centers were Cincinnati, Cleveland, and Philadelphia. There were also important non-union manufacturers in St. Louis and Baltimore. Labor costs in the clothing industry are about 30 per cent of the cost of the product, and wage rates in the union markets in the early twenties were 25 to 50 per cent above the non-union.[1]

During the war and postwar boom, when the demand for clothing was unusually brisk, the union shops had no difficulty in getting business in competition with the non-union. Following the depression of 1921, however, the union shops experienced great difficulty in holding their own. They suffered partly from high labor costs and partly from a change in buying habits which led the public to purchase more cheap suits and fewer high-quality and medium-

---

[1] In 1924 the U. S. Bureau of Labor Statistics found that average hourly earnings of clothing workers in the three principal union markets were: New York, 88.9 cents; Chicago, 86.9 cents; Rochester, 67.2 cents. In the other markets, at this time predominantly non-union, average earnings were: Baltimore, 58.5 cents; Boston, 69.5 cents; Cincinnati, 63.7 cents; eastern Pennsylvania, 36.8 cents; Philadelphia, 61.2 cents. (*Wages and Hours of Labor in the Men's Clothing Industry, 1911 to 1924*, Bulletin No. 387, p. 11.) Of course, the quality of the labor employed in the several markets was not the same. In the non-union markets, where the output was predominantly cheap clothing, most of the operations were machine work requiring less experienced help. But the great difference in production costs (and hence in selling prices) helped produce the shift in the buying habits of the country.

quality suits. Union strength was mainly in shops producing medium-quality and high-quality clothing. The union markets never completely recovered from the depression. Although total employment in the men's clothing industry increased from 165,206 in 1921 to 194,820 in 1923, the number of workers in Chicago remained substantially stationary (decreasing slightly from 29,220 to 29,111), and the number in Rochester dropped from 12,370 to 10,983. New York alone among the union markets had a satisfactory increase—from 32,571 in 1921 to 38,100 in 1923. But New York was in the main a cheap clothing market and one in which union control was far from perfect. Non-union markets, on the other hand, were flourishing. Employment in Philadelphia increased from 8,263 in 1921 to 9,792 in 1923; Cleveland from 3,485 to 4,816; Cincinnati from 5,925 to 7,034; Buffalo from 1,847 to 2,083; and St. Louis from 3,672 to 4,785.[2]

After 1923 the situation of the union shops became worse. A temporary recovery of the clothing business late in 1922 and early in 1923 was followed by a severe slump from which employment in the industry did not recover. The shift of the public from best-quality and medium-quality to cheap suits continued. In fact, between 1923 and 1926 employment in the industry dropped 15.7 per cent.[3] Under these circumstances the union shops found greater difficulty than ever in holding their own. The Chicago market, where the union was strongest, was particularly hard hit. On May 1, 1923, there were 413 union firms employing about 27,000 persons; in December 1926, 206 union firms and 19,000 employees.[4] Not all of this drop of employment in union plants in Chicago was

[2] U. S. Bureau of Labor Statistics, *Wages and Hours of Labor in the Men's Clothing Industry, 1911 to 1924*, Bulletin No. 387, p. 23, and *Wages and Hours of Labor in the Men's Clothing Industry, 1911 to 1926*, Bulletin No. 435, p. 27.

[3] U. S. Bureau of Labor Statistics, *Wages and Hours of Labor in the Men's Clothing Industry, 1911 to 1928*, Bulletin No. 503, p. 28.

[4] The greatest decrease occurred among the contractors. These dropped from 263 employing 6,000 workers in May 1923 to 129 employing 3,000 workers in December 1926. But even among the larger firms belonging to the employers' association there was a considerable decrease—from 61 with 17,000 employees in May 1923, to 36 with 14,500 employees in December 1926. These figures are derived from the records of the unemployment insurance scheme introduced into the Chicago market in 1923. Among the larger Chicago houses which went out of business were Ederheimer Stein, employing about 1,000 people, and Kuh, Nathan, and Fisher, employing about the same number.

a result of their going out of business. A few plants moved to other cities and became non-union.[5] These cases, of course, were a particularly serious loss to the union, because they produced both a drop in union employment and a rise in non-union.

During the depression of 1920-21 the union accepted general wage reductions in order to help union employers compete with non-union and in some cases gave special assistance to employers. For example, in 1921 the large firm of Henry Sonneborn and Company in Baltimore was close to liquidation. Had it shut down it would have thrown 2,000 union members out of work. Drastic reorganization of the shop was effected for the purpose of keeping the firm in business. The executive board of the union reported:

> Our organization has made extraordinary efforts to assist in keeping the firm in business, knowing well that our members thrown out of work by the shutdown of Sonneborn would be thrown on an over-stocked labor market, and would be forced to remain idle for months.[6]

The severe slump in the clothing business, which began about the middle of 1923, led the Chicago manufacturers in the spring of 1924 to demand a substantial reduction in wages. The union refused to concede the reduction, but it was this demand that first made the union leaders realize the seriousness of the problem of non-union competition and the need for the union's acting vigorously and wisely to protect the jobs of its members. From the recognition of this need sprang the policy, first applied systematically in 1924, of assisting union employers to reduce costs.

To quote the words of the union:

> . . . the wage negotiations of 1924 were rapidly converted into a survey of the industry, with a view to discovering all possible sources of saving and means of increasing employment. Prolonged conferences were had with individual firms in which labor costs, overhead, sales methods, shop organization were all discussed and analyzed. The union made suggestions and took under consideration proposals from the employers. The

---

[5] For example, Charles Kaufman and Co., employing about 1,500, moved to Philadelphia, where it became non-union. Another smaller house, Scheyer and Co., employing about 250, also went to Philadelphia and became non-union. Grantert and Rothschild moved to Waukegan, Ill., and became non-union. Other houses attempted to leave the market and to operate with non-union help, but failed.

[6] Amalgamated Clothing Workers of America, *Report of the General Executive Board to the Eighth Biennial Convention*, p. 42.

technically trained deputies of the union worked with the management in devising more economical methods of production; whole new shops, with this effective co-operation of the union, were quickly organized and put into operation without friction and high expense of promotion.[7]

The policy by which the Amalgamated sought to maintain the employment of its members against the competition of non-union plants had five principal parts:

1. The avoidance of strikes in union plants.

2. An attempt to organize non-union plants.

3. Temporary wage concessions on all rates and permanent concessions on specific rates.

4. Extension and enforcement of wage payment by results.

5. Abandonment of restrictive rules and policies which tended to raise the operating costs of employers and were of benefit to only small parts of the union membership.

6. Suggestions and direct assistance to employers with the aim of improving the design of garments, reducing cost of production, and improving quality.

The policy of the Amalgamated with respect to the avoidance of strikes and the organization of non-union plants requires no extended discussion. The leaders of the union realized clearly that strikes would be peculiarly disastrous to union employers because they would create an opportunity for the non-union plants to expand and the union plants would experience great difficulty in regaining their markets. Therefore, the union leaders endeavored to avoid strikes (excepting organizing strikes) and they succeeded to a remarkable extent. In fact the two principal strikes of the decade (outside of organizing strikes), in the International Tailoring Company in Chicago and New York and the Adler Company in Milwaukee, were forced upon the union.

For some years the union had relatively little success in organizing non-union plants. Until the end of the twenties its most important gains were in the Cincinnati market, where the Nash Company was organized in 1924. Not until 1929 did the union succeed in organizing the important Philadelphia market. The organ-

[7] Amalgamated Clothing Workers of America, *Report of the General Executive Board and Proceedings of the Seventh Biennial Convention, 1924-26,* p. 13.

izing efforts of the union, however, may have influenced employers temporarily to raise wages in non-union markets. At any rate, there was some upward movement of hourly earnings in such important non-union territories as Philadelphia and eastern Pennsylvania between 1924 and 1926.[8] This, of course, was helpful to union employers in meeting the competition of non-union markets. After 1926, however, wages in the principal non-union markets dropped.

Aside from these two lines of policy, the major efforts of the union were directed toward assisting its employers to reduce costs.

TEMPORARY OR LIMITED WAGE CONCESSIONS

One of the objectives of the union policy was to prevent wage cuts. Indeed a disposition on the part of the union to accept wage cuts for the purpose of keeping employers in business might easily have had dangerous consequences, for it might have become a method by which the workers were called upon to subsidize incompetent and inefficient managements. Nevertheless, the union recognized that under certain circumstances wage reductions should be made. The wage cuts which the union was willing to accept fell into three principal classes:

1. In some cases firms were urgently in need of immediate relief from competitive pressure. Reductions of costs through improvements in efficiency take time. In a small number of such cases the union consented to temporary general reductions in wages. It was understood that the old rates would be restored as soon as the finances of the firm permitted it.

2. In every piecework shop there are bound to be some rates which are out of line and which yield earnings disproportionate to the skill of the job—sometimes too high and sometimes too low. It had been the policy of the union to resist cuts in rates that were too high and to trade reductions in these rates for increases in rates that had proved to be too low. Now, in order to help union employers find ways of cutting their costs, it modified its attitude toward the high rates. It came to regard them as special privileges accruing to a very few members of the union by which these members profited at the expense of the other members, and hence was willing to accept cuts in such rates.

[8] See the table on p. 527.

3. Recognition by the union that it must help its employers compete with non-union employers led to a marked change in the policy of the union in setting new piece rates. The traditional policy of the union had been to get all that it could in each case. This may not have been precisely the policy approved by the national administration, but it was the policy practiced by local shop committees and business agents. Some of the local business agents were such clever bargainers that they were often able to secure rates which enabled the workers on new lines to earn far more than other workers of equal speed and skill. Thus the cleverness of the best business agents was constantly leading to the creation of new "peak" rates. A well-established part of the bargaining process was for the union shop committee or business agent to keep the rates on new operations unsettled as long as possible. This held back production and raised costs because the workers on unsettled operations naturally restricted their output; they knew that if they produced to capacity they would cause the rate on the new job to be set lower. Delaying the settlement of new rates, therefore, was a method of compelling the employer to consent to a high rate.

When the union recognized that peak rates merely created privileges for a few workers which impaired the employer's ability to give employment to other members of the union, it instructed its business agents to avoid dragging out the settlement of rate cases, to cease attempting to extract the last possible cent or fraction of a cent, and to be content with settlements which would enable the workers, without undue speeding, to earn their customary wages. One result of the new policy was that rate cases, which had formerly come before the umpires in the industry in considerable numbers, virtually disappeared from the dockets of the umpires.

Shifts in the demand for clothing led many houses to introduce new and cheaper lines. These necessitated new piece rates, since the quality of work required was inferior to that on the old lines and, in some respects, changes in the construction of the garments altered the operations. On these new lines the union accepted rates which were substantially below the corresponding rates in the old lines. Technically these new rates were not wage reductions because they represented rates on new jobs rather than cuts in existing rates. Actually the new rates must be regarded as cuts because in proportion to the amount of work in the operations they were lower than the old rates. It was part of the policy of the union to encourage manufacturers to introduce new lines by making very favorable piece prices on the new operations. In a number of instances the union agreed with the employer on a proper piece-rate cost for the entire garment and then assumed the responsibility of distributing this cost among the various operations.

While willing to make substantial concessions in order to encourage employers to put in new and cheaper lines, the union was concerned that the new rates should not reduce the weekly earnings of the workers. As a matter of fact, it was usually possible for the workers on the new lines at the new rates to earn more than the workers on the old lines, because, under the equal-division-of-work rule enforced by the union, the size of the sections on the old lines had not been reduced in proportion to the drop in business, and hence the sections were overmanned. The union was careful not to permit more workers to be transferred to the new sections than could be kept busy there. The union also insisted that the workers be aided in increasing their earnings by favorable operating conditions and methods. For example, it insisted that the work come through in larger lots and that every effort be made to maintain a steady flow of work.

In brief, the position of the union was that it was willing to give the managements rates which meant lower labor costs, provided the managements were willing to co-operate wholeheartedly to make these low rates yield larger earnings than the old rates. Thanks to the better flow of work and favorable operating conditions, the workers on the new lines were able to earn somewhat more than those on the old lines, in spite of the lower piece rates.

EXTENSION AND ENFORCEMENT OF PAYMENT BY RESULTS

One of the first steps which the union took to help employers reduce costs was to extend the use of payment by results, in the form of either piecework or standards of production. Most of the workers who were paid on a time basis were opposed to payment by results—partly because they feared that it would lead to overspeeding and partly because they feared that it would reduce employment. As early as the depression of 1921, before the union fully realized the competitive problem of the union manufacturers, it undertook to extend the use of piecework in the Rochester market. In the New York market, the abuses of subcontracting had aroused among the workers such intense prejudice against payment by results that the union was compelled to proceed slowly. It began by introducing standards of production, but within five years this method of payment in New York had been replaced by piecework.

In Chicago, the union in 1921 had accepted standards of production in the cutting rooms, despite strong opposition from the cutters' local. It had also agreed to the introduction of standards in the trimming department, but these standards had not been put into effect. When the union became clearly aware of the problem of helping union manufacturers compete with non-union, it introduced standards into the trimming rooms. Standards of production in the cutting rooms were by no means working satisfactorily. These standards provided for five rates of pay, the rate received by each cutter depending upon his output. The opposition of the cutters to the system expressed itself in some shops in the form of organized restriction of output. It was common practice in the Chicago market for cutters to limit their output to the amount which would yield them the C rate of pay—this being the middle rate. In some shops practically no cutters produced enough to entitle them to the A or B rates of pay—the two highest rates. The tendency of the cutters to restrict output was reinforced (1) by the general shrinkage in the clothing business and the shift of demand to cheaper grades of suits, because both of these meant less work for the cutters, and (2) by the fact that, although cutters who increased their production sufficiently did receive increases in their hourly rates, these increases were not proportionate to the increase in their production.

The national union had not actively supported the cutters in their restriction of output, but it had pursued a policy which encouraged restriction. The system of standards of production provided that the cutters were to be reclassified at five-week intervals and that cutters who had failed to maintain for a two-week period the output required by their rate of pay were to be reduced to a lower-paying classification. These periods of reclassification were times of more or less commotion in the shop, encouraged to a certain extent by the union deputies (business agents) who undertook to protect cutters against being reduced by urging special reasons why they had been unable to maintain their production.

The union now changed its policy and showed little disposition to contest reductions unless there was a clear reason for doing so. Furthermore, the union now threw its influence definitely against restriction of output by the cutters. Although the process of breaking down the practice was slow, in most shops the union was successful. In one shop, where restriction was especially flagrant and the cutters refused to abandon it, the union penalized them by consenting to an increase in the standard. The cutters also limited production by various rules governing "the height of lay" and the mixing of fabrics in cutting. In some shops this form of restriction lasted for a number of years and in the important shop of Hart, Schaffner, and Marx the last of the important restrictions in the cutting room were not eliminated until 1937.[9]

One important source of waste occurred in bushelling.[10] It had been customary to have the bushellers scattered around the shop, one being attached to each section or group of sections; and because their work was not repetitive, they were paid by the hour. It was customary for them to keep busy by working slowly enough so that they never would run out of something to do. Bushelling costs were especially high in the special order houses where in some cases they ran over 10 per cent of the direct labor cost. The union proposed that the bushellers be placed on piecework and concentrated at one point in the shops where they could be easily supervised. This was done, with a reduction in some cases of 60 per cent in the number of bushellers required.

One of the union rules which, though equitable in principle, had been abused in administration, was the "hour-work" rule. This rule required that pieceworkers under certain circumstances be paid on an hourly basis but at a rate determined by their average piece-

---

[9] See pp. 524-25.
[10] Bushelling consists of doing special repair operations where the work has not been properly performed by the regular operator. The busheller must be able to do any sewing operation on the garment—hence, he must be an all-round tailor.

rate earnings. Naturally this was expensive to the firms because when working by the hour, employees do not ordinarily produce as much as when working by the piece. The necessity for hour work arises in a number of ways. If a new operation is introduced or a radical change made in an old one, the worker may be unable to make his regular piece-rate earnings until he becomes used to the new work. Sometimes it is necessary to transfer a worker temporarily from his regular job to another one with which he may not be familiar.

Since piecework earnings without the necessity of maintaining a piecework pace were attractive to the workers, they demanded hour work whenever a case could be made for it and insisted that they be paid hour work for longer periods than was essential.[11] When the union embarked on the policy of helping union employers to reduce their costs, it undertook to prevent the abuse of hour work. It refused to support its members in the demand for hour work except where there was a clear justification for it and refused to demand it for longer periods than were really needed.

ABANDONMENT OF RESTRICTIVE RULES AND CUSTOMS

When the union recognized that it must help employers reduce their costs, one of the most obvious steps for it to take was to get rid of rules and practices which were uneconomic and burdensome to employers and were beneficial only to small groups of workers. The union took the position that such rules conferred special privileges upon a few of its members at the expense of the other members whose employment suffered from the high costs of the union shops, and that these special privileges must be sacrificed to help the employment of the many. Had the Amalgamated been a craft union instead of an industrial union, it would perhaps have been more reluctant to give up privileges, because in a craft union all members of the trade are likely to benefit from a make-work rule. Since the union included virtually all workers in the plant, most of the members did not benefit from rules and customs which meant extra work or extra compensation for small groups. Hence it was politically

---

[11] During the boom period, when profits were large, the firms did not particularly object to hour work. As a result, hour work in a few cases amounted to 2 or 3 per cent of the total pay roll.

possible for the union (sometimes in the face of rigorous minority opposition) to take a stand in favor of abolishing privileges.[12]

An example of a custom which gave a special privilege to small groups of employees at the expense of the general good was the rule prevailing in the special order houses in the Chicago market which required the employer to pay each cutter called to work on Monday morning an entire week's salary. The employer, of course, could not tell very definitely how many orders would come in during the week, and, therefore, how many cutters he would need. The obvious result was that the firms would sometimes call more cutters than were needed and would be compelled to pay men for doing nothing. This practice was gradually abandoned.

The union was also led to modify its policy with respect to the introduction of labor-saving devices. The policy had been to give manufacturers freedom to introduce new machines provided the machine did not reduce the earnings of the workers, and clauses to this effect had been embodied in the union's agreements. This rule did not necessarily mean that the rates on the new machine jobs must be set high enough to yield as much as the rates on the old jobs, because the requirement that the earnings of the workers should not be reduced might be met by transferring the workers to other jobs which paid as much as the jobs destroyed by the machine. As a matter of adminstrative practice, however, the union had attempted to get rates on new machine jobs set high enough to yield as large earnings as the rates on the old hand jobs. The union was disposed to take this stand even in cases where the machine greatly reduced the skill required.[13]

When the union adopted the policy of helping its employers compete with non-union plants, it abandoned the position that new jobs must yield as much as the old ones. It now permitted the rates on new machines to be set in accordance with the skill of the operation and it limited itself to demanding that workers displaced by

---

[12] Note that the traditional policy of the union had been to create privileges for more and more small groups. The leaders had now come to see the dangers inherent in this policy in the long run.

[13] This was true of seam-piping machines and canvas-padding machines, each of which could be operated by relatively unskilled workers. When done by hand, these operations require considerable skill.

machines be transferred to other jobs which paid equally well. It went out of its way to assist employers in finding places to which the displaced men might be transferred and, instead of making it difficult for employers to make the transfer, it helped them to do it. The union did not even stand inflexibly for the rule that the new job must pay as much as the old. To give such complete protection to the workers displaced by machines at a time when the high costs of union manufacturers were causing them to lose markets would amount to treating them as a privileged class whose earnings were being maintained at the expense of employment of other workers in union plants. Hence the union did not hesitate to permit employers, when necessary, to introduce machines under circumstances which meant an immediate loss in earnings not only to the displaced workers but to other workers as well.[14] For example, the union permitted employers to introduce machines when there were no jobs for the displaced workers and when in consequence it was necessary to give them work by overcrowding sections—to the detriment, of course, of the earnings of everyone in the section.

Another traditional policy of the union had been to fight virtually all cases in which employers sought to discharge workers. There are many twilight zone cases in which it is doubtful whether the worker's fault merits such a severe penalty as discharge. Strong opposition on the part of the union to discharges undoubtedly tends to reduce the number and therefore to add to the worker's security of employment. It also tends, however, to reduce management's control in the shop and therefore to impair efficiency and discipline. When the union realized the competitive difficulties of the union employers, it modified its rigid policy toward discharges. This modification is reflected in the change made in the discharge clause in the Chicago agreement in 1925. The union agreed that it would bring discharge cases for review before the umpire only if, after investigation of the case, it decided that the discharge was clearly unjustified. Obviously, such a clause might in practice have meant little or nothing. As a matter of fact, the union lived up to the

[14] To the extent that the employer's lower costs enabled him to give more employment, the earnings of the workers would not be reduced. So the ultimate result would not necessarily be a drop in the workers' earnings.

spirit of the clause and the number of discharge cases coming before the umpire dropped materially.

In consenting to change its policy the union was undoubtedly influenced by the fact that the shrinkage of employment in union markets caused many competent union members to be out of work. The union took the position that so long as there were more men than places, the jobs might as well go to the men who were most competent to fill them. In fact, the union realized that more men were attached to the industry than could expect to find permanent employment in it. Hence it was a question of who should remain in the industry and who should be forced out. The union took the position that it was in the interest of the workers, the employers, and the union that the best men be retained and the least competent forced out.

In most parts of the industry the union's new policy with respect to discharges had no substantial effect upon efficiency and, therefore, upon the ability of union employers to compete. In a few departments, however, the effect on efficiency was important. The system of standards of production that was introduced into the Chicago trimming rooms provided five rates of pay depending upon the output of the workers. It also provided that the workers must receive at least the minimum rate of pay no matter how little they produced. This, however, did not mean that employers might not discharge workers who failed frequently to produce a minimum amount. Under other circumstances the union might have done its best to find excuses for low producers and to protect them from discharge. But since there were more trimmers than the industry needed, the union allowed employers considerable freedom in getting rid of low producers.

One of the operations that caused considerable trouble to some employers was that of "off-pressing." This is the last pressing which a suit gets before going to the dealer and has much to do with its shape and appearance. The quality of the work done by the off-pressers is difficult to judge and to control. In order to control the quality of off-pressing, it is customary for employers to set a *maximum* limit upon the number of coats which a worker presses in a day. Cases in which employers discharged off-pressers for incompetency or poor workmanship had always been particularly difficult to settle because standards of quality in pressing are indefinite. The change in the union's attitude toward discharge cases was therefore of great assistance to employers in handling off-pressing and it enabled a number of firms substantially to increase the proportion of their off-pressers who were able regularly to press the maximum number permitted.

DIRECT ASSISTANCE TO EMPLOYERS IN REDUCING COSTS AND IMPROVING QUALITY

The abandonment of restrictive rules and policies, helpful as it was, fell far short of giving union employers all the reductions in costs which they needed in order to hold their own with non-union competitors. It was necessary for the union to give some employers more direct and positive assistance in cutting costs and improving quality. Particularly noteworthy is the clearness with which the union leaders recognized this fact and the vigor and efficiency with which they acted on it.

The union had a staff of business agents (usually known as deputies) who were principally engaged in handling piece-rate cases, discharges, and other disputes which arose out of shop operations. The deputies were specialized, some handling coat shops, some cutting rooms, some pressing departments. In the course of their daily work, the deputies acquired an intimate knowledge of operations and production methods in the various shops. In fact, since the work of the deputies took them to all shops in a market, they had a better opportunity to acquire familiarity with methods and practices of clothing manufacturing than anyone else in the business. Equally important, they knew intimately the people in the industry and the difficulties of getting different groups to consent to changes in methods of work. It is obvious that the experience of the deputies made them the logical persons through whom the union could help employers improve their methods and reduce costs. These men, therefore, became the key men in the administration of the union's policy.

Not all of the deputies, of course, were equally good in their understanding of shop practices and in their ability to detect opportunities for improvements. The union leadership, therefore, tended to concentrate the responsibility of improving the efficiency in union shops among those deputies who showed unusual proficiency in this work. In fact, men in some markets, such as Chicago, who had become particularly expert in shop reorganizations, were transferred temporarily to other markets to reorganize certain shops. In this way the union gradually developed a group of experts capable of giving employers an industrial engineering service.[15]

Although the Amalgamated clearly recognized the necessity of helping union employers compete with non-union, it also recognized the danger of "pauperizing" them and of weakening their spirit of initiative, enterprise, and self-reliance. It realized that there was danger that every employer who got into difficulties might expect labor to make sacrifices to get him out. Consequently, the position of the union was that it would help employers who were willing to help themselves, that it would, if necessary, ask the workers to make temporary sacrifices for the purpose of keeping the employer in business, but that it would expect the employer to find ways of making substantial and more permanent reductions in expenses by cutting supervisory staffs, by reducing the amount of space used, or by other methods. In some cases employers were reluctant to make these changes.[16]

The union leaders were well aware that in helping union em-

---

[15] The comment of the general executive board of the union on this policy is of interest: ". . . it has been the policy of the organization to develop among its officers a larger number skilled in the technical and business problems of the industry. It is now possible to find among our local officers more and more men who have added greatly to the strength of the union and to the health of the industry through the application of their practical knowledge of shop management, in most of its many aspects." Amalgamated Clothing Workers of America, *Report of the General Executive Board to the Eighth Biennial Convention 1926-28,* p. 12.

[16] One firm had three coat shops and five contract shops. Often the people in the outside shops had to wait for work from the main plant where the cutting was done. The union was anxious to have these outside shops abolished, and this was done. An additional saving came from combining the three coat shops into one. This eliminated a number of foremen and floor girls. Another firm complained that it was handicapped by high costs. The union suggested that the firm give up one of its three floors, which was done. The vest and pants shops were also combined under one foreman. In another case the space was reduced from nine floors to four. A business of $4,500,000 had been done on the nine floors and a business of $4,000,000 was done on the four. In all, a saving of $300,000 in overhead was accomplished in this case.

ployers meet non-union competition they might be asking workers to make sacrifices that would subsidize inefficient management. The union, therefore, took the position that the management must be competent. In some cases where the management was inefficient, the union insisted on changes. When a tailoring company in Cincinnati was reorganized with the co-operation of the union, the business agent told the firm that it would have to discharge the foreman in the pants shop. This was done, and he was replaced with a man from Chicago recommended by the union.

When employers were guaranteed a definite piece-rate cost on an entire garment, the union made it plain that its guarantee presupposed a certain managerial efficiency. The union was careful to point out that the low piece rates to which it consented in many cases must yield a certain amount per week. Whether they did or not would depend in large part upon the quality of the management. Since the union could not assume responsibility for the quality of the management, it could not make unconditional promises in regard to labor costs; if the management failed to provide a satisfactory flow of work and failed to maintain equipment in proper condition, the union would be compelled to ask for higher piece rates.

SOME ACCOMPLISHMENTS OF THE UNION'S CO-OPERATION

The following scattered examples from many hundreds handled by union deputies illustrate the sort of help which the union has been able to give employers in reducing costs and improving quality:

Each pair of trousers has a strip of canvas around the top between the lining and the goods. It had been the custom in one shop to sew the canvas on after the trousers had been completed. This was done by the man who made the corner—a high-priced, highly skilled operator. The deputy suggested that the canvas could be sewed on to the waistband before it was attached to the rest of the trousers. This method made the operation a simple one, almost a beginner's operation. Instead of paying a skilled operator about 2¼ cents to sew on the canvas, the firm paid a relatively unskilled girl about ¾ of a cent.

The union deputies were often able to suggest ways of rearranging work so as to eliminate or combine operations. For example, a special order house had been basting in, as a separate operation, the piece of wigan between the goods and lining of the vest which gives body to the button holes. The union's deputy suggested that the wigan be sewed in place by the girl who tacked the pockets. A small amount was added to the price of her job to cover this extra work and the operation of basting was eliminated.

In some plants there was urgent need to improve the quality of the work and the union gave valuable assistance in accomplishing this. In the cutting room of a large middle western plant the work was divided between markers, who marked out the job, and choppers, who cut out the work. Marking required more skill than cutting and the markers earned more than the choppers. In fact, the choppers were paid such a low rate that they did hasty, poor work in an attempt to make money. The union wished to combine the two operations in order to improve the quality of the cutting. The markers were opposed because the combined rate would yield lower earnings than the rate on marking. The change was made, however, and as a result the number of returns because of mistakes in cutting was greatly reduced.[17]

Perhaps the best way of showing how the union was able to assist employers to reduce costs and improve the quality of production, and also of showing why the co-operation of the union was advantageous to its members, is to describe briefly what the union did for certain firms.

A large special order house in the Middle West had been specializing on high-grade suits and for several years had not been making money—in fact, had lost several hundred thousand dollars. There was danger that the chief owner would retire and that the firm would be liquidated unless it could be put on a money-making basis. It had been selling three lines of clothing: $30, $32, and $34. It had been losing money on the $30 line, but it had been buying only a small amount of woolens for the cheaper goods and refusing orders as the stock of woolens had been exhausted—

---

[17] The opposition of the markers to the change was considerably reduced by the argument that the cutters would eventually learn to become markers and that the craft would become overcrowded.

in other words, it was using the cheaper lines as bait for the more expensive.

The shift of public demand to cheaper suits convinced the union that this firm would have to be helped to enter the cheap clothing field on a paying basis. The cheaper coats had been costing the firm for direct labor about six dollars. It was agreed between the firm and the union that an attempt would be made to produce a coat with substantially the same specifications as the old one for about four dollars.

In order thus to reduce the labor cost, it was decided to start a new shop. The responsibility for organizing the new shop was assumed in large degree by the union. The union deputy picked the workers for the shop and made the piece rates. The management might, of course, have spent considerable money in organizing the shop, but most of this expense was saved. Despite the fact that the rates in the new shop were lower than in the old one, the earnings of the workers were better. It was realized, of course, that in no other way could the new shop be made a success. As the firm's business had shrunk, there had not been enough work to keep its employees busy. Consequently, its people had lost much time waiting for work. When the new shop was started, it was equipped for a production of 100 coats per week and the management was careful to see that the shop got 100 coats to make. As the business in the low-priced line grew, the force in the new shop was increased, but care was taken not to increase it more rapidly than the volume of orders warranted. The result was that the workers in the new shop lost practically no time waiting for work. This explains why, in spite of lower piece rates, earnings were higher than in the old shop.[18]

In 1924 a clothing firm in a middle western city was on the point of bankruptcy and there was danger that it would retire from business. The company employed about 700 workers. As it was the only large clothing factory in the city, the union felt very

[18] Not only did workers not object to being transferred to the new shop, but a number of them requested to be moved. Of course, as the business in the low-priced line expanded and as more and more work was transferred from the old to the new shop, the earnings of the workers in the old shop diminished. Finally, after about a year the old shop was abandoned.

much interested in its future. If it ceased operations, there were no other shops in the city which could absorb the displaced workers. The union suggested that the firm manufacture a cheaper garment, and the management gave the union a free hand to reorganize its shops with this end in view. The union brought several business agents from Chicago who were experienced in this work. During the next eight months they completely reorganized the coat shop and made radical changes in the pants and vest shops.

In the city of Cincinnati, the union was asked to help reorganize the shop of a small firm which had been losing money for a number of years. The workers had only recently joined the union. Their earnings were low, but the firm felt unable to pay more as long as it was losing money. The owners asked the union to make a survey of the shop and to suggest methods of reducing costs and increasing output. The union brought down three of its expert business agents from Chicago—one to reorganize the coat shop, the second the vest shop, and the third the pants shop. The local manager of the union, a cutter by trade, assumed responsibility for the cutting room.

The union's investigations showed that the flow of work was highly irregular, that there was much unnecessary handling of goods, that there was a lack of proper machinery and equipment, and that the methods of constructing the garments were unnecessarily complicated and laborious. Important changes were made in the construction of the garment, the layout and removing of the work, and the shop equipment. It was found that the different sections of the force were not properly balanced: some had too much work and others not enough. Workers were, therefore, shifted in order to facilitate the flow of work. The old practice had been to require the workers to stay in the factory whether they had work or not. The union insisted that they be permitted to go home when they ran out of work. This compelled the production executives to watch the flow of work carefully and take pains that no section ran out of work.

Of the 187 employees in the operating department, only 92 were regularly working piecework. A schedule of wages in the shop provided for the payment of 30 operations by the piece, but only 20 were regularly paid in this way. The union recommended that all employees be placed on piecework, and with its co-operation this was done.

Many antiquated methods of performing operations were discovered and changed. The workers on an operation in the pants shop which cost the firm about 20 cents were making poor wages. By changing the method, the earnings of these workers were increased from $12 to $14 per week and the cost of the operation to the firm was reduced approximately one-half. The pressing had been done by hand. The union suggested that it be done by machine and six pressing machines were installed.

The wages of the cutters were low in comparison with the rates paid in other markets, but cutting costs were high. The union insisted that the wages of cutters be increased five dollars a week. The union had the order blanks standardized and simplified so that the cutters could read their instructions more easily. The pattern racks had been at one end of the room so that it was necessary for some cutters to walk nearly half a block to get their patterns. The shapers, which give the cutter the shape of the front and the lapel, had been at another spot. The patterns and the shapers were put together in the center of the room. Improvements in the patterns were made, to increase the output of the cutters.[19]

Some of the union executives who had been in the shop many years resented the changes in time-honored methods suggested by the business agents and it was necessary to discharge several of them or let them resign.

Thus by changing the construction of the garment, the layout of the work, the method of wage payment, methods of work, the equipment of the shop, and some of the personnel, the union brought down the costs of the firm to the level of its competitors. The union agents from Chicago gave practically their entire time for several months to the reorganization of this factory. All of this was done by the union without expense to the employer.

Perhaps the most noteworthy of all cases of co-operation between

[19] The old patterns were not marked to indicate the place for the top pockets so that it was necessary for the cutter to measure off in order to locate the place for the pockets. It was often necessary for the cutters to make the coats longer or shorter. In order to make it easier for the cutters to measure this, slots were cut in the patterns and a scale placed in the edge of the slot so that the cutter could change the length of the coat simply by moving the pattern up or down.

the Amalgamated and an employer was that of Hart, Schaffner, and Marx in Chicago. This firm had been primarily a producer of medium-priced suits. Its business had suffered from the shift in demand to cheaper suits. By 1924 it became evident to both the management and the union that the firm would have to adjust its business to new market conditions. Accordingly, it was decided to experiment with a cheaper line of suits made to retail for $35. This line was known as the X line. The union agreed to give the firm a definite labor cost on the suit and to assume the responsibility of setting individual piece rates which would keep the labor cost within the agreed limit. This gave the union deputies an incentive to eliminate every unnecessary operation from the manufacture of the suit. The deputies helped the company design the garment and suggested ways of simplifying its construction and of combining operations in its manufacture. The union also agreed to assume a large part of the responsibility for maintaining quality. This enabled the company to use substantially less than the usual number of examiners.

In order to give the company the desired labor cost, it was necessary to set piece rates substantially below the corresponding rates on old lines. At the same time the union wanted to prevent the earnings of the workers from being reduced by the new rates. It was therefore agreed at the outset that the force which was to make the X line would be limited and would be guaranteed a minimum number of weeks' employment per year, and that production would be restricted to 2,000 suits a week. It was believed that the company would regularly sell this number of suits and thus give unusually steady employment to workers on the X line. The opportunity of the workers to maintain their earnings was also increased by the fact that at the outset the X line contained only two models.

In the cutting room it was not possible for the union to guarantee the firm a definite labor cost. The union, however, did give special concessions to make possible substantial reductions in cutting cost. It is possible for a cutter to cut a number of suits at once by piling the fabric. In the cutting room of Hart, Schaffner, and Marx, the union had limited "the height of lay," as it was called, to 12 layers—that is, a cutter might not cut more than 12 suits at once. In the case of the X line, however, the union permitted the height of lay to be increased to 20. It also permitted the piling of mixed fabrics, which previously had been forbidden by trade custom.

The X line met such a favorable response from the public that the agreement between the firm and the union was soon modified to permit production to be increased from 2,000 to 5,000 a week. The response also led to abandonment of the agreement that the workers on the X line would be assured a minimum number of weeks' employment. It was true that the firm, in view of the low piece rates on this line, recognized a moral obligation to make unusually strenuous efforts to reduce the slack seasons as much as possible and to provide the X-line workers with steady employment. As a matter of definite agreement between the firm and the union, however, the obligation to provide steady work no longer existed. Soon the output on the X line represented 70 per cent of the total production of the firm.[20]

The lower costs made possible to Hart, Schaffner, and Marx on the X line were of great assistance to both the company and its employees in adjusting themselves to changes in the clothing market. True, the adjustments were not sufficient to prevent some shrinkage of business in the face of new and powerful competition. Probably they were not as great as would have been in the interest of both the employees and the firm. Nevertheless, they were of importance in preventing an even greater drop in business and employment.

RESULTS OF THE POLICY OF THE AMALGAMATED AND LATER DEVELOPMENTS

In judging the effects of the union's policy of co-operation, one must bear in mind that even the period before the depression, from 1923 to 1929, was one of decline in the men's clothing industry. Between 1923 and 1929, the number of establishments dropped from 4,607 to 4,202, the number of wage earners from 194,820 to 188,069, the value of products from $1,178,714,731 to

---

[20] The great increase in X-line production created a special problem in the cutting department. Since this line was cut under conditions which permitted the cutters to produce far more suits than before, the cutting force, which even in the beginning was larger than necessary, became more excessive than ever. This led to the creation of a fund of $75,000, described on pp. 131-32, to pay 150 cutters $500 each to give up their jobs.

$1,039,554,283, and the value added by manufacture from $593,910,809 to $515,497,589.[21] In the face of declining markets, competition in the industry, always severe, was fiercer than ever. The tables on this and the following two pages showing the percentage of union membership in several years, hourly earnings for several years by cities, and the number of wage earners in the principal markets of the clothing industry for 1923 and 1929 will be found useful in judging the policy of the union.

NUMBER OF WAGE EARNERS IN THE MEN'S CLOTHING INDUSTRY AND MEMBERSHIP OF THE AMALGAMATED CLOTHING WORKERS' UNION, 1923–31[a]

Year	Number of Wage Earners in the Men's Clothing Industry	Membership of the Amalgamated Clothing Workers	Percentage of Wage Earners in the Amalgamated
1923...................	194,820	134,000	68.8
1925...................	174,332	125,000	72.0
1927...................	186,711	129,000	69.1
1929...................	188,069	110,000	58.5
1931...................	155,053	100,000	64.5

[a] U. S. Bureau of Labor Statistics, *Wages and Hours of Labor in the Men's Clothing Industry, 1932*, Bulletin No. 594, p. 17; Leo Wolman, *Ebb and Flow of Trade Unionism*, p. 100. The percentage of membership is slightly overstated because the union membership contains about 7,000 members in Canada.

1. The policy of helping union employers improve methods of production and reduce costs failed to prevent a drop in the proportion of employees belonging to the Amalgamated from 68.8 per cent in 1923 to 58.5 per cent in 1929.

2. It failed to prevent an increase in the wage differentials between most union markets and non-union markets as measured by hourly earnings. For example, between 1926 and 1930 hourly earnings in Chicago rose slightly from 88.6 cents to 90.0 cents, and in Cincinnati from 65.6 to 71.2 cents. In Rochester, the hourly earnings remained virtually unchanged. On the other hand, in Philadelphia, which had only been organized in 1929, hourly earnings in 1930 were 2.8 cents below 1926; in eastern Pennsylvania they were 7.1 cents below 1926; in Cleveland, 5.4 cents below; and in Baltimore, which had become mainly a non-union market, 11.6

---

[21] U. S. Bureau of Labor Statistics, *Wages and Hours of Labor in the Men's Clothing Industry, 1932*, Bulletin No. 594, p. 17.

cents below. Only in New York, of the principal union markets, did hourly earnings drop in proportion to the drop in hourly earnings in the rest of the industry.

3. It failed to prevent substantial decreases of employment in union markets between 1923 and 1929. The decrease was greatest

HOURLY EARNINGS IN THE MEN'S CLOTHING INDUSTRY IN PRINCIPAL
PRODUCING CENTERS, 1924, 1926, 1930, AND 1932[a]
(In cents)

Producing Center	1924	1926	1930	1932
Baltimore	58.5	57.0	45.4	29.5
Boston	69.5	71.9	69.5	48.0
Buffalo	—	61.9	61.2	37.8
Chicago	86.9	88.6	90.0	64.9
Cincinnati	63.7	65.6	71.2	48.6
Cleveland	—	62.9	57.5	41.0
New York	88.9	87.6	79.9	58.3
Philadelphia	61.2	66.0	63.2	49.0
Eastern Pennsylvania	36.8	39.8	32.7	21.0
Rochester	67.2	71.6	71.1	54.6
St. Louis	—	52.2	49.5	34.9
All	76.0	75.0	70.1	50.6

[a] U. S. Bureau of Labor Statistics, *Wages and Hours of Labor in the Men's Clothing Industry, 1911 to 1924*, Bulletin No. 387, p. 11; *Wages and Hours of Labor in the Men's Clothing Industry, 1911 to 1926*, Bulletin No. 435, p. 7; *Wages and Hours of Labor in the Men's Clothing Industry, 1932*, Bulletin No. 594, p. 7. Differences in earnings reflect partly differences in the character and grade of product made in the several markets and hence differences in the grade of labor employed.

in Chicago where there was a drop of 39.2 per cent, but it was large also in New York and Cincinnati. Only Rochester of the larger union markets succeeded fairly well in holding its own.

4. The policy failed to prevent substantial increases of employment in important markets which were then non-union—such as Philadelphia, Baltimore, and Cleveland.

5. The continued drop of employment in union markets and gains in non-union markets suggest that the union would have been wise to have accepted some decrease in hourly earnings—particularly in view of the fact that between 1926 and 1930 hourly earnings in Cleveland, eastern Pennsylvania, Baltimore, and even Philadelphia were dropping.

Despite all these facts the policy of the union must be regarded as a success. It undoubtedly saved the union from substantial losses of membership and, by keeping up the strength of the union, helped in the organization of non-union markets when favorable opportunities occurred. In 1929, Philadelphia, the largest non-union market, was organized. When the NRA gave the union a golden organizing opportunity, the Amalgamated was strong enough to seize it and by 1935 over 90 per cent of the men's clothing industry had been organized.

NUMBER OF WAGE EARNERS IN THE MEN'S CLOTHING INDUSTRY IN PRINCIPAL PRODUCING CENTERS, 1923 AND 1929[a]

Producing Center	1923		1929	
	Number of Wage Earners	*Percentage of All Workers*	Number of Wage Earners	*Percentage of All Workers*
New York...............	38,100	*19.7*	28,498	*15.1*
Chicago................	29,111	*15.0*	17,706	*9.4*
Rochester..............	10,983	*5.7*	10,647	*5.7*
Philadelphia...........	9,792	*5.0*	10,743	*5.8*
Baltimore..............	9,080	*4.6*	9,363	*5.0*
Cincinnati.............	7,034	*3.6*	5,878	*3.1*
Boston.................	5,286	*2.7*	3,941	*2.1*
Cleveland..............	4,816	*2.5*	5,645	*3.0*
St. Louis..............	4,785	*2.5*	3,946	*2.1*
Total for the United States	194,820	*100.0*	188,069	*100.0*

[a] U. S. Bureau of Labor Statistics, *Wages and Hours of Labor in the Men's Clothing Industry, 1911 to 1926*, Bulletin No. 435, p. 27, and *Wages and Hours of Labor in the Men's Clothing Industry, 1932*, Bulletin No. 594, p. 17.

The gains of the union, of course, greatly reduced the menace of non-union competition. Nevertheless, the union continued, at least until 1939, to assist employers in improving methods of production and in reducing costs. The union had several reasons for continuing this policy. One was that there were always a certain number of union employers who had difficulty in holding their own in competition, whether against union or non-union firms. The local market managers endeavored to help many of these employers in order to save the jobs of the workers.[22] A second reason why the

[22] Some of the employers say that the union does not give help soon enough and that the condition of the employer must be very desperate before the union is willing to move. There is probably some truth in the employers' contention. On the other hand, each market manager was anxious to prevent the growth of unemployment in his locality and he knew that if a firm went out of business, its trade might go to another market.

union continued the policy arose from the problems of newly organized concerns. Some of these concerns got low costs through low wages rather than efficiency. In fact, some of them were more or less isolated from the rest of the clothing industry and, in consequence, were not well informed on the best technical practices. Naturally the newly organized employees expected the Amalgamated to raise their wages, but the union could not do this without threatening the existence of the firm unless it helped the management reduce costs. A third reason for the continuation of the policy was the conviction of the union leaders that industry cannot give its workers a high standard of living if it is burdened with wasteful practices. Finally, the policy was continued because of competition between markets. The manager of each local joint board was anxious to procure a little more employment for his workers. Consequently, there was a tendency for the union managers to make concessions to employers and help them get lower costs in order to win a little more business for the market.

The tendency of the managers of the joint boards to engage in inter-market competition finally led the union, in 1939, to establish a market stabilization department for the purpose of standardizing labor costs in the several markets of the industry and of preventing inter-market competition from taking the form of concessions in labor costs. This step is bound to restrict greatly the activities of the union in helping manufacturers to reduce costs and to improve methods and it may mean the end of the policy.

As a matter of fact, the efforts of the union to introduce uniformity into the labor costs in the several markets goes back to 1933. The movement received great impetus from the large membership gains which the union achieved under the NRA, because these gains reduced the necessity of keeping labor costs low in certain plants in order to meet non-union competition. The union classified garments into various grades and the general executive board established a uniform labor cost for the entire garment in each grade. The minimum labor costs, however, were not rigidly enforced. They represented objectives to be achieved as fast as the local organizations were able to bring up wages in the low-wage communities. Consequently, the local organizations were given discretion to make departures from the established standards. This discretion, however, had the effect of defeating the purpose of the plan. As a result of dissatisfaction within its own ranks over the tendency of inter-market competition to take the form of concessions in labor costs and partly as the result of complaints of manufacturers that discriminatory concessions were being made, the union decided to centralize the administration and enforcement of the program in a special stabilization department in the national office, under the supervision of a director responsible only to President Hillman.[23]

In April 1939, Mr. Hillman appointed a committee of manufacturers' experts to co-operate with the union in working out a program for standardization of labor costs on a national scale. With the help of these experts, garments were classified in the spring of 1939 into six grades based upon the retail price. The two cheapest grades are one and two. It is among these that competition is keenest and the interest of the union and manufacturers in standard labor costs greatest. The characteristics of the garments in grades one and two are specified in detail so that a manufacturer cannot indirectly cut his price by offering some grade two characteristics in a garment sold as grade one. Standard labor costs were established for each grade. Methods of production and piece rates on specific operations may vary from shop to shop, but the total labor cost for each grade must be the same in all shops. For example, the labor cost of a grade one coat was put at $1.70, grade one trousers at 45 cents, a grade two coat at $2.14, and grade two trousers at 55 cents.[24] Only small deviations are permitted to some manufacturers located outside the principal markets who could not compete at the same labor costs with employers in the large markets. Conformity with the standards of quality and labor cost are enforced by in-

---

[23] *Daily News Record*, Apr. 26, 1939, p. 2.

[24] In July 1939, a two-year contract was signed between the Amalgamated Clothing Workers in New York and the Clothing Manufacturers' Exchange of New York, putting this scale into effect. For New York City manufacturers in general, the new labor costs were said to represent a 6- or 7-cent reduction on the grade one coat and the grade one trousers, a 6-cent reduction on the grade two coat and a 4-cent reduction on the grade two trousers. (*Daily News Record*, July 10, 1939, p. 4.) For many out-of-town shops and even for many shops in New York City, the new labor costs required considerable increases in wage rates.

vestigators from the market stabilization department of the union.

Extension of the market stabilization program to the medium- and high-quality clothing may prove impracticable because the characteristics of those garments are difficult to standardize. Furthermore, the demand for application of the program to the higher quality clothing is not urgent because competition in these grades is far less fierce than in the cheap grades. This is fortunate because the market stabilization program deprives the employer of virtually all incentive to improve either his methods of production or the quality of his garments. The gains from improvements in production methods go almost entirely to labor because such improvements are not permitted to reduce the employer's labor cost. Improvements in the garment which would lead an employer to give some grade two characteristics at a grade one price or some grade three or four characteristics at a grade two price simply are not permitted. Because the market stabilization program substantially reduces the employer's incentive to make improvements, it would, if strictly enforced for a considerable period of time, impose stagnation on the union part of the industry, and it would undoubtedly lead to a considerable expansion of non-union production and employment.

CHAPTER XVIII

THE NAUMKEAG CO-OPERATIVE EXPERIMENT

Union-management co-operation in the Naumkeag Steam Cotton Company of Salem, Massachusetts, was started early in 1929.[1] The Naumkeag Company manufactures sheets and pillow cases. It is an old, established concern, having been founded in 1839. In 1929, the company had eight principal competitors, and competition in the business was keen. The company has specialized in quality goods, which it sells under the name of Pequot sheets and pillow cases. This trade name is well known, and the high reputation of the company's goods has protected it in some measure from competition. In 1914 the mill was destroyed by fire. This strengthened the competitive position of the company because the old plant was replaced by one of the most modern construction, equipped with new machinery of the latest design, largely automatic and electrically driven. As a result, job assignments were increased and the company was able to turn out a given amount of product with approximately 25 per cent less labor.

There had been a small union among the loom fixers in the plant for many years, but the mill as a whole was unorganized until the war period. In June 1918, a strike in the spinning and carding department led to organization. The new union received a charter from the United Textile Workers. By the fall of 1919, 75 per cent of the workers were members of the union. A second strike of nearly two months at that time led to the establishment of the closed shop—the only closed shop at the time in the cotton textile industry. The company, unlike most of its competitors, did not reduce wages during the depression of 1921. After the depression its wages were said by both the union and the management to be the highest in any cotton mill in the world. Although

---

[1] For a more complete account of the Naumkeag experiment, see the excellent study by R. C. Nyman, *Union-Management Co-operation in the "Stretch-out."* I have drawn on this study for some factual material. The interpretations and conclusions in this chapter, however, are my own and may not be acceptable to Mr. Nyman.

competition was keen, the company continued to prosper, and in 1923 paid a stock dividend of 100 per cent.

During the twenties competition in the cotton textile industry became increasingly severe. Demand shifted in substantial measure from cotton to silk and rayon.[2] The growing severity of competition caused employers to search desperately for ways of cutting costs. One of the discoveries made was that job assignments could be substantially increased, particularly if the managements took care to see that raw material met certain standards and that equipment was better maintained. Another discovery was that, by changing the methods of work and introducing greater specialization, the need for skilled labor could be greatly reduced. Weavers, for example, could be relieved of filling the batteries with bobbins, cleaning the looms, and removing the finished cloth. The weaver's job then became mainly one of watching the operation of the looms and particularly of tying up broken ends of warped yarn. With better materials, better maintenance, and relief from some duties, a weaver could tend two or even three times as many looms as before. Similar changes could be made in spinning. This was the much-discussed "stretch-out." It will be noted that in part this was a form of labor dilution and produced demotions quite as often as layoffs. In weaving, for example, skilled weavers, often of years' experience, were demoted to helpers. This meant that the dissatisfaction produced by the change was "built into" the force.

The sheeting branch of the cotton industry was less affected by market changes than other parts. The Naumkeag Company remained prosperous until the middle twenties, and its dividend payments of $720,000 a year were the largest in its history. The company continued to make concessions to the union, and the rank and file acquired the habit of expecting concessions. The competitors of the company, however, were introducing the stretch-out and cutting their costs, so that competition became keener. This caused the Naumkeag management to stiffen its resistance to union demands. This began to occur about 1926, when the company failed

---

[2] In 1928 and 1929, for example, the raw cotton consumed in the United States was less than in 1923. In the face of stationary or shrinking demand, the capacity of the industry was increased by the construction of new mills in the South.

by a wide margin to earn its dividend. Although the stretch-out was not proposed by Naumkeag at this time, the union leaders could see that the problem was coming and consequently they felt the need for a well-established co-operative relationship with management.

This situation led the business agent of the union, Mr. John P. O'Connell, to propose a plan of union-management co-operation, similar to those on the Baltimore and Ohio and the Canadian National.[3] The management accepted the plan, and in April 1927 the company and the union signed a formal agreement which stated that the management recognized the union as "desirable to the management, inasmuch as the co-operation of their members is essential to the continued and successful operation of the mills," and that the union agreed to promote the sale of the company's products and pledged "its support in a constructive and responsible way to the end that quantity and quality production may be maintained," and furthermore pledged "its co-operation in effecting such economies in manufacturing as may be brought about by the introduction of improved machinery." Monthly conferences were to be held between management and union representatives to discuss competition, sales, markets, quality and quantity of production, regularization of employment, technical changes, and economies. It was agreed that, in the event of differences over wages, hours, or working conditions, neither side would disrupt production before the expiration of a 60-day period. Meetings were held regularly at first and then irregularly, but this kind of union-management co-operation never became important at Naumkeag.

The year 1927 was one of great prosperity for the company, but the next year proved to be extremely unfavorable. Sales dropped nearly 30 per cent and earnings 75 per cent. The yardage sold was even below the depression year of 1921. The company continued its customary rate of dividends, but nearly half of the disbursements came from surplus. This experience caused a general stock-

---

[3] When the workers in the Naumkeag mill organized in 1918, Mr. O'Connell was secretary of the Salem Central Labor Union and also business agent of the plumbers' union. The Naumkeag workers sought the help of Mr. O'Connell in organizing their union. As a result of his help, he was made the business agent of the new union. Thus, from almost the beginning, the organization had the guidance of a man who, as events proved, was a leader of unusual sagacity.

taking and impressed the management with the fact that its labor costs were substantially above those of its chief competitors. The solution seemed to lie in the introduction of the stretch-out, which had been spreading in the industry since 1923. The mill agent therefore directed department heads to prepare "new schedules of labor and wages" for the purpose of reducing costs. In the weaving department it was proposed to increase the looms operated per weaver from 13 to 24. In December 1928, the new schedules were presented to the union. They would have meant the dismissal of 250 employees.

For over a month there was a deadlock. The rank and file asserted that the management had no proof that the proposed job assignments were fair. Some workers even asserted that the new assignments could not be performed—a very common attitude among workers when increases in the work load are proposed. The union officials, however, were eager to find a way out. On the one hand, they knew that their members, however opposed to the job assignments, did not wish to jeopardize good jobs by striking. They were impressed by the fact that the stretch-out had produced strikes in many plants and that these strikes had been disastrous to the workers. On the other hand, the leaders knew enough of the competitive situation in the textile industry to understand that the mill needed lower costs. They wished the methods of reducing costs, however, to be planned so as to keep displacement of employees to a minimum and to permit the methods to be reviewed by the union.

The business agent of the union had heard something of scientific management and learned that, among industrial engineers, Mr. Morris L. Cooke had shown friendship and sympathy for organized labor. Consequently, the union leaders visited him in Philadelphia and laid their problem before him. He recommended that the union employ an engineer to survey the situation and make a recommendation. Mr. Francis Goodell was engaged. After a two weeks' survey he reported to the executive committee of the union. He confirmed the management's claim that a reduction in costs was needed and that this could be achieved by the more efficient use of labor. The problem was to see that labor was properly safeguarded in devising the new work schedules. This could be done by the union's (1) employing an expert to check the job assignments proposed by the management; (2) employing an expert to supply it with technical material for use in bargaining over new job assignments and piece rates; and (3) inducing management to join with it in sponsoring research on job assignments.

It was on the basis of Mr. Goodell's report that the union proposed to the management the scheme of joint determination of new job assignments which the management, with some modification, agreed to accept. The proposal of January 30, 1929, began by stating that "the union sees the importance of reducing the cost of manufacture and agrees that proposals of the nature of those under discussion mark progress toward this goal." The union leaders pointed out, however, that the changes which the management was seeking to make simultaneously and suddenly should have been made gradually. "By such individual consideration economies are realized earlier and without prolonged friction and relatively few adjustments are forced upon employees at one time." The leaders then pointed out that the company and the union lacked "suitable machinery for bringing up possible waste reductions and for considering and effecting them without disorganization."

The union then proposed that "each question under discussion shall be settled separately and upon the basis of analytical research." This research would be headed by a technician employed by the company. The technician would report to a Waste Elimination Committee composed of several representatives of each side. The duty of this committee would be "to ascertain the facts and to devise methods of co-operation for the elimination of waste and the improvement of working conditions as related to the quality and quantity of production." The committee would "in no case entertain complaints or grievances"[4] but would "concern itself exclusively with constructive suggestions for the promotion of the

---

[4] Of course the Waste Elimination Committee that was later established did consider a multitude of grievances and complaints and did deal with a multitude of conflicts of interests. But the complaints were not those arising under the general agreement but rather that specific assignments were unfair or that specific time studies were erroneous or misleading.

common interests of the parties signatory to this agreement." The committee

should be furnished not only with relevant figures obtained by research but it should also be furnished with factors of major cost and quality problems arising from competition which confront the management. It will then be possible to indoctrinate the employees at each operation with a concrete picture of their part in the goal, to wit, costs and quality which enable "Pequot" to compete successfully.

The union added that it could not endorse a program that would reduce labor requirements per unit unless forward-looking and resourceful efforts were being made to promote sales. Hence it urged "the necessary sales planning" to keep the company adjusted to the changes in the field of distribution. Finally, the union proposed that the company establish an unemployment reserve fund. Such a fund, the union asserted, would stimulate sales administration and "liberate an unprecedented degree of co-operation."

The management regarded the union's proposals as unnecessarily cumbersome and elaborate and, in the case of sales planning, as distinctly impracticable. It knew that "analytical research" into "each question under discussion" meant, among other things, time studies, which it regarded as an unnecessary refinement. The management felt sure that the job assignments which it had proposed were reasonable and could be easily performed. On the other hand, it realized that the union's proposals constituted recognition that cost reductions were necessary and promised a way of reducing costs without provoking labor trouble. The management did not accept the proposals in regard to sales planning and an unemployment reserve fund, but it did decide to accept the proposal that new job assignments be determined by joint research. The union leaders then promptly asked their rank and file whether they would accept the proposal or strike, and the members decided to accept.

INTRODUCTION OF JOINT RESEARCH—INITIAL PROBLEMS

On March 1, 1929, joint research began. Mr. Goodell, the expert retained by the union, was made technician in charge of the research. He was paid by the company but was expected to be a neutral, equally responsible to each side. In conducting the research he was assisted by a staff of two union representatives and two company representatives. Mr. Goodell trained these men in making time studies and they did most of the actual fact-gathering to determine proper job assignments. General supervision of the research work was vested in the Waste Elimination Committee, of which the technician was chairman and on which each side had four representatives, including the above-mentioned full-time research staff. In addition, the union was represented by the presidents of its two locals and the company by the acting superintendent and the plant engineer. Technical questions were to be decided by Mr. Goodell. The results of joint research were to be submitted to the Waste Elimination Committee. On the basis of these results the committee was expected to make recommendations for new job assignments to the union and the management.

Was the arrangement designed to eliminate bargaining in the setting of job assignments or to put bargaining upon a factual basis? Probably both results were intended. The machinery for collecting facts was designed to give each side confidence in them and therefore to make each willing to let facts decide disputes. But likewise the machinery was carefully arranged to permit bargaining in case either side wished to engage in it. Not only did joint representation make bargaining possible in the Committee on Waste Elimination, but the fact that the recommendations of the committee required the approval of the management and the union created additional opportunity for bargaining. Quite properly the entire research machinery was set up to reflect the idea that the determination of proper standards of quality and output are finally a matter of judgment—a matter of valuation rather than of science. The determination of what is a fair day's work depends upon how hard one thinks people should work; there are bound to be some differences of opinion on this point. Even the interpretation of time studies is a matter of judgment. For example, whether abnormal times on certain elements should be included or thrown out depends upon whether one believes the reasons for abnormal times are of such a nature that these times will be repeated in the regular work. But facts scientifically determined were expected to set limits to the play of judgment.

The first task of the technician was to train the members of the research staff to make time studies. The technician was impressed with the fact that the methods of performing operations were not uniform and that working conditions in many respects were not standardized. To set job assignments before conditions were standardized would mean setting them very low in order to prevent them from being too high in some cases and causing dissatisfaction. To set them before the best operating methods had been made uniform throughout each department would also mean that job assignments would have to be too low and that the company would fail to achieve the lowest possible costs. The technician therefore recommended that a firm of textile engineers be engaged to study operating conditions and methods in the plant and to recommend changes in equipment and standard practices, and standards for machine speeds. This was done. After an investigation of several months in the spring of 1929, the engineers made a report recommending many changes in conditions and equipment and methods and suggesting standards for machine speeds, loom stoppage, and end breakage. They emphasized, as the technician had been doing, that the standard job assignments required standard conditions and methods of operation.

Many of the recommendations of the engineers were put into effect. Complete acceptance of their recommendations, however, would have required far greater centralization of management and standardization of practices than the mill agent was willing to approve. Hence many of the engineers' recommendations were ignored. As a result non-standard conditions continued to present difficulties because when individual employees were studied, many variations were discovered in their method of doing a given job. The question was how far to go in standardizing methods. The technician, with his rigorous engineering standards, was in favor of rather complete and detailed standardization of methods; the operating officials of the mill, the workers, and even representatives of each side on the research staff were not. As an example of the difference of opinion, a mill official cites a proposed standard method for cleaning looms which he described as "ridiculous." Loom cleaning is second to the lowest paid job in the weaving department. The technician proposed to show the loom cleaner by a diagram where to start, where to clean next, where next, where to skim over the loom with the air hose, where to blow off the dirt, where to brush it off, where to wipe it off, where to pick it off, and where to scrape it off. The official said that the women who had been cleaning looms for years would not follow a set procedure. They knew what they were expected to do and when a loom was clean.

In strict logic the technician was right: standard job assignments presuppose that everything else is standard. As a matter of practical administration, however, he was wrong. Neither side was ready for the complete and detailed revision of methods which really scientific job assignments required. That would have meant not only much more disturbance of working habits and shop customs than either side had visualized or was prepared to accept, but radical changes in management methods—a centralization of control that no one, least of all the mill agent, desired.

The opposition of officials and workers to interference with time-honored practices and customs compelled the research committee to recommend less scientific and accurate job assignments than the technician would have desired. Later these somewhat rule-of-thumb job assignments caused trouble. More important than this, however, was the mistrust and resentment aroused by the efforts of the technician to achieve high engineering standards by exploring conditions and methods with great thoroughness and by endeavoring to persuade officials and workers to accept standard methods that were very detailed. Furthermore, the extreme thoroughness with which joint research was conducted caused it to be regarded with a certain amount of disrespect on the ground that it was "too theoretical." When these smoldering feelings were fanned into flame by the suffering of the depression, they became important.

PROMISING EARLY DEVELOPMENTS OF JOINT RESEARCH

The Naumkeag experiment falls into two stages: the period prior to the middle of 1931, during which progress was at times promising; and the years from late 1931 to 1935, during which joint research was struggling for survival.

The determination of job assignments. An official of the company criticized the methods of joint research as "too unwieldy, too long, and too tedious." Whether or not this criticism was fair, the methods were certainly thorough. The union was insistent that only "average" workers be timed. After a job had been selected for study, the department head and a union representative selected several average workers. Time studies of these workers were made by a union representative and a management representative on the research committee. Efforts to persuade the union to relinquish its insistence upon participation in the time studies at this early stage were a failure. These preliminary time studies served as the basis of a "job standard" which was worked out by the research staff and which specified the allocation of the duties of the operation and the methods of performing them. This "job standard" was tested by having several workers perform the operation in accordance with the tentative methods. They were timed, and the job standard was revised in the light of the results. Meetings were frequently held to discuss proposed standards with the department overseer and the workers under observation. When the technician and the union and management representatives decided that the job assignment should not be further increased, the standard was submitted to the joint committee on research. If the committee approved, it recommended the standard to the company and the union; if not, it asked the research staff to make further studies.

It is obvious that in practice this procedure gave endless opportunity for conference, discussion, argument, and bargaining and that it was likely to result in standards which reflected not the fastest performances easily possible, but bargaining compromises. At any rate, by the spring of 1930, a year after the scheme of joint research had been adopted, no job assignments had been put into operation and the joint research committee had got no further than a more or less tentative agreement on 20 looms (in place of 12) as a standard job assignment for weavers.

Although the union business agent welcomed the delay provided by the cumbersomeness of the procedure, he saw that uncertainty and suspense over who were to be demoted or dismissed was creating unrest among the workers. He wished the displacements to come in the spring rather than the fall or winter, so that the dismissed workers could find jobs in the expanding summer industries of the New England North Shore. He knew that the joint research had already proved 20-loom assignments to be easily possible and he suspected that the technician, by introducing further improvements into conditions and methods, would show that 24-loom assignments were practicable. He knew that the mill management was impatient over the failure of joint research to produce prompt results in lower costs, and he had an idea that with management in this frame of mind he might be able to drive a favorable bargain. In April 1930 he informed the management that the union was willing to accept a 20-loom stretch-out in the weaving room. To the members of the research staff, 20 looms seemed a low standard. Nevertheless, as the union business agent suspected, the mill agent wanted action, and in order to get it, he accepted the union's offer. Thus, by a bargaining agreement rather than essentially by fact-finding and scientific determination of job assignments, the stretch-out was introduced into the weaving department.

The problem of displacements and demotions. The union leaders had known, of course, that the stretch-out would mean demotions and dismissals, and they had made plans in advance for dealing with these problems. One device was the hiring of temporary workers. All persons hired after the beginning of joint research were put on notice that their jobs were temporary and that they might expect to be dismissed when the stretch-out was introduced. However, a few dismissals of older employees were likely to be necessary and many demotions of these workers were a certainty.

The union was already committed to the principle of seniority and had a seniority rule in its agreement with the company. But this rule was open to more than one interpretation. Suppose a weaver had worked for eight years in the mill—four years at weaving and four years as a helper. Should he be permitted, when demoted, to displace a helper of five years' service? The predominant opinion among the workers was that layoffs should be governed by length of service in the mill rather than on the job. The management and a substantial part of the workers objected to mill or "straight" seniority, as it was called, on the ground that it would permit a number of employees, especially married women, who had means of support other than their jobs, to displace helpers who were solely dependent on their jobs. In order to avoid this result, it was decided to base demotions and layoffs upon length of service on the job (job seniority) rather than upon length of service in the mill. In the illustration above, the weaver with only four years' service on the job could not then displace the helper of five years' service. The union finally agreed that demotions would be governed by seniority on the job.

Early reactions to the stretch-out. The stretch-out reduced the number of weavers from 306 to 183, or 40 per cent, and the number of workers in the weaving department from 589 to 433, or 26 per cent.[5] The union had bargained new wage rates so that the average earnings of weavers were raised from $27.55 to $31.78 per week and the average for the department from $23.22 to $26.78.

The original reactions of both workers and management to the new job assignments in the weaving department were favorable. The assignment of 20 looms for most jobs was low and could be easily performed by the workers. Although there were over 153 dismissals and about the same number of demotions, the former were largely confined to recently hired workers and the number of workers receiving wage increases exceeded the number demoted. The management was pleased because the new job assignments, though rather low, were considerably higher than the old ones and because annual saving on the pay roll in the weaving department promised to exceed $110,000 a year.

During the fall of 1930, the stretch-out was introduced into the warp spinning room and in the spring of 1931 into the weft spinning room. Reorganization of the work and the introduction of some measure of standardization of conditions and methods of operation made it possible to increase the number of "sides" assigned to each spinner from 10 to 18. A member of the research staff described this as "more of a real standard" than the 20-loom standard in weaving. The number of spinners was reduced from 168 to 89, or 47 per cent, but 36 frame-cleaning jobs were created, making a net reduction of 43, or 26 per cent, in the jobs in the two spinning rooms. Labor turnover in the department was considerably higher so that there was a larger percentage of temporary

---

[5] Nyman, *Union-Management Co-operation in the "Stretch-out,"* pp. 75-77.

workers than in weaving. Despite the fact, therefore, that the change to new job assignments was made rapidly, there were practically no layoffs of regular workers in the spinning department. Here the number of workers who received wage increases was about twice the number who were demoted. From spinning, joint research shifted to the carding and cloth inspection departments.

Thus by the spring of 1931 joint research had introduced new job assignments into the two principal departments of the mill. Although demotions were numerous, practically no regular workers had been laid off and advances in pay were more numerous than demotions. The employees were reasonably content with the changes. So was the management, despite the fact that job assignments in weaving were low. The management estimated the net savings of joint research at $185,000 a year; the technicians' estimate was $230,000.[6] The competitive position of the company had been materially improved and in a way that was beneficial rather than harmful to most of the workers.

If business had improved during the summer of 1931, it is probable that the Naumkeag experiment would have gone down in history as a notable success in union-management co-operation. It is important to note this fact because it must be taken into account in judging the success or failure of the experiment, the real causes of its abandonment, and the light which the experiment throws on future possibilities of union-management co-operation.

DECLINE OF THE CO-OPERATIVE VENTURE

The Credit-Anstalt affair on May 11, 1931, the closing of German banks, the run on the pound during the summer, and the abandonment of gold by Great Britain in September were both symptoms and causes of a rapid deterioration in the general business situation. Influenced by the fear that wage cuts would undermine the price structure and induce postponement of commitments, American business enterprises had on the whole maintained wages. As late as May 1931, President Farrell of the United States Steel Corporation had issued a strong public statement against wage cuts. The abandonment of gold by Great Britain, however, ap-

---

[6] The same, p. 75. The difference in the estimates is due to difference in opinion as to expenses properly chargeable to joint research.

parently convinced business leaders that wage cuts would be necessary. The 10 per cent cut of the United States Steel Corporation on October 1, 1931 was the signal for hundreds of other cuts.

By the fall of 1931, the Naumkeag mill was operating only four days a week. This contraction of operations had exceedingly important effects upon industrial relations. In the first place it made all workers dissatisfied with their earnings and, in consequence, disposed to be dissatisfied with everything else. In the second place, it greatly intensified the problem of the demoted workers. These employees, of course, were bound to be critical of joint research because they had suffered from it. When the demoted workers were shifted to lower paying jobs, many of them had hopes that they would soon get back their former jobs at the higher wages which these jobs now paid. This hope at first tempered their dissatisfaction with joint research. In fact, if business had expanded and promotions of the demoted workers had gradually occurred, these employees would not have been a serious problem. When continued contraction of business, however, made it plain that the demoted workers had no immediate prospect of recovering their former jobs, they became more and more hostile to joint research.

The first wage cut and the abandonment of joint research. The continued deterioration of the business situation led the management to feel the need for additional reductions in costs. True, the loss of the company in 1931 was much less than in 1930. In the earlier year the deficit had been over half a million dollars; in 1931 it was slightly more than $50,000. The improvement, however, was due less to better operating results than to smaller inventory markdowns.[7] Total inventories late in 1931 were about the same as in late 1930, but the efforts of the company to give employment to its people had substantially increased its stocks of finished product. Competing mills had already cut wages at least once and most of them twice. Some of them had increased job assignments since the depression started. If the management was

[7] In 1930, the company took markdowns of $1,269,853. Without this shrinkage in raw material in 1930 the management estimated that the company would have made a profit of $734,756.

to follow the policy of attempting to avoid inventory losses by holding its finished stock for liquidation at higher prices and if, at the same time, it was to give its people the maximum possible employment by filling orders from current output, lower operating costs were necessary. In November 1931, the management proposed a wage cut of 10 per cent.

The demand for a wage reduction provoked a critical situation. The workers had already made substantial sacrifices, as indicated above, in the form of demotions and the reduced working week. The continuation of joint research during a time of contracting employment made the workers fearful that it would cause some of them to lose their jobs permanently. This fear was not confined to the departments where joint research was in process or where it had not been started. It existed in the weaving department, where the workers knew that the 20-loom standard was less than both the management and the joint research staff considered possible. Hence, they feared a resumption of joint research.

The union leaders felt certain that the workers would not accept a wage cut while joint research was still in process. They were anxious to preserve good relations with the management and particularly to avoid a strike. They knew that under conditions of depression the union would have great difficulty in winning a strike; they also knew enough of the competitive position of the company to understand that an extended strike would seriously impair the ability of the company to give employment. The union leaders, therefore, offered to ask their members to accept a 10 per cent cut on condition (1) that joint research be discontinued; (2) that the same reduction be applied to the salaries of executives and supervisors; and (3) that no cuts apply to men earning less than $21 a week or women earning less than $15.

These proposals meant that the union leaders who had told their members that joint research was a good thing were now in effect saying that joint research was undesirable. It is true that the union leaders had not in fact abandoned their favorable opinion of joint research. In the eyes of the rank and file, however, the proposal of the union leaders meant that joint research was discredited. The union leaders were labelling it as something that ought to be given up. All of the dislike of the rank and file for having their jobs studied and their methods of work minutely observed, for being told to abandon customary ways of working and to adopt new ones—in short, all of their prejudices against joint research—received official confirmation. All of the educational work of the union leaders and the technician to convince the rank and file that joint research was desirable was undone.

The management, very unwisely, refused to extend the wage cut to executives and supervisors. It also refused to exempt workers earning below given minima. It did, however, agree to abandon joint research if the workers would accept a wage reduction. In January 1932, the research staff was disbanded, the technician was dismissed, and wages were cut. Thus the exigencies of the depression discredited and forced the abandonment of the policy of organized co-operation in increasing operating efficiency.

The second wage cut. Throughout the spring of 1932, orders continued to drop and operations were soon curtailed from four days a week to three and one-half. Additional reductions in cost seemed to be imperative. In April 1932, the management reported to the union that the company was unable to meet the prices quoted by competing mills and make a profit or even come near a profit. It declared that the constant decline in sales would make necessary further curtailment of operations unless competition could be successfully met. On April 29, 1932, the management proposed a second wage cut of 10 per cent (this one applicable to executives and office force as well as operatives) and a further increase in assignments in the spinning and weaving departments. Larger job assignments in spinning and weaving were justified, the management said, by reduced end breakage.[8] The management also asked that the introduction of joint research in the bleachery be considered.

The management's letter of April 29 was a surprise to the union business agent. He prepared an elaborate brief against the demands of the company, partly in hope of dissuading the management from pressing them, partly to impress his rank and file. He attempted to persuade the management to substitute joint research

[8] End breakage refers to the breakage of threads in the loom.

for wage cuts as a means of lowering the cost of production. The management refused to withdraw its demand for lower wages. Furthermore it argued that the data previously collected by the research staff, together with reduction in end breakage, indicated that larger job assignments in the spinning and weaving departments could be made without research. "This," the union business agent said, "simply means the stretch-out system as used in non-union mills."

The refusal of the management to withdraw its demands compelled the union business agent to submit them to a vote of the membership. Instead of asking them, however, whether they would accept larger job assignments, he insisted upon asking them whether they would accept joint research on their jobs. Four questions were submitted and the vote was by secret mail ballot. The results were as follows:

	Yes	No
Will you accept a 10 per cent cut in wages?	520	635
Will you accept research on your job?	134	980
Do you favor a strike if required to accept both No. 1 and No. 2?	575	457
Do you favor a strike if required to accept either No. 1 or No. 2?	341	615

The strategy of the union leaders was obvious. They were endeavoring to limit the concessions either to a wage cut alone or to larger job assignments and joint research alone. The business agent preferred a resumption of joint research because he believed that larger job assignments were inevitable sooner or later. The preference of the rank and file, however, by a very large majority was the other way: wage cuts were much less objectionable to them than joint research. Armed with a vote in favor of striking if the management insisted upon both demands and a vote against striking if the management withdrew one of them, the business agent sought to persuade the company to withdraw its less objectionable demand—larger job assignments. This he succeeded in doing except that the management insisted upon starting joint research in the bleachery, where it had not yet been applied. The 10 per cent wage reduction became effective July 3, 1932. Thus, for a second time, co-operation with the management in introducing larger job assignments had been discredited as a union policy. Although the membership had not made it quite clear that they would strike rather than adopt this policy, they had indicated by an overwhelming vote that they would object less to a 10 per cent wage cut.

The strike of the rank and file against increased job assignments and against the restoration of joint research. The business of the company continued to decline in yardage and even more in dollars. Inventories remained undiminished and by the end of 1932 were equal to more than half the company's annual sales as against one-third in 1929. The company was still operating at a loss. The mangement concluded that further reductions in cost were imperative. The first step was to introduce joint research into the bleachery. The union was represented on the research committee, but the work was directed, not by a neutral technician, but by the superintendent of the bleachery. Furthermore, the union representative, through his previous membership on the research committee in the mill, had lost the confidence of the rank and file. Under the circumstances it was not surprising that the workers promptly complained that the new job assignments recommended by the committee were excessive.[9]

It was in this situation that the management in March 1933 demanded an immediate extension from 20 to 28 on certain types of looms and from 18 to 20 sides per spinner, and other increases in job assignments. The management argued that the larger assignments were justified by reduced end breakage, that less than one-third of the workers would be affected, and that only about 100 out of over 1,200 would be eliminated.

The union leaders (but not all of the rank and file) knew perfectly well that under the improved conditions in the mill the assignment of 20 looms was low. Negotiations with the management convinced the leaders that further cost reductions were needed. The leaders were particularly anxious to avoid wage reductions and, despite the fact that twice the leaders had demanded that the management give up the proposal for joint research or larger job assignments, they still regarded joint research with favor, particularly as a way of avoiding wage cuts. Knowing the

---

[9] The workers seem to have been wrong, but appeal to the union business agent yielded them a slight increase in the rest allowance.

extreme opposition of the rank and file to joint research, the leaders obtained the support of the national union. The national was anxious to avoid a strike, especially against job assignments which were reasonable. It sent on experts of its own to investigate the company's proposals. Negotiations led to a compromise. The weavers were to operate 24 looms instead of 28, but the other job assignments were to be as the management proposed; joint research was to be resumed; layoffs were to be confined to married women without dependents. After the vicissitudes of four years of depression, joint research, after being dropped once at the insistence of the union and again barred by the opposition of the union, was about to be restored with the co-operation of the union in order to help union workers hold their jobs in competition with nonunion mills. Had the rank and file been willing to accept the decision of their leaders, the history of the Naumkeag Company would have been very different.

A meeting to ratify the agreements between the leaders and the company was held on March 29, 1933. The situation of the company was explained and the workers were told that the only alternative to the new job assignments was a third wage cut. They were assured that their national officers regarded the new job assignments as reasonable, that the layoffs would be few—not more than one hundred and possibly less—and that these would be confined to married women without dependents.

The workers were determined to have neither larger job assignments nor a resumption of joint research. Once they had been told that joint research and larger job assignments would help them hold their jobs by helping the company hold its markets. Perhaps the increase in job assignments had done some good, but the workers could not see it. At any rate they knew that the larger assignments had not prevented two wage cuts. Among the workers were two groups particularly hostile to the proposed changes— the group of demoted employees who, of course, had a special grievance against joint research, and the married women (and in some cases their husbands and members of their families) who had been singled out to bear the brunt of the layoffs. The meeting almost unanimously rejected the compromise negotiated by the union leaders. The business agent, however, induced the workers not to make their rejection final until the joint research committee had studied the new job assignments and reported on them.

The committee reported that 24 looms was not an excessive work load. About a month after the first meeting, the proposed agreement was submitted to a second special meeting of the union. Again the workers voted almost unanimously against the agreement. After this second rebuff, the union leaders attempted to persuade the company to concede something besides an assignment of 24 looms instead of 28, but without success. The leaders called a third mass meeting in an attempt to induce the workers to ratify the agreement, but this served only to inflame them against their officers and to arouse the demand for a strike vote and for a promise that the national union support them in a strike. A vote was held and it resulted overwhelmingly in favor of striking—981 to 282. Since the workers were by this time thoroughly distrustful of their leaders who had persistently urged on them a course to which they were bitterly opposed, they elected a special committee of non-officers to conduct the strike.

The national president refused to sanction the strike and came to Salem in an effort to settle it. After he had failed to bring the strike committee into agreement with the management, he called a mass meeting of the union (the fourth) to explain the stand of the national union. The workers demanded that the national support their strike and threatened to leave the union if it failed to come to their aid. With the meeting becoming more and more rebellious, the national president finally declared the strike illegal and adjourned the meeting. The strike had definitely become a revolt of the rank and file against their officers and their union.

The national officers did not abandon their efforts to settle the strike. They knew that their one chance of keeping their union established in the Naumkeag plant was to make a settlement. Furthermore, they were convinced that the strike reflected no more than a temporary feeling of the workers, who had been stirred up by a few radicals and would soon return to their senses. In this belief, however, the national officers were mistaken. Whatever agreement the strikers might be willing to negotiate with the company, they would have nothing to do with their former officers or the national union. By failing to pursue a policy of militant and uncompromising opposition to proposals which competent union experts declared to be reasonable and to represent necessary concessions, the union lost the confidence and allegiance of nearly all of the Naumkeag workers. When the national officers saw this, they withdrew and let the strikers run their own strike.[10]

Thus joint research and large job assignments, which the union had helped bring into the mill in order to preserve the business of the company and the jobs of the employees, eventually destroyed the allegiance of the workers to the union. The union might have destroyed itself by being uncompromising and unreasonable. It adopted instead a policy of reasonableness, but under the influence of depression conditions it lost the allegiance of the rank and file.

At the beginning, the prospects of the strikers seemed hopeless. They lacked funds, discipline, and experienced leaders, and there were radicals in their ranks and among the aspirants for leadership who threatened to divide them. But the strikers were spurred by an almost fanatical opposition to any research on their jobs and to larger job assignments. Hence their ranks held fast.

Late in June and in July the textile industry experienced a sharp boom through the desire of buyers to escape the higher prices which they anticipated from the government's monetary policy, the code, and the restriction of cotton acreage. The orders on the books of the company were increasing and the management was becoming eager to resume operations. It agreed to retain the existing assignments of 20 looms to a weaver and to give all workers except the weavers 48 hours' pay for 40 hours' work. It wished to continue the research program in the bleachery. If this were done, the management agreed to re-study some of the jobs and to accept "straight" seniority. The management pointed out that the growing demand for textiles indicated that the new job assignments would not produce layoffs. The strike committee, however, was adamant on the subject of research and larger job assignments. The

[10] Only among the loom fixers, who for many years had had a local of their own and who were not affected by larger job assignments, did the United Textile Workers retain its members.

management finally offered to postpone all joint research for two years. With this additional concession, the strike committee, and later the workers, agreed to accept the management's terms. The strikers returned to work and shortly afterward formed a new union known as the Independent Sheeting Workers of America. It included about 1,800 of the 2,200 workers.[11]

The strike and wage cut of 1935. The contract suspending research and job extensions expired in the summer of 1935, and again research and job assignments became an issue. The union demanded that there be no stretch-out and no further research, and it presented nineteen other demands. Among them were: (1) the closed shop; (2) a 40-hour week; (3) plant instead of department seniority; (4) a 25 per cent increase in wages. The management refused these concessions and proposed a wage reduction of 15 per cent. The management asserted its right to introduce changes in methods and new job assignments, but offered to give notice of such proposals. The union rejected the management's proposals.

On August 12, 1935, there began a strike which lasted for ten weeks. The union lacked funds, the company was under no great pressure to make deliveries, and by October the question had become, not whether the workers could get their demands, but whether they could prevent a wage cut. The management said that a reduction in wages was necessitated by competitive conditions because it was paying higher wages than any of its rivals and its operatives had smaller job assignments than the employees of its rivals. The management finally offered to compromise on a 11.2 per cent reduction and to open its books to an arbitrator for proof that the cut was justified. On this condition the employees returned to work. An adjuster of the Massachusetts State Board of Conciliation who inspected the books found that even the new wage scale was higher than that paid, on the average, by competing northern mills and far above that paid in the South. He also found that in competing northern mills operatives tended 30 per cent

[11] The continued opposition of the Naumkeag workers to the United Textile Workers' Union, which to them stood for research and the stretch-out, was shown in September 1934. At that time the union called a general strike in the textile industry. Except for the loom fixers, who retained their allegiance to the United, practically all of the Naumkeag employees remained at work.

more spindles with similar yarns and the same kind of machinery, and that weavers tended 60 per cent more looms—32 instead of 20. Thus the compromise offer of the management was upheld.

This settlement meant that for a second time the union succeeded in keeping its existing job assignments, but this time it paid for them by a substantial wage reduction. Plainly the union had become a device for enforcing what was in effect an arrangement for sharing work, for preserving the jobs of a minority at the expense of the standard of living of the majority. This policy of the union is somewhat surprising in view of the fact that the seniority rule in its agreement made clear which workers would be dropped in the event that new job assignments produced layoffs. The explanation is to be found in the fact that job assignments had been an issue so long that the prevention of any further change in them had gradually become for many union members an end in itself.

In the spring of 1940 the assignment issue at Naumkeag remained unsolved. In the summer of 1939, however, an election under the auspices of the National Labor Relations Board was held in Naumkeag and was won by the Textile Workers' Union of America (CIO), which replaced the Independent Sheeting Workers as the bargaining agent of the workers. Under the able leadership of this union there is reason to believe that the job assignment problem of the Naumkeag mill may be solved.

CONCLUSIONS FROM THE NAUMKEAG EXPERIENCE

Does the Naumkeag experience prove that unions cannot afford to help employers reduce costs by increasing job assignments? Do unions destroy themselves when they do this? Does the experience prove that increases in job assignments must be made by employers through the use of their bargaining power and, if necessary, over the opposition of the union?

1. Obviously the Naumkeag experience shows that a policy of union-management co-operation in increasing job assignments is dangerous for a union, even when the new job assignments are determined only after careful study in which the union fully participates and even when the resulting tasks are far from excessive. Such a policy requires that the union members place their long-run interests ahead of their short-run interests; it requires that some

members, at least, make present sacrifices in order that all may achieve future gains. The present sacrifices (demotions mainly in the case of Naumkeag) are definite and tangible; the future benefits are vague, remote, and uncertain. It is not easy for any organization to induce its members to invest heavily in future benefits. Trade unions are no exception.

2. The Naumkeag experience indicates that union co-operation in the introduction of larger job assignments is practicable provided the immediate sacrifices are not too great. The dominant cause of the cessation of the policy of co-operation in the Naumkeag plant was the depression. This conclusion is supported by a review of the situation in the spring of 1931 after new job assignments had been introduced into the two principal departments of the mill. Both sides were then reasonably content with the results. The bitter opposition that subsequently developed among the workers was fundamentally due to the reduced working week, to the management's demand for wage cuts, and to the fear that in a contracting market the continuation of joint research would produce permanent displacement of long-service workers. Had the new job assignments been introduced two or three years earlier or had a recovery of business started in the summer of 1931, the subsequent revolt against joint research would probably not have occurred. One cannot, of course, be sure that this conclusion is correct, and there are some reasons for doubting it. For example, difficulty might have been experienced even during rising markets in inducing the weavers to accept 24-loom or 28-loom assignments instead of 20—a change that would have been inevitable had joint research continued, because in competing northern mills weavers are operating 32 looms.[12] Even during good times southern competition might

---

[12] The job assignments were involved in an arbitration proceeding between the Textile Workers' Union and the company in the winter of 1939-40. In the fall of 1938, when other cotton textile mills in New England cut wages 12 per cent, the Naumkeag management negotiated a 9 per cent reduction with the Independent Sheeting Workers. Under the leadership of the Textile Workers' Union, wage increases of 7.5 per cent in partial restoration of the 12 per cent cut were obtained in many New England mills. The local in the Naumkeag mill sought to obtain a restoration of the 9 per cent reduction of 1938. The management opposed the demand on the ground that the job assignments in Naumkeag were too much below competing mills to warrant the increase. The case went to a board of arbitration. Information on work loads in competing northern mills was submitted

have compelled the management to seek greater concessions than the union leaders could have yielded without provoking a revolt of their members. But despite such grounds for doubt, the probability is great that a normal revival of business in 1931 would have saved the policy of co-operation.

3. All groups connected with the Naumkeag experiment made mistakes and some of them were serious. Furthermore, the machinery for operating the plan left much to be desired—it was too elaborate, cumbersome, and slow moving. The three greatest mistakes were (1) the delay in introducing new job assignments into weaving; (2) the introduction of some inadequate job standards— for example, 20 looms instead of 24, 28, or 32; (3) the attempt to correct low job assignments in the weaving department and to restore joint research in general before improvements in business permitted the company to assure the workers that there would be no layoffs or to offer wage increases in compensation for larger job assignments. It will be observed that these three mistakes are all closely connected—the second was a result of the first and the third was a result of the second. For the initial mistake the management, the technician, and the union must all share the responsibility. The management did not fully realize the implications of larger job assignments and was unwilling to throw its support behind standardization of conditions and methods as fully as was needed, particularly if prompt results were desired; the technician was perhaps over-conscientious and too insistent upon complete and detailed standardization; the union was only too glad to welcome delay. Had the management and the technician been ready to introduce gradually a 24- or 28-loom standard by the beginning of 1930, both sides would have been better off.[13] The company would

to the board by the conciliation service of the Department of Labor. The board declined to order a general wage increase on the ground that most job assignments in Naumkeag were substantially below those in competing mills, but it recommended that wage increases be negotiated in conjunction with a revision of job assignments.

[13] It would have been necessary to introduce the higher standard gradually because many of the workers would have required individual instruction and supervision for a short while. The very fact that the change to 20 looms could be made virtually overnight was in itself evidence that the standard was too low. The larger job assignment would have required the management to assume greater responsibility for the maintenance of standard conditions.

probably still have been compelled to seek wage reductions and the union would still have insisted upon giving up joint research. With more adequate job assignments in weaving, however, it is possible that the company would not have insisted upon restoring joint research in 1933, but would have waited until times were more propitious.

4. The irritation of the workers with joint research was apparently increased by the failure of management to appreciate the importance of maintaining standard conditions. The removal of this source of dissatisfaction, however, would probably have made no decisive difference in the opposition aroused by short time and wage cuts. The workers were looking for something to blame and under the circumstances they were bound to pick on joint research.

5. The union leaders have been criticized for not doing a better job of educating their rank and file to understand the reasons for joint research and its relationship to the interests of the employees. Certainly at no time did a large proportion of the workers acquire a real comprehension of the relationship between the company's competitive position and their own welfare. They knew that the company faced stiff non-union competition, but did not think that this situation affected them as individuals very much.

This criticism of the union leaders, however, is of doubtful validity. In good times the workers could undoubtedly have been led to see in joint research a valuable device for protecting their jobs by improving the ability of the company to compete, and for increasing the power of the union by enabling it to participate in the determination of job assignments. At its inception, joint research was so presented to the workers with success. The very severity of the depression, however, practically made proper educational work impossible. With short time and wage cuts, it was impossible to present joint research to the workers as a policy which gave them additional security and power. The very fact that employment was shrinking at the same time that joint research was progressing led the workers to associate the policy with insecurity of job tenure rather than security. No educational effort could possibly have changed their attitude until conditions changed.

The union leaders did to some extent lose touch with the rank and file and did fail to appreciate fully the intensity of the opposition to joint research. In the fall of 1930 the business agent had proposed a system of departmental union-management co-operative committees and over them a plant committee to consider any matters of mutual interest. The plant management rejected the suggestion, partly no doubt because joint research was moving very slowly at the time and the management feared new committees might slow it up. But better arrangements in some form were needed to bring the grouches and complaints of the workers to the attention of their leaders. There is no reason to believe, however, that such arrangements would have made a decisive difference in the opposition of the rank and file to joint research.

6. The Naumkeag experience strongly suggests that unions should not assume too much responsibility for setting job assignments or production standards. The arrangements for giving the union an opportunity to participate in the determination of job assignments and to protect its members against excessive work loads were unusually complete and thoroughly safeguarded the interests of the workers. But despite the care with which the work was done and the reasonableness of the job assignments (in some cases even their laxity), the rank and file decided that they were excessive. The union's intimate participation in research then became a boomerang. The very fact that the union leaders (and the union time-study experts) assumed joint responsibility with management for the new job assignments created a breach between the rank and file and their leaders. It meant that when joint research was discredited in the eyes of the workers, the union leadership and the union technical experts were also to some extent discredited. The Naumkeag experience suggests that the most practicable arrangement for determining job assignments in union plants is for management to set the assignments and for the union, through its business agents or time-study experts if it has them, to play the role of critic rather than of participant.[14]

7. The Naumkeag experience vividly illustrates how union-management co-operation may create a gulf between the union

---

[14] The workers were always more or less suspicious of their representatives on the joint research committee and the more their representatives got to understand time-study technique the more suspicious the workers became.

leaders and the rank and file. Union-management co-operation turned out to be a process by which the leaders gained such a thorough appreciation of the problems of the company that proposals which seemed quite unreasonable to the rank and file seemed reasonable to the leaders. As a matter of fact, this is a problem of internal union relations which is by no means confined to cases of union-management co-operation, for the leaders are constantly becoming familiar with conditions and problems which the rank and file do not understand. Out of such situations have grown many tragedies of union leadership. In the long run, the interests of the employees of an enterprise are not greatly different from the interests of the concern, because the interests of both require that the enterprise hold its own in competition. Consequently, the union leader who has great foresight and is devoted to the long-run interests of his members is likely to be accused of becoming too close to employers, even of selling out to them. The irony of it is that the leader's very devotion to the interests of his members is the reason for their suspicion.

8. Although the revolt of the rank and file at Naumkeag against joint research enabled them to maintain substantially smaller job assignments than in competing mills, this proved very costly to the members in lower wages. In the twenties, the Naumkeag employees earned substantially more than workers in competing mills and the local union boasted that its members were the best paid workers in the cotton textile industry in the world. In 1940, hourly earnings of Naumkeag workers on the whole were if anything slightly below those in competing northern mills.

One may conclude from the Naumkeag experiemnt that co-operation with management to increase job assignments is not impossible for a union, but that it is likely to produce revolt, particularly at the very time when co-operation is most needed, namely during periods of depression. Job assignments which become obsolete, therefore, should be corrected in so far as possible in times of prosperity. And in so far as possible, the union should let the management assume primary responsibility for job assignments and should confine itself to criticizing the assignments which management proposes.

CHAPTER XIX

ECONOMIC BASIS AND OUTLOOK FOR UNION-MANAGEMENT CO-OPERATION

The instances in which unions have tried more or less systematically to help employers to reduce costs, increase output, or improve quality are not confined to those reviewed in the five preceding chapters. Even in the twenties there were other scattered instances of systematic co-operation between unions and employers in handling problems of management. Among the unions involved were the printing pressmen, the street railway workers, and the hosiery workers.[1] In more recent years the policy has spread. The Amalgamated Clothing Workers has continued to pursue it; the International Ladies' Garment Workers' Union has used it, particularly in the Southwest; the hosiery workers have greatly extended their application of the policy; and the Steel Workers' Organizing Committee has adopted the policy and has issued the small book, *Production Problems,* for the purpose of guiding its locals in applying it. The steel workers have put union-management co-operation into effect in a number of plants.[2] A survey in the winter of 1939-40 revealed 22 enterprises in which an agreement to start union-management co-operation had been made within the last two years.[3] Additional field work would undoubtedly have revealed many more.

[1] A good description of the experience of the printing pressmen by Phillips L. Garman has been published by the American Management Association, *How Organized Labor Can Co-operate with Management,* Personnel Series No. 44. A brief description of the experiment with union-management co-operation on the Pittsburgh street railways was published in the *American Federationist,* December 1927, Vol. XXXIV, pp. 1445-47. The Yeomans Pump Company started a co-operative plan in conjunction with the machinists' union in the late twenties. It was still in operation in 1940.

[2] An excellent description of the experiences of the SWOC will be found in an article by Harold J. Ruttenberg entitled "The Fruits of Industrial Peace," *Harvard Business Review,* Spring 1940, Vol. XVIII, pp. 285-94.

[3] These enterprises included 1 department store, 1 chain store, 6 men's clothing factories, 2 women's clothing factories, 1 hosiery mill, 3 iron and steel mills, 3 metal working establishments, 5 other manufacturing enterprises. As will be pointed out later, not all of these agreements were executed.

Nevertheless, in industry as a whole, the number of unions pursuing the policy of systematic co-operation is small. In fact, they constitute only a minute percentage of all locals in the country. A number of the experiments have been abandoned. Neither the experiment in the Cleveland women's garment industry nor the Naumkeag experiment survived the depression, and of the four principal ventures on the railroads, two have been discontinued.[4] This is not surprising because one must expect the mortality rate in new experiments to be high.[5] What is the future of union-management co-operation in handling production problems? It is likely to continue to grow? Is it ever likely to become widespread?

The traditional view of unions is that getting out production and keeping down costs is the employer's responsibility. In performing these functions, the employer, as they look at it, needs to be checked rather than helped, and also needs to be compelled to share the gains of technological progress as he makes them. Unions have regarded it as their peculiar function to protect workers against methods of increasing output and reducing costs which are injurious to them. Unions also feel responsible for seeing that the workers share promptly in the gains of greater efficiency. Most unions have felt that they have had their hands full doing these two things. Since most unions have been unable, according to their view, to get a fair share of the employer's profits, it has never occurred to most of them that they should help the employer make more money. Likewise, it has never occurred to them that they should endeavor to help management develop new and better methods of production when they already have great difficulty in protecting

---

[4] In some instances union-management co-operation ceased because the intended results had been achieved. This is true of the cases where the Amalgamated Clothing Workers have given special help. This help may be compared to that given by a firm of industrial engineers. After production methods had been modernized and costs reduced, it ceased. It was never intended to continue indefinitely.

[5] The Whitley Councils in England may be regarded as a form of union-management co-operation because they have been designed to deal with matters of common interest rather than with conflicts of interests and matters of bargaining. They function on an industrial rather than a plant basis. Between 1922 and 1930, the number of councils fell from 73 to 42 and, since 1930, there has been a further drop. This heavy mortality suggests that there is little demand for a co-operative agency for an entire industry. This, however, does not preclude the possibility of a good demand for co-operative machinery within single enterprises.

their members from displacement by technological changes.

Is the policy of co-operating to help employers increase plant efficiency likely to continue to be an exceptional one practiced by only a few unions which have special reasons for pursuing it? Or is it likely to spread gradually until it becomes the policy of a large part of the labor movement? What, in short, is the outlook for union-management co-operation? To answer these questions it is necessary to examine the economic basis of the policy of co-operation, trends in the union movement and in industrial relations, and other factors, including the problem of the most appropriate and promising type of machinery for union-management co-operation.

WHY THE POLICY OF UNION-MANAGEMENT CO-OPERATION HAS BEEN SO EXCEPTIONAL

A combination of reasons explains why the policy of union-management co-operation has been pursued by few unions:

1. As indicated above, most unions do not realize that employers need help in reducing costs or improving methods. It seems to most union leaders and members that employers are doing these things pretty fast anyway.

2. Up to the present, unions have been bitterly opposed by most employers and have had to fight for the right to exist. This struggle for existence has necessarily taken precedence over all other concerns of the unions. To the members who must fight for the right to have a union, the idea of co-operating with management has just never occurred. The employer has been an enemy who must be vigilantly watched. One did not think of co-operating with him.

3. Employers must bear considerable responsibility for the limited spread of union-management co-operation. With few exceptions they have not desired or sought the help of unions in increasing efficiency. They have regarded unions as inherently militant and antagonistic organizations with which co-operation was out of the question. They have been opposed to doing anything to improve the prestige or status of the union—and inviting it to participate with plant management would raise its prestige. They have been more interested in keeping unions in their place than in ob-

taining their help. Some employers have simply been jealous of their ancient prerogatives. In their view the worker's function is to execute decisions of management, not to help make them. Arrangements that modified this traditional relationship have been distasteful to managements. A few employers have feared that union-management co-operation would produce friction over the division of gains. In slightly more than half of the cases of union-management co-operation, the initiative in starting the plan came from the union: in the four principal cases on the railroads, in the Naumkeag Steam Cotton Company, and in 12 out of 22 cases where agreements were made to start union-management co-operation during the last two years.

4. As pointed out in Chapter XIV, the interest of unions in cost differentials between union and non-union plants was dulled in the generation ending in 1920 by the rising price level. This had two effects. In the first place, it gave some protection to high-cost plants against the competition of low-cost plants. In the second place, wages tended to lag behind the cost of living. In a period of rising prices, the main problem of the unions was, not cost differentials between union and non-union plants, but the lag of wages behind rising living costs.

5. Finally, and probably most important, many unions have not seen a close relationship between costs and employment, particularly in the short run. They have based their policies upon the assumption that the employer's costs can be substantially raised without producing much effect upon the employment of their members. Certainly the unions have frequently been right in making this assumption, at least for very short periods. Unions, however, are gradually learning to take a long-run point of view in marketing labor and to consider the ultimate effects upon employment in those plants in which costs are high. Of course, the longer the period under consideration, the more elastic is the demand for labor—that is, the more responsive it is to changes in the wage in a plant or an industry. The long-run point of view, however, is only beginning to influence union policy. So long as the union acts upon the assumption that there is no close relationship between an employer's labor costs and the volume of employment which he

gives, it is led to deal with unemployment among its members by pressing for "make-work" rules rather than by pursuing a policy of union-management co-operation. In fact, if the union assumes that there is no close relationship between costs and employment, it cannot consistently pursue a policy of helping the employer reduce costs by labor-saving methods. Such a policy makes sense from the union point of view only in those cases where the demand for labor is elastic—if not immediately, at least in the long run.

REASONS FOR EXPECTING CO-OPERATION TO SPREAD

One must not conclude that simply because the policy of helping managements reduce costs and increase output is contrary to the present traditions of the labor movement and has been adopted by only a small minority of unions, it has no chance of spreading. In studying union policies one must remember that the trade union movement is still young, and that its outlook and policies often reflect inexperience and in some cases have been molded by conditions which are not likely to persist. Hence one must adopt an evolutionary point of view toward trade union policies. Perhaps the policy of union-management co-operation will never be adopted by a majority of American trade unions. Perhaps those which adopt it will pursue it more or less spasmodically—taking it up for a few years, dropping it, and then resuming it. One may predict with considerable confidence, however, that the policy will be pursued more extensively in the future than in the past.

The reason for this belief is that the economic case for the policy is very strong—much stronger than it appears to be at first inspection. Union-management co-operation is well designed to help unions deal with certain problems of more or less permanent importance. Although a few inexperienced unions base their policies upon the assumptions that most employers are making too much money and that the main problem of the union is to get a larger share of swollen profits, most experienced unions find that their toughest problems spring from the fact that a large proportion of employers do not break even. Even in 1929, only 3 out of every 5 of the 509,000 corporations in the United States made money and, in 1937, only 2 out of 5.

The problem of the high-cost employer will always exist. What is a union to do when it is confronted with a management that employs wasteful methods, is inefficient in maintaining quality, fails to make deliveries on time, or is inefficient in other respects? Should the union do nothing, on the ground that a poorly managed company is bound to go out of business? Or should the union help to make the plant efficient—perhaps even by insisting upon changes in managerial personnel? The decision will not be the same in all cases (some managements may seem worth helping and others not), but cases which present this question will never cease to arise. If the union can help the high-cost employer cut expenses, possibly it can save the jobs of its members. Sixteen of the 22 enterprises which agreed to start union-management co-operation during the last two years were high-cost concerns and were faced with serious competitive difficulties.[6]

Likewise, there will always be the problem of the newly organized employer who keeps himself in business, despite poor management, by paying very low wages. When the union organizes such a plant, the employees expect the union to secure a substantial increase in wages. But if it does this, it is likely to drive the employer out of business. Confronted with this dilemma, the union has no alternative except to help the employer improve the management of the plant. The Amalgamated Clothing Workers, the International Ladies' Garment Workers' Union, and the hosiery workers' union (particularly in the seamless branch of the industry) have met this problem again and again in the last five or six years. When the union helps the employer stay in business by giving him expert assistance in reducing his costs, it is simply taking a necessary step to keep the employees of the plant in the union. Rather than lose their jobs by insisting on the union scale, the employees would probably revert to non-unionism.

[6] Among these were a small steel company facing liquidation because of its obsolete and high-cost equipment; a metal working concern seeking a wage reduction in one of its two plants where operating costs were high; a hosiery mill about to shut down its seamless department which had been losing money because of high costs; a stove foundry about to shut down its plant and to move south where labor costs were considerably less; a manufacturer of roofing who, hard pressed by competition, sought a wage cut of 5 cents an hour, and met a refusal from the union but received an offer of co-operation.

As unions mature and gain more experience, they may be expected to deal with the problem of non-union competition more carefully and in more precise quantitative terms—in terms of the cost differential that it is safe to impose on union plants. When the problem is approached in this way, the union will see that it must choose the form of disadvantages which it imposes on union employers; that the greater the disadvantage it imposes in the form of restrictive rules, the smaller the disadvantage it can impose in the form of higher wages.[7] On the other hand, the more the union helps the management reduce costs, the greater the disadvantage which the union may impose on the employer in the form of higher wages. Viewed in this way, the policy of union-management co-operation becomes a method, not by which the union does something for the employer, but by which it achieves for its members the maximum return on their bargaining power.

Finally, unions in selling their labor must consider inter-industry competition and, in the case of durable and semi-durable goods, the competition between the new and the old. Aluminum competes with light steel and copper, cement with brick and wood, cotton with paper and rayon, coal with oil and water power, automobile repairing with automobile manufacturing; railroads compete with trucks and buses, glass containers with cans and paper containers, laundries with the household washing machine; and the several durable consumers' goods industries—radios, refrigerators, automobiles, residential buildings—all are in fierce competition with one another. Likewise, new automobiles compete with old, new furniture with old, new clothing with old, new machines with old, and (most important) new buildings with old. One must not expect trade unions quickly to become well aware of the effects of competition between

---

[7] A rational labor selling policy for a union would require that each member balance the gain that he as an employee would receive from the imposition of additional conditions on the employer against the chance that he might be one of the minority who lose their jobs because of the inability of the employer to give both the new conditions and the same volume of employment. The importance of losing one's job depends, among other things, upon how good a job it is, relative to other jobs which one might obtain. The more successful a union is in raising the compensation of its members above the rate that they could command in other occupations or plants, the greater the interest of its members in avoiding restrictive rules which limit their employment.

industries and between the new and the old upon the elasticity of the demand for goods (and hence for the labor used in making the goods) because employers themselves are only imperfectly aware of these effects—as their pricing policies often indicate. Nevertheless, as unions slowly become aware that competition is more pervasive than it seems to be, their policies will be affected. In so far as the demand for labor is elastic, unions increase the incomes of their members by helping employers reduce costs.

For these several reasons there appears to be a permanent place for at least a limited amount of union-management co-operation. Its main field of application will be in the high-cost establishments where either the equipment is semi-obsolete or the management is poor and where the union needs to do something to help its members hold their jobs. Nevertheless, as unions gain more experience in selling labor and in analyzing the demand for labor, they may be expected more and more to base their policies upon a long-run rather than a short-run view of the market and gradually to become better aware of the various influences, such as inter-industry competition, which make the elasticity of the demand for labor greater than it seems to be. As this occurs, their interest in union-management co-operation may be expected to grow.

SOME PERSISTENT OBSTACLES TO EXPANSION OF UNION-MANAGEMENT CO-OPERATION

Certain more or less permanent obstacles are likely to continue to limit the spread of union-management co-operation. Such co-operation is not likely to develop where the demand for labor is inelastic. The elasticity in the demand for different types of labor varies greatly. Some types are inelastic in demand even when rather long periods of time are involved. The elasticity of demand depends in part upon the unit of bargaining. It is likely to be less for a small part of the force of an enterprise than for the entire force—less for carpenters, for example, than for all of the labor required to build a house. Hence craft unions are more likely than industrial unions to base their policies upon the assumption that the demand for the labor of the members is inelastic. The elasticity of the demand for labor is less for the industry than for any single plant in the industry. Consequently, a shift from bargaining with individual employers to bargaining nationally with all (or nearly all) employers in the industry might be expected to increase the restrictiveness of union rules and to discourage union co-operation with management to cut costs and to increase output. Strangely enough, as indicated in Chapter XIII, it does not. The reason seems to be that national officers take a much longer view of the union's interests than do local officers, and the longer the period of time considered the more elastic is the demand. The higher the proportion of the industry organized, the less elastic will be the demand for labor in the union plants. The pricing policies of employers affect the elasticity of the demand for labor, for obviously if reductions in labor costs do not promptly lead to reductions in the employer's selling price, their effect upon the demand for labor is limited. The pricing policies of a large part of American business leave much to be desired. Until they are altered and prices made more responsive to changes in costs, employers cannot expect a very broad interest on the part of unions in assisting them to reduce costs.

Wherever the union believes that changes in the union wage scale have little effect upon the quantity of labor demanded, it may be expected to pursue restrictive rather than co-operative policies. And if such restrictive policies produce unemployment, the union may be expected to attempt to cure the unemployment by enforcing additional make-work rules.[8] Union-management co-operation to reduce costs under these circumstances would reduce employment unless the union carefully abstained from suggesting any labor-saving devices and suggested only capital-saving ones. Unions will be well-advised, however, as explained in the preceding section, to be extremely cautious in basing their policies upon the assumption that the demand for labor is inelastic, because the relationship between the demand for labor and labor costs always *seems* to be

[8] The fundamental question confronting a union with unemployed members is: "Whose income does the union intend to maximize—the income of all members of the union including the unemployed or only the incomes of those for whom there are jobs without compelling employers to make jobs?" For obviously if the union uses some of its bargaining power to force employers to make jobs, it diminishes its ability to raise wages. One qualification to the last sentence is required. In some instances by moving the unemployed into work the union may raise its bargaining power.

more remote than it really is. The very fact that time is required for changes in labor costs to affect the employer's methods of doing business and for changes in his prices to affect his customers' methods of doing business makes this inevitable.

Not only is the elasticity of the demand for labor easily underestimated, but policies based upon that error are not easily corrected. If a union causes unemployment among its members by misjudging the demand for labor, it may be forced to adopt make-work policies to create jobs for the unemployed. Thus the effort to remedy the trouble accentuates it. Once make-work policies are adopted, moreover, it becomes very difficult for the union to abandon them. However effective such abandonment may ultimately be in increasing the employment of the union members, its immediate effect is bound to be a drop in employment. That is why a union which embarks upon a policy of restriction finds extreme difficulty in shifting to a policy of union-management co-operation.

Finally, even when a union clearly understands that the demand for the services of union members is very sensitive to the labor costs of union employers, it may not adopt the policy of helping employers reduce their costs. Instead, it may seek to protect itself against the competition of non-union plants by invoking the aid of the government. In other words, the union may seek, with the aid of the law, to achieve a monopolistic position. The Guffey Act, covering the bituminous coal industry, illustrates the procedure which may be attempted.

MACHINERY APPROPRIATE FOR UNION-MANAGEMENT CO-OPERATION

The spread of union-management co-operation will depend upon the success of unions in developing satisfactory machinery for conducting the policy. Our examination has revealed three principal types of machinery:

1. Shop committees, supplemented by general committees, as on the Baltimore and Ohio and the Canadian National.

2. Independent experts working with advisers from management and employers, as in the Naumkeag Steam Cotton Company.

3. Union officers who give industrial engineering service to employers, as in the case of the Amalgamated Clothing Workers.

The first arrangement is not incompatible with either the second or the third and could be used with either of them. The second and third could not be used together.

Shop committees collecting suggestions on methods of production, equipment, working conditions, and so forth, are likely to be most useful in repair and jobbing shops where no standard product is made and operations are not highly specialized and repetitive. They have, however, been highly successful in several small steel wills. As a general rule, where each worker does a highly specialized operation on a standard product, the opportunity for the workers to suggest improvements is quite limited. Furthermore, a suggestion which eliminates all or part of some highly specialized operation, necessitates re-setting certain piece rates, and perhaps transfers some workers from one operation to another is likely to provoke discontent within the ranks of the union. Hence in shops where work is repetitive, operations highly specialized, and payment by the piece, the task of getting workers to suggest changes is likely to be very different from the task in shops where the work is non-repetitive, operations are not minutely specialized, and payment is by the hour. Under the former conditions, changes need to be made either by an independent expert or by a union officer.

Where the union wishes to give the management expert assistance in reducing costs and increasing output, it is better as a general rule for the union to develop its own business agents capable of performing this service than to join with the employer in hiring outside experts. The outside expert is usually viewed with suspicion by the rank and file. Furthermore, his very presence dramatizes the process of change and thereby stimulates opposition to it and makes changes more difficult to accomplish. The more nearly the introduction of changes can be treated as a routine execution of union policy carried out by the employer with the co-operation of the regular union personnel, the more smoothly it is likely to proceed. Unions, therefore, should encourage their business agents to become experts on production problems in order that they may be in a position to help the union raise wages without jeopardizing the competitive position of the employer and the jobs of its members.

In a large number of cases, unions are likely to have no business agents capable of giving the employer the kind of technical help he needs. In that event outside experts will be necessary. As a general rule, it seems desirable that such experts be hired by the employer without participation by the union, simply as a normal managerial routine, and that their work be checked by union business agents and the union shop committee just as all proposals by the employer are checked. In other words, it is preferable for the union wherever possible to use its established machinery for protecting the interests of the workers. Special circumstances, however, may require special arrangements. Both the pressmen's and the photo-engravers' unions have their own technical experts who render technical service to the members and their employers. In the case of a few small employers, the women's garment workers' union has itself selected and hired an industrial engineer to help the employer cut his costs. And when the regular union shop committee is not well qualified to work on production and cost problems, a special committee of workers may be necessary to assist the industrial engineer and to check his work.

CHAPTER XX

CONCLUSIONS

This survey of the system of industrial jurisprudence which unions and employers through collective bargaining have built up in a wide variety of industries indicates that its constructive accomplishments have been many. On the other hand, the system of industrial jurisprudence has not been perfected and exhibits deficiencies at some points.

BENEFITS ACHIEVED

Unions have given apprentices a better opportunity to learn trades and have greatly improved apprentice training. To some extent they have reduced the effects of the neglect of employers to train apprentices, for more apprentices are found in union shops than in non-union. Union rules have eliminated some abuses from the hiring of men; and in a few cases they have helped workers in the higher age brackets gain employment.

The efforts of unions to regulate layoffs are still in the experimental stage, but promise on the whole to be useful in helping American workers and industries to adjust themselves to the profound changes that have developed in the labor market during the last twenty years.[1] By the introduction of the principle of equal division of work and by seniority rules, unions have introduced continuity into many jobs where formerly there had been insecurity. One particularly important result of such restrictions on layoffs is to increase the effective working life of a large number of men who, if thrown into the labor market at the age of fifty-five or sixty, would probably be unable to obtain steady work. Unions have reduced in many instances the maladjustments produced by technological changes and market shifts, and they have protected the workers against a multitude of abuses and managerial inefficiencies that arise under piecework.

---

[1] The principal changes are the drop in the rate of expansion of employment and the change in the nature of the movement of labor, which has become forced rather than voluntary.

The recently developed policy of union-management co-operation has been a valuable instrument for labor in the control and improvement of working conditions. It also has helped union members in high-cost plants to keep their employers in business and thus to preserve their own jobs.

SOME SHORTCOMINGS OF THE SYSTEM OF INDUSTRIAL JURISPRUDENCE

Although the contribution which some unions have made to better training of apprentices is great, many unions have done little to develop adequate apprentice training. Apprentice training in some plants encounters many unnecessary obstacles and its cost is too high. A revamping of union rules affecting apprentice training would reduce the cost and increase the ease of training. The number of apprentices taken on each year is too sensitive to the state of business, with the result that few apprentices aie started in periods of depression. Consequently, there is often a shortage of boys finishing their training in years of good demand for men. Particularly great is the need for effective union participation in the training of apprentices. It still exists in only a few plants because of indifference of unions and employers alike.

Although union control of hiring has eliminated some abuses, in a few instances it has created them, particularly where the union requires that men be hired through the union office. National unions, on the whole, have been able to prevent locals from erecting serious obstacles to the movement of labor from one market to another. Nevertheless, the tendency of locals to bar union members coming from other markets is constantly present and needs to be guarded against. In a few instances the closed shop has encouraged excessive initiation fees and restrictive membership requirements./Since the closed shop gives the union, as well as the employer, the right to discharge men, it raises the question whether discharge of men by the union should not be open to the same impartial review as discharge by the employer. The violent fluctuations of employment in some industries have led a few local unions to experiment with devices for controlling hiring which are difficult to defend—particularly the permit system, which becomes a device by which union members exploit non-union members.

The restrictions which trade agreements impose on the employer's freedom to lay off men make it important to have a probationary period in which the employer has ample opportunity to test men before they become members of the permanent working force. The proportion of agreements which provide such probationary periods has increased, but is still small. The layoff policies have not always been adapted to the circumstances of the union and the industry. Policies suitable for long-term unemployment, such as seniority rules, sometimes have been applied to short-term unemployment, and policies suitable for short-term unemployment, such as equal division of work, have in some cases been applied to long-term unemployment. Unions are learning, however, that different kinds of unemployment require different kinds of layoff policy and there is a strong tendency to combine the equal-division-of-work and the seniority principles. This tendency needs to be carried much farther than it has been. In a few cases, the control of layoffs seems to produce insecurity rather than security because it interferes with the transfer of men with their work from one plant or department to another. This is an unnecessary defect in the control of layoffs and can easily be corrected by changing the rule.

Policies for controlling layoffs need to be made in the light of studies of long-run market trends. The policies which are suitable for an expanding industry may not be suitable for a declining one. In fact, if an industry is faced with the problem of the impact of an advancing technology upon a stationary or slowly rising demand (as seems to be true, for example, in the leather industry), union policy for meeting the problem needs to be directed mainly at the control of hiring rather than at the control of layoffs. Otherwise, the union is in danger of becoming an instrument for keeping an excessive number of men in the industry and for reducing the standard of living of its members.

In so far as the efforts of unions to protect their members from displacement due to technological change retard the rate of technological change, they limit the volume of investment and thus limit the amount of employment in the community. Here is a conflict between the interests of particular workers and of labor as a whole. So long as the rate of industrial growth was sufficient to maintain full employment, except for frictional unemployment, the conflict did not exist. Now that a more rapid rate of technological change is needed in order to increase the volume of investment and thus to reduce unemployment, the problem of the optimum rate of technological change becomes more complicated. It is ordinarily said that under competition, the actual rate of technological change exceeds the optimum because the employers who decide upon making changes do not take into account all costs. It is also true that they do not take into account all benefits—the absorption of the unemployed represented by the making of the machines themselves.

SOME GENERAL CONCLUSIONS

A few broad generalizations may be made concerning the system of industrial jurisprudence that collective bargaining has built up:

1. The very fact that the workers have had an opportunity to participate in determining their working conditions is in itself favorable to efficiency. As Mr. Justice Brandeis long ago pointed out, efficiency depends upon consent.[2] Even though the specific rules and policies adopted in particular instances may not be ideal, the process of joint determination of working conditions at least offers the possibility of achieving greater efficiency than could be obtained under rules and conditions dictated by one side.

2. Many problems of collective bargaining have arisen because specific rules and policies have become obsolete as the result of changes in technique, markets, or other conditions. The very fact that a rule or policy is obsolete often makes it more difficult than ever to change. Hence there is need on the part of both labor and management for a definite policy covering the change of rules, in order to guard against their obsolescence.

3. Unnecessary hardships are worked when rules are not flexible. For example, an equal-division-of-work rule which provides that work shall be divided equally "as far as practicable" can be ad-

[2] L. D. Brandeis, "Efficiency by Consent," *Industrial Management*, February 1918, Vol. LV, pp. 108-09.

ministered much more fairly in many plants than one which simply provides for equal division of work. There is need of a definite policy to word rules so as to keep them flexible.

4. It is important to explore carefully all the probable consequences of each prospective rule. The ultimate consequences may be very different from the immediate ones because the intermediate or long-term elasticity of the demand for labor is usually much greater than the immediate elasticity. Unions which fail to notice this difference and which base their policies on wrong assumptions concerning the elasticity of the demand for labor may hurt their members instead of helping them. At least in such cases the union policies may leave the members of the union *as a group* worse off, though the majority who retain their jobs may be better off. Of course, if the demand is elastic and the total income of the group is reduced, the chance that any given member will be better off may not be sufficient to compensate for the chance that he will be worse off. But since the effect of higher operating costs upon the demand for labor takes time to work itself out, wage earners may fail to estimate adequately their chance of losing rather than gaining from the higher costs. In other words, they may suffer from an optical illusion created by the difference between the immediate and intermediate elasticity of demand for labor.

5. The system of industrial jurisprudence should be deliberately designed not to maintain the status quo, but to fit a constantly changing world. For example, in the short run, security for workers may be achieved by imposing obstacles to change—such as obstacles to the substitution of new methods for old—but in the long run, the security of wage earners and employers alike depends upon their adjusting their business methods to a constantly changing environment. It was natural that in the early days of collective bargaining the difference between obtaining security by restriction and obtaining it by adaptation should not have been clearly seen. The dynamic point of view is making rapid progress today.

6. The protection achieved by union rules is not necessarily a net gain to the wage earners. In so far as it involves higher costs for the employer, it also costs the workers something. Since the bargaining power of unions is limited, the increases in costs which

they can impose on employers are also limited. If they choose to impose a cost in one form, say a make-work rule, they are not able to impose the cost in the form of a wage increase. Some unions have not recognized that the cost of working rules limits the wages of their own members and that it is necessary for the union to economize its bargaining power by designing working rules so as to achieve the greatest gain to the union members in return for the least cost to the employer.

7. The success of unions and employers in developing a system of industrial jurisprudence which is adapted to constantly changing conditions will depend partly upon the extent to which both parties are market-minded—that is upon how carefully they consider the effect of working rules and labor costs upon the volume of employment in the plant or industry. This means that unions (including the shop stewards and members of shop committees, as well as business agents and national officers) must have a good opportunity to learn about the market problems of plants and industries —an opportunity which has frequently been lacking, especially in the case of local officers. It means also that managements must maintain a close relationship between their selling policies and their labor policies. When management itself does not promptly translate savings of labor costs into attempts to obtain a larger volume of sales (and hence to bring more jobs into the plant), unions cannot be expected to become market-minded and to be interested in the relationship between labor costs and the volume of employment. As a matter of fact, collective bargaining will produce rules which are more satisfactory to unions and the public if unions show an interest in the price policies of employers. Setting a price means striking a balance between margin and volume. From the standpoint of the business enterprise, the ideal balance is the one that maximizes its profits. If the price is put too high, however, the maximum volume of production and hence the maximum volume of employment compatible with maximum profits are not obtained. There is reason to believe that managements have a tendency to pay too much attention to margins and too little to volume. This is partly because margins are more definite than possible changes in volume. It is also partly because time is required

for demand to respond fully to a change in price. Unions have an interest that employers decide close and doubtful cases in favor of volume rather than margin. Unless managements are willing to give the benefit of the doubt to volume, they must not expect unions to be too interested in the effect of shop rules and policies upon employment.

8. Protecting the status of management and preserving its essential prerogatives have not been a sufficiently definite objective of either union or employer policy in building up our system of industrial jurisprudence. In actual bargaining, the working rules of trade unions are built up gradually one or two at a time. This leads to an atomistic consideration of their effects, which may cause their effects as a whole to be overlooked. For example, in order to prevent the employer from discriminating among union members, his discretion at every point (awarding overtime, promotions, making layoffs) may be so limited that he no longer has proper instruments for encouraging efficiency. Each of the individual rules may seem quite fair and defensible, and yet as a body they may produce an effect which no one intended and which is inimical to the interests of the workers themselves. For the workers, though they have an interest in preventing arbitrary decisions by management, also need to have the management able to maintain reasonable efficiency. If it is not able to do this, then the union's ability to obtain wage increases for its members is restricted. Furthermore, individual members of the union are able to soldier and thus to exploit their fellow workers. It is important to remember that the status of management, however, is just as essential to the success of collective bargaining as an assured status for the union in the form of a closed shop or its equivalent. Furthermore, as our analysis has indicated, the two are closely linked together, because if a union does not enjoy an assured status, it dare not permit much discretion to management.

9. The shop rules and policies of the future will be influenced by union wage policies. Sometimes unions develop their wage policies with little regard to the effect of wages on the volume of employment. When this happens, the union is under great pressure from its unemployed members and the members who fear unem-

ployment to develop shop rules and policies designed to help absorb the unemployed. In other words, wage policies which produce unemployment tend to compel unions to develop make-work rules.

10. The most important economic problem of the country during the next generation is likely to be that of stimulating the expansion of production and employment. This problem becomes of first importance at the very time that the nation has made the encouragement of collective bargaining a matter of public policy. Collective bargaining may be so operated as either to encourage or to impede the expansion of industry. Our survey of trade union shop rules and policies leads to the conclusion that it is possible to develop a system of industrial jurisprudence that effectively protects the essential interests of wage earners without interfering with efficient management. In fact our survey indicates that in important respects trade union shop rules and policies may contribute to more efficient management. They have not always done so, but it is not necessary that the collective bargaining of the future repeat all the mistakes of the past. Whether collective bargaining turns out to be a help or a hindrance in dealing with the outstanding economic problem of stimulating production and employment will depend in large measure upon whether unions are guided by the short-run or the long-run interests of their members. It is often said that in the long run we are all dead, but the majority in most groups of workers expect still to be alive in five, ten, or fifteen years. Consequently, they have a considerable interest in the effect of union policies upon their employment opportunities over such a period. Let us make no mistake, however, about the hard facts of the matter. In a period when the encouragement of growth is a matter of great national concern, the freedom of trade unions would be jeopardized if they were to permit their policies to interfere seriously with the absorption of the new job seekers.

APPENDIX

UNIONS REGULATING APPRENTICES IN 1936[1]

Asbestos Workers, International Association of Heat and Frost Insulators and
Bakery and Confectionery Workers' International Union of America
Barbers' International Union of America, Journeymen
Blacksmiths, Drop Forgers, and Helpers, International Brotherhood of
Boilermakers, Iron Ship Builders and Helpers of America, International Brotherhood of

Bookbinders, International Brotherhood of
Boot and Shoe Workers' Union
Brewery, Flour, Cereal, and Soft Drink Workers of America, International Union of United
Bricklayers, Masons, and Plasterers' International Union of America
Bridge, Structural, and Ornamental Iron Workers, International Association of

Broom and Whisk Makers' Union, International
Carpenters and Joiners of America, United Brotherhood of
Carvers' Association of North America, International Wood
Cigar Makers' International Union
Coopers' International Union of North America

Diamond Workers' Protective Union of America
Electrical Workers, International Brotherhood of
Engineers, International Union of Operating
Engravers and Sketchmakers, Friendly Society of
Engravers' Union, International Metal

Fur Workers' Union of the United States and Canada, International
Garment Workers of America, United
Glass Cutters' League of America, Window
Glass Workers' Union of North America, American Flint
Glove Workers' Union of America, International

Granite Cutters' International Association of America, The
Hatters, Cap, and Millinery Workers' International Union, United (Men's Hat Section)
Horseshoers of the United States and Canada, International Union of Journeymen
Hotel and Restaurant Employees' International Alliance and Bartenders' International League of America
Jewelry Workers' Union, International

Lace Operatives of America, Amalgamated
Lathers' International Union, Wood, Wire, and Metal

---

[1] U. S. Bureau of Labor Statistics, *Handbook of American Trade Unions*, 1936 ed., Bulletin No. 618.

Leather Workers' International Union, United
Lithographers of America, Amalgamated
Machinists, International Association of

Marble, Slate and Stone Polishers, Rubbers and Sawyers, Tile and Marble Setters'
    Helpers and Terrazzo Helpers, International Association of (Marble Polishers)
Masters, Mates, and Pilots of America, National Organization
Metal Polishers' International Union
Molders' Union of North America, International
Painters, Decorators, and Paperhangers of America, Brotherhood of

Pattern Makers' League of North America
Paving Cutters' Union of the United States of America and Canada, International
Photo-Engravers' Union of North America, International
Piano, Organ, and Musical Instrument Workers, International Union of
Plasterers and Cement Finishers' International Association of the United States and
    Canada, Operative

Plate Printers, Die Stampers, and Engravers' Union of North America, International
Plumbers and Steam Fitters of the United States and Canada, United Association of
    Journeymen
Potters, National Brotherhood of Operative
Printing Pressmen and Assistants' Union of North America, International
Quarry Workers' International Union of North America

Railway Carmen of America, Brotherhood of
Roofers, Damp and Waterproof Workers' Association, United Slate, Tile and
    Composition
Sheet Metal Workers International Association
Siderographers, International Association of
Stereotypers and Electrotypers' Union of North America, International

Stone Cutters' Association of North America, Journeymen
Stove Mounters' International Union of North America
Tailors' Union of America, Journeymen
Telephone Workers, International Brotherhood of
Textile Operatives, American Federation of

Textile Workers of America, United
Theatrical Stage Employees and Moving Picture Machine Operators of the United
    States and Canada, International Alliance of
Typographical Union, International
Upholsterers, Carpet and Linoleum Mechanics' International Union of North
    America
Wall Paper Crafts of North America, United

Wire Weavers' Protective Association, American

INDEX